P9-DIB-760

DISCARD

DISCARD

AREA HANDBOOK

for

PORTUGAL

Coauthors

Eugene K. Keefe

David P. Coffin
Sallie M. Hicks
William A. Mussen, Jr.
Robert Rinehart
William J. Simon

Research completed June 1976

First Edition
Published 1977

DA Pam 550-181

Library of Congress Cataloging in Publication Data

Keefe, Eugene K
    Area handbook for Portugal.

    "DA Pam 550-181."
    "One of a series of handbooks prepared by Foreign Area Studies (FAS) of American
University."
    Bibliography: p. 411-435.
    Includes index.
    Supt. of Docs. no.: D 101.22:550-181
    1. Portugal.   I.   American University, Washington, D.C. Foreign Area Studies.
    II.   Title. DP517.K43   946.9   76-608385

First Edition, First Printing, 1977

For sale by the Superintendent of Documents, U.S. Government Printing Office
Washington, D.C. 20402 - Price $7.40

Stock No. 008-020-00630-1

FOREWORD

This volume is one of a series of handbooks prepared by Foreign Area Studies (FAS) of The American University, designed to be useful to military and other personnel who need a convenient compilation of basic facts about the social, economic, political, and military institutions and practices of various countries. The emphasis is on objective description of the nation's present society and the kinds of possible or probable changes that might be expected in the future. The handbook seeks to present as full and as balanced an integrated exposition as limitations on space and research time permit. It was compiled from information available in openly published material. An extensive bibliography is provided to permit recourse to other published sources for more detailed information. There has been no attempt to express any specific point of view or to make policy recommendations. The contents of the handbook represent the work of the authors and FAS and do not represent the official view of the United States government.

An effort has been made to make the handbook as comprehensive as possible. It can be expected, however, that the material, interpretations, and conclusions are subject to modification in the light of new information and developments. Such corrections, additions, and suggestions for factual, interpretive, or other change as readers may have will be welcomed for use in future revisions. Comments may be addressed to:

The Director
Foreign Area Studies
The American University
5010 Wisconsin Avenue, N.W.
Washington, D.C. 20016

PREFACE

On April 25, 1974, a military coup d'etat deposed Portugal's government, which itself had been established after a military takeover forty-eight years earlier. Marcello Caetano, who was prime minister at the time, had ruled for six years, but his administration was a continuation of the regime of António de Oliveira Salazar, who ruled Portugal from the early 1930s to the late 1960s. Both men, however, will be remembered for refusing to face up to the tide of anticolonialism that was sweeping across Africa during their tenures. In the post-World War II era, as the former Belgian, British, French, and Italian colonies in Africa gained independence and became new states and members of the United Nations, the Portuguese leaders remained adamant about holding their colonies. Their intransigence eventually led to colonial warfare, revolution, and decolonization. Portugal not only lost its colonies but was also impoverished by its long, losing effort to hold them. In mid-1976 the new leaders of Portugal were seeking political stability as a platform from which to launch economic recovery and social reform.

The *Area Handbook for Portugal* is intended to provide a concise, objective description of Portugal and the Portuguese. The book covers the historical background and the geography of the country as well as the principal political, social, and economic aspects of the society. There is an inherent danger in writing about a country during the time that it is undergoing a revolutionary experience (six provisional governments, two coup attempts, and two national elections in two years indicate the mercurial nature of the revolutionary regime); however, the authors have made every effort to retain their objectivity while describing the roles played by a multitude of individuals, parties, and interest groups.

The spelling of place names in this handbook conforms to the rulings of the United States Board on Geographic Names except for the use of the conventional spelling of Lisbon rather than the Portuguese Lisboa. Area measurements have been given in hectares rather than acres, and all tonnages are given in metric tons unless otherwise noted.

This study results from the combined efforts of a Foreign Area Studies multidisciplinary team of researchers assisted by the organizational research support staff. The team was chaired by Eugene K. Keefe, who wrote chapter 1 and coordinated the contributions of the other authors. David P. Coffin wrote chapters 12, 13, and 14; Sallie M. Hicks wrote chapters 4, 5, and 6; William A. Mussen, Jr., wrote chapters 8, 9, and 10; Robert Rinehart wrote chapters 2, 7, and 11; and William J. Simon wrote chapters 3, 15, and 16. The authors wish to thank the members of the Portuguese embassy in Washington who have given assistance and advice. Any errors or omissions, however, are the responsibility of the authors.

vi

COUNTRY PROFILE

COUNTRY

Formal Name: Portuguese Republic.
Short Form: Portugal.
Term for Nationals: Portuguese; adjectival form—Portuguese.
Capital: Lisbon.

GEOGRAPHY

Size and Location: Approximately 35,510 square miles including the Azores and Madeira. Continental Portugal occupies about one-sixth of Iberian Peninsula; bounded on north and east by Spain and on west and south by Atlantic Ocean.

Topography: Hills and mountains north of Rio Tejo; rolling plains to the south.

Climate: Varied with considerable rainfall and marked seasonal temperatures in north; dryer conditions and milder temperatures in south.

SOCIETY

Population: Estimated at 8.9 million in 1976; decreasing trend in 1960s and early 1970s probably reversed in the 1975-76 period by slowing emigration and influx of refugees from Africa.

Ethnic Groups and Language: Marked ethnic and linguistic homogeneity; dominated by Mediterranean racial characteristics and Latin language roots.

Religion: Ninety-five percent Roman Catholic; freedom of worship guaranteed.

Education: Free and compulsory for ages seven through sixteen; literarcy estimated at 75 percent.

Mass Communications: Radio and television facilities owned and operated by the state. Diversity of opinion protected in government-financed press. Censorship prohibited.

GOVERNMENT AND POLITICS

Form: Republic.

Government: Parliamentary system. Popularly elected president is head of state; prime minister is head of government.

Politics: Democratic, multiparty.

Administrative Division: Twenty-two districts subdivided into municipalties and parishes (see fig. 1).

Justice: Legal and judicial system based on Roman law and defined in Constitution of April 1976. Administration of justice influenced by French model. Supreme Court of Justice highest tribunal in independent judiciary.

Major International Memberships: United Nations and many of its specialized agencies, North Atlantic Treaty Organization (NATO), Organization for Economic Cooperation and Development (OEDC), and European Free Trade Association (EFTA).

ECONOMY

General Character: Formerly oligarchic and capitalistic; widespread nationalization since April 1974 and new constitutional provisions portend pronounced socialist features.

Gross Domestic Product (GDP): Approximately US$10.7 billion in 1973; GDP per capita, equivalent to US$1,250, lowest in Western Europe.

Agriculture: Yields lowest in Western Europe. Contributes about one-sixth of GDP; employs about one-fourth of work force. Traditional products, cork and wine, provide significant exports.

Industry: Contributes about 45 percent of GDP and employs about 35 percent of work force. Major industries are metal and machine products, textiles, and chemicals.

Economic Planning: Long-range development planning in abeyance pending establishment of new constitutional government.

Foreign Trade: Large annual trade deficits usually offset through 1973 by tourist revenues and emigrant remittances; decline in latter virtually eliminated foreign currency reserve by 1976, but substantial gold reserves remained.

Currency: Escudo—see Glossary.

TRANSPORTATION

Roads: 11,340 miles of national highways and 8,450 miles of rural and municipal roads handle bulk of passenger and freight traffic.

Railroads: 1,750 miles of broad-gauge track incompatible with rest of Western Europe except Spain; 475 miles narrow gauge. Railroads handle about 10 percent of domestic passenger and freight traffic.

Civil Aviation: Three international airfields (Lisbon, Porto, and Faro) served by Portuguese Air Transport (Transportes Aereos Portugueses—TAP), the national airline, and several foreign carriers.

Ports: Lisbon (60 percent of traffic); Porto/Leixoes (30 percent); and Setubal (7 percent).

NATIONAL SECURITY

Armed Forces: Army, 26,000; navy, 12,000 (including 3,000 marines); and air force, 8,000. Reduced from combined strength of almost 220,000 in 1974.

Service Requirements: Eighteen months compulsory national service, scheduled for reduction to fifteen months by late 1976. Inductions take only small fraction of manpower available.

Tactical Units: Brigade-size force committed to NATO.

Equipment: Inventory of mostly obsolete equipment supplied by United States, France, Great Britain, and Italy. Severe reduction in materiel under way in 1976.

Military Budget: About 20 percent of government expenditures in fiscal year (FY) 1975.

Police: Combined strength of paramilitary national police forces about 25,000.

PORTUGAL

TABLE OF CONTENTS

Page

FOREWORD iii

PREFACE v

COUNTRY PROFILE vii

SECTION   I   SOCIAL

Chapter   1. General Character of the Society   1

           2. Historical Setting   13
Lusitania—The Emergence of Portugal—The Expansion of
Portugal—Renaissance Portugal—The House of Bragança (Seventeenth and Eighteenth Centuries)—The Constitutional Monarchy (1822-1910)—The Parliamentary Republic (1910-26)—Salazar
and the New State (1926-74)

           3. Physical Environment   59
Administrative Subdivisions and Boundaries—Natural Features
—The Azores—The Madeira Islands

           4. Population and Living Conditions   81
Population—Work Force—Wages—Migration—Health—Diet—
Housing—Welfare—Leisure

           5. Social System   115
Historical Setting—Social Stratification under Salazar—Chan-
nels of Social Action—The Family and the Individual in Portuguese Society—Postrevolution Developments in Portugal

           6. Religious Life   139
Church and State—Church and Society

           7. Education and the Arts   167
Education—Artistic Expression—Intellectual Expression

SECTION   II. POLITICAL

Chapter   8. Governmental System...   193
Government Before the Revolution—Changes after the 1974
Revolution

           9. Political Dynamics   221
Political Evolution, 1974-76—The Azores and Madeira—Politi-
cal Attitudes and Values—Political Groups and Parties

10. Foreign Relations 257
Basic Objectives to 1974—Conduct of Foreign Relations—
Postrevolution Foreign Policy—Relations with Selected Countries
—Relations with International Organizations

11. Mass Communications 299
Role of Government—The Press—News Agencies—Periodicals—
—Radio—Television—Films—Publishing Houses and Libraries

SECTION III. ECONOMIC

Chapter 12. Character and Structure of the Economy 311
Background—Economic Consequences of the Revolution—
Banking—Foreign Investment—Foreign Aid—Balance of Payments—The Budget—Inflation—Economic Impact of Decolonization—Labor—Currency

13. Agriculture and Industry 333
The Role of Agriculture in the Economy—Major Crops—
Livestock—Forestry—Fisheries—Agricultural Cooperatives—
Agricultural Planning—The Agrarian Reform Movement—Indus-
try

14. Trade, Transportation, and Services 357
Foreign Trade—Domestic Trade—Tourism—Transportation

SECTION IV. NATIONAL SECURITY

Chapter 15. The Armed Forces 373
Historical Background—Mission, Organization, and Operations
—Manpower, Support, and Conditions of Service—The Armed
Forces and the National Economy—Foreign Influence

16. Public Order and Internal Security 397
Police System—Incidence of Crime—Legal Code—1976 Con-
stitution—Judicial Procedures—Penal System

BIBLIOGRAPHY 411

GLOSSARY 437

INDEX 441

LIST OF ILLUSTRATIONS

Figure   Page

1 Portugal, Districts, 1976 xiv

2 Portugal, Roman Lusitania and the Swabian Kingdom 18

3 Portugal, the Reconquest 21

4 Portugal, the Hispanic Kingdoms (1212-1492) 25

5 Portugal, the Portuguese Empire and Routes of Exploration, Fifteenth and
   Sixteenth Centuries 32

6 Southern Africa about 1890 47

7 Portugal, Overseas Territories in Africa, 1974 56

Figure   Page

8   Portugal, the Old Provinces   61

9   Portugal, 1933 Provinces   62

10 Portugal, Mountain Ranges   64

11 Portugal, the Azores   76

12 Portugal, the Madeira Islands   79

13 Portugal, Population by Age and Sex, 1900 and 1970   85

14 Portugal, Density and Percent of Total Population by District, 1970   86

15 Portugal, Percent Population Change Between 1960 and 1970 by Municipali-
    ty   88

16 Portugal, Total Legal and Illegal Emigration, 1886-1973   96

17 Portugal, Transatlantic and Intra-European Emigration, 1950-73   97

18 Portugal, Percent of Total Emigration by District and Region, 1973 103

19 Portugal, Emigrants per 1,000 Population by Municipality, 1973 104

20 Portugal, General Organization of the National Political System, 1933-74 199

21 Portugal, National Governmental (Executive) Structure, March 1974 201

22 Portugal, Judicial Structure, March 1976 204

23 Portugal, Subnational Administrative Structure since 1959 207

24 Portugal, Provisional Cabinet Structure, January 1976 215

25 Portugal, Economic Activity, 1974 336

26 Portugal, Principal Roads, Railroads, Airports, and Ports 369

27 Portugal, Armed Forces, Insignia of Officers' Ranks 392

LIST OF TABLES

Table   Page

1   Portugal, Population Growth, Selected Years, 1801-1976   83

2   Portugal, Labor Force by Sector, 1962-63, 1967-68, and 1972-73   94

3   Portugal, Emigration, 1864-1973   95

4   Portugal, White Population in Angola and Mozambique, Selected Years,
    1930-70   99

5   Portugal, 1975 Constituent Assembly Electorate by District 216

6   Portugal, Major Political Events, 1974-76 222

7   Portugal, Electoral Results, 1975 and 1976 241

8   Portugal, Status of Overseas Territories, February 1976 265

9   Portugal, Leading Newspapers, 1976 302

10 Portugal, Newspapers Affiliated with Political Parties, 1976 305

11 Portugal, Grain-crop Yields Compared with Selected West European Coun-
    tries, 1974 340

12 Portugal, Development of the Secret Police, 1926-74 401

Figure 1. Portugal, Districts, 1976

SECTION I. SOCIAL

CHAPTER 1

GENERAL CHARACTER OF THE SOCIETY

Portugal is one of Europe's oldest states, reckoning its independence from the thirteenth century; it is also Europe's newest state in the sense that the government in mid-1976 had been established by revolution only two years earlier. The future success or failure of Portugal's new revolutionary government will depend to a large extent on *o povo* (the people)—their interests, their aspirations, and their demands. Much has been written about *o povo*—long suffering, stolid, and stoic, bearing the heavy burdens that life dealt them because that was their fate. At least these seem to have been the views of Portuguese leaders down through the centuries. The leadership never seemed to be overly concerned about the terrible inequities of the society, specifically the extreme poverty that was the lot of the vast majority of the people. Kings, nobles, prelates, and dictators were able to accept the fact that their people remained among the poorest and least literate of Europe despite hundreds of years of imperial expansion and immense treasures that poured into Lisbon from its far-flung colonies. Forty-eight years of supposedly efficient fascist dictatorship, from the mid-1920s to the mid-1970s, also did little or nothing to make Portugal into a modern European state. *O povo* still struggled for survival or emigrated.

The Portuguese are one of the most homogeneous peoples in Europe. The area of present-day Portugal has known human habitation since early Paleolithic times, although archaeological finds indicate that the inhabitants of that era were not nearly so numerous as in other parts of the Iberian Peninsula or as numerous as the Neolithic settlers who followed. Iberians appeared sometime in the third millennium B.C., and from that time on many varied peoples visited, invaded, and settled in the area. Among the tribal peoples from whom the modern Portuguese claim descent were the Lusitanians, a branch of the Iberians who chose the western edge of the peninsula as their homeland. After centuries of invasions and occupations by Celts, Romans, Swabians, and Moors and constant intermixing of ethnic groups, the Lusitanians had developed into Portuguese. By 1249 the Moors had been completely driven out of the country that became Portugal, and borders were established that remain essentially the same more than seven hundred years later.

1

Portugal existed as an absolute monarchy for hundreds of years, enjoying sovereignty except for sixty years of Spanish rule from 1580 to 1640 and a few months of French occupation during the Napoleonic Wars of the early nineteenth century. The golden age of Portuguese exploration and imperialism came early in the fifteenth century as daring Portuguese navigators and sailors pioneered trade routes to the Atlantic islands, Africa, Asia, and South America. Great wealth flowed back to Lisbon from the colonies, but that wealth found its way into the hands of a relatively few families surrounding the court, and the bulk of the people were unaffected by the country's new riches. The extensive trade that resulted from exploration and settlement was monopolized completely, society as a whole benefited little or not at all, and there was no growth of a trade-based middle class as in other European mercantile empires. The new wealth, except for paying for the ostentatious life-styles of the aristocracy, was not invested to spur economic growth at home but was reinvested in the colonies, actually inhibiting domestic development.

Portugal lost some of its vast overseas territories to more voracious European imperialists, and in the early nineteenth century Brazil, the jewel of the empire, declared its independence. Even after such losses Portugal's colonies still dwarfed the homeland in size. The centuries of concentration on colonization and neglect of the homeland became obvious during the nineteenth century as the economy stagnated and financial crisis followed financial crisis in never-ending succession. The monarchy, which had been constitutional instead of absolute for about ninety years, finally collapsed in 1910, and a republic took its place. The short, sixteen-year life of the republic, which included unpopular participation in World War I, was filled with political chaos, near anarchy, assassinations, economic disruptions and military intervention in the political process. *O povo* struggled to earn enough money, or to grow enough food, or to catch enough fish to feed themselves—their concern, as always with survival rather than politics.

Portugal's experiment with a republican form of government ended in a military coup d'etat in 1926. Two years later the military rulers asked António de Oliveira Salazar to enter the government as minister of finance. Salazar had taken the same position right after the coup but, when the military refused to give him the authority he deemed requisite to the position, he quit after only a few days in office. The second time he was also given the authority, and from that beginning Salazar made himself the dictator of Portugal.

In 1933, with the promulgation of a new constitution, Salazar established a corporate state, which he called the New State (Estado Novo) and over which he secured his position as authoritarian ruler. For the next forty-one years the country existed under one-man rule. In some ways Salazar did much for Portugal, particularly in the early years of his tenure. He stabilized the financial situation and balanced the budget. He was responsible for such badly needed public works as new roads and improved railroads, and he established new or improved relationships with several foregin countries. But for a man of humble origins, a man of *o povo* , Salazar's lack of accomplishments for the people offset his accomplishments for the state. After exercising power for thirty-five years Salazar left his people mired in poverty and suffering a high rate of illiteracy. Marcello Caetano essentially maintained the status quo during his six years in power.

Salazar's New State was paternalistic. The dictator was certain that he knew what was best for the poeple and, having control of the instruments of repression, he made sure that his personalist views prevailed. Although fascist or at least quasi-fascist, Salazar's rule was low key, and his personal life could not be compared with that of other dictators in Europe, such as Hitler and Mussolini, or even to his contemporary, Francisco Franco, in neighboring Spain. He eschewed the trappings of dictatorship: the military uniforms, the huge displays of military might, the mass rallies, and the haranguing of the people. Instead he rarely appeared in public, avoided notoriety, made few speeches, and led a penurious life. He did, however, use the institutions usually associated with dictatorships. Salazar banned political opposition and established the National Union as the only legal political organization. He also relied on a secret police system, propaganda, censorship, and organizational control of the people through youth movements, veterans' associations, and other such organizations. In all his years as ruler of one of the world's largest empires, Salazar never visited one of his colonies.

When Salazar was incapacitated by a stroke in 1968, he was replaced as prime minister by Caetano, a longtime Salazar associate and former government official who had reportedly fallen out of favor because of disagreements with the dictator. Portugal's dictatorship without its dictator was ineffectual; Caetano, even if he had wanted to, could not have exerted the power and influence of his predecessor. Caetano recognized some of the weaknesses of the corporate state and attempted to institute some governmental reforms; but he could not reform the system without weakening it, and he could not retain the authoritarianism without having the authority to back up his decisions. Faced with an inherently impossible situation, that is, occupying a position of strength without having the power required to sustain it, Caetano's government eventually fell before the forces of a military revolt.

The military coup d'etat that deposed him was perpetrated by the Armed Forces Movement (Movimento das Forças Armadas—MFA). Composed mainly of young military officers, the MFA, because of its diverse membership, was a peculiar instrument of revolution. The movement lacked a common rallying point—an ideology, a popular leader, or a widespread grievance. The raison de'être of the MFA at its inception had been purely professional military. The earlier Captains' Movement, of which the MFA was an outgrowth, evolved principally because some career officers of the army had complaints about pay and promotions. The captains certainly had no thought of overthrowing the government; it is highly unlikely that these officers would even have discussed revolution in 1973; yet only a few months later they had deposed the government.

The actual deposition of the Salazar-Caetano regime was about as peaceful a military coup as could be imagined. There was little bloodshed, and there were no executions; the members of the incumbent government were ousted from office, and the more important ones were sent into exile. Even the hated secret police were protected against violent recriminations and incidents of vengeance (though hundreds of them were imprisoned), but it was at their headquarters that the only shooting of the coup occurred—when the police panicked and opened fire from their windows, killing three and wounding several civilians who were milling about in the streets. In many cases members of the secret police were rescued or protected by military personnel acting out of their desire to maintain the calm and peaceful nature of the overthrow. For the people it was a time of rejoicing. In order to avoid confrontations and possible trouble, the MFA had been broadcasting appeals to the people to remain in their houses and stay off the streets, but they might just as well have requested the Rio Tejo to stop flowing. The people were caught up in the spirit of revolution, and years of repression were falling away in the first joyous surge of freedom.

The coup had been planned and executed by a relatively small group of military conspirators who really had no idea how their actions would be received. As the coup progressed successfully, however, the people came out into the streets—by their presence and vocal support an affirmative vote for the coup leaders. Some of the most memorable photographs of the day's activities show men and women swarming aboard rebel tanks, waving red carnations that soon appeared in the gun barrels and on the uniforms of the rebelling soldiers and inevitably became the symbol of the revolution. What had started as a military coup had become a revolution, and a great number of people were generously and loudly proclaiming their support of the revolutionaries. By evening of that first day the military executors of the overthrow were announcing their intention of bringing democracy to Portugal and stating their desire to turn over the reigns of government to a duly elected body as soon as practical. For the interim the MFA created the Junta of National Salvation, composed of seven senior officers of the army, navy, and air force, to oversee the preparation of the country for free elections and act in the role of a collective executive under MFA supervision.

4

Less than twenty-four hours after the overthrow General António de Spínola, who had been chosen as leader of the junta, appeared on television with the other six members to reassure the people that the government was in stable hands and to guarantee that basic rights (rights that had not been enjoyed in Portugal since the 1920s) would be restored and democratic processes resumed. Still anonymous and remaining in the background were the young officers who constituted the ruling body of the MFA, but the fact that they were there in the background was made unmistakable when General Spínola began his televised statement with the words "in obedience to the mandate conferred by the Armed Forces Movement." Spínola would not have made such a concession if it had not been forced on him by someone with greater authority.

Although originally formed by a group of army captains, the MFA, after expanding to the other services, included some majors and lieutenant colonels plus a smattering of colonels. The high-ranking officers (generals and admirals) of the Junta of National Salvation had been chosen because they were well known to the general public and willing to align themselves with the rebel forces. The MFA leaders thought that their presence in the government would attract support. Spínola particularly was a very popular national hero and, although not associated with the actual coup, was amenable to joining the rebels after the fact. In his opening address to the nation Spínola presented the main points of the MFA program, which included release of political prisoners, dissolution of the secret police, abolition of censorship, and popular determination of the future of the colonies.

The old regime, despite all its years in power and its appearance of stability, collapsed in only a few hours, and few people could be found mourning its passing; however, the Salazar-Caetano legacy would be difficult to accommodate. The euphoria that accompanied the revolution, the camaraderie, and the heady atmosphere that came from the first taste of freedom soon had to give way to reality. Reality was the fascist past to be disassembled, the high unemployment at home, the seemingly endless warfare in the colonies; and, finally, reality was the people, too many of whom were still poverty stricken, still uneducated, and still ranking survival as their highest priority.

Now that the old regime had been overthrown, the new rulers were proclaiming that the revolution was for the people—for o povo —but with so many disparate groups thinking of themselves as o povo no government could possibly satisfy their expectations and demands, some of which were mutually exclusive. The average peasant in the north, for example, owns and farms a miniplot that barely sustains his family, but it is his land and his symbol of freedom. He is generally a staunch Roman Catholic and a militant anticommunist; but too often he can neither read nor write, and his illiteracy holds him in bondage to a system that perpetuates his poverty. He does not use machines because they would be uneconomic on his tiny plot, and to band together with his neighbors in some sort of cooperative would smack of communism and loss of freedom; so he farms the land with animal power and with the strength of his hands and those of his family, just as his forefathers farmed it for generations and centuries past. He is conservative, independent, and accepting of his existence; but his sons, through better education, working abroad, or serving in the army, have seen other life-styles and, if they return to northern Portugal, it is unlikely that they can be as accepting as their fathers.

South of the Rio Tejo the average peasant, in contrast to his northern counterpart, owned no land and was generally a day laborer or sharecropper, working the vast estates of absentee landlords—the latifundists. For the peasant in the south life was primitive as it was in the north but for different reasons. He often lacked machinery to work the latifundios because the owners knew that humans were cheaper than machines and, even when emigration caused shortages of farm laborers, landlords were unwilling to invest the capital that would have been required for modern machinery. Never having had anything to lose but the chains of poverty that bound them to a life of farming someone else's land, the peasants of the south welcomed the underground communist organizers during the Salazar years who at least offered some hope of something better in the future for themselves or for their children. Precipitate expropriation of the vast latifundios by farm laborers after the revolution led to chaos in the agricultural lands south of the Tejo that had still not been remedied in early 1976.

Also included in o povo are the industrial workers—men and women—of Lisbon, Porto, Setúbal, and a few other industrialized areas. These were the employees of Portugal's economic oligarchy—the few families that owned most of the country's means of production—and of the foreign firms that had established branches in Salazar's Portugal because labor was cheap and workers had no rights. Most of the workers lived in slums that had grown up around the cities, and even for the least educated among them it was not difficult to understand that they were the victims of exploitation and received a very minute share of the fruits of their labors. Some workers were Communists, some were even further to the left; and when the revolution came— the revolution that was for o povo—they were ready to make known their demands.

Add to the conservative peasants and the radical peasants and workers the thousands of bureaucrats, technicians, shopkeepers, military, et al, and the scope of the MFA problem can begin to be appreciated. To their credit the more moderate members of the MFA have held to their announced purpose of bringing democracy and eventually returning the country to civilian rule. Perhaps the greatest lesson to be learned about o povo is that they are pluralistic and should never again be taken for granted.

6

From the time of the first announcement of the success of the coup, the political scene in Portugal has been a confusion of personalities, parties, institutions, and interest groups. Prison gates were opened to free political prisoners, political exiles were welcomed back to the country, and a green light was given to the formation of parties, an activity that had been suppressed for almost fifty years. In the two years from April 25, 1974, until April 25, 1976, six provisional governments tried to rule the country, two coups (one right and one left) were attempted and failed, two national elections were held, and countless demonstrations, strikes, and riots seemed at times to bring the country to the brink of civil war. An election for members of the Constituent Assembly (the first free election within memory for most living Portuguese) was held on the first anniversary of the coup. The result of almost a year's labor on the part of the Constituent Assembly, the 1976 Constitution, was promulgated early in April 1976; later that month, on the second anniversary of the coup, Portugal's first freely elected legislature since the 1920s was chosen by the electorate. In both national elections voter turnout was heavy: 92 percent in 1975 and 83 percent in 1976. The Socialists led the voting in both elections, and other relatively moderate parties captured substantial portions of the ballots, indicating that the majority of voters were shying away from extremes of either right or left.

In both national elections four parties won about 85 to 90 percent of the vote. In the 1975 voting for the Constituent Assembly the Portuguese Socialist Party (Partido Socialista Português—PSP) led by Mário Soares finished first. In second place was the Popular Democratic Party (Partido Popular Democrático—PPD) under the leadership of Francisco Sá Carneiro. Third place was won by the Portuguese Communist Party (Partido Comunista Português—PCP) led by its secretary general, Alvaro Cunhal. In fourth place was the Social Democratic Center Party (Partido do Centro Democrático Social—CDS) under party leader Diogo Pinto de Freitas do Amaral. One year later in the elections for the Assembly of the Republic the PSP again led the voting, followed by the PPD; but the CDS, which almost doubled its popular vote, captured third place, and the PCP was fourth.

Of the four major political parties the PCP is by far the best organized, best disciplined, and most ruthless. Communist leaders have no qualms about sending out their strong-arm squads to disrupt meetings of other parties or to interfere with peaceful demonstrations. The PCP operated underground all during the Salazar-Caetano period and gained grudging respect among the people because of its constant opposition to the facist regime. The party has reportedly been well financed from East European and Soviet sources. Cunhal, the party leader, is a tough, wily, and influential leader, respected even in some noncommunist circles. In 1976 he was sixty-two years old, a veteran of the underground battles against Salazar and his secret police. Cunhal spent thirteen years in Salazar's prisons (eight years in solitary

7

confinement) and fourteen more years in exile. He is pro-Moscow, even to the point of supporting the 1968 Soviet invasion of Czechoslovakia, which was unpopular among most Western Communists. He is a neo-Stalinist who proclaims belief in "the dictatorship of the proletariat" but, like Stalin and Lenin before him, Cunhal undoubtedly believes in the party as the vanguard and the secretary general as the ultimate leader, which perverts the so-called dictatorship of the proletariat into a one-man rule.

The PSP was formed in exile in 1973; its clandestine membership in the country consisted of a small group of Marxist-oriented intellectuals who were committed to the liberal social democracy prevalent in much of Western Europe. After the coup the PSP sought to be a party of mass appeal, and it was the party that attracted the most adherents. Having won pluralities in both national elections, the PSP tried constantly to assert its popular strength, but it was often thwarted because of the communist power within the MFA leadership and the government. Soares, in 1976 the fifty-one-year-old leader of the PSP, is the son of a cabinet minister of the short-lived republic that was overthrown in the 1920s. Born and brought up in a liberal atmosphere in which the authoritarianism of Salazar was abhorred, Soares displayed early the radicalism that would lead to frequent arrests and prison sentences. Having escaped from a political prison during the 1960s, Soares left the country and accepted a teaching position at the University of Paris. In that prestigious position he became friendly with various European socialist leaders, including Swedish Prime Minister Olof Palme and the former chancellor of the Federal Republic of Germany (West Germany) Willy Brandt, both of whom visited Soares in Lisbon, lending their support to his party's parliamentary campaign in the spring of 1976.

The strength of the PPD lay principally among the Roman Catholic middle class in the north. It is a reform-minded party similar to many democratic reform parties of Western Europe, advocating limited government intervention in economic affairs combined with private initiative. One of the PPD's major points is closer integration of Portugal into Western Europe.

The CDS is a right-of-center party that sanctions limited government intervention in critical areas of the economy but stresses private initiative and respect for private property. The CDS is oriented toward the Roman Catholic Church, and it was the only party to make major gains in numbers of adherents between the two elections.

The next national electoral contest was scheduled for June 27, 1976, when voters were to choose a president from among several declared candidates. General António Ramalho Eanes, the army chief of staff who played the leading role in putting down the attempted left-wing coup in November 1975, had the backing of all the leading parties except the PCP, which was running its own candidate, Octavio

Pato, a Communist. Also opposed to Eanes in the presidential race were Prime Minister (former admiral) José Pinheiro de Azevedo; Otelo Saraiva de Carvalho, controversial leader in the original coup; and Maria Arlete Vieira da Silva, a Trotskyite. Wenceslau Pompilio da Cruz, a surprise entry who had lived most of his life in Angola, was the candidate of the refugees from Portugal's former African colonies; but he was officially disqualified because of insufficient support.

Of the revolutionary leaders some have shown amazing durability during the two years of turmoil, but others have passed into obscurity or at least into limbo. General Spínola was the first to fall from power. Already a nationally known hero (in a country desperately needing heroes after years of inconclusive and sometimes ignoble warfare), Spínola quickly rose to a position of leadership after the coup, but the generals and admirals in the Junta of National Salvation were supposed to be mere front men for the MFA, and it was not in Spínola's nature to be anybody's puppet. Having ideas that conflicted with those of the MFA leaders—particularly concerning decolonization—Spínola was soon at odds with the young officers who wielded real power. Seeking public support to further his own ambitions, the popular general tried to engineer early elections for the presidency, which he held on an interim basis and thought he could win in an open election. The MFA foiled his plans and forced him to accept Colonel Vasco dos Santos Gonçalves, one of the more left oriented of the original coup leaders, as his new prime minister. Shortly thereafter, in a showdown with the leftists, General Francisco da Costa Gomes refused to back Spínola with the armed forces, and Spínola was forced to resign. Implicated in the right-wing coup attempt of March 1975, Spínola fled the country. In mid-1976 the likelihood of his returning to any position of importance seemed remote.

Spínola's first prime minister, Adelino da Palma Carlos, had sought power from the MFA to exercise his functions as he thought they should be carried out. In league with Spínola he publicly clamored for early popular elections for the presidency to replace the appointed incumbent. Palma Carlos, like Spínola, was sure that the general could command enough popular support to win such an election on his own, which would give him much greater leverage with the MFA. The MFA leaders were in no hurry to hold such elections, nor were the young officers willing to increase the powers of the prime minister. Stymied, Palma Carlos resigned, bringing down the first of six provisional governments.

One of the more enduring leaders has been President Costa Gomes, who took over from Spínola in late 1974. (Spínola referred to Costa Gomes as his "Brutus.") Costa Gomes managed to survive the rise and fall of provisional governments and the wide swings of those governments to the left and back toward the center. Costa Gomes came to be known as "the Cork" because of his ability to stay afloat

9

in the turbulent revolutionary waters. Barring some unforeseeable accident, Costa Gomes should continue as appointed president until the electorate chooses his successor in late June 1976. Leftist Prime Minister Gonçalves also held office over an extended period, serving in the second through the fifth provisional governments. Gonçalves' tenure was stormy, usually because of his constant push toward the left. When Gonçalves was finally ousted by a coalition of opponents led by Costa Gomes, he vanished from the political limelight.

Another politico-military luminary who shone brightly on the revolutionary scene for quite some time was Major Carvalho, whose political fortunes have seesawed drastically. Carvalho, called Otelo by adoring Lisbon crowds, was one of the chief activists of the original coup. He was later promoted to brigadier general and commanded a special military security force, the Continental Operations Command (Comando de Operações do Continente—COPCON). Carvalho is a leftist but not a Communist; he constantly talks about giving power to the people and ruling the country through workers' committees. During 1975 Carvalho attracted a great popular following, and his COP-CON represented the most potent armed force in the country; but in the end the COPCON troops obeyed orders they liked and disobeyed those they disliked. COPCON was eventually disbanded, and Carvalho, linked to the leftist coup attempt of November 1975, was arrested, imprisoned for two months, and demoted to major before being released. In mid-1976 he faced possible trial by a military court, but in the meantime he announced his candidacy for the presidency.

In military affairs other than guerrilla war and revolution, Portugal's membership in the North Atlantic Treaty Organization (NATO) had become practically dormant during the thirteen years of colonial warfare from 1961 to 1974. After the revolution the new left-leaning Lisbon government and the strength of the Communists made other NATO member states wary, and Portugal was excluded from various classified NATO activities. After the failure of the left-wing coup attempt in November 1975, control of the Portuguese armed forces was resumed by the professional military, and by the spring of 1976 Portugal, in effect, was reaffirmed as a NATO member. The size of the armed forces had been cut drastically since the revolution and the end of the colonial wars, and in reducing strength the military hierarchy had tried to eliminate politically undesirable elements. As an example, the paratroop unit (an element of the air force) had been all but disbanded because of the high paratrooper participation in the abortive November coup. As the forces were selectively trimmed, esprit and dicipline were restored, and the major problem of the armed forces in 1976 was obsolete equipment. NATO authorities agreed that only massive foreign aid would enable the Portuguese to modernize their forces.

If the postrevolution political and military situations during 1974 and 1975 were chaotic, the economic situation was just short of catastrophic. The system taken over by the revolutionaries had grave weaknesses: wealth had been controlled by a small oligarchy, industrial production was hampered by poor management, wages were so low as to provide no incentive to workers, and agricultural yields were the lowest in Europe. The bad situation that existed before the revolution became worse after April 1974 partly because of the worldwide recession but more because of the political upheaval and the uncertainty. Rapid decolonization could only have adverse effects on the home economy in the short run, but the withholding of new foreign investment added a serious blow. Revolutionary labor laws, which gave workers bargaining rights that had been denied them for fifty years, took away Portugal's attractiveness to those foreign corporations that had established enterprises in the country simply because of the abysmally low wages and the lack of workers' rights. Some foreign companies ceased operations, adding to the unemployment problem, and new sources of foreign investment dried up. Labor unrest and the nationalization of industries also contributed to the economic chaos and, even though it appeared at times as if nothing less than a series of miracles could help the economy, the calmer political atmosphere of the spring of 1976 portended possibilities of the beginnings of economic recovery. Meanwhile agents of the Ministry of Finance went abroad seeking loans and grants or any assistance to prop up their faltering economy, while agents of the Ministry of External Trade sought new trade agreements.

The country's foreign relations also needed shoring up after the overthrow of the old regime. Salazar and Caetano concentrated almost exclusively on Iberian, European, and Colonial affairs plus, of course, the close ties to Brazil. The communist countries, the developing nations, and much of the rest of the world were virtually ignored, but the picture changed radically after the new revolutionary leaders gave up the colonies and cast off the cloak of semi-isolationism. Relations were established with the communist countries for the first time, and attempts were made to maintain good relations with the former colonies, although not always successfully. New initiatives were also made in other areas of Africa as well as in Latin America and Asia, but the greatest effort continued to be made in Europe, the ultimate objective being membership in the European Communities.

In mid-1976 it was too early to determine how the social system would be affected by the revolution. Obviously some changes are inevitable, but the nature of those changes and the rate at which they will occur depend on a great many variables. Political stability must be achieved, the great influx of returnees from the former colonies must be assimilated, and the economy must be developed in order for the country to take care of its own instead of losing so many of its citizens through emigration. Illiteracy and subliteracy must be eliminated in order that *o povo* may genuinely participate in national affairs. As these needs are met, the country's social system will develop and, given the opportunity to develop without artificially imposed constraints, the system could offer something to all the people rather than to a small elite such as that which previously dominated.

CHAPTER 2

HISTORICAL SETTING

Portugal derives its name from the medieval Latin term *Portucalense,* which designated the country surrounding the Roman town Portus Cale (modern Porto), roughly the northwestern region between the Rio Douro and the Rio Minho. First mentioned in the ninth century A.D., the Portucalense was an administrative area on the frontier of the Christian Kingdom of León, without traditional borders or a previous history as a separate political unit. The Douro-Minho core had been part of larger regions—the tribal lands of the Lusitanians and the Swabian kingdom that had left it with a legacy of isolation and separateness—but until the twelfth century its history was indistinguishable from that of Spain. It was from this core area, however, that the Portuguese state emerged and before the end of the thirteenth century had extended southward to the borders it retains in the twentieth century.

Many historians, Portuguese and Spanish alike, have considered it an accident that Portugal, exposed and peripheral, developed as an independent entity. The country has no distinctive natural borders. Apart from the western littoral its several regions are geographical extensions of larger ones in Spain. In its origins Portugal lacked ethnic cohesion. Its language had a common root with that of the dialects spoken by the people of Galicia, which has never ceased to be a part of Spain. Historians have seen the maintenance of Portuguese independence as resulting from the early development of a colonial empire, an extraordinary political and economic relationship with England, and Spain's untimely preoccupation with matters more urgent than Iberian unification.

Clearly a Portuguese government existed before a Portuguese nation. Nationality developed around allegiance to the king during the twelfth and thirteenth centuries, and from that grew political and cultural unity and a common Portuguese existence for all the king's subjects. The selection of Lisbon as the national capital tied Portugal's future to the Atlantic, making the Portuguese, in the words of the Spanish writer Salvador de Madariaga, "a Spaniard with his back to Castile." Portugal was the first European nation to establish a seaborne overseas empire. Its dominion and civilization were extended to parts of Africa, Asia, and America. Small, poor, and marginal in a

European context, Portugal ensured its continued existence in large measure by its ability to exploit far-flung colonies, and developments in the colonies often had a decisive effect on domestic Portuguese affairs. Throughout its history as a separate state Portugal has had an ambiguous relationship with Spain. It was an imperative of Portuguese policy to resist absorption and the loss of national identity, but nonetheless the history of inter-Iberian relations was marked by repeated efforts by Portugal and Castile to achieve dynastic union. Ironically, in order to maintain the integrity of its empire and its independence from Spain, Portugal became an economic dependency of England.

In the absence of an easily defined national character it is impossible to determine which of the distinct regional characters is authentically Portuguese. Family oriented, generally apolitical, basically conservative and individualistic, the Portuguese is intensely patriotic but not public spirited. Forgetting whatever in it has been unpleasant, he is given to nostalgia for an idealized past. He tends to be phlegmatic but not practical in his political attitudes. Foreign influences are often rejected because they come from a mentality too different from his own to be assimilated.

Contemporary Portuguese historians have been reluctant to study the unstable and weak governments of the early twentieth century. Although proud and boastful of their country's past achievements, they have been embarrassed by the failure of liberal democratic government to take root in Portugal and by the easy resort to authoritarian alternatives.

LUSITANIA

The west flank of the Iberian peninsula has known human habitation for many thousands of years; however, the prehistory of the area is even more obscure than that of most parts of Europe, and the origin of those earliest inhabitants as well as the origins of subsequent waves of migrants who each in turn absorbed their predecessors is a matter of scholarly debate. Archaeological finds in southern Portugal are similar to those excavated in sites stretching across North Africa to the Middle East and are evidence of participation in a common southern Mediterranean Paleolithic culture that had its roots in the African continent. Although later Mesolithic settlers and megalith builders, active before 3000 B.C., probably came into the region from the north, all prehistoric cultures there appear to bear the impress of African cultural influence. Compared with adjacent areas, however, the territory lying within the geographic confines of modern Portugal was an isolated backwater in prehistoric times.

Iberians

During the course of the third millennium B.C. the Iberians spread over the peninsula that came to bear their name. They provided the genetic base for the populations of both Portugal and Spain. Archaeological evidence has been variously interpreted as indicating an African or an eastern Mediterranean origin, the weight of opinion leaning to the latter, but it is likely that the Iberians who emerged into recorded history after 2000 B.C. were an amalgam of several groups of migrants and still earlier inhabitants who after generations of mingling came to share a number of cultural traits and adopt similar modes of social organization. They differed greatly among themselves, however. In some areas a sophisticated urban society emerged based on trade with the Aegean in tin and copper—the components of bronze— and supported by a prosperous agriculture. By contrast the Iberians who settled in the region bounded by the Rio Tejo and the Rio Minho were primitive. Called Lusitanians, they were described by the classical geographers Polybius and Strabo as a loose, quarrelsome federation of tribes, living behind the walls of fortified villages in the hills, engaging in banditry as their primary occupation, and carrying on incessant tribal warfare.

The Lusitanians were marked by their contact with the Celtic herders and metalworkers who moved across the Pyrenees in several waves after 900 B.C. to settle in the northern half of the peninsula. The heaviest concentration of Celts was north of the Rio Douro in Galicia, where they easily adapted to the damp, relatively cool climate similar to that of their Danubian homeland. The Celtic settlers soon were fused racially and culturally with the native Iberians among whom they lived. The degree to which there was a Celtic genetic intrusion south of the Douro is a matter of discussion, but the Lusitanians would seem to have been Iberians who assimilated Celtic culture rather than a racial admixture of Celts and Iberians. Similar though they were in many ways, even in their language, there was nonetheless a clear dividing line at the Douro between the patriarchal bandits of Lusitania and the matriarchal pastoralists of Galicia.

From about 1200 B.C. the Phoenicians, later their Carthaginian colonists, and by 800 B.C. the Greeks moved up the western Iberian coast to Galicia and beyond in search of trade, but the Lusitanian coast held no interest for them. Although they established colonies elsewhere in Iberia, there were no substantial settlements in what later became Portuguese territory, apart from several Phoenician and Carthaginian trading stations exploiting the salt basins and fig groves of the Algarve, at the southern extreme of modern Portugal. The Carthaginians, however, did hire the bellicose Lusitanians as mercenaries, some probably serving under Hannibal during his Italian campaign in the late third century B.C.

Romans

Roman armies invaded Iberia in 212 B.C. to cut Hannibal off from his source of supplies and reinforcement. Resistance by the Iberians was fierce and prolonged, and it was not until 19 B.C. that the Roman emperor Augustus was able to complete the conquest of the peninsula, which the Romans renamed Hispania. The people south of the Rio Tejo, Mediterranean in outlook, were docile in the face of the Roman advance, but it took seventy years to subdue the Lusitanians. Their banditry had a barbarizing effect on areas far beyond their own tribal territory and compelled the Romans to launch repeated expeditions against them. Native chieftains such as Viriato, leading light cavalry skilled in hit-and-run tactics, harried army after army and occasionally decimated them. Viriato, the first of the Hispanic world's caudillos, or popular military leaders, remains one of Portugal's folk heroes.

Once subdued, however, the Lusitanians were quickly and thoroughly romanized. Their fortifications were dismantled, and the tribes moved down from the hills to the more fertile lowlands, where they were introduced to agriculture. So complete was the process of pacification that no troops were permanently garrisoned in Lusitania. Eventually the territory included in modern Portugal was divided into three Roman provinces, but none was coterminous with subsequent Portuguese borders. The capital of Roman Lusitania was at Emerita Augusta, the site of present-day Mérida in Spain. Roman towns of some size were laid out at Baracara Augusta (Braga), Portus Cale (Porto), Pax Julia (Beja), and Olisipo (Lisbon), which according to legend had been founded by Ulysses. Settlers from Italy were few in the north, but large estates or latifundios were staked out in the Alentejo and the Algarve, where the names of Roman villas survive in Portuguese villages.

Unlike other parts of Hispania, Lusitania played no significant part in the history of the Roman Empire. It was neither populous nor prosperous, produced no luminaries of Roman political life or Latin culture, and was without strategic significance. It was for 500 years, however, part of a cosmopolitan world empire, bound together by the Roman road, sharing a common language and legal system, and its people, at peace, united in a common Roman identity and citizenship.

Christianity was introduced in the second century A.D., later than in the rest of Hispania, but an ecclesiastical hierarchy active in church councils had been established by the next century. Despite severe persecution Christianity was popular in provincial towns and cities but made little progress in the Lusitanian countryside until the late fourth century, by which time it had become the officially recognized religion of the Roman Empire. Bishops, who had civil as well as ecclesiastical status, maintained order after government had broken down in that part of the empire in the fifth century.

Swabians

In A.D. 409 the Vandals and the Swabians (Suevi), driven by other Germanic tribes, crossed the Pyrenees into Hispania. The Swabians, never more numerous than 60,000, settled eventually in Galicia and Lusitania. Before the migration they had been peaceful farmers in Saxony and Thuringia, where they had benefited from several centuries of contact with romanized Celts in Helvetia (Switzerland), and they attempted to recreate their former patterns of life in the kingdom that they established in Hispania (see fig. 2). In contrast to the nucleated villages and large estates that survived in the south, the Swabian farms, tilled with heavy quadrangular plows brought from the upper Rhine, were dispersed, single small holdings to be divided among heirs in smaller portions from one generation to the next. They bequeathed few place-names to the land, but they set a pattern for landholding and agricultural technology that persisted in the Douro-Minho area over the centuries.

With large parts of Hispania outside his control, the emperor Honorius in 415 commissioned the Visigoths, the most highly romanized of the Germanic peoples, to restore order there. They compelled the Vandals to sail for North Africa and asserted hegemony over the Swabians, who retained autonomy under their own kings, managing a well-organized government with its seat at Braga, an old Roman provincial capital. The Swabian kings and their Visigothic overlords held commissions to govern in the name of the Roman emperor and, although the emperor's authority was nominal, their kingdoms remained in theory a part of the Roman Empire. The Swabians tilled the land and left the towns to the Luso-Romans. Some towns, such as Coimbra, remained entirely outside Swabian control. Elsewhere Luso-Romans continued to operate the civil administration for the Swabian farmer-warrior elite, and Latin remained the language of government and commerce. By the middle of the fifth century the royal house and most of the Swabians had accepted Christianity.

The Swabians lost their autonomous status within the greater Visigothic state at the end of the sixth century, but by that time they had come to identify their interests entirely with those of the Visigoths. The Swabian kingdom retained its territorial integrity, however, as a viceroyalty traditionally reserved for the heir to the Visigothic throne, but geography served to isolate it from the turmoil of Visigothic politics, of which civil war, usurpation, and assassination were commonplace instruments.

Moors

In A.D. 711 an army of Moors (Arabs and the Moroccan Berbers whom they had conquered and converted to Islam) crossed to Spain

17

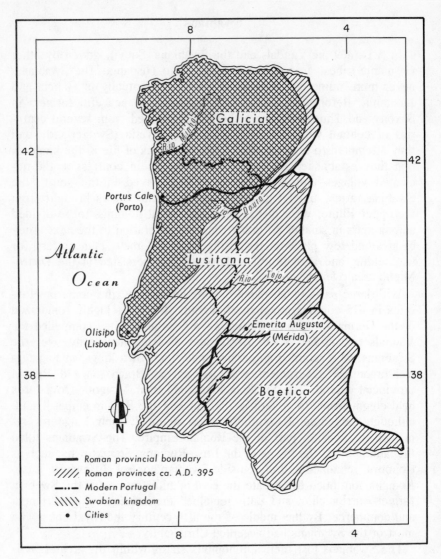

Figure 2. Portugal, Roman Lusitania and the Swabian Kingdom

as allies of Visigothic nobles who had rebelled against Roderic, their king. Having killed the king in battle and decided the issue against the monarchy, the Moors returned home; but the next year Musa ibn Nusair, Muslim governor of North Africa, led the best of his troops back to a Spain bereft of leadership, intent on annexing it to the expanding domains of the caliph of Damascus. By 715 all but the mountainous region of Asturias in the extreme north of the peninsula had been subdued and was in the process of being reorganized as al-Andalus, the name by which Islamic Spain, including its western provinces, was known.

In Lusitania land was apportioned among the Moorish troops. Bad crops, rebellion against their Arab overlords, and dislike for an inhospitable climate put an end to the short-lived Berber colonization along the Rio Douro. The Moors preferred the familiar dry country below the Rio Tejo, especially in the Algarve (from the Arabic *al-Gharb*, the west), an area where the Moorish stamp remained the strongest. An Arab aristocracy assumed ownership of the latifundios or gravitated toward the towns, where they revived lagging urban life. The Berber majority fanned out across the countryside as small farmers. For native rustics the transition from Visigothic to Moorish domination posed no problems. Only superficially Christianized, they readily became Muslims although remaining a caste distinct from Arabs and Berbers. Some Visigothic nobles who held to their Christian faith were reconfirmed by the Moors as local governors, but many others converted to Islam and achieved status in the new society. Jews, who were always an important element in the urban population, continued to exercise a significant role in commerce and scholarship and as artisans. The Christian Luso-Roman urban and landholding classes retained freedom to practice their religion and remained largely self-governing under separate laws and institutions. Called Mozarabs (Arab-like people), they were, however, profoundly affected by Islamic culture and adopted Arab social customs, dress. language, and artistic styles. In almost every respect except that of religion they were integrated into Moorish society.

For 250 years a united al-Andalus flourished under the emirs (later caliphs) who had their capital at Cordova. Nothing in Europe approached Cordova's wealth, power, culture, or the brilliance of its court. But, as the strength of the local nobles increased at the expense of a divided royal house, it became more difficult to hold the state together. The caliphate was torn apart in the eleventh century as rival claimants to the throne, military commanders, and opportunistic aristocrats staked out *taifas* (independent regional city-states), among them the emirates of Badajoz, Mérida, Lisbon, Evora, and a number of lesser states that warred among themselves and made accommodations with the emerging Christian state to the north.

The divided and leaderless Visigothic state had crumbled before the initial Moorish onslaught. Active resistance was limited to small groups of Visigothic warriors who took refuge in the mountain fastness of Asturias in the old Swabian kingdom. There they halted the Moorish advance and, according to tradition, were rallied by the Visigothic chieftain Pelayo (d. 737) to take the offensive, beginning the 700-year-long Reconquest that became the dominant theme in Portuguese as well as Spanish history.

Within fifty years of the Moorish conquest the Christian kings of Asturias-León, who claimed succession from the Visigothic monarchs, had retaken Braga, Porto, Viseu, and Guimarães in the Douro-Minho area, and peasants and craftsmen had gathered for protection around their strongholds. For 200 years the region was a buffer zone across which the frontier shifted back and forth with the ebb and flow of Moorish attacks and Christian counterattacks.

THE EMERGENCE OF PORTUGAL

As the Christians extended the Reconquest, life for Mozarabs in the Muslim-controlled south became precarious. In the late ninth century A.D. a large number of them fled to the north, arriving at a time when the so-called desert zone between Galicia and the Moorish territory was being reorganized, under counts *(comes)* appointed by the kings of León, as the Provincia Portucalense (Province of Portugal), a term first recorded in 883 to designate the Douro-Minho region. Separated from León by the rugged Trás-os-Montes province and called on to deal with the Muslims and Viking raiders by their own devices, the counts, who had their stronghold at Porto, developed local connections and governed with a substantial degree of autonomy. By the mid-eleventh century they had carried the frontier southward to Coimbra (see fig. 3).

Afonso Henriques

In 1096 King Alfonso VI of Castile-León gave hereditary title to the counties of Portugal and Coimbra as a dowry to the crusader Henry of Burgundy on his marriage to the king's illegitimate but favorite daughter, Teresa. Henry was to be sovereign there, but it was recognized by all parties that he held the counties as a vassal of the Castilian king. When Henry died in 1112, Teresa was left as regent for their son, Afonso Henriques. Teresa alienated the Portuguese barons and townsmen by appearing too willing to sacrifice their hard-won liberties and immunities to the designs of her kinsmen in Castile. They turned to Afonso Henriques, whom they encouraged to oust his mother and claim his hereditary right to Portugal.

Afonso Henriques (reigned 1128-85) made war on the Moorish *taifas* to the south, decisively defeating them at Ourique (ca. 1139), a battle acclaimed in legend but its site lost and even its date obscure. Ourique remains an event of great significance in Portuguese national mythology, in which Afonso Henriques, like Constantine, experienced a vision of the labarum, a sign of the cross in the heavens, and so gained assurance of victory on the field of battle.

Backed by his nobles, Afonso Henriques assumed the title of king of Portugal by virtue of his independent conquest of Muslim territory and his direct descent from Alfonso VI. When his cousin Alfonso VII of Castile demanded his homage as a vassal, he refused. Afonso Henriques' assertion of royal dignity and his defiance of Alfonso VII coin-

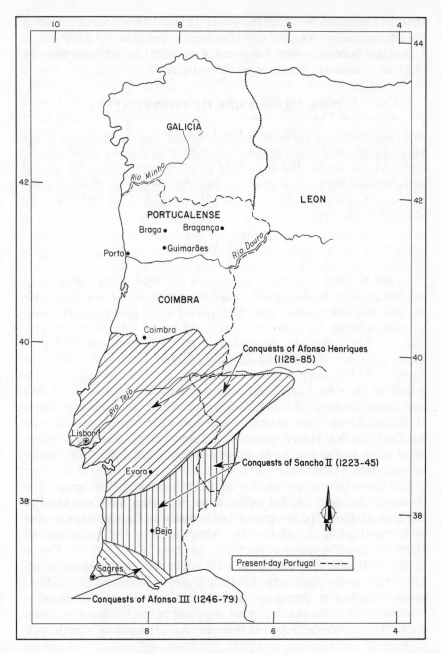

Figure 3. Portugal, the Reconquest

cided with a renewed Moorish offensive that absorbed Castile's energy and limited the king's ability to chastise a recalcitrant vassal. Although later Afonso Henriques reluctantly performed his act of homage, his royal title and Portugal's separate national identity were well
established. He assured recognition of Portuguese political independ-

ence by swearing fealty to the pope, he and his successors holding Portugal thereafter as a fief of the papacy rather than of Castile.

Portugal benefited from 150 years of wise and strong leadership by the line of unusual kings descended from Afonso Henriques, who in his long reign of fifty-seven years laid a firm foundation for subsequent state building. He left a compact kingdom, which grew from a core area—the Douro-Minho—that had a tradition of independence and separateness dating from the Lusitanians and Swabians and a corps of lay and ecclesiastical lords who were tied by allegiance directly to the crown. Using their entrenched royal power his successors founded towns, compiled the law, and carried forward the distinctly Portuguese Reconquest that Afonso Henriques had begun on the field of Ourique.

The Reconquest

To the Moors the Portuguese were the "bravest of the Christians," but the Portuguese Reconquest regularly relied on the aid of crusaders and adventurers from abroad. A papal bull in 1100 called on European chivalry to assist the Hispanic kingdoms in a great western crusade. In 1147, when he succeeded in taking Lisbon, and during an earlier, unsuccessful siege of the city, Afonso Henriques counted as many as 15,000 English, French, Flemish, Rhenish, and Danish crusaders at his side. Many returned home enriched by the booty they had taken during the crusade, and others went on to Palestine after the fall of Lisbon, but some of the crusaders remained as settlers on the land they had helped to conquer. Large tracts in the new territory were given to the knights of military orders to gain their support for future efforts in the Reconquest.

The Alentejo was occupied after 1225 by Sancho II (reigned 1223-45), the weak and divided *taifas* there preferring the Christian Portuguese to the Muslim Berbers who had asserted hegemony over what remained of al-Andalus. The Algarve fell in 1249 to Afonso III (reigned 1246-79), completing the Portuguese phase of the Reconquest. Although the Portuguese were continually called upon to defend the country against the Castilians, they also fought beside them against the Moors. Portuguese knights had served with distinction at Las Navas de Tolosa (1212), a turning point in the Reconquest, where a Castilian chronicler reported that they had "rushed into battle as if at a feast."

Lisbon became Portugal's capital in 1298, finally bringing to rest a peripatetic royal government that had made its seat at Braga, Guimarães, Coimbra, and other points along the road south during the Reconquest. A predominantly Christian city, even under Moorish rule, with an excellent sheltered harbor in the Rio Tejo, Lisbon was already the economic, social, and cultural center of Portugal before it was chosen as its political center. It enjoyed a good climate and a scenic location, and one crusader had described its buildings as "artissime coriglobata" (crowded together with great skill). The prominence of Lisbon ensured Portugal's future orientation toward the Atlantic, but the city, surrounded by the country's most productive area —favored by both Romans and Moors—grew at the expense of the countryside. It was not part of the Portuguese heartland and remained remote from it.

The Medieval Monarchy

King Dinís (reigned 1279-1325) introduced Portuguese as the official language of the realm in place of Latin and imposed its use on the south. Called O Lavrador (the Farmer), he encouraged his nobles to bring their wastelands into cultivation and to take an active interest in agricultural development. It was not an easy step for a warrior aristocracy to settle down as estate managers, and Dinís found it necessary to reassure them that "no baron shall lose caste by dedicating himself to the soil." The new lands in the south, whose development he supervised, provided an abundance of fruits, olives, wine, almonds, and grain that was turned for the first time toward stimulating Portugal's export trade but, despite increased production, Portugal remained a poor country even by medieval standards.

Portugal's kings were fruitful in their children, legitimate and illegitimate. Favors granted by doting royal fathers to their numerous bastard offspring, those of Dinís more plentiful than most, frequently provoked rebellions by legitimate heirs. The daughters of prolific Portuguese monarchs were married well, however, extending Portugal's political contacts to England, Flanders, Burgundy, France, and Denmark, as well as cementing dynastic connections with other Hispanic states.

The Portuguese monarchy had fewer constitutional limitations placed on its authority than those imposed by custom and law on other medieval kingdoms. The king's government was administered by a centralized bureaucracy. The *forais* (charter rights) defined the relationship of individual subjects and communities to the king both directly and through intermediate lords or town corporations. In return for immunities and privileges on their own lands nobles were obliged to provide for the defense of a sector of the country. Rural collectives were encouraged by grants of tax relief and local self-government to farm the poor soil of Trás-os-Montes. The Portuguese Cortes (parliament), composed of representatives of three estates—the church, the nobility, and the towns—had a continuous history beginning in 1254.

Early medieval monarchs were expected to be self-sufficient and to operate the government out of their own resources but, as government became more complex and expensive, they were forced to call on the resources of their subjects as well. In return for a vote of subsidies to the royal government, the estates, through their representatives in the Cortes, compelled the king to listen to their grievances, seek advice, and get their consent for the projects for which the revenues that they granted were intended. The stronger the king, the more willing was the Cortes to provide the funds that he requested; the weaker the king, the more demands were made on him by the estates.

Though feudal terminology was used in charters and deeds in Portugal for lack of a more specific vocabulary, feudalism (that is, hereditary title to the use of land and to legal jurisdiction on that land in return for personal allegiance and service to the donor) did not exist de jure in any developed form in medieval Portugal; in practice, however, situations very much like it did occur. According to Portuguese custom landholders were limited to economic control of the property they held. Legal jurisdiction on that property might be granted, but it was separate from title to the use of the land. All governmental and judicial power was vested ultimately in the crown, but in time it was delegated to landlords acting as the king's agents on their property. As the origin of grants of jurisdiction was obscured by the years, lords assumed that they exercised it as a right, and the crown had to review grants and titles to land continually in order to reclaim and reallocate its own property and authority.

Portugal's borders with Castile were stabilized after 1295 (see fig. 4). But the threat of war with the stronger Spanish kingdom was a constant concern to a succession of kings in the fourteenth century. To keep the tenuous peace, Afonso IV (reigned 1325-57) had ordered the murder of Inês de Castro, heroine of a romance with his heir, Dom Pedro, on suspicion that she was involving Portugal in Castilian politics. When Dom Pedro became king as Pedro I (reigned 1357-67), O Justiceiro (the Judge)—as he was called because he punished the wicked indiscriminately regardless of rank—proclaimed Inês his queen and forced his court to do homage to her corpse, clothed for the occasion in the robes of state. When he died, Pedro was buried with Inês at the abbey of Alcobaça, where his tomb was embellished with the scene in stone of her murderers in hell. Their son, João, became grand master of the military order of Aviz.

Social, Economic, and Cultural Development

The social and economic structure of medieval Portugal differed radically from region to region. A frontier society developed in the north that persisted after the region ceased to be a frontier. Liberties had been granted to soldier yeomen who were willing to take responsibility for defending their holdings. A petty nobility or gentry had risen among those who had succeeded in consolidating their holdings

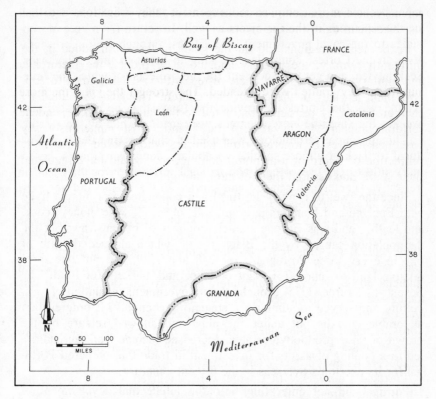

Figure 4. Portugal, the Hispanic Kingdoms (1212-1492)

and those of their dependents, as had a caste of commoner knights
(cavaleiros vilãos) who were granted land to defray their military expenses. But the dominant pattern in much of the north remained that
of the small-holding yeoman farmer who, according to the Germanic
landholding system inherited from the Swabians, divided his land
among all his heirs in plots that shrank in size with each generation.
For the man who possessed it, his land was as much an heirloom as it
was a piece of potentially productive property.

Peasants in the Douro-Minho as well as in Trás-os-Montes formed
collective associations *(pactos de bemfeitoria)* to pay rent on fields
and pastures that went toward the support of the military aristocracy,
which also agreed in the bargain to defend them. Originally they retained full freedom to negotiate contracts with their protector and if
unsatisfied to choose a new lord. As the frontier was pushed forward,
however, peasants were usually tied to one lord. The crown, particularly after Dinís, encouraged family and collective farming by alienat-
ing aristocratic and ecclesiastical land to peasant proprietors.

Above them all was a small number of interrelated great families,
relatively poor in liquid income. From the crown they regularly re-

ceived subsidies that allowed them to meet their obligations and that also tied them tightly to the crown.

In the central regions and on the lands in the south added in the thirteenth century, the military and monastic orders, the hierarchy, and military aristocrats had been vested with vast latifundios to support their services to the crown and church. The land was tilled by sharecroppers, by peasants contracted to the land (though dependent serfdom appears to have been rare) and, most numerously, by wretched masses of itinerant rural laborers who worked without the protection of a lord or a manorial contract that would have regulated their status and assured them of minimal rights.

Since the twelfth century Portugal had conducted a profitable trade with England and Flanders in grain, salt, olive oil, wine, honey, cork, and leather and was Europe's chief producer of broomstraw; but the depopulation caused by the Black Death, which claimed the life of one in every three Portuguese in 1348 and 1349, had put once-productive land to fallow for want of labor and markets for food. The Sesmarias Decree (1375) brought about government regulation of agriculture and served to stimulate a stagnating economy. It ordered that all arable land be put under the plow and allowed seizure by the crown of underproductive estates. Increased income from agriculture led to a pooling of assets for investment in trade that prepared Portugal for its exertions overseas in the fifteenth century.

Portugal did not enter fully into the intellectual development of medieval Europe. Monastic development was geared toward promoting the Reconquest rather than furthering scholarship during the period of cultural flowering elsewhere in Europe in the twelfth and thirteenth centuries. The country did not pick up the impulses that emanated from France in those years and enriched the intellectual life of neighboring lands. Portugal did not have as much contact with medieval Islamic and Jewish culture as was possible in the rest of the peninsula, nor were the Portuguese as interested in transmitting Arabic learning to a Latin audience. Dinís had founded a university in 1290, but it was not highly regarded, and the best of Portugal's scholars studied and made their reputations aboard. Pedro Julião, the only Portuguese to become pope (John XXI, 1276-77), was an eminent teacher in Paris, and Anthony of Padua, the great Franciscan saint born in Lisbon, is identified with his adopted Italy.

The Portuguese church suffered from its very low standards of clerical education. Clerical morals were relaxed, and concubinage among the clergy was common. The hierarchy and many religious houses grew enormously wealthy by Portuguese standards from the lands granted them during the Reconquest, and their wealth often implied great political power as well, which engaged the crown in a running dispute with the church over title to land.

The House of Aviz

Fernando (reigned 1367-83), last of the House of Burgundy, left no male heir, but his daughter was the wife of Juan I of Castile, and it was intended that their offspring should inherit Portugal. Until issue was forthcoming, however, Portugal was to be governed under the regency of Fernando's unpopular widow, Leonor Teles. João, grand master of Aviz, expelled the regent and was proclaimed king as João I (reigned 1384-1433), by a Cortes called at Coimbra in 1385. In response a Castilian army invaded Portugal to uphold the rights of an as yet unborn Castilian heir to the Portuguese throne. What had taken place was a dynastic revolution that had provoked foreign intervention, but the struggle that followed was also a Portuguese civil war. The traditionalist north supported Juan and the cause of legitimacy; the towns and the south where the Order of Aviz was one of the great landholders, backed João. The future of the House of Aviz and, from the perspective of João's followers, the independence of Portugal were decided at the epic battle of Aljubarrota near Lisbon. Fewer than 7,000 Portuguese on foot, under Nuno Alvares Pereira, the "Constable," and a contingent of English longbowmen faced an opposing army of 10,000 infantry and 20,000 cavalry, the cream of Castilian chivalry. As the Constable's men held their positions, the longbowmen shattered the enemy's heavily armored cavalry and won the day for João of Aviz.

English aid to the Aviz dynasty set the stage for the cooperation with England that would be the cornerstone of Portuguese foreign policy for more than 500 years. In 1386 the Treaty of Windsor confirmed the alliance born at Aljubarrota with a pact of perpetual friendship between the two countries. The next year John of Gaunt, duke of Lancaster, son of Edward III and father of Henry IV, landed in Galicia with an expeditionary force to press his claim to the Castilian throne with Portuguese aid. He failed to win the support of the Castilian nobility and returned to England with a cash compensation from the rival claimant, but the war with Castile continued for Portugal until 1411.

John of Gaunt left behind his intelligent and cultured daughter, Philippa of Lancaster, as the wife of João I to seal the Anglo-Portuguese alliance. She introduced an English element at court—an "icy influx," according to the Portuguese, that reformed the morals of their court and imposed uncomfortably rigid standards of behavior on them. More important, Philippa provided royal patronage for English commercial interests that sought to meet the Portuguese desire for cod and cloth in return for wine, cork, salt, and oil through the English-run warehouses at Porto. Philippa also became the mother of an extraordinary line of royal princes who led Portugal into its golden age. For the poet Luís de Camões they were the "marvelous generation," the brothers Durate the king, Pedro the regent, António the crusader, João, and Dom Henrique—Prince Henry the Navigator.

João I distrusted the old aristocracy that had opposed his rise to power. He promoted the growth of a lower nobility attached to the crown and rewarded the urban commercial oligarchy with position and influence in the realm in return for its support of Aviz. He surrounded himself with skilled bureaucrats who professionalized royal administration and extended royal jurisdiction at the expense of the old aristocracy. A strong and confident monarch, João nonetheless summoned the Cortes biennially to approve his legislation and lend legitimacy to the title that he had seized by force. The future of the Aviz dynasty seemed assured by the presence of João's five legitimate sons, but the king also provided for his illegitimate children as he had been provided for by his father. João conferred on his bastard son Afonso the hereditary title of duke of Bragança and endowed him with lands and jurisdiction that amounted to creation of a state within a state supported by a huge reserve of armed retainers. The House of Bragança accumulated wealth to rival that of the crown and assumed leadership of the old aristocracy in opposition to Aviz.

THE EXPANSION OF PORTUGAL

In 1415 the Portuguese seized Ceuta in Morocco, the western depot for the spice trade, and began a campaign that by the end of the century had put them in control of most of Morocco's western coastline. From strongholds on the coast the Portuguese manipulated satellite Muslim states in the interior and provided cover for settlers who had carved out estates in North Africa but derived most of their income from raiding along the frontier between Portuguese and Muslim-held territory. Portuguese efforts throughout most of the fifteenth century were focused on Morocco rather than on exploration by sea and colonization of unknown territory.

Overseas expansion was an extension of the Reconquest, and the same crusading impulses went into exploration abroad that were involved in Moor-killing at home. The Reconquest in Portugal and Spain had been self-sustaining: it lived off its conquests. There was nothing ambiguous about obtaining material gains from crusading. Profit from war was seen as a just reward due those who had fought in a righteous cause; and when the prospects for profit waned, enthusiasm for the campaign lagged, and a period of relative calm and accommodation with the enemy ensued during which newly taken land was assimilated. Men planted on the frontier used banditry to soften up the territory to be taken next. This was the pattern followed throughout the Reconquest, and it has led the Spanish historian José Ortega y Gasset to question whether anything that lasted for 700 years could properly be called a Reconquest.

Aragon had turned to the Mediterranean when its territorial ambitions in Spain had been satisfied. Castile appeared to have an overriding geopolitical claim to the reconquest of Granada, the one remaining Muslim state in the peninsula, which it toyed with for 120 years before crushing. Portuguese attention turned to continuing the crusade in Morocco and at sea. Strategic considerations and concern for making the venture profitable were interlocked. The conquest of Morocco was viewed as a necessary preliminary move to the reconquest of Granada, which had repeatedly received Moorish reinforcements against the Christian powers. Maritime expansion was seen as a weapon in the arsenal for the wars in Morocco. By sea the Portuguese would cut off the flow of gold into Morocco and also link up with the fabled Christian kingdom of Prester John, supposedly on the far side of Africa, to attack the Moors from the rear.

Other factors entered into the process that impelled Portugal, a marginal country in the European context, to become the first European nation to expand its territory outside the continent. There was a deeply felt religious and cultural motivation—the Portuguese gloried in their role as "standard-bearers of the Faith" and readily associated the spread of Christianity by missionary priests with the extension of Portuguese political, economic, and cultural influence. The overseas enterprise provided an outlet for the restless energy of the military aristocracy that had often before disturbed domestic tranquillity. Pursuit of personal honor—as well as fortune—and adventure was an important factor. The exploration of Africa touched on the realization of the ideals of medieval chivalry; for example, Sueno da Costa, alcaide (governor) of Lagos and a veteran of Agincourt, was knighted for his gallantry in Guinea.

Henry the Navigator

Prince Henry the Navigator (1394-1460), to whom much credit for early Portuguese exploration has gone, was not himself a scientist, nor was he well traveled, but he possessed intellectual curiosity and surrounded himself with skillful and imaginative minds at his retreat, the Vila do Infante, on the promontory of Sagres. As master of the Order of Christ, one of the crusading orders, he commanded a permanent military force and had access to substantial resources. His order paid for fitting out expeditions of which the risks outweighed the expectations of profit, and it bore the cost of their failures. Henry prodded his mariners to explore beyond Cape Bojador on the west coast of Africa, a psychological as well as physical barrier that was thought to be the outer boundary of the knowable world. In 1420 Portuguese seamen reached Madeira and by 1427 the Azores. In 1434 Gil Eanes rounded Cape Bojador and reported back to Henry that it was not the end of the world. On succeeding voyages he explored the mouth of the Gambia River and reached the Cape Verde Islands. At first the only material gains produced by the voyages were exotic animals for the market at Bruges and slaves for Henry's estates in the Algarve. The newly found Atlantic islands were settled by Portuguese after 1440, and Madeira soon developed a thriving economy based on wood and cane sugar.

Although Henry's motives were obviously many, he saw exploration primarily in terms of outflanking the Moors and contributing to the success of the conquest of Morocco. His attitudes matured over forty years, however, as his knowledge increased and he began to recognize the separate advantages of overseas expansion. The expeditions he sponsored were better planned and organized, and they began to turn a profit in gold and slaves. By midcentury Portuguese mariners had mapped twenty degrees of latitude south from Cape Bojador and had perceived the curve of the African continent.

Royal Patronage

A conflict over priorities continued to brew between the factions: the old aristocracy, led by the duke of Bragança and demanding expansion in Morocco, and commercial interests in the towns and among the lower nobility, favoring expanded trade overseas and looking to Prince Henry's older brother Dom Pedro for leadership. Pedro was made regent for his young nephew, Afonso V (reigned 1438-81). A scholar and collector of maps, the regent saw the Moroccan wars as a wasted effort and emphasized commercial expansion. In the practical matter of securing profit from exploration Pedro was more effective than his brother Henry. But Pedro's attempts to pull back from Morocco led to armed conflict within Portugal in which the regent died in 1449. An aristocratic reaction took place during the reign of Afonso V, and for a decade after Pedro's fall no further expeditions set sail, but interests revived as even the duke of Bragança saw profit in the importation of slaves from Africa. In fact the renewed wars in Morocco, championed by him, had the desired effect of rechanneling the Sudan gold trade away from North Africa to the Guinea coast, where the gold was picked up by Portuguese ships and conveyed to Europe.

Official patronage of exploration and trade was renewed under João II (reigned 1481-95), and to him belongs credit for the first comprehensive plan for overseas expansion and the idea of rounding Africa to open a new trade route to India. The crown would thereafter take its "royal fifth," or share of the profit, on all chartered commercial ventures, assume direct management of trade, and reap most of the benefits.

The Passage to India

The Portuguese conducted their expeditions in greatest secrecy. Foreign investment, except by the Genoese merchants living in Portugal, was discouraged. The advantages that Portugal derived from advanced ship design and navigational devices and maps, charts, and reports from earlier voyages were carefully guarded. In 1484 Christopher Columbus' recommendation for a westward approach to the Indies was rejected; the Portuguese had an accurate measure of the earth's circumference that had confirmed them in their commitment to finding an eastward route.

New discoveries followed hard upon one another. Between 1482 and 1484 Diogo Cão explored the mouth of the Congo and the coast of Angola and reported home that the way was clear around the southern end of Africa. With three caravels Bartolomeu Dias rounded the Cape of Good Hope in 1487—only to turn back because of the fears of his crews. The next year Pedro da Covilhão began a five-year overland trek to India and East Africa that yielded invaluable information about Asian trade routes. The Portuguese were stimulated by Spanish success in America to vindicate the eastward route, but it was another decade before Vasco da Gama rounded the cape in 1497 and sailed up the coast of Mozambique to Mombasa and from there across the Indian Ocean to the Malabar coast of India, proving the feasibility of the 10,000-mile voyage (see fig. 5).

To head off conflict between Portugal and Spain after Columbus' initial discoveries in America, the Pope's Line of 1493 was devised by Alexander VI, a Spaniard, to divide the world between the two countries, Spain having title west of a line passing near the Cape Verde Islands and Portugal to the east of it. The next year the line was redrawn in the Treaty of Tordesillas and moved more than 1,000 miles westward. Speculation persists that the Portuguese were aware of Brazil's location before Tordesillas. In 1500 Pedro Alvares da Cabral, with thirteen ships following Vasco da Gama's route to India, was reported blown off course and made landfall in Brazil—which lay on the Portuguese side of the revised line. Cabral took the discovery calmly and dispatched one vessel back to Portugal while continuing with the rest for India.

Before the arrival of the Portuguese in the Indian Ocean the South Asian spice trade had been controlled by Arabs, who marketed the goods to Venetian traders holding a monopoly in the Middle East. Military means were required to break that monopoly and assure Portugal of a place in the market. On his third voyage to India, in 1503, Vasco da Gama sailed in a convoy with an escort of fourteen warships, with which he dealt the Arabs a telling defeat. Subsequent victories in the East occurred after Vasco da Gama's and confirmed the Portuguese as the dominant power in the Indian Ocean in the early

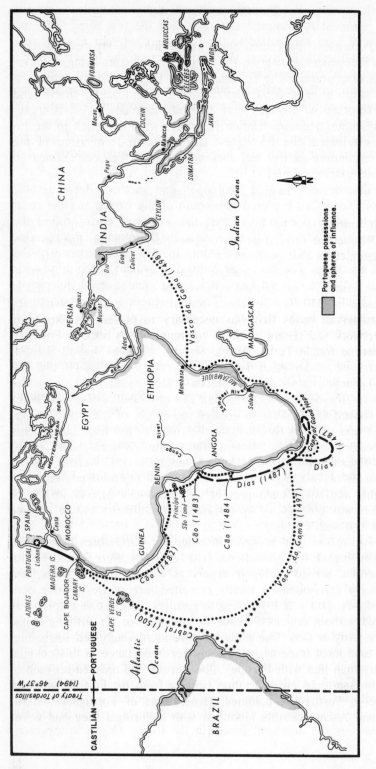

Figure 5. Portugal, the Portuguese Empire and Routes of Exploration, Fifteenth and Sixteenth Centuries

sixteenth century. Yet Portugal itself was weak militarily, a country with a rudimentary domestic economy, and the few ships and small numbers of men who sailed to the East were without hope of reinforcement from their distant homeland. Part of the answer to their success lay, of course, in technological superiority—better ships, better guns—but in those early encounters they also won a psychological advantage over their Asian adversaries with sanguine bravado. The Portuguese were dealing with societies in many ways more sophisticated than their own, but they were feared and respected, and the myth of their near invincibility helped to sustain their position in Asia after actual power to defend their interests had diminished.

Afonso d'Albuquerque

Sheer courage was not enough, however, to hold an empire. Afonso d'Albuquerque arrived as Portuguese viceroy in the East in 1509 and continued in that post until his death in battle in 1515. He was perhaps the single greatest strategic planner in the history of European imperialism. He established a center for operations in the East at Goa, taken in 1510, and set about constructing the string of military and commercial bases that was necessary to protect an expanding trade network and secure a line of communications back to Portugal. Albuquerque fought Turks, Arabs, Malays, and the Moghul Empire. He destroyed an Egyptian fleet—built by the Venetians—in the Red Sea and planned an assault on Mecca, which he intended to hold as ransom for the delivery of Jerusalem. In quick succession his forces seized Ormuz and Muscat to control the mouth of the Persian Gulf. Malacca was claimed to dominate the route to the East Indies. Stations were established in Sumatra, Timor, the Moluccas, and Ceylon. The Portuguese probed the Mekong delta and in 1513 were at Canton in China before making contact with Japan. They obtained commercial rights and later sovereignty in the enclave of Macao. A line of fortresses was constructed up the East African coast and an alliance entered into with Ethiopia.

The Portuguese held enclaves intended for warehouses rather than provinces meant for plantations. The enclaves were stocked with naval stores, served as repair depots as well as trading posts, and were thinly garrisoned by locally recruited mercenaries, native converts, slaves, and a few Portuguese regulars. The Asian empire was governed without direct reference to Portugal—or, in outlying areas, to the viceroy at Goa. The enclaves were increasingly self-sustaining, and in time local trade assumed a greater importance in this colonial economy than that with Europe. Albuquerque had ordered his men to marry in Asia, and miscegenation became from the first an accepted practice in Portuguese colonies. Generations of Portuguese, Eurasians, and Asian converts identified with a Portugal they had never seen.

RENAISSANCE PORTUGAL

João II, called the "perfect prince," was a ruthlessly efficient royal bureaucrat of the kind described by Niccolò Machiavelli. Commercial expansion overseas had altered the political balance of power within Portugal and allowed João and his successor, Manuel I (reigned 1495-1521), enriched by trade, to live on their own without need to seek subsidies or to require advice and consent from the Cortes in order to operate the government. They humbled the long-troublesome old aristocracy, which would survive only as a court-bound nobility, dependent on the crown and incapable of challenging its authority. In addition to being an astute politician Manuel was a man of taste and refinement who used Portugal's new wealth to embellish his court—art and literature, theater and architecture flourishing under his patronage within its narrow circle.

Religion

Although the crown enjoyed patronage over ecclesiastical appointments, the church was the single institution outside its absolute control, largely because of an income at least half that of the king. Portugal was not influenced by the Protestant Reformation, but it was removed from the mainstream of sixteenth-century Roman Catholicism as well. Standards of clerical discipline were low, and there was a tendency to introduce new religious orders—the Society of Jesus (Jesuits) most effective among them—rather than to attempt the rehabilitation of established ones. Parts of the Algarve and the Alentejo remained missionary areas, never properly evangelized after the Reconquest. All the more remarkable considering the condition of the church in Portugal was the prodigious effort put forth by Portuguese missionaries who planted Christianity in Brazil and in small but often fervent communities in Asia and Africa.

A small Jewish community had been protected by the crown in the days when its financial assistance was sought. In 1492 more than 50,-000 Spanish Jews were accepted as refugees on condition that they pay for their transportation out of Portugal within eight months. The price that Manuel paid for an alliance with the Spanish monarchs Ferdinand and Isabella four years later was the adoption of their policy of expelling Jews who refused to become Christians and the enactment of purity-of-blood regulations to restrict those who did: the New Christians. Much attention was paid to replanting family trees as a result. Manuel neglected to enforce his own edicts, accepted even nominal conversions as valid, and eventually removed legal disabilities against converts, but he could not abolish an insidious anti-Semitism that was expressed in popular riots against the New Christians. The Portuguese Inquisition, established by the crown in 1531 as a po-

litical instrument, turned over more than 1,000 of them to the civil arm
for burning in the sixteenth and seventeenth centuries. Many Portuguese Jews emigrated to northern Europe, particularly to the Netherlands, and New Christians were prominent in the settlement of colonial Brazil.

The Portuguese Seaborne Empire

The first half of the sixteenth century was the golden age of the
Portuguese seaborne empire built on the spice trade with the Indies.
Vasco da Gama's first voyage had turned a 600-percent profit. The
average return from the escorted convoy that set off from Lisbon
each February on the eighteen-month round trip to India doubled the
amount of the investment in it, and profits of 300 or 400 percent on
particular ventures were not uncommon. The Casa da India, established in 1503, regulated a monopoly exchanging gold from Guinea for
the spice and pepper carried to Portugal for reexport to markets
throughout Europe.

The Portuguese crown was chief proprietor of a gigantic wholesale
business, and Francis I of France was not off the mark when the
dubbed his brother monarch Manuel the "grocer king." The monopoly was operated with a relatively small amount of new investment
capital, but profits generated by trade were recycled to finance further
expeditions. The court and its bureaucracy were able to operate on a
level far beyond what Portugal's primitive economy could support.
Aristocratic investors and Lisbon's small commercial oligarchy consumed conspicuously on the income from trade. But the economic
benefits of the passage to India, the yearly voyage of the commercial
fleet, had little effect on Portuguese society outside the restricted circle of the court and the city. Surprising for the attention paid to it by
poets and chroniclers, the lore of exploration did not penetrate popular folk culture. Nor did the centrally directed state enterprise, which
shut out independent initiative, serve to create a stable middle class
as more open-ended trade did later in England and the Netherlands.

Indeed success in overseas trade had its detrimental effects. Lisbon, which unlike London and Amsterdam failed to develop its own
industry, grew too large for the hinterland to support and absorbed
more wealth than it siphoned back into the country. Rather than stimulate the domestic economy, overseas trade tended to depress it as
cheaper, more efficiently produced wares and food were purchased
abroad for the home market in exchange for colonial goods.

The success of the monopoly depended upon continuous expansion
of trade to meet demands for reinvestment and imports. Profits
dropped sharply after the middle of the sixteenth century. The volume of Madeira sugar and Asiatic spices put on the European market
drove down prices for these commodities. Lower profits called for

still greater volume, which in turn brought greater demands for investment in ships, men, and exchange goods and for protection. Coincidentally the production of gold that served as exchange declined as well.

Portugal did not have the resources to sustain commercial activity at the pitch of the later fifteenth and early sixteenth centuries or to meet increasing demands on the Casa da India for investment and defense. Vasco da Gama had counseled contraction as early as 1522. Portugal could not build ships fast enough to meet the needs of increased competition or replace vessels lost at sea. The quality of its maritime technology was eroded. By 1560 the Casa da India was bankrupt; the monopoly could not meet its debts and was forced to turn to foreign investors to bail it out, requiring an increasing share of spice trade profits to be distributed outside the country.

The demographic effects of the passage to India on the Portuguese population is an issue for debate. The number engaged in trade overseas was never large at any one time. Never more than 40,000 men were stationed abroad as merchants, soldiers, and administrators. An average of 2,500 Portuguese shipped out each year during the sixteenth century, however, drawn from a country with a population of approximately 1.5 million in 1600, and the rate of attrition among them has been estimated at as much as one-third. From whatever cause, the competency of Portuguese leadership in the East was reduced during the course of the century.

Sebastião (reigned 1557-78) was the sole surviving heir of João III (reigned 1521-57), whom he succeeded at the age of three. Unintelligent and fanatical in his maturity, he launched a campaign in Morocco, where Moorish counterattacks had reduced Portuguese holdings. His 14,000 ill-equipped troops were overwhelmed at Alcázarquivir and destroyed. Sebastião was presumed killed in battle with large numbers of the nobility. More were captured and held for ransom, draining noble households of their substance and of potential investment capital. The natural leadership was depleted, the treasury emptied, and the government at a standstill during the brief interim reign of Sebastião's uncle, the aged Cardinal Henrique (reigned 1578-80).

Habsburg Portugal

The royal House of Aviz died with Henrique. Philip II of Spain (reigned 1580-96 in Portugal as Felipe I) had a better claim to Portugal than any of the several other possible candidates. His first wife and his mother were daughters of kings of Portugal. The master of the greatest military machine and naval power in Europe, he was also the strongest candidate in terms of enforcing his claim. Resistance was slight, and Philip's title was duly recognized by the Portuguese Cortes.

The succession of a Spanish Habsburg king had been anticipated for some years since it became obvious that Sebastião lacked the inclination to perpetuate his dynasty. The union of the Hispanic crowns —Portugal, Castile, and Aragon—had been promoted for generations by dynastic marriages. For a few years at the end of the fifteenth century Portugal and Spain had shared an heir apparent. A carefully negotiated scheme to link Castile with Portugal by the marriage of Isabella of Castile to Afonso V (reigned 1438-81) had been wrecked when she chose instead his rival, Ferdinand of Aragon, and set the course of modern Spanish history.

Philip II inherited several crowns in Spain, Italy, and the Netherlands from his father, the Holy Roman emperor Charles V, and the addition of Portugal fit comfortably into the federal structure of the Spanish Habsburg empire, in which several kingdoms, each retaining its own separate institutions, recognized one king. Contrary to the opinion put forth in some nationalist histories, Portugal was not annexed to Spain and did not lose its independence, nor was it an occupied country during sixty years (1580-1640) under three Habsburg kings. In Portugal Philip II and his successors ruled as kings of Portugal. The government and the Cortes, courts, laws, local customs, and currency remained Portuguese. Taxes were collected by Portuguese for use in Portugal. Portuguese troops manned the garrisons. The colonies were under Portuguese administration, the church under Portuguese bishops. Indeed Portuguese held positions throughout the Habsburg empire out of proportion to their numbers. The Council of Portugal sat in regular attendance on the Habsburg kings wherever they made their capital to advise on Portuguese affairs. For two years (1581-83) Philip II made Lisbon his capital, and in later years it was not Spanish oppression that his Portuguese subjects complained but rather neglect by a distant king.

Union was beneficial economically because it gave Portuguese commerce access to Spanish colonies. Wealthy Portuguese gravitated toward Madrid, and New Christians were frequently employed as tax collectors in Castile. For years before union the economies of the two countries had been intermeshed, and the Portuguese had depended on Spanish-American silver for trade exchange. The Portuguese court had used the language and etiquette of Castile since the fifteenth century, and much serious work had been done in Castilian by Portuguese writers conscious of belonging to a common Hispanic culture.

There was, however, a current of resistance among the masses in the countryside that took form in a messianic cult of the "hidden prince," Sebastião, who they believed did not die in battle but would return again and somehow right all wrongs. Practically Sebastianism has been explained as symptomatic of deep-seated social unrest among tenants exploited by landholders who approved of the Habsburgs and as a demonstration of hostility directed at all forms of authority. Several so-called false Sebastians surfaced in Portugal to claim the throne with the backing of this popular sentiment. Some scholars have seen the origin of the cult in New Christian fears of persecution by the Inquisition. Others have pointed out that nostalgic longing for the unattainable is at the basis of much of Portuguese art and literature or have seen it as a continuing feature of Portuguese political life.

More concrete political and economic causes for the dissolution of the dynastic union can be found in the demands made on Portugal as part of the larger Habsburg empire deeply engaged in European religious and dynastic wars. Portugal was inevitably involved in these wars, for which the Portuguese had little sympathy, and its colonies were exposed to attack by Spain's enemies. The Dutch pounced on Portuguese holdings throughout the East: Ceylon, Malacca, and numerous East Indian islands fell to them, as did the depots in Angola and a large part of Brazil. The Habsburg kings of Portugal were helpless to defend the Portuguese empire.

With Spain at war across Europe and the burden borne almost entirely by Castile, the count-duke of Olivares, chief minister to Philip IV (reigned 1621-40 in Portugal as Felipe III), contrived in the 1630s to give greater direction to the Hispanic states, pooling their resources, integrating their administration, and exploiting untapped manpower. Catalonia rebelled in protest in 1640, and Portugal followed suit when required to assist Philip IV against the Catalans.

João IV (reigned 1640-58), duke of Bragança and nominal commander of the Portuguese forces ordered to Catalonia, reluctantly placed himself at the disposal of his country when called upon by some of the nobility to be king. The move was popular in the countryside, in Brazil, and in the urban merchant community. João IV also had the powerful backing of the Jesuits, who offset the influence of the pro-Habsburg hierarchy. The break with Spain was, however, as much a civil war as it was a revolution.

It was argued that throwing off the Spanish connection would mean peace with Spain's enemies and save the Portuguese empire from destruction at their hands. In fact the Dutch returned nothing they had taken but took more territory after 1640 and demanded concessions in return for support against Spain. Spain did not have the resources to press its cause against the Portuguese, who rated low among Spain's priorities, but neither could the Braganças force recognition of their claim on the Habsburgs. Only in 1668 was peace made between them.

Portugal for its part had chosen to protect its overseas empire rather than participate in a common Hispanic nationhood. Some historians have argued that the choice condemned Portugal to be a small, underdeveloped country dependent on England for survival.

THE HOUSE OF BRAGANCA
(SEVENTEENTH AND EIGHTEENTH CENTURIES)

The House of Bragança was an illegitimate line of the royal family of Aviz and dated from the early fifteenth century. Its dukes had been leaders of the Portuguese aristocracy, and their wealth and holdings in land equaled those of the crown. João IV, who was essentially a businessman in outlook, had profitable interests in the Azores and Brazil and at one point had considered selling Portugal back to the king of Spain. His son Afonso VI (reigned 1656-67) was a degenerate whose brother, Pedro II (reigned 1682-1706), seized control of the government and imprisoned Afonso in 1667 with the aid of the king's wife. He ruled as regent until Afonso's death and then in his own right. Pedro introduced absolutist rule into Portugal after the pattern set by Louis XIV in France, and the Cortes ceased to meet after 1697.

Imperial Development

Despite the losses suffered during the Habsburg period Portugal at the end of the seventeenth century was the pivot of a still-huge empire—in effect, three empires—that focused political concern and commercial interests on Asia, Africa, and Brazil. The reduced Asian holdings were an emporium for commodities ranging from tea and spice to silk and gems, but they had lost their primacy in Portuguese planning. Goa remained an administrative center, the seat of a viceroy, for Portuguese interests in the East Indies and East Africa. Even when Portugal had lost political control of an area, it retained commercial influence; and Portuguese continued to function as the common language of commerce in much of that area. Portuguese Goans had risen to prominence in Mozambique, where traders had settled in the Zambesi region as early as the mid-sixteenth century. They came expecting to find gold but stayed to exploit the fertile soil in an area whose control was contested by rival native tribes. Commanding slave armies, the *prazeiros* (Portuguese overlords) displaced tribal chiefs, assumed their titles and dominion over the tribes, and eventually married into tribal royal families. They kept their Portuguese identity, but political connections with the mother country were tenuous.

In search of the reputed River of Gold in the fifteenth and sixteenth centuries the Portuguese had established a chain of fortresses and depots on the coast of West Africa that through the seventeenth century yielded not only gold but slaves and ivory as well. Alliances formed with African kingdoms included a military pact with Benin, to which the Portuguese supplied troops and arms, and a benevolent protectorate over the kingdom of Congo, whose Christian rulers emulated Portuguese styles at their court.

Angola was first settled in 1575 and organized under seigneurial proprietors licensed by the crown to take title to large tracts of territory that were administered through their deputies, the captains major, in Africa. Attacks by tribal kings against the weak Portuguese footholds along the coast prompted the crown to take direct charge of the colony in 1590 to protect the growing slave trade to Brazil and to Portugal itself, where at one point in the seventeenth century Africans accounted for 10 percent of the population of Lisbon.

The center of gravity of Portuguese colonial interests shifted decisively to Brazil, where the expansion of the coffee-growing plantation economy compensated for losses in Asia. Originally organized as proprietary seigneuries, the Brazilian provinces were converted into crown colonies in the course of the seventeenth century. Brazil played an increasingly important part in domestic political considerations, and Portuguese foreign policy was geared to strengthening the colony's links with the mother country. After the crown's failure to protect them from Dutch incursions, Brazilians became the most vocal opponents of the Spanish connection. It was the settlers themselves who drove the Dutch from the colony in 1654 and recaptured the slave-trading stations in Angola. Because of the discovery of gold in Brazil in 1687 Portugal became in fact the dependent parent of her colonial offspring.

Anglo-Portuguese Relations

João IV had renewed the Anglo-Portuguese alliance during the long stalemate with Spain, and Oliver Cromwell had exacted trade concessions as the price for England's support. The marriage of a Portuguese princess, Catherine of Bragança, to the English king Charles II in 1661 added prestige to the fledgling royal house, and English troops served in Portugal against the Spanish, participating at the decisive battle of Vila Viçosa in 1665. England sheltered the rich but vulnerable Portuguese empire but took in return a mortgage on its economy.

Portugal's domestic economy had been static since the fifteenth century. Crop production never kept pace with the increase in population and, though an agricultural country, Portugal was an importer of grain. No serious attempt was made to organize domestic industries until 1670, when one of the periodic depressions in colonial trade deprived Portugal of the means to pay for manufactured imports. The first effort at industrial development lapsed when colonial trade perked up after 1690.

It was Brazil's apparently bottomless wealth in gold and later in diamonds that assured Portugal of the means to pay for imports and destroyed for several generations the initiative for development at home. Brazilian gold also encouraged England to update its commercial relations with Portugal. The Methuen Treaty (1703) allowed the Portuguese a preferential duty on wine exported to England in return for which Portugal removed restrictions on the importation of English-made goods. The Portuguese market was soon absorbing 10 percent of the English export trade, representing an increase of 120 percent above the quantity of goods imported by Portugal before the treaty. Portuguese exports to England, mainly wine shipped through English merchants at Porto, rose by less than 40 percent. Gold brought in from Brazil went to redressing the balance of Anglo-Portuguese trade. The upswing in state revenues from gold—like that 200 years before from spice—also financed Portugal's baroque flowering in the early eighteenth century (see ch. 7).

Pombal

Eighteenth-century Portuguese government was a highly centralized bureaucracy managed by ministers responsible to the king and exercising as much power as he saw fit to allow them. João V (reigned 1706-50) had been an energetic king until the last years of his reign when he sank into melancholy and turned over his government to ecclesiastical advisers who were not up to the task. His successor, José (reigned 1750-77), was indolent, eager to reign but not to bear the burden of ruling his country and empire. He put direction of his government in the hands of a diplomat, Sebastião José de Carvalho e Melo (1699-1782), later marquis of Pombal, a man of genius and energy at once remarkable for his accomplishments and controversial for the methods he used to achieve them. Pombal became the veritable dictator of Portugal, using the absolute authority of the crown without check and operating the most authoritarian regime known in eighteenth-century Europe.

On November 1, 1755, the feast of All Saints, Lisbon was destroyed by an earthquake, followed by fire and a tidal wave, that killed 60,000 and shook the confidence of "Enlightened" Europe. The direction that Pombal gave in the aftermath of the disaster—"Bury the dead and relieve the living"—brought him to prominence.

Pombal took charge of rebuilding the city. He also undertook the restructuring of state administration to deal with Portugal's recurrent economic problems, stimulating industry—in the face of British opposition—to overcome another trade slump and regulating the export of gold and the production of wine to keep up price levels. Portugal paid a price for the rational government that Pombal sought to give through enlightened despotism. Opponents of his regime were arrested, tortured, and some executed. It was a token of his confidence in his own power that Pombal turned to challenge the position of the church, which had retained a degree of independence from state control and which Pombal despised for its opposition to his reforms. He initiated official anticlericalism in Portugal, intervening in ecclesiastical affairs, confiscating church property, and expelling the Jesuits.

With King José's death Pombal's dictatorship was dismantled as quickly as it had been built. The restrictive monopolies that he had sponsored were suspended, allowing the growth of a class of independent merchants who brought relative prosperity to the country at the end of the century and permitted the Old Regime in Portugal to pass through the revolutionary 1790s unscathed.

The Peninsular War

Portugal resisted participating in the continental blockade imposed in 1804 by Napoleon Bonaparte against importation of British goods. For a short time in 1807 Portugal was occupied by French troops, Napoleon claiming that he had sent an army to liberate the Portuguese people from British economic domination. The royal family —Maria I (reigned 1777-1816) and her son João VI (reigned 1816-34), who acted as regent during her long mental illness that began in 1799 —took refuge in Brazil, where a government-in-exile was established under British protection. A British expeditionary force under Arthur Wellesley, duke of Wellington, compelled a French withdrawal from Portugal and repelled two subsequent invasions. Wellington used Portugal as a base of operations for the offensive that drove the French from Spain in 1813. The Portuguese army was reorganized during the war under British tutelage and put under the command of William Carr Beresford, one of Wellington's officers, who remained in Portugal as regent in the absence of the royal family.

THE CONSTITUTIONAL MONARCHY (1822-1910)

The war passed from Portugal, but the royal family stayed in Brazil, which in 1815 was the political center of the so-called United Kingdom of Portugal, Brazil, and the Algarve. In 1816 João VI succeeded to the Portuguese throne—in Rio de Janeiro.

In Portugal itself discontent at Beresford's regency, the absence of the king, and the country's diminished status in the empire was expressed by the small middle-class intelligentsia and commercial oligarchy, who were identified as liberals and called for constitutional government. The officer corps, which had gained self-esteem during the war, also demanded a larger role in national life. Both groups had confidence that a constitution and a responsible parliamentary government were the remedies needed for curing the country's economic and social ills. Although they wanted to emulate Great Britain's political example, they chafed at the influence exerted by the British in

Brazil. It was the army, however, that took the lead in 1820 by demanding the reestablishment of the Cortes and the writing of a constitution. What followed were years of experimentation with constitutions, a succession of attempts to provide stable government, and repeated foreign intervention in Portuguese affairs.

The 1822 Constitution, written by a Cortes composed mainly of civil servants, academics, and army officers, called for strong central government, a limited monarchy, and ministerial responsibility to a unicameral legislature elected by literate males. João VI, accepting his status as a constitutional monarch in Portugal, returned from Brazil, leaving his heir Dom Pedro behind as co-king. The Cortes was willing to accept representatives from Brazil but would not concede autonomous status within an imperial framework. Having won the fight for a parliament vested with executive authority, the Portuguese liberals did not believe that they could relinquish any sovereignty without compromising the sum of it. More representative of commercial interests than its predecessor, the first Cortes elected under the new constitution attempted to reassert Lisbon's economic control over Brazil. With British support Pedro declared Brazil an independent state and took the title of emperor, but he remained heir to the Portuguese throne.

Opinion was polarized in Portugal in reaction to the loss of Brazil. Politically aware moderates were caught between those who gravitated toward the militantly anticlerical radicals, who demanded a continuing political revolution, and the traditionalists, who were allied with the church and hostile to the drift in affairs under the rule of an urban, middle-class Cortes. Traditionalist juntas, supported by smallholders and peasants, were formed in the north to protect the communal liberties threatened by the liberal central government. Calling for a return to absolutism, the traditionalists found a champion in Dom Miguel, younger son of João VI, who was seen to exult in martial, rural, and Catholic virtues.

If the new emperor of Brazil chose to remain in America, his brother Miguel would succeed their father in Portugal, and there was no doubt that Pedro preferred Brazil. When João VI died in 1826, Pedro reluctantly returned to Portugal, pressured by the British to leave his prosperous Brazilian empire for an impoverished country with an unstable constitutional regime. Backed by the army, which was easily disenchanted by civilian rule, Pedro demanded an accommodation from the liberal Cortes in the form of the compromise Charter of 1826, which replaced the 1822 Constitution and remained substantially in force until 1910. The charter returned executive authority to the king, who governed through a ministry responsible to him. It provided for a bicameral Cortes, consisting of the Chamber of Deputies, elected indirectly by a reduced electorate, and an upper house appointed by the crown.

After the charter was adopted, Pedro returned to Brazil, leaving title to the Portuguese throne to his young daughter Maria da Gloria, later Maria II (reigned 1834-54). Miguel was to act as regent on condition that he accept the new constitution. Miguel duly swore to abide by the settlement, was given command of the army, and promptly seized power, abolished the charter, and appointed an absolutist government that offered him the Portuguese crown.

There had been little resistance to Miguel, but Pedro abdicated his Brazilian throne and recrossed the Atlantic determined to restore the charter and remain in Portugal as constitutional monarch. Leading an expeditionary force from the Azores, where he had established a provisional government, Pedro landed near Porto in 1832 and defeated Miguel with substantial British assistance in a two-year-long civil war that pitted liberals against traditionalists.

The church had overwhelmingly supported Miguel. The government under Mosinho da Silveira, which carried on the regency for Maria II after her father died, purged the hierarchy and abolished the religious orders, about one-third of Portugal's 30,000 clergy. In 1834 the government ordered the expropriation of church property. Intended to raise funds to pay the debt of the civil war, the lands and buildings of 500 religious houses were sold at auction at prices below their market value to approximately 600 new owners who used government credits to make their purchases. The sale of church property resulted in a shift in the ownership of more than one-fourth of all land and created a new class—wealthy landholders who were drawn from the ranks of the liberal political oligarchy and were indebted to the policies of the constitutional monarchy for their position. This group had the dominant influence in the political life of the country throughout the rest of the nineteenth century. Meanwhile local administration was restructured around regional urban centers to increase the power of the liberal urban middle class against that of more conservative small-holders in the countryside.

The Liberal Oligarchy

Anticlericalism, economic freedom achieved through unregulated trade, and an overweening confidence that national honor could be restored through constitutional government were the chief tenets of Portuguese liberalism in the nineteenth century. In reality the governments that it supported came to office through manipulated elections. Revolts by an activist army divided in its political sympathies were regular occurrences. British and French intervention was required to forestall civil war and protect investments. Despite anticlerical legislation the country remained officially Roman Catholic, and royal patronage in nominating bishops was confirmed in a succession of concordats with Rome. The Cortes was representative of a social and economic elite, middle class in its origins, that was determined to retain its position by restricting suffrage. One percent of the population was enfranchised. Property qualifications for candidates limited to 4,500 the number eligible to sit in the Chamber of Deputies. From the Senate, or upper house of the Cortes, a new bourgeois aristocracy emerged, the product of an inflation of titles to encompass the wealthiest of the elite.

Parliamentary politics consisted of working out personal rivalries within the liberal oligarchy. Large working majorities set the stage for arbitrary government by successive liberal ministries that interpreted constitutional guarantees very flexibly. Opposition to the oligarchy was centered in Porto, where the demand for a broader electorate and decentralization was strongest from the industrial—as distinct from commercial and landholding—sector of middle-class opinion. By 1836 a national movement known as the Septembrists had developed around the issue and had entered into loose and unruly coalitions with both radicals and traditionalists, as the disparate extremes of the political spectrum challenged—ineffectively—the entrenched and static center.

An artifical two-party system developed in the Cortes by midcentury. The parties—the Regenerators somewhat the more conservative, the Progressives somewhat the more liberal—agreed on policies and political tactics. Shared patronage was the most cohesive force in keeping the party system functioning. After 1856 the practice of alternating parties in power at regular intervals, called rotativism in Portugal, was all but institutionalized. Because political power was concentrated in so small a group of like-minded men, compromises were easily struck, and reformist factions were quickly absorbed by the established parties. Rotativism produced relatively stable governments that nonetheless failed to come to grips with Portugal's underlying social and economic problems. On the whole, successive governments introduced constructive programs that failed in execution.

Portugal lacked the domestic capital, skilled labor, technology, and raw materials that were necessary for its economy to be industrialized. Up to 80 percent of the country's trade involved reexport of colonial goods. Domestically produced exports were largely confined to fortified wine, olive oil, salt, nuts, and cork. Changes in landholding after 1834 had no effect on the level of agricultural production. Half the state income went to service the debt owed to foreign creditors. Perpetual deficits and defaults in meeting payments brought chronic financial panics. The threat of defaults discouraged long-term investment in Portugal, and speculative investment—much of it from Brazil—caused periodic overheating of the economy and destabilized the currency. Dependent on outside investment, public works projects designed to stimulate the economy led the country deeper into debt. Banking prospered from financing wholesale commerce, but reinvested profits usually went into secure development abroad rather than to Portuguese industry or agriculture.

Despite chronic economic problems later nineteenth-century politics was remarkably free from radical pressures. Socialism and republicanism had little appeal among a people so overwhelmingly depoliticized and untouched by events abroad. The royal family was respected and admired for reflecting the virtues of the liberal oligarchy, and the crown exercised considerable political influence within the framework of the constitution.

Portuguese Africa

The shift to African development after the loss of Brazil was not immediate. In 1826 everyone who had been born in the Portuguese dominions was in theory granted citizenship. It was not until 1836, however, that the legal trade in slaves was halted under pressure from the British government, a measure enforced by the Royal Navy. In fact, except in the coastal areas Lisbon had little control of the territory that it claimed. The development of Mozambique and the port of Lourenço Marques in the 1870s coincided with the opening of the Suez Canal and the establishment of the landlocked Boer republics in South Africa. Mineral deposits in Mozambique were exploited with British financing. The sharpest spur to development, however, was the threat of losing the colonies. The European powers gathered at the Berlin Conference in 1885 had decreed that legitimate title to colonial possessions was determined by "effective occupation." Under that definition Portugal lost its claim to the Congo region, where it had had contacts since the sixteenth century, to Belgium. From the 1870s Portuguese expeditions into the interior, led by the explorer Serpa Pinto and others, crisscrossed the width of southern Africa, and between 1885 and 1935 Portugal won recognition of its sovereignty over 800,000 square miles of territory.

It was the publication of the so-called rose-colored map *(mapa côr de rosa),* showing a Portuguese African empire that stretched overland connecting the Indian and the Atlantic oceans, that led to a serious confrontation with Great Britain (see fig. 6). Based on the Portuguese cross-continental expeditions, it conflicted with Cecil Rhodes' designs to bring the Cape-to-Cairo railroad through a central Africa that was under the British flag. The Portuguese government abjectly acquiesced in a British ultimatum in 1890 and withdrew many of the claims made on the rose-colored map. Pressure resulting from the Boer War (1899-1901) and German colonial expansion subsequently prompted the British to assure the integrity of Portuguese Africa by treaty.

46

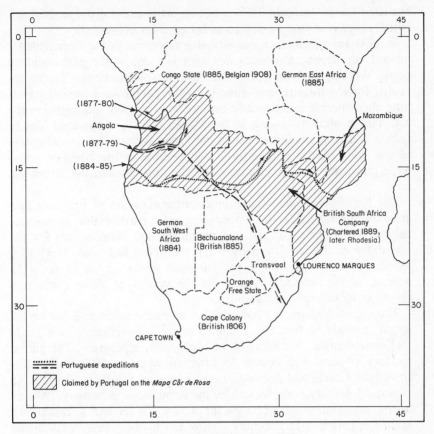

Figure 6. Southern Africa about 1890

João Franco

The year 1890 was a watershed in Portuguese political history. It marked the beginning of a growth in political awareness that contributed to the downfall of the monarchy twenty years later. The government's retreat in the face of the British ultimatum was denounced roundly by the Republicans, who were organized as a political party in 1878. The Republicans' strongest appeal was to nationalism. Portugal, they argued, would never be honored in the world as once it had been until an outworn constitutional monarchy was replaced by a modern democratic republic. Republican propaganda played on fears of Portugal's becoming a British colony or a province of Spain.

The government reacted to the drive for broader suffrage by revising the electoral law in 1896 in order to eliminate minor parties from the Cortes. The king's hand was also strengthened to permit him greater latitude in appointing ministers and dissolving the parliament, but King Carlos (reigned 1889-1908), an artist and a distinguished scientist, refused to rule by decree as his advisers insisted.

In 1900 João Franco, a conservative reformist in the Cortes, led a minority of Regenerator delegates with him out of the parliamentary party. Working to reinvigorate parliamentary institutions, Franco appealed for electoral reform directly to the people—a new and unsettling phenomenon in a depoliticized society. In 1906, although Franco had only a small following in the Cortes, Carlos summoned him to form a coalition government with the Progressives. The unwillingness of one wing of the Progressives to cooperate in the coalition splintered that party just as Franco's defection had broken the Regenerators.

The Republicans were the immediate beneficiaries of Franco's program as prime minister to encourage greater participation in political debate. They turned on the well-meaning king, blaming him for the corruption of the political parties that rotativism had made inevitable. Demands were made for a parliamentary investigation of royal finances, as the monarchy was made the symbol of all that was perceived to be wrong in the country.

The established parties had become so badly splintered that no alternative could be found to Franco's minority government, nor could the prime minister win approval of his legislative program. The parliamentary process had ceased to function when in 1907 Carlos dissolved the Cortes and granted Franco authority to rule by decree. An attempted military coup backed by the Republican in January 1908 led to the cancellation of elections for a new Cortes and a crackdown against opposition. In February Carlos and his heir were assassinated in Lisbon, leaving the eighteen-year-old Manuel II (reigned 1908-10) as king. Manuel could rely only on Franco, against whom all parties were ranged. In an effort to save the young king, Franco called for an election and stepped down as prime minister.

THE PARLIAMENTARY REPUBLIC (1910-26)

The Republicans became the party of urban, middle-class radicalism, nationalistic, libertarian, and intensely anticlerical in temper. Their active ranks included a high proportion of journalists, and the publicity received by the party in the press was out of proportion to its actual size. Republican candidates in the 1908 and 1910 parliamentary elections got a small vote—and that localized in Lisbon—but factionalism prevented the established monarchist parties from forming a stable government capable of resisting them. (Six governments fell during the period between the two elections.)

In October 1910 troops in Lisbon refused to put down a mutiny aboard two warships, and some went over to the dissidents. With no one in a position of authority willing to take charge of the situation and his appeals for advice left unanswered, Manuel II fled with the royal family to exile in England. A provisional government was formed by the Republicans under the presidency of the historian Teófilo Braga and the political direction of Afonso Costa.

The 1911 Constitution

The 1911 Constitution, which formally inaugurated the Portuguese Republic, provided for a parliamentary system of government with executive authority vested in the cabinet and a president, chosen by the parliament, as nominal head of state. It guaranteed individual civil rights and, on paper, provided the basis for the creation of an egalitarian society. Three major parties emerged from the republic's first Cortes: Costa's Democrats, radical and uncompromisingly anticlerical, and moderate parties of the center (Unionists) and the right (Evolutionists), both satisfied with the abolition of the monarchy, intent on reconciling a divided country, and anxious to maintain order.

In 1913 the Democrats formed their first government. Costa, as prime minister, introduced legislation that reduced the electorate by more than half from 850,000 to 400,000, by eliminating illiterates from the voting rolls. Many of those cut were conservative smallholders who had opposed the Democrats at the polls. Costa's party then held a dominant position in the Cortes, except during a short period, for the life of the republic.

World War I

In 1916 Costa brought Portugal into World War I on the side of the Allies, arguing that a German victory would mean loss of the African colonies even if Portugal remained neutral. The expeditionary force that arrived in Flanders in early 1917 eventually numbered 40,000 men in two divisions. The Portuguese suffered heavy casualties defending the Lys sector during the German spring offensive in 1918. Troops were sent to Mozambique to join in the fruitless pursuit of General Paul von Letvow-Vorbeck's German East African colonial army.

There was a genuine lack of enthusiasm for the war. Poor harvests and the war's drain on already meager stocks of supplies caused food shortages and inflation at home. Leftist army and navy units, inspired by the Bolsheviks in Russia, staged mutinies. In reaction a parliamentary coup staged by the center and right and backed by the military succeeded in overthrowing Costa's government in December 1917.

A new government was formed under Sidónio Pais, a diplomat known for his pro-German sympathies. Pais was the republic's first leader to command mass popular backing, and his proposed New Republic with a strong presidential system was approved by plebiscite in May 1918. The opposition, anticipating defeat, abstained.

Pais' New Republic did not find the cure for Portugal's political instability. The National Republicans, a fusion party formed by Pais, won an absolute majority in the new Cortes but immediately fell into factionalism. With universal male suffrage—including illiterates—in effect, the Monarchists, opposed to any republic, won a significant (25 percent) bloc of seats. A wave of terrorism swept the country as extremists took to the streets and troops protested being sent to the front. Pais was murdered in a train station in December by an assassin without any apparent political motivation. Amidst armed anarchist, Bolshevik, and monarchist risings there was a clamor in the leaderless country for a dictatorship. The Cortes restored the 1911 Constitution, however, and in parliamentary elections in 1919 the Democrats regained their majority.

The Republican Record

Machine politics and tinkering with election laws kept the Democrats in power for seven more years but, although they were by far the strongest political party, they were too torn by factionalism to sustain a government in office. The war had had a profoundly unsettling effect on republican institutions. The war debt was insurmountable, and the Versailles Conference, at which Costa had been the Portuguese representative, allotted Portugal only a fraction of 1 percent of German reparations and, in contrast to other combatants, no territory. Successive governments in the early 1920s put forward no comprehensive programs for fiscal and economic recovery. A smaller proportion of the population was enfranchised under the parliamentary republic than during the constitutional monarchy. Total disillusionment with constitutional processes and a quick resort to armed protest against election results usually accompanied defeats at the polls. Military intervention in politics increased, and about half the prime ministers after 1919 came from the armed forces.

The republic never satisfactorily resolved its dispute with the church, against which some of the earliest legislation after 1910 had been directed. Church property was seized, religious orders were once again abolished, and bishops were exiled. Religious observances were discouraged, and a program was launched to wean clergy from their vocations. Churchmen were deprived of the civil and political rights guaranteed by the 1911 Constitution. The church lost its educational and social work facilities. Endowments and contributions were diverted to state-run charities. Official anticlericalism made it impossible for many to accept the republic. It also stimulated the development of a politically involved Catholic intelligentsia in opposition to the parliamentary regime. The apparitions at Fatima in 1917 occurred at the height of Costa's anticlerical campaign and fueled Catholic resentment of it (see ch. 6). There were definite signs in the early 1920s that even the Democrats had seen the political wisdom of coming to terms with Catholic sensitivities.

The pressure of high taxes and inflation on a frightened middle class and a military coup at Braga in June 1926 brought down the parliamentary republic. It had produced, in the words of an economics professor from Coimbra, António de Oliveira Salazar, "government without purpose." Since 1910 there had been seven general elections, forty-five governments—twenty of which resigned after votes of no confidence—eight presidential elections, seven presidents, and eighteen military coups.

SALAZAR AND THE NEW STATE (1926-74)

The right-wing officers' coup that brought down the parliamentary regime in 1926 had been popular. Nothing but a military government seemed likely to survive in Portugal in the short run. A gradual institutional transition to an authoritarian republic was envisaged, and for the time being politics was to be kept out of government in order to allow it to get on with the business of restoring order and reviving the economy. Revolts by leftists only consolidated the military hold on the country. Opponents of the coup, including a number of armed forces officers, were imprisoned or exiled. After some shifting about for a likely candidate, General António Oscar de Fragoso Carmona was named president and held that office until his death in 1951.

The new military government recognized that the most pressing problems confronting it were economic. Salazar (1889-1970), a university professor and leading conservative economist, was brought into the cabinet as minister of finance, but he resigned when not allowed free rein to manage the economy. In 1928 he was recalled to office on his own terms and given the power of veto over all fiscal matters. Salazar made himself indispensable and by 1930 was recognized as the most powerful figure in the government. In 1932 he was named prime minister and introduced a civilian government.

Salazar came from a peasant background. He had studied for the priesthood before turning to economics at Coimbra University, where he earned a reputation as a scholar and writer as well as a leader in Catholic intellectual and political movements. He retained his professorial style as prime minister, lecturing his cabinet, his political followers, and the nation. Austere and ascetic in his tastes, he was a skillful political manipulator with a capacity for ruthlessness who was a respected rather than a popular public figure.

The New State

The period of transition to the authoritarian republic promised after the military takeover in 1926 was brought to an end by the adoption of the 1933 Constitution dictated by Salazar that created the New State (Estado Novo), in theory a corporate state representative of interest groups rather than of individuals. The constitution provided for a president directly elected for a seven-year term and a prime minister appointed by and responsible to the president. The relation of the office of prime minister to the presidency was an ambiguous one. Salazar, continuing as prime minister, was head of government; exercised executive and legislative functions; controlled local administration, police, and patronage; and was leader of the National Union, an umbrella group for supporters of the regime and the only legal political organization.

A legislature, the National Assembly, restricted to members of the National Union, could initiate legislation but only concerning matters that did not require government expenditures. The parallel Corporative Chamber included representatives of cultural and professional groups and of the official workers' syndicates that replaced free trade unions.

Women were given the vote for the first time, but literacy and property qualifications held the enfranchised segment of the population to about 20 percent, a greater percentage than under the parliamentary regime. Elections were held regularly, without opposition.

In 1945 Salazar introduced so-called democratic measures, including an amnesty for political prisoners and a loosening of censorship, that were believed by liberals to represent a move toward democratic government. In the parliamentary elections that year the opposition formed the broadly based Movement of National Unity, which brought democrats together with fascists and communists. The opposition withdrew before the election, however, charging that the government intended to manipulate votes. A candidate opposing Carmona in the 1949 presidential election pulled out on the same grounds. In 1958 the eccentric General Humberto Delgado ran against the official candidate, Admiral Américo Tomás, representing the National Union. Delgado pointedly campaigned on the issue of replacing Salazar and won 25 percent of the vote. After the election, rules were altered to provide for the legislature to choose the president.

Salazar's was a low-keyed personalist rule. The New State was his and not a forum for a party or ideology. Although intensely patriotic he was cynical about a Portuguese national character that made the people easy prey for demagogues. He avoided opportunities to politicize public life and appeared uncomfortable with the political groups that were eventually introduced to mobilize opinion on the side of the regime's policies. Politics in Salazar's Portugal consisted of balancing power blocs within the country—the military, business and commerce, landholders, colonial interests, and the church. All political parties were banned. The National Union, officially a civic association, encouraged public apathy rather than political involvement. Its leadership was composed of a small political and commercial elite, and contacts within ruling circles were usually made on an informal, personal basis rather than through official channels. Within the circle it was possible to discuss and criticize policy, but there were no channels for expression outside it.

The National Union had no guiding philosophy apart from support for Salazar. The tenets of the regime were said to be authoritarian government, patriotic unity, Christian morality, and the work ethic and, despite a great deal of deference paid to the theory of the corporate state, this was essentially the extent of the regime's ideological content. Although the regime indulged in rallies and youth movements with the trappings of fascist salutes and paraphernalia, it was satisfied to direct public enthusiasm into "fado, Fatima, and football"—music, religion, and sports.

A devout Catholic, Salazar sought a rapprochement with the church in Portugal. A concordat with the Vatican in 1940 reintroduced state aid to Catholic education, but Salazar resisted involving the church—which he called "the great source of our national life"—in political questions. His policies were aimed essentially at healing the divisions caused within Portuguese society by generations of anticlericalism. Although the church had consistently supported Salazar, the regime came under increasing criticism by progressive elements in the clergy in the 1960s. One such incident led to the expulsion of the bishop of Porto.

Fiscal Policy

Whatever may be said of his political methods, Salazar had an exceptional grasp of the techniques of fiscal management and, within the limits that he had set for the regime, his program of economic recovery succeeded. Portugal's overriding problem in 1926 had been its enormous public debt. Salazar's solution was to achieve financial solvency by balancing the national budget and reducing external debt. This required the action of a strong government capable of cutting public expenditures and reducing domestic consumption by raising taxes and controlling credit and trade. What Salazar singlemindedly accomplished in a few years was a solvent currency, a favorable balance of trade, and surpluses both in foreign reserves and in the national budget, but the bulk of the Portuguese people remained among the poorest in Europe.

The austerity that Salazar's fiscal and economic policies demanded lay most heavily on the working class and the rural poor, forestalling the development, his critics argued, that would raise their standards of living. Outside the cities there was little alteration in traditional patterns of life, especially in the conservative north, which had been stabilized by evenly distributed poverty and was a stronghold of support for the regime. To create an atmosphere of rising expectations without having the means to satisfy them, Salazar argued, would return the country to the chaotic conditions Portugal had known earlier in the century.

Stable government and a solvent economy would eventually attract foreign investment regardless of the attitude abroad to the nature of Salazar's regime. Cheap labor and the promise of competitive prices for Portuguese-made goods provided an incentive for investment, particularly in labor-intensive production, which was becoming uneconomic in northern Europe. Priority was given, however, to colonial development, Salazar insisting that the overseas territories be made to pay for themselves and also to provide the trade surpluses required by Portugal to import the essentials that it could not produce itself. In essence he updated Portuguese mercantilist policy: colonial goods sold abroad to create a surplus at home.

Foreign Affairs

In the years before World War II Salazar cultivated good relations with all major powers except the Soviet Union. Intent on preserving Portuguese neutrality, he had entered into a nonintervention convention with the European powers during the Spanish civil war (1936-39); however, Soviet activity in Spain and the leftward course of the Spanish Republic persuaded him to throw support to Francisco Franco's Nationalists, with whom more than 20,000 Portuguese volunteers served. The war in Spain also prompted Salazar to mobilize a political militia, the Portuguese Legion, as a counterweight to the army.

Although he admired Benito Mussolini for his equitable settlement of Italy's church-state conflict, Salazar found the "pagan" elements in German nazism repugnant. He opposed appeasement, protested the German invasion of Poland in 1939, and would appear to have been among the first—with Winston Churchill—to express confidence in ultimate Allied victory as early as 1940. Portugal remained neutral during World War II, but the Anglo-Portuguese alliance was kept intact, Great Britain pledging to protect Portuguese neutrality. The United States and Great Britain were granted bases in the Azores after 1943, and Portuguese colonial products—copper and chromium—were funneled into Allied war production. Macao and Timor were occupied by Japan from 1941 to 1945.

Portugal was a charter member of the North Atlantic Treaty Organization (NATO) in 1949, and in 1971 Lisbon became headquarters for NATO's Iberian Atlantic Command (IBERLANT). Portugal also maintained a defensive military alliance (the Iberian Pact) with Spain that dated from 1939. Admission to the United Nations (UN) was blocked by the Soviet Union until 1955. In 1961 Indian armed forces invaded and seized Goa, which had been Portuguese since 1510.

Africa

Into the early twentieth century the European settler communities in Portuguese Africa had virtual autonomy, and colonial administrations were perpetually bankrupt. Lisbon's concern in Angola and Mozambique was to make good the Portuguese claim to those territories, and pacification of the interior was still under way in the 1930s. Control over the colonies was tightened under Salazar.

The Colonial Act of 1930 stated that Portugal and its colonies were interdependent entities. The New State insisted on increased production and better marketing of colonial goods to make the overseas territories self-supporting and to halt the drain on the Portuguese treasury for their defense and maintenance. New land was opened for settlement, and emigration to the colonies was encouraged.

Portugal ignored the UN Declaration on Colonialism in 1960, which called on the colonial powers to relinquish control of dependent territories. African possessions were made provinces with the same status as those in metropolitan Portugal by constitutional amendment in 1951 (see fig. 7). Portugal, as Marcello Caetano liked to point out, was an African as well as a European country.

Armed resistance to the Portuguese colonial administration broke out in Angola in 1961 and had spread by 1964 to Mozambique and Guinea. By 1974 Portugal had committed 80 percent of its available forces to Africa: approximately 140,000 troops, 60 percent of whom were African. Portuguese combat casualties were relatively light, and fighting consisted of small-unit action in border areas at a distance from population centers. Only in Guinea did rebel troops control substantial territory. Portuguese forces appeared to have contained the insurgencies and, although large numbers of troops were required to hold the territory, Portugal seemed to some observers capable of sustaining military activity in Africa indefinitely. From a military standpoint these same observers considered that the wars had been won.

The wars did not interrupt the colonial production on which Portuguese economic stability depended. Indeed they had provided a windfall to economic development in Angola and Mozambique, both with large settler communities. A large rural development project was under way in the Carbora Bassa region of Mozambique, as was the exploitation of oil in Cabinda near Angola. More colonial income was being diverted into social services for Africans and Europeans, and in areas of medicine and education better facilities were thought to be available in Luanda and Lourenço Marques than in Lisbon; however, forced native labor remained a factor in the economic development of Portuguese Africa into the 1960s. Foreign investment capital often came to the colonies from countries whose governments had officially condemned Portuguese colonialism.

Marcello Caetano

No man except Pombal left so broad a mark on modern Portuguese history as Salazar. For nearly forty years he completely dominated Portuguese government and politics. His departure was prosaic—he

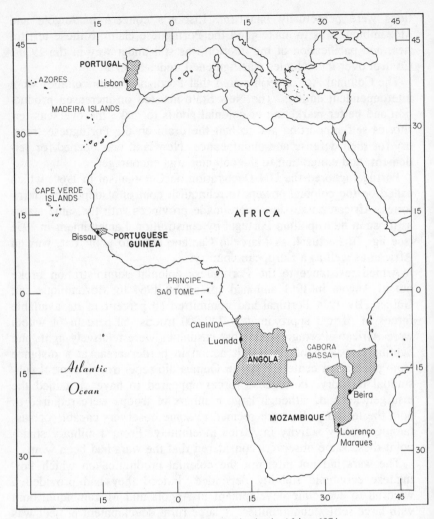

Figure 7. Portugal, Overseas Territories in Africa, 1974

suffered an incapacitating stroke in June 1968 after a freak accident and died, still in a coma, more than a year later.

President Tomás appointed Marcello Caetano to succeed Salazar as prime minister, although it required some time for the regime to admit that Salazar would not be returning to power. Caetano was a teacher, jurist, and scholar of international reputation who had been one of the drafters of the 1933 Constitution. Considered a moderate within the regime, he had taken unpopular stands in opposition to Salazar. He had resigned as rector of Lisbon University in 1960 in protest over police repression of student demonstrations. Unlike Salazar he had come from the upper middle class, was ebullient and personable, and sought contact with the people.

It was clear from the start that he was a different sort of leader. He spoke of "evolution within continuity," change fast enough to keep up with expectations but not so fast as to antagonize conservatives. He introduced technocrats into government and eased police repression. The elections held in 1969 were the freest in decades. He altered the nomenclature of the regime—the New State became the Social State—but his remained an authoritarian regime.

In contrast to Salazar, Caetano advocated an expansionist economic policy and promoted rapid development and increasing consumption without, however, supplementing the means of production. The consequence of liberalization was the first perceptible inflation in years, reaching 15 percent on such working-class staples as codfish and rice.

Caetano had inherited Salazar's office but not his power nor, apparently, his skill as a politician and economist. President Tomás, meanwhile, had emerged with greater authority, as Salazar's death put him in a position to exercise the constitutional authority of the presidency to the fullest. Deeply conservative and supported by an entrenched right wing within the official political movement, Tomás employed threats of an army coup to oppose Caetano's policy of liberalization. Caetano took a harder line on Africa in an effort to head off opposition by the president and the officers close to him.

As the events of spring 1974 were to demonstrate, the regimes of Salazar's New State and Caetano's Social State had depended on personalities. In existence for more than forty years, the institutions of the corporate state had never put down roots in Portuguese political soil. Apathy had not implied support. On April 25, 1974—known since as the Day of the Red Carnations—the officers and men of the Armed Forces Movement (Movimento das Forças Armadas—MFA) ousted Caetano and Tomás, paving the way for a junta under General António de Spínola to take command of the Portuguese Republic.

* * * * * * * * * * * * * * *

Stanley G. Payne's *A History of Spain and Portugal* (two volumes) provides a solidly researched and clearly written introductory survey of Portuguese history by an outstanding American scholar. Harold V. Livermore's older and more detailed *A New History of Portugal* is also useful, particularly for earlier periods; and the analytical approach of A.H.R. de Oliveira Marques in *A History of Portugal* (two volumes) can be recommended for readers with some previous background in Portuguese studies. Marques' brilliantly conceived *Daily Life in Portugal in the Late Middle Ages* is considered a classic work of European social history. Sarah Bradford and Charles E. Nowell have written briefer popular surveys, both titled *Portugal,* that were up to date in 1973. For the history of Portuguese exploration and colonial expansion there are no better English-language sources than John H. Parry's *The Age of Reconnaissance* and Charles R. Boxer's *The Portuguese Seaborne Empire, 1415-1825.* Hugh Kay's *Salazar and Modern Portugal* offers objective insights into the personality and policies of that public figure as well as a political history of Portugal in the twentieth century. A detailed account of Portugal's colonial wars in the 1960s and 1970s is found in Neil Bruce's *Portugal: The Last Empire.* (For further information see Bibliography.)

CHAPTER 3

PHYSICAL ENVIRONMENT

Portugal is one of the smaller countries of Europe, its continental portion occupying 34,312 square miles, or about one-sixth of the Iberian Peninsula. Historically Iberia has been considered a remote compartment of Europe, culturally separated, even isolated, from the rest of the continent by the Pyrenees between France and Spain. For Portugal, on the far western edge of the peninsula with the vastness of Spain between it and the continent, the isolation was even more pronounced and gave the country an Atlantic orientation from the earliest days. A reminder of this geographical and historical orientation is the fact that two Atlantic Ocean archipelagoes—the Azores, about 800 miles due west of Lisbon, and the Madeira Islands, about 600 miles to the southwest—are part of metropolitan Portugal. Including the Azores (nine major islands and several islets covering about 890 square miles) and Madeira (two major and several minor islands covering about 308 square miles), metropolitan Portugal has a total land area of about 35,510 square miles. Portugal also exercises jurisdiction over the Selvagens, a group of small uninhabited islands about 145 miles southeast of Madeira.

Portugal has several distinct geographical regions where the culture of the people has been markedly influenced by the physical environment in which they live and work. Northern Portugal is a mountainous, rainy region, characterized by vineyards and small farms; in the central coastal region, largely consisting of dunes and pine forests, farmers often supplement their incomes and diets by becoming part-time fishermen; the greater Lisbon area is a mixture of small farms and intensive industrialization; the interior agricultural areas with small to medium-sized farms and some mining and light industry form a transitional zone into the Alentejo, the region south of the Rio Tejo, where large-scale agriculture and grazing are predominant; finally in the extreme south the Algarve is a dry region of small holdings where animal grazing and fishing are the chief occupations of the inhabitants. The outstanding influence in Portugals's geography is not a land feature or any combination of features; rather it is the Atlantic Ocean, and many Portuguese have traditionally turned to the sea for their livelihoods.

ADMINISTRATIVE SUBDIVISIONS AND BOUNDARIES

Regional and Administrative Subdivisions

For administrative purposes metropolitan Portugal is divided into districts (*distritos*). For several hundred years after becoming an independent state the country was divided into six provinces for administration (see fig. 8). In 1833 the provinces were abolished as such, and the country was divided into districts patterned after the French departmental system. The new districts were named after their capital cities, but the old province names—Minho, Trás-os-Montes, Beira, Estremadura, Alentejo, and Algarve—remained in common use as regional designations. One hundred years later the 1933 Constitution reintroduced the province as an administrative subdivision, superimposing eleven provinces over the existing eighteen districts (see fig. 9). There was almost immediate dissatisfaction with the new administrative breakdown but, because the system had been incorporated into the constitution, it remained in force for several years. Meanwhile the district continued as the major administrative subdivision, and in 1959 the province classification was again abolished. In early 1976 there were twenty-two administrative districts—eighteen in the Iberian homeland, three in the Azores, and one consisting of the Madeira archipelago (see fig. 1). Province names, usually of the six old provinces but often of the eleven later provinces, continue in use as regional designations.

Portugal's twenty-two districts are divided into municipalities (*concelhos*—see Glossary), which in turn are subdivided into parishes (*freguesias*—see Glossary). In Lisbon and Porto there is an intermediate level, known as the ward (*bairro*), between the municipality and the parish. In mainland Portugal there are more than 300 municipalities and almost 4,000 parishes. The three districts of the Azores are divided into nineteen municipalities and 189 parishes; Funchal District (Madeira) is divided into eleven municipalities and fifty-three parishes.

Boundaries

Portugal's boundaries are the Atlantic Ocean, along which it has a coastline of 523 miles, and Spain, with which it shares a northern frontier of about 210 miles and an eastern frontier of about 540 miles. The Spanish-Portuguese frontier is easily traversed overland, and rivers form the boundary in many places. The boundaries of modern Portugal were fixed by treaties in 1864 and 1906, and in early 1976 there were no disputes, nor were there serious Portuguese claims to Olivença and Juromenha, two Alentejo towns seized by Spain in 1801 and not returned despite an agreement in 1815.

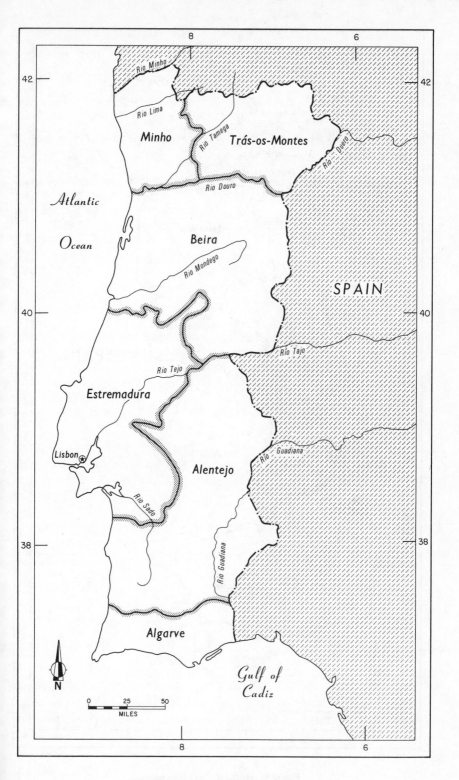

Figure 8. Portugal, the Old Provinces

Figure 9. Portugal, 1933 Provinces

In the north the border follows the Rio Minho from its mouth on the Atlantic coast for forty-six miles to the point where the Minho divides Portugal from Spain. The deep valley formed by the river creates a natural frontier between the Spanish region of Galicia and the Minho region of Portugal. From the Rio Minho the border traverses a series of rugged mountain ranges, crossing several tributaries of the Rio Douro before reaching the point where that river enters Portugal.

The eastern boundary with Spain runs in a generally north-south direction, occasionally changing to an east-west direction for relatively short distances before ending at the mouth of the Rio Guadiana on the Gulf of Cadiz. For seventy-four miles the boundary follows the Rio Douro which, like the Rio Minho, forms a deep gorge, making it another natural dividing line. At Barca d'Alva, the upper navigation limit for small craft on the Douro, the river turns west, but the border continues southward through the thinly populated Serra das Mesas. Continuing in a southwestern direction, the boundary reaches the Rio Tejo valley and follows the Tejo for thirty miles west before turning sharply to the southeast. In this region there is more population than along the northern frontier. The boundary follows small rivers until it reaches the Rio Guadiana, whose course it follows through the Elvas-Badajoz area, a rolling countryside that has no natural obstacles and through which Portugal was often invaded in earlier eras.

The boundary leaves the Guadiana and juts eastward for about seventy miles to the Rio Chança, which it follows westward through a sparsely populated area before returning to the Guadiana. The boundary is formed by the Guadiana until it reaches the ocean at Vila Real de Santo António. As there are no bridges across the river, the only connection with Spain on the lower Guadiana is by ferry.

NATURAL FEATURES

Topography

Portugal, a small country, has a wide variety of landforms, climatic conditions, and soils. The topography changes from area to area, but the most notable differences are those between the north and the south; the Rio Tejo forms a convenient dividing line between the hilly to mountainous regions of the north and the great rolling plains of the south (see fig. 10). Within these two major geographic regions there are subdivisions that further reflect the vast differences in the country. The names of the six provinces that existed from medieval times until the nineteenth century are used to designate the various geographic regions. Three of these regions—the Minho, Trás-os-Montes, and Beira—lie completely north of the Tejo. Three-quarters of Estremadura is also north of the river. The remainder of Estremadura, the Alentejo, and the Algarve lie south of the river.

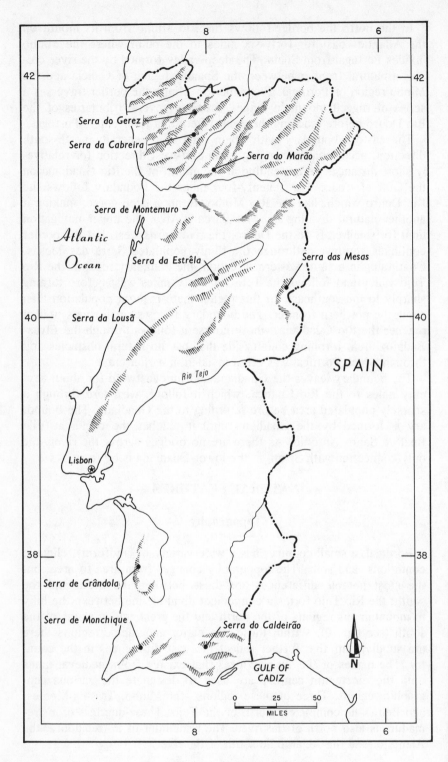

Figure 10. Portugal, Mountain Ranges

The Minho occupies the northwest corner of the country between the Rio Minho in the north and the Rio Douro in the south. The Minho's western boundary is the Atlantic Ocean. The coastal plain in that part of the country generally does not exceed five miles in width and by the mid-1970s had not attained the economic importance of the southern coast. From the narrow coastal strip the land rises steeply to levels 1,000 to 2,000 feet above sea level. The Minho's eastern boundary is delimited by a range of mountains, forming a ring that separates it from Trás-os-Montes (literally, beyond the mountains). When the old provinces were subdivided in 1833, the Minho was divided into the districts of Viana do Castelo, Braga, and Porto. The overall favorable climate and abundant rainfall support the most intensive agriculture in the country, and the Minho is very densely populated despite heavy emigration. The emigration has resulted from the fragmenting of family farms through inheritance over several generations until the small plots have become unprofitable and too small for further subdivision. Many young men have chosen to emigrate rather than remain landless in their homeland.

Trás-os-Montes, the northeasternmost area of Portugal, encompassing the districts of Vila Real and Bragança, is bounded on the north and east by Spain, on the south by the Rio Douro, and on the west by the mountains that separate it from the Minho. The mountains cause the clouds moving toward Trás-os-Montes to precipitate, and as a result this region is arid and parched in comparison with the lush green of the Minho. On the western side of the mountains the average annual rainfall approaches 100 inches, but on the Trás-os-Montes side the average is less than twenty inches. The dryness and the composition of the soils have made this a region of cereal cultivation, principally rye, and animal grazing. The famous port wine area of the Rio Douro is situated on the terraced slopes of that river along the southern boundary of Trás-os-Montes. The terraces on which the vines are grown were hand cut into the slopes down to the Douro valley by generations of Portuguese peasants. Trás-os-Montes is sparsely populated, particularly as compared with the Minho.

The Beira region is much larger than the two northern regions, stretching from the Spanish border in the east to the Atlantic coast in the west and from the Rio Douro in the north as far south as the Rio Tejo. When the provinces were subdivided, Beira was made into five districts: Aveiro, Coimbra, Viseu, Guarda, and Castelo Branco. Aveiro and Coimbra districts are commonly referred to as Beira Litoral (Coastal Beira), Viseu and Guarda as Beira Alta (Upper Beira), and Castelo Branco as Beira Baixa (Lower Beira)—the 1933 province names.

Beira Litoral and Estremadura to the south as far as Lisbon are unique among the landforms of the Iberian Peninsula in that the area is younger geologically and contains sandstone, limestone, and volcanic rock rather than the granite and schist that are predominant in other areas. The Beira coastal plain, which extends inland up to thirty miles from the ocean as opposed to the very narrow coastal strip of the Minho, contains salt marshes and alluvial deposits and stretches of sand dunes sometimes two to five miles in width. Around the lagoon known as the Ria de Aveiro there is a fertile region of land reclaimed from the sea. The lower course of the Rio Mondego crosses a fertile area of Beira Litoral that, taken as a whole, is one of the more fertile regions of the country and features rice, corn, grapes, and forest products among its varied produce. Fishing is also important to the economy of the coastal region, which supports a much larger population than the interior.

Beira Alta contains the Serra da Estrêla, Portugal's major mountain range (the highest peak is 6,532 feet). The Serra da Estrêla, which stretches across the country for about seventy-five miles and averages about thirty miles in width, forms a barrier in the center of Portugal. Communication can only be effected easily along the coast or on the relatively lower land east of Guarda. The more humid western half of Beira Alta is densely populated, and its terraced slopes are noted for a variety of crops, including corn, cabbage, and grapes. To the east the population is less dense and, where cultivation is possible, there are more cereal crops. Summer pastures on the Serra da Estrêla have long been important to the widespread sheep raising in the area.

Beira Baixa is a dry and windswept region that is similar to Trás-os-Montes in its economy and population density. This area is an extension of the Spanish plateau and rises to an average height of about 2,000 feet. The economy is mixed—stockraising and cereal-crop cultivation combined with some mining and manufacturing. The southern portion of Beira Baixa is a transitional area that begins to resemble the rolling hills of the Alentejo and is covered with cork oak plantations and olive groves.

Estremadura, part of Portugal's unique coastal region, includes the Tejo estuary, the capital city of Lisbon, and the important Tejo valley area known as Ribatejo. The old province was divided into the districts of Leiria, Santarém, Lisbon, and Setúbal. Estremadura's fertile soils and moderate climate support an intensive agriculture and a dense population. The region is known for its grapes, and its wines are considered among Portuguese to be second only to those of the Douro. The Setúbal area is also noted for its orange groves, and in the northern Ribatejo cattle breeding is an important sector of the economy. Lisbon, situated on the Tejo estuary, is the country's political, cultural, and economic center.

The Alentejo (literally, land across the Tejo) is a vast area of gently rolling hills generally rising to about 600 feet but occasionally reaching between 900 and 1,500 feet. Although the Alentejo is remarkably and monotonously similar in its topographic appearance, it is usually divided into two subregions, Alto Alentejo (Upper Alentejo) encompassing the districts of Portalegre and Evora and Baixo Alentejo (Lower Alentejo) being conterminous with Beja, the largest district in the country. Until the revolution of 1974 the Alentejo was the land of latifundios or estates of up to 1,000 acres in size. They were vast in comparison with the family farms of the Minho and were often owned by absentee landlords. Wheat and rye are grown on the plains of the Alentejo, but the area is also known for its large ranges of cork oak and its olive groves. Cattle raising and pig raising are also important to the economy. The Alentejo is one of the driest regions in the country, and it also experiences rather wide extremes of temperature, particularly in the east along the Spanish border. The kind of farming, the climate, and the bleakness of the land have all served to hold down the population and, particularly when compared with most regions north of the Tejo, the Alentejo is very sparsely populated.

The Algarve is a distinct region, not only geographically but also culturally because of a persistent Moorish influence. This was the last area of the country to be taken from the Moors, and its towns and buildings as well as the speech of its inhabitants all reveal evidences of its Moorish background. The Algarve is separated from the Alentejo by two mountain ranges, the Serra de Monchique in the west and the Serra do Caldeirão in the east; these mountains also serve to differentiate the hilly interior of the province from its low coastal plain. Much of the mountainous area is covered by scrub growth and poor soils and is very sparsely populated, whereas the coastal lands are fertile and densely settled. Stock grazing and grain production are important in the dry areas of the western Algarve, but to the south corn is widespread in cultivable areas, and tree crops become predominant. Cork oak and olives are grown, but the climate is particularly favorable for the growing of fruit trees; and the sunshine, meager rainfall, and warm winters of the coastal plain have aided the production of almonds, carobs, figs, oranges, and pomegranates. The proximity to the sea has ensured that many inhabitants of the Algarve earn their livings from fishing, and there are many engaged in agriculture who also work part time in the fishing industry. When the six provinces were subdivided into districts in 1833, the Algarve's boundaries were left intact, and the province became the district of Faro.

There are several zones of intense seismic activity as well as major geological faults in Portugal. The largest zones are concentrated in the Algarve, the greater Lisbon area, and the Rio Tejo estuary as far as Benavente. Smaller zones fan out from Porto along the rim of the mountainous amphitheater of the Minho region. There are other, scattered zones in Portugal. Large faults crisscross the Minho region, and larger ones extend into Spain along the north side of the Serra da Estrêla. Faults in Estremadura reach into the Lisbon area. In southern Portugal there is a triangular fault along the eastern edge of the Serra de Grândola (near the coast, west of the Rio Sado) and another extending from Beja in a southwestern direction.

The disastrous earthquake of November 1, 1755, killed an estimated 20,000 people in the Lisbon area and caused extensive damage in the lower portion of the old city. In the south Setúbal, Lagos, Portimão, and Faro suffered considerable damage as well. Lisbon was subsequently rebuilt, and architecture designed to resist further earth tremors was employed in the lower portion of the city. Almost all of the reconstructed area remained intact in 1976. Seismic activity in the twentieth century has centered in the northern Minho region rather than in Lisbon, although tremors were felt in Lisbon in 1969.

Climate

Climatic differences have a marked effect on the lives and work of the Portuguese people. Essentially there are northern and southern climatic zones, using the Rio Tejo as the boundary. Within these two zones there are climatic subregions that are uniquely Portuguese and others that are extensions of the climatic regions of Spain. The rainy north, an extension of the climatic zone of Spanish Galicia, is a heavily populated zone of small holdings where family labor produces a wide variety of crops. The semiarid, sparsely populated zone of latifundios in southern Portugal begins gradually midway through the country. The Algarve, a zone that is often as dry as Spanish Andalusia, is noted for its small farms and cultivation of tree crops.

The rainy north is generally defined as the interior of the Minho, the western portion of Trás-os-Montes, and the coastal plain extending from Porto to Lisbon. These regions have an average annual rainfall exceeding thirty-nine inches. The city of Braga, for example, almost consistently receives from fifty-nine to seventy inches of rainfall annually. The Coimbra area receives only about half as much as Braga—from twenty to thirty-nine inches.

Temperatures in rainy, mountainous northern Portugal are considerably lower than those in the south, and northerners must have protective clothing during the winter months. Winter snows in the Serra da Estrêla and the Serra do Gerez frequently block roads, but warm, humid air currents off the Atlantic tend to modify the cold along the northern coast. Mean temperatures at Braga (627 feet above sea level) range from 48°F in January to 65°F in August. Viana do Castelo, on the coast, has virtually the same temperature range, but its precipitation level is usually nine inches in December whereas Braga's is twelve, because the moist air passing over the coast is cooled and precipitated as it reaches the mountains.

The northern interior, comprising the district of Bragança and the eastern portions of the districts of Vila Real, Guarda, and Castelo Branco, is cut off from the Atlantic rains by mountains. The plateau of Bragança has a bleak, windswept aspect, and the land is mainly given over to grazing and rye growing. Vila Real, the center of the port wine region, often has summer temperatures in excess of 100°F. Normal precipitation in the northern interior at Mirandela (situated almost in the center of Trás-os-Montes) is barely one inch in July and little more than three inches in January. The usual temperature range in that area—from 40°F in January to 75°F in August—does not appear to be extreme, but the lack of rainfall and the consistent wind combine with the isolation of the region to make life bleak and harsh.

Southern Portugal has a Mediterranean climate with a low annual rainfall and many sunny days. The region closely resembles interior Spain, and the Algarve appears more like some parts of North Africa than Europe. The dry climate and warm temperatures favor olive growing and cattle grazing. The Algarve, which is separated from the Alentejo by the Serra de Monchique and the Serra do Caldeirão, is considered a distinct subregion within Portugal. Its only rainy months are in the late fall and winter, under the influence of the North Atlantic low-pressure system. Summer drought reflects the influence of the Azorean high-pressure system. At Caldas de Monchique (666 feet above sea level) the temperature is 50°F in January, and the rainfall is eight inches; but in July the rainfall is only one-tenth of an inch and the temperature 75°F. Algarvian coastal towns show similar temperature patterns. Because of the summer drought the region's farmers have traditionally depended on intensive irrigation.

The various climatic zones of the country are essentially influenced by a combination of factors: the North Atlantic low, the Azorean high, and the weather extremes of the Spanish Meseta. Winter and summer seasons are noticeably different in both the northern and the southern climatic zones. Along the coast the force of the prevailing winds has caused trees to grow at an angle. The prevailing winds at Lisbon are northerly, albeit with a westerly bias. In northern Portugal winter winds are southerly or easterly, and continuing through the summer they bring the dust of the Spanish Meseta and North Africa. An old Portuguese proverb states: "From Spain, neither a good wind nor a good marriage."

Summer weather conditions are generally favorable along the coast, but in the interior of the Alentejo and the Algarve there are frequent droughts. In the north the intense summer heat of the Douro valley (over 100°F) makes work almost impossible in the terraced vineyards. These conditions are caused by the consistent Azorean high, which extends into the Bay of Biscay. By winter the influence of the Azorean high diminishes in favor of the North Atlantic low, which brings humid sea air into contact with the land, causing heavy rainfall, particularly in northern Portugal. Drizzles and showers are frequent, and torrential rains occur occasionally. Because almost all of Portugal with the exception of the Algarve consistently receives more rainfall than Spain, the climate in general is milder and more pleasant.

Drainage

Of the ten major rivers in Portugal five have their origins in Spain and at one or more points in their courses toward the Atlantic Ocean form part of the Spanish-Portuguese frontier. The remaining five are entirely within Portugal and are not very long, the longest being the Rio Sado, whose course is only 108 miles. These rivers have numerous tributaries, and since the mid-1920s numerous flood control, navigation, irrigation, and hydroelectric projects have been constructed on Portuguese rivers.

The Rio Douro is of great importance to the commerce of northern Portugal. It originates in Spain and flows 584 miles before reaching the Atlantic Ocean at Porto. The Douro is navigable by small craft for its full course in Portugal (124 miles) from Porto to the frontier at Barca d'Alva. Ocean tides are felt as far as eighteen miles above the river's mouth. The mouth itself is blocked by a sandbar, and an artificial harbor was built at Leixões to handle oceangoing ships. In general the Douro is narrow, shallow, and difficult to navigate, and only the smallest craft can pass beyond Peso de Régua, fifty miles above Porto. The *barco rabelo* (literally, boat with a tail), a picturesque rivercraft of the past, is now rarely used to bring casks of port wine to Porto. The river, its steep banks terraced for vineyards, gives a distinct character to the region. The river undergoes three sharp drops before reaching Porto: from 4,800 feet at its source to 1,500 feet at Zamora and 600 feet at Barca d'Alva, always in a deep, winding gorge. The area of the Douro basin in Portugal is 7,200 square miles.

The Rio Minho rises in Spanish Galicia and is 211 miles long; 165 miles are in Spain, and forty-six miles form the Spanish-Portuguese frontier. Some barges and other small craft can navigate the Minho for twenty-eight miles upstream, although most are unable to proceed beyond eighteen miles. Tides are felt as far as Moncão, twenty-five miles upstream. There is a dangerous sandbar at the mouth of the Minho. Only thirty square miles of the Minho's 8,680-square-mile basin are in Portugal. The Minho has one major tributary in Portugal, the Coura, entering on its left bank.

Of the other three rivers in the old Minho province only the Lima originates in Spain. The Cávado and the Ave are entirely within Portugal. The Lima flows from the Spanish Province of Orense to its mouth at Viana do Castelo. In Portugal its length is thirty-eight miles; it forms the Spanish-Portuguese frontier for two miles. Over half of its 850-square-mile basin is in Portugal. The Lima is navigable twenty-five miles upstream. The Ave, flowing fifty-three miles from the Serra da Cabreira to its mouth one mile south of the Vila do Conde, is navigable only one mile upstream. Its basin is 540 square miles. The Cávado flows seventy-three miles from northwestern Trás-os-Montes to its mouth at Esposende and is navigable for four miles. Its basin is 620 square miles.

In Beira the Rio Mondego and the Rio Vouga are the principal navigable rivers, and both are entirely within Portugal. The Mondego rises in the Serra da Estrêla and meanders 136 miles, making a long, U-shaped turn in the mountains and eventually entering the Atlantic Ocean at Figueira da Foz. It is navigable for fifty-three miles upstream, at which point it meets its principal tributary, the Rio Dão. The Atlantic tide is felt for twelve miles upstream. The Mondego basin is 2,630 square miles. At Figueira da Foz, an important fishing port, a sandbar restricts navigation, but there is local lighter and barge traffic. The Mondego flows past the historic medieval capital city of Coimbra, noted for its university. The Vouga flows eighty-four miles to the Ria de Aveiro on the Atlantic coast, a wide expanse of salt marshes and ricefields, long known as a haven for waterfowl. The Vouga silted the Ria de Aveiro by the sixteenth century, ruining the fishing industry; but in the early nineteenth century a canal was constructed, allowing the river to flow freely into the estuary, and the Aveiro fishing industry was revived. The Vouga is navigable thirty-one miles upriver, and its basin is 1,430 square miles.

The Rio Tejo, is Portugal's longest river and the most important economically, and it has the largest drainage basin. It is an important Spanish river as well, and it is the longest of the Iberian Peninsula rivers with a total length of 621 miles. In Spain the Tejo is called Rio Tajo, and in English texts it is usually referred to as the Tagus River. The Tejo drops from 4,800 feet above sea level at its point of orgin to barely 100 feet at the Spanish-Portuguese frontier. Although the Tejo extends 142 miles into Portugal, it is navigable by shallow-draft vessels only about fifty miles upstream to Santarém. Most river traffic stops at Vila Franca de Xira. It is possible to proceed farther upriver in shallow-draft vessels past the Spanish-Portuguese frontier, but the irregularity of the river's flow makes this impractical. The Atlantic tide is felt upriver fifty-eight miles. During a drought in 1798 it was possible to walk across the riverbed at Santarém; yet at the peak of floods the river level has risen twenty feet.

The Tejo basin in Portugal is 9,620 square miles. The river deposits an enormous quantity of silt, making the Ribatejo near Santarém a rich wheat-, rye-, and olive-growing region and making it possible to convert the island of Lezíria, downriver near Vila Franca de Xira, into a rice plantation. The most striking feature of the Tejo is its estuary, encompassing ninety-seven square miles in the Lisbon region. The estuary, the Mar da Palha, is one of the world's great natural harbors, providing ocean access for exports of the Portuguese chemical industry at Barreiro on the estuary. The National Steelworks (Siderurgia Nacional) at Seixal, south of Lisbon, uses the water resources of the Tejo and its tributary, the Coina. The drydock at Cacilhas is the largest in the world.

In the Alentejo and the Algarve the major rivers are the Sado, the Mira, the Arade, and the Guadiana, only the last of which flows outside Portugal. The Rio Sado flows 108 miles northwest, forming the Sado estuary on the Atlantic Ocean west of Setúbal. The area around the estuary and its marshes has been settled since ancient times, and the inhabitants have developed a prosperous salt industry. The name of Alcácer do Sal, a town on the Rio Sado, means "Salt Fortress," attesting to its importance in the salt trade during the Moorish period. The Sado is navigable for small craft as far as Porto do Rio, forty-three miles upstream.

The Rio Guadiana is the major river south of the Tejo. The Guadiana rises in Spain and flows about 340 miles before it reaches the Portuguese-Spanish border. The river then forms the border for about forty miles, flows through the Alentejo for slightly over ninety miles, then forms the border again for thirty miles before emptying into the Gulf of Cadiz near the Algarve port of Vila Real de Santo António. That last stretch of the river is navigable by ships displacing up to 1,000 tons; small craft are able to navigate an additional fifteen miles upstream. Ore-carrying barges on the Guadiana have been important in the exploitation of copper mines at São Domingos, about twenty-seven miles upriver. The area around the mouth of the Guadiana has become important as a truck-farming region for supply of vegetables to the Lisbon market. Vila Real de Santo António is one of the chief fishing ports of the Algarve.

Soils and Vegetation

Most soil systems in Portugal are extensions of Iberian systems, the exceptions being the coastal soils and some soils in the Algarve. Most soils of Portugal can be classified as having a volcanic origin. The dominant types are sandy, arid, and acid, as are most of the soils of the Iberian Peninsula from the western end of the Pyrenees to central Portugal.

The soils north of the Rio Tejo are generally lacking in carbonates; they sometimes resemble moorlands but have not developed the peat bogs generally associated with moorlands. The soils of southern Portugal are predominantly sandy and are also lacking in carbonates and soluble salts. Parts of the Alentejo, Estremadura, and the Algarve have calcareous and semicalcareous soils that are kept dry by the meager rainfall and the summer drought. These soils would be able to support more intensive agriculture, as do similar but better watered soils of the north; however, because of the lack of rainfall the land is given over to grazing and tree-crop plantations, and the population density is low. Alluvial soils are important in river valley agriculture, and saline soils in estuaries have been reclaimed for rice production.

One-quarter of Portugal is covered by forests, and the total rises to one-third when such cultivated tree crops as olives, cork oak, almonds, and citrus and other fruits are included. The north is characterized by forests of pine and deciduous oak. The uplands are covered with oak, sweet chestnut, and a low growth of lavender. Sage and scrub prevail on the dry, eastern mountain slopes. Pines are prevalent up to about 3,000 feet and make up half of the forest cover in the north. The rough, stony river valleys and dry, cold interior plateaus do not lend themselves to the olive or the cork oak of the south. Sweet chestnut, holm oak, deciduous oak, elm, and poplar predominate above 4,500 feet but are gradually replaced by birch and yew. At higher altitudes the vegetation cover gradually changes to heather and myrtle.

Central Portugal, the region between the Mondego and Tejo rivers, is a transition area for vegetation cover. The changes are mainly attributable to climate, although soil types play a role. This zone is best typified by a mingling of Portuguese oak and holm oak. The predominant limestone-influenced soils of the transitional region differ markedly from the soils of the north and favor growth of the oak, which flourishes. The English oak is more common in the wet coastal region, and the Portuguese oak grows well in the limey soils of the interior. The interior also contains stands of heath and gum cistus scrub, especially south of Coimbra and east of Leiria. Fruit trees are common, and orange groves extend southward from Condeixa near Coimbra. Toward the district of Castelo Branco there are large zones of *matorral* (scrub growth) for grazing and cork oak forests, as well as stands of cluster pine and scarlet oak.

The region south of the Tejo is characterized by dry soils, lack of rain, mild temperatures, and a decidedly Mediterranean pattern of vegetation. The Italian stone pine is found from south of Setúbal to the northern end of the Algarve. In the plateaus and uplands of the Alentejo the cork oak and holm oak predominate along with cultivated olive trees. In central and southern Alentejo, heath and rough pasturage (suitable for sheep and goat grazing) form the heavy vegetation cover; in the west and south large cork oak forests cover much of the region. Large stands of such bushes as the gum cistus are also common south of the Tejo.

In the Algarve the vegetation cover varies, and agriculture requires intensive irrigation. The western area is covered with heath and gum cistus, stretching across the Serra de Monchique. Along the coast the limestone escarpments above the beaches are covered with pine, olive groves, and cork oak. The area around Faro is mainly dunes and salt marsh. Farther inland, reaching to the foothills, is the region of the most intense cultivation of figs, almonds, grapes (for both raisin and wine production), carobs, and other fruits that are dried, prepared, and shipped for export. Many of these groves of fruit trees extend into the Alentejo as well as north into Estremadura, but the Algarve is the area of the most intense cultivation. Citrus fruits, such as oranges, lemons, and grapefruit, are common to the Algarve and the Alentejo.

Wildlife

Generally the fauna resembles that of central Europe and North Africa. In remote mountain districts, especially the Serra da Estrêla, there are wild goats, deer, foxes, and wild boar. Wolves are less frequently encountered. The lynx is common in the Alentejo. Quail, ducks, and other game birds such as pheasant are common, as are such predatory birds as the hawk and the eagle. Freshwater trout remain common in northern Portuguese rivers, and the Rio Minho is considered the southern European limit for salmon. Only one species of poisonous snake is known (*Pelias berus*), but there are many nonpoisonous species. Wildfowl and hares shot in the Alentejo are considered delicacies and are often sold in Lisbon markets during the fall. Hunting, once restricted to nobles, is still controlled.

Natural Resources

Although geological surveys had not been completed for all areas of Portugal in early 1976, most mineral resources were believed to have been located (see ch. 13). High-grade alluvial deposits of kaolin, crucial to the china and pottery industries, are found at Porto, Aveiro, and Santarém. Building stone, such as granite, limestone, and basalt, and decorative stone, such as marble and alabaster, mined from large quarries, are economically important in the Alentejo and in the Sintra-Mafra area near Lisbon. The monastery and royal residence at Mafra were built with locally quarried marble.

For the most part Portugal is deficient in hydrocarbon fuels. There are virtually no commercially exploitable petroleum deposits, although small deposits have been discovered near Coimbra. A consortium of Portuguese and foreign firms has begun offshore exploration for petroleum and natural gas. There are anthracite coal mines at Pejão and São Pedro da Cova, both near Porto, and at Moinho da Ordem near the Sado estuary. Lignite is found north of Figueira da Foz at Cabo Mondego and at other, scattered locations. Despite the exploitation of coal deposits, considerable amounts are imported from the United States, Poland, and Western Europe.

Copper mines in southern Portugal have been exploited since prehistoric times, and significant deposits are still found in the Alentejo at São Domingos, Chança, and Aljustrel. High-grade iron ore (hematite) and tin are mined in the Bragança district, but most of the tin deposits are in the Serra da Estrêla. Tin is often mined with titanium and wolframite. There are numerous tin deposits in Guarda, Viseu, and Castelo Branco districts. During World War II Portuguese production of wolframite was the highest in the world. Production continues on a reduced scale from deposits at Panasqueira, where it is mined in conjunction with tin, and at Borralha, near Vila Real.

There are deposits of manganese near Beja and Porto, antimony is found in the Serra de Estrêla, and small deposits of gold and silver are located in Vila Real. The products of these deposits are not sufficient to satisfy domestic consumption. Sulfur, used in the Barreiro chemical industry, is found at São Domingos in the Alentejo. There are uranium deposits near the Rio Mondego in the district of Viseu. Zinc and titanium are found at Guarda and Castelo Branco in small amounts. Lead is mined in Aveiro. Although Portugal is able to export some secondary minerals, it is largely mineral deficient and must import semimanufactured metal products. The development of the National Steelworks was designed to utilize the bulk of the national iron and coal production. Coke for the blast furnaces, however, must be imported from the United States, and in 1976 Portuguese iron ore resources were not expected to last many more years.

Salt extracting in the Ria de Aveiro, the Sado estuary, and along various channels of the Tejo; at Figueira da Foz and Alcácer do Sal; and in the Algarve at Faro, Tavira, and Vila Real de Santo António is important to the chemical industry, to the cod fishing fleets, for human consumption, and for export. The salt-extracting industries on the Vouga and Sado estuaries have their origins in pre-Roman times.

The Atlantic coasts of Portugal provide the nation with an exceptional natural resource: an abundance and variety of fish. What Portugal lacks in agriculture and minerals it partially makes up with its wealth of sardines, tuna, and other fish. Sardine fisheries are especially important, providing over half the value of the total annual catch. The industry began in its modern form in 1880 with the establishment of a French-financed cannery at Setúbal. Tuna account for 3 percent of the total annual value of fish caught, and about 10,000 tons are exported annually. The main tuna fishing ports are in the Algarve. Whiting, mackerel, and other varieties of fish are caught close to the shore. The Portuguese have also been fishing the Grand Banks and Labrador since the fifteenth century. Rising costs in the 1970s have made the Portuguese fishing fleet less competitive with those of other countries, and pollution of both rivers and coasts by expanding industry as well as oil spills has caused concern over the continued marketability of fish caught in Portuguese waters.

THE AZORES

The Azores archipelago is a group of nine inhabited islands and the Formigas Rocks, several uninhabited islets, in the Atlantic Ocean about 800 miles west of Portugal (see fig. 11). The islands have a total land area of 890 square miles and in 1976 had a population of about

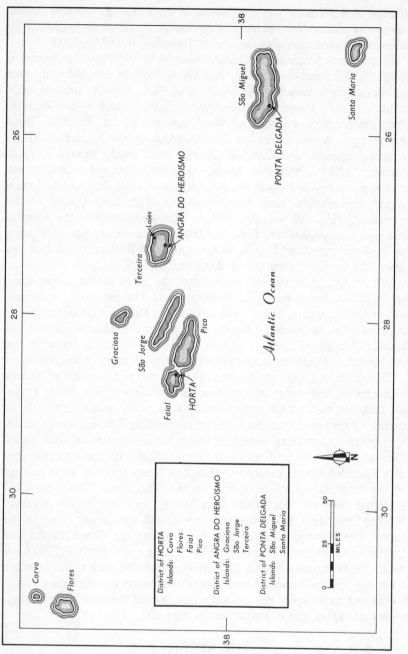

Figure 11. Portugal, the Azores

District of HORTA
Islands: Corvo
Flores
Faial
Pico

District of ANGRA DO HEROISMO
Islands: Graciosa
São Jorge
Terceira

District of PONTA DELGADA
Islands: São Miguel
Santa Maria

MILES

0   25   50

Corvo

Flores

Graciosa

São Jorge

Faial

HORTA

Pico

Terceira

ANGRA DO HEROISMO

Lajes

São Miguel

PONTA DELGADA

Santa Maria

Atlantic Ocean

N

38

38

26

26

28

28

30

30

300,000. The Azores are scattered over tens of thousands of square miles of the Atlantic; Corvo, the smallest of the islands, is about 360 miles from Santa Maria, the easternmost island. The name Azores is derived from *açores* (hawks), which were sighted in great numbers by Portuguese navigators who visited the islands in the early fifteenth century.

The climate of the Azores is moderate. The temperature rarely exceeds 80°F in the summer and does not often go below 50°F in the winter, but the winter months can be rainy and unpleasant. There are considerable variations in annual rainfall between the eastern and western islands of the archipelago. Flores, for example, averages sixty inches of rainfall annually, whereas São Miguel registers only twenty-nine inches. Summer and winter seasons provide marked contrasts in that July is characterized by days of total calm whereas December is often a month of rain and gale-force winds. Sea swells during the winter often prevent transport of passengers and cargo to Flores and Corvo.

Although most of the original forest growth of *faia* a kind of beech, still survives, most of the islands' flora and fauna were brought by European settlers. There were no mammals before the introduction of domesticated European varieties, although birds, eels, wingless beetles, other insects, and seventy species of indigenous mollusks were found in the islands.

With the exception of Santa Maria Island, the Azores are volcanic in origin. One of the islands, Pico, has a volcanic peak, O Pico (7,615 feet). Erosion of mountains and lava flows by wind and rain has produced a rich volcanic soil. Craters provide natural reservoirs for rainwater, which seeps into springs through underground streams. The agreeable climate and volcanic soil have combined to produce favorable conditions for agriculture. Although the islanders are self-sufficient in terms of their food needs, they depend exclusively on imported coal and petroleum products. Wooded mountain slopes are carefully reforested as timber is used for fuel. Intensive agriculture is practiced on family holdings throughout the islands, producing a wide variety of crops, including cereals, vegetables, pineapples, sugarcane, tobacco, and wine grapes.

The Azores produce more than enough food for internal consumption and export the remainder to continental Portugal. São Jorge Island is a dairy and meat production center. Inhabitants of the smaller islands of Faial, Graciosa, Flores, and Corvo rely on a mixed economy of cattle raising, small-scale agriculture, whaling, and fishing for a livelihood. São Miguel has larger holdings, as the terrain permits grazing as well as intensive farming on small holdings. The joint Portuguese and American air base on Terceira provides additional employment for many Azoreans.

Second to agriculture as the chief occupation of the Azoreans, the fishing industry employs thousands of islanders in catching, processing, and exporting fish. Many fishermen journey thousands of miles to fish the Grand Banks, and others work in coastal waters. Although the whaling industry has lost the important position it held in the nineteenth century, it still employs many men who hunt whales from longboats, which are launched whenever whales are sighted.

The small holdings and relative isolation of the islands have tended to preserve the traditional ways of the islanders. Most people live in villages; on some of the islands there are no cities, and those that do exist—the three district capitals of Ponta Delgada, Horta, and Angra do Heroísmo—are very small. In 1976 the estimated population of Ponta Delgada, the chief port and the economic center of the Azores, was only about 25,000. The lack of available land has been one of the chief causes of emigration of Azoreans, principally to the Americas.

THE MADEIRA ISLANDS

The Madeira archipelago (the Funchal district), about 600 miles southwest of Lisbon in the Atlantic Ocean, consists of the islands of Madeira, Porto Santo, and the uninhabited Ilhas Desertas (see fig. 12). The islands have an area of 308 square miles and had a population of about 252,000 in 1973. The island of Madeira is severely overpopulated, and a large number of its inhabitants emigrate each year to Europe and the Americas.

The volcanic origin of the island of Madeira is reflected in its rich soil, rugged terrain, high peaks, and lack of beaches or a coastline suitable for landings. The semitropical climate and the rich soil combine to provide near ideal conditions for raising bananas, pineapples, vetetables, citrus fruits, and the grapes from which the famous Madeira wine is made. The upper slopes of the mountains are covered with pine and other evergreens. Although most of Madeira's agriculture is concentrated along the island's coastal fringe, there is some cereal growing and cattle grazing. The semifeudal forms of land tenure and water rights inhibit agricultural growth, obliging islanders to turn to the sea for their livelihoods in the fishing and whaling industries. The lack of sufficient cereal or meat production necessitates costly imports.

Small-scale cottage industries, such as embroidery and the manufacture of wicker furniture, are also sources of income for the islanders. Tourism has become important in Madeira because many Europeans are attracted by the mild climate. As there are no beaches on Madeira, many islanders and tourists visit Porto Santo, where there are extensive beaches. Most of the inhabitants of Porto Santo are fishermen, although some work in the island's limestone quarries.

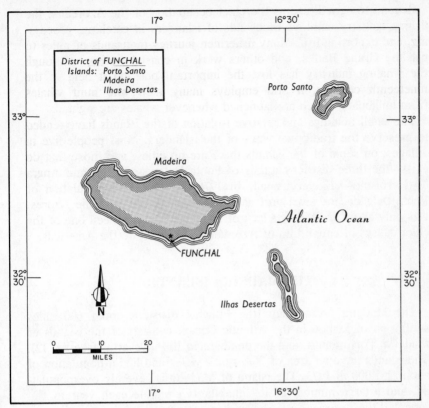

Figure 12. Portugal, the Madeira Islands

CHAPTER 4

POPULATION AND LIVING CONDITIONS

By the time of the official census in 1970 the resident population of Portugal was 8,663,252, a decrease of 226,140 from the total population in 1960. Unusually heavy emigration during the decade accounted for the decline. Districts have experienced uneven patterns of growth; the population in certain districts has increased as much as fivefold since the first official census in 1864, whereas that of others has decreased or increased only slightly. In general districts along the coast have shown the greatest population growth since 1864.

Between 1960 and 1970 district capitals and urban-industrial centers along the coast were the only areas where population rose. The great influx of migrants to the cities created acute housing shortages and forced many workers into substandard housing or into peripheral areas where transportation was poor. Within the cities *barracas* (shantytowns) sprang up. Sanitation was poor both in these *barracas* and throughout the country.

The proportion of women in the total population and in the working force was growing as was the number of persons in the upper age-groups. The emigration of young men seeking work in Western European industrial countries was the major reason for this change in the population structure. In the 1960s most of these young men were agricultural workers, and their departure caused agricultural wages to rise. More men from the industrial and services sectors had begun emigrating by the 1970s, and the departure of these skilled workers was becoming a serious deterrent to internal development. Most emigrants were from northern Portugal. Before 1960 Brazil had been the most favored destination, but during the 1960s and 1970s the majority of emigrants—both legal and illegal—went to European countries.

Many young men left Portugal to seek higher wages, but many others, particularly from the north, left because there was no alternative. Excessive fragmentation of the land dictated that the eldest son inherit the property to ensure its economic viability. Other sons were forced to seek their fortunes elsewhere. This created a shortage of men that in turn affected patterns of marriage and fertility. Many women were forced to remain single or to spend long periods of time separated from their husbands.

81

Birthrates and infant mortality rates in Portugal were among the highest in Europe—testifying to the poor health conditions still prevalent in 1970. Fatal diseases common among the young were enteritis, diarrhea, and pneumonia. Whereas death rates were about average by European standards, life expectancy was lower. Contagious diseases (among them tuberculosis, typhoid fever, and diphtheria) still existed in Portugal despite vaccination and eradication programs conducted by the government.

Although the numbers of doctors and medical facilities had been increasing since 1960, by European standards they were small, and there was maldistribution of personnel and facilities. Over half of all doctors were located in the cities of Lisbon and Porto. Folk medicine continued to play an important role in the lives of rural Portuguese but did not preclude the use of modern medical practices.

By early 1976 rampant inflation had affected most consumer goods. Meat had become very expensive, and there were shortages of butter and milk. Even fish and eggs, staples of the Portuguese diet, had become scarce and had risen in price. In many cases rising wages were not sufficient to keep pace with inflation; in others, too sharp an increase in wages coupled with a general decline in productivity resulted in large-scale layoffs and closure of some factories. Unemployment was high—a situation aggravated by the return of about 800,000 Portuguese settlers from Africa.

The welfare system was undergoing a transformation in 1976. Before the revolution of April 1974 welfare benefits were unevenly distributed. Traditionally almsgiving and stealing substituted for the lack of social assistance programs in the rural areas.

POPULATION

The first official census of the Portuguese population was taken in 1864. Further censuses were taken at irregular intervals until 1920, when the National Institute of Statistics (Instituto Nacional de Estatística) regularized the collection of data and began conducting a census of the population every ten years. In addition to the official census the institute compiles volumes of annual and monthly statistics summarizing demographic, social, and economic data. Many of the figures presented are abstracted and estimated from more specialized volumes of statistics on emigration, housing, and the like. Until the census of 1970 two separate sections of statistics were compiled. The first covered metropolitan Portugal, including Madeira and the Azores, and the second dealt with Portugal's overseas territories.

Population Structure

The estimated population in 1976 was 8,944,000, an increase of more than 280,000 since the official census of 1970. The increase was attributed to the large number of settlers who had returned to the homeland from Africa during the period. The overall population was more than double that of 1864, the year of the first census. Since that date more than 90 percent of the total has resided in continental Portugal.

Until 1960 the population increased, although the rate of growth was not always steady (see table 1). The period between 1960 and 1970 is particularly significant in that Portugal witnessed a drop in population. Apparently the decrease was unanticipated. Annual estimates had indicated an increase to over 9 million by 1969. Unusually heavy emigration, however, drew off a large portion of the population. More than 46 percent of all emigrants since 1864, or 1,033,030 people, left Portugal during the period from 1960 through 1970. The restricted job market in Portugal and the desire of many young men to avoid compulsory military service in the colonial wars had a bearing on the heavy emigration of the 1960s, but the booming economies of many Western European countries and the liberalization of United States and Canadian immigration requirements also accounted, in part, for the dramatic increase in the number of emigrants.

A more detailed look at population data over time and by district reveals that population trends were by no means uniform throughout Portugal. Two districts decreased in absolute numbers from 1864 to 1970: Guarda, a district in the northern interior (the Beira Alta region), decreased slightly, and Horta, a district in the Azores, lost approximately one-third of its population. The populations of only seven of the remaining twenty districts increased by two times or more. Of

Table 1. Portugal, Population Growth, Selected Years, 1801-1976

Year	Population (in thousands)	Average Yearly Growth (in percent)
1801	3,115	. . .
1864	4,287	0.6
1878	4,669	0.6
1890	5,103	0.8
1900	5,447	0.7
1911	5,999	0.9
1920	6,080	0.2
1930	6,802	1.2
1940	7,755	1.4
1950	8,510	0.9
1960	8,889	0.5
1970	8,663	-0.3
1976*	8,944	. . .

*Estimate.

Source: Based on information from Anuário Estatístico, 1962, Lisbon, 1963, p. 9; Anuário Estatístico, 1973, Lisbon, 1974, p. 9; and Massimo Livi Bacci, A Century of Portuguese Fertility, Princeton, 1971, p. 31.

those on the continent, all lay on the coast except for Santarém, which had an outlet to the sea through the Tejo estuary. All were also part of what could be termed Portugal's industrial belt. The populations of Aveiro, Leiria, and Santarém more than doubled; that of Porto tripled; Lisbon's population increased by approximately four-and-one-half times; and Setúbal had a population in 1970 more than five times greater than its 1864 total. Of the island districts Funchal (in Madeira) increased by nearly two-and-one-third times. The mainland districts in the far north and the northern interior witnessed the least overall population increase. Viana do Castelo, Vila Real, Bragança, and Viseu grew by less than one-half. The island districts of Angra do Heroísmo and Ponta Delgada in the Azores also grew by less than one-half.

The generalized 1960 to 1970 population decline affected almost all districts. Only five, again those in coastal areas, recorded an increase during that decade—Braga, Porto, Aveiro, Lisbon, and Setúbal. Internal migration to urban areas and transatlantic and intra-European emigration explain, in large measure, the marked population growth of a small number of districts and the relative depopulation (in terms of a percentage of the total population) of most other districts.

Age and Sex Composition

Since the time of the first census women have constituted a larger portion of the Portuguese population than men. This holds true for individual districts as well as for Portugal as a whole. Only in particular municipalities (*concelhos*—see Glossary) are there instances where the number of men is greater. Of the 304 municipalities in 1970, there were only twenty-two (four in the north and eighteen in the south) where women did not form the majority. The northeast and center of the country were the areas where the ratio of women to men was highest—most probably a result of the pattern of heavy emigration from the north.

The Portuguese are an aging population (see fig. 13). From 1900 to 1970 there was a gradual decrease in the relative size of the age-groups under thirty (that is, the number of males and females in the age-group as a percentage of the total number of males and females respectively) and a rise in the relative size of the other age-groups. Moreover, although in the 1970s the relative size of the age-group thirty to forty-four had increased from its 1900 level, it had decreased from its 1960 level. In other words, between 1960 and 1970 the aging of the Portuguese population, particularly the male portion, was accentuated, and there was a rise only in the relative size of the population forty-five and over. Again emigration provides an important part of the explanation. Young people, attracted by the greater economic opportunities outside Portugal, have chosen to leave.

Some interesting variations existed among districts and municipalities in the sex and age structure of the population in 1970. The district

84

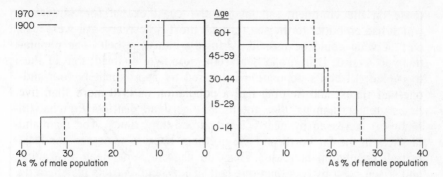

Source: Based on information from *Anuário Estatístico, 1973*, Lisbon, 1974, p. 13; and
Anuário Estatístico, 1962, Lisbon, 1963, pp. 14-15.

Figure 13. *Portugal, Population by Age and Sex, 1900 and 1970*

of Braga, in the Minho region of the north, for example, had an unusually large proportion of those fourteen years old and younger. This
age-group accounted for over 35 percent of the female population and
over 40 percent of the male population. Guarda, a district on the
Spanish border in the Beira Alta region, was characterized by a relatively small proportion of young adults—those between the ages of
fifteen and forty-five—and a larger proportion of the young and the
aged. The district of Lisbon, lying on the coast, had a comparatively
large young adult population. The proportion of those falling into the
age-groups zero to fourteen and thirty to forty-five was about equal.
These differences in the sex and age structure were even more pronounced among municipalities.

One Portuguese demographer identified several broad areas of the
country that corresponded to the different patterns of age structure
reflected in the 1970 census data. Young people under twenty years of
age predominated on the coast north of Lisbon and in the north generally. This trend was more pronounced in the male population. The
aged (those sixty-five years of age and over) formed sizable proportions of the populations in the center and interior. This trend was
more accentuated among females. Finally the population between the
ages of twenty and sixty-five was located primarily in the districts of
Lisbon, Santarém, and Setúbal and along the southern coast between
Lisbon and the Algarve. Parts of Evora and Portalegre also shared
this pattern.

Settlement Patterns

In 1970 Portugal had an average population density of 244.9 persons
per square mile. The population, however, was not distributed evenly
throughout the country (see fig. 14).

It is possible to divide Portugal into several zones that reflect variations in demography and settlement patterns. Such zonal divisions
provide a useful, if somewhat oversimplified, classification. For exam-

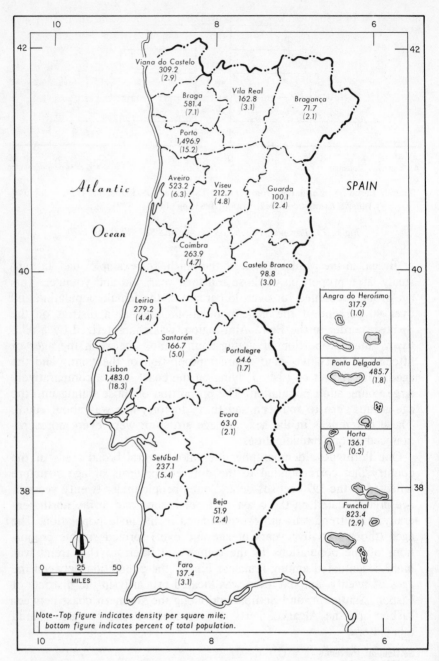

Figure 14. Portugal, Density and Percent of Total Population by District, 1970

ple, the northern interior regions of Portugal, including the Trás-os-Montes e Alto Douro as well as the northeasterly section of Beira Alta all have certain common features (see ch. 3). In this area the population density is low, and the population is grouped into villages and small rural clusters. The Minho region, Douro Litoral, the northwest part of Beira Alta, and the northern part of Beira Litoral constitute another zone. Here there is a high population density; the land is divided into small, fragmented holdings; and the nonurban population is dispersed throughout the countryside. A high population density also characterizes Estremadura, the sections of the Ribatejo that lie along the Tejo and north of it, most of Beira Litoral, and the southern half of Beira Alta. This high density is particularly pronounced in urban areas along the coast, although the population remains relatively well distributed throughout the rest of the area. Population density is exceptionally low in the area that includes the southern half of Beira Baixa and everything south of the Tejo except the Algarve. Traditionally this has been the land of the latifundios, large estates owned by wealthy and often absentee landowners. The population has had a tendency to settle in large villages that are relatively isolated from each other. Finally the Algarve constitutes a marked contrast to most of southern Portugal. Although density is not as high as in parts of the Minho and the urbanizing areas along the coast, it is still relatively high. The population in this zone consists primarily of small landowners.

The majority of Portugal's population in 1970 could be classified as rural. Urban areas of any size or consequence, in terms of major industrial activity, were located along the coast. If urban is used in a very loose sense to indicate areas in which industry has been overtaking agriculture, then it is also possible to classify municipalities in the interior—primarily the district capitals—as urban. Most of these municipalities, however, are small—sometimes including populations of under 10,000 people.

Between 1960 and 1970 there was increasing urbanization—both on the coast and in the small urban areas of the interior—which was underscored by the general population decline during those years and the internal migration of the population (see fig. 15). While most of the country was losing population, urban centers were the only areas gaining population.

As might be expected, the municipalities toward the interior of the country, where climate and soil conditions are poorest, registered the heaviest population losses (see ch. 3). Seventeen of the forty-six municipalities that had population decreases of 25 to 47 percent were on the Portuguese-Spanish border, and most of the remaining twenty-nine were located nearby. In the south the district of Faro (in the Algarve) lost 14 percent of its population between 1960 and 1970, all but three of the municipalities losing more than 5 percent.

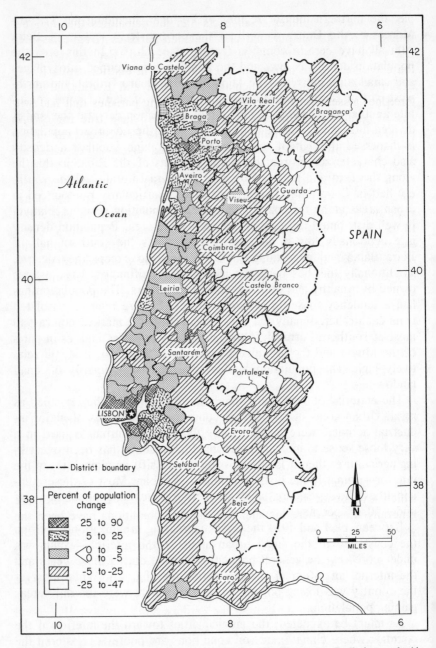

Source: Based on information from Jorge Gaspar, "Os Resultados Preliminares do 11.
Recenseamento da População" (The Preliminary Results of the Eleventh Census of the Population), *Finisterra*, Lisbon, VI, No. 12, 1971, p. 298.

*Figure 15. Portugal, Percent Population Change Between 1960 and 1970
by Municipality*

There were a number of districts and municipalities that had net losses of population but that also included parishes (*freguesias*—see Glossary) in which the population had increased. For the most part these parishes were urbanizing areas located in district capitals. For example, the southern municipalities of Beja and Evora had registered net losses; yet both contained urbanizing parishes that had witnessed population increases. The same pattern held true for certain parishes in the central municipality of Castelo Branco and the northern municipalities of Bragança, Vila Real, and Viseu—all of which are capitals of districts having the same names.

The pull of the urban centers along the coast was greater than elsewhere in the country and was primarily responsible for the dense population pattern and the high rate of growth in this area. Attraction to the cities of Lisbon and Porto was the strongest. This did not necessarily result, however, in population increases within the boundaries of these cities. Instead there was a trend toward suburbanization. The city of Lisbon, for example, evidenced a 3-percent population decrease while the parishes surrounding Lisbon all recorded population increases.

It would be necessary to look at the conditions prevailing in the individual parishes within each of the cities in order to assess the reasons for suburbanization, but in general several causes can be discerned. First high rents and lack of low-income housing forced a sizable portion of the population into peripheral areas (where sanitary and housing conditions were often less favorable) even though there were dwellings within the city that remained unoccupied. This appeared to account partially for the suburbanization around Lisbon, Guimarães, and Coimbra. Second there has been a trend—particularly marked in the cities of Lisbon, Aveiro, Porto, and Braga—toward the depopulation of old neighborhoods and the growth of new ones, some of which lay outside the cities proper. The old parts of the cities are generally those where housing and sanitary conditions have been the worst. This has created a desire to leave for reasons essentially the reverse of those in the first case. Finally expansion of economic activity has often squeezed out housing. In Lisbon, for example, the central part of the city has been largely taken over by growth in the services sector. It was for this reason that the parishes of São Sebastião de Pedreira and Arroios in the center of the city lost 19 percent and 27 percent of their populations respectively from 1960 to 1970.

Transportation played an important role in determining which of the municipalities and parishes located near Lisbon increased most. For example, the municipalities of Mafra and Benavente each recorded an overall loss of population. Yet Malveira, a parish in Mafra, gained 61 percent because its bus and train facilities provided easy access to Lisbon and because there was some local development in the industrial and services sectors. Samora Correia, a parish within Benavente, recorded a 32-percent increase—again because of its access to Lisbon and its own industrialization. A third case was that of the municipality of Vila Franca de Xira, which rose in population by 33 percent. It contained some parishes that recorded decreases of 7 percent or more, which were much less accessible to either Lisbon or the urbanized strip in general. Porto, where employment opportunities in industry were more widely dispersed outside the city proper, witnessed a similar suburbanization process although to a lesser degree.

Population Dynamics

Births

In the early 1970s birthrates in Portugal were higher than in most other European countries. The estimated birthrate for 1973, for example, was 20.1 per 1,000 of the population, whereas the European average was only 15.5 per 1,000. Albania, Ireland, and Iceland were the only European countries during that period that experienced a higher birthrate than Portugal.

Throughout the nineteenth century birthrates in Portugal had been among the lowest in Europe. In the late 1800s they averaged approximately thirty-three per 1,000—a figure that was markedly low for that era and similar to that found only in England and Scandinavia at the time. Massimo Livi Bacci, who has extensively investigated patterns of Portuguese fertility, attributes the relatively low birthrates during this period to the low marriage rate, among other factors. With the onset of what is known as the secular decline, however Portugal failed to evidence the same sharp drop in birthrates as most other European countries.

There was a great amount of fluctuation in Portugal's birthrates from 1900 to the late 1920s. A high of 38.6 per 1,000 was recorded in 1911. It was only after World War I that the birthrate began an overall decline. In contrast Italy and Spain, which had experienced much higher rates than Portugal before 1900, had begun to register sharp decreases by the turn of the century. For Portugal the sharpest decrease came between 1930 and 1940, when the rate fell from nearly thirty births per 1,000 to just over twenty-four. A low rate of 19.3 was registered in 1970.

Since 1950 districts in the north of Portugal have consistently experienced the highest birthrates—well above the continental average. Braga, Porto, Vila Real, and Aveiro ranked among the five highest in the censuses of 1950, 1960, and 1970. Braga, in the Minho region, ranked first in all three census years: 31.7 per 1,000 in 1950, 32.2 in 1960, and 26.8 in 1970.

Greater variation has existed in the districts recording the lowest birthrates since 1950, but for the most part those in the south and

90

southern interior have registered the lowest rates. Evora, Faro, and Portalegre had 1970 birthrates of 14.1, 14.6, and 14.7 per 1,000 respectively and were among the five lowest from 1950 to 1970.

The proportion of illegitmate births in Portugal is high in comparison with such other southern European and predominantly Roman Catholic countries as Spain and Italy. The apex was reached in 1937, when approximately 16 percent of all births were illegitimate. Since 1940 the proportion has been declining, and in the early 1970s it had fallen to just over 7 percent. In part the high proportion of illegitimate births can be explained by the prevalence of cohabitation without marriage in the south of Portugal. Religion is not accorded the same high respect in the south as in the north. Church weddings have never been as important, and couples are often unwilling or unable to pay the necessary fees for civil ceremonies. The overall decline in illegitimacy in the country during the twentieth century has been attributed to its decrease in the north, where marriage rates have risen and illegitimate births have decreased. Few changes in the proportion of illegitimate births and in marriage rates have been found in the southern districts.

Marriage and Fertility

Since the beginning of the twentieth century marriage rates have fluctuated from just over five per 1,000 to just under ten per 1,000. They were at their lowest between 1910 and 1920. Although there was a sudden surge upward in the early 1920s, the marriage rate did not really start showing an upward trend until the 1940s. By 1973 it had reached a high of 9.9 per 1,000. The drop in the marriage age—that is, the increasing number of women between the ages of twenty and twenty-four who have been marrying—has been cited as the reason for the increase.

As the marriage rate has increased, regional patterns have undergone changes. In nineteenth-century Portugal the tendency for women to marry young was greatest in the south and least in the north. Purportedly, however, this trend was reversing itself in the 1960s, although general nuptiality in the north was still considered low. Livi Bacci, borrowing from the observations of Paul Descamps, has offered two explanations for the traditionally low nuptiality of northern Portugal—emigration and patterns of landholding and inheritance. Emigration has always been heaviest from the north. Thus, as Livi Bacci concludes, "it is obvious that the permanent emigration of many young men has lessened the opportunities for women to marry, and made female celibacy a common phenomenon." The north and more specifically the Minho region contained the largest proportion of unmarried women between the ages of fifty and fifty-four. Even after 1960 the proportion in certain areas was greater than 30 percent.

Customary patterns of inheritance have further reinforced female celibacy by forcing a portion of the young male population to migrate or remain single. At one time land in the north was divided equally among the male offspring. This resulted, however, in an excessive fragmentation of the land into plots of such small size that it was impossible to secure even a minimal livelihood. In order to guard against this fragmentation, the eldest son would often inherit the property, and the others would either take up another occupation or leave the area. Although the legal institution supporting this inheritance pattern was abandoned in the 1800s, it is still customary in parts of northern Portugal for younger sons to relinquish their claim to the family properties, thus ensuring the economic viability of the land. For those young men who are excluded from inheritance there is little choice but to emigrate or to remain single.

The divorce rate in Portugal is negligible. In 1973 it was approximately 0.1 per 1,000, among the lowest in Europe.

Deaths

By 1973 the death rate in Portugal had reached the level of 11.1 per 1,000—about average for a European country. Regional variations in death rates were not apparent although, in very general terms, those districts with the lowest rates were spread along the coast from Setúbal to Braga. In the censuses of 1950 and 1960 districts in the north had registered the highest death rates, but in the census of 1970 this was no longer the case. Porto, for example, had topped the list of districts registering high death rates in 1950 and 1960 but by 1970 ranked among the lowest.

WORK FORCE

Age and Sex Composition

According to International Labor Organization (ILO) statistics, the work force in the 1970s included 39.2 percent of the total population (3,395,850 people). The Organization for Economic Cooperation and Development (OECD) recorded a lower number—approximately 2,-943,000 for the 1972-73 period.

An increase in the number of women employed and a slight aging of the economically active male population characterized the working force between 1960 and 1970. ILO noted that females accounted for over a quarter of the work force in 1970. This was an increase of 7 to 8 percent over their 1960 total. Figures gathered by OECD show a lower proportion of working women for the same period, but the increase is only 1 percent less, and the fact remains that women have been gradually assuming a greater role in the work force.

Emigration was probably the major cause of this upsurge in the proportion of working females. The active male population was lured away from Portugal to such countries as France and the Federal Republic of Germany (West Germany), where remunerations were higher. In addition there was a rise in the number of employable males serving in the armed forces. This number grew from 1960 to 1970 as a result of increased military forces in certain of the Portuguese territories and a lengthening of the term of active duty. Thus women in certain parts of the country were forced out of their traditional domestic sphere and assumed a more active economic role.

Over three-fourths of the active male and female population fell in the age range of fifteen to fifty-four years. Nearly half of the working males, however, were between the ages of thirty and fifty-four, and nearly half of the working females were between the ages of fifteen and twenty-nine. From 1960 until 1970 the proportion of working males in the higher age categories increased; that is there was a slight aging of the male work force. OECD's *Portugal* (Economic Survey) of 1974 also cites an annual average decrease in the work force of 0.6 percent for the 1962-63 to 1972-73 ten-year period.

Distribution of the Work Force

The most profound changes in Portugal's work force by the 1970s were in the variations of employment by economic sector. The proportion employed in the primary sector, including agriculture, hunting, forestry, and fishing, had dropped dramatically from previous years. According to ILO statistics, in 1950 the primary sector employed 48.4 percent of the active population; in 1960 the proportion had dropped to 42.3 percent; by 1970 the primary sector accounted for only 29.5 percent. According to OECD information, in the 1972-73 period agricultural workers constituted 28.6 percent of the active population. OECD noted that from 1962 through the early 1970s two of every three workers who had abandoned agriculture had not moved into industry and services but rather had left the country to take up employment opportunities abroad. Only the proportion of the active female population employed in the primary sector increased.

ILO and OECD information conflict as to the proportion of workers employed in the industry and services sectors, probably a result of a slightly different breakdown of sectoral activity, but the trends indicated from both sets of data are the same (see table 2). From 1960 through the early 1970s the industrial work force increased but only by a small amount. OECD reported an annual average increase of 0.7 percent. The number of workers employed in services, in contrast, had a larger rate of growth (OECD placed the figure at 2 percent), although not large enough to account for the decline of those employed in the primary sector.

In 1970 the largest number of females was found in the services sector, followed by the industry and agriculture sectors respectively. For the active male population the order was reversed and the sectoral distribution somewhat more even.

Sector	Number (in thousands)			Percent		
	1962-63	1967-68	1972-73	1962-63	1967-68	1972-73
Agricultural, fishing, and mining ..	1,235	1,030	843	39.8	34.0	28.6
Industrial	936	964	1,000	30.2	31.8	34.0
(Processing industries) ...	(677)	(695)	(717)	(21.8)	(22.9)	(24.4)
(Construction)..	(222)	(237)	(254)	(7.1)	(7.8)	(8.6)
Services	929	1,036	1,105	30.0	34.2	37.6
TOTAL....	3,100	3,030	2,948	100.0	100.0	100.2*

*Figures do not add to total because of rounding.

Source: Based on information from Organization for Economic Cooperation and Development, *Portugal* (Economic Surveys), Paris, July 1974, p. 12.

Using yearly figures on job applications and vacancies provided by the Portuguese Ministry of Labor, the OECD found that in 1973 the services sector received the highest number of applications, mostly from officeworkers and sales personnel, but the largest number of vacancies occurred in the industrial sector, particularly in certain skilled occupations in the clothing and building industries. Shortly after the revolution in April 1974 the number of applicants had grown, but registered vacancies had fallen. By 1976 unemployment had reached an estimated 15 percent (see ch. 12).

WAGES

Before the revolution wages in all sectors of the economy were low, and the distribution of income was grossly uneven. A postrevolutionary estimate by the Portuguese government in 1975 indicated that the annual per capita income of Portugal in the early 1970s was the lowest in Europe, 12,900 escudos (for value of the escudo—see Glossary). From 1970 to 1972 Portugal spent the lowest proportion of its national income on the compensation of its employees of any European country except Greece.

Low wages in agriculture were responsible for the exodus of emigrants in the 1960s, and by the 1970s wages began to rise, albeit slowly, as a result of the shortage of labor this exodus created. From 1968 to 1973, for example, the average daily wages of agricultural workers rose from fifty-nine to ninety-five escudos for men and from thirty to sixty-one escudos for women. This rise in wages (12.5 percent), however, did not keep pace with price increases (20 percent) for the same period. Thus while nominal wages increased, real wages, in terms of buying power, fell.

The index of industrial wages in the cities of Lisbon and Porto had risen by 1973 to 235.9 and 265.9 respectively (1963 equal to 100). Yet in January 1974 about 81 percent of the population not in agriculture or public administration were still earning less than 4,800 escudos per month, and only 7 percent were earning above 7,200 escudos per month.

Because the fluctuation of wages and prices since the revolution continued in early 1976, it was difficult to comment on the state of wages and purchasing power. One report in early 1976 claimed that the average household head was earning 5,600 escudos per month. Wage and price freezes had been imposed, lifted, and reimposed. Initially the institution of a minimum wage worked to the laborers' advantage, but in January 1976 the government was forced to raise prices on most consumer goods.

MIGRATION

Emigration has had the single greatest impact on Portugal's population structure in the twentieth century. Portugal's tradition of exploration and colonization has always accorded emigration a historic role, but it was not until the late 1800s and the 1900s that mass emigration occurred. With the exception of Ireland, Portugal has registered the highest net population loss, more than 2 million people from 1864 through 1973 (see table 3; fig.16). The rate of emigration has acceler-

Table 3. Portugal, Emigration, 1864-1973[1]

Destination	Number of Emigrants	Destination	Number of Emigrants
France	800,000	Zaire	20,000
Brazil	620,000	Belgium	12,000
United States	160,000	Australia	8,000
South Africa	140,000	Southern Rhodesia......	8,000
Canada	110,000	Netherlands	6,000
West Germany[2].......	110,000	Switzerland	2,500
Venezuela	95,000	Bermuda	2,000
Argentina	40,000	Netherlands Antilles	1,500
Spain	26,000	Italy	1,500
Great Britain	24,000	Sweden	1,500
Luxembourg	24,000	TOTAL	2,212,000

[1] The prerevolution Portuguese government did not count population movement to the former overseas territories (for example, Angola and Mozambique) as emigration.
[2] Federal Republic of Germany.

Source: Based on information from *Boletim Anual 1973*, Lisbon, 1974, p. 229.

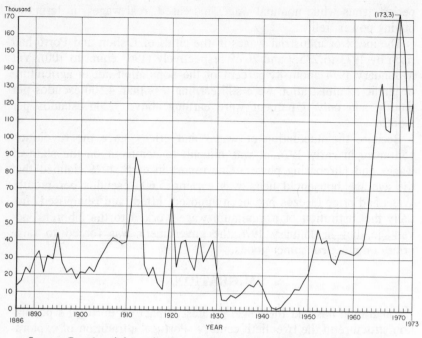

Source: Based on information from *Boletim Anual 1973*, Lisbon, 1974, pp. 4-7.

Figure 16. Portugal, Total Legal and Illegal Emigration, 1886-1973

ated since the end of World War II, nearly 64 percent of all emigration (1,409,222 people) taking place between 1960 and 1973. The aging of the Portuguese population, the predominance of females, the negative population growth despite high birthrates, and the depopulation of certain sections of the country can all be explained in part by emigration.

Emigration to America

From the time of the first census until the early 1970s, emigration to the Americas accounted for 46 percent of total emigration from Portugal. Although such a high proportion is impressive, the figure was even higher before the 1960s (see fig. 17). From 1950 to 1954, for example, nearly 97 percent of all legal emigrants sailed for the Americas. By the 1965-69 period the proportion had plummeted to 27 percent and, if illegal emigration is taken into consideration, the figure drops even further to 15 percent for the 1970-73 period. Emigration figures for the mid-1970s were not available in early 1976, but it is likely that emigration to North and South America had picked up in view of the numbers (many of them professional people) leaving the country since the revolution of April 1974 and of the economic situa-

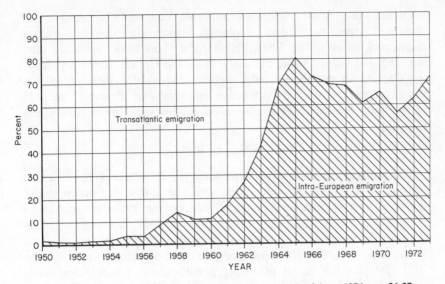

Source: Based on information from *Boletim Anual 1973*, Lisbon, 1974, pp. 26-27.

Figure 17. Portugal, Transatlantic and Intra-European Emigration, 1950-73

tion in Europe and the tighter immigration restrictions in the mid-1970s.

Traditionally Brazil has been the favored point of destination outside of Europe. Approximately 28 percent of Portugal's net emigration between 1864 and 1973 was to Brazil. Brazil's attraction lay in its favorable climate, the comfortable blending of its populations, and the special relationship it enjoyed with Portugal even after gaining independence in 1822. Since 1970, for example, citizens of Portugal and Brazil have had the reciprocal privilege of participating—as both candidates and voters—in each other's elections.

The height of emigration to Brazil came in 1952 when that country received nearly 88 percent (41,518 people) of the year's total. Emigration to Brazil began declining in the late 1950s, and its sharpest decline was registered in 1963 and 1964. An economic depression in 1963 led the Brazilian government to impose restrictions on the importation of unskilled workers. In 1972 emigrants to Brazil were only 1 percent of the total. With the fall of the Marcello Caetano government in Portugal in 1974, General António de Spínola's abortive coup, and the exodus of refugees from the Portuguese African territories in 1975, however, the flow of emigration to Brazil increased, even if only temporarily. Some estimates placed the number of emigrants to Brazil since the Portuguese revolution as high as 40,000 (not all of whom had registered with the Brazilian authorities), but others maintained that the increase over the yearly average of 2,000 in the early 1970s was slight.

Of the other South American countries Venezuela has ranked second and Argentina third in popularity. Emigration to North America began picking up in the 1960s; its sharpest gains were registered during 1965 and 1966. During the early 1970s the United States was leading Canada in popularity only slightly. From 1971 through 1973 a yearly average of 15,300 Portuguese emigrants, or almost 13 percent of the total for those years, were bound for the United States and Canada.

Emigration to Europe

The shift in emigration patterns away from overseas countries to European countries did not come until the 1960s; but when it did come, it was sudden and dramatic. Before the 1960s emigration to Europe had been negligible. From 1965 to 1969, however, Europe became the preferred destination—receiving 70 percent of all legal Portuguese emigrants for those five years and 65 percent from 1970 to 1973. Despite the threat of heavy penalties and possible imprisonment, clandestine emigration, most of it to Europe, also became a common phenomenon in the 1960s and 1970s. If the number of clandestine emigrants is added to the total of legal emigrants, it can be said that nearly 82 percent of all Portuguese emigrants from 1970 to 1973 went to European countries.

Of the Western European industrialized countries, France and West Germany have admitted the largest number of Portuguese. French and West German figures differ from the Portuguese, but the overall pattern is the same. The surge of emigrants to France began in 1962, slackened slightly from 1967 to 1968, and dropped again after 1970. According to one source about 8 percent of the Portuguese population (700,000 people) resided in France in 1972.

Emigration to West Germany also grew markedly in the 1960s although on a considerably lesser scale than that to France. Again there was a slight dip in the 1966-67 period, but the rate of emigration, after decreasing in 1971, had risen again by 1973. OECD placed the number of Portuguese in West Germany at 115,000 in 1973.

In 1974 it appeared that the number of emigrants to Europe was on the downswing. The economic milieu was becoming less inviting, and regulatory measures had been effected. Portugal and France entered into a bilateral manpower agreement that was meant to curb the number of Portuguese workers bound for France. West Germany took steps in 1973 to limit the importation of foreign migrant labor from countries that were not members of the European Communities (EC).

Emigration to Africa

Emigration to the former Portuguese African territories had never been popular despite government efforts to encourage large-scale settlement there (see table 4). From 1950 until the early 1970s, when the African colonies were granted independence, emigration to Africa accounted for less than 4 percent of total Portuguese emigration. Still by 1970 estimates placed the number of Europeans in Angola at 350,000 (including the Portuguese military forces stationed there) and the number in Mozambique at 170,000. Guinea-Bissau (formerly Portuguese Guinea), whose hot and humid climate produced less favorable conditions, had never been an attractive site for settlement.

Policies of the Portuguese government aimed at directing and promoting the flow of emigration to Africa date from the early 1800s. After Brazil gained independence in 1822, the Portuguese government began introducing a variety of measures designed to lure emigrants to Africa. These measures included allowing prisoners to work off their terms by settling in the African colonies, providing free passage, and offering land grants and stipends to prospective settlers.

Efforts at settlement were particularly stepped up in the 1950s and the 1960s not only for economic but also for political reasons. One policy statement issued in 1953 made the Portuguese objectives quite explicit: "The economic and social life of the overseas provinces is regulated and coordinated in accordance with the colonization of the region, especially through the settlement of national families, by regulating the emigration of labor and the systematic control and protection of emigration and immigration." Angola and Mozambique provided convenient outlets for surplus Portuguese labor, thereby alleviating the potential social conflict that threatened Portugal from the large segments of the population that were unemployed. At the same time emigration to the African territories was meant to satisfy international criticism by demonstrating that Portugal did indeed effectively control its overseas territories.

Table 4. *Portugal, White Population in Angola and Mozambique, Selected Years, 1930-70*
(in thousands)

Year	Angola	Mozambique
1930	30.0	19.8
1940	44.1	27.4
1950	78.8	48.2
1960	172.5	97.2
1970	350.0	170.0

Source: Based on information from Eduardo de Sousa Ferreira, "The Present Role of the Portuguese Resettlement Policy," *Africa Today*, 21, No. 1, Winter 1974, pp. 47-55; and S.J. Bosgra, "Colonization and Settlement in Portuguese Africa," *Migration Today*, Geneva, 15, Autumn 1970, pp. 34-42.

In the early 1960s, as anticolonial unrest in Africa had grown to alarming proportions, the Portuguese government established provincial settlement boards. The major objective of these boards was to instigate wider dispersion of small Portuguese settlements (*colonatos*). Land grants and credit were offered to those willing to pioneer such projects. In particular the government campaigns were directed toward ex-soldiers who had served in the African territories. These ex-soldiers were to settle the territories and, at the same time, act as a kind of paramilitary force. In a sense the settlements were supposed to form buffer zones between the Portuguese population and militant segments of the African population. The provincial settlement board in Angola offered to train ex-servicemen as social workers and to provide them with employment opportunities. The overall program of soldier settlements, however, was not a success. About 4,800 former servicemen had emigrated to Angola by the end of 1966, and only 152 had settled in the outlying settlements.

In addition to encouraging former military men to make the territories their permanent home, the Portuguese government promoted general European emigration to Africa. As one observer remarked: "While the policy of settling ex-servicemen demonstrates the military and strategic character of Portuguese population policy, the recruitment of non-Portuguese Europeans makes plain its discriminatory character." Government plans meant, in many cases, the forced resettlement of large segments of the indigenous population. In the 1960s it was estimated that Europeans in Angola controlled over 60 percent of the arable land.

Even so-called plans for the economic development of the overseas territories were tinged with the ulterior motive of luring Portuguese and other European emigrants to Africa. The Cunene Dam project in Angola and the Cabora Bassa Plan in Mozambique were meant to bring open lands under cultivation. At the same time, however, officials had hoped that the former project would bring as many as 500,000 Portuguese by 1980 and that the latter would eventually attract as many as 1 million settlers.

Returnees from Africa

With the sudden decolonization of Portuguese African territories after the revolution of 1974, metropolitan Portugal found the ranks of its resident population swelled by returning war veterans, African refugees and, most important, the Portuguese settlers whom the governments of António de Oliveira Salazar and Caetano had sought so vigorously to entice to Africa. In mid-1976 estimates placed the number of returnees as high as 800,000. Civil conflict and fear of reprisals were the major reasons why most had decided to flee to Portugal and, although many of them originally expressed the hope of returning to Africa, by 1976 that hope had grown more and more remote.

The Portuguese government made a considerable effort to direct the flow of refugees and to lend them whatever social assistance was possible. Yet anger and frustration were apparent among the refugees. At one time encouraged to emigrate, they felt betrayed by Portugal—especially the more radical elements of the government whom they blamed for the rapid decolonization policy and for the slowness in providing them with safe passage out of Africa.

By the end of 1975 it was estimated that at least 40,000 Portuguese had emigrated to Brazil since the revolution of April 1974. This total included many of the wealthier refugees from Portuguese Africa as well as self-exiles from the homeland who chose to flee the revolution. The poorer returnees from Africa who were repatriated to mainland Portugal had no choice as to where they might settle. Without money for transportation they could only remain in Africa or take one of the free flights to Portugal offered primarily through the efforts of the Portuguese government and the United States.

Most of the returning refugees originally came from northern Portugal, and in 1975 and 1976 the government was encouraging them to return there—particularly those who still had relatives. The returnees were recognized as a potentially reactionary political force, and it was the desire of the government to discourage their migration to, and concentration in, the larger urban areas. Nevertheless as of early 1976 many of them were refusing to evacuate the temporary relief centers in Lisbon and its environs. The luckier ones were accommodated in hotel resorts along the coast, but other were crowded into unfinished and substandard housing or were living with relatives.

As of 1975 the refugees were not eligible for unemployment compensation although the government had made provisions for resettlement aid and special monthly stipends. Each adult refugee was permitted to transfer less than 5,000 escudos (the equivalent of US$200) of his savings from Africa. Although government aid was out of necessity limited, one source indicated that the government spent the equivalent of US$70 million from June to September 1975 to cover the cost of food, shelter, and clothing.

In addition to the refugee problem in general, there were overtones of a prejudicial nature—vis-à-vis the returnees as a group but also vis-à-vis racial subgroups. Many of the refugees were bitter over the treatment accorded them in the urban areas especially. As one remarked, "We are colons, not colonizers, but they hate us." Information on the racial composition of the refugee population was difficult to obtain; however, one estimate placed the number of persons of mixed blood in preindependence Angola at 100,000. These persons were considered to be Portuguese citizens, and many of them fled to Portugal. Even before the revolution of April 1974 the number of Africans working in mainland Portugal had increased. At the end of 1973, for example, an estimated 20,000 Cape Verdeans were living and working in Portugal. The plight of the refugees, together with the political and social tension they portend, promises to be among the most formidable problems facing postrevolutionary governments in Portugal.

Emigrants' Places of Origin

Emigration from Portugal has been and continues to be preponderantly an emigration from the north and from the so-called adjacent islands (see fig. 18; fig. 19). Whether one looks at the total or chooses to look at district emigration rates, the pattern is basically the same. Aveiro, Braga, Coimbra, Leiria, Porto, Viseu, Ponta Delgada (the Azores), and Funchal (Madeira) have each averaged more than 5 percent of the total emigration from 1950 through 1973. Lisbon has been the only other mainland district that can make the same claim. In 1973 Leiria registered the highest rate of emigration of the mainland districts—17.3 per 1,000 of the population—followed by Vila Real (12.6), Viseu (12.5), Aveiro (11.3), Bragança (10.5), and Coimbra (10.2). All island districts recorded rates exceeding nineteen per 1,000.

Traditionally emigration from the north was encouraged as a kind of safety valve to halt the already excessive fragmentation of the land. Since Portugal's industrial and services sectors were unable to absorb the supply of labor, emigration seemed to provide the only alternative. In the south, where wage workers and tenant farmers predominated, emigration has been negligible because there have always been seasonal shortages of labor. Where migration has occurred, it has usually been an internal migration to the cities or a seasonal migration to Spain and North Africa.

If place of origin and place of destination are considered together, some generalizations can be made. In the 1960s and early 1970s North and South America received the largest proportion of emigrants from the islands. The majority of France's Portuguese population originated in the north, but the trend in West Germany was moving toward a predominance of emigrants from central Portugal. Over half of those entering West Germany in 1972 were from this region.

HEALTH

Health Conditions

Although improving, health conditions in Portugal were still among the poorest in Europe. According to early 1970 estimates the life expectancy for males was approximately sixty-five years. Only males from Luxembourg and Albania had a lower life expectancy. Women fared somewhat better, having a life expectancy of seventy-one years.

102

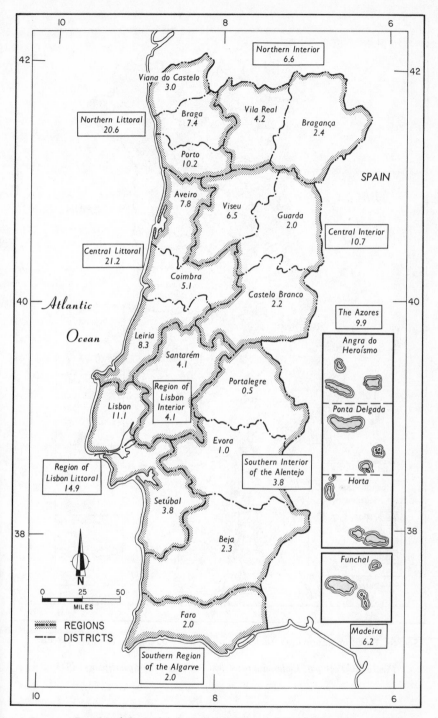

Source: Based on information from *Boletim Anual 1973*, Lisbon, 1974, pp. 68-69.

Figure 18. Portugal, Percent of Total Emigration by District and Region, 1973

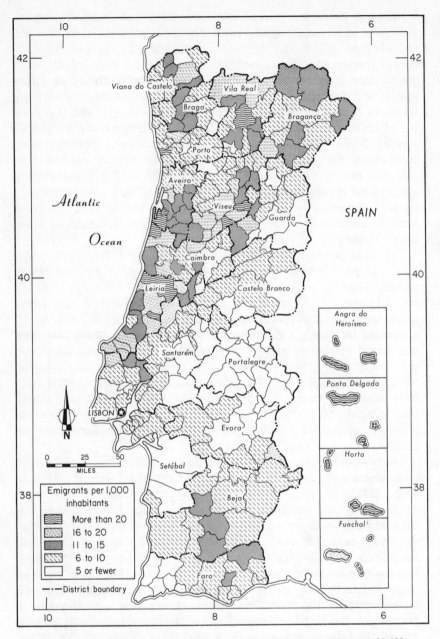

Source: Based on information from *Boletim Anual 1973*, Lisbon, 1974, pp. 108-109.

Figure 19. Portugal, Emigrants per 1,000 Population by Municipality, 1973

Although Portugal's rate of infant mortality had dropped from its 1970 level of fifty-eight deaths per 1,000 of the population, in 1973 the rate (44.8 per 1,000) was still among the highest in Europe. Only Albania experienced a higher rate. Mortality rates for male infants were greater than those for females. The dissemination of child care information and the wider availability of medicines and medical care allayed, to some extent, fears concerning child survival, and the number of children born to couples during the 1960s and early 1970s was smaller. Nevertheless, as José Cutileiro, a Portuguese anthropologist, commented, children are valued in Portuguese society, and few couples risk having only one. An expression still in vogue particularly among rural people is that "children are very difficult cattle to raise." Custom dictates that women are to wear mourning only upon the death of children over seven—attesting to the high frequency of child deaths in the past.

The most common causes of death among the young were infectious and parasitic diseases, followed by diseases of the respiratory system. Together they accounted for over half of all deaths of those under fourteen years of age in 1973. Enteritis, diarrhea, and pneumonia were the most prevalent of these diseases. Tuberculosis, which accounted for nearly a quarter of all infectious and parasitic ailments, was found primarily among the population over fourteen and more specifically among those over thirty. For people over thirty diseases of the circulatory system accounted for the most deaths—increasing from nearly 18 percent for the population between thirty and forty-four to nearly 50 percent for those over sixty. Cerebrovascular complications accounted for over half of all deaths from circulatory ailments.

The fewest deaths occurred among the age-group fifteen to twenty-nine, where only 2,188, or 2.3 percent of the total, were recorded in 1973. Accidents, poisoning, and violence were responsible for about 45 percent of the deaths in this group, and other diseases were distributed fairly evenly. Accidents, poisoning, and violence were also the major causes of death for those between the ages of thirty and forty-four. It was at age thirty, however, that diseases of the digestive tract began to be significant causes of death. For those between thirty and forty-four and those between forty-five and fifty-nine, diseases related to the digestive system accounted for approximately 10 percent of the deaths. Cancer, more particularly stomach cancer, caused the highest proportion (31.4 percent) of deaths for Portuguese aged forty-five to fifty-nine. Respiratory diseases—bronchitis, emphysema, asthma, and pneumonia—were important causes of death for those over sixty.

If ill-defined causes of death are ignored, the major fatal diseases in 1973 were diseases of the circulatory system, cancer, and diseases of the respiratory system. Age distribution at time of death constituted a sort of inverted bell curve until the age of sixty. Deaths of those under fourteen accounted for 11 percent of the total, of those between fifteen and twenty-nine for 2 percent, of those between thirty and forty-four for 4 percent, and of those between forty-five and fifty-nine for 11 percent.

Cases of typhoid fever, cerebrospinal meningitis, hepatitis, diphtheria, scarlet fever, whooping cough, and acute sleeping sickness (encephalitis), in descending order of prevalence, have been regularly reported even in the 1970s. In 1972 alone the combined number of cases reported was 2,840, but it is likely that not all cases were reported. In 1973 typhoid fever, diphtheria, whooping cough, scarlet fever, and infectious meningitis were still listed among the causes of death. There were vaccination programs in progress in the 1970s to prevent some of these diseases.

Facilities

The number of doctors and professionals in medical-related fields in Portugal has been increasing. The number of doctors increased from 5,845 in 1950 to 7,075 in 1960 and 8,156 in 1970. The number of medical-related professionals rose even more dramatically from an overall total of 16,355 in 1960 to 26,294 in 1970. Nevertheless in 1970 the mainland averaged only one doctor per 1,000 people; only Lisbon, Porto, and Coimbra had more than one doctor per 1,000. All island districts averaged less than one doctor per 1,000. The same maldistribution held true for nurses and other medical professionals. The mainland average was 1.2 nurses per 1,000; only Lisbon, Porto, and Coimbra on the mainland and Funchal in Madeira had more than the mainland average. Porto, Lisbon, and Coimbra had more than five medical-related professionals per 1,000, and every other district had under three.

The highest number of doctors were specializing in general surgery, stomatology, pediatrics, gynecology, and obstetrics, which together included 46.5 percent of all specialists. Medicine was predominantly a male profession. Women constituted only 15.7 percent of the total number of doctors nationwide and 21.2 percent in the cities of Lisbon and Porto. The most popular specializations for women were obstetrics (where they made up 41 percent of the total), gynecology (38 percent), and pediatrics (30 percent). In fifteen of the thirty specialties listed by the Portuguese health authorities, there were fewer than five women.

In addition to the increase in the number of medical professionals there has been an increase in the number of health facilities. For the size of the population, however, the number was not impressive. By 1973 more than 600 health facilities with and without beds had been added to those in operation ten years earlier. There were also over

2,100 pharmacies in the country. There appeared to be no pattern to the distribution of health facilities. The north had more medical establishments than the south, but the number per 1,000 people was slightly higher in the south.

Folk Health

In a society with as few medical facilities and personnel as Portugal folk medicine continues to play an important role—particularly in rural areas. Cutileiro reports that most rural villages have healing mediators, who are usually poor old women. These women are not actual healers but rather agents in the healing process. According to Cutileiro, "None of them is considered as holy or is supposed to perform miracles; they are mere officiants and, when the desired intervention is supposed to have occurred, it is attributed to the saint whose aid has been invoked and, ultimately, to God." Their services extend to all age-groups and include assisting at childbirth and preparing the dying for the afterlife. Treatment of disease consists of diagnosing the disease and offering special prayers to a saint (there are usually different prayers and practices for each affliction).

Even with the advent of modern medicine and the dissemination of health information, traditional medical practices have changed very slowly among the rural population. Modern medicine exists alongside folk medicine, neither one preempting the other. All precautions are taken in times of sickness. Thus a folk healer and a doctor may both be consulted; and in addition the usual prayers may be offered to a saint. If the patient survives, all are given credit—completing the mixing of the modern with the folk, the natural with the supernatural.

What is distrusted is the unfamiliar. Cases have been recorded in which the government provided certain rural municipalities with free medical services and doctors. Yet the rural people refused to take advantage of the services and frustrated efforts to compile health statistics. In one case the people actually turned to a private physician, despite the fees charged, in preference to the public doctor. The private doctor had grown up in the municipality, spoke the local dialect, and was considered a part of the community. In contrast the doctor assigned to the municipality by the health authorities was always considered an outsider. He spent little time meeting the people, and his speech reflected his urban and educated tastes.

DIET

Eating follows a fairly regular schedule in Portugal—a light breakfast of coffee and rolls in the morning, the main meal in the afternoon, and a moderate supper at any time from 7:30 P.M. to 10:00 P.M. The Portuguese enjoy eating, and they may spend as much as two hours consuming their afternoon meal.

A three-course meal is the norm for the most Portugues families, whatever their income. The first course is soup. Portuguese soups are thick and filling, and each region of the country tends to have its own special variety. Coastal regions are particularly noted for their fish soups, the Alentjo for its *açords* (bread soup), the Algarve for its *gaspacho* (cold soup), and the north for its potato soups and its *caldo verde* (green cabbage soup).

Fish usually forms the second course of the afternoon meal. It is a staple in the Portuguese diet and is eaten almost every day. Fish is cheaper than meat (among the cheapest in Europe before the revolution), and the ratio of consumption of fish to meat is about ten to one. The most common and popular fish among all segments of the population is *bacalhau* (dried and salted cod). It is known as the faithful friend (*o fiel amigo*). The yearly average of cod consumed is said to be 100 pounds per person. It is not surprising therefore that even before the revolution it was necessary to import cod from other countries. Cod forms a part of every traditional Christmas supper. It is used in over 300 dishes. Over 200 other kinds of fish and seafood are sold throughout Portugal. It is possible to find sardines, eels, tuna, mullet, hake, clams, oysters, lobster, and octopus. Grilled sardines are a favorite among the poor. In 1975 and 1976 shortages of fish had developed, and the variety of fish offered for sale had diminished. Even cod, the faithful friend, was affected by the overall shortage.

The third course of the afternoon meal usually consists of a meat dish followed by a dessert. The poor, who can rarely afford to eat meat, often substitute eggs or a vegetable stew as their third course. During the early 1970s before the revolution, however, a growing proportion of the population were eating meat and dairy products— indicating a rise in living standards. For the most part the quality of meat was low, and there was little variety. Pork, kid, veal, chicken, and hare are among the more common choices, varying more or less according to the region. Food shortages appeared to hit the meat market particularly hard after the revolution. In early 1976 in Lisbon steak was reportedly being sold for as much as ninety-nine escudos (US$3.60) a pound and a boiling fowl for a total of 220 escudos (US$8.00).

Eggs are another important staple in the Portuguese diet. Often they form an alternative to fish or meat as a main course. Many of the thick soups and most Portuguese desserts are prepared with eggs.

In the early 1970s shifts in the food tastes of the Portuguese were occuring—primarily because of the slight increase in the standard of living. There was less consumption of starchy foods, such as bread and beans. The food shortages of 1975 and 1976, however, were likely to lead once again to heavier consumption of starches.

In addition to the shortages of meat and fish, supplies of butter, milk, and imported foods were dwindling. Coffee, a favorite among the Portuguese, had risen sharply in price. In January 1976 the overall price of food had risen over 50 percent from its 1975 level. The headline of one Portuguese newspaper expressed in a nutshell the overall situation at the end of 1975—"Christmas—The Last Supper?"

HOUSING

Reliable housing statistics are difficult to obtain. Those published before the revolution tended to mask the extent of substandard housing and poor sanitation. There appeared to be a calculated absence of information, designed to give the impression that in 1972 housing in the cities of Lisbon, Porto, and Coimbra all contained, at the barest minimum, electricity, running water, and a sewage system and that most also contained indoor plumbing, Outside reports clearly indicate, however, that this was not the case. The influx of migrants from rural areas to urban-industrial centers during the 1950s and more markedly during the 1960s created a housing shortage and soaring rents—forcing poorer families into substandard housing.

Barracas (shantytowns) sprang up within and around the larger cities such as Lisbon. Figures obtained since the revolution on the numbers of such dwellings and the people accommodated there vary considerably. One source placed the number living in Lisbon's *barracas* at 30,000. In contrast a postrevolution governmental source estimated that by 1970 shanties had doubled from their 1960 total of 10,918 and that the number living in them had grown from 43,470 to approximately 70,000. Few *barracas* had running water, waste disposal systems, or paved streets. Speculation in *barracas* housing had even begun to be practiced in the 1970s; shanties were bought at a low price and rented at a higher one.

Evidently attempts were made in the late 1960s and early 1970s to rid Lisbon in particular of its unattractive *barracas*. Little consideration, however, was given to the people living there. Teams were sent, reportedly without warning, to demolish the units and to rehouse portions of the population—particularly the elderly and the single—in higher rent housing. Although residents of some *barracas* managed collectively to resist such moves, those living in the more visible ones were literally carted off to prefabricated dormitory-style housing on the periphery of the city and their shanty homes torn down. When persons refused such housing, they crowded together into apartments—sharing expenses that were more than they could afford by themselves. A 1974 estimate records 150,000 people living in dormitories, cramped quarters, and *barracas* near Lisbon.

The countrywide housing situation in the mid-1970s was grim. Conditions were among the poorest in Europe. Since electricity companies were private, many villages had no electricity. Sewage systems were absent from about 80 percent of housing; about 33 percent lacked running water or readily available pumped water; and garbage-collecting services were nonexistent for close to two-thirds of the dwellings.

The construction of residential housing grew in the early 1970s; an estimated 41,923 dwellings were built in 1973. This was still among the lowest number constructed per 1,000 of the population of any European country. About half the new units had uncontrolled rents. In 1974 housing needs were placed at over 500,000 units. Housing construction has been mainly a private enterprise, the state contributing under 10 percent to total housing construction.

The housing shortage is only part of the housing problem. High rents have placed housing in urban areas beyond the reach of a great percentage of the people. According to United Nations statistics and using 1970 as the base year (100), the rent index had risen to 185 by 1973. This was the second highest increase for that period registered by any European country. Moreover it was the smaller units (those with fewer than five rooms) that were hardest hit by the increases. The average monthly rent in 1973 was 1,000 escudos per room.

The government hoped to provide middle-and low-income housing for 100,000 people during the 1975-76 period and to escalate the building program between 1975 and 1994 to average some 76,000 residential units yearly. What is likely to hamper the government's plan, however, is inflation, the depressed building industry, lack of credit, and the high cost of land. In the meantime steps have been taken to improve life in the *barracas* by providing electricity and more wells. Housing problems were compounded, however, by the return of the Portuguese-Angolan refugees in 1975 and the slowdown of emigration.

WELFARE

Before the advent of modern social security systems, almsgiving was the traditional and institutionalized form of assistance and relief among the rural poor, particularly in the south of Portugal. Landowners felt a sense of responsibility for the welfare of their workers. In times of economic crisis or seasonal unemployment, they helped to alleviate the plight of their workers with gifts of food and other charitable donations. During seasonal unemployment groups of unemployed workers and their families roamed about asking for food. Such seasonal beggars were socially acceptable, unlike those who made begging their yearlong vocation, because there was no alternative for those persons who were able and willing to work but could not find jobs.

When wealthy landowners died, their wills stated as a matter of course that a portion of the inheritance was to go to the poor. In the present day the relatives of newly deceased wealthy landowners from certain rural areas continue to distribute money, clothing, and food to the poor even though distribution of such gifts is no longer specified in wills. Almsgiving was not entirely motivated by unselfish motives but stemmed from the acceptance of a necessity for well-being based on mutual advantage. Unless workers enjoyed certain minimum standards of health and welfare, the large landowner ultimately suffered. In their charitable donations the landowners were also inspired by certain religious and prestige-oriented motives. Alms were, as Cutileiro has noted, "a loan to God, and served as an atonement for sins committed in this world while at the same time helping to ward off social unrest." They lent the wealthy added prestige by acting as a means for displaying generosity.

Stealing was sometimes an alternative to begging. Despite the social acceptability of begging, many rural folk found the practice demeaning, for it publicly exposed their inability to provide for their families. Landowners were less sympathetic to stealing, but they were expected to release those caught with little more than a severe verbal reprimand.

As the government gradually began providing social services to the public and as the landowners began experiencing greater financial difficulties, the traditional bond of commitment between worker and landowner began to disappear. Landowners no longer felt obliged to give assistance since other agencies had been set up to protect the workers. Government programs, however, were poorly administered.

The houses of the people (*casas do povo*) were established in rural areas to dispense unemployment and sickness benefits. Landowners were required by the government to contribute a certain monthly portion of their taxable incomes, and workers were expected to pay monthly membership dues. Benefits included free medical service, discounts on drugs, and old-age pensions. For fishermen the counterpart scheme was the houses of the fishermen (*casas dos pescadores*). Welfare schemes for industrial workers were generally better administered and the benefits more inclusive. The Agency of Social Welfare and Family Assistance (Caixas de Previdência e Abono e Familia) was charged with dispensing benefits for industrial workers.

Before the revolution the Ministry of Corporations was the overseer of social welfare programs. Since the revolution the separate Ministry of Social Affairs has been organized and charged with developing better nationwide health and insurance schemes. In 1976 pressing political and economic problems had pushed the development of social programs into the background.

LEISURE

The Portuguese delight in many of the traditional pastimes of their ancestors. Although some forms of modern entertainment—notably films and soccer games—have become popular in recent years, traditional forms of leisure activity continue to play an important role in the lives of most Portuguese. They include gathering at coffeehouses, attending bullfights, listening to fados (certain urban Portuguese folk songs), and attending festas, or celebrations.

Sitting in cafés sipping coffee is a common and widespread practice among Portuguese men. At almost any time of the day, but most often between midmorning and midafternoon, groups of men can be found frequenting the coffeehouses. Although men may stop in cafés simply to taste the renowned Portuguese coffees (special African and Brazilian blends), more often than not they are also interested in exchanging news and gossip. Before the revolution in particular, coffeehouses were important sources of political information. Their social and communications function continues to be the most important. If Portuguese women have a counterpart to the coffeehouse, it is perhaps the *pastelaria*, or pastry shop. Like the coffeehouses the *pastelarias* serve as a kind of marketplace for the trading of information and gossip.

Bullfighting is among the oldest Portuguese activities. Although the soccer match has begun to rival the bullfight for spectator attention, neither has preempted the other. There are four parts to the classical Portuguese bullfight. It begins with the *courtesias*, or parade to the ring. The bulls are driven through the streets of the city or town by a group of men on horseback. The parade is an integral part of the total performance, and no amount of ceremony is spared in its execution. When the bulls arrive at the ring, the *toureiros* (bullfighters) enter. These are men who confront the bull on foot and with capes. Essentially their stunts are meant only to set the stage for the main attraction—the *cavaleiro* (horseman) versus the bull. The art of Portuguese bullfighting lies in the demonstration by the *cavaleiro* of agility and equestrian skill. The *cavaleiro* must strategically place six *bandarilhas* (lances) of progressively shorter lengths along the bull's neck muscle. Each maneuver brings the rider closer and closer to the bull. The successful *cavaleiro* is one who has properly placed his *bandarilhas* into the bull without allowing his horse to be gored in the process. In reality danger is kept at a minimum. The bull's horns are padded, and he is not killed in the ring. (In contrast Spanish bullfighting pits one man on foot against a bull in what becomes an act of daring and a display of courage; and the killing of the bull is part of the performance.) The last part of the Portuguese bullfight is the *pega de cara* (literally, grabbing the face). In it, a group of men (usually eight) on foot enter the ring to challenge the bull to one final bout. They attempt by sheer numbers to surround and subdue the bull. After the *pega de cara* the bull is led out of the ring—to be either slaughtered or returned to the pasture as a breeding bull.

Easter marks the opening of the bullfighting season, which generally runs for six to seven months. Classical bullfights are most popular in southern Portugal, and both the bulls and the specially trained horses are bred in the Alentejo and Ribatejo regions. There are regional variations in bullfighting. In the Azores, for example, bullfighting is an amateur's activity in which the whole village participates. A long rope controlled by a group of men is attached to the bull. Except for this one restriction the bull is let loose in the streets of the town. The more daring of the young men attempt to confront the bull and evade its charges to impress the onlookers—that is, those who have retreated behind the wooden barriers erected for protection.

Listening to fados is another favorite Portuguese pastime. The singing of fados is something unique to Portugal. Literally, fado means fate. The fado is a song that expresses a kind of melancholy longing, intermingled with sadness and resignation. The origin of the fado is unknown although it is thought to date from the late 1700s and early 1800s and to reflect a mixture of Moorish, African, and indigenous influences. It is known, however, that this style of music evolved among the urban poor. The *fadista* (singer of the fados) is usually a woman clothed in black—the traditional garb of the poor. Two guitarists accompany her in mournful and soul-felt tunes. The singers in the old sections of the city of Lisbon are said to render the most authentic versions of the fado.

Festas are popular in Portugal. Usually they are held in honor of a village or parish patron saint, although other events, such as the harvest, are also cause for celebration. Religious beliefs and rituals are directly connected and continue to play an important role in most festas, although the Portuguese church is dominating these activities less and less. Men from each of the communities are annually selected to organize and collect money for the festive occasions. The women participate in any ritualistic activities connected with the various festas. The number of small, local festas has increased since the early part of the twentieth century, and the festa is becoming an important means whereby each village affirms its separate territorial identity.

The best known of the festas internationally is the *círio* (literally, large candle). The name derives from the fact that images were molded in wax to represent saints. The *círio* marks the journey of the saints from one parish to the next. Large groups of people gather to bid the saint farewell and to accompany the statue as it is carried to the parish church that will house it for the coming year. The procession proceeds through the parish area gathering followers as it stops to rest in each of the villages. *Círios* are found in the Estremadura region of Portugal.

* * * * * * * * * * * * * * *

There is a dearth of information on population and living conditions in Portugal both before and after the revolution of April 1974. The Portuguese government conducts a census of the population every ten years and compiles an annual volume of general statistics that includes demographic, economic, and social data. The figures presented appear to be reliable and are used by the United Nations, the International Labor Organization, and the Organization for Economic Cooperation and Development. There have been few detailed analyses, however, of the population data—the notable exception being the somewhat technical work by Massimo Livi Bacci, *A Century of Portuguese Fertility*. The yearly Portuguese government publication *Boletim Anual* of the Secretariodo National de Emigração is a thorough compilation of emigration data, and various issues of the journal *Migration News* (Geneva) contribute additional useful information. Sarah Bradford's *Portugal* and José Cutileiro's *A Portuguese Rural Society* both provide a useful but very general overview of living conditions in Portugal. (For further information see Bibliography.)

CHAPTER 5

SOCIAL SYSTEM

The most distinctive feature of Portugal's social structure has been its remarkable continuity—surviving through time nearly unaltered. Except for distinctions based on class, Portugal has historically been characterized by few cleavages. The country was consolidated and unified in the thirteenth century, achieving nationhood at a time when most of the countries of modern-day Europe had not yet been created. It was never plagued by the ethnic, religious, and linguistic conflicts that marked the development of many of its European neighbors. Mainland Portugal is one of the most culturally homogeneous nation-states in the world. Ironically the very stability—indeed the stagnation—of Portugal's social structure may well have been a product of the country's homogeneity.

In early Portugal social prestige, political power, and economic prosperity all depended on ownership of land. Such ownership was concentrated in the hands of the few. Initially the aristocracy and the clergy held the rights to the land. During the eighteenth and nineteenth centuries they were gradually replaced by a nouveau riche class who amassed wealth by investing in land. The great majority of the peasants, however, remained isolated and unaffected, and the actual structure of the society changed little. In the early 1970s Portuguese society still comprised a small, wealthy upper class, a somewhat larger middle class, and a massive, predominantly rural lower class.

The prerevolution Portuguese elite formed a conscious and self-perpetuating group. Among them they controlled all centers of power —the government, the church, industry, agriculture, finance, education, and the military. There was evidence of horizontal mobility from the top echelon of one segment of the elite to the top of another. Education seemed to provide the only channel of upward mobility, although the ability to attend the university was itself a function of economic prosperity.

The middle class in Portugal was small compared with its West European counterparts. Urbanization and industrialization were beginning to create new occupational categories, resulting in the growth in the 1960s and 1970s of a lower middle class of skilled workmen and technicians. The middle class appeared to be in a state of flux, and the relative prestige of some of the more traditional middle-class occupations was changing. Lack of information, however, made it impossible to give other than an impressionistic account of this class.

The people *(o povo)* were not a homogeneous group. In the rural areas differences of outlook based on region, patterns of landholding, and village social organization were apparent. In general peasants in the north tended to be small landowners who were strongly attached to their land and who were thought to be politically conservative. Within their villages there was little social differentiation. In contrast peasants in the south tended to have less access to the land and were thought to be more politically active. Because they often worked for latifundists, large landowners, they were daily confronted with and reminded of the uneven distribution of wealth.

Before the revolution of 1974 the Portuguese state was based on a corporative system. Corporative bodies *(organismos corporativos)*, organized according to occupation, roughly corresponded to social class divisions. In theory the interests of the different classes were viewed as essentially harmonious, and the corporative bodies were to provide channels of class articulation. In reality these bodies were thought by members of all social classes to be ineffective and to stifle expression. They were bypassed in favor of personal and individual channels of communication. In order to make their voices heard the elite were able to rely on friendships; the people had to rely on the patronage of the rich.

The hierarchical structure of Portuguese society before the revolution extended all the way down to the level of the family and the individual. The ideal family was one based on the authority of the husband-father. It was often made strikingly explicit in legal codes that gave the male head of the household a virtual monopoly on all economic and political decisions. In real life, however, variation in kinship patterns and family relations was evident. The wealthy tended to approach the ideal type more closely; economic necessity often dictated that the poor deviate from the model.

In mid-1976 it was too early to tell the extent to which the revolution would affect the traditional attitudes of the Portuguese and alter the social structure of the country. The social changes that had been set in motion and speeded up in the decade before the revolution—urbanization, industrialization, and temporary and seasonal emigration—promised to have far-reaching social implications. The revolution, however, had essentially been implemented from the top. Although many people saw the need for social change, many others were staunchly opposed to radical reforms. It was left to the postrevolution government to strike a balance between tradition and modernity.

HISTORICAL SETTING

The historian Stanley Payne has characterized early Portugal as a three-tiered hierarchically structured society. The military aristocracy formed the top layer. In wresting the land from the Moors the Portuguese monarchs had relied heavily on the military aristocracy and for services rendered gratefully offered them large tracts of land. The aristocracy was small—Payne has estimated "a half dozen truly powerful and influential aristocratic families." They were allied to the crown through blood relations and shared in royal revenues. The circulation of wealth and influence among such a small, related ruling clique perpetuated the social, economic, and political dominance of that group. To the upper class aristocracy should also be added the military-religious orders of the Roman Catholic Church. Having acted as soldiers of the crown, they had acquired vast estates as gifts—particularly in central and southern Portugal. The large stores of wealth built up from these tax-exempt lands early accorded the church a significant economic and political role in Portugal—a fact that quickly led to friction between various monarchs and the church hierarchy (see ch.6).

A group of *cavaleiros vilãos* (commoner knights) formed the next rung on the social ladder. They shared neither the social heritage nor the vast wealth of the noble class, but through their military services to the crown they had managed to secure special favors. Land grants, supplementary allowances from the crown, and tax exemptions allowed them over time to amass substantial wealth.

At the bottom of the social scale—separated from the two higher strata by a wide gulf of poverty—were the peasants. Their poverty set them apart as a class; but despite the generic term, the "peasants" were neither a solidified, class-conscious group nor an undifferentiated mass. They included a group (primarily in the north) who enjoyed certain hereditary renting rights over the land, a group of sharecroppers whose access to the land was somewhat more regulated and restricted, a group who worked as laborers on larger estates but were sometimes allowed to cultivate small plots, and a group of landless laborers (primarily in the south).

In the ancien régime land meant economic and political power and social prestige. The aristocracy and the clergy retained control over most of the land until the mid-eighteenth century. Neither of the two groups, however, was particularly interested in working or managing the land. Members of the aristocracy, for example, preferred to dabble in the lucrative trading opened up by exploration and exploitation of new lands in South America and India. Many had been given land grants and political jurisdiction in the overseas territories. Thus large tracts of land in Portugal were left uncultivated—maintained as country estates, hunting preserves, or monastery lands. Proprietors leased the remaining lands, and many became quite wealthy and locally influential by cultivating part of the land themselves and inviting sharecroppers to sublet other tracts.

The first concerted attempt at limited agrarian reform came under the dictatorship of the marquis of Pombal, prime minister to King José from 1756 to 1777. Neither the aristocracy nor the church hierarchy fared well under Pombal's dictatorship. Many of the religious orders were expelled, and ecclesiastical lands were confiscated and resold by the crown. The political power of the aristocracy and its jurisdiction over the overseas territories were also curbed. Unfortunately the peasants were not the main benefactors of Pombal's reforms. The land merely changed hands at the top, primarily benefiting the proprietors who had managed to accumulate enough capital to invest in land. If Pombal had further plans for land reform, they were laid to rest with the fall of his government in 1777.

In the area of trade Pombal had relied heavily on state-regulated and -sanctioned monopolies. Such policies stifled the development of a middle class. Still, profitable trade possibilities had emerged with the goods flowing in from the overseas territories, and by the end of the 1700s a class of wealthy merchants of nonaristocratic origin had developed in Portugal. They attained recognition as a group though their numbers were small, and their political influence was limited. They and the liberal professionals made up what middle class existed in Portugal. Yet despite some shifts in landownership and the emergence of a middle class, by the early nineteenth century the structure of Portuguese society had changed little from the ancien régime. The aristocracy, the wealthy bourgeoisie, and the clergy numbered about 3 percent of the population and the mercantile class and the professionals about 9 percent. Separated by abysmal poverty were the people.

The eighteenth and nineteenth centuries were a time of social upheaval for much of Europe, but Portugal remained isolated and largely unaffected. The peasantry was oblivious to the kinds of changes occurring outside Portugal, and the middle class lacked the capability and the class consciousness to spearhead social change. The aristocracy, therefore, felt little pressure from below. Neither the brief occupation of Portugal by the French in 1807 and 1808 nor the 1832-34 civil war portended a dramatic alteration of the pattern of society. The liberal governments of the nineteenth century auctioned off more church land, but again there was only a change of landowners, not an improvement of the peasant's lot. In fact with partition of the common lands—access to which peasants had shared as a community—the peasant became relatively worse off. Payne noted that in the mid-nineteenth century there was a proliferation of aristocratic titles but only because they were granted with greater frequency and less discretion. The nouveaux riches had begun to replace the traditional aristocracy, but just before the end of the century the wealthy upper classes still accounted for only a minuscule proportion of the population—perhaps 1 percent. The middle classes had grown—albeit slowly in comparison with the increase in the number of their counterparts in Europe—to 15 percent. The overwhelming majority remained poor and rural, although an urban proletariat had also begun to evolve.

The parliamentary republic that came into being in 1910 was looked to with hope by those who saw the need for social change and a better distribution of wealth. At first the middle class profited from land reform but mostly to the detriment of the lower class. What common lands had been left intact were parceled out during the republican period. Peasant holdings continued to decrease. Toward the end of the republic the economic situation had rapidly worsened and was marked by rampant inflation and high taxation. Initially many of the people approved the fall of the republic in 1926 and the eventual rise to power of António de Oliveira Salazar.

SOCIAL STRATIFICATION UNDER SALAZAR

The Salazar government did little to remedy the social inequalities prevalent in Portugal. The vast majority of the population remained rural and was left outside and untouched by the slowly developing economy. Salazar recognized that much of his strength lay in the conservative peasantry (particularly in the north, where the people were strongly attached to the land); thus he was not anxious to introduce changes, such as intensive literacy campaigns, that could have had far-reaching implications. Under his New State (Estado Novo), social status remained ascriptive—that is, based on birth. His own philosophy on the distribution of wealth and opportunity was manifest in the statements attributed to him that "God had given him 'the privilege of being poor'" and that "education, health, and economic reform 'would not create happiness.'"

During his tenure in office industrialization and urbanization proceeded at a pace much slower than elsewhere in Western Europe. Salazar's success in keeping Portugal out of World War II had given the country an advantage relative to the rest of Europe immediately after the war. Portugal failed, however, to obtain as high a growth rate as the rapidly recovering countries of Europe, which had accepted and benefited from United States aid through the Marshall Plan. Neither Salazar nor his successor, Marcello Caetano, pursued a vigorous social and economic development program. When the regime finally fell in April 1974, Portugal remained by many indicators—level of gross national product (GNP), urbanization, literacy—one of the most underdeveloped regions of Europe.

Social structure appeared to have changed little from what it had been a century earlier. Basing their conclusions on 1960 census data on income and occupation, two Portuguese writers, A. Sedas Nunes and J. David Miranda, confirmed the pyramidal social structure evident in Portugal in the 1960s. They discovered a very small upper class atop a small middle stratum. Despite limited industrialization and urbanization the two groups displayed few signs of growth. Separated from them by a substantially lower standard of living were those at the bottom, consisting predominantly of the rural poor but also including a growing urban proletariat. The authors linked the persistence of an archaic and ascriptive social structure to the low level of economic development and the mass emigration, which although providing a safety valve for excess labor had only delayed necessary internal development.

In another study also based on census data Miranda found evidence to suggest four levels of social status in Portugal. He divided the population according to occupational criteria. An upper stratum composed of large-scale industrialists (owners and managers), professionals (doctors and lawyers), university professors, and high-level government administrators accounted for 3.8 percent of the population; a middle stratum of rural proprietors, military officers, industrialists heading small-scale enterprises, and high-school teachers constituted 6.9 percent of the population; an intermediate level designated lower middle or upper lower consisted of small entrepreneurs, lower civil servants, and primary-school teachers and made up 27.2 percent of the population; and the largest group—62.1 percent of the population —were "workers not self-employed." Interestingly Miranda also found that 84 percent of the university students in Portugal in the early 1960s had come from the two highest strata, which together had constituted only a little over one-tenth of the population.

These two studies confirmed the estimates of class size in the 1960s and early 1970s determined independently by another Portuguese writer, Herminio Martins. Using a range of socioeconomic indicators— among them level of education and percentage of surtax payers within particular income-occupational groups—he found that the upper echelon of Portuguese society constituted about 1 percent of the population. A middle class identified according to occupation, tax information, and voting privilege was estimated at 15 to 25 percent of the economically active population (6 to 10 percent of the total). Thus at least 75 percent of the population remained members of the lower class.

If there was a change in the Portuguese social structure during the time of Salazar's New State, it was perhaps the emergence of a class that had achieved a degree of comfort above a bare subsistence level. These were the clerks, lower civil servants, and others who made up what might be termed an upper lower class or lower middle class. There remained, however, a large gulf in wealth and prestige between this group and the two upper strata.

The Elite

Some have called prerevolution Portugal a "classist dictatorship," that is, one based on the existence and perpetuation of a small elite group representing a spectrum of interests. Indeed the upper class in Portugal before the revolution of April 1974 formed a group that was aware of its influence and status and whose members recognized a shared unity based on common values and attitudes. Similar educational experiences and the tendency to intermarry had formed what might be called a common culture. Among the elite ranks were the largest landowners, the directors and owners of the major industries, high-ranking government officials, leading financiers, top-level military officers, the Catholic church hierarchy, university professors, and the elite of the professions (medical specialists and leading lawyers). The upper class recognized these careers as the most prestigious. When a sample of businessmen, for example, was asked to rank occupations according to prestige, "the businessmen ranked university professors as the most prestigious profession, followed by medical specialist, businessmen heading an enterprise employing more than 450 workers, director-general of a ministry, government engineer, and lastly, colonel with a command."

With the growth of industry (albeit small relative to other West European countries), businessmen rose to a position of special preeminence. The increasing importance of industry to the national economy (industry contributes more than any other sector to GNP) and the rapid growth of urban centers contributed to the influence and power of business leaders, especially during the 1960s. One impressionistic account of social status in Portugal maintained that the owner or director of a large-scale enterprise had "in general become an almost mythical figure, whose status . . . [was] higher than that of almost everybody else in Portugal except for two or three of the most highly placed officials in the nation."

Harry M. Makler, an American sociologist, studied the business elite of northern and central Portugal extensively during the 1960s. His sample included a group of about 300 industrialists heading manufacturing and service enterprises that employed from fifty to 1,000 workers. His sample was specially designed to include almost all of the men heading the largest industries. The typical businessman, he found, was drawn from a middle-class family. The vast majority were sons of businessmen, professionals, or property owners. They were a highly educated group, and a substantial proportion had pursued advanced, university degrees. Education in Portugal was one of the few channels of upward social mobility, but it was very expensive and thus itself a sign of economic prosperity. Before the revolution, as one critic of the regime noted, "secondary and higher education . . . [was] amongst the scarcest and most unequally distributed goods in the stratification system."

Familism in business was still evident in Portugal before 1974. It was more pronounced in the north, where small businesses predominated, but even the larger industries tended to be family owned and operated. It has been estimated that 80 percent of the economy was dependent on eight families, most of whom had secured their fortunes and positions of influence before Salazar's regime. Heads of enterprises employed relatives as a matter of course. Even the directors of large-scale modern industries hired members of their families, so that there appeared to be a direct relation between the size of the firm and the number of family members employed.

There was evidence to indicate a substantial amount of horizontal mobility from the top ranks of various occupations into big business. Such movement reinforced the unity of values and group consciousness among members of the upper stratum and also facilitated open channels of communication between those influential in the economy, the polity, the military, and the educational network. Some of the directors of the largest industries in the 1960s had entered big business through the upper levels of other prestigious occupations. Makler found that "the typical career path to a large modern corporation in Portugal started with an assistant professorship at a university, particularly under the tutelage of a well-known catedrático [university professor], movement into an undersecretarial (deputy minister) position and then either from there to a top industrial post or continuation in the government, moving into a ministerial position, and then into industry."

The latifundists of southern Portugal were a traditional part of the upper stratum of Portuguese society before the revolution. They had experienced a decline in relative social prestige, however, in the twenty years before the revolution. The southern landowner had faced a rise in wages (although agricultural wages were still well below the West European norm), a decrease in prices for agricultural products, and a depreciation in the value of land (according to some estimates, up to 75 percent). Thus their income had remained steady or had declined while that of the industrialist had risen. Most latifundists, however, were absentee landlords who owned land in several parishes. They also maintained firm links with the upper urban stratum, often investing in industry.

The latifundists had more in common socially and culturally with their urban counterparts than with other groups in rural Portugal. Most of them had never worked on the land they owned, and they displayed an aversion to manual labor. Many resided in urban areas, leaving the day-to-day business of agriculture in the hands of estate managers. They adopted the speech and the dress of urbanites and tended to accentuate their differences in order to distance themselves from the people. Although many of the latifundists had come, four or five generations earlier, from modest origins, they often attemped to mask this fact by tracing their ancestry to the aristocracy. The republican government had prohibited the use of titles during the early part of the twentieth century, but even in the 1960s titles continued to be used unofficially.

Like the industrialists, the latifundists had attended the university and encouraged their children to pursue formal education. By and large they had been loyal supporters of the New State and its ascriptive social system. They had secured and maintained their large landholdings by intermarrying among themselves or with the urban industrial, political, and professional elite whose wealth was equal to their own. Although they had not necessarily been able to enact legislation, they had been able to affect its outcome. Thus when a minor agrarian reform program had been proposed in the early 1960s, the latifundists as a group had been able effectively to forestall it.

Those in the professions enjoyed a special prominence in Portuguese society because of their education and their scarcity. There was, for example, less than one doctor—generalist or specialist—per 1,000 of the population in the early 1970s, and most doctors were concentrated in the two largest cities, Lisbon and Porto. Law was one of the more popular professions among Portuguese university students, and together with the military and the professoriate it was generally considered a means of attaining entrance to a high-level government career. According to one account, "well over half the civilian Cabinet ministers during the period 1932-68 graduated in Law." Incomes were roughly equal for persons in high positions in the military and government and at the university.

One of the best examples of interclass mobility and overlapping interest among the Portuguese elite was that provided by Caetano, prime minister until the revolution of 1974. As one author pointed out, Caetano had come from a modest socioeconomic background. Given the opportunity to pursue a university education, he was eventually able to secure a position as a prominent law professor. He then shifted to a political career, serving in a variety of capacities including cabinet member. He later married into a wealthy industrial family.

The Middle Class

The middle class in Portugal was ill defined and difficult to describe. It was small relative to comparable groups in other European countries and included, in its broadest conception, a wide range of income-occupational groups. Among the members of the traditional middle class were small-scale entrepreneurs, those in the professions, and university teachers below the level of professor. Most of these people were quite well-off and often had more in common with the upper class than with the mass of the population. During the 1960s and 1970s, however, another group had begun to achieve a modicum of comfort and economic security. This group could be classified as lower middle class or upper lower class and included skilled technicians, clerks and employees in the developing services sector, midlevel business executives, schoolteachers, and lower to midlevel civil servants.

Urbanization and industrialization brought changes to traditional occupations and affected their relative prestige by creating new career alternatives with new pay scales. In the past, for example, many moderately prosperous landowners had entered government in order both to supplement income from the land and to enhance their social prestige. By the late 1960s government employment was no longer considered well paying, benefit laden, or socially prestigious. Many government employees had found it necessary to hold two jobs in order to maintain their accustomed standard of living, and according to João Baptista Nunes Pereira Neto, a Portuguese social scientist, "those at the bottom of the ladder now sell smuggled goods, work as doormen at theaters, do little bookkeeping jobs and door-to-door selling, collect bills." College graduates appeared to be drawn away from government and into business.

The shopkeeper was another member of the middle class whose social prestige and real income suffered during the 1960s and early 1970s. In the smaller towns he once played an important and influential role. Through his extension of credit he often managed to build up a substantial body of customers who were tied to him from one annual agricultural cycle to the next. He was gradually being replaced, however, by larger companies that, with lower overheads, could afford to sell comparable goods at reduced prices. As it became less necessary to enter into patronage relationships with the shopkeeper-middleman, his status declined accordingly.

In contrast technicians and skilled workmen were among those whose standard of living improved rapidly in the ten to fifteen years before the revolution. Much of their newfound wealth was spent in conspicuous consumption in an effort to enhance their social prestige.

If there was a middle class in rural Portugal, it perhaps comprised medium-sized landowners. The devaluation of land and the opening of new career opportunities in the factories, however, had caused them to suffer a decrease in relative prestige and wealth during the 1960s. They were distinct from the latifundists not only because their incomes were generally smaller but also because those incomes were derived entirely from the land they owned, worked, and lived on. They did not display an aversion to manual labor; most had worked in the fields and had taken an active part in the management of their farms. They tended to live comfortably but not ostentatiously and, although their prosperity was evident, they were less concerned with maintaining social appearances. Their dress and speech tended to reflect their provincial origins, and they frequently interacted with their

124

poorer neighbors—if not socially, then in amiable work relations. Most of the power and influence of the proprietors was limited to a local level. Generally they were less well educated than the latifundists, although educational opportunities were available to them, and they encouraged their children to pursue university education.

The People

It is tempting to characterize social differences within Portugal in terms of oversimplified contrasts. Cleavages based on wealth (rich and poor), region (north and south), and economic activity (urban and rural) are all important distinctions that need to be taken into account simultaneously in describing the people. Among the upper classes wealth seemed to be the single most important criterion of membership, but within the lower class a common bond of poverty had not fostered a shared consciousness. In the early 1970s there were at least three distinct groups of the poor: the small landholding peasant (concentrated primarily in the north), the peasant with limited or no access to the land (concentrated primarily in the south), and the urban worker.

Before the revolution of April 1974 patterns of landholding continued to be the standard indicator of social stratification, especially in rural Portugal. Land still meant prestige, even though its value was decreasing. Many were deserting the countryside to find work in the city and abroad, but their intent was not to escape the land through emigration but rather to earn enough money to return and invest in the land.

One survey indicated that 78 percent of the farms were less than four hectares (one hectare equals 2.47 acres) in size and covered only 15 percent of the total land area. Most of these small farms were located in the north, where the majority of the population resided. The south was the land of latifundios (large estates), and the majority of the peasants there had only partial access to the land or were completely landless. In addition to regional variations in patterns of landholding, there also seemed to be important regional variations in village social organization. Social differentiation, for example, was less visible in the north but was confronted almost daily in the south. This in part explained the often repeated generalization that the peasants in the north were politically more conservative than the peasants in the south.

Two anthropological studies illustrated the extent of regional differences based on landholding patterns and intravillage organization. The anthropologist Joyce F. Riegelhaupt found a total absence of class distinctions in the Estremadura parish where she conducted her fieldwork. The majority of the population were small-scale farmers. Poverty was equally dispersed throughout the village. Class distinctions

125

were only brought into fine relief in the villagers' contacts with outsiders, mostly wealthy Lisbonites. Contacts with these wealthy people were not infrequent, but they were ephemeral and did not encroach on the day-to-day life of the village. Women traveled to Lisbon to sell their products (chicken, eggs, bread) and to work temporarily as domestic servants. Men seldom left the village and spent most of their day in the fields. Thus class contrasts were distant. The villagers were aware of their importance on a national level, but everyone in the locality shared the same benefits, the same problems, and the same frustrations.

In contrast the Alentejo parish studied by the anthropologist José Cutileiro was hierarchically structured. At the top were the wealthy absentee landowners who either rented out their lands or hired someone to manage them. Next were the proprietors, local men who had built up sizable holdings but had continued to operate the land themselves with the help of hired laborers. Below these two groups were the rural poor—the small landowner, the sharecropper *(seareiro)*, and the landless laborer. In Cutileiro's parish these groups were in continual contact with one another, if only indirectly. Class distinctions were emphasized, particularly by the upper stratum. On the one hand the disdain of the latifundists for manual labor and on the other the ambivalence of the small farmers and laborers toward the rich (whom they resented yet desired to emulate) meant that class tensions lay seething beneath the surface.

Even among the rural poor Cutileiro found that a kind of social hierarchy existed—again based on access to the land. In the hierarchy of the poor those who owned land were accorded the highest prestige, the sharecroppers came next, and the landless laborers were at the bottom. At one time demarcations of status within the lower class were supposed to have been as rigid as those between social classes. Each group, for example, had its own marriage circle. With the devaluation of land and the rise in agricultural wages, however, distinctions tended to blur. Moreover many small landowners found it necessary to supplement their incomes with wagework, and some so-called landless peasants were able to purchase small plots with their meager earnings.

Differences in prestige had to do with the sense of security derived from ownership of land rather than with actual differences of wealth. Traditionally the landless laborer was the least secure. He was subject to seasonal employment and, when a harvest was poor, he was apt to find himself unemployed for an indeterminate length of time. Despite a rise in wages during the 1960s, he was still among the poorest paid of all Portuguese. The work of the rural laborer was least envied and ranked lowest in social prestige. Rural laborers in the Alentejo were referred to as *trabalhadores* (workers)—a term applied solely to agricultural wagework and one that carried with it a low

126

status valuation. Sharecroppers and small landowners did the same kind of work as *trabalhadores,* but they were self-employed. *Trabalho* implied manual labor—working with one's hands—and even those who ran machinery felt themselves to be one step above the *trabalhadores.*

Despite these intraclass differentiations there were some signs of solidarity among the poor. Proprietors and small landowners who managed their own land were accorded more personal respect than the absentee latifundists, even though the position of the latter was considered more prestigious. Cutileiro observed that "labourers feel obliged to work harder for the small landowners, with whom they have a closer personal relationship and who are not as rich as the latifundists." In his opinion the laborers' manipulation of their own productivity in this way was a mild form of social protest.

Urbanization and the consequent development of an urban working class were relatively recent phenomena in Portugal. Between 1960 and 1970, however, the large industrial centers along the coast were the only areas on the mainland that recorded a growth in population (see ch. 4). The proliferation of shantytowns indicated that it was primarily an increase of the urban poor. The new industrial laborer was drawn from the ranks of the landless peasants. Factory workers generally earned more than rural laborers, and once employed they were not subject to the same kind of seasonal layoffs; yet within the bounds of the city they too occupied the lowest level on the social scale.

The author Sarah Bradford has stressed the contrast between urban and rural Portugal, describing it as not only a difference in geography and economic activity but also a difference in time. She was in fact characterizing an important difference in attitude between the rural and the urban Portuguese. The countryside was thought to be the stronghold of tradition, where the peasant lived much as he had centuries earlier—wedded to the land, unaware of the wider world, and fearful of change. In contrast the city was thought to be the symbol of all that was modern. Martins noted, however, that the shift from rural to urban in Portugal had been a "highly mediated" one—an indication that the outlook of the urban poor remained essentially parochial. Many of the poor had continued to live in rural areas while working in the factories; some had made a graduated move to the city (from village to town to city); and others were insulated within the city by their network of kin relations, which limited their exposure to new people and ideas.

CHANNELS OF SOCIAL ACTION

Formal Channels

The New State was established as a corporative system. In theory, corporatism *(corporativismo)* held that the interests of the various social classes were essentially harmonious. Although differences were bound to arise, the interests of the urban worker and the industrialist as well as those of the rural laborer and the landowner were not seen as conflicting. Rather disagreements were considered likely to be misunderstandings that could be readily resolved through the corporative organizations. The state was to oversee these organizations but only in order to ensure that each group was adequately represented.

The corporative bodies concerned with economic activity were most reflective of social class division. They were organized along occupational lines. In urban areas industrialists and small entrepreneurs were organized into guilds *(grémios)* depending on the branch of industry and its location. Urban workers were organized into syndicates *(sindicatos)*, roughly comparable to trade unions. In the rural areas there were landowners' guilds *(grémios da lavoura)* and, for farm laborers, houses of the people *(casas do povo)*. These organizations, particularly the guilds, were meant to regulate relations among members as well as to act as representative bodies in relations with the other corporative groups and with the government. Industrial guilds, for example, dealt with the concerns of individual members as well as with worker-management and government-management relations. The houses of the people served diffuse functions including the distribution of health and welfare benefits, and membership was compulsory for landowners (see ch. 4).

Corporative bodies, designed as channels for class articulation and social action, were considered ineffective or a least inefficient by the vast majority of the population at all social levels. To the rural laborer the houses of the people were synonymous with the landowners' interests since landowners usually controlled the governing boards. The houses rarely upheld the laborer who had the audacity to complain about unfair treatment from a landowner. In the Alentejo parish studied by Cutileiro, the people looked on the house of the people as an organization "alien to their interest, and . . . in fact, a cross between a tax collecting office and a charity organization." To the urban laborer the syndicates meant a usurpation of the right to freely elected trade unions.

But the lower classes were not alone in their condemnation of the corporative organizations. Both industrialists and landowners viewed them as needlessly bothersome and inefficient for achieving specific goals. Holding a corporative office depended on political reliability, but the associations were rarely instrumental in pushing through government legislation. In interviewing the Portuguese business elite, Makler found that few turned solely to the guilds to resolve business problems or to secure government attention despite the fact that almost half the men in his sample held either a governmental office or a position of leadership in a corporative body. Questions over leadership and administrative responsiveness, doubts concerning the actual authority of the guilds and the effectiveness of a corporative system, and competitiveness among members were often-cited complaints.

It was interesting that both landowners and industrialists considered their guilds of dubious value and that a government largely supported by these elites should have sought to contain their expression. What Makler observed in the 1960s of industry-government relations held true also for landowner-government relations: "This was a group to which the regime was beholden but wished to keep at arm's length, a group on which the regime's power was based but which was accorded little power of its own. . . . It appears that the regime attempted through compartmentalization both to maintain and contain the traditional class structure."

Thus the corporative bodies of the New State were little more than networks of state surveillance and control, and they were recognized as such by all members of society. Through these associations the government sought to dilute and diffuse any real interest group or class-based action. At the bottom levels they were seen as instruments of repression, at the top as circuitous mechanisms for social action. In order to make their interests known, th Portuguese traditionally turned to informal and individual communication networks.

Informal Channels

It was difficult to speak of social or class action in Portugal before the revolution of April 1974. Whenever administrative or other help was sought, it was sought through individual and personnal channels. One's facility and resourcefulness in getting things done were a product of whom one knew. Obtaining favors from an equal depended on friendship; obtaining favors from one higher up on the social ladder depended on patronage. Both were seen as relationships based on give-and-take; reciprocity, albeit uneven, was expected in all transactions. The poor did not resent having to pay the rich for services rendered, for it reassured them they were not mere recipients of charity. Ideally both sides were to retain a semblance of power so that a favor was returned with a favor. Such mutual leverage, however, was often more illusory than real.

Friendship and patronage networks were the cement of Portuguese society and the primary means of communication within and between social classes long before the government of Salazar appeared on the scene. Formal class and political organizations have come and gone, but friendship and patronage have remained the basic avenues of social action.

The obvious alternative to the lack of formal channels for latifundists and industrialists was the network of friendships acquired from university days, through intermarriages, and through contacts developed within the social circuit of the elite. It was not unusual for those in the upper stratum to bypass bureaucratic machinery and go directly to the top with problems. Many of the businessmen in Makler's sample admitted circumventing the corporative bodies and getting in touch with the administration directly. Those in the most advantageous position were the directors of large industries, many of whom held or had held national offices in the government. Big business often recruited executives from the high levels of government, and it tended to benefit from the contacts these new employees brought with them.

Likewise the latifundists often derived more benefits and were able to exert more political pressure on a personal level than through the guilds. While Cutileiro was doing his fieldwork in an Alentejo parish, the minister of economy paid a visit to the area to discuss the agricultural situation. He met with the latifundists privately but did not consult the guild. Similar observations led Cutileiro to conclude that "the relevant exchanges preceding government measures relating to agriculture may not take place in Parliament or in the appropriate government departments, but over dining tables or in the course of the shooting parties given by the latifundists."

The small-scale entrepreneurs and medium-sized landowners were perhaps the groups that felt least able to articulate their interests. Their frequent competitiveness with the more wealthy precluded the kinds of patronage relationships open to the poor, and they often did not have the necessary connections to deal with the administration directly. Locally they tended to be influential, often holding municipal office, but in matters requiring national attention they were no match for the large industrialists and the latifundists. They sometimes benefited from the policies pursued by these elites, but they were rarely consulted about them. When Makler asked small industrialist-entrepreneurs how they solved business problems requiring action at the national level, a common response was: "I do nothing." Realizing the inherent limitations of the guilds and lacking friendship connections outside the locality, both the small industrialist and the medium-sized landowner experienced a sense of impotence on extralocal issues.

The peasant could rely on friends for help with day-to-day problems and small favors, but repayment in kind was expected. Close friendships, however, were often precluded because the peasants were in competition for scarce resources. In the south, for example, where seasonal unemployment was common, employment for one laborer sometimes meant unemployment for another. The camaraderie evident in the taverns and during local fiestas tended to hid a deeper sense of ambivalence growing out of economic insecurity. Outwardly convivial relations were maintained. Yet envy over the economic prosperity or good fortune of a fellow peasant was widely held to be the reason for casting the evil eye that brought sickness upon the family (especially the children) of the envied. This kind of envy was not directed toward members of different social classes but only toward those considered equals.

In circumstances that threatened the economic livelihood and integrity of the family, the peasant turned to people higher up on the social ladder, those most able to provide social assistance themselves or to apply the necessary leverage where it counted. Cutileiro noted that the people did not think of patronage as a patterned whole, although to the outside observer these networks of personal relations appeared to be an almost institutionalized part of society. When the Portuguese sought help through personal connections, they usually spoke of "inserting a cunha" (literally, wedge). Cunha refers both to the process of obtaining a needed favor and to the person who acts as the patron in a particular situation. The word concehimentos (contacts) is also used in the context of seeking help through another's intervention.

In the 1970s the vast majority of the population continued to be involved in patronage relationships. Personal connections, however tenuous or ephemeral, were a kind of insurance in times of crisis. People seldom established a permanent patron-client relationship with only one person but rather attempted to establish many such connections, which could be called into force during different situations. Women were often the intermediaries. For example, as domestic servants in the homes of the wealthy, women sometimes formed the closest link between the poor and the rich.

The need to rely almost exclusively on personal relations in order to maintain or better one's position and to receive proper attention and treatment was symptomatic of a society based on inequality. At the same time it served to reinforce and lend legitimacy to the social order. As Cutileiro noted, "The social conditions that create the need for patronage are perpetuated by patronage itself. The basic assumption behind the search for patronage is that the individual can only get what he needs from an unjustly organized society by opposing its apparently hostile and inefficient mechanisms (designed for the common good though these supposedly are) with a series of operative personal relationships with those who are in a position to manipulate the mechanisms of society most effectively." Although patronage had been a traditional aspect of Portuguese society, under the New State it failed to operate effectively while the government provided the masses with no other channel of articulation and action. For example, with the expansion of governmental control and the partial erosion of the landowner's prestige (and hence power), the landowner was less willing and sometimes less able to adopt the kind of patriarchal position toward his workers that he once enjoyed. At the same time the government did not effectively fill the gap created in such areas as social assistance (see ch. 4).

131

THE FAMILY AND THE INDIVIDUAL IN
PORTUGUESE SOCIETY

The family in Portugal is the primary unit of social interaction. In the 1933 Constitution Salazar formalized the role of the family as a channel for social action by basing his corporate state system on it. Section III, Article 12, stated: "The State shall ensure the formation and protection of the family as the source of the maintenance and development of the race, the first and elementary basis of education, discipline and social harmony, and, by its association and representation in the parish and the town, the foundation of all political and administrative order." Theoretically the family was to participate in the national government through representative boards elected locally by the heads of the households in each parish (see ch. 8). In reality government was an institution remote from the majority of the population. Yet there was a certain consonance evident in the organization of the state and the family. Portugal's authoritarian governmental system to some extent had its counterparts at all levels of society, and the family was not an exception. Authority was vested in the head of the household, who legally represented the family in all economic and political affairs. Other members were to trust his judgments and accept his decisions.

Although a patriarchal and nuclear family was the norm in Portugal, a wide array of kinship patterns existed within the society, varying primarily with social status and region. The kinship pattern of the upper classes, both urban and rural, displayed the greatest country-wide uniformity. The father tended to be the focal point of kin relations, and his children—whether married or single—continued to recognize his authority as long as he was alive (and retained control of the wealth). The family unit was generally a cohesive, supportive group. Kin relations outside the nuclear family were closely maintained where they enhanced family prestige and conveniently forgotten where they detracted from it. Holidays, such as Christmas and Easter, and family celebrations were important occasions for confirming kinship ties.

Marriage customs among the elite served to segregate them socially from the people and perpetuate the concentration of wealth in the hands of the few. Before the twentieth century wealthy rival kin groups often vied for political power at the local level. The choice of marriage partners was confined not only to a specific social class but also to a specific geographic area and sometimes to particular kin groups within that area. The peasants were often the pawns in the political maneuvering of the rival groups, who sought their votes or support in return for patronage benefits. During the days of the New State, however, the elite tended to form one "family," united and sharing in political influence, if not power. (The peasant, however,

132

lost what little political leverage he had when free elections were suppressed.) Marriages cut across regional and occupational lines but remained limited to members of the same class. Indeed marriages were often instrumental—a matter of economics as much as sentiment. Although marriage outside one's class was discouraged if not openly opposed, the choice of marriage partner was left open within class boundaries.

The kinship pattern among the poor differed in certain essential respects from that of the elite and displayed more interregional variation. Generalizations were risky, however, and no overall pattern predominated throughout rural or urban Portugal. There seemed to be more evidence of an orientation toward the maternal side of the family. Names and property in northern Portugal were often passed on through the female line. This practice was partially attributable to the high rate of emigration, which had left many villages without a young male population. In the Alentejo, when a marriage outside the village occurred, the couple tended to reside in the village of the wife. Relations between sisters and between mothers and daughters tended to be more permanent and stable than other familial relations, but there were many deviations.

The families of the landed peasantry (particularly in the north) were more close knit than those of the rural laborer and the urban worker. Marriages between members of the same village were the norm. Even as late as the 1960s the thought of permanently leaving the parish, or even the village, of one's birth was inconceivable to the vast majority. Young girls were sometimes forced to seek work outside the village as domestic servants, and young men were sometimes forced to seek wagework in nearby factories or abroad; but all hoped and were expected to return to the village to marry and raise a family.

In parts of northern Portugal a kind of joint household prevailed. The eldest son inherited the land and was responsible for supporting his brothers and sisters, who remained unmarried and continued to work the land or to emigrate and send back money. This system of entail had traditionally been effective in coping with the scarceness of fertile land and, although the younger children were legally entitled to a share of the family property, they recognized that further division was uneconomic. By the mid-twentieth century contacts and experiences outside the village (resulting primarily from emigration and military service) had made young people less willing to remain single. Those who returned to the villages began marrying and, with their savings, setting up households on previously uncultivated lands. The results were beginning to be shown in the erosion of traditional village organization, which had been based on hereditary rights to common pasturelands and in the village council. The newcomers held none of these rights and were thus accorded lower prestige.

133

Among the rural landless and the urban poor, kin relations outside the nuclear family were weak. Except for the parent-child relationship, there were no sets of rights and obligations formally or uniformly observed among relatives. Once married, a son no longer felt subject to a father's authority. Relations between friends were sometimes held above relations between brothers. Marriage partners still tended to be found among social equals, although there was more flexibility and the child of a sharecropper, for instance, might marry the child of a laborer. In general, however, there was little preoccupation with building economic alliances since there was no wealth to be shared. Likewise tracing descent did little to enhance prestige since in most cases one's ancestors had been just as poor as oneself.

Although the oriental attitude of Portuguese men toward their women has perhaps been overemphasized, there was some truth to the conception of the protected, subordinate, and somewhat secluded Portuguese female. Women from upper class families tended to approach the stereotype more closely than those from poorer families. Even as late as the 1930s cases were observed in rural Portugal in which the wealthy did not allow their women on the streets unless accompanied by a female servant or a male member of the family. Women were cut off from contacts with men outside the family—particularly those of a different social rank—although some freedom was allowed between men and women who belonged to kin groups where marriage was considered appropriate. Young couples were chaperoned closely.

Women from the poorer classes deviated most from the traditional conception of the woman in Portuguese society. Among the urban and rural poor, avoidance of unrelated men was often impossible. Economic necessity dictated that women spend part of their time outside the home—helping with the agricultural work, making purchases for the family, and marketing produce not channeled through government agencies. In parts of northern and southern Portugal where emigration or seasonal migration had become a way of life, the long absence of men forced women to assume greater responsibilities.

Nonetheless, whatever the social rank, Portuguese familial stability was conditioned on the hierarchical arrangement of family members. Before 1970 the superordinate status of the male had been formalized in Portuguese legal codes. The woman had few political, economic, or even personal rights. As a subordinate member of the family she was not allowed to vote in local elections, that right being reserved for her husband, the legal household head. (She was able to vote in national elections under certain circumstances, but the literacy requirement was more stringent and the fee higher.) She could not dispose of family property or enter into economic transactions without her husband's consent. She was required by law to reside with her husband

and was not permitted to hold a passport or travel abroad without special authorization.

Such legal discrimination based on sex survived into the 1960s. It was made strikingly explicit in a remark by the minister of justice in 1966 quoted by Riegelhaupt in her anthropological study of the Portuguese woman. The minister, when discussing proposed changes to the Portuguese Civil Code of 1867 that were supposedly meant to upgrade the status of women, commented that the revisions did "not go to the extreme absurdity of proclaiming the juridical equality of married people. This would end by destroying family unity, ignoring the profound natural inequality of the two sexes which is at the basis of matrimonial union."

Legal sexual discrimination reflected and reinforced what were felt to be the traditional and ideal roles of men and women. Only at marriage did a boy become a man, for at that stage in life he established himself as a new center of authority with all the rights and obligations such a position entailed. To the man marriage represented the ability and responsibility to provide a family with the necessities of life. The woman was expected to lend moral fiber to the family through the realization of her role as a faithful and obedient wife. She was expected to defer to her husband on all matters. Cutileiro, conducting his fieldwork in southern Portugal in the 1960s, recorded instances where women still followed several paces behind men when walking in public and still ate separately when male guests were present. Adultery was often an acceptable part of male behavior (the ability to keep a mistress was a sign of prosperity), but women caught having an affair brought shame upon themselves and their families.

The actual economic and political power of women, however, was often far greater than a cursory glance at legal codes and ideal stereotypes might have suggested. Riegelhaupt found that women, at least among the rural poor, were the hub of the communication network—a fact that allotted them a degree of influence beyond that usually assumed. Their daily tasks brought them into close contact with one another and, in marketing produce and accepting work as domestic servants, they were able to establish advantageous relations with wealthy persons outside the village. The activities of men, in contrast, kept them in the fields and isolated from the mainstream of information. They were forced to rely on their wives not only to keep abreast of village news but also to activate the vital communication link between poor and rich. Thus the woman's role as the intermediary in patronage relationships was often politically more important than the man's right to vote. Among the poor Riegelhaupt also discovered that the woman, through her buying, selling, and trading contacts, had considerable influence in the economic sphere. The family budget was often maintained by the woman.

In the 1960s and early 1970s being confined to the home and not having to work remained signs of status for many rural Portuguese women, and young girls still aspired to become "ladies"—the designation that such a life of leisure implied. The effects of modernization and a broadening of contacts were, however, slowly beginning to erode the restrictive attitude toward women and to extend their own aspirations. Although there was still a large discrepancy between women's wages and those of men (both in agriculture and in industry), women were employed in a variety of fields—as schoolteachers, nurses, and civil servants. Women also went to nightclubs and attended the university. According to one estimate they formed about half the student body at Lisbon University in the early 1970s.

Under the Caetano regime a limited upgrading of the status of women had become apparent. Uniform voting requirements for men and women were instituted but only after, as one critical account reported, "the Corporative Chamber has issued a resolution concluding that 'it has been verified that women are more conservative than men, and much more afraid of adventure and change.'" Since the revolution of April 1974 a woman's liberation movement has developed. In early 1976 it appeared that traditional attitudes concerning sex roles would be slow to change. Legal discrimination based on sex, however, had been eliminated by the Constitution of 1976, which stated that "the couple have equal rights and duties regarding civil and political capacity."

POSTREVOLUTION DEVELOPMENTS IN PORTUGAL

Despite its apparent stability Portugal in the 1960s was the scene of some important social processes that helped earn acceptance of, if not pave the way for, the revolution of April 1974. During the 1960s urbanization, emigration, and involvement in colonial wars in Africa had all accelerated to an unprecedented degree, and by the early 1970s the lives of most Portuguese had been touched in one way or another by at least one of these processes. The most important effect of each was the opportunity for exposure to new people and ideas that was given to a Portuguese people heretofore largely isolated from the world outside their villages.

Part of the success of the Salazar and Caetano regimes had been an ability to minimize the contacts and exposure of the people; yet in an effort to maintain an archaic and closed society Salazar and, to a lesser extent, Caetano were led to pursue policies that in the long run could delay change but not stop it. Emigration, for example, was seen as a means of alleviating the pressure of a work force that could not be accommodated within the existing economy. Indeed Martins considered emigration one of the key reasons for the stability of the social structure in Portugal. It siphoned off a young male population that

might have filled class leadership roles; it delayed internal development; and it gave the people an illusion of mobility by enabling them
to better their standard of living without at the same time having to
learn new skills. The result, in Martins' opinion, was to direct the
people's attention away from the unjustness in their own society.

In the long run, however, emigration could only prove destabilizing,
especially to a country such as Portugal with an extremely high rate
of emigration (see ch. 4). The 1960s and 1970s, moreover, saw two
important shifts in emigration. One was its acceleration: over 1.4 million Portuguese emigrated between 1960 and 1973. The other was the
destination of emigrants: over 65 percent of all emigration between
1965 and 1973 was to other European countries, whereas emigration
to North and South America had previously been most popular. Intra-
European emigration was often seasonal and, when it was not, it still
provided the emigrant with more frequent opportunities to return to
his homeland. The emigrant, exposed to migrant laborers from other
countries very much like himself, found many opportunities for the
kind of social dialogue that had been impossible in Portugal. These
new ideas he took with him on his visits home.

In much the same way the colonial wars in Africa were beginning
to impinge on the lives of the Portuguese during the 1960s. The colonies in Africa had long served as a source of pride for all Portuguese,
rich and poor. Portugal had in fact been able to survive as an underdeveloped country in Europe largely because of the rich resources
provided by the African colonies. The intensification of civil violence,
however, brought the Portuguese face to face with the situation as
never before. A major part of the taxpayers' money was being used
to fight a costly and distant war, and more and more families were
being forced to give up their sons to the armed services.

Migration to urban areas in Portugal—to the urban-industrial coastal
strip—also speeded up between 1960 and 1970. It was a migration
primarily of the rural poor, who went to the city without skills and
with little education. Crowding together in makeshift shantytowns,
they came to know people from other parts of the country and were
beginning to experience the meaning of a shared bond of poverty.

It was not the people themselves, however, who initiated the revolution of April 1974, although once under way it was largely carried
out in their name, and many of them welcomed the fall of the old regime. In the aftermath of the revolution press reports drew attention
to the expropriation of estates in southern Portugal by workers'
commissions, the takeover of factories in Lisbon, and the institution
of student-run university departments. The mood of the country appeared to be one of *saneamento* (purge or cleaning up)—getting rid of
all vestiges of the old, repressive regime, including the people that
had served it.

As the provisional governments began to nationalize the banks and certain key industries, a flight of the middle and upper classes out of Portugal became apparent. The country, already having a scarcity of professional and educated people, felt the loss. By the end of 1975 it was estimated that over 80,000 skilled workers, technicians, professionals, and businessmen had left for Brazil alone. They had little difficulty in finding high-level employment abroad. A popular Lisbon saying toward the end of 1975 summarized the situation concisely: "Portugal used to send its legs to Brazil, but now we are sending our heads."

In mid-1976 it was still too early to tell what the net impact of the revolution would be on social structure in Portugal. Several events indicated, however, that it would not be as far reaching as press reports and interested obervers had believed in 1975. Changes appeared to be taking place in Portugal but, as one account aptly commented, they were taking place "among a lot that hasn't changed." Structures were perhaps easier to replace than the attitudes that ensured their viability. Leftist groups had failed to make an impressive showing in the first two elections after the revolution. There seemed to be a growing recognition that many people, particularly in the conservative north, did not fit into the simple dichotomy of laborer versus landowner or proletarian versus bourgeois and that reforms would therefore have to be tailored to the variability that existed within the country. Moveover by early 1976 many factory owners and managers were being discreetly invited back to reassume their positions, and promises were being made to landowners to reinstate illegally expropriated land.

Yet changes had been set in motion by the revolution that in 1976 appeared irreversible. It would require perhaps another generation before such changes would make themselves felt in the social system of Portugal.

* * * * * * * * * * * * * * * *

Any discussion of social structure in Portugal necessarily suffers from a lack of published material. The historical summary in this chapter was drawn from the excellent presentation in Stanley Payne's *A History of Spain and Portugal* (volumes I and II). The discussion of structure and dynamics in the New State relied on a diverse collection of sources: Harry Makler's studies of the business elite, the anthropological writings of Joyce Riegelhaupt and José Cutileiro, and the more general examinations of class and status in Portugal by Herminio Martins and João Baptista Nunes Pereira Neto. Most studies of family and kinship were outdated, but the piece on kinship by Emilio Willems and the material presented in Riegelhaupt's and Cutileiro's village studies were useful. It was necessary to rely almost solely on news accounts (which were primarily preoccupied with politics and economics) in discussing the impact of the revolution of April 1974 on Portuguese social structure. (For further information see Bibliography.)

CHAPTER 6

RELIGIOUS LIFE

The history of Portugal is in many respects a history of church-state relations—characterized at times by cooperation and at other times by conflict. Portugal achieved independence and assumed a position as a world power with the help of the Roman Catholic Church. Missionaries accompanied Portuguese explorers in their quest for new territories and played a crucial role in securing these lands by practicing what they considered to be their civilizing mission. The state repaid the church for its support by sharing wealth and, to some extent, political power with the church hierarchy. Despite minor disruptions, a mutually reinforcing and beneficial relationship persisted until the mid-eighteenth century.

Strong anticlerical sentiments surfaced in the late 1700s and continued nearly unabated through the early 1900s, presenting a powerful challenge to the authority of the church. Anticlericalism, brought on by church corruption, also reflected a changing political climate. During the republican era of the early 1900s measures restricting church influence were carried to extremes and created a counterreaction. By allying himself with the church, António de Oliveira Salazar was able to profit politically from the counterreaction; in 1932 he became prime minister, and he held this office until incapacitated by a stroke in 1968.

Salazar rescued the church and promoted a religious revival. Although church and state were nominally separate and freedom of worship was guaranteed under Salazar, the Catholic church was accorded special recognition and privilege. In return Salazar expected implicit, if not explicit, support for his domestic and foreign policies. Except in isolated instances he received that support. It was only toward the end of his tenure that dissatisfaction became evident.

During the late 1960s and early 1970s the situation in Portuguese Africa had rapidly worsened. Criticism of the Portuguese regime—primarily from Roman Catholics outside Portugal—increased, and pressure was placed upon the Portuguese church hierarchy to clarify its relationship with the state. The hierarchy, however, was also under pressure from the state and chose to remain silent.

Church response to the revolution of April 1974 was mixed and cautious, reflecting divisions within the Catholic ranks and general uncertainty. In early 1976 the church was showing itself willing to accept and adjust to change provided that such change did not threaten its survival. A government that would not accommodate the church within its system appeared unlikely to survive long in Portugal.

According to baptismal statistics over 95 percent of the population is Catholic, but some surveys reveal that only a small percentage of people attend Sunday mass—the implication being that there is a growing indifference to religion. Such an implication, however, tends to mask the rold of religion in the lives of the predominantly rural population. Many religious practices take place outside the church. Although these expressions of faith may not always be condoned by the clergy, they are nonetheless associated with Catholicism in the minds of the people. Superstition also has a place in the people's religious framework. Religious piety in northern Portugal is usually accompanied by belief in magic and witchcraft.

The religion of the rural folk is a personal and familiar religion. The people often form intimate relations with saints, parallel in many respects to their relations with human beings. The priest is usually considered a temporal agent, not a spiritual mediator. The anticlericalism of the common people is different from the anticlericalism of the educated: it is apolitical; it does not question the conflict between the temporal and spiritual roles of the clergy; and it does not indicate an opposition to religion.

Only a small number of Protestants (less than 1 percent of the population) and an even smaller number of Jews resided in Portugal in the mid-1970s. The Protestants in Portugal have never been a significant minority, but they have enjoyed greater freedom than their counterparts in Spain. The Jews prospered in early Portugal, but many left the country in the decades after the decree of 1497 that called for expelling all Jews who refused to convert. Many others left during the heyday of the Inquisition in the sixteenth and seventeenth centuries.

CHURCH AND STATE

Historical Background

Christian history predates the formation of Portugal as a country, but it was under Afonso Henriques (reigned 1128-85), the first king of Portugal, that the Catholic church and the Portuguese state established a lasting and mutually beneficial partnership. Partially to ensure recognition as an independent country, Afonso declared Portugal a vassal state of the pope. Afonso, determined to extend his kingdom southward and expel the Moors from the Iberian Peninsula, found the church a useful ally. For its support and execution of his policies, he rewarded the church generously. The clergy began amassing great

140

wealth, mostly in the form of tax-exempt land grants, and enjoying many special privileges. At the same time the state asserted its supremacy over the church—a supremacy that it has maintained, albeit with varying degrees of success.

During the thirteenth and early fourteenth centuries the economic— and consequently the political—power of the clergy increased and began to rival that of the nobility and the crown. Various monarchs attempted to curb the influence of the church, and a series of personal and legal battles between the clergy and the crown followed. The state ordered investigations of titles to properties held in perpetuity. The church, however, held firm and was able to maintain its wealth and power. Despite these disagreements, which arose from each side's desire to guard its own authority, overall relations between church and state were amiable and stable.

The Great Western Schism (1378-1417) saw an erosion of the church's political and social influence. The state began extending its jurisdiction over the church—papal bulls, for example, had to be submitted to the king for approval before publication in Portugal. Disagreements over which claimant to the papacy to recognize weakened and divided the Portuguese clergy. After some initial indecision the crown supported the Roman rather than the Avignon line. The choice was a political one and reflected traditional enmities and alliances. Spain and France supported the claimant in Avignon; but Portugal joined with England, its longtime friend, in recognizing the Roman pope.

During the fifteenth and early sixteenth centuries the church enjoyed a religious revival resulting primarily from successful overseas expansion. As Portugal extended the boundaries of its kingdom to include territories in Africa, Asia, and America, the crown and the church shared in the glory and the profit. The clergy, a number of whom belonged to military religious orders, were literally soldiers of the crown.

The late sixteenth and the seventeenth centuries witnessed dramatic changes with respect to the position of church and state. The Inquisition, established in Portugal in 1531, succeeded in draining much of the vitality from the Portuguese nation. In particular, its relentless pursuit of the Jews and the Moors destroyed the intellectual, economic, and cultural resources that these populations offered. In 1540 the Jesuits entered the country. Much of the secondary and university education then available in Portugal was under the direction of the Jesuits, and many of the finest scholars of the day were among their ranks. The Jesuits and the Inquisition officials—mainly Dominicans—were not always in agreement on religious and social policies, although historians have often confused the two groups. The Jesuits, in fact, had supported the Jewish cause.

The defeat of King Sebastião in 1578 in the battle of Alcázarquivir in Morocco signaled the decline of Portugal as a great world power. Overseas missionary activity decreased rapidly in the seventeenth century.

The 1700s and 1800s witnessed mixed relations between church and state. After the marquis of Pombal became prime minister in 1756, the state entered its first serious period of anticlericalism. Pombal broke diplomatic relations with Rome, banished the Jesuit order, and brought education under the purview of the state. Although many of Pombal's reforms were reversed by the traditionalist government that immediately succeeded him, he had managed to set in motion an anticlerical trend that gradually diminished the economic and political power of the clergy. Still more reforms were instituted in 1820 and 1834. The Inquisition was dismantled, and clerical favors were curbed, religious orders banned, church properties auctioned off, and diplomatic relations with the Holy See once again severed. Toward the middle of the century relations with the church became more stable, and religious orders were permitted to return, but the church lost most of its wealth and much of its influence.

The revolution of 1910 ushered in a second great wave of anticlericalism. The church became the symbol of the old order, and anticlerical reforms were introduced and sometimes reached extreme proportions. Properties were confiscated, diplomatic relations with the Vatican again broken, and religious orders abolished. Separation of church and state was affirmed, and education was secularized. In addition, however, the ringing of church bells during certain times of the day was prohibited, processionals and folk celebrations were discouraged, and priests were forbidden to appear in clerical apparel on the streets.

Limiting the power of the church was perhaps necessary; but the extreme measures taken were unrealistic, antagonized an essentially apolitical people, and served to unite opposition to the government. The avid anticlericalism of the republic hastened its demise. Initially it also provided one of the issues that enabled Salazar to secure and maintain support for his regime.

The Church under Salazar

During Salazar's gradual ascent to power, the church in Portugal began to experience a revival. The apparitions at Fatima in 1917 had breathed spiritual life into the ailing church, and after 1933 Salazar provided the state support necessary for the church to pursue a vigorous religious revival.

Salazar's policies with regard to both domestic and foreign relations were shaped and colored by his own religious background. He had once studied for the priesthood and, while in office, he was often referred to as "the monk and the priest of the fatherland." Indeed his life-style was based on his religious outlook, and he cultivated the image of his life as one of abstinence and seclusion. Throughout his tenure in office Salazar also maintained personal contacts with members of the clergy. His friend and former classmate Manuel Gonçalves Cerejeira became cardinal patriarch of Lisbon. In many respects their careers paralleled one another. Between them they controlled the two most powerful positions in Portugal. Salazar died in 1970, and Cardinal Cerejeira retired the following year.

Many of the reforms that Salazar adopted in the state's relations with the church after 1933 were based on ideas he had long nurtured during the years of the parliamentary republic (1910-26) and during his career as an economics professor. At that time he had become involved in Catholic Action groups that were attempting to bolster the position of the church in Portuguese society and to moderate the prevailing anticlericalism. In fact Salazar was once elected as a Catholic deputy to parliament. Disillusioned with this first political experience, however, he served only a short term before retreating from public life. During the early 1920s, long before any of his political ambitions were realized, Salazar spoke out in favor of a state founded on Catholic principles. At the same time he promoted church recognition of state supremacy in all activities connected with politics.

One of Salazar's first acts as prime minister was to undertake the development of a new constitution, which was promulgated in 1933 and contained a section dealing with the government's position on religion and religious rights (see ch. 8). The traditional and historical role of the Catholic church in Portugal was noted, but the separation of church and state effected in 1911 was maintained—at least in theory. The document further ensured "freedom of worship," although only the Catholic church was mentioned by name.

The Concordat of 1940 between Portugal and the Holy See clarified the separate but special relation that the Catholic church was to enjoy under Salazar's tutelage. In an often quoted statement issued after the concordat was concluded, Salazar revealed his strong Catholic sense of history: "We return, with all the force of a nation reborn, to the great source of our national life . . . and, without any sacrifice of the material progress of our time, we aim to place ourselves on the same spiritual level as eight centuries ago." The concordat reversed many of the republican reforms that had been aimed at making the separation of church and state more than nominal. The church was given exclusive control over religious instruction in the public schools. Upon special request children whose parents claimed affiliation with another religion (or no religious affiliation) could be excused from such instruction, but in practice this rarely happened. In addition the Catholic church was entrusted with the moral instruction and care of those serving in the military and those relying on state supervision and public support (orphans and prisoners, for example). The church was also permitted to maintain private educational institutions.

One of the most radical reforms of the republic had been recognition of the right to obtain a divorce. Under the concordat divorce was again prohibited for persons married in the Catholic church. Only those Catholics married before the concordat were excepted. Moreover Catholic marriages and civil ceremonies became the only ones acknowledged as legally binding.

For legal and financial purposes the church was granted a juridical personality. Such recognition was useful, for it allowed the church as an institution to incorporate and own property. Salazar also restored much of the property that had been expropriated from the church by the republican government. Members of the clergy, at least on the mainland, were not financed by the government, and they had to rely on the generosity of their parishioners for their livelihood. They were exempt from many taxes, however, and the state promised indirect financial support in the way of gifts and grants.

It was in the sphere of politics that Salazar desired to restrict the actions and privileges of the church. There was no doubt in his mind that the church should and would remain subservient to his state. According to the concordat, appointments to the Portuguese church hierarchy had to be submitted to the government for approval; although the state did not propose candidates, it did exercise a veto power over all appointments. In practice the separation of church and state was applicable only to political affairs, and then only when it suited Salazar's purposes. He expected church support for his political policies, but he would not tolerate political meddling by the church. Salazar made his views explicit when he said: "The State will abstain from dealing in politics with the Church, and feels sure that the Church will equally refrain from any political action in relation to the State. . . . It must be so, because political activity corrupts the Church."

Under Salazar's heavy hand of protection, the church and state in Portugal maintained a comfortable and mutually reinforcing friendship, despite minor and isolated disagreements. Salazar had lifted the church out of an abyss, and he expected gratitude, in the form either of silence or of political support for his policies. He dealt with dissenters quickly and harshly. It is true that toward the end of his tenure in office individual members of the church were displaying signs of restiveness but, while Salazar was alive, the church as an institution dared not raise its voice against his regime.

The Church in the Overseas Territories

If the Catholic church achieved a position of special privilege in Portugal, it achieved near hegemony in Portuguese Africa. The church's range of privileges in Africa extended far beyond that accorded it in Portugal; its institutions and policies permeated and colored every aspect of life.

The relations between church and state in the overseas territories were regulated by the Missionary Agreement of 1940 (concluded at the same time as the Concordat of 1940) and the Missionary Statute of 1941. In effect these documents delivered the spiritual domain of Portuguese Africa into the hands of the Catholic church. It was usual for all Catholic missions to come under the purview of the Congregation for the Evangelization of Peoples in the Vatican. The Portuguese missions, however, were permitted to remain outside the congregation's dominion. They were essentially treated as government enterprises and received substantial subsidies.

The missionary agreements were meant to ensure that all of Portuguese Africa was adequately served by Catholic priests. If Portuguese clergy were not available, foreign Catholic missionaries could be invited. Their selection, however, required the approval of the Portuguese government as well as the Vatican. Foreign missionaries also had to relinquish the protection of their national hierarchies and agree to abide by the rulings of the prelates in Portuguese Africa.

The Missionary Agreement and the Missionary Statute further stipulated that the church in the overseas territories was to remain firmly and unmistakably Portuguese. Top positions in the church hierarchy in Portuguese Africa were reserved for Portuguese citizens; in 1972 all but three of the top twenty positions were held by prelates born in Portugal, and only one was held by an Angolan black. Moreover it was not until 1969 that an episcopal conference was organized for Angola and Mozambique. Previously the church officials in Africa had been considered an appendage of the hierarchy in Portugal.

Missionaries, Portuguese or foreign, were required to demonstrate facility in the Portuguese language and to teach and use it in the schools. They were allowed to conduct religious services in native languages, but in reality only foreign missionaries attempted to do so. Education was understood as the integration of Africa and Africans with Portugal.

The state granted special privileges to missionaries. Land for mission stations was freely available to the church. Clergymen did not have to pay duties and special taxes, and they received free transport to and from their stations. The missionaries in effect received all the benefits of state civil servants.

The historic idea of the church and state as civilizing agents never really died in Portugal. National mission was equated with spiritual mission, and national security became synonymous with religious conformity. Such ideas had their roots in the concept of *padroado* (patronage). *Padroado*, first granted to the Portuguese crown in 1514, was official recognition by the Holy See that the ruler of Portugal was entitled to all the lands discovered by his nationals. At the same time the Portuguese crown was charged with bringing the native peoples into the Catholic fold. The degree of association between church and state that such a practice entailed meant that the Catholic clergy inevitably became identified as soldiers of the state. Indeed when the military religious order of the Knights Templar was abolished by the pope in the fourteenth century, King Diní́s of Portugal (reigned 1279-1325) was permitted to retain its services. Later it was reorganized as the Military Order of Christ and acted in effect as a military reserve unit.

The continuation of the *padroado* idea was evidence as late as 1961 during the uprisings in Angola, at a time when most of the rest of the world had already acknowledged the right of peoples to self-determination. The Portuguese hierarchy, in a pastoral letter, wrote:

> For many centuries, the providential guidance of our history has made us the Lord's instrument for the evangelization of a considerable part of the world. At a time when the West seems to have lost its sense of purpose, Portugal remains conscious of its evangelizing and civilizing mission. And it pains us to see that this mission is under attack, that there are people in the world who oppose the union of our missionary action and the mission of the Portuguese State, a union which has always been declared indissoluble. . . . Our missionaries are Portuguese citizens who work on the soil of their own Fatherland—a single Fatherland which is spread over different continents.

The statements and actions of the Portuguese Catholic church were interpreted by the third world as approval for the policies of the state. The church attempted methodically to destroy the African culture and value system and replace it with a European system; rather than africanizing its institutions to take into account the uniqueness of African history and tradition, the church attempted to accommodate the Africans to the Portuguese way of life. The reward to Africans who cooperated and accepted these new values, if only superficially, was limited social advancement—but only within a Portuguese framework. Complete integration was never achieved. Dissenters and those suspected of ties with activists were dealt with ruthlessly by Portuguese authorities.

In 1976 it appeared that the protection and favors afforded the church by the Portuguese government had damaged its position in the newly independent African countries of Angola and Mozambique. The image of the church as the servant of a colonialist power would not be easy to change.

Relations with the Roman Catholic World

Relations with the Catholic world outside Portugal have been marked by periods of relative calm and periods of cold aloofness. Throughout most of Salazar's term in office the Vatican supported his government by condoning—or at least remaining silent on—Portugal's domestic and international policies. Because of the special position that Salazar had accorded to the Catholic church in Portugal, the Vatican was favorably disposed toward his regime and experienced only minor difficulty in overlooking the social injustices prevalent in Portugal and the overseas territories.

During the 1960s and early 1970s, however, the Vatican found itself increasingly caught between two poles. The rapidly changing world political situation forced the Vatican to reassess its role as an international institution. The younger and more progressive members of the Catholic clergy were pressing for church reform. On the one hand the church wished to retain these ecclesiastics within the Catholic fold and to assure itself a place in the newly emerging nations of the world. On the other hand the Portuguese hierarchy was among the most conservative—partially a result of its isolation from events outside of Portugal and its domination by the Portuguese state. The Vatican did not want to lose these members of the church or the special privileges it received from Salazar by antagonizing him. The two extremes posed a very real dilemma for the Holy See.

The first signs of a rift between the Vatican and the Salazar government followed the exile early in 1959 of Dom António Ferreira Gomes, the bishop of Porto, for publicly disagreeing with Salazar's domestic policies. At approximately the same time a newly appointed papal nuncio had arrived from Rome. Salazar, in an effort to make clear his disapproval of any political dilettantism on the part of Catholic clergymen and to warn the Catholic world against displaying political partisanship, kept the nuncio waiting for several months before officially accepting his credentials. A series of incidents expressive of growing discontent followed in the early 1960s. The famous encyclical *Pacem in Terris* (Peace on Earth) issued by Pope John XXIII in 1963, which dealt with human rights and the relation of the individual to the state, was censored in Portugal and the overseas territories. When Pope Paul VI visited India in 1964, the government of Salazar regarded it as a political insult. Only a few years earlier India had annexed the Portuguese territory of Goa. The mass media in Portugal were prohibited from mentioning the pope's visit. The Portuguese hierarchy remained silent, and only a handful of Catholic laymen dared question the state's position. A quick rapprochement, nonetheless, was always possible—especially when the state could turn it to its political advantage. Thus, when Pope Paul VI visited Portugal on a pilgrimage to Fatima in 1967, he was given a hero's welcome. As one critical foreign source noted, the state experienced no difficulty in declaring the visit "an official blessing on its [the state's] 'most Christian' policy."

What threatened to widen the gap between the Holy See and the Portuguese government beyond reconciliation were the Vatican's changing attitudes toward the countries of the third world and its increasing involvement in the fate of Portugal's African possessions. The pope's 1967 encyclical *Popularum Progresso* (Development of the Peoples), touching as it did upon the issue of self-determination, was

147

received with hostility by the Portuguese government. Copies of the message that made their way into Portuguese Africa were bought up and destroyed by the Portuguese secret police. The audience that Pope Paul VI granted to three African liberation leaders in 1970 further angered the Portuguese government, and diplomatic relations between Portugal and the Vatican were jeopardized.

The Vatican, however, continued slowly to increase its contacts with the peoples of the third world. Its main impetus came from foreign Catholic missionaries to Angola and Mozambique. During the early 1970s their increasingly frequent reports of torture and massacres became impossible to ignore. In addition international Catholic service groups and Protestant organizations began mounting a campaign against the Portuguese colonialists. The World Council of Churches, for example, raised funds to provide medical and educational assistance to African activists and to help young Portuguese men who wanted to escape military service. An international Catholic peace movement, Pax Christi, urged the Vatican to expose and protest alleged atrocities. Finally, after prolonged delay, the Holy See issued a statement in 1973 decrying war crimes and disavowing any implicit support for Portuguese actions in Africa that might be inferred from its "ecclesiastical and missionary" agreements with the Portuguese government.

Roman Catholic Opposition

The unofficial marriage of church and state in Portugal has not been beyond the criticism of some church officials. Dissent among Portuguese Catholics, however, has centered on isolated incidents and has involved individual church leaders rather than the church as an institution. The church did not in any organized or collective sense oppose the policies of the prerevolution state or become involved in the social and political questions of the day.

Opposition by individual church leaders to government policies did not surface until the last half of Salazar's dictatorship. The republican years had left a lasting impression on the minds of the clergy, and the church was slow to recover. For the church to prosper Salazar's support was necessary, but it was conditional and easily withheld whenever the church overstepped the limits drawn by Salazar.

In the 1950s, nonetheless, growing discontent became more visible. Dissatisfaction with government policies focused on workers' rights and welfare. The first serious challenge to Salazar's social policies came from Bishop Gomes of Porto. He wrote to Salazar in July 1958 to express concern over the laws prohibiting strikes, the ineffectiveness of social programs in meeting the needs of the poor, and the inability of the people to participate politically under the existing system. The bishop expressed dismay over the increasingly low esteem accorded the church by most workers and youth, and he blamed it on the apparent collusion between church and state. Rather than being identified as the champion of the poor, the church was increasingly regarded as the instrument of the rich. At the conclusion of his letter to Salazar the bishop requested state approval for organizing and encouraging Catholic participation in the sociopolitical life of the country.

When the contents of the letter were made public, Salazar was furious. In his mind the letter constituted an indictment of his regime. The hierarchy attempted to placate Salazar and protect itself by issuing a pastoral letter in January 1959 that reaffirmed the church's obligation to the moral and social well-being of the people but also made clear that the church did not intend to become involved in partisan politics. In essence the letter echoed Bishop Gomes' cry for increased individual liberty, but it rejected involvement in politics by the church as an institution. Criticism of the corporate state system and Salazar's application of it was avoided, and the independent action of Bishop Gomes was neither condoned nor condemned (although the bishop signed the pastoral letter).

Later in the year Bishop Gomes left the country, and he remained in exile for the next eleven years. It is difficult to assess the degree of support that the sentiments expressed in his letter received from the hierarchy. At a subsequent meeting of the Second Vatican Council in Rome, Bishop Gomes was ostracized by the Portuguese delegtaion (whether by choice or from state pressure) and was forced to seek lodging with the South American bishops.

The state's condemnation of the independent action of Bishop Gomes aroused resentment among members of the lower clergy. Protest, however, continued to come from individuals and small ad hoc groups. Individual clergymen were subjected to increased scrutiny by public authorities. In March 1959 a Catholic priest and nearly 300 other people were implicated in an alleged communist conspiracy against the regime. In 1963 two priests from Porto were arrested when they refused to serve a tour of duty as military chaplains in Portuguese Africa. Another priest from Porto was detained, reportedly for using pacifist language in his sermon. Such incidents, however, were sporadic, and disunity within the clergy was apparent. In 1965 over l00 Catholic laymen issued a public statement condemning Salazar's authoritarian state and supporting freedom of speech, the right of association, and the principle of self-determination for the people in the overseas territories. Three days later over 100 conservative Catholics issued a counterstatement reaffirming faith in the policies of the government.

During the latter half of the 1960s and the early 1970s Catholic opposition was building against Portugal's policies in the overseas territories. The two most serious events were the 1971 withdrawal of the

White Fathers, an international Catholic missionary group, from Mozambique and the 1972 reports of an alleged massacre in Mozambique. Both directed worldwide attention to conditions in Portuguese Africa, both involved non-Portuguese Catholic missionaries in opposition to the Portuguese government, and both stimulated a mixed response from the Portuguese Catholic authorities.

In 1971 the White Fathers decided to leave Mozambique in protest against government treatment of the native population and government curtailment of their missionary activities. The White Fathers, who had operated in Portuguese Africa since 1946, favored adapting Catholic liturgy to the prevailing African culture and promoting an African Catholic identity.

The situation in Mozambique was steadily worsening in the early 1970s as Portugal's control over the overseas territories became more tenuous. Catholics from outside Portugal recognized the necessity for the church to dissociate itself from government policies; church silence could only be interpreted as tacit support. Moreover a number of Portuguese priests had become government informers. The White Fathers demanded public clarification of the relations between church and state in Portuguese Africa. In presenting their case to the world they declared: "Facing a silence which we do not understand, we feel in conscience that we do not have the right to be accused of complicity in sustaining officially, as the hierarchy seems to do, a regime that uses the church precisely to consolidate and perpetuate in Africa an anachronistic situation." Before the White Fathers could leave Mozambique of their own volition, as they had intended, they were expelled by the Portuguese government. Official explanations justified the action by claiming that certain statements and policies of the White Fathers encouraged "acts of terrorism" and constituted "subversive activity."

The second important incident reflective of Catholic opposition to Portuguese overseas policies concerned an alleged massacre in Mozambique in December 1972. Again it was foreign Catholic missionaries who directed world attention to the event. Nearly 400 African villagers were said to have been brutally killed by Portuguese troops frustrated in their antiguerrilla campaign. The Marcello Caetano government at first denied the atrocity but was later forced to admit that certain excesses might have occurred.

Only a minority of Portuguese Catholics spoke out in support of the foreign missionaries and against government policy. Among them was Bishop Manuel Vieira Pinto of Nampula, Mozambique. He publicly defended the action of the White Fathers, stating: "We are sorry indeed that many of our traditional catholics . . . used the events . . . to confuse deliberately the love of the gospel with political attitudes. . . . We prefer a church that is persecuted but alive to a church that is generously subsidized but at the price of a damaging connivance at the behaviour of the temporal powers." The bishop's stand did not earn him immediate exile, but he became suspect in the eyes of the government. Bishop Pinto openly favored a political rather than a military solution in Portuguese Africa, as did General António de Spínola (see ch. 9). Shortly before the revolution of 1974 the bishop was expelled from Mozambique for subversive activities and his support of so-called insurgent foreign missionaries.

The response of other Portuguese prelates was markedly conservative. Not until March 1974 did the Portuguese Catholic authorities as a group voice even weak disapproval of government action. They protested the dismissal of Bishop Pinto but reminded their clergy once again to remain neutral on political questions.

The Church in the 1970s

In the early 1970s the Caetano regime closely monitored any signs of political activism on the part of the church and dealt harshly with opponents. On questions relating to the overseas territories Caetano held firmly to the precedent set by Salazar and did not tolerate opposition from the church or individual clergymen. At the same time Caetano favored a limited liberalization of domestic policies. The bishop of Porto was allowed to return to Portugal and resume his post, which had been temporarily assigned to an apostolic administrator. The bishop's political zeal was notably toned down, although he continued to speak out in favor of press freedom, workers' rights, and the right of people to participate in the political life of their country. When Cardinal Cerejeira retired in 1971, he was replaced by a young, liberally oriented but politically acceptable bishop, António Ribeiro. Caetano's regime was short lived, however, and his limited liberalization program may even have hastened his downfall.

Church response to the revolution of April 1974 was mixed and cautious. Upon General Spínola's assumption of power the church issued a statement: "We call upon all Portuguese Catholics and other men of good will to support the new military leaders. We are glad that the dictatorship has been overthrown, as this is in the interests of the Portuguese nation. We share the desires and hopes of the people, at this time, and pledge our collaboration, insofar as we are competent, for the construction of a social order founded on truth, justice, freedom, love and peace." For some members of the clergy such a statement was a sincere expression of their sentiments; for others it was an accommodation to political realities.

With Spínola's political demise and the apparent leftward swing of the government, however, the church was forced into a contrary political position. In the "dynamization" programs of the Armed Forces Movement (Movimento das Forças Armadas—MFA), soldiers scattered throughout the countryside to educate the people and orient them toward the goals of the revolution (see ch. 9). In reality the programs were often conducted as antireligion and antichurch campaigns. The church, having remained remarkably silent, finally voiced open criticism during the election of April 1975. The MFA had encouraged the people to cast blank ballots if they were undecided as to which political party to support. These were to be counted as votes backing the MFA and its programs. Priests, however, directed their parishioners to vote according to their conscience but not for any program or "any party . . . incompatible with the Christian ideals of man and society." Blank ballots constituted only 7 percent of the total, and at least part of the reason for such a small proportion stemmed from the church's opposition.

What appeared to portend a possible crisis in relations between the church and the postrevolution governments was the expropriation of the church's national radio station in Lisbon, Radio Renascença, by leftist workers. The church refused to relinquish its legal right to the station and frustrated efforts to nationalize it. The issue became particularly heated in June and July 1975. Certain members of the government supported church claims on the station, but the armed forces disagreed. To many Portuguese Catholics the seizure of Radio Renascença was an attack on tradition and religious values; it was not a political issue. Such collective challenges to the role of religion in society elicited strong reactions. The church finally regained control of the station after the more leftist-oriented elements of the government and military were expelled in November 1975. Other radio and television stations were reorganized and nationalized.

In early 1976 it appeared inevitable that the church in Portugal would accept some far-reaching political and social reforms. An agreement had already been signed in 1975 that permitted Catholics to obtain divorces. In July 1975 the equality of religions was ensured under a constitutional provision. A new concordat with the Vatican also seemed imminent. At the same time the postrevolution governments and leaders of various political parties recognized the need to proceed cautiously in attempting to redefine the role of the church in Portuguese society. Reaction against the intense anticlericalism of the republican era had been partly responsible for the eventual rise of Salazar, and few wished to repeat history. The people and the church appeared willing to accept change—but gradual rather than radical change.

CHURCH AND SOCIETY

Roman Catholics in Portugal

Census figures and baptismal statistics indicate that Portugal is an overwhelmingly Catholic country. The proportion of Catholics is among the highest in Europe; approximately 95 percent of the people are baptized Catholics. The traditional importance of the church in the lives of the Portuguese is evident in the physical layout of almost every village in Portugal. Churches are often located in the center of the village or on hilltops in close proximity to and in view of the village. Many of the smaller churches and chapels, built in the fifteenth and sixteenth centuries and even earlier, have been allowed to fall into ruin or disuse, but they often come to life for the yearly celebration honoring the village patron saints.

Church Organization

The Concordat of 1940 specified the organization that the Catholic church in Portugal still maintained in mid-1976. The country was divided into three ecclesiastical provinces roughly along geographic lines—north, central, and south. In the north an archbishopric located in the municipality of Braga claimed as suffragan sees (subordinate dioceses) seven bishoprics—Bragança, Vila Real, Porto, Lamego (ir the district of Viseu), Aveiro, Viseu, and Coimbra. A patriarchate was located in Lisbon, and in addition to the bishoprics of Guarda, Leiria, and Portalegre it included ecclesiastical jurisdiction over the remainder of the central region. The bishoprics of Angra do Heroísmo and Funchal (in the Azores and Madeira respectively) were also part of the metropolitan see of Lisbon. The third area, southern Portugal, included an archbishopric in Evora and bishoprics in Beja and Faro. Immediately evident was the concentration of the church hierarchy in the north, where the population was denser and the piety of the people allegedly greater.

Each of the seventeen sees was further divided into *paróquias* (parishes), the smallest ecclesiastical subdivision. In the urban areas a city may be divided into several *paróquias*, but in rural areas several villages may be grouped together into one *paróquia*. The *freguesia*, which also translates as parish, is a political subdivision that corresponds to the ecclesiastical *paróquia*. The number of *paróquias* had increased only slightly over the years. In 1873 there were reportedly 3,788 parishes; according to the *1976 Catholic Almanac* the number in 1975 was 4,314.

The church in Portugal in the mid-1970s was understaffed for a predominantly Catholic country. The hierarchy consisted of three cardinals (including the patriarch of Lisbon), three archbishops, and seventeen bishops. (Some members of the hierarchy held more than one title.) It was at the parish level, however, that the clergy was under strength. There were only 4,105 diocesan clergymen in 1975, and some *paróquias* were without the regular services of a priest. Portugal was reputed to have the lowest ratio of priests to population of any Catholic European country. The distribution of clergy throughout Portugal was extremely uneven: in the north, for example, there were nearly two priests per 1,000 Catholics; in central Portugal there was one priest for approximately 4,500; and in the south the ratio was even smaller—in some areas of the south a priest might have as many as 12,000 people within his jurisdiction. The outlook in 1976 was not promising. The number of those graduating from seminaries and entering the priesthood had declined and was one of the lowest in Europe. One source reported that in the two most populous dioceses (Lisbon and Porto) fifty-seven new priests were ordained between 1958 and 1960 but only twenty-four between 1968 and 1970. The dropout rate of seminarians was considered alarmingly high in the early 1970s.

The proportion of men and women attached to religious orders also was smaller than in other Catholic European countries. According to the *1976 Catholic Almanac* there were 889 priests and 1,707 other men belonging to religious orders and 7,119 nuns in 1975. Among the orders claiming the highest membership were the Jesuits (men only), the Dorotheans (women only), and the Dominicans, Franciscans, and Carmelites (men and women).

Religion and the People

Those skeptical of the role of religion and the church (particularly the Catholic church) in the modern world and those who would see its gradual decline have pointed out the gap between the number of baptized Catholics and the number of practicing Catholics. In the early 1970s between 15 and 35 percent of the Catholics in Portugal regularly attended church—although the percentage varied in particular regions or districts. The north, for example, had always been considered the most devoutly religious area of Portugal, and over 90 percent of the people participated in mass every Sunday. *Promessas* (vows) to the various saints and penance for transgressions often assumed masochistic form: rural folk have been known to climb to hilltop chapels on their knees in order to fulfill *promessas*. The piety of the people (at least as measured by church attendance), however, was much less apparent in the center and the south. In the central section of the country (the archdiocese of Lisbon and its metropolitan suffragan sees) fewer than 20 percent attended Sunday services, and in the south only 5 to 10 percent were regular churchgoers.

The Catholic church in rural areas was becoming increasingly the domain of women and children. This pattern was more evident in the south, but even in the north it was the women who attended church more regularly and participated in the Catholic rituals. While the women were at church, the men could often be observed frequenting the taverns and coffeehouses.Men attended church only irregularly (in the north) or rarely (in the south) except on such religious holidays as Christmas and Easter. Certain sacraments corresponding to crises in the life cycle—such as birth and marriage—were also occasions for church attendance by both men and women. When men did attend ceremonies, they often displayed little respect. An outsider attending

154

Christmas services at a rural parish church in the Alentejo found men crowded in the back of the church, smoking, talking, and noisily recovering from their sojourn to the tavern.

The low level of attendance at mass and the apparent lack of respect for church ceremony, particularly in the south, have caused most Protestant missionaries, many foreign Catholics, and even some members of the Portuguese hierarchy in the north to classify areas of the Alentejo and the Algarve as mission fields. Parish priests tried to compensate for low attendance and justify their presence by broadcasting Sunday sermons over radio and television. Many of the smaller villages were equipped with loudspeaker systems through which the priest was able to reach the whole village—whether or not the villagers wanted to hear the sermon.

The decreasing number of practicing Catholics as measured by church attendance would seem to portend a gradual decline of the Catholic church in Portugal. Reaching fewer and fewer people, the church seemed to be losing control over the majority of Portuguese. When the revolution of April 1974 succeeded in ending a state dictatorship, many leftist thinkers predicted the demise of the church as well. Critics of the church, however, have failed to grasp the role of religion and the church in the everyday lives of the people. Just as census and baptismal statistics do not measure the piety of the people, so church attendance records do not adequately reflect the depth of religious sentiment.

Much of the religious life of the Portuguese people lies outside the formal structure and the official domain of the Catholic church. Nonetheless, the peasant identifies his religion with the Catholic church and associates both with his identity as a Portuguese citizen. To be Portuguese is to be Catholic. For most rural Portuguese the two are inseparable.

The attitude of the Portuguese toward the parish priests with whom they interact daily is one of ambivalence. It is a result of the contradiction between the ideal of the priest as spiritual guardian and bearer of religious tradition and the reality of the priest as a mortal man with all the weaknesses and vices of any other human being. On the whole the people have accepted this contradiction. Only when the delicate balance between the ideal and the real has been upset have the people expressed their disapproval through violent anticlericalism. The existence of a temporal as well as a spiritual role for the clergy has never really been questioned. Scholars who have studied rural Portuguese attitudes believe that enmity toward clergymen is apolitical despite the close connection that existed between church and state for many years.

The religion of the Portuguese people is highly personal. In a country where for centuries people have earned their livelihood from the land, where good health is a luxury, and where national institutions have remained distant, people have attempted to place religion on a level that they can manipulate and comprehend. The rural Portuguese establish intricate networks of relations with various saints that are in many ways parallel to their human relations. God, like the state, is a remote and awe-inspiring figure. In order to reach him the people cultivate relations with patron saints who can intercede on their behalf. These relations are not based on equality; but neither are they based on dependence, for they involve reciprocity—payment for deeds done or services rendered. Payment usually takes the form of fulfilling *promessas* or giving alms to the poor. In temporal life attempts to relate to the state assume many of these same characteristics. Contacts are established with influential people or civil servants in order to link the citizen with high government authorities. The rural folk seek out the parish priest as a temporal mediator but rarely as a spiritual mediator.

Although a community has a patron saint, most persons (especially women) find it convenient and emotionally satisfying to form an intimate relationship with a particular saint. This saint acts as a lifelong spiritual guardian. Men do not form as close contacts with the saints as women do, and they may even belittle women for doing so. Nevertheless, when a crisis arises, the men are never completely willing to forsake the possibility of spiritual help. If the problem involves health, for example, men seek the advice of a medical doctor when one is available, but they also seek the protection of the saints. Their sporadic and apparent religious skepticism is rooted only in the desire to mask their reliance on women or to deny any appearance of being subordinate to women.

In the religious world of the rural folk women are accorded a strategic role. The path separating man from God is marked by the presence of woman, and it is to woman (in both human and spiritual form) that man must go in order to reach his God. The Virgin Mary is the most popular of the spiritual mediators, and some critics have claimed that she is held in greater esteem than Jesus. *Romarias* (pilgrimages) and *círios* (religious processions; literally, large candles— named for waxen images carried in these processions) usually involve the celebration of a virgin patron saint. Relations with the saints are neither mystical nor formidable. Respect is present, but spiritual mediators are thought to have some of the same emotions and foibles as human beings.

The Catholic church has criticized folk religion for dividing man from his God. The church seeks to establish a direct link between man and God, but in the process it also promotes spiritual atomization. The people, however, prefer their belief system because it is a system they understand and participate in every day of their lives. The very humanization of the patron saints allows the individual to rationalize disappointments and excuse unfulfilled spiritual bargains.

At the same time belief in a God of grace and goodness remains undiminished. Disappointments are blamed on the fancies of a mischievous saint or the neglect of a minor ceremonial detail and not on the insensitivity of God.

The humanization of religion by the Portuguese has given God a face of love despite his remoteness. Unlike the Spanish, the Portuguese picture God and his saints as serene beings. They see God in his ectasy rather than his agony. Mary is a virgin and a saint but still a woman. In Spain the expressions on the faces of statues reveal pain and anguish; in Portugal they reveal calm complacence.

The Dark Side of Religion

There is another side to the folk religion of the Portuguese that focuses on beliefs in witchcraft, magic, and the existence of benevolent and malevolent spirits. Catholics who proudly acclaim the intense devoutness of northern Portugal admit that superstition also finds a haven there. Formal religion, popular beliefs and practices, and superstition mesh completely, and all are part of being a Catholic in the minds of some Portuguese. The rural people seeking to cover all contingencies, allow folk beliefs to exist alongside formal religion just as the art of folk healing exists alongside modern medicine.

Women, who more often than men are religious mediators, are also thought of as possessing the ability to do great evil. One author, W.J. Barnes, counted nine classifications of women versed in the art of magic, based on their varying degrees of power. Cases of witch burning were still reported as late as the 1930s, and women were still practicing their magical skills in the mid-twentieth century. Modernization and contact outside the village have signaled the decline of many folk beliefs—especially those connected with rites of exorcism.

In the late 1960s those women classified as healing mediators were the most numerous. They were called on to administer cures, and their methods usually consisted of a mixture of pagan and Christian ritual and invocations. As José Cutileiro has noted, they were in effect unordained priestesses. They had no formal role within the church, but the people had faith in their knowledge and in times of crisis sought their help rather than that of the priests.

Common beliefs include the belief in werewolves and spirits who inhabit the forests and countryside. The belief in the evil eye is widespread and has been likened to the Christian belief in the Devil. Small children are considered particularly susceptible to the evil eye and, while they are young, parents protect them with special medallions (either pagan or Christian). Women cast the evil eye—unconsciously or consciously—and envy of another's prosperity or good fortune is usually thought to be the reason.

Folk beliefs have been sustained in rural Portugal because of the precarious nature of life and the isolation and underdevelopment of many countryside villages. The fear of disease and death and the unavailability of modern scientific alternatives have kept traditional practices alive. Returning emigrants who have been exposed to better living conditions and more modern medical practices, however, are beginning to affect the attitudes of their countrymen. It is likely that, as integration with the national society becomes a reality and health and living conditions begin to improve, belief in and reliance upon folk practices will decrease rapidly.

Celebrations and Pilgrimages

Festas, celebrations, and pilgrimages are an integral part of rural religious practice. When the Catholic church first entered Portugal, it found a people whose culture and rituals were tied to the land and derived from day-to-day experiences. The church originally took advantage of the prevailing traditions and practices and integrated its ceremonies with those already existing. In time the two systems became fused into one. The Catholic church of the twentieth century is finding it difficult to rid itself of this pre-Christian dimension despite efforts to purify the ritual. In Portugal during the early 1970s two broad categories of religious rites could be observed—those that the church approved and supported and those that were still popular with the people although not endorsed by the church.

The church has promoted those celebrations and rites that place it in a central role and give it the central seat of authority. Most popular festivities express communal feelings and the belief in a shared destiny. Thus the church has attempted to weaken the individual's link to his community and strengthen instead his relation with the church.

Baptisms, weddings, funerals, and the observance of special religious holidays, such as Christmas and Easter, are encouraged by the clergy. All involve the priest as the prime officiator and usually require church attendance. All also involve individual or family participation. Most rural Portuguese, regardless of their attitude toward the church, partake in the sacraments connected with crises in the life cycle. Cutileiro studied a village in southern Portugal that had been without the services of a priest for several years. He noted that the villagers, because they could not afford to bring in a priest from a neighboring area, often had dispensed with baptisms and church weddings. When a priest was present, however, the people took the opportunity to secure the church ceremony. In other words, they were not disturbed by the inability to observe the sacraments of the church, but they preferred them when available.

Birth, marriage, and death are intimate family occasions. To the villagers they also have a wider significance. Birth is the entry of a new member into the community; marriage is the establishment of a new economic unit; and death calls for a final valediction. Baptisms, weddings, and funerals are often followed by communal celebrations. The

158

observances of Christmas and Easter are also family affairs, but families attend church services and then depart to enjoy the holidays in the privacy of their own homes.

Pilgrimages to special shrines are still supported and encouraged by the church, but only to those shrines that are specifically Catholic in origin. The shrine of Fatima (in the district of Santarém) is the most popular and enjoys an international reputation, It has been called "a symbol of the renaissance of the Portuguese Church." Pilgrims from around the world visit the site, on which three rural children claimed to have seen the Virgin Mary. The first vision allegedly occurred on May 13, 1917. In the thirteenth day of each of the following five months, the Virgin is said to have revealed herself to the children. By October, the last month, large crowds had gathered to witness the event. Many thousands professed to have seen the sun "dancing" in the sky. Only the children, however, saw the Virgin Mary, who reputedly disclosed several prophecies to the oldest girl. The two youngest children died only a few years after the alleged apparitions. The oldest became a Carmelite nun and lived in seclusion. The drawing power of the shrine at Fatima can be seen in the throngs of pilgrims who continue to visit it annually.

For the church in Portugal, greatly weakened during the republican era, Fatima was a means of mobilizing the public and launching a spiritual revival. The Fatima incident also enabled the Salazar government to reinforce its position since one of the reported messages of the Virgin referred to the dangers of communism. This message, which seemed to lend a certain air of legitimacy to Salazar's policies and mode of administration, was given wide credence, despite the many skeptics who voiced doubts about the authenticity of the Fatima phenomenon in its entirety, and the anticommunist prophecy in particular.

Dependence upon the productivity of the land and the fortunes of the weather shaped and influenced all aspects of the lives of the predominantly rural Portuguese people. Thus many so-called religious holidays corresponded to agricultural events. Religion became tied to the agricultural cycle, and the two have for centuries remained virtually indistinguishable. The reckoning of time, for example, is evidence of the traditional importance of religion and agriculture in the lives of the people. Cutiliero has pointed out that months of the year are rarely referred to by their proper names; instead June becomes Harvesttime or the month of São João. Even economic transactions are calculated according to the religious or agricultural calendar.

Religious folk holidays and festivals, in addition to having agricultural significance, are expressions of community identity and solidarity. One community distinguishes itself from another by the celebration of its village patron saint. In fact different patron saints were and are associated with different degrees of inclusiveness: each individual has his or her patron saint, each village its patron saint, and each parish its patron saint. The celebration of particular saints varies with the desire to express solidarity or distance at any given moment. In Estremadura, the central coastal region of Portugal, a number of parishes occasionally acknowledge their unity during *círios*. In these celebrations a waxen image, sculptured to represent a particular saint, is carried from one parish to another where it will be housed for one year. Large crowds gather to bid the saint farewell. Each parish through which the image and its followers wend their way honors the saint with a festival, and the crowds grow larger and larger as the procession continues.

The three best known and most widely honored saints are São João, Santo António, and São Pedro. Each is a combination of saint and folk hero, and their degree of popularity varies with the region. São João, most popular in northern Portugal, is hailed as the matchmaker. He symbolizes true love, guards and blesses the harvest, and bestows good health upon the people. On the eve of his day young girls act out a series of rituals that are supposed to foretell the future courses of their love lives. Rainwater and dew collected on São João's night is considered to have important healing power.

In the center and south of Portugal Santo António rivals São João in popularity. Santo António, better known as Anthony of Padua, was a Franciscan friar. Born in Lisbon near the end of the twelfth century, he is particularly dear to the Portuguese and is the patron saint of all Portugal. In popular lore he is noted for guiding people to lost possessions. Like São João, he watches over lovers and heals the sick. His feast day falls on the anniversary of his death, June 13.

São Pedro is most revered by coastal villagers in Portugal—those who earn their livelihood from the sea. His day marks the beginning of a new year for the fishermen. During the festivities the villagers carry his image down to the shores to bless the boats.

The church has sought to downplay the significance of religious folk holidays and has begun to withdraw its institutional and financial support. Other factors have also begun to detract from the popular and local celebrations. The mass media have started to rival festivals for the people's leisure time. Transportation, emigration, urbanization (and subsequent deemphasis of agriculture), and modernization are expanding the boundaries of the rural folks' world and are constantly pushing toward national integration at the expense of community loyalty. Evidence from the mid-1960s suggests that folk celebrations (particularly those that are localized) are declining in number but are not disappearing altogether. Some festivals remain as testimony to religious and folk tradition; others are being kept alive as commercial attractions for the tourists.

Minority Religions

There has been no non-Catholic minority of any size or consequence in Portugal in modern history. In the census of 1960 the Portuguese people were grouped in four categories—Catholics, non-Catholic Christians (Protestants), non-Christians, (Jews, Moslems, and others), and those without a religion. Those who claimed no religious affiliation—less than 5 percent—constituted the largest proportion of the population after the overwhelming Catholic majority. Some were older intellectuals who had been deeply affected by the liberal trends of the republican era. Others were younger people who had grown disillusioned with the church and its ability to effect sorely needed social change.

Protestants

Only 38,000 non-Catholic Christians (0.4 percent of the Portuguese population)—that is, Protestants—were listed in the 1960 census data. A Protestant source claimed 45,000 adherents in 1975. The figure was not impressive, but the growth of Protestant congregations in the twentieth century has nonetheless been substantial. Between 1910 and 1975 the number of Protestants increased more than elevenfold. Protestant sources claimed a wider membership by including among their ranks the families of communicants and those who attended Protestant services regularly without officially joining a particular sect.

What there was of a Protestant movement in Portugal did not emerge until the 1800s. The Reformation of the sixteenth century never really extended beyond the Pyrenees and into Portugal, isolated physically and culturally as it was from the rest of Europe. Various scholars and artists, such as the famous Portuguese humanist Damião de Góis (1501-74) and the playwright and poet Gil Vicente (ca. 1470-1536), alluded in their writings to the need for church reform. Early reformers and theologians never appeared in Portugal—as John Wycliffe did in England and John Huss in Bohemia—to pave the way for the Protestant movement.

Consequently the history of the Protestant church in Portugal is essentially a history of missionary activity and foreign influence during the nineteenth and twentieth centuries. The first Protestant churches in Portugal were operated by and for the British. Because of England's special relationship with Portugal, British subjects were allowed a certain amount of religious freedom. Not until the 1800s, after the abolition of the Inquisition and the establishment of liberal state reforms, did other foreign missionaries enter Portugal to establish churches and seek adherents. Most groups were organized after 1860. The Lusitanian Evangelical Church, the Methodist Church, the Church of the Brethren, and the Congregational Church are among the oldest denominations; until the late 1950s they also enjoyed the largest followings. Fundamentalist faiths—the Pentecostals, and the

Baptists, for example—grew rapidly after 1960, however, and in the early 1970s they had the largest number of communicants.

Protestants in Portugal never experienced the systematic persecution that plagued their counterparts in Spain. The Constitution of 1933 guaranteed freedom of worship. Protestants were allowed to establish churches, and in the early 1960s there were well over 600. They were also free to establish their own primary and secondary schools and religious training centers. Although until the early 1970s the Catholic church was charged with providing moral instruction in all public schools, Protestant parents could request that their children be withdrawn from such classes. Ostensibly Protestants were afforded the same opportunities for professional advancement as Catholics. They could secure military posts, teaching positions, and government jobs. Protestants were also free to conduct their own marriage and burial services, although Protestant marriages were not recognized as legal, and civil ceremonies were also necessary.

There were, however, subtle pressures for Protestants to conform to the religious norm. Since they did not have juridical status, Protestant groups could not incorporate, and their ability to own property and obtain building permits was handicapped. Groups new to Portugal, such as the Assembly of God, were particularly affected by the lack of legal recognition. In addition Catholic priests enjoyed privileges not extended to their Protestant counterparts. Unlike the latter, priests were exempt from taxes, they were issued professional identity cards entitling them to special discounts, and under the Concordat of 1940 they were excused from military service. The media generally sided with the Catholic clergy, and Protestants found it difficult to secure broadcasting time or newspaper space to issue rebuttals when disagreements arose.

In addition to extralegal factors the Protestant groups have had to reckon with the prevailing international political climate and their own internal divisions. The rebellions in Portuguese Africa during the 1960s made the government and the people highly suspicious of foreign-based organizations. Protestant missionaries in both Portugal and Africa were critical of Portuguese colonial policies. The government therefore tended to label Protestant leaders as political agitators. The Protestants, moreover, were not united. Many different denominations were represented in Portugal, and often the various sects were in competition with one another. Divisions centered on differences of theology, organization, and country of origin. During the 1960s and 1970s, however, interdenominational associations had begun to develop, among which were the Portuguese Inter-Ecclesiastical Commission and the Evangelical Alliance. Finally, the Protestant groups have been handicapped by the reluctance of the Portuguese people to affiliate themselves officially with any one group. The 1962 *World Christian Handbook* listed over 42,000 Protestant communicants, but it also estimated that 110,000 people regularly attended or participated in Protestant activities.

In the early 1970s the government of Prime Minister Caetano began to loosen extralegal restrictions. A proposed bill no longer required students in public schools to participate in religious classes and allowed young adults to determine their beliefs independently. The Catholic hierarchy, intensely jealous of any attempts to contract its institutional authority, objected strongly to these new measures.

Since the revolution of 1974 many religious reforms favorable to Protestants have been carried out. Protestant groups have been recognized as corporate entities. They have been granted, along with other kinds of groups, the right to assemble and to hold open-air meetings. Alternate service has been made available for those who register as conscientious objectors.

Jews

The number of Jews in Portugal in 1975 was even smaller than the number of Protestants. The *Jewish Year Book, 1975* recorded 500, although other sources estimated nearly 700. Jews had resided in Portugal even before the establishment of the first Portuguese kingdom. Under early Portuguese rule Jews lived much as they had under Moorish rule. They maintained segregated communities, often by choice, and suffered only minor restrictions. The prevailing mood was one of tolerance, and from the twelfth century until the end of the fifteenth century Jews prospered and contributed to the development of the cultural, economic, intellectual, and professional life of Portugal. Most of the rulers of Portugal considered the Jews a valuable resource; many of the monarchs employed Jews as personal physicians, court astrologers, financiers, and civil servants. The marriage of Christian noblemen to the daughters of wealthy Jews was common.

Afonso Henriques, the first king of Portugal, gave the Jews a wide degree of autonomy, and under Afonso III (reigned 1246-79) the jurisdiction of the Jews over their own internal affairs was extended. The Jews were concentrated into *judiarias* (ghettos). A rabbi *mór* (chief rabbi) was chosen to oversee these Jewish communities and regulate their affairs. He was primarily responsible for ensuring that all special taxes were paid to the state. Payments included a poll tax, a personal or family tax, customs and road taxes, and taxes on all income and expenditures. Other special taxes were levied according to the whims and the needs of the crown at a particular time. The rabbi *mór* selected seven chief justices to act as legal authority in the seven administrative division into which Portugal was then divided. Each community over a certain size was required to choose a rabbi.

There was considerable animosity toward the Jews, partly related to envy of their economic prosperity. In 1350 this went so far that the Jews were blamed for the plague that ravaged Portugal. The protection of the crown, however, prevented violence.

163

During the fifteenth century emotion against the Jews finally erupted into violence. In 1449 the *judiaria* in Lisbon, the largest Jewish community of the time, was stormed by an angry mob under the direction of a group of Dominican friars. The king dealt severely with the culprits, but the stage had been set for further anti-Jewish action.

When Ferdinand of Aragon and Isabella of Castile expelled the Jews from Spain in 1492, many sought refuge in Portugal. João II agreed to allow, for a fee, more than 50,000 of these Jews safe passage through Portugal, provided that they leave the country within a few months on ships that he promised to supply. The sea transport was never provided, and many of the Spanish Jews were passed into slavery or torn from their families and sent to populate Portugal's island territories.

When Manuel I mounted the throne in 1495, he initially showed great respect for the Jews and attempted to reverse anti-Semitism or at least to compensate the Jews for their misery. He and his advisers recognized that the Jews constituted one of the most enlightened and productive segments of Portuguese society. Manuel's political ambitions to rule all of the Iberian Peninsula, however, led him to issue a decree in 1497 expelling the Jews. As a result he won the hand of Isabella, the daughter of Ferdinand of Aragon and Isabella of Castile, in marriage. Manuel attempted to circumvent his own ruling and to keep the Jews in Portugal by having many of them forcibly baptized and then issuing special laws of protection. The forced converts were known as New Christians or Maranos (secret Jews), and many continued to practice their religion secretly. Those who were able, however, emigrated at the first opportunity.

When the Inquisition was introduced in 1531 during the reign of King João III, Jews speeded their departure from Portugal. Those who had not converted and who did not escape the country went into deep hiding. Be the time the Inquisition was suppressed in Portugal in 1820, it was generally thought that no Jews were to be found in the country.

During the late nineteenth century Jews began resettling in Portugal, albeit slowly. Foreigners were allowed freedom of worship under the charter of 1826, and most of the Jews who came to Portugal during this period were foreign merchants. One Jewish source claimed that many of the nearly 700 Jews who were residing in Portugal in the early 1970s were foreign (Polish, French, or American). There were no rabbis serving the Jewish communities of Lisbon and Porto in 1975, although each city had a synagogue.

In the early twentieth century small communities of Maranos were discovered in the north of Portugal—predominantly in the regions of Trás-os-Montes and Beira Baixa. These Jews had not been counted in the religious censuses of the population, and in 1976 no accurate estimate of their numerical strength existed. They still lived much as they

had during the days of the Inquisition. To outside observers they acted as Christians—attending Catholic church services and partaking in
the Catholic sacraments. With the greatest of secrecy, however, they
continued to celebrate their religion. When these communities were
discovered, worldwide Jewish organizations began to raise money in
order to bring them back into the fold. Success was limited. The
Maranos were difficult to reach; their distrust of outsiders made them
wary even of fellow Jews, and they seemed to believe that they were
the only pure Jews remaining.

Anthropologists working in the mid-1960s still found Marano communities living in semi-isolation, cut off from most of the developments in the world and in their own religion. The estimate of the
number of these Jews was revised downward, and they appeared to
be disappearing. Decades and even centuries of intermarriage were
evidenced in the poor health of community members. Most were poor
and earned their livelihoods as wandering tradesmen. Those who had
managed to achieve upward mobility had achieved it through marriage
outside the group and subsequent departure from Jewish tradition.

****

There are no comprehensive works in English on religious life in Portugal. It is possible, however, to gain some useful insights into the historical, political, social, and cultural aspects of religion in Portugal by consulting a variety of sources. The articles
"Portugal" in both the *New Catholic Encyclopedia* and the *Jewish Encyclopedia* provide concise historical summaries. Hugh Kay's *Salazar and Modern Portugal* is helpful
in explaining Salazar's relations with and attitude toward the church. A controversial
work concerning church and state relations in Portugal and the overseas territories during the years of Salazar is the critical review *Freedom and Catholic Power and Spain
and Portugal* by the anti-Catholic polemicist Paul Blanshard. The Pro Mundi Vita Society has produced the most useful and comprehensive monograph to date on the role of
the Roman Catholic Church in the overseas territories. For information on Portugal and
the Catholic world, Catholic opposition to Portuguese domestic and colonial policies,
and the role of the church in the 1970s one is forced to rely almost entirely upon news
accounts in various religious journals (*America, Commonweal, Christian Century,* and
Christianity Today), as well as articles from the *New York Times,* the *Washington Post,*
and the *Financial Times.* Descriptions in this chapter of the social and cultural aspects
of religious life, particularly in rural Portugal, are based on and owe much to the work
of two anthropologists, Joyce Riegelhaupt and José Cutileiro. (For further information
see Bibliography.)

CHAPTER 7

EDUCATION AND THE ARTS

Portuguese education had been in a state of gradual transition in the early 1970s, its deficiencies generally recognized by government officials and educators; but the political and social pressures unleashed in 1974 by the revolution brought the educational system to a state of chaos from which it had not emerged at the end of the 1975-76 academic year. Traditionally, low priority was given to education and, as a percentage of gross national product (GNP—see Glossary), Portugal's budgetary allocations for education were the lowest in Europe. Schooling was not a critical concern in the lives of most Portuguese. A large segment of the population had been excluded from full participation in the formal educational process and was suspicious of it or even hostile. Portugal had the lowest rate of literacy in Europe.

Despite reforms undertaken since 1964, education was essentially class oriented and aimed at meeting the requirements of an academically adjusted middle-class constituency. Teaching was formal and innovation discouraged. A large proportion of the teaching personnel did not possess officially required pedagogical training. There were substantial discrepancies in standards of education between urban and rural areas. Scientific and technical training was inadequate for the needs of future economic development. Statistics available in 1976 relating to education were dated and inadequate and did not reflect existing conditions.

Portugal has not been a pacesetter in the arts except in lyric poetry. Patronage of the arts came almost entirely from the court and the church until late in the eighteenth century. The arts in the nineteenth century mirrored the taste of the bourgeoisie. Even in the third quarter of the twentieth century, Portugal lacked cultural solidarity. Despite the work of exceptionally gifted artists and the periodic flourishes of creative activity—which directly paralleled periods of prosperity in the sixteenth and eighteenth centuries—Portuguese literature, architecture, music, and the plastic arts have been derivative of foreign styles and techniques. Outside Portugal the sixteenth-century poet Luís de Camões is perhaps the only widely known Portuguese artistic figure. The Portuguese have been sensitive to what some observers have felt was a national inferiority in formal culture, and they have tended to be apologetic about their country's artistic expression. Art-

167

ists have accepted cultural subservience to international styles, which often were adopted in Portugal a generation after the rest of Europe. The Portuguese public has usually preferred books, art, and music by foreign writers and artists to those by their countrymen.

EDUCATION

Cathedral and monastic schools trained the clergy that provided Portugal with its civil bureaucracy as well as its ecclesiastical and intellectual leaders in the Middle Ages. Lisbon University, founded under the patronage of King Dinís in 1290, remained Portugal's only university until the sixteenth century. In common with all medieval universities, it was chartered as an autonomous corporation, dependent on the church—and ultimately under the jurisdiction of the pope —rather than the Portuguese crown. The university failed to attain a position of respect even among Portuguese scholars, many of whom —in the cosmopolitan atmosphere of medieval university life—went abroad for their education, especially to Salamanca, where a substantial portion of the student body was Portuguese, and to Paris, the center of later medieval intellectual life, where a residence was set aside for them.

The university's site was shifted permanently to Coimbra in 1537 and its charter reformed under royal aegis, more to curb corporate privileges than to advance learning. The humanist and pedagogical innovator André de Gouveia undertook in the mid-sixteenth century to reform teaching methods and revamp the curriculum in Portuguese schools; however, he died before he could accomplish his task, and his faculty, recruited abroad, was scattered by the Inquisition. The Jesuits thereafter until the eighteenth century exercised a virtually unchallenged monopoly of education through their schools for boys and the university that they founded at Evora in 1557 and by dominating the faculties at Coimbra. The expulsion of the Jesuits in 1759 and the closing of their schools were the first steps in the reform of education initiated by the marquis of Pombal, who had become virtual dictator of the country (see ch. 2). Under his guidance the curriculum at Coimbra was expanded to include mathematics and natural science, and professional schools were instituted in commerce, administration, technology, design, and the arts.

A system of public secondary school education was established in 1821, but the church operated all primary education. It took Portuguese education the rest of the nineteenth century to recover from the abolition of the religious orders in 1834 (see ch. 6). By 1900 the state was supporting nine schools for every 10,000 people in a population of approximately 5 million, but the rate of illiteracy in that year was estimated at almost 75 percent. Successive governments gave enthusiastic support to the principle of educational reform and expansion but little money to support it, and until 1964 only four years of education were required for Portuguese children, the lowest such figure in Europe. João de Deus (1830-96) pioneered preprimary education in Portugal in the 1870s, and his concepts of early childhood education were officially accepted, but the country remained without a state-supported preschool program.

Disproportionate attention was paid to a system of higher education that was in practice reserved for a few students, and secondary education was geared almost exclusively to preparation for university. Coimbra, waggishly referred to as the best medieval university in the modern world, rated poorly academically, without competition and the incentive to improve. An initial act of the Portuguese Republic was to break Coimbra's monopoly on higher education and establish new universities in 1911 at Lisbon and Porto. In 1931 the Technical University of Lisbon was founded. University programs remained inflexible, particularly in curriculum. Courses of study were static, and degrees, earned after an indefinite period of study, led only to specific professions. Although the country suffered from a shortage of skilled labor, owing in large part to the paucity of vocational training available, there was a surplus of university graduates.

The Prerevolution Educational System

In 1964 the period of compulsory education was raised from four to six years to include children between the ages of seven and thirteen, but in practice it was impossible to enforce these requirements in rural areas. Four years of primary education and an additional two years of secondary school were free. Emphasis was put on essentials —reading, writing, and arithmetic—but most schools also taught literature, music, and civics and provided for some form of physical education. Religious instruction was available if specifically requested by parents for their children. The Ministry of Education claimed to reach nine out of ten children with the compulsory primary school program; however, one-fifth of the students who began at age seven had left school before completing the full six years. At least one-third of those finishing the required program were judged unqualified to continue to the noncompulsory secondary level. Primary-school teachers received their pedagogical training at the secondary school level at which Portuguese teacher training schools operate.

The second level of secondary education, or senior high school, was not free in 1974, although state subsidies were granted to qualified students for tuition and expenses. The program of studies was conducted on two tiers, the first tier for three years and the second tier for two years, intended to prepare students for admission to university. Senior high school students, especially those from outlying rural districts distant from schools, were required to live away from home. Despite subsidies, the additional expenses and the loss of students' labor to their families discouraged many from continuing their education after the compulsory cycle or caused others to discontinue the secondary level studies that they had begun. In 1974 approximately 40 percent of the population between the ages of thirteen and seventeen were enrolled in secondary schools, approximately 75 percent of them in the initial three-year tier. A relatively high number of students failed to meet the academic standards to pass to the second tier for university preparation, and not more than 30 percent of those who entered senior (academic) high schools completed the full five-year course. In theory secondary-school teachers were expected to have university degrees.

Technical and vocational training was available at state-supported schools, which offered three-year programs after the six-year compulsory cycle as well as three- and four-year courses at an advanced level to students who completed the first tier of senior high school. Areas of training included industrial arts, agriculture, business and commerce, nursing and midwifery, and social work. Also operating as secondary schools were conservatories for music and art and teacher training schools for prospective primary level and physical education teachers.

Four universities offered advanced degrees in 1974—Coimbra, Lisbon, Porto, and the Technical University of Lisbon. The Catholic University of Lisbon, chartered with pontifical accreditation in 1968, was scheduled to begin operation in 1974; and three regional universities whose administrations were established in 1973—Aveiro, Evora, and Minho (at Braga)—were assembling faculties in expectation of admitting students to degree programs in the 1975-76 academic year.

Faculties, or academic departments, were self-regulating within the structure of the university administrations. Coimbra, Lisbon, and Porto maintained faculties of arts and letters, medicine, science, and pharmacy. Coimbra and Lisbon also had law faculties, and Porto had an engineering department. The Technical University of Lisbon offered programs leading to degrees in engineering and technology. A growing number of polytechnic institutes provided nonuniversity higher education in engineering, industrial arts, and business and public administration; traditional academies and institutes outside the university structure were responsible for education in architecture, economics, sociology, veterinary medicine, and agronomy. Schools at postsecondary levels also gave specialized training in the arts, journalism, public relations, business and commerce, physical education, nursing, and agriculture. Adult education courses, both on the job and by correspondence, emphasized industrial arts and were designed to overcome Portugal's chronic shortage of skilled labor.

The quantitative growth of Portuguese education in the 1960s and early 1970s was impressive, but its qualitative improvement was subject to question. Teaching methods were considered outmoded and, despite efforts at several levels to correct the deficiency, scientific and technological training remained insufficient to meet the needs of the country's economy. Many new primary and secondary schools were constructed, a large number of them to replace older and inadequate facilities. The number of students in schools at all levels in 1970 was nearly 1.5 million out of a national population estimated then at 8.7 million. Two-thirds were enrolled in the compulsory six-year program, representing an increase in that sector of 10 percent since 1960.

The greatest growth was in secondary education; 265,000 students were enrolled, more than two-and-one-half times the number in school at that level in 1960. The bulk of private education, almost all of it in church-operated schools that received state support, was at the secondary level. In the past students had been attracted to the private schools by the favorable student-teacher ratio. With the striking increase in public facilities, however, the number of students in private high schools decreased from 60,000 to 45,000 between 1960 and 1970. Vocational training was provided to 135,000 students in 1970 in schools paralleling the senior high schools; these schools were producing approximately 10,000 graduates annually, one-third more than ten years before.

The 46,000 students working for advanced degrees at the four universities in 1970 was double the number in 1960. It was estimated that there were 60,000 holders of university degrees in 1970—a figure up by 18,000 in ten years—accounting for 2 percent of the labor force. With more than 3,000 university students taking degrees in 1970, it was projected that the total number of degree holders in the labor force by 1975 would represent an increase of 137 percent over that in 1960.

According to 1970 statistics Portuguese schools employed 70,000 teachers, 58,000 of them in public institutions, or more than half again as many as were in the profession in 1960. This in turn was twice the number that had been teaching in 1950. The average teacher-to-student ratio in primary and secondary schools in 1970 was one to twenty-four; the ultimate goal was set at one to seventeen. Teaching methods, however, were considered by international observers to be ill adapted to contemporary needs. Teacher training schools for primary-school teachers provided an alternative to academic secondary schools and were understood as being inferior to them. Certificates in primary education were in effect second-class high school diplomas and adversely affected the self-image and prestige of primary-school teachers. Separate specialized training, also on the secondary level, was provided in physical education and in the care and education of abnormal children. An advanced university degree, the equivalent of a master's degree, was required for teaching personnel in secondary schools. It was estimated in 1974 that three-fourths of secondary-

171

school teachers were without the formal pedagogical training also required of them. Among these, however, were a large number of engineers, lawyers, and other university-trained professionals who entered teaching because they could not secure jobs elsewhere.

The budget for 1974, prepared by Marcello Caetano's government, called for a public expenditure of 9.7 billion escudos (for value of the escudo—see Glossary) on education, approximately 15 percent of the total budget and 2.5 percent of GNP. This was more than three times the amount spent on education in 1960 but was only a fractionally higher proportion of GNP.

In the 1960s Portugal participated in the Mediterranean Regional Project on education undertaken with Spain, Greece, Turkey, and Yugoslavia under the sponsorship of the Organization for Economic Cooperation and Development (OECD). The objectives of the research project were to suggest means for increasing the percentage of GNP allocated to education and to provide a master plan for long-range educational reform and growth. Particular attention was paid in Portugal to reducing regional disparities, making educational opportunities independent of students' financial means, modernizing curriculum, and updating teaching methods. The OECD plan for revamping the Portuguese educational system was adopted by the Caetano government in 1971. It called specifically for expanding, individualizing, and diversifying education as resources became available. The period of compulsory school attendance was lengthened in the plan to eight years with the object of keeping in the classroom all Portuguese children between the ages of six and fourteen. More flexible secondary and university programs were recommended, and emphasis was put on upgrading pedagogical training. By 1973 the Caetano government had begun implementation of the OECD plan.

Postrevolution Education

The broad lines of the OECD educational reform package were not challenged by the new government after the April 1974 revolution or by subsequent governments; however, the implementation of many programs set in motion before 1974 was postponed because of scarcity of funds and preoccupation with political revolution in the schools, the universities, and the communist-dominated Ministry of Education. Priority was given to removing teachers who had been too closely identified with the Caetano regime and to replacing textbooks with material that reflected changed political conditions. The result, in many instances, was to leave classrooms without either teachers or books, and the routine of education was disrupted.

In guidelines laid down by the Ministry of Education in 1975, students and teachers were encouraged to assume a more active role in school administration. The integration of previously neglected portions of the population into the educational process was emphasized through projects that made use of radio and television. Literacy programs were stressed, often with the cooperation of the Armed Forces Movement (Movimento das Forças Armadas—MFA, see Glossary), political parties, and trade unions. More attention was to be paid to creativity, less to academic subjects, and the value of manual and productive labor emphasized in secondary schools. No overall policy for education was proposed, however, and specified programs that were introduced were not enforced in any determined fashion. In certain schools, university faculties, and local jurisdictions, separate and uncoordinated reforms were undertaken; some succeeded in their aims, especially in areas of community action. In many areas the process of politicization of education was pervasive, and administrators were often appointed whose credentials were political rather than professional. Remarkably, however, the majority of schools appeared to operate as before in the same facilities, with the same personnel, teaching the same subjects according to the same standards.

The authority of the Ministry of Education to deal with independent actions taken by various schools and universities was weakened by frequent changes in ministers. The ministry itself was as politicized as the school system that it was supposed to administer. Theoretically the ministry exercised control over the universities, but in practice its directives were disregarded on the university campuses, and its involvement was limited to providing funds and offering advice. Even within the universities, central administration was ineffective. Academic government rested with student-teacher assemblies in the separate faculties, and intradepartmental politics surfaced in the form of struggles for control of the assemblies between communist and Maoist factions. It was recognized in 1975, for instance, that Maoists dominated assemblies controlling the faculties of medicine and letters at Lisbon and the law faculty at Coimbra and that the law faculty at Lisbon was a communist preserve. Student committees elected instructors and decided on curriculum, and their decisions were regularly rubber-stamped by the Ministry of Education.

A genuine effort was made to reform the outdated university curriculum, but many courses—among them required courses—added by the student-teacher assemblies were heavily ideological in content and reflected the political attitudes of the factions in control of the departments. Scheduled courses often did not get off the ground. Classes were frequently interrupted by the political activities in which students and teachers were engaged, and lecture halls lay empty during much of the 1974-75 academic year. At the opening of the 1975-76 academic year in October 1975, Prime Minister José Pinheiro de Azevedo criticized "students who do not study, teachers who do not teach," but the criticism appeared to have little effect.

Expanding educational opportunities to meet the aspirations of the largest possible number of Portuguese students became an important issue after the revolution and, in dealing with it, reality was sometimes subordinated to political requirements. The new government was obliged to take hastily conceived measures to ensure that increased demand for places in universities could be met. When the Ministry of Education failed to get approval for a modified system for selection of students entering university in 1974, it conceded to a politically motivated scheme not only to open admission to all high school graduates—as proposed in the OECD plan—but also to grant administrative passes without final examinations to all seniors in the class of 1974. Unquestionably the last weeks of the academic year had been irreparably disrupted by the enthusiasm generated by the April revolution.

A so-called social service year, planned as an introduction to university, was seen as a means to forestall the onslaught of as many as 28,000 potential entrants (no one knew how many high school graduates to expect), or more than double the number of first-year graduates admitted in 1973, for whom teachers, courses, classroom space, living accommodations, and study materials had not been made available. In effect first-year university studies for the 1974-75 academic year were suspended. It was anticipated that the students released from classroom requirements during the first year at university would engage in socially beneficial fieldwork provided by the government and prepare for the next academic year through television and correspondence courses. At the opening of the·academic year in October 1974, however, the social service program remained in the planning stage.

Students who could afford it went abroad to continue their studies. Many other eligible students barred from immediate admission appeared to have dropped out to enter the labor market. Others repeated their senior years in high school, and as a result facilities at that level were severely crowded. The extreme left condemned social service as forced labor, calling it a "bourgeois ruse" to prevent admission of the working class to university. Others, sympathetic to the government's dilemma, refused to cooperate because the program had been poorly thought out and was ineffective in providing either interim education or meaningful jobs. The Socialist Youth Movement pointed out that cleaning parks and painting school buildings had no social value for students and in fact did harm to an already depressed labor market.

Officials at the Ministry of Education interviewed late in 1975 believed that, with added facilities for higher education, graduates from 1974 could be absorbed at university in the 1975-76 academic year, especially in the absence of a second-year class; it was not clear how high school graduates from 1975 would be accommodated when they arrived after their social service year to begin studies in October 1976. The opening of the new universities at Aveiro, Evora, and Braga was speeded to meet the crush of new students. University colleges were planned as branches of established universities to bring higher education nearer potential students in more remote parts of the country. The New University of Lisbon, created to relieve the burden on Lisbon University, opened in 1976, as did the long-promised facility for higher education in the Azores. Innovative open universities were already holding classes in 1975 to bring academic and technical courses to workers.

Despite the activity of student-teacher assemblies, there had been no real reorganization of existing universities by the end of 1975. Examinations as a means of indicating student achievement were eliminated in some faculties, however, and individual performance in studies was no longer considered a decisive factor in advancing students to a higher level. Students' qualifications were judged on the basis of their observed interaction in collective projects. Concern was expressed by professional associations over the credentials of graduates being turned out under this approach, particularly by medical and engineering faculties.

Literacy

By any standard of measurement Portugal had the lowest rate of literacy in Europe in 1974. The new government sought to demonstrate that the country's continued backwardness in this area was the result of negligence by the old regime. In fact the 60 percent literacy rate claimed by the old government in 1960 contrasted with only 30 percent estimated in 1930.

Figures on Portuguese illiteracy vary widely according to the source of the survey, the segment of the population sampled, and the definition applied to literacy. Some Portuguese who were taken as illiterates in certain surveys had basic reading skills but were unable to compose a letter or to fill out a form—one of a number of tests of literacy. Official Portuguese sources after the revolution estimated that 28 percent of the population above the age of fifteen were illiterate, as was 37 percent of the population over thirty-five years of age. Illiteracy was lower in metropolitan areas—12 and 14 percent in Porto and Lisbon—but rose to 40 percent in the Alentejo. Other estimates by non-Portuguese sources were considerably more positive. A World Bank (see Glossary) survey from 1970 put the illiteracy figure at 20 percent of the "active" population.

Foreign observers familiar with Portuguese affairs attempted to make the point that the gradually increasing rate of literacy, although slow, matched the growth of awareness of the problem among the general public and the increased accessibility of primary education.

Traditionally there was no social stigma attached to illiteracy, and there was no organized constituency demanding programs to attack it. Other sources explained that public indifference to illiteracy and the more prevalent subliteracy was but another symptom of the estrangement of the mass of the Portuguese people from education. Despite criticism of the inadequacy of adult literacy programs undertaken by the old government, no overall program to combat illiteracy was in operation in 1975. Ambitious but uncoordinated projects were devised by the MFA, political parties, and trade unions in parts of the country. In urban industrial and collectivized rural areas, the MFA in particular conducted consciousness-raising sessions to convey an awareness of the advantages of literacy by first stimulating an interest in literature and the written word. Projects differed from place to place in their goals, methods, and success depending on leadership and the quality of instruction provided.

Government efforts to organize programs were plagued by delays, usually the result of political rivalries among participants. Although some notable literacy projects met with considerable success, especially those conducted by trade unions and professional associations, the dropout rate from existing adult programs in 1975 was reported to be discouragingly high. This apparent failure to sustain the interest of adult illiterates in improving their condition was laid generally to the enthusiastic but amateurish approach toward the projects, the poor quality of instruction offered, and the slow progress inevitably made by enrollees unfamiliar with classroom procedure, which had the effect of reinforcing their indifference. Some educationists concluded that attention should focus on teaching basic reading skills to children.

ARTISTIC EXPRESSION

Language and Literature

Portuguese is spoken as a native language by more than 100 million people in Portugal and Brazil, as well as in the former Portuguese colonies in Africa and India. A pidgin Portuguese is used in the East Indies, a reminder of the days when Portuguese was the language of commerce in that part of the world. The language evolved from the rustic Latin spoken on the western coast of the Iberian Peninsula more than 1,000 years before the Gallego-Portuguese dialects emerged as a language distinct from other Hispanic tongues in the tenth century. Portuguese is the most archaic of the Romance languages, and an educated reader can cope with thirteenth-century Portuguese without difficulty.

Portugal and Galicia had a common literary heritage and, as written languages, Portuguese and Galician were indistinguishable until the fifteenth century. The formal Portuguese language was enriched by the classical learning of humanists who used it as a medium of intellectual exchange at a time when the impress of Castilian as a written language had relegated Galician to the status of a regional dialect. Some of Portugal's finest authors and poets also wrote in Castilian when the occasion suited its use. The process of castilianization at court and among the nobility preceded the Spanish Habsburgs in Portugal by a century and resulted from Portuguese and Castilian identification with a common Hispanic culture rather than from political pressures (see ch. 2). Contemporary educated Portuguese read and understand Spanish without difficulty.

The literature of Portugal contains a wealth of lyric poetry, part of a tradition to which Portuguese poets have returned over the centuries as their most effective mode of expression. Portugal has also excelled in its historical writers and has produced a small number of excellent novelists in the late nineteenth and the twentieth centuries. Yet few Portuguese writers—except for Luís de Camões, the author of an acknowledged European classic, *Os Lusíadas* (The Lusiads, 1572)—have attracted the attention of an audience outside their own country. The Portuguese experience has been too far from the European mainstream to be understood easily, and the simplicity of the characters presented by Portuguese writers has often discouraged readers abroad.

An emotional theme repeated throughout Portuguese literature, the feeling of *saudade*, a sense of unremitting nostalgia and impossible yearnings for the past, has been described as the most characteristic trait of the Portuguese personality. In a present that was intolerable and with a future that was uncertain, the past became a refuge—but one that was unattainable. Sebastianism, the messianic faith that a lost king would return to redeem the country and return it to its past prosperity and glory, has also been explained as a political manifestation of this Portuguese phenomenon (see ch. 2).

The country's illiteracy and lack of interest in literature have frustrated many serious writers and led José Maria de Eça de Queirós, perhaps the greatest of Portugal's novelists, to complain of his language that it was the "tomb of my mind," because of the limited reading public that it allowed him. Censorship and the high cost of books printed in small press runs have also had a stultifying effect on the development of writers.

The manuscript collections of *cancioneiros* (song books) contain *cantigas* (lyric songs) dating from the twelfth century. These lyrics are the earliest known examples of Portuguese literature but are evidently a more highly developed form of a much older oral poetic tradition. The songs in the *cancioneiros* were composed by professional court troubadours, by the socially inferior public entertainers, and—important in Portugal—by the aristocrats and clerics who turned a hand to

177

poetry. The tradition in which they wrote was courtly in every sense —not only for the court but in the court as well. Alfonso X (the Wise), king of Castile, composed his *Cantigas de Santa Maria* (Songs of the Virgin) in the dialect that he had spoken as a child in Galicia, deferring to Gallego-Portuguese as the fashionable language for lyric poetry. The highest state of lyric art was achieved at the court of Alfonso's grandson, Dinís of Portugal (reigned 1279-1325), to whom the largest collection of *cancioneiros* is attributed. The decline of the tradition after Dinís demonstrated the extent to which courtly poetry depended on the patronage of the court.

The *romanceiro* (Castilian ballad) displaced the *cantigas* in popularity at court. A reawakening of interest in Portuguese as a medium for poetic expression after the battle of Aljubarrota (1385) resulted in a Portuguese version of the Arthurian legend, but it was only with the collection of the *Cancioneiro Geral* by the humanist Garcia de Resende (ca. 1470-1536) that the lyric tradition was revived. Bernardim Ribeiro (1482-1552), called the last of the troubadours, carefully catalogued the many nuances of romatic love in the *Menina e Moça* (Little Girl and Maiden), one of the last lyrics to be done in the old manner.

Portuguese prose originated in anonymous chronicles from the fourteenth century. The motivation for these and later chronicles by court bureaucrats was political, but the achievement was of a high order as literature. The first of the great chroniclers, Fernão Lopes, was commissioned by King Duarte (reigned 1435-38) to compile a record of the rise of the House of Aviz (see ch. 2). A notary employed in the royal archives and a superior storyteller, Lopes underscored the indebtedness of the dynasty to the townsmen and artisans who supported João I against the old aristocracy that had been content to allow a Castilian succession. Lopes' successor as royal chronicler, Gomes Eanes de Zurara, reflected the changed political atmosphere under Afonso V (reigned 1438-81) in the stress he laid on the role of the nobility in building the nation.

The attention of sixteenth-century chroniclers was directed toward the passage to India and the growth of the seaborne empire. João de Barros used the records of the Casa da India (India House), where he was treasurer, to research his *Décadas*. Fernão Lopes de Castanheda published the first of ten volumes of his history of the conquest of India in 1551, just ahead of Barros' work. The archivist of Coimbra, Castanheda wrote against the background of his observations during years of service in India. As "official" histories, the Indian chronicles were flawed by the defects of the genre. Gaspar Correia (1495-ca. 1565) and Diogo do Couto (ca. 1543-1616), both of whom had spent the greater part of their lives in the East, left unauthorized commentaries on life in Portuguese India that denounced abuses of authority by colonial officials and condemned the rapaciousness of their countrymen. Correia and Couto concluded that the colonial experience had robbed the Portuguese of their better instincts. Their histories were suppressed and left unpublished for 250 years. Probably the most widely read of the numerous travel books and chronicles that appeared in the sixteenth century was the *Peregrinaçam* (Pilgrimage) of Fernão Mendes Pinto (ca. 1514-83). Called the "Father of All Lies," Mendes Pinto put his vivid imagination to work in recording the sights and observations of his twenty years in the Orient. There was general critical agreement that the *Peregrinaçam*, although unreliable as historical narrative, was the prose masterpiece of its time.

Portuguese theater was the creation of Gil Vicente (ca. 1470-1536), poet to the court of King Manuel I (reigned 1495-1521) and a figure as momentous in the cultural history of his country as was William Shakespeare in England. For more than thirty years no court occasion could be marked appropriately without the performance of one of Gil Vicente's *autos* (religious dramas) or farces, which were written and performed for a bilingual audience in both Portuguese and Castilian. Gil Vicente's plays fell entirely within the medieval tradition. With little sense of plot, he called down heaven to put to right the wrongs of this world. His stereotyped characters allowed for the sharp contrast of virtue and vice on stage. Slapstick did not detract from the religious intention of the *autos*, which was to impart a moral lesson, and the clergy as well as women and courtiers—the large part of the audience for whom he wrote—were the butt of Gil Vicente's satirical, frequently ribald wit. Before the end of the sixteenth century the Inquisition had put a stop to the secular theater, and even the *autos* of Gil Vicente were brutally expurgated.

The first of Portugal's Renaissance poets, Francisco de Sá de Miranda (1481-1558), returned to his country after many years in Italy to challenge the medieval conventions of the *cantigas* and *romanceiros* with the Petrarchan sonnet form, to which he shaped the Portuguese language. Sá de Miranda deplored the cupidity of the court and looked back with nostalgia in his pastoral verse to the heyday of the landed aristocracy, which he took to be a time of rustic simplicity. The impact of the verse style that he introduced to Portuguese was felt throughout the rest of the sixteenth century.

Os Lusíadas, by the adventurer-poet Camões, holds the highest place in Portuguese literature. It is a lyric chronicle of Vasco da Gama's voyage and a recounting of Portuguese history. Modeled on the *Aeneid* of Vergil, *Os Lusíadas* reflects Camões' experiences during more than twenty years in the East and in Africa. Camões is revered as a national hero, and his poem is considered Portugal's national epic; however, the poet died in penury, and his work in a sense marked the end of Portugal's heroic age. Camões' lyric sonnets were published only after his death in 1580. His poetry introduced new words and expressions into common usage, enriching the Portuguese language and leaving his mark on it. Modern critics have judged

Camões the greatest Iberian lyricist, a poet who was master of every verse form.

Castilian was the preferred language for literary expression among many Portuguese writers during the Habsburg period (1580-1640), and Francisco Manuel de Melo, the finest prose stylist in Portugal in the seventeenth century, was the product of a bilingual culture. A polymath poet, historian, essayist, and statesman in the service of both the Habsburgs and the Braganças, Melo wrote his most important work, a history of the Catalan rising of 1640, in Castilian. Only a handful of writers sustained the integrity of Portuguese against the preference of their contemporaries for Castilian. The best known work by a seventeenth-century Portuguese writer, however, was published in French and, although presumably written originally in Portuguese, belongs to the literature of Portugal only in translation: *Lettres portugaises* (Portuguese Letters), five letters believed to have been written by Sister Marianna Alcoforado, a nun from Beja, to her lover, the French conde de Chamilly—describing their affair with intense lyric passion—was published in 1669 in Paris. Enormously popular, this work was the foundation for the epistolary novel of the next century.

The early eighteenth century witnessed an unequal struggle between the attempt to contrive literary styles distinctive to Portugal and subservience to French canons of criticism. Portuguese writers penned prosaic poetry and arid prose, and only a few stood out as a cut above the average in what has been called a neoclassic wasteland. The poet Pedro António Correia Garção (1724-73) was dedicated to uprooting Castilian influence in Portuguese literature. His literary rival, Filinto Elisío (pseudonym of Padre Manuel do Nascimento, 1734-1819), was a hero to a generation of Portuguese writers, more in sympathy with his radical politics, however, than in admiration of his neoclassic poetry.

The preromantic poet Manuel Maria Barbosa du Bocage (1765-1805), whose provocative verse surpassed anything written in Portugal in the eighteenth century and was not surpassed in the nineteenth, was encouraged by Filinto Elisío, although Bocage rejected the older poet's formalism in favor of freer forms influenced by the Ossian poems of James Macpherson. Jailed for his radical views, Bocage capitalized on his image as a rascal. His somber, brooding poetry went beyond self-pity and verged on masochism.

Two figures—the poet-playwright visconde de Almeida Garrett and the historian-novelist Alexandre Herculano—dominated Portuguese letters in the first half of the nineteenth century by their criticism, patronage, and political activism as much as by their own considerable literary efforts. Readers deferred to their taste, and the work of other writers was judged by the standards they set. Proposing to modernize Portuguese society by putting their isolated country in touch with Europe through literature, Almeida Garrett and Herculano fixed the romantic strain in Portuguese liberalism, and their success was symbolic of the cultural as well as the political triumph of the bourgeoisie.

The naturalist reaction to romanticism came first from Antero de Quental (1842-92), an aristocratic intellectual and poet from the Azores. The influence of French positivism led him to reject romanticism with its individualistic values and to proclaim in *Odes Modernas* (Modern Odes, 1865) the overriding social function of literature. Quental was the moving spirit behind the Generation of 1870, a group of like-minded scholars and writers—the historians Teófilo Braga and Joaquim Martins, the novelists Eça de Queirós and José Ortigão, and the poet Abílio Junqueiro—who arrived at their artistic maturity during the decade of the 1870s. Quental drifted into socialism but was disillusioned when he discovered that the Portuguese working class did not live up to the ideal image of it that he had projected in his poetry. In search of a supportive ideology, he dabbled in esoteric philosophies and oriental mysticism without satisfying his quest. Quental died by his own hand.

Portuguese fiction in the mid-nineteenth century was influenced by the work of Sir Walter Scott, Victor Hugo, Charles Dickens, and William Thackeray, but the novel was late in being adopted by Portuguese writers. The bohemian journalist Camilo Castelo Branco (1825-95), a prolific short story writer, became Portugal's first successful novelist with the publication of his immensely popular *Amor de Perdição* (Love of Perdition, 1862). Castelo Branco was interested in style rather than in structure and never came to grips with the genre that he apparently initiated. The distinction between the novel and the extended story also eluded Júlio Dinís (pseudonym of Joaquin Guilherme Gomes Coelho, 1839-71), whose serialized fiction marked a transition from romanticism to realism in popular literature.

Eça de Queirós, one of the Generation of 1870, was Portugal's most original and forceful novelist, from the standpoint of both his objective style and his narrative abilities. In his early realistic social novels, devastating in their effect, he exposed the vices of the middle class and clergy and the foibles of women. *O Crime do Padre Amaro* (The Sin of Father Amaro, 1875) and *O Primo Basílio* (Cousin Basílio, 1878) are the best of his novels from this period. A diplomat, Eça de Queirós lived mostly abroad, and distance gave him a perspective on his country. Although he deplored Portugal's backwardness, a common element in his satire was criticism of the presumption that European values could be imposed on the Portuguese people. The signs of his fading idealism were clear in his later impressionistic novels, but many readers were left uncomfortable by his perception of society.

Disillusionment was the common experience of others associated with the Generation of 1870. Ortigão lost faith in social reform and became a *vencido da vida* (one defeated by life), a stock character in Portuguese literature. António Duarte Gomes Leal, whose fascination with sin and longing for an unobtainable purity pervaded his verse masterpiece, *Claridades do Sul* (Brightness of the South, 1875), abandoned his once violent anticlericalism and was reconciled to the church.

Portuguese readers found the nostalgic poetry and historical fiction of the Romantic revival of the 1890s more congenial than the unsettling work of naturalist writers. Teixeira de Pascoais, whose neoromantic verse was the finest of the period, explained *saudade* as the key to understanding the Portuguese soul and concluded that progress was not possible for a people whose past would always be more attractive than their future.

The influence of the work of Fernando Pessoa (1888-1935) on modern Portuguese literature is comparable with that of T. S. Eliot on English. Although in his lifetime Pessoa published only one slim volume of poems, *Mensagem* (Message, 1924), which was indifferently received, he has come to be recognized as the greatest Portuguese poet since Camões. A futurist who saw art as an entity divorced from its creator, Pessoa wrote under various pseudonyms giving to each persona a distinct style that represented a different aspect of his own personality.

Pessoa remained the model for a school of poetic stylists who were published in literary journals and magazines in the 1940s and 1950s. The poetry of Alexandre O'Neill and Jorge de Sena won praise for its intellectual content. Sena, who migrated to Brazil, translated Eliot into Portuguese. Mário Cesarinez de Vasconcelos' surrealist verse pointed to the absurdity of the intellectual's existence in modern Portugal. A group of Catholic philosophical poets, influenced by Pessoa's technique, emerged under the leadership of Sofia de Mello Breyner Andersen. The introspection, subjectivity, and intellectuality of Pessoa's verse were paralleled by Raul Brandão in novels and short stories that were philosophical meditations in which the author delineated the distinction between the real, inner being (ego) and the public, social being (persona).

Aquilino Ribeiro was the author of more than seventy novels, collections of short stories and essays, popular histories, and children's books. Generally described as a regional writer, his earlier novels depicted rustic life in Beira and were difficult reading for outsiders. Indeed the richness of his vocabulary necessitated publication of a glossary. Ribeiro admired the wit and doggedness of his peasant and working-class characters, and his treatment of physical love among them was advanced for its time. Much of his work was banned after its first printing, and criminal charges—later dropped—were brought against him after publication of his last novel, *Quando os Lobos Uivam* (When the Wolves Howl, 1958). Miguel Torga, a regional writer from Trás-os-Montes, dwelt on the brevity and harshness of existence and ridiculed sacrifice and striving as futile gestures. His most representative prose work, *Bichos* (The Beasts, 1940), is peopled by animals with human emotions, trapped in the natural cycle of life over which they have no control.

Neorealism attracted writers who found fault with the abstract and metaphysical preoccupations of Pessoa and his followers. Under the influence of Ernest Hemingway, John Steinbeck, and John Dos Passos, such Portuguese novelists as José Maria Ferreira de Castro and Fernando Namora developed an interest in the realistic portrayal of workers, migrants, and peasants. Ferreira de Castro based *Emigrantes* (The Emigrants, 1928), the first important social novel in Portuguese, on his experiences on Brazilian rubber plantations. He won international recognition with his treatment of the same theme in *A Selva* (The Jungle, 1930). In later novels he dealt with the moral dilemmas posed by war and with the conditions of the socially underprivileged. Namora is well known outside Portugal for *The Fields of Fate,* an omniscient narrative on the hardships of the peasants of the Alentejo.

No Portuguese writers—possibly since Marianna Alcoforado—have attracted the notoriety of the "Three Marias," the collective authors of *Nova Cartas Portuguesas* (New Portuguese Letters), which was banned at the time of its publication in 1972 on grounds of obscenity. Taking Sister Marianna's letters as their point of departure, Maria Teresa Horta, Maria Isabel Barreno, and Maria Fátima Velho da Costa compiled an exchange of stories, letters, poems, and pastisches that had as a common theme the repression of women by men and by the social institutions that men create. Hailed by some critics as a landmark in feminist literature, the book has circulated widely since 1974.

Music

Fragments of the music for the liturgy of the cathedral of Braga, part of a Hispanic tradition distinct from that of the rest of the Latin church, date from the twelfth century. The secular lyrics of the *cantigas* were set to tunes of Provençal origin or were sung in chant. Portugal had an established native musical tradition in the fifteenth century, and notations in Burgundian and German manuscripts appear to indicate that distinctively Portuguese techniques for voice were adopted elsewhere in Europe. The *ars nova,* the fashionable polyphonic style introduced from Flanders and France, was not at first encouraged at the Portuguese court: Afonso V complained that the music of Guillaume Dufay reminded him of the howling of dogs. Early in the sixteenth century, however, the cathedral chapter of Coimbra was a center for polyphonic music and produced composers and choirmasters of recognized ability, among them Fernão Gomes Correia and

Vasco Pires. The Portuguese carried their musical tradition with them on their quests overseas. A choir was established in Goa shortly after the city's conquest in 1510. Portuguese music was sung in Ethiopian churches in the sixteenth century and at the court of the kings of Congo. Gil Vicente's religious dramas included incidental music, and some can be described as musical plays. To a greater degree music was an integral part of the Jesuit tragicomedies.

Formal musical training was in the hands of the church, and the clergy dominated the field of composition through the seventeenth century, first under Flemish and Spanish and later under Italian influence. The choral pieces of Frei Manuel Cardoso, Duarte Lobo, and Frei Francisco de Santiago show the debt of their composers to the Italian Giovanni Palestrina. The Portuguese church also fostered an outstanding tradition of composition for the organ; Frei Eurico Gama was the best known of the school. After 1640 Evora—with its cathedral and university and with the frequent residence of the court—developed as a center for the study and performance of music.

The eighteenth-century courts of João V and José had the most lively musical life of any in Europe. Both kings lavished money and attention on music teachers, composers, and virtuosos and on the chapel choir and court opera. Carlos Seixas, perhaps the best known Portuguese musical figure, composed for organ and keyboard. José da Silva, a Brazilian Jew, was a popular operatic composer before he fell victim to the Inquisition. It was Domenico Scarlatti's tenure as court choirmaster, however, and the founding of a conservatory in Lisbon under his aegis, that had the greatest impact on music in the eighteenth century; Scarlatti's influence ensured the triumph of Neapolitan styles in Portuguese church music and opera.

King José's musical interests were secular, and the opera flourished under his patronage. João de Sousa Carvalho was one of the most popular composers of opera and musical drama in Europe in the second half of the eighteenth century, and his influence on the operatic stage continued into the next century through the performances of his many students, one of whom, António Fonseca, achieved celebrity status in Italy.

João Domingos Bomtempo (1775-1852), a prolific composer in his own right, influenced two generations of musicians as head of the National Academy of Music and ensured the ascendancy of the classical style in Portugal well into the Romantic era, in preference to the more original music of Joaquim Casimiro Júnior and Angelo Frondoni. Romantic music from abroad was more readily accepted, and it was only with the performances of the successful operas of Alfredo Keil, a student of Franz Liszt, that Portuguese Romantic music can be said to have come into its own. Keil remained Portugal's only Romantic composer of consequence, and his patriotic hymn, A Portuguesa, was adopted as the national anthem.

Opera remains the most popular serious musical form in Portugal (for discussion of fado, see ch. 4). Lisbon is a regular stop on the itineraries of major European companies, which perform before enthusiastic audiences at the Teatro São Carlos. Domestic opera companies, despite the very high quality of their performers, have been at a disadvantage in competing for audiences. The Portuguese Opera Company performs in Lisbon at the smaller Teatro da Trinidade, and its repertoire regularly includes the popular Italian fare. Contemporary works are also staged and, by custom, at least one Portuguese opera is performed each season. The company relies in part on government subsidies and faced an uncertain future as the government, in an economy measure, threatened to withhold funds for the 1976-77 opera season.

The Lisbon Philharmonic performs at the Teatre Municipal de São Luiz, and the symphony orchestra of the National Radio System (Emissora Nacional de Radiodifusão—ENR) gives concerts at the Tivoli in addition to its broadcasting schedule. The Gulbenkian Orchestra and Chorus performs at the Gulbenkian Foundation's auditorium.

Painting

The art of painting came late to Portugal. Its development in the fifteenth century was encouraged by Flemish craftsmen brought to the country by João I. The dominance of the Flemish primitive style was confirmed by the sizable contingent of Portuguese craftsmen who served their apprenticeships in the workshops of Flanders. On brightly colored panels these painters strove to portray every aspect of life with precisely drawn figures and detailed iconography that was at the same time sumptuous and severe in execution. The patronage that determined taste was made possible by the profits from trade in colonial goods with Flanders, from whose great markets—Bruges, Ghent, and Antwerp—cultural influence flowed back into Portugal until the mid-sixteenth century.

The retable of Saint Vincent, among the finest of late Gothic paintings, is attributed to Nuno Gonçalves, court painter to Afonso V in the fifteenth century. The six-paneled altarpiece, a panoramic representation of fifteenth-century society, depicts the patron saint of Lisbon receiving homage from the court and people of Portugal.

No one after Nuno Gonçalves matched the standards of excellence that he set, but his contemporaries and followers produced skillful illuminations and miniatures. The charts and atlases of the Goan mapmaker Fernão Vaz Dourado raised cartography to a high art form. Two schools of Portuguese painting after the Flemish fashion were recognizable in the early sixteenth century: the Lisbon-Evora school of Jorge Afonso, who as court painter to King Manuel created portraits of high quality, and the Viseu school of Grão Vasco Fernandes,

185

whose work was characterized by earthy themes and a vigorous, sometimes awkward, style.

Portuguese taste shifted after the mid-sixteenth century to Italian mannerism, the style of the late Renaissance, complementing a similar move away from the Gothic in architecture; but Portuguese painters did not share in the architects' success in adapting to the changed demand. Portugal reflected none of the magnificence of Spanish art during the period of union. Only Domingos Vieira achieved anything approaching the psychological insight sought by the mannerists. The late seventeenth century witnessed an increasing Dutch influence, and most paintings executed during this period were deficient in originality and imagination. Nothing except the modest efforts of Bento Coelho da Silveira and the repetitive still lifes of Josefa de Obidos bears mentioning.

Domingos António Sequeira (1768-1837) was the only Portuguese painter after Nuno Gonçalves to merit recognition outside the country. His earlier works, subsidized by the court, were allegorical religious and historical paintings done in an academic neoclassic style, technically on a par with what was being done elsewhere in Europe. In his later paintings—particularly his portraits—however, Sequeira's technique was similar to that of his Spanish contemporary Francisco Goya, although his work was more serene and lacked Goya's impact. There is no evidence that the two ever met or that Sequeira was familiar with any of Goya's work. Sequeira's charcoal drawings, done near the end of his career, were his finest accomplishments.

The heavy hand of academic neoclassicism lay on Portuguese art through the first half of the nineteenth century. António Manuel da Fonseca and his students at the Academy of Fine Arts, founded in 1836, provided pompous canvases imitative of the Italian masters that were admired by the cultural establishment. Miguel Lupi led the Romantic revolt against the academicians. His elegant portraits made him the most sought after artist of the second half of the century.

Portuguese artists at the end of the nineteenth century were unable to keep up with the pace set by their contemporaries abroad. Their parochialism was largely self-imposed as they strove for a nationalist style, and this attempt had the effect of keeping a hackneyed Romantic tradition alive in Portugal into the 1920s. Among the most popular painters of the period were Silva Porto, a landscapist; João Malhoa, a folklorist; Sousa Pinto, a pastelist; and Columbano Berdal Pinheiro, a portraitist and the most gifted of the group. These artists and others of their generation are well represented in Portuguese galleries.

A few innovative Portuguese painters lived in France. The most successful of them was Amadeu da Souza Cardoso, a companion of Amedeo Modigliani and Georges Braque and a student of Paul Cézanne, whose influence was clear in Cardoso's early cubism before he evolved as an expressionist.

Official advocacy of a national style during the Salazar years led to nothing in painting except by way of reaction. Portugal's most promising painters moved abroad. Generally acknowledged as the greatest living Portuguese artist, Maria Helena Vieira da Silva (1908-) has lived in Paris since 1929. Although her style is cosmopolitan, Silva's use of colors is sometimes reminiscent of that in traditional *azulejos* (wall tiles).

Painters working in Portugal complained of the public's reluctance to accept contemporary art, the absence of critical attention and, until the late 1960s, the lack of facilities for exhibitions of new art. In fact the work of Portuguese artists was not of a high order. In the 1940s and 1950s rival groups—neorealists, geometric abstractionists, surrealists—were more concerned in their artistic manifestos with the ethical value of their work than with its aesthetic merit. Júlio Resende was the best known artist to come to creative maturity during those years. During the 1960s and early 1970s there was a trend back toward academic training in the arts.

All of the artistic tendencies found in the international marketplace were present in Portugal in 1976. Op art, pop art, and mech art were popular in Lisbon. Abstractionism prevailed among artists in Porto. Some of the artists whose work was exhibited were op artists Noronha da Costa and Eduardo Nery; abstractionist Manuel Baptista; António Palolo, a metaphysically inclined pop artist; and Fátima Vaz, a neofigurativist strong in graphic ability, whose work was influenced by Vasili Kandinski and Walt Disney. Since 1974 strides have been made in poster art and graphic design. Illustrations by João Abel Manta, appearing in *Sempre Fixe* and other periodicals and reproduced as posters, were among the best art inspired by the April revolution, of which his *Primavera* (Spring) became a symbol.

Architecture

Although Portugal is not rich in antique ruins, the Temple of Diana, built in the second century A.D., is the best preserved Roman building on the Iberian Peninsula. Only traces of Byzantine and Visigothic architecture remain, and there is only sparse evidence of direct Moorish influence in surviving architecture aside from fortifications. There was considerable castle building, particularly in the Alentejo, in the twelfth century; the largest structure of its kind in Portugal, the spectacular citadel at Bragança, was begun in 1187. The impressive fortifications at Amieira and Lisbon were erected at the end of the fourteenth century. A quadrangle with a rectangular tower at each corner, Amieira was modeled on the crusader castles in Syria. Lisbon's fortifications are similar to Italian city fortresses of the same period.

Four great Romanesque cathedrals—Porto, Lisbon, Evora, and Coimbra—plus hundreds of village churches were built in the twelfth and thirteenth centuries. The finest example of the style in Portugal is the church at Bravães. The Cistercians brought their austere architecture—a transition between Romanesque and Gothic—from France in the twelfth century. Deprived by the strict rule of their reformed monastic order from adventurous decoration, the Cistercians cultivated a functional architecture that aimed at simplicity of design. The monastery at Alcobaça is considered the purest example of Cistercian architecture surviving anywhere in Europe. The earliest Gothic structures date from the late thirteenth century and are found in reconquered areas in the south not committed to Romanesque. The monastery of Batalha, one of the most representative examples, was begun by João I to commemorate his victory at Aljubarrota and to serve as pantheon to the House of Aviz. It was built by English stonemasons and clearly bears the stamp of their style.

Although all styles of architecture common throughout Europe can be found in Portugal, few examples exist—like Alcobaça—in anything approaching their original state. Most of the greater medieval ecclesiastical buildings present a melange of architecture and decoration in styles representative of the twelfth through the eighteenth centuries. Construction on medieval structures continued from one generation to the next as kings vied with forebears to leave the impress of their reigns on national monuments. Church interiors and facades were continually "modernized," embellished successively in Manueline, Palladian, and baroque styles.

Manueline design—named for the monarch (Manuel, reigned 1495-1521)—was unique to Portugal and compared as a local development of late Gothic style to English perpendicular. It was Portugal's most original contribution to European artistic expression. Apart from its use in the Jeronimite monastery at Belem, built to commemorate Portugal's entry into India, the Manueline style was employed as decorative architecture in porches, portals, windows, and interiors to reshape old monuments rather than to create new ones. The Manueline style was the exuberant and opulent expression of the spirit of Portugal's age of discovery and expansion. It was willfully eccentric and meant to startle and astonish. Appropriately called Atlantic Gothic, it set out to provide an iconography for exploration and trade and with contorted columns and writhing stone portrayed nautical motifs and the life of the sea among figures of angels and knights in armor. The first use of Manueline concepts was in the Church of Jesu at Setúbal, but the most striking examples of its use are in the Tower of Belem, the Convent of Christ at Tomar, and the unfinished cloister at Batalha, one of the clearest examples of architectural invention in Europe.

The introduction of "plain architecture," as the Renaissance style was called in Portugal, marked the triumph of geometry over extravagant embellishment. The use of the more modest proportions and humane scale of Renaissance building, which persisted through the seventeenth century, was dictated both by Portugal's declining fortunes after 1550 and by the influence of Italian craftsmen brought in under Habsburg patronage. The altered taste of the late sixteenth century is seen in the hall church of São Vicente de Fora in Lisbon and in the architecture of the Jesuit university at Evora. Barrel-vaulted Portuguese Palladian was sometimes archaeological in its imitation of antique prototypes. Portuguese taste acted on Italian suggestions in plain architecture with the convention of contrasting white plaster with dark granite trim. The rather severe taste of the early Bragança period imitated Dutch and English styles that made their only real impact in the building of country houses.

Because of the patronage of its bishops, Braga became a center for baroque architecture, the international style of the early eighteenth century. Relatively few churches were constructed in the Baroque, whose restless but controlled structural convolutions and elaborations were preferred for decorative effects, as at Bom Jesus in Setúbal. Mafra, the royal palace and monastery built by João V as Portugal's response to Spain's Escorial, was the extravagant product of the prosperity ushered in by the discovery of gold in Brazil. More than 30,000 craftsmen labored between 1717 and 1730 to construct a complex of buildings in a monotonously classical style that was relieved by the statues and baroque embellishment of Joachim Machado de Castro. Rococo, a refinement of the baroque, was robust and provocative in Portugal, especially in the hands of Nicolau Nasoni who was active in Porto and Braga. After the earthquake of 1755 Pombal dictated rebuilding central Lisbon in severe neo-Palladian architecture along a checkerboard of geometric squares and straight streets running back from a grand plaza at the waterfront. The Pombaline style, which bore an official stamp of approval for more than twenty years, was the comprehensive and systematic architecture of bureaucrats and military engineers, a style lacking in grace except for rococo details and interiors. The neoclassicism that succeeded it was arrived at by stripping away decorative overlay to emphasize the Palladian effects of the Pombaline, as in the Teatro São Carlos (1793). The eclectic architecture of the nineteenth century was obsessed with the imitation of historical styles.

There has been little encouragement for innovative modern architecture. Urban planning as well as the quality of construction and materials has been very poor. Housing projects, constructed since the mid-twentieth century, have taken the concrete-block design common throughout Europe as a norm. Some exceptions, however, are the João de Deus and Infante Santo projects in Lisbon, the latter having a Mediterranean design using polychrome *azulejos,* and the Exhibition Hall and Gulbenkian Foundation complex also in the capital.

Sculpture and Crafts

Late medieval sculpture exhibited the mannered realism typical of the best Gothic art. The two outstanding examples from the period are the tombs of Pedro I and Inês de Castro at Alcobaça (ca. 1360) and those of João I and Phillipa of Lancaster completed two generations later at Batalha. The stonecutters at Coimbra used Ança stone from nearby quarries for their bas-reliefs in the Old Cathedral, and their style was imitated throughout the country, but much of Portugal's earlier ecclesiastical stonecarving was done by English and French craftsmen.

Portuguese sculptors and stonecutters accomplished little more than the ordinary after their impressive exertions of imagination and craft in architectural embellishment during the Manueline epoch. An exception was Machado de Castro, who designed the statuary at Mafra and executed the equestrian statue of King José in Pombal's Praça do Comércio (commonly called Black Horse Square) in Lisbon. A school of sculpture was instituted at Mafra under his direction.

Official preference in sculpture in the nineteenth and twentieth centuries was by turns for the neoclassical, the Romantic, and the heroically monumental. A cut above a mediocre average, however, was the work of Soares dos Reis (1847-89), who tried to express *saudade* in stone, and Teixeira Lopes (1866-1918), whose portrait busts of children had considerable appeal. Francisco Franco (1885-1955), a futurist, has been the outstanding Portuguese sculptor of the twentieth century. Two of the most prominent works of twentieth-century sculpture are the *Padrão dos Descobrimentos* (Monument of the Discoveries), erected in 1960 beside the Rio Tejo to commemorate the five-hundredth anniversary of the death of Henry the Navigator, and the *Christ in Majesty*, a gigantic stela overlooking the Tejo estuary.

The Portuguese found wood a more congenial medium to work in than stone. In the fifteenth century the fine woods brought from Madeira and the East and later the exotic woods of Brazil were used to create the *talhadourada* (carved wood) interiors that covered bare Gothic walls after the Flemish fashion; altarpieces; ceilings in Italian-styled mannerist buildings; and the ornamental overlay in the ornate baroque of the seventeenth and eighteenth centuries. Outstanding earlier examples of *talhadourada* were the interior of the Old Cathedral at Coimbra and the Jesuit-style retables accomplished by the Coelho family in the late sixteenth century. The craft reached its climax in the eighteenth century in the spectacular apse of the Dominican convent at Aveiro (1725). The Portuguese skill in woodworking was also turned to the manufacture of furniture.

Portuguese ceramics are esteemed for both their functionalism and their beauty. *Azulejos* have been an important form of Portuguese creative art and a fixture in interior and exterior decorative design since they were introduced from Andalusia in the fifteenth century. Portuguese ceramicists retained polychromatic Moorish geometric designs that were modeled after those found on Persian rugs. Late in the seventeenth century, however, ceramicists restricted themselves to Delft blue and white after the Dutch fashion (in part to counter Dutch competition on the Portuguese market) and introduced figurative design into ornamental wall covering, in which each tile was an organic part of an overall scene. Muted color was reintegrated into the *azulejos* in the first half of the eighteenth century, the high point in the development of the craft. *Azulejos* were mass produced after the 1755 earthquake to meet the demands of rebuilding. Their use was integral to the design of Pombaline public buildings, churches, and houses. Although viewed more from the standpoint of utility than of art, the *azulejos* remained a distinctive feature of Portuguese architectural design.

The weaving of Arraiolas rugs in delicate patterns taken from Persian designs flourished in the eighteenth century and persists in present-day Portugal, but the craft dates from the sixteenth century, when Moorish women in the Alentejo were encouraged to engage in it. Portuguese craftsmen have also earned a reputation for their skills as cabinetmakers, leatherworkers and metalworkers, bookbinders and printers, and basket weavers.

INTELLECTUAL EXPRESSION

Preoccupation with the Reconquest limited the ability of the church in Portugal and, in particular, of the religious orders to enter into the mainstream of the intellectual developments of the twelfth and thirteenth centuries, in which they took the lead in other countries. The great thirteenth-century Franciscan saint Anthony of Padua was a native of Lisbon—although he is identified outside Portugal with the Italian city of his adoption. Anthony's learned theological discourse caused him to be numbered among the Doctors of the Church. Pedro Julião, the only Portuguese to be elected pope (John XXI, 1276-77), wrote the *Summalae Logicales*, which remained a standard textbook in logic at universities in the sixteenth century.

In the sixteenth century Portugal produced a small but significant group of humanists, schooled in logic, grammar, dialectic, and rhetoric, who sought—usually in the service of the church or the state—to make the use of language more effective. Aires Barbosa made his mark as a grammarian, and André de Resende as a philologist. Resende, whose interests extended to poetry, music, antiquities, and archaeology, perhaps better than any other Portuguese fitted the description of a Renaissance man. Better known as a historian, Duarte Nunes de Leão also wrote extensively on Portuguese spelling and morphology, and another historian, João de Barros, prepared a Portuguese grammar for use by East Indians. Heitor Pinto, a Jeronimite monk who covered Europe in his travels, absorbed the Neoplatonic humanism of Florence. His Latin commentaries on biblical prophecy earned him a place of importance among contemporary theologians, but he was best known in Portugal for his dialogues, the *Imagem da Vida Cristã* (Image of the Christian Life, 1563). The Jesuits, preeminent at Coimbra University after 1550, edited the *Conimbricenses*, a continuing series of commentaries on Aristotle that was acclaimed in both Catholic and Protestant Europe.

A few Portuguese humanists attracted attention abroad. Damião de Góis (1501-74), the most prominent, was a courtier employed at the Portuguese depot in Antwerp and on diplomatic missions that took him as far as Russia. Encouraged by his friend Erasmus of Rotterdam, Damião studied at Padua, where he joined some of the foremost humanists of his day. Settling later at Louvain, he turned his pen to many and varied subjects—commentaries on the Ethiopian church and on the Lapps, a description of the siege of Diu, a translation of Cicero into Portuguese, and a defense of the character of the Hispanic peoples. He was an accomplished musician and a discerning art collector. Damião returned to Portugal to become historiographer to the court. Always suspect in Portugal because of his foreign connections, Damião was at one time imprisoned by the Inquisition and narrowly escaped execution.

The history of Portuguese humanistic scholarship, apart from historical studies, is a wasteland after the sixteenth century, and in the twentieth century only a few scholars of international consequence bear noting. Philosophical studies were hampered both by uncreative teaching in the universities and by a hostile government attitude during the Salazar years.

* * * * * * * * * * * * * * * *

Essays on art and literature in *Portugal and Brazil* (1953), edited by Harold V. Livermore, are dated, but the book remains the best survey available in one volume. A detailed, scholarly presentation of literary history until 1910, Aubrey Bell's *Portuguese Literature* (1922, reprinted 1970) is a standard reference for students already acquainted with the subject, and brief biographical sketches of important Portuguese writers are found in *The Penguin Companion to European Literature* (1969) edited by Anthony Thorlby. Robert C. Smith's *The Art of Portugal, 1500-1800* covers the whole range of his subject from major architecture to crafts. Articles of interest are published in every issue of the *Journal of the American Portuguese Cultural Society*. Portuguese literature available in translation is cited in the bibliography provided in this volume. (For further information see Bibliography).

SECTION II. POLITICAL

CHAPTER 8

GOVERNMENTAL SYSTEM

A nation's constitution and its formal political system do not necessarily reflect political reality. The 1933 Constitution—still in effect in March 1976 but only in a limited transitional sense—established a detailed political structure comprising a head of state and three branches of government: executive, legislative, and judicial. The constitution further provided for certain checks and balances between branches and formally established liberal constitutional guarantees for Portuguese citizens. In actual practice the constitution served primarily to ensure António de Oliveira Salazar's control over the Portuguese state. This nullified many of the formal constitutional provisions regarding the structure and operation of government. The constitution had been written with Salazar's paramount role in mind; he was given official authority and power through his post as prime minister. That formal position partially obfuscated, and partially contributed to, his personal influence and power as dictator of Portugal.

Salazar's successor, Marcello Caetano, ruled for six years. His apparent success seemed to indicate that he, too, was a capable, authoritarian dictator or perhaps that some of Salazar's personal power had been successfully institutionalized in the office of prime minister. Caetano's regime, however, was brought to an abrupt end by the Portuguese military in 1974. There followed a confusing period during which several different loci of military and governmental authority attempted to administer the Portuguese state (see Changes after the 1974 Revolution, this ch.) (see ch. 9).

Not until a particular group could establish lasting control within and over the military could a reasonably unified authoritative system of government be implemented in Portugal. By March 1976 it appeared that a relatively moderate element within the military was emerging with such control. Press reports indicated that the mixture of prerevolution and postrevolution authoritative organs that constituted the transitional government would be replaced by a system to be established by a new constitution. Only with the passage of time will it be determined whether true constitutional government has been implemented and accepted by the major political parties and persuasions as well as by the military in Portugal.

GOVERNMENT BEFORE THE REVOLUTION

Corporatism

From 1932 to 1974 Portugal's government was a manifestation of Salazar's political and social philosophy as reflected in his concept of corporatism. He believed that the political state was subjected to two basically incompatible, divisive forces. The first of those forces disregarded tradition in favor of the new and different. It emphasized change, which was automatically, but often falsely, equated with progress. In contrast the second force found value only in the traditional past and feared change and the future. Salazar indicated that the first force was a combination of generous intentions and naive inexperience that would result in irrationalism and that the second force wrongly opposed every attempt at innovation and reform. Consequently a middle course had to be found, and this was the role of Salazar's corporate New State (Estado Novo).

Corporatism emphasizes the importance of national stability and unity. It is based on the idea of functional representation; that is, an individual is represented in the political system through membership in functional associations. The associations are usually based on the location of members' residences and on their occupations. Thus corporate associations usually comprise municipal, vocational, and professional groups. To these Salazar added the family, which he believed to be the basic Portuguese social unit.

The corporative groups pursue the somewhat diverse interests of their members but always on the basis of what is best for the state as a whole. The state can be seen as a large family whose members are the functional groups. Adjustments between groups are possible, but the groups themselves and the framework within which they operate temper group demands. The role of the corporate functional groups is different from that of pluralistic interest groups and traditional political parties. A corporatist system does not involve multiple interests that compete and eventually cooperate through compromise. Instead, based upon extensive economic organization, it mutes many diverse, pluralistic interests by reducing them to the simplest common denominator, function. It creates a minimal number of different functional groups and provides an institutional framework within which their interests can be satisfied, always limited by the greater good of the whole state.

Any system that emphasizes and even attempts to institutionalize stability, sacrificing pluralism for a form of enforced unity, is inherently conservative and risks becoming authoritarian. Furthermore a system that emphasizes the good of the state as an entity separate from the good of the nation (the state's citizens) risks becoming a dictatorship. This is because there are few practical methods for interpreting what is best for the state in such a situation. Usually an individual assumes the task and becomes a dictator in the process. Portugal fell victim to these dangers. Salazar defended the status quo and brooked no organized opposition. Assuming power soon after a period of chaos and near anarchy, he decided that unity and stability were of primary importance both as values and as goals. Furthermore he created a whole governmental and extragovernmental framework through which those objectives could be pursued and institutionalized.

Authoritarian though it was, Salazar's corporatism and the political and economic organization it fostered never approached ·the authoritarianism of Mussolini's Italy, much less of Hitler's Germany; even less did Portugal approach the totalitarianism of post-World War II East European communist regimes. Salazar remained a traditional, even paternalistic, authoritarian rather than evolving into a modern, twentieth-century totalitarian dictator. Despite official attempts to organize and mobilize the people in support of the New State, no real attempt was made to force the passive or the apathetic individual into some positive, active form of citizenship. Those who did not oppose Salazar were left alone for the most part.

The New State's constitution and the planning that followed its adoption included provisions for extensive economic organization; however, despite Salazar's long tenure in office, detailed economic organization was never fully completed. To Salazar corporatism and the political and economic structures based on it were but means to an end. The end was a unified, stable state. So long as it appeared that the end had been achieved, further development and maturation of the means were unnecessary and thus not pursued to fruition. The stability and unity that had been attained, however, were artificial and contrived. Increasing dissension within the Portuguese society and particularly within the military (a cornerstone in any aurhoritarian regime), underscored and exacerbated by the colonial wars, ended Salazar's New State with the April 1974 revolution (see ch. 9).

Salazar equated multiple interests or pluralism (pursued in most Western systems by individual political parties) with the divisive competitiveness that he felt threatened the Portuguese state. He thus banned all political parties and in their place created the National Union (União Nacional) in 1930. Not a political party, the National Union was more a general movement or national interest group. Its primary function was to educate the public and foster support for the New State. It did not attempt to encourage actual citizen participation in the political system. In 1936 Salazar established the Portuguese Legion, a kind of home guard devoted to the ideals of Portuguese corporatism and the National Union. The Portuguese Youth (Mocidade Portuguesa), a movement dedicated to the same purpose, was also created that year.

The establishment of these extragovernmental bodies was part of Salazar's attempt to create and instill unity and stability in Portugal. The official institutional framework, established through the constitution, was clearly directed toward the same objectives.

1933 Constitution

Salazar, Portugal's finance minister from 1928 to 1930, became prime minister in 1932. In that year a draft constitution was presented to the public. Opposition to the draft was significant but not well organized. Republicans felt that it was not liberal enough, Socialists wanted more concentration upon economic and social reform, and some Roman Catholics believed more emphasis should have been placed on the social role of religion. The opposition was clearly seen in the results of the March 19, 1933, plebiscite on the draft. Of the registered electorate of 1,214,159, only 5,955 voted against the draft, but 488,840 abstained. Some 719,364 voters approved the document, which then became Portugal's constitution.

The constitution provided, to a considerable extent, for a system of checks and balances. The system was based on the incompatibility of concurrent service by an individual in more than one branch of the government or in both national and subnational governmental bodies. Furthermore the constitution provided for both exclusive and shared powers among and between the three branches. For example, the executive negotiated international treaties, but the legislature approved them. The executive was responsible for fiscal and tax matters but only with legislative authorization. Both the executive and the legislature initiated bills, the legislature passing them into law in general form and leaving the details to the executive. The legislature determined the constitutionality of laws. The judiciary ruled on abuses of governmental authority and could disqualify candidates for office in the other two branches. In theory the overwhelming power of the president of the republic, positioned above the branches, could have nullified these checks and balances. In practice they were nullified by the dominant power of the individual who occupied the position of prime minister.

The constitution established that the Portuguese state was a unitary, corporate republic and vested sovereignty in the nation. The document included several very liberal guarantees. Portuguese citizens, for example, were assured of the right to life and personal safety, the right to work, religious liberty, the free expression of thought in any form, freedom of teaching, judicial due process, and the freedom of meeting and association. At the same time very basic limitations clearly illustrated the authoritarian nature of Salazar's corporate state. The constitution stipulated that "special laws shall govern the exercise of the freedom of expression of opinion, education, meeting and

196

of association." The special laws were to "prevent, by precautionary or restrictive measures, the perversion of public opinion in its function as a social force." The constitution also permitted imprisonment without formal charge of persons caught in flagrante delicto and for crimes committed "against the safety of the State." These included, among others, counterfeiting, willful homicide, robbery, arson, and the manufacture, possession, or use of explosives.

Interpretation and Revision

The 1933 Constitution charged the National Assembly, or legislative branch, with safeguarding "the observance of the Constitution and the laws" and with examining "the acts of the Government [executive branch] or the administration." More specifically the National Assembly was given the power of determining the "formal constitutional illegality of ordinances promulgated by the President of the Republic . . . either on its own initiative or on that of the Government."

The constitution was relatively easy to amend, or more properly to revise, and revisions have been approved on several occasions. Again it was the National Assembly that was given this power. The procedure called for the introduction and passage of bills of constitutional revision in the legislature. The major limitation was one of time: revisions were only to be allowed every ten years, counted from the date of the last revision. In certain situations the constitution could be changed more frequently, as it was, for example, each year from 1935 through 1938.

Head of State

The constitution provided that only citizens more than thirty-five years of age who had always possessed Portuguese nationality were eligible to become president of the republic. It gave most governmental power and authority—either individually or in conjunction with other bodies—to the president, who was designated head of state. Among other powers the constitution gave him the authority to appoint and remove the president of the Council of Ministers (the prime minister), the ministers themselves, and their secretaries of state and under secretaries of state. The president of the republic could also dissolve the National Assembly and call for new elections. He was charged with directing foreign policy and concluding international agreements, which had to be approved by the National Assembly.

Although the president could dismiss ministers and dissolve the legislature, neither the executive nor the legislative branch had similar powers over him. This was because the president was solely responsible to the nation, which originally meant that he was responsible to the national electorate. The president was elected for a seven-year term, and most presidents succeeded themselves for one or more additional terms. In 1959, however, after an electoral campaign in which an unsuccessful opposition candidate ran on a platform of replacing Salazar as prime minister, the constitution was revised so that the president would in the future be elected by an electoral college (see ch. 2). The electoral college comprised members of the National Assembly, the Corporative Chamber, municipal representatives, and administrative representatives from the overseas territories. The constitutional revision decreased the already remote chance that someone not to Salazar's liking might attain the presidency.

The president of the republic was assisted by the Council of State. An advisory and consultative body, the council comprised the presidents of the Council of Ministers, the National Assembly, the Corporative Chamber, and the Supreme Court of Justice (Supremo Tribunal de Justiça) as well as the procurator general of the republic and "ten public men of outstanding ability," appointed for life by the head of state.

As head of state the president of the republic was above, rather than a part of, the regular governmental system. Thus the Portuguese system was not actually a presidential form of government. Daily administrative and governmental responsibilities were in the hands of the prime minister and his cabinet, not in those of the president. The system was even less a parliamentary form of government, however, for the prime minister and his cabinet were not members of the legislature, nor were they responsible to that branch. Likewise the prime minister could not dissolve the National Assembly. Thus Portugal had what might best be termed a strong executive form of government with almost all power formally vested outside and above the general governmental structure in the presidency of the republic (see fig. 20). In practice, however, the president exercised his authority at the behest of the prime minister, who was the most powerful element in the Portuguese political system.

Branches of Government

Executive Branch. The executive branch, generally and constitutionally referred to as "the Government," was charged with countersigning acts of the president of the republic, formulating decree laws, appointing governors of overseas territories, and general superintendence of "public administration as a whole, ensuring that the laws and resolutions of the National Assembly are carried out, [and] controlling the acts of administrative bodies and of corporate entities of public administrative utility." It included the Council of Ministers—in effect a cabinet—comprising the heads of the administrative departments or ministries usually found at the national governmental level. The executive branch was headed by the president of the Council of Ministers, an office much like that of a prime minister in administrative terms. (Some English sources refer to the council president as a premier, but the term *prime minister* is used herein.) The prime minister was as-

198

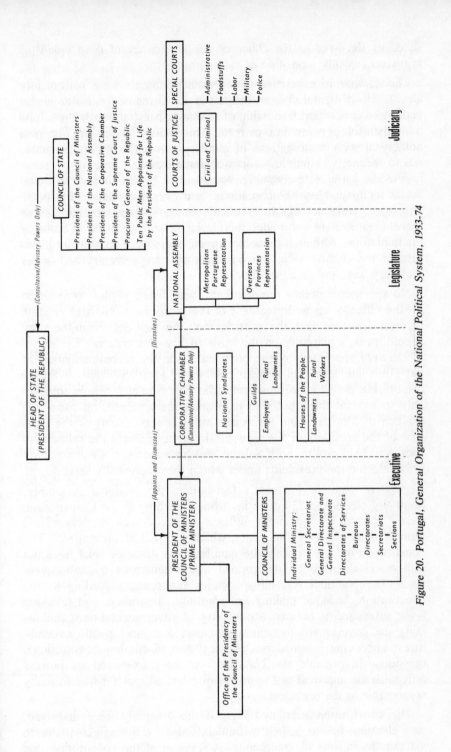

Figure 20. Portugal, General Organization of the National Political System, 1933-74

Head of State (President of the Republic)

(Consultative/Advisory Powers Only)

Council of State
- President of the Council of Ministers
- President of the National Assembly
- President of the Corporative Chamber
- President of the Supreme Court of Justice
- Procurator General of the Republic
- Ten Public Men Appointed for Life by the President of the Republic

(Dissolves)

(Appoints and Dismisses)

Judiciary

Courts of Justice
- Civil and Criminal

Special Courts
- Administrative
- Foodstuffs
- Labor
- Military
- Police

Legislature

National Assembly
- Metropolitan Portuguese Representation
- Overseas Provinces Representation

Corporative Chamber
(Consultative/Advisory Powers Only)
- National Syndicates
- Guilds
  - Employers
  - Rural Landowners
- Houses of the People
  - Landowners
  - Rural Workers

Executive

President of the Council of Ministers (Prime Minister)

Office of the Presidency of the Council of Ministers

Council of Ministers

Individual Ministry:
- General Secretariat
- General Directorate and General Inspectorate
- Directorates of Services
- Bureaus
- Directorates
- Secretariats
- Sections

sisted by the head of the Office of the Presidency of the Council of Ministers, usually a position of cabinet rank.

The number of ministries varied as departments were periodically elevated to or demoted from cabinet level. Often one minister would undertake concurrent leadership of two ministries, although the ministries themselves were not merged. This paired leadership occurred notably in such combinations of ministries as national defense-army, finance-economy, public works-communications, interior-overseas provinces, agriculture-commerce, and public health-corporations and social security. These combinations, and even the names of specific ministries, were subject to frequent change. A variable number of secretaries of state and under secretaries of state assisted in some of the ministries. Although those occupying them were technically members of the civil service, the positions of state secretary and under secretary were political (see fig. 21).

No specific eligibility requirements were listed in the constitution for the office of council president or the positions of minister or state secretary, except that the president of the republic filled them by appointment, apparently on the basis of his own criteria. The secretaries were appointed by the president upon the recommendation of the prime minister. Those who held these positions were in theory responsible only to the president, who was formally empowered not only to appoint them but also to dismiss them at will; on paper the Council of Ministers and the prime minister served only at the pleasure of the president of the republic. In practice it was the prime minister who held power; both Salazar and his successor, Caetano, carefully selected the presidents under whom they technically served.

Legislative Branch. Portugal's legislature, the National Assembly, originally comprised 130 deputies who, according to the Constitution, were "elected by the direct suffrage of the citizen electors. Their term of office shall be four years, which may not be prolonged." The constitution did not specify the qualifications deputies must have but rather left them to be determined and enumerated by subsequent laws. The National Assembly's major functions, according to the constitution, included making, interpreting, suspending, and revoking laws; safeguarding the constitutionality of governmental acts; authorizing the government to collect revenues and meet public expenditures; approving international treaties; and discussing constitutional revisions. In practice the National Assembly exercised its powers only with the approval of the prime minister, although it was formally responsible to the president.

The constitution stipulated that, if the assembly were dissolved, new elections had to be held within sixty days, a period extendable to six months in time of emergency. A revision of the constitution that took effect in 1973 expanded the membership of the National Assem-

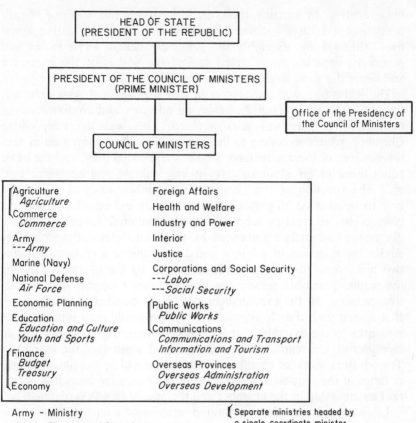

```
              HEAD OF STATE
          (PRESIDENT OF THE REPUBLIC)

         PRESIDENT OF THE COUNCIL OF MINISTERS
                    (PRIME MINISTER)
                                              Office of the Presidency of
                                              the Council of Ministers
           COUNCIL OF MINISTERS
```

⌠Agriculture	Foreign Affairs
Agriculture	Health and Welfare
⌡Commerce	Industry and Power
Commerce	Interior
Army	Justice
---*Army*	Corporations and Social Security
Marine (Navy)	---*Labor*
National Defense	---*Social Security*
Air Force	⌠Public Works
Economic Planning	*Public Works*
Education	⌡Communications
Education and Culture	*Communications and Transport*
Youth and Sports	*Information and Tourism*
⌠Finance	Overseas Provinces
Budget	*Overseas Administration*
Treasury	*Overseas Development*
⌡Economy	

Army – Ministry
Army – Secretary of State for
---*Army* – Undersecretary of State for

⎰ Separate ministries headed by
  a single coordinate minister.

Source: Based on information from *The Europa Year Book, 1974: A World Survey*, I,
London, 1974, p. 1154; and *International Year Book and Statesmen's Who's Who 1974*, London, 1974, p. 344.

Figure 21. Portugal, National Governmental (Executive) Structure, March 1974

bly to 150 deputies, 116 representing metropolitan Portugal and thirty-four representing the overseas provinces.

Decisions of the National Assembly were by absolute majority vote. The right to introduce legislation rested equally with the executive branch and any assembly deputy. Bills approved by the assembly were called decrees; if signed by the president of the republic within fifteen days, they became laws. If a decree was not signed in the stipulated time but was again approved in the assembly by at least a two-thirds majority vote, the president had no choice but to sign it into law. Despite such formal ultimate power, the actual legislative authority of the National Assembly was severely limited. According to the constitution, "laws voted by the National Assembly must be confined to the examination of general legal principles of the enactments." More specific aspects of any legislation passed into law were left to the executive. In practice, then, the legislature's role was one of ratification of executive-initiated proposals, not one of legislative initiative. Although the assembly did genuinely debate some issues and programs, deputies rarely voted against the wishes of the executive and never did so in large numbers.

The legislature was unicameral in that the National Assembly was the only legislative organ; however, an advisory and consultative but nonlegislative body was also involved. This was the Corporative Chamber, which according to the constitution was "composed of representatives of local autonomous bodies and social interests, the latter being those of an administrative, moral, cultural and economic order." The function of the Corporative Chamber was "to report and give its opinion on all proposals or draft bills and on all international conventions or treaties submitted to the National Assembly, before discussion thereof is commenced by the latter." Should the chamber advise the rejection of a bill, it could recommend a replacement; the two bills would then be considered jointly by the assembly. During the regular assembly session the chamber could suggest such legislative measures to the executive branch as its members felt advisable. If it agreed with the chamber, the executive could then introduce the measures to the assembly for legislative action. The chamber was to meet during the regular three-month annual session of the assembly. The advisory work of chamber committees could be continued at other times at the request and direction of the executive branch. Concurrent membership in the chamber and the assembly was prohibited.

Laws passed after the constitution established a number of corporative representative bodies below the chamber. Urban workers and employees were organized into national syndicates (sindicatos nacionais). These so-called national syndicates operated only at district level and, although separate district syndicates were permitted to federate, the emphasis on the district level kept labor fragmented in terms of national organization. Two kinds of guild were also developed: compulsory employers' guilds (grémios), initiated by the state in the industrial, commercial, and agricultural sectors; and rural landowners' guilds (grémios da lavoura).

A house of the people (casa do povo) was established at the local or parish level and comprised both rural workers and landowners. Structured so as to ensure landowner control over decisionmaking, the original role of the body was one of providing welfare, relief, and educational services, not one of employer-employee representation. After the rural landowners' guilds were formed, however, bargaining was undertaken between the guilds and the houses of the people. In such situations landowners from the houses of the people, representing the workers, negotiated with landowners from the rural guilds. The Portuguese corporative system was thus one that enhanced employer domination of the employee and state control over the employer-employee relationship.

202

Judicial Branch and Legal System. The constitution provided for the Supreme Court of Justice and courts of first and second instance. It gave the judiciary considerable independence by stipulating that "judges of the ordinary courts are appointed for life and cannot be removed." The constitution's judicial section also reiterated that only the National Assembly could determine matters of constitutionality; the courts had no jurisdiction in this area. Laws passed after the adoption of the constitution established that, after examination by a board of legal experts, judges would be appointed by the Higher Council of Judicature, a body comprising the president of the supreme court and the presidents of the appeals courts *(tribunais de relação).*

The Portuguese legal and judicial system was based on Roman civil law and was heavily influenced by the French model. The system distinguished between civil (including commercial), criminal, military, labor, administrative, and fiscal law. Two court systems were established. The courts of justice system had trial and appellate jurisdiction over civil and criminal cases. Equivalent jurisdiction over military, labor, administrative, and fiscal law was exercised by the special courts system.

The principle of habeas corpus was recognized as a protection against abuses of authority. Capital punishment was prohibited except in time of war. The state was represented in all courts and tribunals by an agent of the national attorney general. The minister of justice acted as an intermediary between the government and the judicial system. His ministry was responsible for administrative services including the attorney general's department, prison services, and the judicial police (who functioned much like the investigatory personnel of an American district attorney's office).

The popular consensus before the April 1974 revolution seemed to be that, at least for nonpolitical crimes, the legal system was fair and impartial. Members of the upper classes could possibly expect better treatment than the poor but no more so than in most established judicial systems. The major criticism was that the Portuguese system was overburdened and outdated. The judicial process required long periods of time; furthermore it was not consistent in dealing with relatively new or unprecedented social problems, such as drug-related crimes.

The courts of justice system was multitiered (see fig. 22). The municipal courts *(tribunais municipais)* at the lowest level handled relatively minor civil and criminal cases. Above the municipal level were the district courts *(tribunais de comarca).* The Portuguese Republic was divided into 171 judicial districts. District courts had original jurisdiction over both criminal and civil cases. They also had appellate jurisdiction over municipal court decisions.

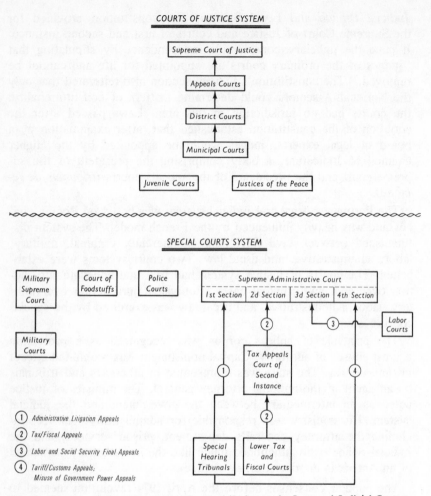

COURTS OF JUSTICE SYSTEM

Supreme Court of Justice

↑

Appeals Courts

↑

District Courts

↑

Municipal Courts

Juvenile Courts   Justices of the Peace

SPECIAL COURTS SYSTEM

Military Supreme Court	Court of Foodstuffs	Police Courts	Supreme Administrative Court			
			1st Section	2d Section	3d Section	4th Section

Military Courts

Labor Courts

Tax Appeals Court of Second Instance

① Administrative Litigation Appeals
② Tax/Fiscal Appeals
③ Labor and Social Security Final Appeals
④ Tariff/Customs Appeals;
　Misuse of Government Power Appeals

Special Hearing Tribunals   Lower Tax and Fiscal Courts

Source: Based on information from "Portugal," chapter in *Law and Judicial Systems of Nations*, Washington, 1968.

Figure 22. Portugal, Judicial Structure, March 1976

The appeals courts occupied an intermediate position between the district courts and the supreme court. Before the dissolution of the empire there were six appeals courts: three in metropolitan Portugal— in Lisbon, Porto, and Coimbra—and three overseas—in Luanda, Lourenço Marques, and Goa. Each appeals court had a number of sitting judges, headed by a presiding and an associate presiding judge, called the president and vice president of the court. The appeals court could sit in full or could be divided into sections. It had appellate jurisdiction over district court trials and original jurisdiction over cases involving crimes by lower court judges and prosecutors.

The highest court in the courts of justice system was the Supreme Court of Justice in Lisbon. Its jurisdiction, covering metropolitan Portugal and all overseas provinces, was confined to matters of law in both civil and criminal cases. It was headed by a chief justice, or president.

The district, appeals, and supreme courts all maintained pools of eligible judges from which working bodies of judges were periodically selected for given periods of time. District and appeals courts handling more serious cases would ordinarily utilize panels of three judges drawn from their respective working bodies of magistrates. The supreme court could function with all working judges acting as a single body, or it could be divided into three chambers, each with five justices. In such a situation two chambers would handle civil cases, and one would handle criminal cases. In municipal and district courts less serious cases were handled by a single magistrate.

The courts of justice system also included the juvenile supervision courts (tribunais tutelares de menores) and the justices of the peace (juízes de paz). Juvenile courts were specialized tribunals for cases involving juvenile delinquency and domestic relations. The justice of the peace occupied the lowest rank in the judiciary. He was more an administrator than a judge, although he did have the power, when individuals were caught in the commission of a crime, to bind them over to a higher court (see ch. 16).

The special courts system covered military, labor, administrative, and fiscal justice, as well as traffic offenses and violations of food and drug regulations. Courts of military and naval justice tried offenses committed by members of the armed forces and in some cases by members of the merchant marine. The courts were headed by the Military Supreme Court (Supremo Tribunal Militar), which had both judicial and advisory functions. It also acted as the final appellate court for cases begun in the lower military courts. The jurisdiction of the military courts was governed by the Portuguese Code of Military Justice.

Labor courts heard cases involving the interpretation and execution of collective contracts, employer-employee conflicts, and social security matters. The labor courts were independent and autonomous, but for administrative purposes judges and other court personnel were placed under the supervision of the Ministry of Labor.

Special hearing tribunals (auditorias administrativas) had jurisdiction over administrative litigation, tariffs and customs duties, and abuses of power by government agencies and corporations. There was an administrative court, or tribunal, in each judicial district. A number of separate, lower level tax and fiscal courts existed, their jurisdictions based on geography and the relative seriousness of the cases they heard. Above them was an intermediate appeals court of second instance for tax and fiscal matters.

The Supreme Administrative Court (Supremo Tribunal Administrativo) in Lisbon headed the administrative and fiscal court system. It comprised a presiding judge and twelve associate judges and was divided into four sections. The first section heard appeals from the hearing tribunals regarding general administrative matters. The second section had appellate jurisdiction over cases originating in the tax and fiscal appeals court of second instance. The third section had final appeallate jurisdiction over labor and social security cases. The fourth section had appellate jurisdiction over the hearing tribunals on customs and tariff matters and heard appeals regarding the misuse of government authority by ministries, agencies, and government corporations. The Supreme Administrative Court could also sit as a single body and did so, for example, when reviewing judgments rendered by any of its separate sections.

Together with its various judicial duties, the Supreme Administrative Court also served as an advisory body to the executive branch. In this capacity it judged the validity, interpretation, and execution of administrative contracts to which the government or any agency thereof was a party.

The special courts system also included the Court of Foodstuffs (Tribunal dos Géneros Alimentícios) and police courts (juízos de policia). The foodstuffs court had jurisdiction over cases involving violations of weight and measurement standards, food and drug laws, and public health and sanitation. The police courts dealt with such things as disorderly conduct, prostitution, minor property losses, and traffic violations.

Portuguese attorneys were divided into trial lawyers (advogados) and court agents (solicitadores). Five years of law school, a law degree, and the completion of an eighteen-month practical training period under an established attorney were necessary before one was permitted to practice law. Attorneys had to be more than twenty-one years of age. In order to argue a case before the Supreme Court of Justice an attorney had to have practiced law for a minimum of ten years.

Court agents served as clerks and to some extent as legal advisers. They had to possess a bachelor of laws degree and pass both oral and written examinations covering civil and criminal legal procedures, legal briefings and forms, judicial fees, and the like. An agent had to be more than twenty-one years of age and had to serve a practical training period under an established agent of at least five years' experience. Court agents were licensed, and their number was limited in each judicial district.

Portuguese trial attorneys have an organized bar association, the Order of Advocates. The association outspokenly supported the principles of the rule of law concerning individual rights and procedural guarantees both before and after the 1974 revolution.

Division of Powers

Because of Portugal's establishment as a unitary republic, all political and administrative authority was vested in the central or national government. Such subnational units as districts *(distritos)* or municipalities *(concelhos)* had no authority of their own but were delegated their authority from the national government (see fig. 23). That delegated authority was under continuous scrutiny; Article 127 of the constitution stipulated: "The administrative life of the local autonomous bodies is subject to inspection by agents of the [national] Government and the solutions of the relative administrative bodies may be subject to the authorisation or require the approval of other organisations or authorities and be submitted to referendum."

The constitution designated the subnational governmental units, from more to less powerful, as provinces *(províncias)*, districts, communes or municipalities, and parishes *(freguesias)*. An additional

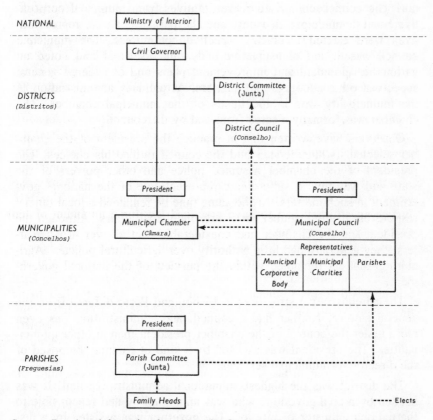

Source: Based on information from Marcello Caetano, *Manual de Direito Administrativo*, Lisbon, 1965, pp. 418-421, 429-430, 433-438.

Figure 23. Portugal, Subnational Administrative Structure since 1959

207

administrative unit, the ward *(bairro)*, was placed between the parishes and the municipalities in Lisbon and Porto. A constitutional revision in 1959 discontinued the use of the province as an administrative unit (see ch. 3).

The lowest governmental unit, the parish, almost always corresponded to an existing ecclesiastical parish. It comprised all of the families who lived in an area and were members of the parish. Each family's interests were represented by the family head. Administrative duties were carried out by a parish board or committee (junta), headed by a president. Theoretically the parish committee could take considerable initiative in planning and instituting local public works projects; its real powers were severely limited, however, because of the parish's usual lack of funds and almost complete dependence on the municipality.

The administrative organs of the municipality comprised a council *(conselho)* with its own president, a chamber *(câmara)*, and the president of the chamber, who was appointed by the district civil governor. The council comprised representatives from municipal corporative bodies, municipal charities, and the parishes. Parish representatives were elected by their respective committees. The municipal council was a kind of legislative body that discussed and voted on various development and improvement plans and considered general aspects of other administrative matters. Actual daily administration of the municipality was in the hands of the municipal chamber. The chamber was formally elected from and by the council.

Observers have written that in practice the president of the chamber selected its membership and the council ratified his choices. The president of the chamber assumed police and other powers of the state and was thus a subordinate representative of the national government in such matters. At the same time he remained a local official responsible to the chamber on clearly municipal affairs. Although the president and the chamber had considerable control over urban matters, they generally had little authority over agricultural policies. Agricultural matters remained within the purview of the national government.

The administrative structures in Lisbon and Porto differed from the general pattern. Neither had a council, and administration was even more under the control of the chamber president than in other municipalities. The president was assisted by a kind of cabinet composed of the directors of municipal services.

The district was the highest subnational administrative unit. It was headed by a civil governor, who was appointed by and responsible to the national minister of interior. The governor was assisted by a district council and a district committee. The council comprised procurators or agents from each municipality, chosen by their municipal

208

chambers. The committee, elected by the council, supervised district services and in many ways was analogous to the municipal chamber.

National Elections

The 1933 Constitution provided for national elections to fill the office of president of the republic and to determine the membership of the National Assembly. The electorate comprised adult males who were literate or who paid a predetermined minimum amount in annual taxes and literate adult women who paid a higher minimum tax or who possessed a secondary education. With relatively few exceptions these requirements limited the franchise to male heads of households. The size of the 1933 electorate was between 1.2 and 1.3 million of a total population of 7 million. By the mid-1960s the electorate had grown to only 1.5 million. During the same period the population had increased by 2 million, and the illiteracy rate had been halved. Obviously a number of qualified voters did not register or were deprived of their voting privileges. Accusations have been made that retention on the voting lists depended upon how one voted in the previous election. In any event the Portuguese government never encouraged large electoral turnouts, a policy that may have contributed to voter apathy.

Further contributing to voter apathy was the fact that only the National Union, later changed to the National Popular Action (Ação Nacional Popular—ANP), could propose candidates for the National Assembly and for the presidency of the republic. Realistically then the voter had the choice of supporting the Salazar government candidate or simply not voting; he had no chance to vote in favor of an alternative candidate. The government for the first time did allow opposition candidates to run for the National Assembly in 1945. It did not, however, allow the opposition the time needed to organize for the electoral campaign. Not until the relatively more liberal regime of Salazar's successor, Caetano, were opposition candidates permitted actively to organize electoral campaigns.

CHANGES AFTER THE 1974 REVOLUTION

The 1933 Constitution was not suspended by the Armed Forces Movement (Movimento das Forças Armadas—MFA) after the April 1974 revolution. Specific constitutional provisions were replaced by applicable sections of the MFA program, but the overall constitution was left in force temporarily until a new one could be written.

The MFA Program and Governmental Structure

The MFA envisioned a period of three to five years during which the military would remain active in politics, exercising, if not total control, at least a veto over the actions of governmental bodies. A provisional government or executive would exist during this so-called transitional period. That government and a similarly transitional legislative assembly would be dissolved toward the end of the three- to five-year period, and a new legislative assembly would be elected. After the legislative assembly revised the new constitution previously formulated by a special constituent assembly, the transitional period would formally end, and the military would withdraw from politics.

Plans for the actual organization and structure of governmental authority during the period of transition were confused and subject to change. Those changes were in turn subject to, but not limited to, changes in the MFA command structure. Originally the MFA apparently planned that authority and power would be exercised by a constituent assembly, the president of the republic, the Junta of National Salvation, the Council of State, the provisional government, and the law courts. The Corporative Chamber had been dissolved immediately after the 1974 revolution.

The Constituent Assembly's power was indirect, limited solely to drafting and approving a new constitution. The office of the president of the republic included powers similar to those it held before the revolution: the president could appoint members of the government, negotiate international treaties, grant judicial pardons, ensure that constitutional rules and laws were fulfilled, and the like. He presided over the Council of State and the Junta of National Salvation and was chosen by the latter from among its members.

The Junta of National Salvation—military figures sympathetic to, but not members of, the MFA—existed for almost a year after the revolution. The junta's purpose was to coordinate military influence within the transitional power structure. It was originally intended to function until a president of the republic and a legislative assembly had been elected at the end of the transitional period.

The powers of the Council of State, at least theoretically, were increased somewhat over those it possessed before the revolution. It was to sanction the decrees of the provisional government, designate new members of the Junta of National Salvation, and generally act as an advisory body to the president of the republic. The council's new composition was to include the members of the junta, seven additional armed forces representatives, and seven citizens selected by the president.

The provisional government comprised the prime minister, ministers without portfolio (limited to four in number), and the ministers of national defense, cooperation (also called interterritorial coordination), internal administration, justice, finance, economy, foreign affairs, social equipment and environment, education and culture, labor, and social affairs and social communication. Secretaries of state and under secretaries would assist various ministers. All members of the

210

government and of the other authoritative bodies had to be identified with or support the MFA. The prime minister and his department ministers were responsible for daily government and administration just as they had been before the revolution.

The law courts continued for the most part to function as they had before the revolution. The MFA did not alter the judicial system or the court structure, although new military tribunals were established to handle political crimes.

In short the provisional power structure was a combination of some of the older authoritative bodies retained from before the revolution and a new military body. The older structures included the office of the presidency of the republic, the Council of State, the government —that is, the prime minister, departmental ministers, state secretaries, and under secretaries—and the court system. In all cases the memberships of these bodies were completely changed from those of their prerevolutionary predecessors. The new military organ was the Junta of National Salvation.

The numerous loci of MFA authority, regular military channels, and the various bodies exercising national governmental authority presented a confusing situation. There was considerable overlap in the memberships of all the groups, and in practice no clearly established hierarchical structure of authority existed to which all adhered. Authoritative bodies and individual persons often competed, and groups of various political persuasions jockeyed for position, particularly within the MFA. In short there existed so many loci of decisionmaking that a crisis of authority developed in which directives were often ambiguous and resolute action frequently lacking.

The attempted coup d'etat by sympathizers of General António de Spínola in March 1975 led to an effort to centralize decisionmaking to facilitate effective government (see ch. 9). The Council of the Revolution (often referred to as the Supreme Council in the Western press) was established on April 25 and, according to the Ministry of Mass Communication, would "fill the gap of a slow-working composite Government which has at times shown itself to be unpragmatic at the level of executive decision and control." The new council replaced the Junta of National Salvation and the Council of State as well as two internal MFA bodies: the MFA Coordinating Committee and the Council of the Twenty (see ch. 15).

After the MFA and governmental reorganizations that followed the March 1975 coup attempt, the MFA and the major political parties negotiated an important agreement. The pact, signed by the parties on April 11, 1975, established the new transitional power structure and recognized the continued participation of the military in Portuguese politics for the transitional period. It stipulated that the president of the republic, Council of the Revolution, MFA assembly, legislative assembly, government, and courts would be "the organs of sovereignty of the Portuguese Republic . . . during the period of transition."

The president was to be the ex officio chairman of the Council of the Revolution and would preside over its meetings. He was empowered to dissolve the legislative assembly on decision of the council. The president was to be elected by an electoral college comprising the MFA assembly and the legislative assembly.

The Council of the Revolution was by far the most powerful of the loci of sovereignty in terms of formal powers. Among other things it was empowered to define "the necessary programmatic orientations of home and foreign policy"; determine the constitutionality of laws; appraise and sanction legislation emanating from both the executive and the legislature regarding economic and social policy and foreign relations; exercise several legislative powers in urgent situations when the legislature and government were unable to act; "exercise legislative powers in military affairs"; and "express its opinion to the President of the Republic on the choice of the Prime Minister and of the Ministers who must enjoy the confidence of the [MFA]." The composition of the council has been subject to change. Under the revised pact between the MFA and the political parties approved by the Constituent Assembly in early 1976, the council membership was to include the president of the republic, who would preside; the chief and deputy chief of the armed forces general staff; the chiefs of the three military branches; the prime minister when he held military rank; and fourteen additional officers—eight army, three air force, and three navy—to be appointed by their respective branches. In practice the president of the republic assumed a position of leadership, though not one of dominance, over the Council of the Revolution.

The composition and duties of the government were left unchanged for the most part after the March coup attempt. The president could not select the prime minister, however, without the advice of the Council of the Revolution "and such political parties and forces as it thinks fit." The prime minister not only was responsible to the president, as had always been the case, but also would be made politically responsible to the legislature.

The MFA assembly was given little direct governmental authority or power. Originally it was given some indirect power in that it formed half of the presidential electoral college. The assembly, consisting of 240 representatives of all ranks and services, mainly functioned to provide input, particularly to the Council of the Revolution, from the MFA rank-and-file membership.

The legislature, or more specifically the legislative assembly, had not yet been elected, but its election date was later set for April 25, 1976. The pact between the MFA and the political parties, revised in early 1976, stipulated that the assembly would have the "power to pass a vote of no confidence in the Government. The approval of two motions of no confidence at intervals of not less than thirty days shall make a ministerial re-shuffle obligatory." Whether the prime minister would have to relinquish power in such a situation was unclear.

Constituent Assembly

The task of drafting and approving a new constitution fell to the special Constituent Assembly elected by popular vote on April 25, 1975, in the first postrevolution national election. This was the third time in Portuguese history that a constituent assembly had been formed to draft a new constitution: preceding occasions were after the revolutions of August 1820 and October 1910. In practice the assembly frequently functioned as a forum in which controversial political issues were freely debated. The debate usually reflected the views of the major political parties represented in the assembly. Party disagreements and jockeying for the inclusion of advantageous constitutional provisions caused the work of the assembly to take longer than expected, and its original time limitation of a few months was extended. The work of the assembly was also delayed by the effort of the MFA and the political parties to revise their April 1975 pact in an attempt to redefine the role of the military in Portuguese politics. Talks began in late 1975, and provisions of the new agreement were to be included in the constitution. The Constituent Assembly was reconvened in early March and completed the new constitution before the legislative assembly election planned for late April. The Constituent Assembly was to be dissolved upon its approval of the new constitution.

Provisional Government, January 1976

The political action plan of the MFA, approved by the Council of the Revolution on June 21, 1975, stated that "the present State machinery is extremely heavy and bureaucratic, and is clearly unsuited to the dynamism of the present revolutionary process. It can only respond slowly and incompletely to the demands made of it." Consequently the MFA felt it necessary to "eliminate excessively bureaucratic and complex procedures within the State machinery, replacing them by rapid, revolutionary methods able to meet the pressures of demand, attributing full responsibility to those who execute such a policy and such measures."

The MFA briefly attempted to institute a new scheme of representation to determine and coordinate the will of both civilians and the military. Each representative unit was to elect delegates to a next higher unit beginning with the so-called basic organization, through local people's assemblies, municipal people's assemblies, district people's assemblies, regional people's assemblies, and finally the national people's assembly. The plan would in effect have created a system parallel to a combination of already existing national and subnational governmental systems. How the new system was to implement its decisions was unclear. Although numerous assemblies were established, particularly at the local level, the overall plan was never fully implemented. The plan of the people's assemblies appeared to reflect only the views of a specific group within the MFA. In reality it represented more an attempt to circumvent the organized political parties in the Portuguese political process than purposely to create a new system of government.

Despite the MFA political action plan that called for more revolutionary governmental machinery and the ill-fated people's assemblies, the MFA shied away from attempts to alter the structure of the national executive branch radically. Some ministries were demoted from cabinet-level status, names of others changed, and entire new ones added. (The prerevolutionary regimes of Salazar and Caetano had frequently engaged in similar cabinet shuffling.) In January 1976 the cabinet of the provisional government comprised fifteen ministries, each headed by a different minister. Most ministers were assisted by one or more secretaries of state (see fig. 24).

A major difference from prerevolutionary governments was that neither the Ministry of Defense nor any of the armed forces was represented in the provisional cabinet. Military and defense considerations had reverted to the regular military chain of command. At the same time the president of the republic and the Council of the Revolution were jointly placed at the top of the military command structure, and together they coordinated governmental and military administration. The president was the supreme commander of the armed forces, and the council exercised legislative power in military affairs.

Elections

Electoral Law

The electoral law for the 1975 election for the Constituent Assembly was drafted by a committee of jurists and approved by the provisional government and the Council of State in November 1974. The electoral law was particularly significant in that it vastly extended the franchise. All Portuguese citizens over eighteen years of age were given the right to vote. Restrictions based on literacy, sex, and head-of-household status were removed. An emigrant was allowed to vote provided that he or she had children under eighteen years of age living in Portugal or a spouse habitually resident in Portuguese territory, had been a continuous resident in Portuguese territory for five years preceding the publication of the electoral law, or had been living in Portuguese territory for more than six months at the time of the elec-

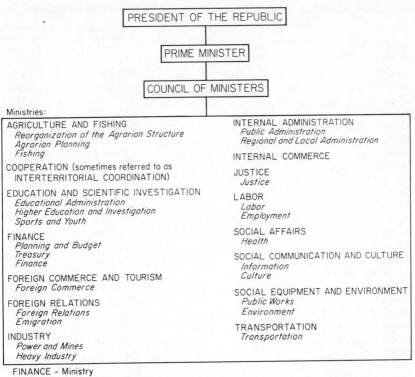

Figure 24. Portugal, Provisional Cabinet Structure, January 1976

tion. The exact number of potentially eligible voters was not known; however, just under 6.2 million voters were placed on the electoral roll of a total population of nearly 9 million.

The electoral law established proportional rather than majority representation as the system to be used in the Constituent Assembly. The proportional system provides for representation of different parties in a ratio roughly equivalent to their respective strength among the electorate in each constituency. All concerned apparently agreed that this was preferable to the winner-take-all result of majority representation because the assembly's task was to formulate a constitution, or basic law of the land. The d'Hondt form of proportional representation was utilized. Named for its developer, Victor d'Hondt, and first used in late nineteenth-century Belgian elections, the d'Hondt system is weighted in favor of the party that finishes strongest in any given constituency. Only candidates affiliated with one of the political parties taking part in the election were eligible to receive votes (see ch. 9). For electoral purposes Portugal was divided into twenty-two constituencies that coincided geographically with the administrative districts. There was to be one assembly member for every 25,000 electors or a remainder of 12,500 or more in each constituency (see table 5).

Table 5. *Portugal, 1975 Constituent Assembly Electorate by District*

District	Eligible Voters	Number Elected
Aveiro	358,885	14
Beja	139,357	6
Braga	367,055	15
Bragança	109,866	4
Castelo Branco	167,905	7
Coimbra	295,849	12
Evora	135,144	5
Faro	227,468	9
Guarda	137,790	6
Leiria	264,487	11
Lisbon	1,371,559	55
Portalegre	107,813	4
Porto	889,295	36
Santarém	321,957	13
Setúbal	402,339	16
Viana do Castelo	156,884	6
Vila Real	156,507	6
Viseu	261,218	10
Angra do Heroísmo	49,812	2
Horta	25,749	1
Ponta Delgada	84,365	3
Funchal	141,133	6
TOTAL	6,172,437	247*

*Three additional seats representing Macao. Mozambique, and Portuguese emigrants respectively bring total to 250 members.

Source: Based on information from Portugal, Ministry of Mass Communication, *Portugal Information*, No. 1, Lisbon, March 1975, p. 17.

Assembly of the Republic

On December 24, 1975, after a decision by the Council of the Revolution, the government announced that the election for the Assembly of the Republic (formerly called the National Assembly) would be held no later than April 25, 1976. At a later time April 25, the second anniversary of the revolution, was set as the actual election date. The election was to be by direct, secret, universal suffrage for a body of no more than 250 members, later expanded to 263. Like the earlier election to the Constituent Assembly, the Assembly of the Republic election used a proportional representation system based on multiple representatives from the various administrative district electoral constituencies.

216

President of the Republic

The president of the republic was originally chosen by the Junta for National Salvation. By mid-1975 the major political parties and the MFA signed an agreement that included a provision for the election of the president by an electoral college. The electoral college was to comprise the MFA assembly and the legislative assembly. By the end of the year, however, it was decided that the president should be popularly elected. In January 1976 the minister of internal administration was reported to have consulted the political parties represented in the Constituent Assembly regarding the order of future elections. Agreement was reached that the April assembly election would be held as scheduled. At least one political party, the Popular Democratic Party (Partido Popular Democrático—PPD), wanted the presidential election to be held at the same time. Its views notwithstanding, the Council of the Revolution and the other political parties agreed that the presidential election should follow the legislative election, probably in early summer, and would be followed by local elections.

Further Effects of the Revolution

Civil Service

Senior-level civil servants, such as ministers and their state secretaries and under secretaries, have always been political appointees in the Portuguese system just as they are in many other countries. Recruitment to the middle and lower levels of the civil service has usually been on the basis of the candidate's documented qualifications rather than by competitive examinations. The prospective candidate would apply to an individual ministry or public service in writing; his qualifications and references would be reviewed by a board in the personnel department of the ministry or public service; and the more eligible candidates would later be interviewed and the selection made.

This kind of recruitment system was less impartial than one based on competitive examinations. Friendships and personal influence undoubtedly played a part in some appointments. Despite this the middle and lower levels of the civil service have generally been professional and careerist. During the tumultous period in Portuguese history just after the beginning of the twentieth century, the civil service provided the only continuity and ongoing administration that existed. After the rise of Salazar members of the civil service had to support, at least nominally, the goals of the ANP. Outspoken opponents of the movement could be dismissed without the procedural protections usually afforded in disciplinary situations. For the most part, however, members of the middle and lower levels of the civil service remained apolitical, far more interested in administration than in politics.

217

The 1974 revolution had little effect on the civil service. Caetano's ministers, state secretaries, and under secretaries were removed from office, as were the few political appointees below the senior level. According to a postrevolution Portuguese government representative, only a few nonpolitical career service members were dismissed. When dismissals occurred, outspoken opposition to the revolution and its goals was usually involved. In short, dismissal from the career civil service apparently occurred on a fairly isolated, individual basis, rather than as an attempt to purge and replace whole sections or levels of the service.

At the local level, although apolitical administrators were generally not affected by the revolution, elected and appointed officials often fared less well. Many parish councils and municipal councils and chambers were dissolved and replaced by nonelective committees. Communist-oriented parties usually initiated the changes, but whether the situation was uniform across the country is questionable. Some sources noted that locally elected officials were purged en masse. Other sources indicated that whether local officials were replaced had much to do with their prerevolution popularity and with the strength of communist-oriented groups in their area.

Judiciary

No immediate attempt was made after the revolution drastically to alter the judicial system, but some reports indicated that by March 1976 plans were being formulated for the implementation of trial by jury within the regular courts. Other reports maintained that the judicial police had taken over some of the investigatory duties of the old prerevolution secret police and were functioning something like the American Federal Bureau of Investigation (see ch. 16). The judicial system has not been used for showcase political trials.

Criminal cases have continued to be processed in the court system, albeit slowly, much as before the revolution. There have been few, if any, complaints by attorneys regarding violations of defense rights or judicial procedure. The courts also continued to exercise their civil law jurisdiction. Civil procedure has been interrupted, however, for political reasons, particularly regarding property rights and land seizures by various groups. Some reports indicated that the work of the already overloaded judicial system was complicated as a number of judges and lawyers left Portugal after the revolution. In some cases local revolutionary committees in neighborhoods and factories usurped judicial authority, and the rule of law undoubtedly suffered.

The MFA first planned to use the regular judicial system in prosecuting political crimes, ruling out the creation of special courts for the purpose. Under the prerevolutionary military justice code the military part of the special courts system had been given authority over many categories of crimes that might be termed political. That jurisdiction was continued after the revolution by various decree laws. The established military courts, however, apparently continued to try only more exclusively military cases. Reports in both August and November 1975 indicated that the Council of the Revolution had reversed earlier policy and decided to establish special military tribunals to try political crimes.

Despite their long-term incarceration and the unpredictability as to how or when their cases would finally be resolved, political prisoners apparently have not been physically abused. Most reports, including those of released prisoners, indicated that there had been no attempt to torture or otherwise physically harass political detainees. The question of judicial due process, however, has been another matter. During the summer of 1975 the Portuguese Order of Advocates called for the establishment of several principles that were, it stated, then being violated. The principles included detainment only on the basis of some offense against preexisting laws, access to an attorney, fair trial by independent courts, strict adherence to rules of detention, and the right of habeas corpus, which had been denied by decree law to those under military jurisdiction since August 1974. The Council of the Revolution reportedly accepted the principle of the right of access to attorneys in November 1975. As late as March 1976 the other points raised by the Order of Advocates and the more general issues of military authority, political crimes, and judicial procedure were unresolved. The final resolution of these matters probably depended to a considerable extent on the forthcoming constitution and the elections for the Assembly of the Republic and the presidency, all due to occur by early summer of 1976.

Ombudsman

After the April revolution the Ministry of Justice decided to create a national ombudsman. The first ombudsman was sworn in by President Francisco da Costa Gomes in March 1976. The president stated:

> The function of the ombudsman is to insure justice and legality to the public administration through informal means by investigating complaints made by citizens against the aforementioned administration.
>
> By drawing attention to omissions, defects and deficiencies in the laws and to the existence of inadequate or untimely provisions, the ombudsman may suggest the revision or coordination of a whole set of state laws, adjusting them to the needs of national life.

Future appointments to the office of ombudsman were to be made by the Assembly of the Republic.

Military-Government Relationship

The 1933 Constitution established a particular political structure with various authoritative institutions. In reality power and authority were held by an individual, Salazar. Similarly the postrevolution MFA program and its subsequent modifications established a detailed structure of overlapping political and military authority. Again the formal structures did not always accurately reflect reality, and ultimate authority generally rested with the strongest MFA faction at any given time.

Thus the military in general and the MFA in particular could be expected to decide to what extent the new constitution and the formal structures of political authority it establishes will actually operate. The MFA was not, in March 1976, a monolithic movement; many political differences existed among its leaders and within its rank and file. In December the MFA initiated talks with party leaders in order to change the pact between them signed in April of that year. That pact had, in effect, legitimized military plans to dominate the political system for the next three to five years. In February 1976 press reports indicated that the draft of the revised pact included provisions for the Council of the Revolution to relinquish power to a popularly elected president of the republic. The council would then become a strictly advisory body. Further provisions called for the council and other military leadership organs to come under the authority of political institutions established by the new constitution. By March 1976 it appeared that the power of professional military figures, either politically moderate or perhaps even relatively apolitical, was increasing within the MFA. Thus there was a chance that the military would voluntarily withdraw from politics, making true constitutional government for Portugal a possible result (see ch. 9).

* * * * * * * * * * * * * * * *

For those with a reading knowledge of Portuguese, former Prime Minister Marcello Caetano provides the most authoritative source on government and administration before the 1974 revolution in *Manual de Direito Administrativo*. Hugh Kay's *Salazar and Modern Portugal* is a good examination of the government and of Salazar's corporatist theories. More detailed information on the Portuguese corporatist system is found in *Corporatism and Public Policy in Authoritarian Portugal*, by Philippe C. Schmitter. Although primarily a cultural and sociological study, José Cutileiro's *A Portuguese Rural Society* provides insight regarding the operation of the Portuguese administrative system on the local level. The Secretariado da Propaganda Nacional has published an English-language edition of the 1933 Constitution under the title *Political Constitution of the Portuguese Republic*. Complete sources on governmental organization and operation after the revolution were lacking in mid-1976. Information on these subjects could be obtained from the popular press, various political yearbooks, and English-language publications of the Portuguese Ministry of Mass Communication. Some of the ministry's more helpful publications include *Political Action Plan of The A.F.M.* and *Portugal Information*, numbers 1 and 2. (For further information see Bibliography.)

CHAPTER 9

POLITICAL DYNAMICS

On April 25, 1974, officers of the Armed Forces Movement (Movimento das Forças Armadas—MFA) overthrew the ruling regime in Portugal. The regime had dominated Portugal for almost fifty years, first under António de Oliveira Salazar, then under his successor, Marcello Caetano. The coup of April 25 was referred to as a revolution by the Portuguese, and indeed that was what it became. The MFA began, however, not as a revolutionary body but as the outgrowth of a group of young careerist military officers who had professional grievances. Long tours of duty in indecisive African colonial wars, coupled with exposure to their opponents' revolutionary ideology and a growing awareness of Portugal's social, political, and economic stagnation, contributed to the officers' perception that changes were needed. The jubilant, enthusiastic reaction of the people to the MFA immdiately after the coup helped that event become a real revolution, not simply a transfer of ruling power. Clearly the MFA and most of the public looked forward to fundamental changes for Portugal in the future.

A general consensus existed on such specific policy matters as the necessity of ending the colonial wars. For the most part, however, there was little agreement as to where, or how, the broader revolution was to proceed. While the postcoup military authorities and the government attempted to consolidate power, preserve public order, and grapple with immediate economic problems, a plethora of political parties and movements emerged with different, often conflicting plans for Portugal's future. They ranged politically from far left Marxist-Leninist and Maoist groups to far rightist armed groups operating from Spain. In between were moderate parties that generally resembled West European conservative, liberal, and social democratic counterparts. Between the moderates and the far leftists there existed the polemical, Moscow-oriented Portuguese Communist Party (Partido Comunista Português—PCP).

The period between the 1974 coup and May 1976 saw six provisional governments, an attempted right-wing coup, an attempted left-wing coup, two national elections, and the promulgation of a new constitution, while the power of various groups and ideologies waxed and waned and the military decided voluntarily to retire from politics (see

221

table 6). Portugal's political future was not at all sure in May 1976, but stability seemed to be increasing and with it at least some chance for the success of a democratic, pluralistic, political system apparently desired by both the leaders and the people.

Table 6. Portugal, Major Political Events, 1974-76

Year	Month	Event
1974 ...	May	General António de Spínola appointed president of Portugal
	July	First provisional government dismissed; second government formed by Vasco dos Santos Gonçalves as prime minister
		Continental Operations Command (Comando de Operações do Continente—COPCON) formed
		Spínola announces right of Portuguese overseas territories to independence
	September	General Francisco da Costa Gomes replaces Spínola as president
	December	Third provisional government formed; Gonçalves retains post as prime minister
1975 ...	January-February	Leftist groups harass numerous meetings of moderate political parties
	March	Unsuccessful right-wing coup attempt; Council of the Revolution created as final government and military authority
		Fourth provisional government formed; Gonçalves remains prime minister
	April	Pact signed between Armed Forces Movement (Movimento das Forças Armadas—MFA) and political parties
		Constituent Assembly election results in victory for moderate parties
	May	Leftist labor groups seize daily newspaper *República*
	June	MFA publishes direct democracies plan based on people's assemblies
	July	Portuguese Socialist Party (Partido Socialista Português—PSP) withdraws from cabinet; government dissolved
		Triumvirate of Costa Gomes, Gonçalves, and COPCON head, Otelo Saraiva de Carvalho, formed to run government and military

Table 6. Portugal, Major Political Events, 1974-76—Continued

Year	Month	Event
	August	Moderate MFA group issues Document of the Nine
		Gonçalves forms fifth provisional government, excluding all political party representation from cabinet
		Civilian and military opposition to Gonçalves increases; Gonçalves resigns as prime minister to accept appointment as armed forces chief of staff
	September	Gonçalves forced to decline chief-of-staff appointment and is dropped from Council of the Revolution membership; triumvirate ceases to exist
		Sixth provisional government formed with José Pinheiro de Azevedo as prime minister
	October-November	Political unrest continues, particularly in the north
	November	Azevedo and his cabinet refuse to continue governing without increased support from military
		Unsuccessful left-wing coup attempt
	December	MFA leaders meet with representatives from political parties to decide future political role of military
1976 ...	February	New pact between MFA and parties signed
	April	Constituent Assembly completes new, liberal constitution
		Legislative election results in victory for moderate parties
		Portuguese government approves statutes for the creation of autonomous regions of the Azores and Madeira
	May	Azorean leaders reject Portuguese plan and demand increased autonomy

Despite indications of increasing political stability after the failure of a left-wing coup attempt in November 1975, the prospects for continuing peaceful political evolution were clouded by several extremely serious economic problems. By mid-1976 the country's balance-of-payments deficit was increasing at an annual rate estimated at US$1 billion, unemployment was estimated at 15 percent, and productivity and investments were significantly depressed. The rapid nationalization of several economic enterprises, together with the purge of many qualified directors and administrators, had caused severe management problems, which the government had attempted to solve by inviting some of the managers to return.

An estimated 800,000 colonial refugees severely taxed social services and exacerbated many of the other economic problems. The refugees tended to polarize into a conservative, increasingly activist political element. Portugal had early looked to cooperative postindependence relations with its former overseas possessions to help solve some of its economic problems by providing increased markets and raw materials for Portuguese industry. By mid-1976, however, relations with most of the former colonies were worsening significantly.

Portugal's economic problems required strong, austere measures. The results of the legislative election, in which no party gained a majority, complicated the implementation of such policies; the public's patience with irresolute policies or with austere ones that were not immediately successful was an unknown quantity. Another serious problem was the continued existence of well-armed, highly organized, and highly motivated radicial groups on both ends of the political spectrum. Finally a significant element within the armed forces still advocated a continuing political role for the military. Exceptions notwithstanding, the majority of Portuguese leaders, as well as most of the public, increasingly appeared to favor the institutionalization of a pluralistic, democratic political system coupled with some form of socialist economics. The success or failure of such a system in Portugal could not be predicted with any certainty in mid-1976.

POLITICAL EVOLUTION, 1974-76

Competition for Power, May 1974-March 1975

On May 15, 1974, three weeks after the coup, General António de Spínola was sworn in as president of Portugal, and the first provisional government was appointed. Spínola had been deputy chief of staff of the armed forces until the previous month, when he had been fired by Prime Minister Caetano. A highly decorated and very popular national hero, Spínola was offered the presidency by the leadership of the MFA, who correctly assessed that his personal popularity would be valuable in rallying support for the new regime. There began a confusing period in which authority was shared between the president, the Council of State, the predominantly civilian government, the Junta of National Salvation—the ultimate leadership body of the MFA, composed of officers supportive of but not originally identified with the movement—and the broader MFA, which included several overlapping authoritative and policymaking bodies. Almost immediately a dual struggle for power began involving military versus civilian authority and political leftists versus political moderates in both the government and the military.

During the months of May and June labor unrest, intensified by leftist rhetoric, led to strikes, inflated wage demands, and the firing of hundreds of industrial managers and directors. So-called workers' committees attempted to take over the duties of the deposed managers. A similar process of *saneamento* (cleansing or purging) occurred at the local political level, where numerous officials identified with the Salazar-Caetano regime were sacked, usually at the instigation of local Communists and their allies.

The prime minister of the first provisional government was Adelino da Palma Carlos, a liberal law professor who chafed under the Council of State's control of the cabinet. With no power of its own, the cabinet was unable to preserve public order. In July Palma Carlos requested more governmental power to deal with labor unrest and proposed that a presidential election be called within three months. A popularly elected president would have had an independent political base from which to counter the power of special interest groups. Also, as the people's representative, he might have been better able to curb the labor and social unrest. Failing to win the Council of State's approval, Palma Carlos resigned; Spínola had no choice but to dismiss the rest of the cabinet.

On July 12 the Continental Operations Command (Comando de Operações do Continente—COPCON) was formed as an elite military group charged with protecting the revolution and the MFA program. It was headed by Brigadier Otelo Saraiva de Carvalho, one of the leaders of the April coup. Carvalho was a man of militant but inconsistent leftist views. Later in the month the MFA pressured Spínola to form the second provisional government with procommunist Vasco dos Santos Gonçalves as prime minister. Despite his widely known views regarding a gradual decolonization process ending in some form of confederation, Spínola again gave in to MFA pressure on July 27 and announced Portugal's official recognition of the rights of its overseas territories to total independence.

Spínola had apparently attempted to build a following among the nonradical political parties, conservative military units, and moderate sectors of the public. The events of July, however, showed his influence to be waning. Spínola's supporters were usually less visible than the Communists and far left groups, and they became known as the silent majority. In August and September they held numerous demonstrations supporting Spínola and opposing Gonçalves and the PCP. Spínola's speech of September 10 against "extremist totalitarians that fight from the shadows" was widely interpreted as an appeal for support to counteract increasing leftist influence in Portugal. A mass rally of the so-called silent majority was scheduled for September 28, but communist and far leftist groups organized and blocked access to Lisbon by Spínola's supporters. As the possibility of direct and violent confrontation increased, the MFA forced Spínola to cancel the demonstration. He resigned on September 30. The Portuguese government later charged that the events surrounding the canceled September 28 silent majority demonstration were part of an attempted countercoup by conservatives. Whether the charges were justified was questionable, but there was little doubt that small right-wing extremist groups had been planning to launch violent attacks on leftists in conjunction with the demonstration.

Spínola was replaced by another general, Francisco da Costa Gomes, a popular MFA leader of unknown political persuasion. After Costa Gomes' appointment to the presidency the military more openly dominated the government. During the late summer and fall of 1974 the MFA sent psychological action teams into rural areas of Portugal to encourage public support for the movement and the revolution. The teams operated mainly in the north. Using modern audiovisual equipment, military bands, and even parachute jumps, they spread propaganda about the evils of capitalism and the precoup regime and the benefits of the idealism of the MFA. They also discussed local problems and attempted to convey to the local populations the necessity of an alliance between the people and the MFA, irrespective of the government in general and the political parties in particular.

The third provisional government was formed in December 1974, and procommunist Gonçalves retained his position as prime minister. The MFA was not a monolithic body, and by the end of the year various factions were debating the movement's role in the future election for the Constituent Assembly, the body that would be charged with drafting a new constitution. Some thought the MFA should have a bloc of seats in the assembly; others believed it should operate through the existing political parties; and still others felt the MFA should withdraw from politics altogether.

Before and immediately after the April 1974 coup the PCP enjoyed considerable organizational strength within the trade unions. In the following months, however, it began to lose significant amounts of that strength to the Portuguese Socialist Party (Partido Socialista Português—PSP) and to numerous far left groups. By the end of 1974 the Communists were pressing the MFA to make the Intersindical—an organization composed of numerous unions and craft groups in the Lisbon, Porto, and Setúbal areas, which they dominated—the single official body for organized labor. Despite the opposition of some MFA members, the Socialists, the slightly left-of-center Popular Democratic Party (Partido Popular Democrático—PPD), and the Roman Catholic Church, the MFA and the government passed the required legislation in January 1975. The plan, however, did not immediately go into effect.

In January and Febuary a number of moderate party rallies and meetings of the PSP, PPD, and Social Democratic Center Party (Partido do Centro Democrático Social—CDS) were harassed and interrupted by far left groups. A Marxist-Leninist party, the Movement for the Reorganization of the Party of the Proletariat (Movimento Reorganizativo do Partido do Proletariado—MRPP) took credit for most of the incidents, and the PCP officially dissociated itself from the incidents. The MRPP and a somewhat more moderate leftist group, the Movement of the Socialist Left (Movimento da Esquerda Socialista—MES), also demonstrated against Portuguese participation in North Atlantic Treaty Organization (NATO) maneuvers.

While the Communists were attempting to consolidate their control over the trade unions through the Intersindical and the far leftist groups were interfering with the political meetings of relatively moderate political parties, moderates within the MFA appeared to be gaining strength over military leftists. From Spínola's resignation as president to the early months of 1975 Portuguese military politics were based on attempts by moderates and leftists to win the allegiance of different military units and garrisons; each side strove peacefully to amass decisive military power. By March 1975 the moderates seemed to be gaining the advantage. Their advocacy of holding the Constituent Assembly election as scheduled became the official MFA policy, much to the chagrin of leftists who, in the light of dwindling public support, desired to postpone the contest. Furthermore elections in each of the military service's MFA advisory councils during early 1975 had seen several moderate, even pro-Spínola, representatives replace leftist counterparts.

Communist Ascendancy, March-July 1975

Right-Wing Coup Attempt

The evolution toward moderate control of the MFA was interrupted by an attempted coup on March 11, 1975, undertaken by moderate and conservative military elements. Units loyal to Spínola attacked a leftist unit in Lisbon. The attack caused several casualties and very possibly cost the coup leaders nonleftist support they otherwise could have expected. By the end of the day COPCON units and civilian crowds persuaded the rebels to end their insurrection. Spínola flew to Spain and later was granted political asylum in Brazil. Fifteen military officers who apparently organized the coup also fled the country.

The extent of Spínola's actual involvement in the coup was unclear. He was known to have maintained his political and military contacts after his presidential resignation. A number of reports placed him at the air force base from which the rebels began their attack just before or during the coup attempt. Spínola has, however, denied participation in the coup, but the Portuguese government, after some initial hesitation, accused him of involvement.

The motives for the coup, especially when moderates seemed to be gaining strength within the MFA, were also unclear. Several observers indicated that the coup was triggered by rumors of an operation with the code name of the Great Easter Massacre, in which some 1,500 Spínola supporters, both military and civilian, were to be arrested and perhaps executed. One scenario, generally accepted by 1976, was that the Communists, worried about their declining influence within the MFA and their lack of public support for the approaching election, lured right-wing elements into a premature coup attempt by circulating false rumors about an impending, but in reality fictional, massacre plan.

The immediate result of the coup was an antirightist reaction that enhanced the leftists' positions in the military and the government, caused anticonservative public demonstrations, led to the arrests of businessmen, and saw the implementation of leftist economic policies. Many moderate and conservative officers were purged from military councils and MFA decisionmaking bodies. Most important the Council of the Revolution was created, with a predominantly leftist membership, to exercise final authority over both the MFA and the government.

On March 25 the fourth provisional government was installed. PSP leader Mário Soares was demoted from foreign minister (his position in the previous cabinets) to minister without portfolio. PCP representation in the cabinet was increased from one to two, and two other ministerial posts were given to members of the Portuguese Democratic Movement (Movimento Democrático Português—MDP), a leftist party espousing views very close to those of the Communists. At least one independent cabinet member was also known to have pro-communist sympathies. Seven military officers were given cabinet appointments, but most of the economic positions at the cabinet level and just below went to the Communists and other leftists. Whereas the left wing definitely emerged in a stronger governmental position than it had previously possessed, the change was made less significant by the government's increased subservience to the military and especially to the new Council of the Revolution.

The postcoup, antirightist reaction was reflected not only in formal MFA and government reorganization but also in public demonstrations. Mobs burned the Lisbon headquarters of the PPD and the Porto headquarters of the relatively rightist Christian Democratic Party (Partido da Democracia Cristã—PDC). Immediately after the coup attempt vigilante groups, many of which identified with the PCP, blocked roads and searched cars for escaping so-called reactionaries.

228

Industrialists and bankers were suspected of complicity in the attempted rebellion. President Costa Gomes described them as having formed "certain capitalist and privileged sectors, unable to adapt to the new political and social conditions." At least sixty leading businessmen were reported arrested.

Just before the coup, unions in Lisbon, Porto, and Coimbra closed the banks, demanding their nationalization to put "the economy at the service of the Portuguese people." The MFA and the government had not originally planned complete nationalization of the banking industry, but on March 13 they acceded to the union demands. A few days later insurance companies were also nationalized. By the end of April approximately fifty major domestic firms in the financial and industrial sectors had been placed under public ownership. Foreign companies, however, were excluded from nationalization. The Portuguese state was ill prepared to assume the management of so many enterprises, a fact that aggravated the already unsettled economic situation.

The MFA and the government also planned to institute land reform based upon the redistribution of holdings over 120 acres. Before a coordinated program could be put into effect, however, communist and other leftist groups began taking over landholdings in the central and southern regions of the country, frequently by force. The seizures, beginning soon after the revolution and lasting well into 1975, totaled as much as 2.5 million acres.

The leftward shift in Portuguese politics was also reflected in foreign relations. Together with the extension of diplomatic ties with several European nations, on March 15 Portugal confirmed that it was considering a Soviet Union request for the use of merchant marine refueling facilities on Madeira (see ch. 10). Reports of a similar, earlier request in January 1975 had been denied by the Portuguese government. NATO authorities, especially the United States, began publicly voicing concern regarding Portugal's dependability as an ally.

Constituent Assembly Election

The Constituent Assembly election was preceded by a formal pact between the MFA and the political parties. The signing of the pact on April 11 was the culmination of negotiations that had begun in early 1975. The March coup interrupted the negotiations, and the military later in effect imposed the agreement on the parties; indeed, although the major parties signed, several minor groups refused to accede to the pact. The pact established certain points that were to be incorporated in the constitution to be written by the Constituent Assembly. In effect it institutionalized the Council of the Revolution as the supreme governing body and legitimized continued military control over Portuguese politics for a transitional three-to-five-year period.

The PSP, PPD, and CDS reluctantly signed the pact but were disturbed by the provision for the president of the republic to be elected

229

by the legislative assembly and the MFA assembly, rather than by universal suffrage. The PCP, MDP, and another leftist group close to the PCP, the Popular Socialist Front (Frente Socialista Popular— FSP), enthusiastically agreed to the MFA pact. The groups who refused to sign the pact but participated in the Constituent Assembly election included the rightist Popular Monarchist Party (Partido Popular Monárquico—PPM) and the leftist but self-proclaimed non-Leninist MES. Also included were four far left organizations: the Communist Electoral Front/Marxist-Leninist (Frente Eleitoral de Comunista/Marxista-Leninista—FEC-ML), the International Communist League (Liga Comunista Internacionalista—LCI), the Popular Unity Party (Partido da Unidade Popular—PUP), and the Popular Democratic Union (União Democrática Popular—UDP).

Three additional parties were barred from participating in the election by the MFA on March 18. These were the rightist PDC, suspected of having supported the March 11 coup, and two far left groups, the MRPP and the Alliance of Workers and Peasants (Aliança Operária Camponesa—AOC). Both leftist groups were bitter opponents of the PCP, which may have contributed to their electoral prohibition.

Sporadic incidents in which far leftist groups attacked meetings of more moderate parties in northern Portugal appeared to be atypical considering the generally calm, peaceful campaign and voting process. Almost 92 percent of the registered electorate of over 6 million cast votes. The results were a clear victory for the relatively moderate parties. The PSP received 37.9 percent of the vote and 116 seats in the assembly and the PPD 26.4 percent and eighty-one seats, making the moderate left-of-center vote total 64.3 percent, for 197 of the 250 seats. The moderate right CDS received 7.7 percent of the vote and sixteen seats. The PCP polled 12.5 percent of the vote for thirty seats, and its ally, the MDP, 4.1 percent, for five seats. Clearly the PCP's strength within the MFA and the government was out of proportion to its public support.

Emigrants who had left Portugal within the previous five years were allowed to vote in the Constituent Assembly election, but relatively few participated. The exact number of eligible emigrant voters was unknown but, of more than 2 million Portuguese living abroad at the time of the election, only about 50,000 registered to vote. These included approximately 22,000 emigrants in Brazil, the United States, and Western Europe, who elected a PPD candidate as their representative. The PSP was the only party to run a candidate to represent the 600,000 Portuguese emigrants living in Mozambique, where only about 25,000 registered to vote. The overseas territory of Macao had an electorate of less than 4,000, which elected a local party candidate as their representative.

Leftist radicals within the MFA had sought to minimize the expected moderate victory by urging the electorate to cast blank ballots.

They had hoped that up to 40 percent of the electorate would comply, indicating confusion or lack of support for any political party, and thus provide the MFA with a popular mandate to govern. Only about 7 percent of the electorate turned in blank or invalid ballots, and even some of these were undoubtedly owing to mistakes having nothing to do with the MFA plan. The MFA, however, was still able to interpret the election results as a victory for the movement. By totaling the votes cast for parties that were represented in the fourth provisional government coalition, together with votes cast for unrepresented but leftist parties, the Ministry of Mass Communication concluded "that the [MFA] got over 80 percent of the votes."

Demise of the Fourth Provisional Government

On May 19 members of the communist-dominated printers union seized the socialist-oriented daily newspaper *República* (see ch. 11). The PSP demanded the return of the newspaper to its editors and owners and later boycotted cabinet meetings over the issue. The Council of the Revolution decided that the issue should be settled in the courts. PSP leader Soares sharply disagreed and accused MFA authorities of favoring the PCP. He warned that the PSP would quit the coalition government if communist takeovers of the media were not ended. He further demanded that secret elections be held to determine true communist strength in the labor unions and that local elections be held to replace Communists who had seized parish and municipal political power after the 1974 coup.

Tension was increased when some MFA leaders began openly to speak of the possibility of eliminating future political party conflicts by forming a new all-military government. A rally by approximately 50,000 socialist supporters was held in Lisbon on May 22. The next day PSP and PCP leaders met separately with President Costa Gomes and the Council of the Revolution, but with little apparent result. Within a week, however, the PSP suspended its cabinet boycott, suggesting that a solution to the *República* issue was near. The PSP's other demands were apparently placed in abeyance. By the first week of June the Council of the Republic had approved the return of *República* to its editors, and the PSP announced its intention to remain in the government.

By mid-June the Socialists' concern over *República* again came to the surface, against a background of increasing, sometimes violent, public demonstrations. Despite the Council of the Revolution's decision, the newspaper remained in the hands of the communist printers. COPCON units sent to implement the ruling refused to force the issue and sided with the workers. Relations between the moderate parties and MFA authorities were further strained toward the end of the month with the release of the MFA's political action plan. The plan included provisions to establish direct democracy through a system of people's assemblies of civilian and military representatives, which would bypass much of the existing polictical institutional framework and thus the existing political parties (see ch. 8).

There was, however, dissension within the MFA. A moderate faction that opposed people's assemblies and communist control of the media emerged and attempted to force the resignation of procommunist Prime Minister Gonçalves during early July. Its efforts failed, and on July 10 the PSP withdrew from the fourth provisional government. The cabinet was dissolved one week later when the PPD followed suit, denouncing the MFA's direct democracy plan and the media situation and repeating the PSP's earlier calls for union and local political elections. The MFA rebuked Soares after a large socialist rally on July 19 at which the party leader demanded Gonçalves' resignation. Demonstrations by the supporters of the PSP, PPD, and PCP continued for several days. A number of PCP headquarters were attacked in several northern towns.

On July 25 the MFA assembly approved, as the Council of the Revolution had earlier, a plan to entrust governing power to a triumvirate of leading MFA generals: President Costa Gomes, Prime Minister Gonçalves, and COPCON chief Carvalho. Debate on the triumvirate within the assembly was reportedly bitter, although the moderate, anti-Gonçalves faction, led by Ernesto Augusto de Melo Antunes (the foreign minister in the fourth provisional government), had been inexplicably absent. Approval of the triumvirate plan was interpreted by some observers as an indication that the relatively moderate Costa Gomes was losing control to the left wing within the Council of the Revolution and the government. Others saw the triumvirate as part of a clever plan by Costa Gomes: by placing Carvalho and Gonçalves in the triumvirate, the far leftist Carvalho would be balanced against the more doctrinaire Communist, Gonçalves, resulting in the neutralization of both and supposedly in a dominant position for Costa Gomes.

Moderate Reaction and Leftist Decline, August-September 1975

Document of the Nine and the Fifth Provisional Government

On August 7 the so-called Document of the Nine, a political manifesto signed by Melo Antunes and eight other moderate MFA officers, was delivered to President Costa Gomes. Other copies reportedly made their way to various members of the Lisbon diplomatic community, including the United States ambassador, Frank Carlucci, and to the foreign and domestic press. One Lisbon newspaper published a special edition with the full text of the document. The document criticized increasing MFA involvement in the political bickering between the parties. It also criticized "uncontrolled and anarchical forms of exercising power [that] were gradually introduced everywhere (even in the armed forces)." The statement rejected "the East European model of socialist society to which we will inevitably be led by a political . . . 'vanguard' resting on a very narrow social base" and that resulted in "bureaucratic control" by "totalitarian regimes." Also rejected was "the Social Democratic model of . . . Western Europe, because . . . the great problems of Portuguese society cannot be surmounted by repeating the classical schemes of advanced capitalism in our country."

The alternatives advanced by the signers of the document were generalized. They desired "a socialist society" that would be classless, "where the exploitation of man by man will be ended." Such a society was to be "achieved at a rate suited to the concrete social reality of Portugal, so that this transition will be made gradually and peacefully without convulsions." Finally, the Document of the Nine stressed that "this model of socialism is inseparable from political democracy. It must therefore be built in a context of political pluralism, with the participation of the parties prepared to support this national plan. This model of socialism, moreover, is inseparable from fundamental freedoms, rights, and guarantees."

The governing triumvirate officially denounced the authors of the document, and Melo Antunes and three other signers were temporarily suspended from the Council of the Revolution. The authors of the document were not otherwise punished, however, and two, who were military region commanders, retained their posts. The document was circulated among military units and received considerable support, particularly in the north.

The Document of the Nine overshadowed the announcement of the formation of the fifth provisional government on August 8. Prime Minister Gonçalves eliminated all political party representation from his new cabinet, which consisted primarily of unknown military men —thought to be procommunist—and of civilians who were leftists but not identified with specific parties. The PSP and PPD condemned the new government, as did Melo Antunes' group and other MFA moderates. It was reported that Costa Gomes referred to the new government at the time as transitory.

Ouster of Vasco dos Santos Gonçalves

During August opposition to Gonçalves increased within the military, particularly among army and air force units. Within the government Carvalho, leader of COPCON, opposed Gonçalves, whereas Costa Gomes apparently maintained a neutral position. Outside the government the PSP and PPD continued their condemnations of the fifth provisional government and demanded Gonçalves' resignation. Political violence between moderate parties and the Communists and far leftists increased, particularly in the north. Press reports indicated that over fifty PCP headquarters were ransacked or destroyed. By late August it had become obvious that Gonçalves could not continue as prime minister. Costa Gomes then offered Gonçalves the position of chief of staff of the armed forces if he would resign his government post. He had little choice but to accept the offer, resigning as prime minister during the last week of August.

Far from quelling the turmoil, Gonçalves' change of posts only made the situation worse, at least within the military. By September 3 both the army and the air force chiefs publicly declared against Gonçalves as chief of staff. The army's MFA assembly was reported to have opposed Gonçalves and also to have opposed a meeting of the MFA General Assembly, called by Costa Gomes to consider the Gonçalves appointment. The army's representatives felt that the broader body was unfairly packed with procommunist delegates. Faced with such concerted opposition, Gonçalves was forced to decline the appointment. The same day, September 5, he was dropped from the Council of the Revolution and thus was effectively removed from all political bases of power. The triumvirate ceased to exist, and moderates replaced several leftists on the Council of the Revolution.

The role played by Costa Gomes in Gonçalves' ouster was unclear. Some observers indicated that the president's appointment of Gonçalves to the chief-of-staff post was a clumsy mistake. Most of the press reported that he had strongly supported Gonçalves, perhaps up to the point where his own position had become endangered. Some journalists, however, have suggested that the entire incident was part of a plan by Costa Gomes to oust Gonçalves in such a way as to prevent him from rallying support as a martyr and preserve the facade of MFA unity. According to this scenario Costa Gomes baited Gonçalves out of the prime ministership with the offer of the post of chief of staff, all along believing the military would not accept the appointment.

Sixth Provisional Government

Costa Gomes appointed José Pinheiro de Azevedo, the navy chief of staff, to replace Gonçalves as prime minister. On September 6 members of the fifth provisional government resigned. Over the next several days Costa Gomes and Azevedo conferred with party leaders in an attempt to find a satisfactory basis for representation in the new government. The PCP demanded it be given at least as many ministers as the PPD; the PPD and PSP pressed for party representation roughly proportional to the results of the Constituent Assembly election. The sixth provisional government, formed September 19, was so proportioned. Cabinet membership included four Socialists, two Popular Democrats, and one Communist together with a number of military men and civilians with no party affiliation. Among the military members of the cabinet were Melo Antunes as foreign minister and Vitor Alves, another signer of the Document of the Nine, as education minister. Party leaders, apparently desiring to be free to criticize the new government, did not join the cabinet, leaving the seats to be filled by their party lieutenants.

Continuing Unrest, October-December 1975

The removal of Gonçalves from power and the formation of the sixth provisional government did not quell political dissension. Several public political demonstrations, frequently punctuated by bomb incidents and other violence, were held during the fall of 1975. A leftist military unit temporarily rebelled near Porto. The PPD and PCP continued to demand each other's expulsion from the cabinet. The chaotic political situation was exacerbated by repeated warnings of impending leftist coups from the PSP and PPD and impending rightist coups from the PCP. Several far left groups had secured large quantities of small arms from dissident military units, and far right groups were also well armed. In an effort to minimize the continuing violence the Council of the Revolution and the government ordered civilians to relinquish all unauthorized weapons to the proper authorities. Compliance with the government order was negligible, however, and the potential for continuing violence and instability remained.

In mid-October the government was forced to grant large pay increases to thousands of construction workers who had laid siege to Azevedo's home and the Constituent Assembly's building. The prime minister was in effect held prisoner, for neither regular troops nor COPCON units moved to end the siege. Claiming that the military was not providing the support necessary for effective government, Azevedo and his cabinet announced on November 20 that they would not govern until the required support was forthcoming. The Council of the Revolution condemned the move. At the same time, however, the council resisted intense leftist pressure to dismiss the sixth provisional government. It replaced Carvalho as commander of the Military Region of Lisbon, although he retained his post as head of COPCON. Any encouragement that moderates might have felt because of Carvalho's loss of the regular military post was nullified when the council assigned him the new duty of developing the institutions necessary to implement the MFA people's assemblies plan.

Left-Wing Coup Attempt

The deteriorating political situation, marked by the governmental stalemate between the Council of the Revolution and the cabinet, reached a climax on November 25. In an ill-fated coup attempt leftist paratroop units took over four air force bases and the headquarters of the national television network and appealed to workers to join their cause against the government. Soon confronted by superior forces, the isolated rebel units surrendered with a minimum of bloodshed, and the coup was over by nightfall. On November 27 Costa Gomes was able to declare that "the politico-military coup in which a false Left convinced itself it would succeed in mystifying and manipulating the working masses and peasants has been overcome."

In January 1976 a military commission investigating the coup implicated the PCP, which immediately denounced the charge. Despite the
finding the PCP retained its membership in the government. A number
of far leftist groups were implicated, including the UDP and the Revolutionary Party of the Proletariat-Revolutionary Brigades (Partido
Revolucionário do Proletariado-Brigadas Revolucionárias—PRP-BR).
Allegations from other sources were made against the United Revolutionary Front (Frente Unidad Revolucionária—FUR), which included
the PRP-BR and five other leftist groups. Complete details on the
coup and its participants were not available by mid-1976, but in retro-
spect it appeared likely that, whereas far leftist groups had participated, involvement by Carvalho and the PCP was less sure. Carvalho
and the PCP were probably willing to ride the crest of a successful
leftist coup but apparently remained aloof from direct participation
in what early became an obviously lost cause. Carvalho was arrested
for his involvement in the coup but was released for lack of evidence.
In May 1976 he reportedly stated that conservative military leaders
had engineered the coup situation so as to have an excuse to end the
leftist threat and thus end dissension within the MFA and the government.

Coup Aftermath

The attempted coup resulted in a purge of leftists from the media,
which the Council of the Revolution accused of having helped to incite the rebellion. The broadcast media, both radio and television,
were nationalized, with the exception of the Roman Catholic Rádio
Renascença (see ch. 11). The purge of communist and leftist military
leaders included the army and navy chiefs of staff and extended down
the ranks to colonels, majors, and naval commanders (see ch. 15). On
January 20, 1976, the Council of the Revolution issued a decree law
that provided for the expulsion from the armed forces of military personnel who had deserted their posts during or after the coup or had
refused to report when summoned by superiors for investigatory purposes. Expulsion was to include the loss of political rights for twenty
years.

Increasing Stability, January-April 1976

Agricultural and Industrial Policies

During January 1976 several protests were held by farmowners who
objected to land seizures by leftists and to the government's agrarian
reform program. The farmers wanted the program replaced with a
new one to be decided by their associations and the political parties
and approved by the legislative assembly that would be elected later
in the year. The government modified its program and limited legal
expropriations to the southern region of the country. The farmers
were not satisfied, and demonstrations continued into February. The

government defended its program but stressed that it would also take steps to end the illegal farm seizures and occupations. A final solution to the controversial agrarian reform issue was not likely to emerge until after the legislative and presidential elections scheduled for later in the year and until the new government was formed based on those elections.

Decreasing productivity and fear of factory closings and resulting unemployment caused the government to discontinue state intervention in some of the nationalized economic firms by February 1976. Despite a PCP campaign against "the return of the bosses," who would "recover privileges and positions lost with the overthrow of fascism," the government also began inviting previously fired managers and administrators to return to the failing factories.

New Pact Between the MFA and the Parties and the New Constitution

A few days after the attempted leftist coup the Council of the Revolution began reassessing the military's role in politics. It subsequently decided to hold talks with leading political parties in order to modify the 1975 pact between the MFA and the parties that had given dominant political power to the military. In December 1975 the military was divided into two basic groups: the professional or operational group, who wanted the military out of politics, and the political group, headed by Melo Antunes, who desired a continuing, albeit more limited, political role for the armed forces.

By early February 1976 the military professionals and the party representatives were near agreement on a plan to end armed forces dominance of political affairs and replace it with predominantly civilian rule for a four-year transitional period. The Council of the Revolution was to become an advisory body to the president, who was to be elected by popular suffrage. It was agreed that the new pact, once signed by the parties, would be incorporated into the constitution then being written by the Constituent Assembly. The new pact would in effect form the section of the constitution that provided for government organization over the transitional period. The pact was signed by the military and the major parties on February 28.

The Constituent Assembly completed and approved the draft of the new constitution on April 1. The next day that draft officially replaced the 1933 Constitution as the basic law of the land, after being promulgated by the president. Most observers agreed that the new Portuguese Constitution was one of the most progressive in the world regarding human rights and the social and economic rights of the workers. In fact the Lisbon daily newspaper *Diário de Notícias* was reported to have stated that the Constitution was so detailed on the subject of human rights as to be obsessive. The newspaper further explained that this was an understandable reaction to almost fifty years of dictatorship followed by a government of several months under a procommunist prime minister.

The document was very lengthy, containing 312 articles. The influence of the PSP, which had a large plurality in the Constituent Assembly, was obvious in the Constitution. The first article committed Portugal to a "transformation into a classless society." The second guaranteed basic rights and liberties, free expression, and free political organization. It specified, however, that for the good of the state it was necessary "to assure the transition to socialism by creating conditions for the democratic exercise of power by the working classes." Centrist and rightist parties objected to the commitment of the state to socialism, and even some Socialists were reported to have thought that such goals should be subject to renewal through popular vote, not part of the basic law of the land. The Constitution was also controversial in that it prohibited amendments during the four-year transitional period.

Five governmental bodies were to exist during the transitional period: the president of the republic, the Council of the Revolution, the legislative assembly, the government (cabinet), and the courts. The role of the MFA general assembly, established by the first pact between the MFA and the parties, was eliminated (see ch. 8). Most of the power was placed in the office of the president, who was also the chairman of the Council of the Revolution. The council retained much of the power it had been given under the first pact, though technically the power was now consultative. Before the president could take action in most matters of importance, however, consultation with the council was mandatory. The council retained legislative authority only on purely military affairs.

The Council of the Revolution could declare new laws unconstitutional before they were promulgated by the president. In this situation the president had no choice but to veto the legislation. A cabinet decree was then dead, but assembly-initiated legislation could still be passed into law if the assembly again approved it by a two-thirds vote of those present. The president had no choice but to promulgate such legislation. (When constitutionality was not involved, the legislature could override a presidential veto by a positive vote of an absolute majority of its total membership.) The council could also determine the constitutionality of existing laws but only when requested to do so by the president of the republic, president of the legislature, prime minister, attorney general, or ombudsman.

The actual work of determining constitutionality was to be undertaken by a new body that would assist the Council of the Revolution in this regard. The new body was the Constitutional Commission. It was to be chaired by a member of the council and to consist of four judges plus four additional members of merit, one each appointed by

238

the president of the republic and the legislature and two members appointed by the council.

The president was to appoint and dismiss the prime minister after consultation with the Council of the Revolution. The cabinet would be responsible to the legislature. The passage of a censure motion or the failure of a piece of major governmental legislation to pass in the legislative assembly would end the tenure of a given government. The legislature would exist for the four-year transitional period, after which it would be replaced by a second legislative assembly empowered to revise the Constitution. The transitional period would end when a revised constitution went into force. In short, then, except for the existence of the Council of the Revolution, the new Portuguese governmental structure appeared to resemble the model of the French Fifth Republic, in which day-to-day governing was the function of a parliamentary or cabinet system and overall guidance was in the hands of a president located outside and above the general governmental framework. This was much like the model established in theory, but not in practice, by the 1933 Portuguese Constitution (see ch. 8).

Legislative and Presidential Elections

The campaign to elect members to the legislative body, the Assembly of the Republic, began officially on April 4. Fourteen parties originally planned to run candidates. These were the PSP, PPD, PCP, CDS, UDP, PPM, FSP, MES, and LCI, all of which had participated in the 1975 election; the AOC, MRPP, and PDC, all of which had been banned in that election; and two parties that had not previously attempted to run candidates, the Portuguese Communist Party/Marxist-Leninist (Partido Comunista Português/Marxista-Leninista—PCP-ML) and the Revolutionary Workers' Party (Partido Revolucionário dos Trabalhadores—PRT). Three parties that ran in 1975—the MDP, FEC-ML, and PUP—did not field candidates for the Assembly of the Republic. Just before the election the PCP-ML withdrew in an apparent attempt to prevent the fragmentation of the far leftist vote.

Most of the parties emphasized the economy as the basic campaign issue. The PSP wanted to establish basic rules and end such excesses as the illegal land seizures. It stressed close ties with Western Europe. The PCP defended the revolution's accomplishments—nationalization and agrarian reform—which it wanted continued. It advocated a wage-price policy that would favor the working class. The PPD stressed the need for a mixed economy, defending private initiative if it were socially useful. It wanted farmers to have a say in future agrarian policy. The CDS advocated the free enterprise economic system and an end to agrarian reform. Two rightist parties, the PPM and PDC, ran basically negative campaigns against almost all aspects of the revolution and its aftermath. Among the far leftist parties, the UDP demanded that Portugal withdraw from NATO, reject American aid, and ally itself with the third world of developing nations. The MRPP also wanted an end to all foreign bases on Portuguese territory. The far leftist parties in general professed some form of Maoist or Marxist-Leninist dogma, advocated people's power and direct democracy, and stressed workers' control. Most spent a considerable amount of time condemning the 'Communists as false leftists and social fascists.

The campaign was more violent than that which preceded the 1975 election. Serious incidents included several fights and bombings, and the PSP, PDC, PPD, and CDS had rallies disrupted, headquarters attacked, and workers mobbed. At least five people were reported killed in campaign-related incidents. The most publicized incident, attributed to various far right groups, involved the bombing of the Cuban embassy in Lisbon, in which two people were killed.

With one major exception the results of the 1976 legislative election resembled those of the Constituent Assembly that preceded it. Of the parties that ran in both elections, the PCP vote increased by 2 percent of the total vote cast; the vote of each of the other leftist and far leftist parties increased or decreased by less than 1 percent of the total. The PSP's vote decreased by just under 3 percent and the PPD's by just over 2 percent. The rightist PPM's vote was virtually unchanged, but the larger, center-rightist CDS increased its share of the total vote by more than 8 percent. The combined poll of the five parties that ran candidates for the first time in 1976 was less than 2 percent of the total vote cast (see table 7). Just over 83 percent of those eligible voted—down 9 percent from the 1975 turnout but still high by America,-standards.

Under the 1976 Constitution the president, after consulting with the Council of the Revolution, was to choose a prime minister on the basis of the election result and, with the advice of the prime minister, would also choose the cabinet. This selection process would await the election of a new president during the summer, and the sixth provisional government was to remain in power in the interim. PSP leader Soares announced that his party would attempt to form a minority government. He rejected a coalition with either the Communists or the centrist parties but did not rule out the inclusion of independents and military men in his future cabinet. Some Western press reports also indicated that Soares might attempt to undermine the PPD by appointing members of a splinter group from that party to his government.

PPD leader Francisco Sá Carneiro demanded a coalition government that would include the Popular Democrats; he threatened that the PPD would leave the sixth provisional government unless Soares agreed but later decided that his party would remain in the interim cabinet. The CDS also pressed for a coalition government but avoided threats. The Communists argued for a PSP-PCP coalition "govern-

240

Table 7. Portugal, Electoral Results, 1975 and 1976

Party	Constituent Assembly May 1975			Assembly of the Republic May 1976			Percent Popular Vote Change
	Votes	Percent of Popular Votes	Delegates	Votes	Percent of Popular Votes	Delegates	
Portuguese Socialist Party	2,145,618	37.9	115	1,887,180	35.0	106	-2.9
Popular Democratic Party	1,495,017	26.4	80	1,296,432	24.0	71	-2.4
Social Democratic Center Party	433,343	7.7	16	858,783	15.9	41	+8.3
Portuguese Communist Party	709,659	12.5	30	785,620	14.6	40	+2.1
Popular Democratic Union	44,546	0.8	1	91,383	1.7	1	+0.9
Popular Socialist Front	66,163	1.2	0	41,954	0.8	0	-0.4
Movement of the Socialist Left	57,695	1.0	0	31,065	0.6	0	-0.4
Popular Monarchist Party	31,809	0.6	0	28,163	0.5	0	-0.1
International Communist League	10,732	0.2	0	16,235	0.3	0	+0.1
Portuguese Democratic Movement	233,380	4.1	5	Did not run	.....	.....	.....
Marxist-Leninist Communist Electoral Front	32,519	0.6	0	Did not run	.....	.....	.....
Popular Unity Party	12,996	0.2	0	Did not run	.....	.....	.....
Alliance of Workers and Peasants	Banned	.....	.....	15,671	0.3	0	.....
Movement for the Reorganization of the Party of the Proletariat	Banned	.....	.....	36,237	0.7	0	.....
Christian Democratic Party	Banned	.....	.....	28,226	0.5	0	.....
Portuguese Communist Party/Marxist-Leninist	Did not run	.....	.....	15,801[1]	0.3	.....	.....
Revolutionary Workers' Party	Did not run	.....	.....	5,182	0.1	0	.....
Null and blank ballots	393,219	6.9	.....	No data	.....	.....	.....
TOTAL	5,666,696	100.0[2]	247[3]	5,137,932	95.3[4]	259[5]	.....

[1] Withdrew before election.
[2] Figures do not add to total because of rounding.
[3] In addition Portuguese Socialist Party obtained one seat for Portuguese in Mozambique; Popular Democratic Party, one seat for other Portuguese emigrants; and one independent seat for Macao. This made for a total of 250 seats.
[4] Discrepancy due to lack of data regarding null and blank ballots.
[5] Four additional seats for Portuguese emigrants for a total of 263 seats.

ment of the left," justifying their membership on the basis that of the parties that formed the sixth provisional government only the PCP had increased its vote in 1976 over what it had received in 1975.

By May 1976 the army chief of staff, António Ramalho Eanes, appeared to be the leading contender for the presidental election scheduled for June 27. Along with considerable military support the PSP, PPD, and CDS had indicated that they would back Ramalho Eanes. The PCP initially indicated it would support a military candidate but later decided to run one of its own leaders, Octavio Pato. The sixth provisional government prime minister, Azevedo, was also a candidate. Most party politicians probably would have preferred a civilian president; however, they apparently felt a military president was necessary in view of the continuing importance of the armed forces in political matters. There were also other political considerations. Press reports indicated, for example, that Soares was reluctant to run in the presidential campaign for fear that the PSP's left wing would gain control of the party.

Still another possible factor in presidential politics was the unconfirmed but persistent rumor that former president Spínola planned to return to Portugal after the legislative election, perhaps to run for the presidency. Carvalho, the former head of COPCON, declared himself a presidential candidate despite continued controversy over his possible involvement in the November 1975 left-wing coup attempt. The colonial refugees attempted to run Wenceslau Pompilio da Cruz as their presidential candidate, but he was disqualified in early June by the Supreme Court of Justice, reportedly because of irregularities in his list of 7,500 supportive signatures. The candidates were required to submit such a list to prove that they had at least a minimal amount of popular support.

THE AZORES AND MADEIRA

Politics, 1974-76

There has long been resentment in the Azores and Madeira against what the islanders feel has been exploitation by mainland Portugal. The mainland has heavily taxed both imports from and exports to the islands and, their citizens feel, provided little in return. Island businessmen have also complained that Portuguese authorities limit local commercial concerns to prevent competition with mainland enterprises.

The Azorean and Madeiran populations are predominantly Roman Catholic and politically conservative. These factors, combined with the economic resentment, caused increasing unrest during the summer of 1975 when it appeared that the Communists and other leftists were emerging as the dominant political force in Portugal. Leftist ideology was anathema to most islanders. In addition Azoreans feared a leftist mainland government would end the United States use of island military facilities, which contributed a significant amount to the local economy. Many emigrants from the Azores live in the United States, a fact that added to the feeling of Azorean-American affinity. By mid-July independence movements in both island groups were winning local support and causing concern in Lisbon. The majority of the populations of both island groups wanted greatly increased regional autonomy. Observers generally agreed, however, that total independence would be preferred only if the Communists succeeded in a complete takeover of the mainland government.

In late August 1975 Portugal relinquished Azorean administration to a junta of local political leaders. Together with local governing duties the junta was charged with formulating a plan for increased island autonomy to be considered by the Lisbon government. A similar administrative and planning junta was approved for Madeira in December. The juntas of both island groups wanted far-reaching monetary reforms in their relations with the mainland government. The reforms included an end to mainland taxes on the islands' exports and imports, the local use of the islands' tax revenues, and an end to Lisbon's receivership of the islands' foreign currency revenues. The Azores junta further demanded that a regional Azorean assembly be created and empowered to make, interpret, and suspend laws applying to the island group. Madeira's leaders wanted even greater monetary autonomy through the creation of a Madeiran currency.

After the juntas submitted their plans for autonomy, the Portuguese government and the Council of the Revolution approved, on April 30, 1976, provisional statutes to establish the Autonomous Region of the Azores and the Autonomous Region of Madeira. Under the Lisbon statutes each island group would have a regional legislative assembly to be elected later in the summer. The Portuguese president, on recommendation of the prime minister, would appoint a separate regional minister for each island group. The minister would then appoint the island's local government; he would also have the power to veto legislation passed by the island's popularly elected assembly.

Press reports indicated that Madeiran authorities tentatively accepted the Lisbon plan with reservations. Azorean leaders, however, rejected it, accusing the mainland government of having made "profound alterations" in the junta's original proposals. The Azorean junta was particularly critical of the Lisbon-appointed regional minister's wide powers. The Portuguese plan had also rejected the request that the islands be permitted to keep foreign revenue for local use. Another point of contention was the composition of the Azorean regional assembly. Azorean authorities had wanted each of the group's nine islands to have equal representation; the Lisbon plan called for proportional representation. Proportional representation would give the group's most densely populated island, São Miguel, greater representation than the other islands, something the junta wanted to avoid because of interisland rivalries. The Azorean junta also believed that proportional representation would give unfair advantage to the PSP, which had strong support on São Miguel but was less popular elsewhere in the island group. Lisbon's prohibiting the islands' 600,000 emigrants, most of whom were politically conservative, from voting in the assembly election was also interpreted as an attempt to give the PSP an unfair electoral advantage. Soon after the rejection of the Lisbon plan Prime Minister Azevedo, in an attempt to meet the junta's demands, reportedly decided to limit the powers of the regional minister and assure island emigrants of a voice in local Azorean affairs. The issue of the autonomous regions was clearly unsettled in early May 1976.

Activist Organizations

The two major Azorean separatist groups were the Movement for the Self-Determination of the Azorean People and the Azores Liberation Front (Frente Libertação Açores—FLA). Portuguese authorities banned the Azorean self-determination movement in March 1975. The FLA became particularly active during the summer of 1975 in reaction to increased communist power on the mainland. In July 1975 the group established a clandestine provisional government of the Azores and asked the United Nations General Assembly for an independence referendum for the island group. The PPD in the Azores has been linked to the FLA, a connection the political party denies. At least one antiseparatist group, the Patriotic Action League of the Azores, had been formed. Its October 1975 leaflets stated; "We are against separatism and the exploitation of the workers, and we stand for freedom and democracy."

Madeira had several small separatist groups including the Revolutionary Brigade for the Independence of Madeira, the Madeira Liberation Army, and the Independence for Madeira Movement. Several groups attempted to merge into a united front called the Front for the Liberation of the Madeira Archipelago. The front sought independence from Portugal because of the mainland's communist tendencies. It suggested a possible federation of Madeira, the Azores, and the Spanish Canary Islands. The front has been blamed for a number of bombing incidents during 1975 and 1976. Most observers felt its claim of support from 80 percent of Madeira's population to be very inflated.

In April 1976 former members of the outlawed Azorean self-determination movement formed the Democratic Union of the Atlantic, which purported to unite autonomist elements from the Azores and Madeira. Its first announced goal was to gain majorities in the regional assemblies of both island groups and use them to obtain as much autonomy as constitutionally possible.

244

POLITICAL ATTITUDES AND VALUES

Portugal's contemporary political history—almost fifty years of dictatorship, a revolution, and two years of instability—prevent any conclusions regarding the attitudes and values of the people. Tentative generalizations, however, may be hazarded on the basis of certain events that have occurred since the 1974 revolution.

The high turnout in two national elections (92 percent of the electorate in 1975, 83 percent in 1976) was an indication that the public was interested in participating in the political process, at least where it thought that participation was meaningful. The results of both elections clearly showed a preference for the relatively moderate parties: the PSP, left of center, more militant but still similar to other West European democratic socialist, working-class-oriented parties; the PPD, slightly left of center, similar to other West European liberal, reformist parties; and the CDS, further to the right, similar to other West European moderate conservative parties. Despite Portugal's historical isolation the political values of its people, as represented by electoral choices, appeared to lie well within the political mainstream of Western Europe.

The three major moderate parties differed on economics and more specifically on the demarcation of the private and public sectors of the economy. All appeared, however, to be genuinely committed to a pluralistic, democratic, institutionalized political process and to civil liberties and human rights. Together these parties polled 72 percent of the vote in the 1975 election and 75 percent in 1976.

Concomitantly the high electoral turnouts and their results seemed to indicate a rejection of violence as a method of attaining political goals. Some violence did occur in both electoral campaigns but appeared to be used, or at least usually initiated, by the minor extremist groups—many of which rejected institutional politics and none of which had, or was likely to gain, a large public following. The one exception has been the PCP, which has used violence, or often merely the threat of violence, as political tools and which has attracted a significant political following (15 percent of the electorate in the 1976 legislative election). The PCP has been extremely opportunistic in temporarily subverting its dogma to the specific political realities of the time. It has also been under considerable pressure from other West European communist parties to moderate its dogma and cooperate genuinely with other parties in a pluralistic political system.

Finally there was the extraordinary phenomenon of the military's apparently relinquishing political power voluntarily. Although the process was to be slow—the military would retain significant power during the transition period—it still would seem to have underscored a commitment to institutionalized civilian politics by the dominant portion—at least in May 1976—of the armed forces. An observer, Stan-

245

ley Plastrik, may have best summarized the Portuguese people's political feelings and aspirations when he wrote: "While the euphoria of
the early weeks of the revolution has worn off, the momentum of the
rediscovery of political freedom is still present. Given half a chance
to assert themselves, the Portuguese will not return to any form of
totalitarianism, Left or Right." The Salazar and Caetano regimes
were authoritarian, not totalitarian; Plastrik's point was otherwise
well taken.

POLITICAL GROUPS AND PARTIES

From 1932 to 1974 political parties were banned in Portugal. A few
parties, notably the communist and to a lesser extent the socialist and
some far left groups, operated clandestinely. These organizations,
together with many new ones, formed the plethora of political parties
and movements that emerged after the 1974 revolution. The large
number of far leftist groups, usually identified with Marxist-Leninist,
Maoist, or even anarchist ideology, caused concern in the West until
it became clear that their differences were so serious as realistically to
preclude any extreme-Leftist unity. Furthermore the far left denounced and helped to undermine the PCP, the one leftist organization
that offered a potential threat to pluralistic politics generally and to
the moderate political parties electorally.

Electoral Parties, April 1976

Thirteen political organizations ran candidates in the 1976 Assembly
of the Republic election; a fourteenth withdrew at the last moment
but still received votes. The five parties that won representation to
the legislative assembly were the PSP, PPD, CDS, PCP, and UDP.

Portuguese Socialist Party

In terms of electoral strength the Portuguese Socialist Party (Partido Socialista Português—PSP) has been the most popular party in
Portugal. Its leader, Soares, was generally regarded as the country's
most popular political figure. The party was formed in 1973 and was
affiliated with the Socialist International. The PSP was a mass party,
enjoying its strongest support in Porto and other urban areas. Although not as popular in rural areas, it has still attracted significant
support from peasant landowners and other segments of the rural
population. The party's basic program, as of February 1975, stressed
that the "foundation of public freedoms is the defense of the interests
of the workers and that the exercise of their freedom is a condition of
the full participation of citizens in political, social, economic, and cultural life." The PSP advocated a vastly expanded public sector of the
national economy and a foreign policy of national independence and

246

cooperation with all peoples. It favored eventual dissociation from political and military blocs, leading to a policy of nonalignment that would prevent "Portugal from becoming embroiled in quarrels which concern the superpowers." It did not, however, advocate an immediate Portuguese withdrawal from NATO, and it looked forward to a close economic relationship with Western Europe.

In relative terms the PSP was representative of the leftist or militant wings of most West European social democratic parties. Soares has written:

> I should be the first to emphasize that none of the Socialist systems now in being seems to me wholly adequate. Communism, like all the people's democracies, has sacrificed the great essential, liberty, to the conception of the totalitarian state—a conception I abhor—while the para-Socialist experiments in those countries of Western Europe where Social Democrats have come to power, either alone or in coalition, have, in my view, lacked consequence and the strength of their own convictions, and so nearly always end up as the faithful agents of capitalism.

Soares has also written that the socialist tradition has never been strong in Portugal. As a political ideology it found Portuguese proponents in the latter half of the nineteenth century, but they were intellectuals, relatively isolated from the masses. Attempts to establish a socialist underground during the period of opposition to the Salazar and Caetano regimes were largely failures that lacked public support. During these years Socialists joined several opposition confederations or common fronts, including, among others, the Republican and Socialist Alliance (1932-34), the Socialist Front (1950-54), and the Republican and Socialist Resistance (1955-64). The PSP developed from still another broad group, the Portuguese Socialist Action.

Soares believed that the major obstacle to the formation of a meaningful socialist party was the impossibility of uniting Roman Catholics and non-Roman Catholics into one group. Since 1966 Socialists have attempted to unite the noncommunist left into a movement flexible enough to attract not only various forms of socialism but also both Catholics and non-Catholics. Such a movement would not be inherently anticommunist. According to Soares the Socialists would be willing to work with the Portuguese Communists so long as the latter respected democratic forms of government, as other West European communist parties seemed increasingly willing to do. Soares felt that a pluralistic Portuguese political system would also require the representation of Christian Democrats and liberal-republican organizations capable of mobilizing centrist and moderate rightist support.

Concerned over reports in 1975 that the Soviet Union and other East European nations were aiding the PCP with up to US$10 million per month, Social Democratic Party leaders from Sweden, Great Britain, the Federal Republic of Germany (West Germany), France, Austria, Norway, Denmark, and the Netherlands met in August 1975 and agreed to support the PSP, a move later repeated by the Socialist International. The PSP established an education fund, which could legally accept foreign cash contributions according to Portuguese law. The largest amounts of aid reportedly came from the Netherlands and West Germany. Swedish district socialist parties adopted Portuguese counterparts to which they were to send aid. Total West European assistance amounting to a few million dollars was apparently much less than that received by the PCP from its sources.

Popular Democratic Party

The Popular Democratic Party (Partido Popular Democrático—PPD) was formed a few weeks after the April 1974 coup by its secretary general, Sá Carneiro, together with Francisco Balsemão and Joaquim Magalhaes Mota, all former members of the liberal faction in the old, precoup National Assembly. The party's main support came from the politically and socially conservative, usually Catholic, middle class in northern Portugal.

The PPD was similar to other West European liberal, reform-oriented parties. It stressed the importance of a free society, human rights, and equality, to be accomplished through a redistribution of national income and state economic intervention. The will of the people, expressed through the ballot, was paramount to any future Portuguese society. The PPD favored subordination of economic power to political power and of private interests to the common good. It supported nationalization of such key segments of the economy as utilities and other natural monopolies. At the same time it defended what it termed socially useful private initiative. In the foreign policy field the PPD favored Portuguese relations with all peoples and especially desired progressive Portuguese integration into the West European community and membership in the European Economic Community (EEC, also called the Common Market).

In December 1975 Jorge de Carvalho Sá Borges, then social affairs minister, led three other PPD members of the government and twenty-one Constituent Assembly deputies out of the party. The dissidents complained of the growth of Sá Carneiro's personal power and the party's rightward shift, symbolized by its increasingly anticommunist stance after the ill-fated November leftist coup attempt. The PPD dissidents formed a new group, the Social Democratic Movement, in February 1976.

Social Democratic Center Party

The Social Democratic Center Party (Partido do Centro Democrático Social—CDS) was formed after the April 1974 coup by officials of the precoup regime, including party leader Diogo Pinto de Freitas do Amaral, Adelino Amaro, and Valentin Pintado. The CDS was a member of the European Christian Democratic Union, the rough equivalent of the democratic socialists' Socialist International, and has reportedly received aid from West Germany's Christian Democratic

Union and Great Britain's Conservative Party. Some Western press reports indicated that major Portuguese banks have backed the party. The CDS has sought electoral alliances with the PSP and PPD for the purpose of running joint candidates, but a permanent CDS merger with either party is unlikely. The CDS sanctioned limited government intervention in key segments of the economy; however, it stressed respect for private property and initiative. It has supported worker participation in the management of economic enterprises based on the social doctrine of the Catholic church, not on socialist economics. Of the parties that ran in the elections of 1975 and April 1976 only the CDS significantly increased its support.

Portuguese Communist Party

The Portuguese Communist Party (Partido Comunista Português—PCP) was founded in 1921 and became a clandestine organization in 1926 after the republic was overthrown. It attempted to form common fronts with Socialists, Liberals, and Republicans from the 1930s to the 1960s. Salazar was an extreme anticommunist, and his secret police made special efforts to eliminate the PCP. Those efforts contributed to the PCP's near-folklore status as the main opponent of the Salazar and Caetano regimes. That and the party's strong organization contributed to its considerable public support immediately after the April 1974 coup. Some reports indicated that after the coup the PCP was assisted in its organization by several specially trained, foreign (primarily Czechoslovakian), Portuguese-speaking agents. The PCP also received financial assistance totaling several million dollars during 1974 and 1975 from East European sources.

The PCP was a cadre party of 3,000 to 5,000 when it emerged in 1974; within a few months it claimed a membership increase of over 100,000. It reportedly retained, however, its unique structure, based on a network of cells. The cells were established in places of work, both urban and rural, and each cell comprised four to six members. Despite its rapid increase in growth, the party was said to have continued to use a careful screening process to eliminate unreliable new converts. The party's main strength was in a so-called red belt in the southeastern Alentejo region, sixty miles west-southwest of Lisbon. The area was composed of large landholdings; the majority of its population, landless peasants, were naturally receptive to communist propaganda regarding agrarian reform. The PCP also enjoyed considerable support in some labor unions.

The PCP was Moscow oriented and ideologically dogmatic, the only major West European communist party to support the 1968 Soviet invasion of Czechoslovakia. At the same time the PCP was very opportunistic in attempting to improve its position relative to that of the other Portuguese parties. It attempted, for example, to become the ideological wing of the MFA, hoping to utilize what was clearly the dominant postcoup movement as a vehicle to further its doctrines.

The PCP supported the first provisional government and the MFA authorities, declaring against the working-class strikers for higher wages in the summer of 1974; it justified its position on the basis that economic turmoil would help reactionaries regain power. The PCP was highly critical of the Council of the Revolution just before the ill-fated November 1975 left-wing coup but, when that insurrection was obviously failing, the PCP disavowed its leftist connections and issued a statement calling for a peaceful solution to the problems at hand and recognizing errors committed by the rebelling leftist elements. The PCP has repeatedly called the PSP fascistic, but it looked to an electoral alliance with the Socialists in February 1976 as a means of increasing its poll; after the legislative election the PCP advocated a coalition of the left with the PSP against the other moderate parties.

The leader of the PCP, Alvaro Cunhal, was imprisoned for several years during the Salazar regime. Reputed to be a communist ideological thinker of international importance, Cunhal has often been called one of Europe's last Stalinists.

The PCP has claimed to recognize the importance of freedom because of its experiences during the years of clandestine opposition to Salazar. It has stated that no democratic society could be established in Portugal without the PCP. This was because, according to the party, "opposition to the P.C.P. is opposition to the working class and the people as a mass." When questioned by the Italian journalist Oriana Fallaci regarding the PCP's poor showing in the Constituent Assembly election, Cunhal stated that "Communists do not accept the game of elections." Revolutionary dynamics were important, but "the election process is only marginally complementary to these dynamics." The views of the PCP regarding pluralism and a competitive political party system were evident in 1975 in its support for an MFA direct democracy plan that would have circumvented the political parties in representing the people within the Portuguese political process.

The Armed Revolutionary Action (Ação Revolutionária Armada— ARA) has been identified by some observers as the militant, armed wing of the PCP. Formed during the 1960s, by late 1975 its membership numbered as high as 20,000. According to some press reports its members included leftist militants from Cuba, Chile, Spain, and Uruguay. The ARA was blamed for several terrorist attacks on NATO facilities in Portugal before the 1974 coup, but its activities were said to have been suspended by the PCP when the larger party became a member of the first provisional government. The PCP has carefully avoided taking a public stand on Portugal's future relationship with NATO.

Carlos Aboim Ingles was reported to be the leader of a moderate PCP faction, but as of May 1976 a moderate split seemed unlikely. The PCP has, however, spawned several minor far leftist splinter groups in recent years, most of which continually condemned the PCP for having become bourgeois and social fascistic. The PCP had also been criticized by a number of other national communist parties, particularly in the West, for its negative attitudes toward democratic, pluralistic, institutionalized politics in general and toward popular suffrage and cooperation with socialist and other noncommunist parties in particular. The Spanish, French, Greek, Yugoslav, and Romanian communist parties have urged restraint on the PCP. Italian Communists, in the midst of negotiating a so-called historic compromise with Christian Democrats, have been particulary embarrassed by the PCP. The policies of Western communist parties, which increasingly call for cooperation with noncommunist parties and independence from the Moscow line, have been called Euro-Communism. For his part Cunhal has reportedly commented, quite simply, that "there is no Euro-Communism."

Popular Democratic Union

The Popular Democratic Union (União Democrática Popular—UDP) was formed in 1974 by Stalinist hardliners from the PCP who were upset by what they perceived to be the party's revisionism. Not a single party, the UDP was a common front for three organizations: the Committee of Support for the Reconstruction of the Marxist-Leninist Party, the Marxist-Leninist Revolutionary Union, and the Marxist-Leninist Revolutionary Communist Committee. The UDP's support in the 1976 legislative election almost doubled the 1975 figure, but it still amounted to less than 2 percent of the total votes cast.

Other Political Parties

Nine other organizations ran candidates for the Assembly of the Republic but failed to win representation to that body. These included five relatively far left groups, two leftist groups, and two rightist groups.

The far left groups included the AOC, a Marxist-Leninist body banned from the 1975 election, which attacked the PCP as often as it did parties of the right and had strong support in a few labor unions; the LCI, a Trotskyite group that demanded the formation of workers' councils and was penalized campaign media time by the Council of the Revolution for using expressions that might constitute insurrection or slander; the PRT, which polled only 5,000 votes; and the MRPP, founded in 1970, which condemned the PCP as revisionist and the Council of the Revolution as reactionary. Most popular of what were generally termed Marxist-Leninist groups, the MRPP enjoyed considerable student support. It condemned both the United States and the Soviet Union. The MRPP armed itself by seizing weapons from the old Portuguese Legion. Also banned from the 1975 election, it suffered internal dessension later in the year when its major theoretician,

J.L. Saldanha Sanches, criticized it for becoming increasingly counterrevolutionary.

The fifth far left group, the Portuguese Communist Party/Marxist-Leninist (Partido Comunista Português/Marxista-Leninista—PCP-ML), withdrew from the 1976 campaign just before the election was held but still received almost 16,000 votes. Recognized by the People's Republic of China, the PCP-ML's main function seemed to be to spawn such splinter groups as the AOC, the PUP, and the Portuguese Communist Marxist-Leninist Organization.

The more moderate leftist groups were the FSP, led by Manuel Serra António Lobo Villela and founded as a leftist splinter group from the PSP, perhaps at PCP instigation, and the MES, led by Victor Wengorovius and Alfonso de Barros, which attempted to occupy a position between the PSP and PCP while supporting the MFA. Variously described as non-Leninist and Catholic Marxist, the movement's ideology included tenets of anticlericalism, the abolition of all private property, and an absolute dictatorship of the proletariat. It approximated more the communist than the socialist viewpoint.

The rightist parties were the PPM, founded in 1974, which tempered its somewhat reactionary call for a king (similar to democratic monarchs of Western Europe) with the advocacy of very limited nationalization, and the PDC, which was formed just after the 1974 coup, banned from the 1975 election, and revitalized after the ill-fated left-wing coup attempt of November 1975. Its founder was Eduardo Sanches Osorio, a supporter of Spínola, who was implicated in the March 1975 right-wing coup attempt and who, with Spínola, fled the country. Osorio reportedly returned to Portugal in the spring of 1976 to test Spínola's popularity. In January 1976 the PDC selected Antero Silva Resende as its new secretary general. Three months later the party declared itself against the processes of decolonization and agrarian reform, the new pact between the parties and the MFA, and the Marxist content of the Constitution. It reportedly had some following in rural areas where the Catholic Church was particularly influential, but it did poorly in the April 1976 elections.

Other Electoral Parties

Three parties participated in the 1975 Constituent Assembly election but did not run candidates in 1976. These included two far left groups and one less extreme left group. The far left groups were the FEC-ML and the PUP.

The less extreme leftist party was the MDP, which developed from the Democratic Electoral Commission (Comissão Democrática Elitoral —CDE), the organization that ran communist candidates in the 1969 National Assembly election. Uniting elements of both the PCP and the PSP, the movement was headed by Francisco Pereira de Moura and José Manuel Tengarrinka. It established joint platforms with the PCP on several issues and has been referred to by some observers as a communist front party. It was probably the group most responsible for the purge of local officials immediately after the April 1974 coup. In March 1976 the movement announced it would not participate in the Assembly of the Republic election because it believed right-wing parties would exploit the results.

Other Active Political Organizations

Several political groups existed in mid-1976 that attracted varying degrees of popular support but failed to compete in either the Constituent Assembly or Assembly of the Republic elections. Most of them were extremist and consequently important, if for no other reason than their potentially dysfunctional effect on the developing Portuguese political system. The most important of the far leftist groups were the United League for Revolutionary Action (Liga de União e Ação Revolucionária—LUAR) and the PRP-BR. LUAR was one of the oldest antifascist groups, having led much of the armed struggle against the Salazar and Caetano regimes. Headed by Herminio da Palma Inacio, LUAR was also opposed to the PCP and sometimes operated with the MRPP. It attempted to remain aloof from major party organizations.

Like LUAR, the PRP-BR had engaged in armed resistance to the Salazar and Caetano regimes; it was especially opposed to Portugal's colonial program. The group financed its existence by robbing banks. It was headed by Isabel do Carmo, who was a friend of former COPCON chief Carvalho. Carmo's connection with Carvalho reportedly enabled her group to obtain weapons diverted from Portuguese troops returning from the African wars.

The PRP-BR was formed in 1970 and broke with the PCP on two issues. First, it saw violence as necessary to combat fascism (despite its contacts with the ARA, the PCP did not officially advocate violence); second, it wanted to skip the transitional step of a national, democratic revolution, necessary in PCP ideology, and proceed immediately with the socialist revolution. The PRP-BR refused to accept the revolutions and other political experiences of foreign countries as valid models for Portugal. It stressed the need for workers' management and control and was dedicated to the establishment of autonomous organizations, based on the workplace, through which the proletariat would exercise its dictatorship. The PRP-BR's autonomous organizations, called the Revolutionary Councils of Workers, Soldiers, and Sailors, were thus much broader in scope than the workers' councils, which developed soon after the April 1974 coup and were aimed only at managing the workplace.

According to its theory the PRP-BR would coexist with the autonomous councils for an undetermined period of time. The PRP-BR justified its own existence as necessary to analyze the social, political, and economic situation and to coordinate the struggle to eliminate the class society. It was, in short, "the body which is capable of making a synthesis between theory and revolutionary practice." After the councils were fully developed and the class society ended, the PRP-BR would disappear. In fact it reportedly disappeared much sooner, going underground in October 1975 to challenge the Council of the Revolution's order that all civilian weapons be relinquished to the proper authorities.

Other far leftist groups included the Cry of the People (O Grito do Povo), which operated in the Porto area and remained aloof from other Marxist-Leninist organizations; three minor splinter groups that reportedly emerged from a 1964 split within the PCP—the Marxist-Leninist Communist Union, the Communist Revolutionary Committee, and the Marxist-Leninist Union to Reconstruct the Communist Party; the Antifascist Intervention Brigade, established in March 1976 to "try all counterrevolutionaries and execute on the spot the main fascists"; and the Portuguese Liberation Movement, a group of militant anarchists.

Many of the various leftist groups and splinter groups attempted to organize into common fronts. Two of the larger fronts were the Unified Socialist Movement, founded in April 1976 by LUAR and other less radical leftist dissidents to form a revolutionary vanguard in the historical Marxist sense, and the FUR, formed in August 1975 to advance the cause of a government composed exclusively of representatives from autonomous local organizations. Finally there was the Union of Portuguese Antifascist Resistance, which encompassed all antifascists regardless of their political or ideological beliefs.

The far right also had its violent, militant groups. These included the Democratic Movement for the Liberation of Portugal (Movimento Democrático para a Libertação de Portugal—MDLP) and the Portuguese Liberation Army (Exército de Libertação Português—ELP), two armed, rebel Portuguese groups operating from Spain. In May 1976 the Spanish government was reported to be restricting the ELP, which numbered 200 to 300 and claimed credit for a December 1975 bombing incident near the Portuguese embassy in Paris. Leadership of the MDLP was assumed by Spínola in August 1975. Other groups included the Commandos for the Defense of Western Civilization, which claimed credit for the autumn 1975 bomb attacks against the PCP's headquarters in Porto, and the Portuguese Anticommunist Movement, reported to comprise two dozen former members of Salazar's secret police, who claimed responsibility for bombing the Cuban embassy in Lisbon just before the 1976 legislative election.

Interest Groups

In addition to the groups that were primarily concerned with politics there existed several broader interest groups. Catholic intellectuals founded the Society for the Study of Social and Economic Development (Sociedade de Estudos de Desevolvimento Economico e Social—SEDES) during the Salazar regime to function as a source of social planning and constructive criticism. Its original membership primarily comprised Christian Democratic technocrats, but it later included PPD and CDS members as well as some Socialists. Two of its members, Sá Carneiro and Magalhaes Mota, were founders of the PPD. Also involved with social thinking and criticism but focusing on the Catholic church have been newer, postcoup groups, such as the Christians in Permanent Reflection (in Guarda), and the Group for Reflection, Action, and Intervention (in Porto). Both organizations consisted primarily of lay people and were extremely critical of the church's past identification with the Salazar and Caetano regimes.

The Democratic Women's Movement was founded before the revolution. Its members, who were also members of the PSP and PCP, organized the group in 1968 to study and discuss women's issues; it was not what would generally be called a militant feminist group. Activist groups were also formed within the military, primarily for political reasons but also with the goals of improving the working and living conditions in the armed forces and minimizing military discipline. The best known of these groups was the semiclandestine Soldiers United Will Win (Soldados Unidos Vencerão—SUV), later changed to the Revolutionary Organization of the Armed Forces (Organização Revolucionária de las Fuerzas Armadas—ORFA) (see ch. 15).

The two most powerful interest groups in mid-1976 were probably the farmowners and the colonial refugees. The farmowners organized into the Confederation of Portuguese Farmers and have clashed repeatedly with leftist groups occupying land in the central and southern regions of Portugal. The farmers' confederation has demanded a return of illegally seized land, an end to the government's agrarian reform program, and the formulation of a new program based on the farmers' view. It threatened to cut Lisbon's food supplies if its demands were not met.

By late 1975 the colonial refugees had grown impatient with what they felt to be the government's inadequate measures to help assimilate them into the Portuguese society. The refugees demanded housing, employment, food subsidies, and payment for land they had lost in the overseas territories. They occupied the Ministry of Social Affairs in February 1976 to dramatize their grievances. In May 1976 they occupied luxury hotels and the parliament building after the government imposed restrictions on the refugee food subsidy program.

The refugees organized the Independent Social Center as a political party in February 1976. The party was to run candidates in the legislative election as well as in the presidential and local elections that would follow. It did not, however, participate in the April legislative election. The refugees' presidential candidate, Cruz, was disqualified by the Supreme Court of Justice in early June 1976 (see Political Evolution, 1974-76, this ch.). Several of the established parties, including the PPD, PDC, PPM, and CDS, have included refugees among their candidates in an apparent attempt to court the refugee vote. The PCP established an organization for returnees in Lisbon. Along with the far left, the established party incurring most of the refugees' wrath has apparently been the PSP. PSP leader Soares presided over the start of the decolonization process as foreign minister in the first three provisional governments.

* * * * * * * * * * * * * * * *

A number of good sources on the 1974 Portuguese revolution are available, including Neil Bruce's *Portugal: The Last Empire;* Thomas C. Bruneau's "The Portuguese Coup: Causes and Probable Consequences" in *World Today;* and Norman A. Bailey and William J. Simon's "Portugal: Four Myths of a Curious Revolution" in *Columbia Forum.* For information on Portuguese politics from the revolution to the end of the fifth provisional government in September 1975, see the Institute for the Study of Conflict's *Portugal: Revolution and Backlash* (especially "The Quest for Democracy" by Hugh Kay); George W. Grayson's "Portugal and the Armed Forces Movement" in *Orbis,* and Kenneth Maxwell's "The Thorns of the Portuguese Revolution" in *Foreign Affairs.* An excellent, broad examination of the Portuguese political situation from before the revolution through the summer of 1975 is found in Michael Harsgor's *Portugal in the Revolution.* The People's Translation Service of Berkeley, California, has provided an invaluable research aid in *Portugal: Key Documents of the Revolutionary Process.* Very few scholarly sources on Portuguese politics since September 1975 had become available by mid-1976, necessitating an overreliance on popular press coverage for the preparation of some parts of this chapter. (For further information see Bibliography.)

CHAPTER 10

FOREIGN RELATIONS

The foreign relations of Portugal since António de Oliveira Salazar's consolidation of power as Portuguese prime minister in 1932 have reflected to a considerable extent the historical isolation of the Iberian Peninsula. Bilateral and multilateral relations were minimal, limited primarily to defense matters and involving Western nations almost exclusively. Some relations were also established with Latin America, but Eastern Europe and the underdeveloped or third world nations of Africa and Asia were generally ignored. Instead Portugal devoted itself to the maintenance of its overseas territories, a vast colonial empire nearly 500 years old that included numerous possessions in Africa and the Far East.

All of this suddenly changed after the Portuguese revolution of April 25, 1974. Within a few weeks Portugal began to establish relations with communist and third world nations. Within twenty months all but two relatively insignificant colonial holdings had been given independence. Such drastic changes in its long-established foreign policy might have been seen as evidence that Portugal was little more than an anachronism, a country whose previous cold war fears and past colonial greatness offered little comfort or guidance for an uncertain future.

To the Portuguese government and the Armed Forces Movement (Movimento das Forças Armadas—MFA), however, the period after the revolution has not been a time of defeatism or memories of things past in the realm of foreign relations. Speaking to the Conference on Security and Cooperation in Europe held in Helsinki in July and August 1975, Portuguese President Francisco da Costa Gomes remarked that the postrevolution period for Portugal had been one in which

we have proclaimed and we have clearly pursued a foreign policy based as much on respect for our former international undertakings as on a total opening up to all the peoples of the world, with full respect for the principles of sovereign equality of rights, non-intervention in the internal affairs of others, and the recognition of the right of all peoples to freely choose for themselves.

Having cast off its traditional colonialism and isolationism, Portugal attempted to approach its future foreign relations without preconceptions. In the process it began to conceive and perhaps develop for itself a new international role, and it attempted to increase foreign trade as a means of improving its weak domestic economy.

Foreign policy, like other aspects of Portuguese government and politics, was under the firm control of Salazar during his long tenure as prime minister from 1932 to 1968. Because of the chaotic state of Portugal's finances during the first part of the twentieth century. Salazar's primary concerns were fiscal. Domestic economic development was considered far more important than an active foreign policy. Not only did Salazar seek to preserve the status quo in foreign relations, but he and other leaders of his conservative, authoritarian regime were suspicious of foreign influences in Portugal. Their attempts to discourage such influences led to Portugal's further isolation from the world community. In addition to this general isolationism Portuguese foreign policy until the April 1974 revolution was based on two fundamental objectives: maintenance of the Portuguese empire and opposition to communism.

Maintenance of the Empire

While pursuing an isolationist policy in relation to most of the rest of the world, Portugal actively sought to maintain its colonial empire. As late as 1960 the 500-year-old Portuguese colonial empire comprised the African territories of Angola, Cabinda, Mozambique, Portuguese Guinea (present-day Guinea-Bissau), the Cape Verde Islands, São Tomé and Príncipe, and São João Baptista de Ajudá, a small enclave in Dahomey (present-day Benin); the Portuguese State of India, which included the enclaves of Goa, Damão, Diu, Dadra, and Nagar-Aveli; Macao, an enclave in the People's Republic of China (PRC); and the eastern half of the island of Timor, in the Arafura Sea northwest of Darwin, Australia (the western half belonged to Indonesia) (see fig. on Portuguese empire, ch. 2). Dahomey gained its independence from France in 1960 and soon began pressing the Portuguese to relinquish São João Baptista de Ajudá. By that time the Portuguese holding was limited to the governor's residence and the land on which it stood. Rather than cede the residence to Dahomey, however, the last Portuguese governor burned it to the ground before returning to Lisbon.

An even better indication of Portugal's tenacity in clinging to its empire was demonstrated by its reaction to India's armed takeover of Goa and the other Portuguese Indian enclaves in 1961. More than a decade after the event not only had Salazar refused to recognize Indian sovereignty over the enclaves, but official Portuguese literature and maps showed them as temporarily occupied Portuguese territories. Representatives of the Portuguese State of India also continued to be seated in the Portuguese National Assembly.

Most European colonial powers drew a sharp distinction between the homeland and the colonies, which were unrelated, subservient dependencies. Though metropolitan Portugal (European continental Portugal and the North Atlantic Ocean islands of the Azores and Madeira) firmly controlled the affairs of its colonial territories, they were not considered subservient dependencies. On the contrary, the fundamental principle upon which the Portuguese empire was built was that the overseas territories *(ultramar)* were an integral part of the homeland. In 1951 the unitary relation between metropolitan Portugal and its overseas territories was formalized in a revision of the 1933 Constitution. Before 1951 the territories were referred to as colonies, a term that could denote a dependent, non-self-governing status; therefore the term *colonies* was replaced by the term *provinces*. This change meant that, at least legally, the overseas territories were integral parts of a unitary state, all parts being governed by the same constitution. As Article 135 of the constitution stated, "The Overseas Provinces, as an integral part of the Portuguese State, are united as between themselves and with Metropolitan Portugal."

Anticolonial pressure within the United Nations (UN) increased during the 1950s on the basis of Article 73 of the Charter of the United Nations. That article called on colonial powers to assist in the development of free political institutions in their non-self-governing territories and to submit to the secretary general statistical data on the economic, social, and educational conditions of those areas. Portugal refused to submit the information or to make changes in the overseas territories' political institutions, claiming on the basis of its 1951 constitutional change that those areas were integral parts of Portugal. A UN committee of six nations studied the Portuguese colonial situation in 1959, and in 1960, upon its recommendation, the General Assembly passed a resolution rejecting the Portuguese argument and declaring the overseas territories to be non-self-governing and thus covered by the UN charter. The Portuguese responded that the overseas territories were regulated by a national constitution over which the UN had no control and thereafter ignored anticolonial actions by the UN.

There were a number of reasons why Portugal so tenaciously clung to its overseas possessions even after other colonial powers relinquished theirs. Portugal, a small, poor country, found some of its possessions profitable. This was particularly true of Angolan natural resources. The overseas territories were also valuable as receivers of large numbers of Portuguese settlers. Perhaps most important were the unique historical circumstances of Portuguese imperialism, which caused it to become part of the national identity. The Portuguese truly believed that they had an imperial mission that went far beyond simple exploitation. Furthermore it involved the protection and extension of the Christian faith, particularly to the East. These enlightened aspects of Portuguese imperialism were never fully realized. Nevertheless they became embodied in Portuguese culture and politics, as seen in Article 133 of the 1933 Constitution, which stated: "It is in-

trinsic in the Portuguese Nation to fulfill its historic mission of colonization in the lands of the Discoveries under their sovereignty and to
diffuse among the populations inhabiting them the benefits of their
civilization, as also to exercise the moral influence enjoined upon it
by the Patronage of the East" (see ch. 2).

Finally it must be recognized that most Portuguese leaders, even as
late as the 1960s, were firmly convinced that a Portuguese decolonization policy, particularly if rapid, would have serious negative consequences for the native peoples involved. To a considerable extent the
Portuguese themselves had contributed to the validity of this point by
failing to prepare the populations of their overseas territories for independence. Portuguese leaders also believed that their country's loss
of its overseas holdings would seriously weaken the general defense
of the Western alliance. They thought that, as Portugal withdrew
from its colonial holdings, power vacuums would result in which other foreign powers would compete to establish their influence in the
vacated areas.

Salazar's successor, Prime Minister Marcello Caetano, did institute
some limited colonial reforms. Angola and Mozambique were given
the status of states, which increased their autonomy. Even more significant, locally elected assemblies with real power to pass legislation
affecting their territories were established in the overseas provinces.
Such reforms, however, proved insufficient to meet the demands of
the various independence movements already fighting in the field. The
colonial wars, begun in the early 1960s, continued and increasingly
contributed to the discontent that eventually led to the April 1974
revolution.

Anticommunism

The second basic objective of Portuguese foreign policy was opposition to communism and particularly to its spread to the West. Salazar's fear of communism was something of an obsession, caused at
least in part by Soviet intervention in the Spanish civil war (1936-39).
He considered communism a threat to Portugal's corporatist form of
government, to its Roman Catholic religion, and to the society he attempted to foster. Salazar declared Portuguese opposition "to all
forms of internationism, Communism, Socialism, syndicalism and
everything which may divide or minimize or break up the family. We
are against class warfare, irreligion, and disloyalty to one's own country; against serfdom, a materialistic conception of life, and might over
right."

Salazar worried about both a domestic communist underground and
a foreign communist threat. He instituted state censorship primarily
to limit the influence of communism in Portugal. In short Salazar believed that communism waged "a latent war" and represented "a foreign invasion which is ever imminent."

The anticommunist policy also contributed to the country's isolation. Before the 1974 revolution no diplomatic relations at the ambassadorial level were maintained with any communist country. Portugal did, however, have diplomatic relations with Cuba at the chargé d' affaires level. It also maintained relatively minor trade arrangements with some East European nations including the Soviet Union.

Portugal's anticommunist attitude was manifested in a firm commitment to the defense of the West. Despite economic and social isolationism and notwithstanding some West European objection to its domestic dictatorship and colonial policies, Portugal was welcomed into the Atlantic defense community and became a charter member of the North Atlantic Treaty Organization (NATO). The Portuguese have also permitted the United States to use important air and naval facilities in the Azores.

CONDUCT OF FOREIGN RELATIONS

Portuguese foreign relations have been the responsibility of the Ministry of Foreign Affairs and a professional foreign service. Before the 1974 revolution foreign relations were nominally directed by a foreign minister, but policy was clearly under the close scrutiny and overall direction of the prime minister in both the Salazar and Caetano regimes. Traditionally the foreign service has been a career service. By January 1976 Portugal had established relations with almost all foreign nations. Of its numerous senior foreign service officers with ambassadorial rank fewer than twelve were political appointees. Recruitment to the Portuguese foreign service has usually been by an examination that tests diplomatic history, international law, economics, geopolitics, and foreign languages. Consequently careers in the foreign service were usually limited to members of the upper class or at least to the university educated. A foreign service career has traditionally been considered prestigious within Portuguese society.

The overseas territories, each legally autonomous, were under the general direction of the Ministry for Overseas Provinces. The overseas minister was empowered to make policy decisions and issue decrees in situations involving more than one territory. Except in times of emergency he had first to consult with an advisory group, the Council for Overseas Territories. The Portuguese National Assembly was also empowered to pass special legislation pertaining to the overseas territories, and the metropolitan government retained the right to issue decree laws pertaining to whole territories or to some aspect of the relations between a territory and metropolitan Portugal.

A highly organized, professional administrative service, together with co-opted local native leaders, was responsible for the actual governing of each overseas province. Junior administrative officers were trained at the Higher Institute for Overseas Studies (Instituto Superior de Estudos Ultramarinos) in Lisbon. These officers filled posts in comparatively small administrative units *(concelhos)* and very underdeveloped or outlying areas *(circumscrições)*. If considered dependable and loyal, native leaders would also be paid by the Portuguese to exercise authority in their behalf. Each of the small administrative areas was headed by a Portuguese administrator who directed its internal affairs. Several such areas formed the larger district, which was headed by the district governor, a senior administrative official. The overall territory or province comprised several districts and was headed by the provincial governor. After the outbreak of the colonial wars the provinces were often placed under the command of high military officers. Responsible for both civil and military affairs, their title (when of general rank) was governor general.

POSTREVOLUTION FOREIGN POLICY

Decolonization

The 1974 revolution did not outwardly affect the conduct of Portugal's foreign relations. The organization and operation of the foreign ministry and the foreign service were not substantially altered, although the country assignments of some ambassadors were reportedly changed. Senior Portuguese diplomats were not replaced except when they appeared hostile to the revolutionary regime. Thus in July 1975, more than a year after the revolution, the Portuguese UN representative, José Veiga Simão, was dismissed after he made what were regarded as critical observations on the Portuguese government's attitude toward human rights.

Recruitment for the foreign service was liberalized after the 1974 revolution. The requirement that a candidate have advanced knowledge in the fields of law and economics was deemphasized. Furthermore women were reportedly being given greater consideration for foreign service careers.

The mechanics of Portuguese international relations may have been basically unchanged, but the future of its actual foreign policy, particularly regarding the colonies, appeared to be quite unsettled. Much of the discontent that led to the revolution was an outgrowth of dissatisfaction with the wars Portugal had been fighting to preserve the empire. Although the Portuguese government could possibly have continued to finance the colonial wars, expenditures had reached a point where they were consuming approximately 50 percent of the national budget and placing a considerable strain on the country's social services. Student unrest, particularly in Lisbon, had increased; more and more young Portuguese refused to be inducted into the army and contributed to an increase in the rate of illegal Portuguese emigration to other West European countries.

There was general agreement on the part of those involved in the revolution that these conditions could not be allowed to continue. Clearly the traditional objective of maintaining the empire had to be altered to end the colonial wars. The question was exactly how this should be accomplished, and here the consensus ended. On April 26, 1974, the revolutionary regime dismissed all governors general and civil governors in the overseas territories. Yet except for the vague recognition in the MFA program that a "solution for the wars in the overseas territories is a political one, not military," the MFA itself had provided no firm direction on which to base future colonial policy. Decolonization had become the official policy, but there was considerable disagreement over precisely what that term meant.

The main disagreement was between President António de Spínola and most of the MFA leaders. Spínola had been the first major Portuguese leader to suggest publicly that the country's overseas problems required political rather than military solutions. His plans for the overseas provinces, as stated in his influential book *Portugal and the Future*, published not long before the revolution, were relatively well developed and ambitious. He was very critical of what he considered the myth of Portugal's civilizing mission. Spínola saw three possible approaches for Portugal to take in its relations with its foreign provinces: it could simply and unconditionally abandon them; it could continue its traditional policy of repressing their independent development; or it could fundamentally modify the basis of the relationship between metropolitan Portugal and its overseas provinces. Spínola rejected the first two alternatives in favor of the third, in which he envisioned the development of a Lusitanian community (Lusitania being the classical name for Portugal) comprising metropolitan Portugal, the overseas provinces, and the former Portuguese colony of Brazil, all enjoying autonomy from the whole but all retaining specific ties to the whole for mutual benefit. Such a community of nations could have been most significant, for it could possibly have dominated the South Atlantic, eastern South America, and parts of sub-Saharan Africa. Spínola emphasized self determination, through which the native populations of the various territories would be free to decide their future relations with Portugal in referenda.

As their program indicated, the MFA leaders agreed with Spínola as to the necessity of a political solution to Portugal's overseas problems. They were not enthusiastic, however, about a Lusitanian community, and no progress was made toward implementing such a plan. Instead the MFA rather quickly decided upon complete decolonization, each overseas province to be granted total independence. Self-determination was not a consideration except for Timor. In May 1974, less than a month after the revolution, Portuguese leaders began various talks with independence leaders from Guinea-Bissau, Mozambique, and Angola. Talks with the leaders of independence movements in the other provinces followed soon thereafter. The provinces' right to independence was officially recognized in a speech by President Spínola on July 27, 1974 .

The MFA did not in fact desire a complete break with the provinces even after they had achieved their formal independence. Instead, as the Portuguese government declared, "The originality of the . . . decolonization process is to be found in the fact that it is not a withdrawal or an act of abandonment, but a progressive transfer of powers, which implies a policy of co-operation and aid, based on an exchange that will, once and for all, wash out any vestige of racism or neo-colonialism." MFA leaders envisioned some form of special, cooperative relations with the former provinces but nothing so formal or grandiose as Spínola's Lusitanian community. Still their desire for amicable postindependence relations and their willingness to support the new nations as much as their own domestic economy would allow signified that Portugal's leaders believed that much of the country's future depended upon its relations with the underdeveloped third world. The Portuguese decolonization process was symbolized by the demise of the old overseas ministry and its eventual replacement by the Ministry of Cooperation.

Guinea-Bissau

The only important independence movement in the territory of Portuguese Guinea was the African Party for the Independence of Guinea and Cape Verde (Partido Africano da Independência de Guiné e Cabo Verde—PAIGC) (see table 8). Another group, the Front for the Liberty and Independence of Portuguese Guinea (Frente para a Libertação e Independência da Guiné Português—FLING), was a weak confederation of several nationalist groups. A relatively moderate group, it never became a serious rival of the avowedly Marxist PAIGC.

On September 26, 1973, PAIGC representatives proclaimed the independence of the Republic of Guinea-Bissau. They further announced the organization of an independent government in a so-called liberated area of the territory. On the same date the Portuguese UN representative denounced the PAIGC proclamation as propaganda and stated that the independence movement operated exclusively from neighboring countries and had no hope of establishing a permanent presence within Portuguese Guinea. Within four weeks, however, approximately seventy nonaligned and communist countries, including most of the members of the Organization of African Unity (OAU), recognized the PAIGC regime. In November the UN General Assembly adopted a draft resolution welcoming the independence of Guinea-Bissau. These political successes had little effect on PAIGC's limited guerrilla war against Portuguese forces, and the fighting continued until after the April 1974 revolution.

PAIGC had been considered the best example of a unified independence group operating in the Portuguese territories. Like many of

264

Table 8. Portugal, Status of Overseas Territories, February 1976

Territory	Date Granted Independence	National Leader	Independence Parties[1]	Lesser Groups	Remarks
Guinea-Bissau	September 10, 1974	Luis Cabral	PAIGC	FLING	Early cordial relations with Portugal rapidly dissolved
Cape Verde Islands ...	July 5, 1975	Aristides Pereira	PAIGC	UDCV; UPICV	Close relations with Guinea-Bissau; future unification possible
Mozambique	June 25, 1975	Samora Machel	FRELIMO	GUMO; COREMO; FICO	Unsuccessful coup December 1975; antiwhite campaign December-January; strained relations with Portugal
São Tomé and Príncipe	July 12, 1975	Manuel Pinto da Costa	MLSTP	– –	Relatively peaceful transition to independence; amicable relations with Portugal
Angola	November 11, 1975	– –	MPLA versus FNLA and UNITA	FLEC	Latter stages of civil war, major factions originally supported by foreign powers; MPLA recognized in February 1976 by over eighty nations including Portugal; enclave of Cabinda also involved
Portuguese State of India	December 31, 1974 (retroactive to 1961)	– –	– –	– –	December 1974 agreement led to resumption of Portuguese-Indian diplomatic relations

See footnotes at end of table.

Table 8. Portugal, Status of Overseas Territories, February 1976—Continued

Territory	Date Granted Independence	National Leader	Independence Parties[1]	Lesser Groups	Remarks
Timor	— —	— —	APODETI and UDT versus FRETLIN	ASDT; ADITLA	Civil war; Indonesian invasion in support of one faction December 1975; still claimed by Portugal
Macao	— —	— —	— —	— —	Continued as Portuguese possession with PRC[2] sufferance; granted increased autonomy by Portugal January 1976

— —means not applicable.
[1] For full names of parties—see Glossary.
[2] People's Republic of China.

the other groups, however, it suffered from internal dissension. There was a dichotomy within the organization between its Cape Verde leaders and its Guinean rank and file. Adding to PAIGC's problems were several military reversals suffered after 1968, when General Spínola was placed in command of Portuguese forces in Portuguese Guinea.

Still PAIGC, led by its secretary general, Aristides Pereira, was the only organized, disciplined group in the province with which the Portuguese had to deal after proclaiming the policy of decolonization for the overseas territories. PAIGC's founder, Amilcar Cabral (assassinated in 1973) had long preached that the group's fight was with colonialism, not with the Portuguese people. This position had made Portuguese contact with the independence movement easier after the 1974 revolution. In May 1974 Mário Soares, then Portuguese foreign minister, met with Secretary General Pereira in Dakar, Senegal. Negotiations were continued, first in London and later in Algiers. A final cease-fire agreement was signed in August, and Portugal officially recognized Guinea-Bissau as an independent republic on September 10, 1974. The United States recognized Guinea-Bissau, and the new state was admitted to the UN. The Portuguese government stressed the positive nature of its postindependence relationship with Guinea-Bissau, relationship based on "the development of active cooperation, especially on economic, financial, and technical matters, on a basis of independence, mutual respect, equality and reciprocity of interests and harmonious relations between the citizens of the two republics."

Guinea-Bissau has received postindependence aid from Sweden, the Netherlands, and many of the nations that supported its guerrilla war effort, including the Sovet Union, Cuba, and Yugoslavia. Relations with Portugal were amicable for several months. The Portuguese sent more than 100 advisers to Guinea-Bissau to assist the new country as teachers, medical technicians, and communications specialists. Vasco Cabral, first ambassador to Portugal from Guinea-Bissau, noted in April 1975 that the two countries were "linked by a common ideal and a special solidarity." The Guinea-Bissau commissioner for transports and communication visited Lisbon in late spring 1975 to discuss Portuguese economic aid. Under consideration was a Portuguese loan of 200 million escudos (for value of the escudo—see Glossary) to be used in developing air and sea tranportation and fisheries. In June Pereira met with President Costa Gomes in Lisbon. They signed an agreement of cooperation and friendship regarding the economic, cultural, legal, and consular aspects of relations between Guinea-Bissau and Portugal. The positive nature of these relations was evidenced by the remarks of the PAIGC leader and Guinea-Bissau's president, Luis Cabral, both of whom were quoted in June as saying that Portugal was the number one ally of Guinea-Bissau and the Cape Verde Islands.

By March 1976, however, relations between the two countries had significantly deteriorated. At issue was Guinea-Bissau's claim to approximately 1 billion escudos in gold and hard currency reserves held by Portugal's overseas issuing bank (Banco Nacional Ultramarine—BNU). Guinea-Bissau froze all BNU assets, and Portugal retaliated by ordering the Bank of Portugal (Banco de Portugal) and the BNU to discontinue all payments to the BNU branch in Guinea-Bissau. The former colony also planned to issue its own currency in place of the escudo, issued by the BNU before independence.

Cape Verde Islands

The colonial settlement of the Cape Verde Islands involved the movement of a mixed Portuguese-African mainland population to an unpopulated area rather than the suppression of an already existing native population. This unusual historical circumstance, combined with the necessary preoccupation of eking out an existence in a difficult and drought-stricken land, may have contributed to lack of interest in independence movements in the Cape Verde Islands until after the Portuguese revolution. After the revolution, however, PAIGC (which had always considered itself representative of the Cape Verde Islands, as its name indicated) became entrenched in the islands.

PAIGC's domination of the Cape Verde Islands was opposed by two main groups: the Democratic Union of the Cape Verde Islands (União Democrática do Cabo Verde—UDCV) and the Union of the Peoples of the Cape Verde Islands (União dos Povos das Ilhas do Cabo Verde—UPICV). The major issue on which these groups opposed PAIGC was the eventual unification of the Cape Verde Islands with Guinea-Bissau, a basic PAIGC goal. Those against such unification argued that because of the Cape Verde Islands' unique history, population, and culture they should remain independent. Most organized opposition to PAIGC ended with the independence of the Cape Verde Islands from Portugal. The Portuguese government negotiated an amnesty for UDCV and UPICV members, and several of them accompanied the last Portuguese troops to be withdrawn from the islands on July 6, 1975.

From December 30, 1974, until June 30, 1975, the Portuguese shared a transitional government with PAIGC represnetatives. Members of the United Nations Decolonization Committee reported in March 1975 that the Portuguese and PAIGC representatives were cooperating and that the decolonization process, begun with the signing of an agreement on December 18, 1974, was proceeding. Further talks between the Portuguese government and PAIGC were held in May and June 1975 on economic, social, financial, and legal cooperation between the two countries.

The election for a Cape Verdean legislative assembly was held on June 30, 1975. Running virtually unopposed, PAIGC candidates received over 95 percent of the vote. The Cape Verde Islands became

268

independent on July 5, 1975, and a member of the UN shortly thereafter. The National Assembly elected Secretary General Pereira of PAIGC as first president of the Cape Verde Islands. As it did in the case of Guinea-Bissau, Portugal attempted to implement a positive postindependence relationship with the Cape Verde Islands. Before independence Portugal was planning to extend economic aid totaling 525 million escudos to the islands.

After June 30 committees of the national assemblies of Guinea-Bissau and the Cape Verde Islands formed the Council of Unity to study the future unification of the two countries. That fact, together with the close ties between political leaders in the two countries, led to considerable speculation that unification between the Cape Verde Islands and Guinea-Bissau would occur with little delay. Yet as the Cape Verde Islands' independence approached, PAICG requested that foreign governments recognize that country as separate and independent. Many nations, including the United States, did so. President Luis Cabral of Guinea-Bissau, long an advocate of unification, stated that the two nations would remain independent for an indeterminate period of time. By early January 1976 the Cape Verde Islands were still an independent member of the UN. Their future relationship with Guinea-Bissau was probably destined to be close, perhaps culminating in unification.

Mozambique

The guerrilla operations of the Front for the Liberation of Mozambique (Frente de Libertação de Moçambique—FRELIMO) were in the ascendancy in early 1974, especially in the central Tete region of the territory. For this reason Prime Minister Caetano recognized the United Group of Mozambique (Grupo Unido de Moçambique—GUMO) as the official group with which Portugal would negotiate. GUMO was a multiracial party that favored an autonomous Mozambique, but it was far more moderate and less ideological than FRELIMO.

GUMO failed to attract much popular support, and FRELIMO's other competitors were no more successful. The competitors included the Revolutionary Committee for Mozambique (Comitê Revolucionário para Moçambique—COREMO), a small Maoist guerrilla group that operated primarily from Zambia, and a white settlers organization that resisted native political aspirations. The white extremist group, the Front for Independence and Continuity with the West (Frente para Independência e Continuidade com o Occidente—FICO), advocated a Rhodesian form of political and social structure for Mozambique. In the fall of 1974 FICO participated in an ill-fated coup that was quickly put down by Portuguese forces of the transitional government.

The white separatist group offered no real alternative to native-led independence for Mozambique, and FRELIMO had rather easily neutralized its GUMO and COREMO competition. Consequently FRELI-

MO was clearly the group the Portuguese had to deal with after their decision to grant independence to their colonies. The first Portuguese-FRELIMO talks were held on May 12 and 13, 1974, and were followed by further meetings later that month and in June. The Lusaka (Zambia) talks of September 5-7, 1974, produced a formal recognition of Mozambique's right to independence and a cease-fire agreement. On September 15 a transitional or provisional government, comprising representatives of both the Portuguese government and FRELIMO, took office. The Portuguese high commissioner for Mozambique, Admiral Victor Crespo, noted FRELIMO cooperation during the decolonization process in an interview with a Lisbon newspaper in early February 1975. He also spoke optimistically about the future relations between Portugal and Mozambique after the latter's independence. The same general views were echoed later in the month by Joaquim Carvalho, a high FRELIMO official then visiting Lisbon.

Mozambique became independent on June 25, 1975, and was accepted as a member of the UN in September. There was some bitterness in the former Portuguese territory toward Western nations, particularly the United States, because of what the Mozambique government believed had been at least tacit support for Portuguese colonialism. In any event the United States did recognize Mozambique, and after protracted talks the two nations agreed to exchange representatives in 1976.

In an attempt to foster a good postindependence relationship Portugal agreed to bear Mozambique's international debts (estimated as high as US$920 million in mid-1975) until its former territory could assume part of the fiscal burden. Portugal also relinquished control over its nationalized banks and insurance companies in Mozambique to the FRELIMO government. Before Mozambique's independence the Portuguese government made public its plans to negotiate a loan of 500 million escudos for Mozambique. It also founded the Portugal-Mozambique Association to recruit the technicians needed for Mozambique's social and economic planning. Another goal of the association was the familiarization of Mozambique with Portuguese literature, drama, and music. There were early indications that the Mozambique government was receptive to the idea of an amicable postindependence relationship with Portugal. Just before his nation's independence Mozambique's president, Samora Machel, declared in a speech to FRELIMO's central committee, "We shall develop relations with Portugal. We have no complexes, no feelings of rancour or hate; quite the contrary, the people of Portugal are our allies."

Dissident elements of Mozambique's army and police forces staged an unsuccessful coup attempt in early December 1975. Later in the month reports began circulating of a government-inspired racist campaign against those whites who had remained in the country. Soldiers,

FRELIMO members, and a new security force responsible only to President Machel were all reported to be involved in the arbitrary harassment and arrest of whites and the confiscation of their property. Estimates of the number of white settlers who left Mozambique as independence approached varied. One report put the figure at about 100,000, or half the preindependence white population. By early 1976 only about 50,000 whites remained in the country.

The plight of the white Portuguese population in Mozambique was a major cause of the strained relations between the two countries that became public in mid-January 1976. The outward manifestation of the new turn in Portuguese-Mozambican relations was the suspension of regular Portuguese airline flights to Mozambique. The official reason given for the suspension was the failure of the two countries to reach an air transport accord. At least two other factors, however, were involved according to unofficial press reports. The first of these was Portuguese concern regarding the fate of while settlers still in Mozambique, particularly of those taken into custody. The second was the Mozambique government's attempt to get Portugal to recognize the Popular Movement for the Liberation of Angola (Movimento Popular de Libertação de Angola—MPLA) as the legitimate regime of that country. Despite the strained relations, however, the Portuguese government announced its intention of continuing its program of technical assistance to and cooperation with Mozambique.

That intention notwithstanding, relations between the two countries continued to deteriorate. In early February Mozambique's government decided to nationalize all privately owned houses and rental apartments. The Portuguese government declared that decision to be "an unfriendly act to Portugal" and stated that it disregarded "the spirit of the accord signed between the two countries." Portugal called for urgent, high-level talks with Mozambique to define their future relationship. In early March it dispatched a government delegation to Mozambique to investigate continuing reports of mistreatment of Portuguese there.

São Tomé and Príncipe

The independence movement in São Tomé and Príncipe, like that in the Cape Verde Islands, did not include the violence found in the movements of Portugal's other African territories. The movement, the Freedom Movement for São Tomé and Príncipe (Movimento para a Libertação de São Tomé e Príncipe—MLSTP), was formally organized well before the Portuguese revolution. Before its legalization in São Tomé and Príncipe MLSTP was based in Gabon, and its views were represented in the islands by an organization called the Civic Association. Representatives of the Portuguese government and MLSTP met in Algiers in November 1974 to negotiate decolonization, and independence was set for the summer of 1975. A five-member transitional government comprising four MLSTP members and one

Portuguese government representative was installed in December 1974. A Portuguese high commissioner oversaw the overall decolonization process.

Dissension within MLSTP became public in March 1975 when two of its four transitional government members were dismissed by party leaders. The dissidents were accused of calling for islanders to work only after independence had actually been achieved and of attempting to incite race hatred against whites in direct contravention of a long-established MLSTP multiracial policy. Secretary General Manuel Pinto da Costa of the MLSTP remained in control of the party and continued to command the support of most of the population. The Portuguese high commissioner concluded that despite a few dissidents all elements of the society were strongly united as independence approached.

São Tomé and Príncipe became independent on July 12, 1975. The islands have been recognized by the United States, and they joined the UN in September 1975. Representatives of the governments of Portugal and São Tomé and Príncipe initialed the Agreement on Cooperation and Friendship on July 12, 1975.

Angola

Portugal had only one independence movement or a least a clearly dominant one, to deal with in most of its African territories. Angola, with three separate movements, proved a perplexing exception. The three movements were the MPLA, led by Agostinho Neto and supported by the Soviet Union; the National Front for the Liberation of Angola (Frente Nacional de Libertação de Angola—FNLA), led by Holden Roberto (brother-in-law to President Mobutu Sese Seko of Zaire) and supported by Zaire, the PRC, and the United States, as well as by a dissident MPLA faction led by Daniel Chipenda; and the National Union for the Total Independence of Angola (União Nacional para a Independência Total de Angola—UNITA), led by an FNLA defector, Jonas Savimbi, and supported to some extent by the United States, the PRC, and South Africa. Cuba and South Africa sent combat units to the former Portuguese territory in support of MPLA and UNITA respectively.

The three movements fought the Portuguese for Angolan independence but also battled each other in what amounted to a civil war based as much on tribal differences and personality clashes between leaders as on differences in ideology. UNITA was militarily weak and rarely provoked clashes with the other groups. MPLA and FNLA, however, engaged in continual conflict both before and after Portugal declared its decolonization policy. The Portuguese policy on Angolan decolonization was threefold: recognition of all three independence movements, complete neutrality in dealing with those movements, and support for a postindependence national or coalition government for Angola. Charges were made by FNLA and UNITA and corrobor-

272

ated by some Western observers that Portuguese authorities in Angola favored MPLA during the period of increasing communist influence in the Portuguese government that followed the revolution. Because of clashes between Portuguese and MPLA forces in mid-July 1975, however, MPLA demanded the early withdrawal of Portuguese troops from Angola. With some exceptions on the part of highly placed Portuguese officials, Portugal's government attempted to be neutral in dealing with the three independence movements, especially after July 1975. In implementing its neutrality policy and in an attempt to eliminate foreign intervention, the Portuguese government on January 6, 1976, banned the use of the Azores as a transit point for military aid destined to any of the warring factions in Angola.

After its decision to decolonize Angola Portugal negotiated ceasefires with UNITA in June and with FNLA and MPLA in October 1974. After several unsuccessful attempts to form a common front, the three independence groups met at Mombasa, Kenya, in January 1975 and agreed to conduct negotiations concerning Angolan decolonization with Portugal later in the month. It was at this later meeting, known as the Algarve (Portugal) summit, that all parties agreed to November 11, 1975, as the date for Angola's independence. They also formally agreed to a coalition transitional government headed by a Portuguese high commissioner.

In February 1975 the transitional government was sworn in, but within days localized conflicts between MPLA and FNLA forces began again. In March delegations from the three independence groups reaffirmed the Algarve agreements but with little effect on the renewed fighting. In June UNITA forces joined in the struggle with the other groups. Despite its commitment to decolonization the Portuguese government seriously considered reinforcing its troops in Angola in an attempt to maintain order but eventually decided against such a move, at least on a large scale.

The continued fighting led to an exodus of white Portuguese settlers, which accelerated as independence approached. The refugees, eventually numbering as many as 800,000 according to some sources, became a serious drain upon Portuguese social services. In reponse to an appeal by the International Committee of the Red Cross for humanitarian assistance, in September 1975 the United States contributed US$200,000 for the relief of Angolans displaced by the factional fighting. The United States also provided two chartered civilian aircraft and crews for an indefinite period to participate in an airlift of Angolan refugees to Portugal. A new American aid program for Portugal of US$85 million was announced the next month. It included US$35 million in grant aid for the resettlement of Angolan refugees in Portugal.

Along with the social problems caused by the refugees who returned to Portugal there were implications for Portuguese politics.

There was widespread speculation, for example, that the refugees might interject a significant conservative, anticommunist element into Portuguese politics, possibly altering Portugal's decolonization policy to one sympathetic to the more Western-oriented FNLA and UNITA movements in Angola. Certainly refugees took part in Lisbon demonstrations supporting those two groups. Both FNLA and UNITA were far more sympathetic than MPLA to the postindependence position of the Portuguese settlers. During the summer and fall of 1975 there was also speculation that Portuguese Communists and other leftists might attempt to force a change in Portugal's decolonization policy in favor of MPLA, even to the point of staging a coup. Although no leftist coup was actually attempted until after Angola had achieved independence, the press reported that the Angolan issued had divided the Portuguese government. The socialist-dominated cabinet favored the long-established position of neutrality regarding the three Angolan factions. Communists in the government and some younger, more militant armed forces officers supported the recognition of MPLA. President Costa Gomes took no public stand but was reported to have proposed that an Angolan coalition of MPLA representatives and independents be recognized. Apparently enough moderates on the Armed Forces Revolutionary Council supported the Socialists, and the official policy of neutrality was continued. Neither rightist nor leftist pressures had any appreciable effect on the decolonization process, and Angola became independent on November 11, 1975, as previously agreed.

On independence day the warring factions controlled separate geographical areas in Angola, leaving the former colony with no central governmental authority to which the Portuguese could relinquish control. Consequently Portugal ceded independence to the people of Angola. FNLA and UNITA then announced that they were forming a coalition to fight the Luanda-based MPLA. They named the territory they controlled the Democratic People's Republic of Angola; MPLA called its territory the People's Republic of Angola.

The status of the small, oil-rich territory of Cabinda further complicated the Angolan situation. The three Angolan groups agreed that Cabinda was an integral part of Angola. Portugal has consistently taken the same stand. Cabinda, however, is not contiguous to Angola. It is a coastal enclave north of Angolan territory, surrounded by the People's Republic of the Congo (Congo) to its north and Zaire to its south. Zaire President Mobutu asserted that Cabinda was not part of Angola and called for self-determination for the enclave.

MPLA clashed with the Cabinda independence movement, the Front for the Liberation of the Enclave of Cabinda (Frente para a Libertação do Enclavo de Cabinda—FLEC), in November and December 1975. FLEC, headed by Henriques Tiago Nzita, was militarily weak and ineffectual. It first proclaimed Cabinda independent in August 1975 but was unable to follow its declaration with any decisive action. MPLA maintained its control over Cabinda into 1976.

Portugal continued its policy of condemning all foreign intervention in Angola through January 1976. On January 6 it banned the use of the Azores as a transfer point for men and supplies destined for Angola. Despite the ban Cuba was reported to have continued using the Azores for several days while supporting MPLA forces.

In January 1976 the OAU met in Addis Ababa for the purpose of finding a solution to the Angolan situation and ending the strife there. The OAU had unsuccessfully attempted to mediate a settlement between the factions on numerous occasions during the period of Angolan decolonization. The Addis Ababa meeting also came to naught as a stalemate developed among the OAU member states, an equal number supporting two conflicting resolutions. The first resolution, introduced by Senegal, called for a coalition government of national unity; the second, by Nigeria, called for official recognition of MPLA. According to the OAU secretary general, William Eteki Mboumoua, all of Portugal's former African territories (Cape Verde, Guinea-Bissau, Mozambique, and São Tomé and Príncipe) had recognized the MPLA regime as Angola's legitimate government before the January OAU meeting. In mid-February, after a number of MPLA victories over FNLA and UNITA forces, the OAU recognized the Soviet-backed faction as Angola's official government.

In the actual Angolan fighting MPLA, with Cuban troop support, emerged as the dominant military power in Angola. Conventional armed clashes appeared to be near an end by early February, but FNLA and UNITA pledged to continue waging guerrilla warfare against MPLA. By the end of the month more than eighty nations had recognized the MPLA as the legitimate Angolan government. Families of the Cuban soldiers who had fought for MPLA were reported to be joining their husbands in Angola. Unofficial estimates predicted that the Cuban community in Angola, primarily members of Cuba's mulatto population, would eventually number as many as 40,000 people.

The Portuguese government officially recognized MPLA on February 22. Its decision followed an extraordinary all-night cabinet meeting in which the socialist and communist parties joined in support of the move. Portugal's second largest party, the Popular Democratic Party (Partido Popular Democrático—PPD), remained adamant against MPLA recognition, as did the large number of Angolan refugees. Critics felt that recognition should have been left to the National Assembly, for which elections were to be held on April 25. Opponents of the government's policy noted the deteriorating relations that followed recognition of the leftist regime in Mozambique and the harassment of Portuguese still living there. Government supporters countered that Portuguese interests in Angola could best be protected by Lisbon's recognition of the ruling faction there. The presidential recognition statement continued the Portuguese postcolonial policy of attempting to establish positive relations with its former overseas territories. It called for friendly relations "based on noninterference, equality and mutual respect" between the two countries.

Portuguese State of India

India's invasion of the Portuguese State of India territories (Goa, Damão, Diu, Dadra, and Nagar-Aveli) and Prime Minister Salazar's refusal to recognize their loss caused a break in Portuguese-Indian relations that lasted from 1961 to 1975. The postrevolution Portuguese government, in an attempt to mend diplomatic fences and in recognition of the reality of the Indian state situation, decided to alter the Salazar-Caetano stand on the issue.

In September 1974 Portugal and India signed an agreement in which Portugal agreed to relinquish all claims to the territories involved in the dispute. On December 31, 1974, the Portuguese foreign minister, Soares, signed a treaty in New Delhi. The treaty stipulated Portuguese recognition of Indian sovereignty over the Indian state territories from the dates of their incorporation into India according to that nation's constitution. It also provided for the immediate resumption of diplomatic relations between Portugal and India.

Timor

Independence movements did not begin to organize in Timor until after the Portuguese revolution. The new Portuguese government did, however, affirm its intention of applying the decolonization process to Timor as soon as the wishes of the Timorese people could be determined.

Three major Timorese political groups developed in the months after the Portuguese revolution. These were the Timorese Democratic Union (União Democrática Timorense—UDT), the Revolutionary Front for an Independent East Timor (Frente Revolucionária para Timor do Leste Independente—FRETLIN), and the Timorese People's Democratic Association (Associação Popular Democrática Timorense—APODETI). UDT, primarily representing commercial interests, began as a moderate group that sought the institution of a Western-style government and the retention of some ties with Portugal. FRETLIN was leftist and wanted a totally independent Timor. APODETI advocated that East Timor become an autonomous Indonesian province. Two minor parties were also formed. These were the Timorese Social Democratic Association (Associação Social Democrática Timorense—ASDT), which wanted total Timorese independence but only after a transition period of a few years in which to prepare the Timorese people, and a pro-Australian party, the Democratic Association for the Integration of Eastern Timor in Australia (Associação Democrática para a Integração do Timor do Leste na Austrália —ADITLA).

276

In October 1974 Portuguese representatives visited Jakarta to discuss the future of Portuguese Timor with the Indonesians. A Portuguese spokesman announced his government's belief that total independence for Timor was unrealistic because a majority of the people wished to retain some ties with Portugal. He also stated that further decolonization measures would be based on the results of a Timorese referendum to be held in March 1975, but the referendum was later canceled.

In June 1975 delegations from two of the three major Timorese groups met with Portuguese government representatives to discuss decolonization and the eventual establishment of self-rule on Timor. FRETLIN boycotted the talks because of APODETI's participation. Portugal and the two other Timorese parties agreed on decolonization as an eventual goal. They further agreed that elections would be held in October 1976 for a people's assembly that would formulate political and administrative statutes for the territory. A transitional Portuguese-controlled government was to be installed that would last until October 1978.

Two months later, in August 1975, UDT unsuccessfully attempted to gain complete power in Timor, and a civil war followed. There were reports that the Portuguese governor of Timor had used UDT in his personal struggle with leftist officers recently arrived from Portugal who were training and encouraging FRETLIN. In any event what may have been an unplanned coup attempt by UDT was quickly followed by a more successful countercoup by FRETLIN. FRETLIN troops pushed APODETI and UDT forces to the border of West (Indonesian) Timor during the rest of August and September. The Portuguese governor and most other administrators withdrew from Timor during the hostilities. In late August a special Portuguese envoy visited Indonesia and Australia in an unsuccessful attempt to end the Timorese crisis, but no agreement could be reached among the three governments.

By late October UDT had joined APODETI, and with considerable Indonesian aid the two groups began to push FRETLIN forces back toward the East Timor capital of Dili. On November 28, while its forces were in general retreat, FRETLIN unilaterally declared East Timorese independence. One day later the pro-Indonesian movements responded by declaring East Timor part of Indonesia. Indonesia initially rejected the claims of both FRETLIN and APODETI forces and declared that East Timor still belonged to Portugal. Portugal made no immediate statement but requested the assistance of the UN in negotiating a peace settlement on the island.

The already unsettled Timorese situation was drastically altered on December 7 when Indonesian forces invaded East Timor and captured Dili from FRETLIN troops. Reports that Indonesia might be considering invading East Timor had begun to circulate at least as early as February 1975. Indonesia was known to be concerned about the proximity of an unstable or, even worse, a communist regime to its eastern islands, an area that frequently chafed under the Javanese domination of the Indonesian nation. Indonesia apparently also questioned whether the FRETLIN group truly represented East Timor's population and pointed to some 40,000 refugees who had fled to West Timor after FRETLIN's takeover of the East Timorese government.

After the invasion Foreign Minister Adam Malik of Indonesia stated that his country's troops had been committed to the Timorese fighting in response to requests from APODETI leaders for assistance in ending the bloodshed. He also stated that Indonesian troops would remain in East Timor only as long as it took to determine the real desires of the Timorese people regarding their territory's future. In a second announcement, on December 8, Malik stated that the pro-Indonesian Timorese groups had established a provisional government in Dili. FRETLIN forces were reported to have retreated to the mountains south of Dili, where they planned to wage a guerrilla campaign.

Portugal responded to the Indonesian invasion by immediately breaking relations with that country, relations that had previously been broken in 1964 and reestablished only after the 1974 revolution. In a communiqué issued after an emergency cabinet meeting on December 7 the Portuguese government stressed that it still considered Portugal the administrative power in East Timor; the Indonesian invasion, it said, "brutally altered the process of decolonization." On December 8 Portugal requested an urgent UN Security Council meeting to consider the Timorese situation.

The colonial committee of the UN General Assembly voted on December 11 to demand that Indonesia withdraw all of its military forces from Portuguese Timor and desist from "further violation of the territorial integrity" of the former colony. In an unrelated incident Ocussi Ambeno, a small Portuguese enclave on the northern coast of West Timor, was incorporated into Indonesia on December 13. The enclave had not been involved in the fighting in East Timor.

On December 22 the Security Council unanimously approved a resolution that called on Indonesia to withdraw its military forces from Portuguese Timor. The resolution also called for those measures necessary to ensure self-determination for the people of the former Portuguese colony. The Indonesians and the Timorese parties they supported continued to engage FRETLIN forces into early January 1976. FRETLIN lost all of the larger towns it had held before the Indonesian invasion. UN Secretary General Kurt Waldheim was reported to be attempting to arrange an inspection tour of Portuguese Timor in conformance with the December Security Council resolution, but plans for such a trip had not been completed by mid-January.

As it had done for the State of India territories, the postrevolution Portuguese government attempted to modify the situation involving Macao in the light of diplomatic reality. The Macao territory, comprising a small peninsula and two islands, had long existed under Portuguese rule only at the sufferance of the PRC. There had been no direct diplomatic contact between Portugal and the PRC for several years before the Portuguese revolution, and as late as 1972 the Peking government had claimed sovereignty over the Macao territory.

The press reported that the revolutionary government decided to cede Macao to the PRC. It formally recognized the PRC in January 1975 and a month later broke relations with the Republic of China (Nationalist China). The response of the PRC could not have been what the Portuguese expected. Not only did the PRC ignore the Portuguese revolution, but it apparently ignored the reported overtures about a change in Macao's sovereignty. Furthermore the Peking regime failed to reciprocate Portuguese recognition.

The Portuguese government had gone on record as early as October 1974 as being willing to negotiate on Macao whenever the PRC wished to pursue the matter. A Portuguese government spokesman admitted, however, that Peking had not shown any interest in changing the status of the enclave. There were reports that the PRC, unofficially through the chairman of the Macao Chamber of Commerce, had indicated satisfaction and even a preference for maintaining the status quo.

Peking's position was based on both political and economic considerations. The Portuguese allowed a considerable gambling operation to flourish in Macao. That operation was controlled by Chinese interests and provided the PRC with a rare source of foreign capital. Furthermore Communist Chinese leaders may have been worried that a change in Macao's status might adversely affect the PRC relationship with the British colony of Hong Kong. Hong Kong had long been the PRC's major access point to the Western world, though its importance in this regard may have diminished in the face of continuing direct contact between the PRC and the United States.

In early January 1976 the Portuguese government ended eight months of consultation with Macao officials and approved a new statute for the territory that greatly increased its autonomy. The statute provided that Macao be administered by a governor appointed directly by the Portuguese president rather than by the Ministry for Overseas Provinces, as had previously been the case. The governor would be assisted by a cabinet and a seventeen member legislative assembly (six delegates directly elected, six elected by Macao interest groups, and five appointed by the governor). The assembly would be empowered to formulate laws for the territory. Furthermore Macao would be able to contract for its own foreign loans, appoint its civil service, and control its security force. To a considerable extent, however, the new statute simply formalized many rights Macao had long possessed in practice. Macao's autonomy had been greater than that of other Portuguese territories because of its distance from Lisbon, its relative unimportance, and Chinese influence in its affairs.

East European Relations

With the end of the Caetano regime the basic Portuguese foreign policy tenet of almost automatic and universal opposition to communism became obsolete. If there was early postrevolution confusion about how to change Portugal's colonial policy, there was none about pursuing a new foreign policy toward communist states. The most obvious diplomatic manifestation of Portugal's new policy was the rapid extension of official relations to a number of communist nations. Portugal maintained its relations with Cuba and on June 3, 1974, established diplomatic relations with Romania. Within the next four weeks diplomatic relations were also established with the Soviet Union, Yugoslavia, Hungary, Czechoslovakia, the German Democratic Republic (East Germany), and Bulgaria.

The opening of diplomatic relations was followed by substantive negotiations between Portugal and a number of East European states. The results of these negotiations indicated that Portugal was implementing a policy that emphasized trade and economic cooperation. Notwithstanding the obvious political implications of these expanded relations, Portugal appeared to be utilizing its international relations, or the trade and economic value derived therefrom, to aid its ailing domestic economy.

A five-year pact between Portugal and Hungary was signed on January 23, 1975. The intent of the agreement was to increase trade and to develop economic, industrial, and technical cooperation. Under the agreement Portugal expected to export to Hungary such goods as agricultural produce, canned fish, timber, cork, metal ores, chemicals, and raw textile materials. The same kinds of exports were expected to figure in a similar trade and economic agreement signed with East Germany on January 25. Still other agreements included a long-term trade pact with Czechoslovakia to increase the level of exchange between the two countries, a similar agreement with Bulgaria, a trade and tourist agreement with Yugoslavia, and a trade agreement with Poland that concentrated on the development of mutual interests in engineering and industrial chemicals, sea transportation and fisheries and, especially, shipbuilding.

The minister of industry, João Cravinho, visited Poland in June and concluded a ship construction contract that was expected to provide considerable work for Portuguese shipyards—a depressed sector of the Portuguese economy—until 1978. An East German trade delegation also visited Portugal later in the month. That visit ended with East Germany's agreement to purchase significant amounts of wine and to use Portuguese shipyards for the repair of a number of its vessels.

Also in June 1975 President Costa Gomes visited Romania, repaying the earlier visit of President Nicolae Ceausescu, the first national leader to pay a state visit to Portugal after its revolution. Costa Gomes was warmly welcomed by the Romanian government. Substantive agreements stemming from his visit provided for projects to increase tourism between the two countries and to establish mixed associations to study further economic cooperation, particularly in industrial chemical production, livestock management, and agriculture. Portugal expected Romanian assistance in organizing agricultural cooperatives. There was also discussion regarding future coordination of Portuguese and Romanian scientific and technical research.

Soviet-Portuguese diplomatic relations, resumed after the April revolution, were amicable through mid-1975. It was during this period that the influence of the Portuguese Communist Party (Partido Comunista Português—PCP) was increasing in the Portuguese government, the military, and the trade unions (see ch. 9). Soares, the leader of the Portuguese Socialist Party (Partido Socialista Português—PSP), visited Moscow while still foreign minister. So, too, did PCP leader Alvara Cunhal in November 1974, when he was a minister without portfolio. The Soviet Union appeared to be cognizant of Western fears regarding its relationship with Portugal, and perhaps for this reason its leaders reportedly received these early visits with some restraint.

During the early months of 1975 Portugal and the Soviet Union initiated a number of cultural and tourist exchanges. In early March the Soviet national airline, Aeroflot, began flights between Moscow, Lisbon, and Havana. Heavily subsidized package tours for Portuguese tourists going to either communist capital were included in the Aeroflot service. By the spring of 1975, less than a year after the formal establishment of relations, the Soviets increased the size of their Lisbon embassy staff to well over 100, roughly equivalent to the size of the United States mission. As good relations continued and the fortunes of the Portuguese Communists apparently were in the ascendancy, the Soviet Union enthusiastically welcomed the visit of the Portuguese labor minister, José da Costa Martins, in late March 1975. Martins returned to Lisbon with word that the Soviet Union and the Warsaw Pact countries offered a sizable amount of economic aid to Portugal, primarily in the form of generous credit terms and other advantageous trade agreements. The Portuguese had already concluded an agreement to purchase 1 million tons of Soviet crude oil. The two countries had also agreed on the establishment of a Soviet trade mission as an integral part of the Soviet mission in Lisbon.

A major Soviet goal in maintaining cordial relations with Portugal was the Portuguese concession of maritime refueling facilities on the island of Madeira. An informal request for such rights was confirmed by the Portuguese Ministry of Information in March 1975. The Soviet Union's request for port facilities caused considerable concern within NATO circles, particularly because it occurred at a time when the power of the Portuguese Communists seemed to be increasing. The Portuguese, however, never granted the Soviet request. Portugal's April 1975 elections demonstrated little mass support for the communist party. At the end of August the procommunist prime minister, Vasco dos Santos Gonçalves, was forced from office as the moderate-centralist shift in Portuguese politics and in the ruling regime began (see ch.9).

The moderate shift in Portuguese politics was apparently accompanied by a concomitant cooling in Soviet-Portuguese relations, at least on the part of the Soviet Union. In late September 1975 President Costa Gomes visited Moscow. Despite Soviet praise for the Portuguese revolution the atmosphere was reported as reserved, perhaps even somewhat strained. More significant was the apparent lack of substance in the agreements signed between the two nations. These included a declaration of principles that was primarily a reaffirmation of the European security conference agreements signed in Helsinki in the late summer. There were also commercial, scientific, and cultural exchange accords. These agreements, however, reportedly only confirmed that such ties between the two countries existed and broke no new ground.

The cooling in Portuguese-Soviet relations, if indeed it did occur, did not indicate a renewed anticommunist outlook by the Lisbon government. On the contrary Portugal still pursued positive, cooperative relations with East European states. In late October 1975 President Ceausescu of Romania again visited Lisbon. It was reported that the Portuguese government was particularly interested in Ceausescu's interceding with Soviet and perhaps PRC leaders to end the Angolan conflict. Two months later, in December, Portugal and Romania concluded the latest in a series of trade agreements. The new pact was valued at 500 million escudos.

Though the shift in the Portuguese attitude toward communism and relations with communist states was a major innovation, it was not a total reversal of earlier policy. That is, although the Portuguese government negated the anticommunist foreign policy of its predecessors, it did not subsequently invoke a procommunist, anti-Western foreign policy. Rather than favor one international bloc over the other the Portuguese desired positive, cooperative relations, particularly in the economic sphere, with the nations of both. In fact the new Portuguese leaders apparently visualized an intermediary role for Portugal to play among nations. During a June 1975 visit to France Presi-

dent Costa Gomes declared that Portugal was concerned with superpowers and blocs "to the extent that we may serve as a link, a point
of encounter, a buffer to reduce tensions, a multilateral friend always
ready to collaborate in the tasks of peace and concord in building a
better, juster world." Portugal's Ministry of Mass Communication
also noted the view of Portuguese leaders that "our country would
like to serve as a kind of bridge between the industrialized powers
and the Third World."

RELATIONS WITH SELECTED COUNTRIES

Brazil

Portugal's closest international relationship has been with Brazil, a
former Portuguese colony that proclaimed its independence in 1822.
Economic, cultural, linguistic, and religious ties between the two
countries have been so strong as to form the basis of the so-called
Luso-Brazilian Community, a relationship far exceeding the so-called
special relationship that exists between other friendly nations (see ch.
2). Portuguese documents have traditionally referred to Brazil as a
sister nation. The Luso-Brazilian Community has also included novel
political ties. Existing agreements between the two countries have
provided for annual joint consultations between their foreign ministers. Brazilians living in Portugal have been granted Portuguese citizenship status. The status has included, after five years' residence,
the right to vote in local Portuguese elections and to hold local Portuguese political office. A reciprocal agreement has entitled Portuguese citizens living in Brazil to similar political rights there.

In 1966 Portugal and Brazil concluded agreements that provided for
joint financial and technical cooperation. Private enterprise was to initiate the activities with the active encouragement of both governments. The Luso-Brazilian Center for Economic Cooperation was
established in 1969. Two of the larger Portuguese and Brazilian banks
later merged. Brazilians have also invested in the Portuguese tourist
industry and in Portuguese real estate. The strengthening of the Luso-
Brazilian Community and of economic and other cooperative ties
between the two nations was known to have been a particular goal of
Prime Minister Caetano's foreign policy after he replaced Salazar.

Brazil was the major source of colonial riches for Portugal, and
even after its independence trade with the former colony continued to
be of considerable importance to the Portuguese economy. Brazil has
traditionally been considered a land of opportunity by the Portuguese,
and it was consequently the major destination of Portuguese emigration until the 1960s, when it was replaced by Western Europe. Because of political and social turmoil and worsening economic conditions, Portuguese emigration to Brazil again increased after the April
1974 revolution.

The exact nature and extent of Brazilian involvement in the Portuguese revolution had not become clear by early 1976. Some reports, however, indicated that before the revolution the Brazilian ambassador in Lisbon exchanged intelligence information with Caetano's secret police. Other observers had noted the strange movements of General Spínola's principal aide-de-camp between the Brazilian embassy, Portuguese army headquarters, and the Portuguese prime minister's office just before the revolution. Whether or not it was actually involved in the revoluation, Brazil has long been motivated by a desire to expand its influence generally throughout the South Atlantic area and more specifically to derive economic benefits from relations with nations in southern Africa. Such goals might well have been attained within the framework of the Luso-Brazilian Community, especially if Portugal had retained strong ties with the Portuguese African territories. Both Caetano and his successor, Spínola, envisioned the maintenance of such ties, albeit in different forms.

The Brazilians have appeared to view postrevolution Portugal and the removal of Spínola from the Portuguese political scene with caution and perhaps some perturbation. Both Spínola and Caetano were granted political asylum in Brazil. The Brazilian government prohibited any political activity by Caetano, but it allowed his book, *Depoimento* (Deposition), to be published. In the book he defended his regime and warned of the increasing communist influence in the Portuguese government.

The staunchly anticommunist Brazilian government did not censor reports about the rise of the PCP. A number of Brazilian newspapers began to specialize in Portuguese news after the revolution, and Portuguese emigrants in Brazil were reported to be avidly following developments. The Brazilian government, however, threatened to deport any Portuguese citizen who became directly involved in Portuguese politics.

A serious misunderstanding arose between Portugal and Brazil in the spring of 1975 over Portugal's nationalization of banks. Along with the nationalization plan the Bank of Portugal announced in April that it would place so called delegates in Portuguese branches of foreign-owned banks. The Brazilian foreign minister informed the Portuguese ambassador that Brazil would sever diplomatic relations if there were any intervention in the Lisbon branch of the Bank of Brazil. The Portuguese government subsequently responded that its delegate scheme constituted not intervention but merely some degree of control over normal banking operations. It also noted that the Brazilian government used a similar procedure. Brazil thereupon accepted the Portuguese explanation, and further crisis was averted. Such misunderstandings and Brazilian apprehension over the Portuguese situation notwithstanding, no move within either government to alter, much less to interrupt, the special Luso-Brazilian relationship had become evident by early 1976.

Spain

Spain, like Brazil, has traditionally been referred to as a sister nation by the Portuguese. At the same time, the Spanish dynastic union with Portugal (1580-1640) and the numerous wars between the two countries have contributed to lasting suspicions on the part of many Portuguese, suspicions that varied from fears for Portugal's independence to more restrained views of Spain as simply an overshadowing big brother. Spanish economic investment in Portugal in recent years has helped keep fears of undue Spanish influence over Portugal alive.

A major aim of the foreign policies of both Salazar and Caetano was Iberian solidarity. The governments of both men consequently attempted to establish closer relations with Spain despite the fears or suspicions of some Portuguese. The attempt to foster better Portuguese-Spanish relations began with, and to a considerable extent was based on, the close personal friendship of Salazar and the Spanish head of state, Francisco Franco. The two men shared many simular views, and both felt the need to oppose communism. In 1939 they concluded the Iberian Pact, a treaty of friendship and nonaggression that served for many years as a major basis for the foreign policies of both countries. Salazar's successor, Caetano, also had numerous personal and political friends in Spain. Under his regime Portugal and Spain concluded a number of cooperative agreements. One of these, for example, dealt with cooperative development of the Iberian fishing industry.

A strain in Portuguese-Spanish relations developed over Spain's refusal to support Portugal's colonial policy. This refusal has been attributed in part to Spain's desire to court third world opinion in support of its claim to Gibraltar. The end of the Caetano regime and the postrevolution decolonization policy of Portugal removed the colonial issue as a stumbling block in the way of Portuguese-Spanish relations.

Relations between the two countries after the revolution were dormant but not officially suspended. The Spanish government was hesitant to pursue relations with Portugal until it became clear which faction would emerge to dominate the political system. Spain was all the more cautious and disturbed during the period because it appeared that the most powerful faction in Portugal might turn out to be the Communists. In the fall of 1975 Franco died, and his successor, King Juan Carlos I, has been more concerned with consolidating his power and preserving authority and stability in Spain than with foreign relations. Both countries continued to concentrate on internal affairs into January 1976.

Although Iberian relations may have been temporarily placed in the background, neither country appeared to desire any upset in their relationship. In the spring of 1975 the Portuguese accused two extreme rightist groups, the Portuguese Liberation Army (Exército de Libertação Português—ELP) and the Democratic Movement for the Liberation of Portugal (Movimento Democrático para a Libertação de Portugal—MDLP), of making armed attacks in northern Portugal. The Portuguese government also charged that the groups operated from Spain and made subversive radiobroadcasts from that country. At the same time, however, Portugal did not accuse Spain of any complicity or responsibility in the affair. The Spanish government in turn has declined to become involved in postrevolution Portuguese politics. When the former Portuguese president Spínola attempted to visit Spain in January 1976, he was promptly expelled. Press reports have linked Spínola with the MDLP. Clearly future Portuguese-Spanish relations will depend to a considerable extent on the restoration of internal stability in both countries.

On February 12, 1976, the Portuguese and Spanish foreign ministers met in Guarda, Portugal, to discuss future relations. It was reported that common problems were discussed, including the opposition and activities of extremist groups in both countries. The Portuguese secretary of state for foreign affairs, José Medeiros Ferreira, noted that bilaterial relations were becoming quite positive after a period of rising tension that had culminated in the sacking of the Spanish embassy in Lisbon after Spain's execution of Basque nationalists in the fall of 1975. He stated that Portugal's goal in its future relations with Spain was to create an "area of stability" in the Iberian Peninsula based on mutual noninterference in each other's internal affairs.

Great Britain

In 1373 Portugal and England signed a treaty of alliance. That treaty, reinforced and updated by further treaties, has remained in force for more than 600 years, making the resulting alliance the longest in the history of Western nations (see ch. 2). The long-term impact of the Anglo-Portuguese economic relationship, an outgrowth of the original military alliance, was still evident in the early 1970s, when most of the foreign companies conducting business in Portugal were British owned. The British have invested in several sectors of the Portuguese economy, including wine, transportation and, until nationalized by the Caetano regime, the Lisbon telephone system.

During the first half of the twentieth century the Anglo-Portuguese relationship continued with little interruption. The British, however, became increasingly intolerant of Portuguese colonial policy. British disapproval of the Salazar dictatorship also grew. That disapproval was particularly evident during periods of British Labour Party government.

The most serious strain in Anglo-Portuguese relations occurred during the Indian seizure of Portugal's Indian state territories in 1961. One the basis of the traditional alliance Portugal immediately requested the use of British airbases so that Portuguese reinforcements could be sent to Goa and the other enclaves. The British failed to answer the Portuguese request until the swift campaign waged by India made plans for further Portuguese action academic. Salazar reportedly never forgave the British for their refusal to honor promptly their traditional agreements with Portugal.

Anglo-Portuguese relations were again strained in 1964 when Southern Rhodesia unilaterally declared independence from Great Britain. Increasingly under attack for its colonial policies by black African nations, Portugal was sympathetic to the white Southern Rhodesian regime. Furthermore the Mozambique port of Beira profited economically as a major shipping point for Southern Rhodesian imports and exports. Although Salazar reportedly attempted to intercede personally with Ian Smith, the Southern Rhodesian leader, to encourage a settlement with Great Britain, the Portuguese refused to participate in the economic and trade sanctions requested by the British. Ill feeling between Portugal and Great Britain was heightened when the British implemented a naval blockade of Beira to prevent petroleum shipments to Southern Rhodesia.

Since 1964 Anglo-Portuguese relations have encountered few new problems. British displeasure with the Portuguese dictatorship as a form of government continued, as did differences over British sanctions against Southern Rhodesia. Nevertheless a considerable amount of trade was carried on between the two countries. That trade, however, and mutual cooperation within the framework of NATO were about the only areas left in which Great Britain and Portugal still had significant contact. The passage of time, the disintegration of their overseas empires, and the reduction of their strategic responsibilities have made the Anglo-Portuguese relationship less important than it once was.

France

During the 1960s the French significantly increased their investment in and trade with Portugal. It was during this period that Portugal shifted its attention from Great Britain toward France, as France appeared to offer more potential for assisting the Portuguese in improving their relations with Western Europe. France was also more sympathetic than the British to Portugal's colonial problems.

Since the 1974 Portuguese revolution France, like most other West European nations, has adopted a cautious, wait-and-see attitude toward the Portuguese turmoil. In June 1975 President Costa Gomes paid a state visit to France and attempted to convince the French that stability based on liberal, democratic principles would be maintained in Portugal. He also reaffirmed his nation's intention of remaining in the Atlantic alliance. Although the French president, Valéry Giscard d'Estaing, welcomed Costa Gomes' assurances, the press reported that he was not fully convinced. Skeptical about the future course of Portuguese politics, he reportedly warned Costa Gomes that a violent swing to the left by Portugal would rule out French aid.

Costa Gomes requested French assistance in obtaining advantageous arrangements with the European Economic Community (EEC, also called the Common Market) to increase Portuguese exports and improve Portuguese chances of acquiring community loans. He also desired French help in securing improved social security arrangements for Portuguese emigrant workers in EEC countries. The French were reported to be noncommittal in responding to the Portuguese requests. Because of the high level of French unemployment, they refused to remove their eleven-month ban on the immigration of foreign workers to France. France's reluctance to be more helpful was in part due to the Portuguese situation's having become an issue in domestic French politics. There was considerable disagreement among French leftists (particularly between the French socialist and communist parties) as to which Portuguese parties deserved their assistance. The Portuguese shift toward more moderate politics that followed the unsuccessful leftist coup in November 1975 had not visibly affected Franco-Portuguese relations by the end of January 1976, but closer relations between the two countries were a likely result (see ch. 9).

United States

Toward the end of World War I the United States was permitted to share the use of a naval base at Ponta Delgada in the Azores with the British. During World War II the Portuguese, again at the behest of the British, granted the United States the right to use air and naval bases in the Azores. Military and defense matters have been at the center of American-Portuguese relations since the war, relations that included aid for Portugal through the European Recovery Program (Marshall Plan) during the late 1940s and early 1950s and subsequent military grants and economic assistance under the United States mutual security program. The security accords between the two countries have been in the form of both treaties and executive agreements.

American-Portuguese relations became severely strained during the John F. Kennedy administration when the United States took an anticolonial stand that prohibited the use in Portuguese African Territories of military supplies given to Portugal within the framework of NATO. In response Portugual refused to renew the Azores bases agreement with the United States that had expired in 1962, though the

American navy and air force continued to use the facilities on an informal basis. In response to a shift in American policy during the Richard M. Nixon administration, which provided for specialized training of Portuguese military personnel, Prime Minister Caetano renewed the Azores bases agreement in the fall of 1971. The American arms embargo, however, continued in effect, with minor modifications, until the African territories achieved independence in 1974 and 1975.

American intelligence officials testified publicly before the House of Representatives Select Committee on Intelligence in October 1975 that the United States had no preknowledge of the April 1974 Portuguese revolution. After the revolution the United States generally favored the extension of aid to Portugal except when communist influence within the Portuguese government seemed to be in the ascendancy. American policy thus varied to some extent with the vagaries of internal Portuguese politics.

The United States did not seem especially perturbed by the Portuguese revolution when it occurred nor by the Armed Forces Movement (Movimento das Forças Armadas—MFA) program. The program was rather vague and not inherently damaging to American interests, and General Spínola, correctly perceived to be pro-Western, had quickly risen to the forefront of the postrevolution MFA regime. American-Portuguese relations remained amicable. The United States was among the first to recognize the new government, and the American ambassador in Lisbon was the first foreign envoy to call on the new president. When the first postrevolution cabinet was formed in May 1974, the United States appeared little concerned that it included members of the PCP. On May 14, the same day Prime Minister Adelino Palma Carlos' cabinet was sworn in, the United States and Portugal concluded a pact on the peaceful uses of nuclear energy under which Portugal was to receive nuclear fuel for power plants.

On June 12 President Nixon, en route to the Middle East, met with President Spínola at the American air base in the Azores. Public accounts of Nixon's remarks indicated that he was quite supportive of the Portuguese revolution and offered American assistance in general terms. Despite press reports of increasing American concern over the ascendancy of communism in Portugal during the fall, the State Department officials announced in December a new aid program for Portugal as "a positive demonstration of United States support and confidence in Portugal's future." The aid program included guaranteed loans totaling US$20 million for low-cost housing and US$15 million in loans and technical assistance grants. The announcement also noted that the Export-Import Bank would give sympathetic consideration to financing American exports to Portugal. Finally Department of State officials stated they would support a proposed amendment to the congressional foreign aid bill that would give Portugal another US$50 million.

An ill-fated right-wing coup was attempted on March 11, 1975. The immediate result was the flight from the country of Spínola, who had been living in retirement since his resignation from the presidency the previous September. The attempted coup increased the visibility and activity of numerous left-wing groups. The PCP's influence within the government also increased.

Department of State officials testifying before the House of Representatives Subcommittee on International Political and Military Affairs on March 14, three days after the coup attempt, presented a generally moderate, constructive view of the Portuguese situation. One of the officials reemphasized United States "support of Portugal's own stated policy of transition to democratic processes of government. We have also made that position consistently and firmly clear in all our contacts with the present Portuguese leadership and we will continue to do so." The same official saw congressionally appropriated economic assistance to Portugal as a further demonstration of American support. That assistance had amounted by March to US$25 million (US$10 million of which had been appropriated under a resolution that expired in February) to be spent on feasibility studies, technical assistance, low-cost housing loans, and assistance to the Portuguese African territories (primarily the Cape Verde Islands), in addition to the US$20 million in low-cost housing investment guarantees announced the previous December.

United States concern over communist influence within the Portuguese regime was reflected, however, in the remarks of Secretary of State Henry Kissinger later in March. In a press conference with West European correspondents in April Secretary Kissinger reiterated his concern over communist influence within Portugal and the possibility that Portugal's government might become fully communist.

The Portuguese election for the Constituent Assembly empowered to write a new constitution was held on April 25, 1975, one year after the revolution. It resulted in a victory for the moderate democratic socialist parties, the PCP receiving only 12.5 percent of the vote (see ch. 9). The United States deputy assistant secretary of state for European affairs, L. Bruce Laingen, in testimony before the House of Representatives Subcommittee on International Political and Military Affairs on May 1, was cautiously optimistic about the election results, though he correctly noted that "their practical impact in the short term . . . has been limited by the prior action of the Armed Forces Movement in laying down the essential outlines of the constitution."

Despite the election results, which he recognized as hopeful, President Ford was concerned over continuing communist influence within Portugal and that nation's relationship with NATO. In an interview with several West European correspondents on May 23, the president raised the question of Portugal's continued membership in NATO when he stated:

290

> I am concerned about the Communist element and its influence in Portugal and therefore Portugal's relationship with NATO. . . . I don't see how you can have a Communist element significant in an organization that was put together and formed for the purpose of meeting a challenge by Communist elements from the East.

By the end of the summer the communist surge of power had apparently run its course. Much of the communist influence in Portuguese labor unions had been lost to the Socialists and to a lesser extent to parties of the far left. Anticommunist demonstrations were increasingly held, especially in northern Portugal. Perhaps most significant, the procommunist prime minister, Gonçalves, was forced from office in August (see ch. 9)

Secretary Kissinger was cautiously optimistic about the new trend in Portuguese politics after August 1975. In a September 9 press conference he stated, "We cannot yet fully assess what is taking place within the military movement. But, on the whole, we believe that the events of the last two weeks have been encouraging." A moderate Portuguese government was subsequently formed with party representation based on the results of the April election. Although the left was by no means routed, the moderate political parties seemed to be slowly and carefully consolidating power. On October 10 the United States Department of State announced a US$85 million emergency economic assistance program for Portugal including US$35 million for resettling Angolan refugees. Secretary Kissinger described the program as a first step in "United States support for the political evolution in Portugal." Foreign Minister Ernesto Augusto de Melo Antunes expressed gratitude for the support and looked forward to future cooperation between the two countries and additional economic assistance from the United States.

In late 1975 United States foreign policy attention to Portuguese-related matters turned to the Angolan situation. The success with which the moderates put down the attempted leftist coup in Portugal in November, however, and their continued consolidation of power could not but augur well for future American-Portuguese relations. Indeed in an early December interview with one of his country's newspapers Ferreira, the Portuguese secretary of state for foreign affairs, underscored the positive nature of the relations between the United States and Portugal at that time.

A major consideration of American-Portuguese relations still unsettled in early 1976 was United States use of military facilities in the Azores, particularly of the Lajes air base. The importance of the Lajes base to American strategic planning was emphasized during the October 1973 Middle East war when United States cargo planes refueled there en route to Israel. Prime Minister Caetano was reluctant at first to permit such refueling, but he eventually allowed it. Though his successor, President Spínola, assured the United States that Portugal intended to remain in NATO, he was noncommittal about American refueling rights at the Lajes base.

Negotiations over a renewal of the agreement allowing American use of the base were begun in September 1974 but were soon suspended. On April 8, 1975, Prime Minister Gonçalves announced that the United States would not be allowed to use the Lajes base for refueling in the event of another Middle East war. The apparent reason for this action was Portugal's desire to foster closer relations with several Arab nations, relations that had been established after the 1974 revolution. A formal renewal of the Azores Agreement had not been concluded by late January 1976.

The Third World

Portuguese President Costa Gomes has declared that Portugal's "basic interests link [it] with Europe and with the Third World." Ties with Western Europe were traditional, and relations with Eastern Europe were an outgrowth of the 1974 revolution. The new Portuguese emphasis on the third world was another result of the revolution. Recognition of the importance of the third world to Portugal was evidenced in the Portuguese decolonization policy and in its attempt to establish cordial, cooperative relations with its former colonies after their independence. Still another manifestation of Portugal's new attitude was the extension of Portuguese diplomatic relations to several third world nations.

Within a few months of the April 1974 revolution Portugal established diplomatic relations with many Arab states, including Egypt, Morocco, Tunisia, Syria, Kuwait, Algeria, and Iraq. Later Algeria also gave Portuguese civil aircraft the right to overfly its territory.

Because of Portugal's announced decolonization program and its recognition of Guinea-Bissau's independence, a number of African states established relations with Portugal. These included Senegal in September 1974 (the month Guinea-Bissau gained independence) and the Congo, Ivory Coast, and Gabon in January 1975. These countries broke the ban the OAU had placed on the establishment of diplomatic relations with Portugal. Foreign Minister Soares visited President Mohamed Siad Barre of Somalia (then president of the OAU) in December 1974 and requested that the OAU's ban be removed in the light of Portugal's decolonization policy. The OAU granted Soares' request in February 1975, and relations with a number of other African states were subsequently established. These included Burundi in February, Mauritania in March, and Tanzania and Zambia in April.

The establishment of relations between Portugal and Senegal led to the conclusion of a trade agreement between the two in 1975. Portugal and Zambia developed what appeared to be a particularly cordial relationship. President Kenneth Kaunda of Zambia visited Portugal in

May 1975. Continued references to feelings of solidarity between the Portuguese and Zambian peoples were made in the talks between the representatives of the two countries, and President Costa Gomes accepted an invitation to visit Zambia. Plans for the establishment of mutual diplomatic missions were completed, and a further agreement regarding future joint negotiations on trade and cooperation was signed. Discussions were also held on the possibility of making grants available to support Zambians studying the Portuguese language. The possible exchange of technical personnel was also studied. Kaunda had been instrumental in bringing Portuguese and FRELIMO representatives together to negotiate the decolonization of Mozambique. The Zambian leader's assistance was also sought in settling the Angolan situation.

RELATIONS WITH INTERNATIONAL ORGANIZATIONS

United Nations

Portugal was admitted to the UN on December 14, 1955. The subject of a number of UN resolutions condemning its colonial policy both before and after its admittance, Portugal usually ignored such condemnation on the basis that its overseas territories were integral parts of Portugal and thus not subject to UN action (see Basic Objectives to 1974, this ch.). Portugal also joined most of the UN specialized agencies including the International Labor Organization, Food and Agriculture Organization, World Health Organization, International Monetary Fund, World Bank (see Glossary), International Finance Corporation, International Civil Aviation Organization, Universal Postal Union, International Telecommunications Union, World Meteorological Organization, General Agreement on Tariffs and Trade, and International Atomic Energy Agency. Portugal was also a member of the United Nations Educational, Scientific and Cultural Organization (UNESCO); it left that body in 1973 and rejoined it in 1974. Portugal did not join the International Development Association or the Intergovernmental Maritime Consultative Organization (both specialized agencies), nor did it join either the United Nations Children's Fund (UNICEF) or the United Nations High Commission for Refugees (the former a standing committee, the latter a commission), both of which reported to the General Assembly's Economic and Social Council, as did the specialized agencies.

International Economic Associations

Other Portuguese international commitments have included membership in the Organization for Economic Cooperation and Development (OECD). The OECD was established on September 30, 1961, to replace the Organization for European Economic Cooperation, which had been founded in 1948 to administer the Marshall Plan and allocate American aid. The goals of the OECD were to achieve the highest possible economic growth and employment consistent with financial stability, to aid developing countries, and to help expand world trade on a nondiscriminatory basis. To administer its assistance to developing nations the OECD created the Development Assistance Committee. Portugal was a member of this committee but withdrew in October 1974.

Portugal was also one of seven Western nations that signed the Stockholm Treaty (July 4, 1960) establishing the European Free Trade Association (EFTA). Its basic goal was the abolishment by 1970 of tariffs on industrial products among the EFTA states. External tariffs between individual EFTA and non-EFTA members were left to the states involved. In a wider sense, of course, the EFTA was intended to be something of a counter to the establishment of the European Economic Community (EEC). The transitory nature of EFTA was recognized by its members, who agreed to remain in that organization while each examined the possibility of entering into direct relations with the EEC.

This was precisely the course taken by Portugal. It continued its EFTA membership but, particularly after Great Britain's conversion from EFTA to EEC membership, found it advisable to seek a relationship with the EEC that would provide preferential tariff treatment. This was especially necessary for Portugal, which has long been the poorest West European nation.

The state of Portugal's economy prevented the country from becoming a full member of the EEC. Portugal did, however, apply under Article 238 of the Treaty of Rome (March 25, 1957) for associate member status, but action on that application was interrupted by the Portuguese revolution. The immediate reaction of the EEC to the revolution and to subsequent Portuguese requests for economic assistance was one of caution. The EEC external affairs commissioner, Christopher Soames, visited Portugal in February 1975, but he had not been empowered to negotiate EEC aid or terms of Portuguese association with the EEC.

The foreign ministers of the EEC nations met in Dublin, Ireland, on May 26, 1975, and agreed that the community should increase its trade and economic assistance to Portugal so long as these actions appeared to contribute to the maintenance of democracy there. The EEC offer to adjust to Portugal's advantage the agreements that had been in effect since early 1973 was thus conditional, and its statement was in fact a warning against future actions of the antidemocratic elements of Portugal's leftist movements and military. Some individual EEC members, particularly West Germany, and EFTA had already agreed to increase aid to Portugal earlier in the month. A number of Western governments and political parties also aided Portuguese moderate parties just as East European nations had aided the leftist Portuguese factions (see ch. 9).

By mid-July a special EEC commission had developed an economic assistance plan for Portugal amounting to approximately US$700 million to be implemented from 1976 to 1978 (see ch. 12). The plan, however, was jeopardized by the collapse of Portugal's fourth postrevolution cabinet and the subsequent governmental crisis in mid-July. Press reports indicated that President Giscard d'Estaing of France had decided against aid to Portugal and that West German Chancellor Helmut Schmidt and British Prime Minister Harold Wilson were having second thoughts.

Because of lessening communist influence in the Portuguese government beginning in August 1975, the chances for a closer EEC-Portuguese relationship were improved. They continued to improve with the left's unsuccessful coup in November 1975 and the Portuguese moderates' subsequent consolidation of power.

North Atlantic Treaty Organization

To Portugal, before its 1974 revolution, participation in NATO had been a major method of guarding against communism, one of its traditional prerevolutionary foreign policy objectives. Although vigilance against communism may not have been as important after the revolution, the various Portuguese governments that followed consistently repeated Portugal's continuing support for NATO. President Spínola reportedly attempted to assure President Nixon of this support during Nixon's visit to the Azores in June 1974. Portugal also voluntarily relinquished its turn to serve on NATO's Nuclear Planning Group in deference to concerns of some NATO members regarding security and Portugal's leftist orientation.

In late March 1975 Secretary of State Kissinger publicly warned of the danger to NATO posed by Portugal's apparent swing leftward. Five other NATO countries—West Germany, Belgium, the Netherlands, Denmark, and Italy—reportedly delivered similar warnings to the Portuguese after the American concern had been expressed to the Lisbon regime. Secretary Kissinger was reported to have aired further views on Portugal and NATO, including the possibility that continued Portuguese participation in that body would weaken or compromise it, in a press conference with West European newsmen on April 16, 1975.

Press reports stated that the United States was not simply concerned about the possible loss of NATO facilities but also the possible compromise of NATO secrets and a possible Soviet naval presence in Madeira. Such a presence could have had considerable impact upon NATO operations in the North Atlantic and especially in the

Mediterranean. United States worry over Portugal and NATO reached something of a climax on May 23 when President Ford publicly questioned continued Portuguese membership in the defense alliance. Despite concerns of their own, some West European NATO members reportedly criticized the American position as premature and an overreaction.

During the NATO meeting in Brussels in late May Prime Minister Gonçalves repeatedly reassured other alliance members in the strongest terms of Portugal's intention of honoring its NATO obligations. He indicated that Portugal would not be a Trojan Horse for NATO. The political turmoil that followed the PSP's withdrawal from the cabinet a month later did nothing to allay NATO fears. Portugal's future in NATO seemed increasingly questionable until August.

With the ouster of Prime Minister Gonçalves from office and the general reduction of communist influence within the government, Portugal's relations with its NATO allies began to improve. On September 19 the sixth Portuguese postrevolution cabinet was sworn in, its composition proportionally based on the results of the April election. On September 23 a West German representative, appearing before a NATO political committee meeting in Copenhagen, urged NATO members to begin immediate economic assistance to Portugal. More improvement in Portuguese-NATO relations was noted in December after the unsuccessful attempted leftist coup on November 25. According to press reports Secretary of State for Foreign Affairs Ferreira was well received at an early December NATO meeting in Brussels, where Portugal was urged by other members to remain in the alliance. A senior Portuguese official at that meeting was quoted as having spoken of "a new climate of confidence" within NATO. "Our relations with NATO have been unblocked," he was reported to have said. In early 1976 the future of the Portuguese membership in NATO looked brighter than at any other time since the April 1974 revolution.

****

Few reliable, detailed sources are available on Portuguese foreign relations, particularly for the period after the 1974 revolution. Major newspapers must thus be consulted as sources, and *Keesing's Contemporary Archives* is especially helpful in this regard. Hugh Kay's *Salazar and Modern Portugal* and Sarah Bradford's *Portugal* provide some general foreign relations information to 1970 and 1973, respectively. The United States, Congress' *United States Policy Toward Portugal* and *Portugal in Transition* provide information on American-Portuguese relations both before and after the revolution. The journalist Tad Szulc contributes a critical review on the same subject in "Lisbon and Washington: Behind the Portuguese Revolution" in *Foreign Policy* (Winter 1975-76). Material on Portuguese colonial affairs is abundant. Along with articles in various journals, two excellent sources are David M. Abshire and Michael Samuels' *Portuguese Africa: A Handbook* and Neil Bruce's more recent *Portugal: The Last Empire*. Portugal's traditional argument is well presented by its former United Nations representative, Franco Nogueira, in two works, *The United Nations and Portugal* and *Portuguese*

Foreign Policy, and in *Portugal Replies to the United Nations*, published by the Portuguese Ministry of Foreign Affairs. An English translation of António de Spínola's interesting book *Portugal and the Future* is also available. (For further information see Bibliography.)

CHAPTER 11

MASS COMMUNICATIONS

The mass communications media, restrained under nearly fifty years of authoritarian government, underwent a radical transformation in the revolutionary period after the coup d'etat of April 25, 1974. Any material compiled about the Portuguese press, radio, and television before that date is useful in a historical sense but has been made obsolete by subsequent events. One of the first acts of the revolutionary government was to abolish the censorship that had prevailed since 1926, but the habit of government interference in the flow of information was difficult to break. Freedom of the press was restricted in several areas under interim laws that were maintained by successive provisional governments, supposedly in the interests of public order, military discipline, and the promotion of ideological pluralism in the media. After a turbulent period of experimentation with worker participation in management of the media and the formulation of editorial policy, the status of the press, radio, and television and their relations to the state were regularized in the Constitution that went into effect in April 1976.

Through the Ministry of Social Communication and Culture the government can exert influence on the operation, management, and political direction of the state-owned newspapers and news agency, the public radio network, and television. The state acquired financial control over eight daily newspapers in Lisbon and Porto when it nationalized the banking houses that had previously owned them and had been operating them at a loss. A heavy public subsidy has since been required to keep these newspapers in business. Only three nationally circulated dailies and an increasingly popular weekly press remained in private hands. Prompted by an attempted left-wing coup in November 1975, the provisional government headed by Prime Minister José Pinheiro de Azevedo dismissed the editorial staffs and temporarily suspended publication of several state-owned Lisbon newspapers on grounds of biased reporting. The staffs were subsequently reorganized, and the newspapers resumed publication. Since the beginning of 1976 the state-owned press has operated under a unique system devised to provide ideological balance, under which political orientations were assigned by the government to particular newspapers.

299

Television service is provided by Portuguese Television (Radiotelevisão Portuguesa—RTP), established in 1959 as a semiprivate enterprise and nationalized in 1975. The Portuguese Radio System (Emissora Radiodifusão Portuguesa—ERP), which is a public corporation modeled on the British Broadcasting Corporation, and the Roman Catholic Rádio Renascença have a monopoly on radiobroadcasting.

Private film studios produce a small number of feature-length motion pictures each year for domestic consumption, as well as television films and commercial advertising. Increasing attention has been given to upgrading the artistic and technical standards of Portuguese filmmaking through cooperative endeavors financed by foundation grants and public subsidies.

With restraints imposed by the former regime removed, Portuguese publishers have done a thriving business since 1974 in the sale of new titles and the distribution of books that had been banned from the market. Portugal's book-reading public is smaller in proportion to population than those in other West European countries, however, and printings seldom run to more than a few thousand copies.

ROLE OF GOVERNMENT

The Portuguese press enjoyed unlimited freedom of expression under the parliamentary republic (1910-26), but sources have noted that the politicized newspapers of that era so abused their liberty with irresponsible polemics that they bore much responsibility for the disorders that preceded the dictatorship. Under the regime of António de Oliveira Salazar newspapers were subject to prepublication censorship, and fines and suspension followed hard upon infractions of restrictive press laws. In 1972 Salazar's successor, Marcello Caetano, revised the law to make writers legally responsible for censoring their own work, although press runs were examined selectively by a panel of censors composed largely of military officers. Contempt for law and institutions, demoralization of family life, and obscenity and pornography were the usual causes for bureaucratic red-penciling.

Isolated from the world press under the Salazar and Caetano regimes, the Portuguese media were used to promote an image of tranquillity and stability in Portugal that was intended to attract tourism and investment. The deadening effect of censorship was to demoralize the press and to discredit it in the eyes of Portuguese readers. The revolution and the legal end to censorship could not alter a tradition in which the government viewed writers and the media as national assets to be used in the national interest; criticism of the government, officials, or the military was seen after April 1974 as a betrayal of the revolution. A revealing example of this logic is seen in the June 1975 statement attributed to Navy Commander Jorge Jesuino, controversial minister of social communication and culture, that "to pursue a real

300

information policy in Portugal today is to fulfill the government's priorities [to which] the press must be synchronized."

On the day after the coup that toppled the Caetano regime, Portuguese newspapers carried the legend "Not Submitted to Censorship" prominently on their mastheads; however, the revolutionary government, which in one of its first acts had abolished censorship, soon imposed interim media laws to serve as guidelines for the press and radio until permanent legislation could be formulated. Infractions were punishable by fines and suspension. An ad hoc committee was set up to monitor the media and to enforce the interim laws; nominally under the Ministry of Social Communication and Culture, it was composed largely of military officers who took it as their mandate to curb so-called ideological aggression; reports of dissension within the military or the government, labor unrest, popular opposition to government policy, and publication of unauthorized interviews fell into this category. The ministry was generally ineffective in muzzling the press, however, and the penalties imposed for infractions of the interim laws were often rescinded. Creation of a military-controlled censorship committee, proposed by Jesuino, was blocked by opposition from the media, which refused to abide by ministry directives. The ad hoc media committee was suspended, and the interim media laws were superseded by the enactment of legislation, modeled on British press statutes, that was subsequently embodied in the 1976 Constitution.

The 1976 Constitution guarantees freedom of expression and citizens' right to access to the news media. Censorship is categorically prohibited and is made punishable in civil courts. Journalists are allowed to determine the political orientation of newspapers and periodicals that are not controlled by the state or by political parties. Employees are not permitted to impede publication of newspapers in disputes over editorial policy. All persons and groups are granted the right to reply to material appearing in the public media. Cooperative groups, profitmaking publishing companies, and political organizations can own and operate independent newspapers and periodicals unrestrained by the state or by competing organizations. Ownership of media enterprises, however, is restricted to Portuguese citizens. Financial pressure on the independent press for the purpose of exerting influence over it is illegal; newspapers may not be shut down for failure to pay debts, nor may advertisers use the threat of withdrawing their business to protest editorial policy.

THE PRESS

The nationalization of Portuguese banks in March 1975 gave the state financial control of eight daily newspapers and a number of periodicals that had been owned by the banks. These included the

morning *Jornal do Comércio, Diário de Notícias,* and *Século* and
the evening *Diário Popular, A Capital,* and *Diário de Lisboa* in *Lisbon*
and the *Porto* morning *Jornal de Notícias* and *O Comércio do Porto*
(see table 9). The government also gained control of the weekly
Sempre Fixe and the popular newsmagazine *Vida Mundial.* Of the
major Lisbon dailies only *República* remained independently owned.
Athough proprietorship of the state-owned press continued to be exercised by nationalized companies rather than by a government agency, management was transferred to military officers and press workers, whose leftist sympathies were at odds with the Azevedo government. *António Almeida Santos,* minister of social communication and
culture after August 1975, was quick to point out the contradictions
inherent in a situation in which the state-owned press attacked the
government that subsidized it. In the aftermath of the attempted *left-
wing coup in November 1975,* state-owned Lisbon newspapers were
shut down and their editorial staffs dismissed (see ch. 9).

During a period of suspension that was extended for nearly six
weeks, the affected newspapers were reorganized in accordance with
a plan for achieving political balance in the press. Major *political parties* were called on to recommend editors and journalists to staff
state-owned newspapers each of which would be assigned a political
orientation by the *Ministry of Social Communication and Culture.*
Under the plan, for instance, *Diário de Notícias* and *A Capital* supported the center-left policies associated with *Mário Soares* and the

Table 9. Portugal, Leading Newspapers, 1976

Newspaper	City	Founded	Frequency	Estimated Circulation (in thousands)
Expresso..........	Lisbon	1973	weekly	110
Tempo	—do—	1975	—do—	110
Diário do Notícias *. .	—do—	1864	morning	106
O Comércio do Porto *	Porto	1854	-do-	100
Jornal do Comércio *	Lisbon	1853	—do—	100
Jornal Novo	—do—	1975	evening	100
A Luta	—do—	1975	—do—	80
Jornal de Notícias *. .	Porto	1889	morning	75
Diário Popular *	Lisbon	1942	evening	73
O Primerio de Janeiro	Porto	1889	morning	70
A Capital *	Lisbon	1968	evening	60
O Jornal	—do—	1975	weekly	60
O Século *..........	—do—	1881	morning	40
Diário de Lisboa *. . .	—do—	1921	evening	38

*Owned by the state.

Source: Based on information from *The Europa Year Book, 1976: A World
Survey,* I, London, 1976.

Portuguese Socialist Party (Partido Socialista Português—PSP); *O Século*, jokingly dismissed as "Portugal's *Izvestia*" for its adherence to a communist line before its suspension, adopted a moderate, broadly progovernment stance; *Diário de Lisboa*, slated to be communist oriented, reflected instead a wide range of left-wing views. It was intended that state-owned newspapers be identified with the political tendencies in Portuguese society rather than with specific political parties.

Guidelines proposed for eliminating bias in reporting made a distinction between news and editorial analysis of news. Different standards of reporting were also applied to newspapers whose role was to report the news and to the party-owned press that by its nature reflected partisan viewpoints. Party publications and the editorial policies of the independent press were exempted from regulation.

Diário de Notícias barely retained its position in 1976 as Portugal's largest daily; its circulation considerably dimished from the more than 150,000 claimed before the revolution. For many years *Diário de Notícias* ranked as the country's most prestigious and reliable newspaper and was set apart from its competition by a format that featured classified advertising on the front page in the tradition of the *Times* of London. During the Salazar years the newspaper was generally considered an unofficial government mouthpiece, but with the revolution it changed editors and adopted a new format and an aggressively procommunist editorial stance. Before its suspension in November 1975, however, a majority of journalists of *Diário de Notícias* petitioned the government to expel the leftist minority that had dictated editorial policy; the state-owned newspaper resumed publication in 1976 with a socialist editor and a moderate, progovernment orientation.

The other leading morning newspapers, *O Comércio do Porto* and *Jornal do Comérico*, are relied on by the business and professional community for their extensive coverage of financial news. The circulation of *O Século*, which has undergone several changes in editorial policy since 1974, has lagged as has that of all the state-owned press in Lisbon. An official daily government gazette, *Diário do Governo*, has been published since 1820.

The quality newspapers *Jornal Novo* and *A Luta*, established with private capital in 1975, quickly moved ahead of state-owned tabloids in evening circulation. They are Lisbon's only independently managed dailies of consequence. Attractive in its makeup and well written, *Jornal Novo* boats of its objective reporting and educated analysis of the news. *A Luta*, an independent socialist newspaper staffed by journalists who had worked for *República*, was outspoken in its hostility to the extreme left. *O Diário*, a sedate tabloid employing leftist journalists purged from *Diário de Notícias* and *Diário de Lisboa*, was communist oriented but independent of party connections. Editorial comment was kept separate from news content, but the newspaper has not succeeded in attracting a significant readership. The larger state-owned evening tabloids, *Diário de Lisboa* and the breezier *Diário Popular*, showed declining circulations in early 1976.

The subject of political controversy in 1975, the socialist-oriented morning newspaper *República* was the property of its more than 3,000 shareholders and had been the only major Lisbon daily to escape nationalization in the government sweep of bank-owned newspapers. In April 1975 press workers, whose union was part of the communist-dominated Intersindical (Portugal's all-inclusive trade union organization), went on strike in protest against articles appearing in *República* that had revealed alleged communist tactics for gaining control of the media; the press workers demanded Raul Rêgo's removal as editor.

Although the interim media laws clearly reserved policymaking for management in consultation with the journalists, the Ministry of Social Communication and Culture under Jesuino made a fruitless attempt to mediate the dispute and suggested a comprise acceptable to neither side. When the press workers seized the newspaper—with the cooperation of army units dispatched to expel them—and resumed publication of *República*, the conflict was brought into the street by socialist and communist demonstrators. In July the Council of the Revolution appointed an army commander as editor against assurances previously made to Soares that *República* would be returned to its owners. In protest members of Soares' PSP and the liberal Popular Democratic Party (Partido Popular Democático—PPD) withdrew from the government, an action that hastened its fall.

In grave financial difficulty, *República* was returned to its shareholders early in 1976. Rêgo—who had in the meantime begun the successful daily *A Luta* —announced that *República*, its circulation at less than 20,000, would be kept in publication as a weekly "for sentimental reasons."

The liberal *Expresso* was the most widely read newspaper in 1976 and was considered to contain the Portuguese press' most balanced and authoritative reporting. First appearing as a mass-circulation weekly in 1973, *Expresso* was modeled in format and style on the *Observer* of London. It was from the start a one-man operation; Francisco Balsemão, the editor, owned a majority of the stock and reserved the remainder for select shareholders. Balsemão, who emerged after the revolution as a leading figure in the PPD, gave *Expresso* a liberal orientation; but he and his youthful staff insisted on editorial pluralism, and readers regularly found contrasting opinions published on the same page. *Expresso* was Portugal's best source of foreign news. Harassed by the Caetano regime in the first year of its publication, *Expresso* was fined by the revolutionary government for contravention of the interim media laws.

An immediate success after it began publication in 1975, *O Jornal* is a left-wing cooperative weekly owned jointly by its journalists, who elect their editors for one-year terms. *O Jornal* takes a serious approach to the news, specializes in exhaustive analysis of particular issues, and has been outspoken in its criticism of the Armed Forced Movement (Movimento das Forças Armadas—MFA). An independent right-wing weekly, *Tempo* has taken a similar adversary position and enjoys increasing popularity. *Liberdade*, representative of center-left opinion, has attracted attention for its investigative reporting and printing of news not found in other newspapers, but its circulation has remained small. The satirical illustrated weekly *Sempre Fixe*, one of the brightest additions to the Portuguese press after the revolution and famous for its graphics and color photography, suspended publication for an indefinite period after its nationalization in August 1975.

The weeklies and some Lisbon dailies command a national readership. Porto newspapers circulate throughout northern Portugal and, after the revolution, won an audience in Lisbon as well. The provincial press has a limited circulation. Political parties and movements publish an array of partisan weeklies that are exempted from the legal provisions imposed on the independent press to ensure plurality of opinion and allow for staff determination of editorial policy (see table 10).

NEWS AGENCIES

The Portuguese News Agency (Agência Noticiosa Portuguesa—ANOP) was acquired by the government in 1975 through the nationalization of the privately owned News and Information Agency (Agência de Notícias e de Informações—ANI) and is operated by the Ministry of Social Communication and Culture. It is the only domestic wire service serving the Portuguese press. ANOP, which distributes more than 40,000 words in Portuguese daily, maintains a branch office in Rio de Janeiro and employs stringers in other news centers. ANOP shares special services with several other European news agencies under agreements made by ANI. United Press International (UPI) also

Table 10. Portugal, Newspapers Affiliated with Political Parties, 1976

Newspaper	Affiliation
Avante!	Portuguese Communist Party
Democracia 74	Social Democratic Center Party
Povo Livre	Popular Democratic Party
Portugal Socialista	Portuguese Socialist Party
Unidade	Portuguese Democratic Movement

Source: Based on information from *The Europa Year Book, 1976: A World Survey*, I, London, 1976, pp. 1030-1031.

provides economic and shipping news that is sold to subscribers and provided to state-owned newspapers and banks. Lusitania (Agência Lusitania), a Lisbon-based nonprofit cooperative that had provided a daily service to Portuguese-language newspapers abroad and distributed news from the former African provinces to the metropolitan press, was closed down in 1975 by government order.

All major Western news agencies, including the Associated Press and UPI of the United States, have offices in Lisbon. Since 1974 the Soviet Union's TASS and agencies from other communist countries have also been represented.

PERIODICALS

More than 300 periodicals are published in Portugal. The thrice-weekly sporting magazines command the most avid audiences; *Bola*, with an average sale per issue of over 100,000 copies, leads in circulation. *Motor* is a popular mass-circulation weekly for automobile enthusiasts; *ACP*, the twice-monthly journal of the Portuguese Automobile Club, has 70,000 subscribers. Weekly women's magazines, of which *Crónica Feminina* and *Eva* are the best sellers, feature a mixture of fashion news, homemaking hints, and light fiction.

The weekly newsmagazines *Vida Mundial* and *Flama*, both with circulations approaching 50,000, offer summaries of current events and opinion similar to those in *Time* and *Newsweek*. Published every two weeks, *Plateia* covers the theater and cinema, *Etc* art and current literature. *Brotéria,* a serious journal, appears monthly in two editions, one a review of cultural activities and the other devoted to the natural sciences. Also a respected part of the Portuguese intellectual and cultural scene, *Seara Nova* is valued for its monthly commentaries on politics, sociology, and literature. *Jornal Português de Economia e Finanças* and *Notícias do Comércio* are the leading economic and financial periodicals. A large number of professional and scholarly journals dealing with the arts, medicine, science, and the social sciences are published under the auspices of the universities, libraries, museums, foundations, and professional associations. Illustrated supplements are included in the weekend editions of some newspapers.

RADIO

Radiobroadcasting developed in Portugal around public, private, commercial, and church-affiliated stations that operated side by side and provided a broad variety of programming to Portugal and its Atlantic islands from twenty-five national and local stations broadcasting over more than sixty amplitude modulation (AM) and frequency modulation (FM) transmitters to more than 1.5 million receivers. In the early 1920s private radio clubs interested in the commercial possibilities of the medium began transmission on frequencies assigned and regulated by the Post and Telegraph Administration. By 1929 individual stations had begun to form cooperatives, pooling resources and sharing facilities to cut costs. The most successful of the cooperatives, Rádio Clube Português, built a nationwide network of commercial stations, which, along with other private stations, was taken over by workers after the 1974 revolution. All commercial broadcasting facilities, except those belonging to the church, were nationalized in November 1975.

Rádio Renascença has been operated under the auspices of the Roman Catholic hierarchy in Portugal since 1932; its independence and immunity from government censorship were guaranteed in the Concordat of 1940. Studios in Lisbon and Porto broadcast commercial programming thirteen hours daily from AM, FM, and shortwave transmitters.

A state broadcasting system, the National Radio System (Emissora Nacional de Radiodifusão—ENR) was established in 1933 as an autonomous public corporation managed by a government appointee and supported from license fees paid by commercial stations and owners of radio receivers. In addition to regular programming over two channels, ENR operated an educational station and a shortwave international service. In 1974 ENR was put under the direct control of the Ministry of Social Communication and Culture preliminary to its reorganization in 1975 as the state-owned ERP, which incorporated the facilities of ENR with those of nationalized private commercial stations. Worker participation in management, a point of contention in the private stations after the revolution, was prohibited in the state system.

ERP broadcast over four channels in the Home Service, which reached all of continental Portugal. Rebroadcasts and local programming were provided in Madeira and the Azores. Network I and Network II continued the same kinds of noncommercial programming that had been furnished by ENR, Network I on a twenty-four-hour schedule. Network II, specializing in cultural programming, broadcast seventeen hours on both AM and FM circuits. The other two channels were being gradually integrated into the nationwide system as commercial stations featuring news and light entertainment. One newsroom served all four channels.

The International Service of ERP broadcast in Portuguese to Timor and Macao and to Portugal's former African provinces, as well as to Brazil, North America, and the fishing fleet at sea. Shortwave transmission in five foreign languages including English, was beamed to selected points on a limited schedule. Portugal's Radio Liberty, founded as Radio Trans-Europe in 1970, used a high-powered shortwave facility to transmit programs from the ERP Home Service to Portuguese workers abroad. Radio Canada International, Deutsche

Welle of the Federal Republic of Germany (West Germany) and Radio Free Europe leased relay facilities in Portugal. An adjunct of ERP, Rádio Estundantil, was on the air two hours daily. It was operated by a student group using the facilities of the former ENR educational service.

TELEVISION

Television service was furnished by Portuguese Television (Radiotelevisão Portuguesa—RTP), a state-owned commercial network with eight transmitters and thirty-eight relayers that reached approximately 90 percent of the population in metropolitan Portugal, the Azores and, since 1972, Madeira. Programs emanated from studios in Lisbon and Porto. The RTP's black-and-white system utilized a 625-line transmission compatible with those of other systems in the Eurovision linkup, which Portugal had joined in 1966. Color television, although under study, had not been introduced in 1976. RTP was being financed by direct government subsidy and out of revenue from commercial advertising and from annual license fees levied on receivers, which numbered more than 700,000 in 1975.

Regular television programming was introduced in 1956, when RTP was established under a twenty-year license as a private corporation in which the state was a principal shareholder. The Ministry of Social Communication and Culture assumed responsibility for RTP's management in 1975, when its license came up for renewal. Shares in the corporation not already state owned were subsequently nationalized.

The 1976 Constitution provided for the Television Advisory Council to ensure that the technical operation of the state-owned network would not be disrupted by its employees or by the government in power. Members of the council represented a political cross section of the legislature and had as one of their duties the periodic review of television programming for ideological content. In contrast to the ERP situation, representatives of the television workers' assembly shared responsibility for supervision of RTP's management, financing, and programming with the Ministry of Social Communication and Culture and the legislature. Workers were cautioned, however, not to mix politics with their professional duties.

Viewers had a choice of two channels. Program I provided a variety of films, sports, light entertainment, popular and classical music, and live drama, as well as news and documentaries, during seven and one-half hours of regular daily programming; an additional four and one-half hours were reserved for school programs. Program II offered two and one-half hours in prime time of serious music and drama.

One frequent complaint against the revolution heard in parts of rural Portugal was that it had "ruined television," the only form of entertainment available in many villages. "In the old days we used to have lots of bullfights, soccer, and plays," one farmer with other grudges against the new regime was reported by the *New York Times* to have grumbled; "now there's almost nothing but politics."

FILMS

An average of only four or five feature-length films, few of which rise above the ordinary, were being produced annually by the Portuguese film industry, but by 1974 four major studios, all located in Lisbon, were making more than 300 short films and documentaries a year, many made for television, as well as commercial advertising spots. Feature filmmaking has been hindered by a number of factors, the most pressing of which have been high production costs and the limited appeal of Portuguese motion pictures even in Portugal. Portuguese films have not attracted a market abroad.

Popular foreign-made films appeared in Lisbon cinemas soon after release. Nearly 40 percent of the approximately 300 films imported annually came from the United States.

Standards of censorship have been relaxed considerably since 1974, and films that would have been banned for political or moral reasons before that time formed a large portion of the films shown across the country in 1976; however, fully half of the thirty or more films being shown at a given time may have admission restricted to patrons over the age of eighteen. Relatively few films, in fact, were open to general admission. Attendance at Portugal's 500 cinemas, only 100 of which operate on a full-time schedule, was 28 million in 1974, making the per capita attendance the lowest in Europe.

PUBLISHING HOUSES AND LIBRARIES

The publishing industry in Portugal dates from at least 1489, when Jewish printers are known to have been operating the presses in Lisbon and Faro that turned out the country's earliest incunabula in Hebrew. Several of the fifty-seven publishing houses located in Lisbon, Porto, and Coimbra in 1976 have been in business for a century or more. The oldest of them, Lisbon's Livraria Bertrand, was founded in 1732 and had branches in several cities; the largest house, Moraes Editores, had 374 titles in print in 1975. Many publishers directed their business toward specific markets; some also owned bookshops and sponsored book clubs. Owing to the high rate of illiteracy and the low level of education of a large part of the population, books were not as significant a means of communication in Portugal as in other European countries, and publishers seldom invested in initial press runs of more than 3,000 copies; as a consequence books, even in paperbound editions, were expensive.

Prepublication censorship of books was not usual under the Salazar regime, which chose instead to ban books of which it disapproved

309

after they had been put on the market. According to the Portuguese Association of Publishers and Booksellers, more than 3,600 Portuguese and foreign titles were suppressed in this manner during the years of the dictatorship, among them the works of some of Portugal's foremost novelists. Within a year of the revolution almost 100 suppressed works of fiction were reprinted, and books seized or stored by publishers were put into circulation.

Portuguese readers in 1974 and 1975, however, had a particular craving for nonfiction; books on politics, contemporary history, sociology, and religion were among the best-sellers. Every major party leader or revolutionary figure published a political testament for a receptive audience. Taste among readers—at least those who were purchasing books—in the spring of 1975 leaned heavily toward works about Marxism or by Marxists; in April four of the best-selling authors, as reported by Lisbon booksellers, were Marx, Lenin, Rosa Luxemburg, and Alvaro Cunhal. One year later the best-seller list included, in addition to several works of current fiction, the Portuguese editions of books by Andrei Sakharov and Wilhelm Reich as well as George Orwell's *Animal Farm*.

Public libraries at the municipal and district levels contained approximately 5 million volumes in the mid-1970s and also served as local archives. The largest of these was the Municipal Library at Porto. The National Library in Lisbon, with over 1 million volumes in its collection, occupied a position in Portugal similar to that of the Library of Congress in the United States. Among other important research facilities in Lisbon were the Ajuda Library, founded in 1756, and the 600-year-old National Archives of Torre do Tombo, which housed a collection of 60,000 manuscripts, the oldest of them dating from the ninth century A.D.

310

SECTION III. ECONOMIC

CHAPTER 12

CHARACTER AND STRUCTURE OF THE ECONOMY

When the regime of Marcello Caetano was overthrown on April 25, 1974, there were immediate economic repercussions. The existing economic structure, which was a reflection of a half-century of authoritarian rule, had become increasingly out of touch with the European economic scene. Although much of the economic difficulty of the country was attributed to the burden of colonial wars, which certainly played a part, there were more fundamental weaknesses that clamored for correction. These included an oligarchic structure of control over the economy, a growing gap between the privileged and the poor, and an inadequate and backward agricultural sector producing the lowest yields in Western Europe. Although there was a considerable modern industrial sector, it was handicapped by a dearth of managerial and technical talent and offered little opportunity for a large number of the country's untrained youths, who were forced to seek employment abroad. The result of these weaknesses was an economy that outranked only Turkey in most of the indexes of economic well-being among the noncommunist countries of Europe. The only bright spot was an ample hoard of foreign exchange and gold reserves, fed by tourist revenues and remittances from Portuguese workers abroad and carefully husbanded by a government still under the spell of the forty-year rule of conservative economics professor-dictator António de Oliverira Salazar.

Although Portugal has been classified as an industrial country by the World Bank (see Glossary) and by the International Monetary Fund (IMF), this designation reflected its role as a donor of development aid (in Portugal's case to its overseas possessions) rather than its degree of economic development. By most statistical measurements it lagged behind Spain and, by some, behind Greece, both of which were classified in 1975 as developing countries by these international bodies. In 1973 its gross domestic product (GDP) was the equivalent of US$10.7 billion at current prices, which ranked it twenty-first among the twenty-four member countries of the Organization for Economic Cooperation and Development (OECD), ahead of only Ireland, Luxembourg, and Iceland. In GDP per capita Portugal's estimated US$1,250 ranked twenty-third, surpassing only Turkey among

311

OECD countries and following immediately after Greece and Spain, twenty-first and twenty-second respectively.

Other indications of Portugal's comparatively low rank among OECD members in economic development and well-being included its rank of twenty-third in per capita gross capital investment (about US$250) and in private per capita consumption expenditure (US$900). Living standards were correspondingly low (see ch. 4). Portugal ranked twenty-third among the twenty-four members in energy consumption and in telephones per 1,000 inhabitants.

During the first two years after the April 1974 coup the course of the economy was sharply downward. Although in some degree this reflected worldwide economic conditions, it was also the result of colonial disengagement and the internal upheavals within metropolitan Portugal. Labor, freed from the restrictions of the previous regime, was quick to make demands for wage increases and shorter hours, job security, and a voice in enterprise management. Hopes for orderly reform of the archaic land tenure system foundered with the precipitate takeover of the large estates. The widespread nationalization of farms and factories, though accomplished with surprisingly little serious violence, resulted in considerable disruption of productivity and loss of investor confidence.

In early 1976 tentative figures for economic performance in 1975 revealed the serious state of the national economy. Overall output had dropped by 10 to 15 percent; manufacturing had dropped by 15 percent and construction by 20 percent. This was alleged by the London *Financial Times* to be "a European record for negative growth." Capital investment, chronically low in Portugal in the best of times, was 50 percent below the figure forecast in the 1975 budget. Unemployment was at an estimated 15 percent, not including the 500,000 or more who had returned from Africa. Inflation, in spite of vigorous price control measures, was running at 25 to 30 percent, and the prediction for 1976 was for 50 to 100 percent. The trade deficit of 43 billion escudos (for value of the escudo—see Glossary) was outrunning the usually offsetting tourist income and emigrant remittances, and there was an adverse balance of payments of about US$1 billion.

On the positive side it appeared in mid-1976 that the precipitate takeovers of enterprises and agricultural holdings, whether under official sanction or by mob action, that had characterized the first two years of the revolution, had run their course. Although a number of established foreign firms had departed, many remained in spite of harassments and the lack of immediate prospects for economic gain. New foreign investment—which had virtually halted—was again being sought with assurances of government protective guarantees, and foreign aid offers were being tendered, encouraged by renewed hopes for orderly government. Some observers saw a danger of a return to the restrictive and reactionary policies of the Salazar-Caetano

period, but the 1976 Constitution indicated that the economic structure would have a pronounced socialistic cast (see ch. 9). Given the
results of the April 1976 parliamentary election, however, there appeared to be a good possibility of Portugal's establishing an economic
system that could be accommodated within the existing economic patterns of Western Europe.

BACKGROUND

The Pre-Salazar Economy

The economic history of Portugal since the fifteenth century had
been dominated by the country's attempts to live up to its role as a
colonizing power. The effort to establish and maintain an overseas
empire was for centuries as much a burden as a benefit in terms of
economic development at home. Domestic production was neglected
in favor of imported goods, creating an undue dependence on the colonies. This dependence, though reflecting in some degree the limited
resource base of continental Portugal, created a policy orientation
that resulted in neglect of the potential for domestic development.
Even national dietary tastes reflected an overseas bias, depending
more on codfish from the far-off Grand Banks of Newfoundland than
on the more accessible fish in nearby waters.

The dependence on the colonies, although it received a blow with
the loss of Brazil in the early nineteenth century, continued into the
twentieth century as attention turned to exploitation of the African
territories. Failure to develop industrially at home was encouraged by
traditional ties with Great Britain, which often appeared to be treating
Portugal economically as one of its own colonies by supplying low-
cost manufactured goods in return for wine and other agricultural
products. This is not to say that there were no economic advances in
the nineteenth century. British economic incursions and the loss of
Brazil encouraged in a small degree the development of manufacturing, first in the Porto area and later in the Lisbon region. Other economic patterns were also changing. Many of the Roman Catholic
Church, noble, and royal landholdings were broken up and sold, creating a class of bourgeois landowners and increasing the land under
cultivation as well as agricultural output (see ch. 2).

Public works, primarily road and railroad construction, were undertaken. Starting with the founding of the Bank of Lisbon in 1821, a
banking system was established, and foreign investment was encouraged. Both domestic and foreign investment, however, tended to seek
opportunities in commerce and services rather than industry. Meanwhile the burden of public expenditures was borne largely by excise
taxes that fell on the poorer classes. The landowning and commercial
classes, who effectively controlled government policy, managed to

313

escape much of the tax burden and thus consolidated their position of economic power. This imbalance of economic control continued and became a major factor in the stormy course of the first republic (1910-26). It was also reflected in the oligarchic dominance and authoritarian politics of the Salazar-Caetano period and in the economic upheavals since the overthrow in 1974.

At the beginning of the twentieth century Portugal's economy was still primarily agricultural; over 60 percent of the work force was engaged in farming and fishing. Industry was largely confined to textiles, leather goods, and the processing of such traditional Portuguese products as cork and wine. There was a lack of skilled labor and industrial raw materials as well as capital for industrial development. The supply of raw materials and the provision of shipping and other commercial services and much of the development of industry had been left in foreign, largely British, hands.

There was, in comparison with the rest of Europe, only a small urban working class. By 1910 only about 20 percent of the work force was engaged in manufacturing, and of these only 20 percent were employed in factories of ten or more workers. The chronically depressed conditions in agriculture, rather than causing a flow of rural poor to the cities, resulted in considerable emigration, mostly to Brazil and increasingly in the twentieth century to North America.

Although the overthrow of the monarchy in 1910 was sparked by liberal and democratic ideals, the revolution failed to bring to the surface the talents and discipline needed to cope with the political, social, and economic problems that had caused it. The economy went from bad to worse. Severe inflation, which brought the national currency down to less than one-thirtieth of its par value in sixteen years of the republic, was accompanied by bank failures and continuing labor unrest. The political and social turmoil of the period was exacerbated by Portugal's participation in World War I. The demands of war contributed heavily to inflation and the continuing economic crises.

Economic Developments under Salazar

The end of the republic came in 1926 through a military coup. The new military leaders, casting about for guidance in bringing the country out of bankruptcy, requested Salazar—Portugal's best known economist—to leave his post as professor of political economy at Coimbra University and assume control of the Ministry of Finance. His initial tour as minister lasted only a week, because the military declined to give him the absolute control over the nation's finances that he felt was necessary. Two years later, as the situation appeared more desperate, he was asked to return and was offered the complete budgetary control that he had initially requested.

314

During forty years of personal rule—four as minister of finance and thirty-six as prime minister—Salazar made an indelible mark on the economy of Portugal. He was an uncompromising advocate of balanced budgets and fiscal solvency and of corporate free enterprise within the limits of strict state control. His faith in the gold standard and in a stable currency backed by gold and substantial foreign exchange reserves was unshaken even in the worst days of the worldwide depression and war during the 1930s and 1940s. These policies were apparently effective in bringing the country through the depression with only moderate disruption of its stable, albeit static, economy. At the end of 1933, for example, when the rest of the world was suffering from widespread unemployment, registered unemployment in Portugal was less than 1 percent.

Although Portugal emerged from the difficult periods of depression and war in Europe in better economic condition than its West European neighbors, except perhaps for Switzerland, it remained a backward nation. Little progress had been made in improving living standards, which had been the lowest in Europe, and Portugal returned to that ranking as soon as economic recovery, spurred by Marshall Plan aid from the United States, spread through the rest of the area. Portugal, though a charter member of the North Atlantic Treaty Organization (NATO) and a participant in the Marshall Plan, asked for and received few benefits from Marshall Plan economic aid or from United States economic assistance extended during the operations of the Mutual Security Act. Its total receipts of economic and military aid from the United States in the 1946-65 period, allowing for repayments and interest, amounted to less than US$500 million of more than US$40 billion extended to Europe during this period. Even Spain, a late starter in this respect and a political pariah in Europe during the 1950s, was able to share more fully in the prosperity of Western Europe. By 1958 Portugal's per capita national income of the equivalent of US$216 was significantly outranked by Spain at US$305 and Greece at US$326, and its average annual increase in the 1950s was only 3 percent.

The principal stumbling block in the path of Portugal's sharing in Western Europe's growing prosperity in the 1950s was the inflexible economic philosophy of Salazar. His insistence on a stable currency, a positive balance of payments, and a balanced budget and his suspicion of foreign aid and foreign investment outweighed the arguments of those who would have preferred a more dynamic attack on the low living standards and static economic development. Salazar's critics have alleged that he failed to extract the maximum advantage in economic aid as the price for United States use of the Azores and the other contributions that Portugal has been able to make as a member of NATO. Moreover opportunities to attract foreign investment, which could have been realized because of Portugal's strong and secure monetary record and its low costs and politically stable labor supply, were largely ignored in this period.

The concept of national economic planning was first adopted by Portugal in the mid-1950s with a series of six-year development plans. These were basically outlines of official goals and guidelines, following the indicative planning models popularized by the French. The First Development Plan (1953-58), the Second Development Plan (1959-64), and the subsequent Interim Plan (1965-67) were geared primarily to public investment projects and were modest in scope. In spite of some emphasis on hydroelectric and irrigation projects, the latter have progressed slowly. Investment in the modernization of agriculture was given low priority, and agriculture failed to contribute to the otherwise favorable growth of the 1960s.

The Third Development Plan (1968-73) forecast an average annual growth of the GDP of 7 percent; actual growth exceeded this goal. Tourism was expected to reach an average annual growth rate of 20 percent, manufacturing 9 percent, and construction 8 percent. These goals were also achieved, but agriculture, as usual the economic stepchild, failed to meet its projected 3-percent growth rate.

The Fourth Development Plan (1974-79), which was soon discarded by the revolutionary government, called for a minimum annual growth of the gross national product (GNP) of 7.5 percent and continued emphasis on investment in infrastructure projects and basic industries (see Economic Consequences of the Revolution, this ch.). The continuing industrial bias at the expense of agriculture was shown by the planned slowing of agricultural growth from 3 to 2 percent. The major project was to be the building of a US$1.2 billion industrial and port complex at Sines, south of Lisbon (see ch. 13).

In the 1960s a policy reorientation with respect to foreign economic relations became evident. For a variety of reasons, among which was presumably the recognition of a need for a bulwark against communism and a strengthening of the hold on the colonies, Portugal decided to take on closer economic ties with the noncommunist world. It became a charter member of the European Free Trade Association (EFTA) in 1959 and followed in the early 1960s with memberships in the General Agreement on Tariffs and Trade (GATT), the World Bank, and the IMF. These steps served to lower trade barriers and to open up both metropolitan Portugal and the overseas territories to foreign investment. These factors, together with a great increase of migrant workers to northern Europe and a consequent flow of remittances plus the discovery of Portugal as an inexpensive vacation spot by northern European tourists, brought a marked increase in the economic growth rate.

Although GNP grew at an average rate of 6.2 percent per annum during the 1960s, the benefits of this growth were largely confined to the industrial and service sectors in the urban areas. The agricultural

316

sector grew by only 1.3 percent annually, while industry, construction, and services grew by 9.0 percent, 8.1 percent, and 5.9 percent respectively. Visible signs of modernity, such as the Salazar Bridge, the Lisbon subway, the massive supertanker construction and repair facilities at Lisbon and Setúbal, and the luxury hotels in Lisbon and in the oceanside resort areas, contrasted with the inadequate housing, small and obsolete enterprises in many traditional manufacturing and service activities, an inadequate and obsolete fishing fleet, and the most backward agricultural sector in Western Europe. After forty years of rule by the world's first economist-dictator, Portugal remained, as it had been on his accession in the 1920s, Western Europe's poorest nation.

Caetano, who became prime minister after Salazar suffered a stroke in 1968, gave indications that he recognized the need for a more responsive approach to economic problems and adopted a number of cautiously liberal policies. Wages were allowed to rise at a faster rate than in previous years, and foreign investment was given greater encouragement. Unfortunately inflation became a greater problem, and worldwide inflationary trends and the 1973 oil embargo contributed to internal problems. The cost of living in the year preceding the April 1974 coup rose by 30 percent, far outrunning increases in personal income, which in any case were enjoyed by only a minority of workers. In the meantime the African wars were not only creating disaffection within the military but also contributing to economic problems. Although the coup d'etat that removed Caetano from office was the direct result of military disaffection, the long-standing economic inequities played a contributing role and were leading factors in the ready acceptance of the change among the Portuguese people.

ECONOMIC CONSEQUENCES OF THE REVOLUTION

Economic Policy Orientation

On May 15, 1974, three weeks after the April coup, the economic policy orientation of the new government was revealed in the issuance of Decree Law 203-74. The broad scope of this decree included economic and social welfare measures that provided a preview of major changes in the character of the Portuguese economy. The economic measures called for an income equalization program that combined minimum wages with salary ceilings and tax reform to ease the burden on lower income groups and reduce tax evasion in the higher brackets. Anti-inflation measures included a freeze on prices for essential goods, rents, and other services. Labor was to have a stronger voice in enterprise management and to receive greater protection in employment rights. Banking and credit reforms were promised, including the nationalization of the banks of issue. The stock exchanges

317

at Lisbon and Porto were closed and transactions in securities suspended. The Fourth Development Plan was to be shelved, and new development priorities were announced. These included more regional development and assistance to smaller industries, as well as increased investment in infrastructural projects, low-cost housing, and education. The elimination of monopolistic practices and the promotion of cooperative movements and other marketing improvements were promised.

Economic Planning

The discarded Fourth Development Plan—which presumably would have had little chance of survival because of its identification with the old regime—was in any case ill suited to the new economic situation because of its heavy emphasis on private-sector financing, which was expected to provide funds for 87 percent of the planned projects. One of the first economic decisions set forth in the May 15, 1974, statement of economic, financial, and social policies was a promise to revise the Fourth Development Plan. This was also an indication of the new policy orientation as well as a recognition that the economic climate was hardly conducive to large-scale private investment.

Subsequent policy statements have indicated that a new development plan for the 1976-79 period was in preparation, but as of mid-1976 no comprehensive plan had appeared. There were instead a series of elaborations of the policies announced on May 15, 1974, combined with emergency decrees designed to stem inflation, reduce unemployment, and solve other economic problems. In addition from time to time announcements have been made with respect to long-term public investment plans for separate sectors of the economy. For example, it was announced in February 1976 that some 300 billion escudos would be invested in state-owned and state-controlled concerns between 1976 and 1980, of which between 76 and 80 billion would be invested in 1976. The latter figure is higher than the entire budgeted revenue figure for 1976 (see The Budget, this ch.). It appeared probable that such announcements were designed for their public relations effect rather than as an indication that a coordinated and realistic development plan had been prepared.

Starting in July 1974 the second provisional government announced major steps to control runaway inflation and boost production by a series of draft decrees restricting strikes, controlling prices, prohibiting lockouts, promising credit to threatened businesses, and offering incentives for low-cost housing construction and foreign investment. Strikes were to be delayed during a mandatory thirty-day negotiation period. Other laws made it virtually impossible to lay off workers. Wages came under government control; in May 1974 the basic minimum wage was doubled, and in July 1975 an additional 20 percent

318

was added. In June 1975 a ceiling was put on salaries. Anti-inflationary measures included restrictions on consumer credit and steep sur-. charges, ranging between 20 and 30 percent, on a wide range of imports.

Fuller elaboration of policy goals appeared in the three-year program for economic and social reform issued by the government on February 20, 1975, calling for government aid to business, improved social services, and a price and incomes policy monitored by a cost-of-living council. Such basic industries as mining, oil, gas and petrochemicals, electricity, tobacco, and arms were to have their controlling interests held by the government. These fields would be closed to foreign investment, as would cement, chemicals, fertilizers, brewing, pharmaceuticals, paper and pulp, heavy engineering, transportation, insurance, banking, and advertising. Foreign investment, however, would be encouraged in other fields. For example, repatriation of capital up to 15 percent annually would be allowed for foreign participants in export-oriented industries.

Nationalization of Enterprises

The most far-reaching economic action of the revolutionary regime has been the widespread nationalization of major sectors of the economy. This appears to have happened not as the result of a long-range plan or of carefully developed policy decisions but rather as a reaction to an attempted rightist coup in March 1975. The only actual nationalizations that were anticipated in the economic and financial policy announcements of May 15, 1974, were of the banks of issue, and those were put into effect in the fall of 1974. Although it was made clear then that the state would play a much more active role in economic decisionmaking, the May 1974 program gave assurance that government intervention in the economy would be without prejudice to the legitimate interests of private enterprise and that incentives for private investment would be created. Between May 1974 and February 1975, when a more detailed set of economic and social guidelines was issued, the nationalization of the banks of issue was the only formal government action of this kind, although there had been a number of worker takeovers and interventions in industry that the government had done little to prevent. The February 1975 program foresaw only limited and partial nationalizations involving the extension of existing state participation in such semipublic enterprises as basic steel, oil, and public utilities.

The apparent moderation of this program had been welcomed by the Confederation of Portuguese Industry, and it would presumably have been followed but for the abortive coup attempt of March 11, 1975 (see ch. 9). Charges that the attempt had been financed, if not masterminded, by the oligarchic leaders of the previous regime led to a wave of strikes and demonstrations. The bank workers' union in particular demanded the nationalization of all domestic banks and insurance companies. These nationalizations were carried out on March 13 and 15. This meant in practice that large segments of industry also came under state control because of the close control held by private banks over most of the major industrial enterprises (see Banking, this ch.). The nationalization of the financial institutions was extended in April and May to electricity, oil, steel, railroads, the national airline, road transport, cement plants, shipbuilding, heavy engineering plants, wood pulp, and tobacco.

The nationalizations had been designed primarily as an attack on the family-owned financial and industrial conglomerates that had dominated the economic structure of Portugal before the coup. Of these the largest was probably the United Manufacturing Company (Companhia União Fabril—CUF), owned by the de Mello family. This company, involved in industry, shipping, banking, and insurance, has been estimated to have controlled about 20 percent of all Portuguese industry and to have been responsible for about 10 percent of the entire economy through its 186 subsidiaries. Another important conglomerate was the Champalimaud Group, which had large holdings in the cement and steel industries. Other well-known family-dominated enterprises included those of the Espírito Santo family, with large African interests, and those of the Borges Irmão and Quina families. Family ties of these financial and industrial oligarchies extended to the large landowning families, whose estates, known as latifundios, occupied most of the agricultural land in the southern half of the country. The positions of privilege in Portugal before the coup were enjoyed by members of between 100 and 200 families; of these only about twenty held most of the economic power.

Because of the interlocking ties between these families and the few large private banks and insurance companies, the takeover of the latter meant that in a precipitate action more than half of Portuguese industry had been acquired by the government. Since the action was followed within months by a takeover of those activities that had somehow escaped the first wave of nationalization, except for the carefully exempted foreign holdings, estimates of the portion of the economy in government hands by the end of December 1975 have run as high as 65 percent.

Press accounts have not made clear the fate of the family members involved or the impact of these actions on their futures. Hasty departures for Brazil and France have been reported, and it is evident that some arrests, mostly temporary, were made. In spite of these sweeping actions, however, the voice of private industry was not completely stilled. Press accounts indicated that the Confederation of Portuguese Industry, headed by António Vasco de Mello of the CUF, was still in operation in March 1976.

In addition to the 117 companies that were nationalized and the additional 201 that came under state control because of the nationalization of their parent financial institutions, a large number of companies were placed under state administration because of financial difficulties that threatened their continued existence. Under a decree law of March 27, 1975, the Institute for State Participation (Instituto das Participações do Estado) was established to provide this administration and to coordinate the activities of companies in both categories. According to press reports this organization lacked an adequate staff to function effectively; other press reports indicated that workers' committees, which took de facto control of many enterprises before and after formal nationalization, have placed heavy burdens of wage and fringe benefit demands on the companies, thus exacerbating management problems.

As a result of the hasty actions of nationalization and other less formal kinds of intervention, it was evident that one of the most pressing problems in the Portuguese economy was the loss of managerial skills through the purge *(saneamento)* of company directors and managers by the hastily organized workers' committees in factories, service companies, and public corporations. Reportedly the worst hit were the postal and telephone services, railroads, electric companies, and the national airline. The entire management of these essential services was reportedly deposed in the months after the coup. The situation became so severe that the Portuguese Communist Party (Partido Comunista Português—PCP), which largely controlled the workers' committees, was obliged to serve as a moderating influence to prevent strikes in banks and shipyards and to suggest that workers in other areas moderate their wage demands, which were driving some companies to bankruptcy.

In spite of the evidence of disruption of the economy, these developments received formal sanction when the Constitution, which became the basic law of the land on April 2, 1976, set the stage for the progressive establishment of a socialist economy (see ch. 9). Article 9 of the new Constitution stated that among the fundamental duties of the state was the socialization of the means of production, and subsequent articles affirmed the right of workers to intervene in management through workers' commissions. The Constitution also affirmed the legality of the nationalizations of property that had taken place in the two years since the coup.

BANKING

Throughout the 1960s and early 1970s the banking system was under the supervision of the General Inspectorate of Credit and Insurance of the Ministry of Finance. The four principal kinds of institutions performing banking functions during that period were: the banks of issue, the state credit institutions, the special credit institutions, and the commercial banks.

The principal bank of issue was the Bank of Portugal (Banco de Portugal). It acted as state banker and government adviser on monetary and exchange matters and as agency for the management of treasury funds, gold, and foreign currency reserves and for the regulation of money markets and credit. Its operations, which covered continental Portugal, Madeira, and the Azores, were duplicated for the overseas possessions by the Bank of Angola (Banco de Angola) and the National Overseas Bank (Banco Nacional Ultramarino). These banks differed from most European central banks in that they had some private shareholders and carried out some commercial banking operations. The banks of issue were nationalized in the fall of 1974.

The two state credit institutions were the General Bank for Deposits, Credit, and Social Security (Caixa Geral de Depósitos, Credito e Previdência) and the associated National Credit Bank (Caixa Nacional de Crédito). The former was the depository of funds paid in to the social security system and the state pension fund and also served as a savings bank for small depositors. The two institutions extended credit to government organizations and private firms for industrial and agricultural purposes. Development projects and other creditworthy ventures approved by the Ministry of Economic Coordination (created after the revolution) were among the primary recipients of loans from these sources.

Among the special credit establishments the principal institution was the National Development Bank (Banco de Fomento Nacional), which was established in 1959 to encourage social and economic development projects and specifically to channel available funds to projects included in the national development plans. Another special credit bank, the Portuguese Building Credit (Crédito Prédial Português), specialized in mortgages for industrial, commercial, and residential building. The Portuguese Finance Society (Sociedade Financeira Portuguêsa) was founded in 1969 to investigate and carry out a variety of special investment activities, with emphasis on encouraging foreign investment, mergers, reorganizations, and formation of consortia. Regional special credit establishments included the Economic and Cooperative Funds (Caixas Econômicas e Cooperativas de Crédito), established to attract and invest small savings in local development projects. This category also included nineteen savings banks and several special funds established to encourage tourism, agrarian improvement, and the merchant marine and fishing fleets.

Among the large commercial banks the leading seven were linked to major industrial and commercial groups through interlocking directorates. Their functions were similar to commercial banks elsewhere, but there is little doubt that they favored the groups with which they were associated. Except for the banks of issue, which were nationalized in the fall of 1974, banks and insurance companies were specifically exempted from the nationalization projections of the economic and social plan óf February 20, 1975. In the reaction to the aborted coup attempt of March 1975, however, these exemptions were ignored, and the banks and insurance companies were nationalized on March 13 and 15 respectively. The only exceptions were the savings banks, some agricultural loan institutions, and the three foreign banks then operating in the country: the Bank of Brazil, the Bank of London and South America, and the French-Portuguese Credit Bank. The take-overs were accompanied by arrests—temporary in most cases—of a number of highly placed bankers, including members of the prominent de Mello, Champalimaud, and Espírito Santo families. The Council of Ministers decided on August 20, 1975, that the nationalized banks were to be gradually reduced in number through mergers from twenty-two to twelve.

The Bank of Portugal has been required to carry out massive rediscounting operations in order to provide the other banks with sufficient funds to keep their major industrial and commercial subsidiaries in operation. Rediscounting was reported to have reached 100 billion escudos in March 1976 from a low of 8.8 billion in 1973. The bank was also taking more complete control of foreign exchange operations by closing down private dealers and concentrating operations in the nationalized banks. Other measures to conserve foreign exchange and restore depositor confidence in the banks included special deposit accounts for emigrant remittances with a six-month renewable option to keep them in the currency of the depositor's choice.

FOREIGN INVESTMENT

For much of his period of rule the isolationist policies of Salazar called for the accumulation of investment capital from domestic sources rather than from foreign investment. Foreign aid was to be avoided, which explains why Portugal failed to share in the benefits of Marshall Plan aid in the post-World War II period to any significant degree or to attract an economic quid pro quo from the United States in return for the use of bases in the Azores. Foreign capital was barred in large measure from the overseas territories as well.

A loosening of restrictions on foreign capital in the early 1960s brought a flood of foreign investment and foreign-based firms into the country, attracted by low wages and by a labor force that appeared to accept the repressive labor conditions of the Salazar regime. Such large multinational firms as International Telephone and Telegraph, Timex, Ford, Firestone, and Heinz and such European firms as Renault, Grundig, and British Leyland brought foreign investment in Portuguese industry from an estimated 1.5 percent in 1960 to 27 percent in 1970. The rapidity with which the country acquired a dependence on foreign investment was revealed by the jump in the foreign investment component in planned capital outlays between the first and second development plans. The plan for the 1953-58 period called for foreign investment of only 5.8 percent, the plan for the 1959-64 period for 25 percent. The annual net inflow of private capital averaged almost US$40 million from 1962 to 1965 and rose to an average of US$80 million from 1971 to 1973. Although the United Kingdom had been the leader since the nineteenth century, by 1973 the Federal Republic of Germany (West Germany) was the principal investor with about US$33 million, followed by the United Kingdom with about US$22 million and the United States with about US$10 million. As of mid-1976 there were reportedly some 100 to 125 American firms in Portugal with a total investment estimated to be between US$200 and US$250 million, placing the United States third among foreign investors.

After the coup the provisional governments were careful to avoid actions that would discourage foreign investment. In virtually all cases of nationalization and other forms of intervention foreign interests were officially exempted, but all foreign firms felt the impact of the economic difficulties of the period. In addition some foreign agricultural holdings were swept up in the overenthusiastic expropriations of estates that characterized the first eighteen months of the revolution (see ch. 13). In spite of the apparent effort to avoid frightening off foreign investment, political developments and economic difficulties have been discouraging elements, and new investment dropped off markedly after the coup. With some notable exceptions, however, most foreign firms attempted to continue operations in Portugal during 1974 and 1975 and have continued to be subject, along with domestic firms, to rising material and labor costs, labor interference, and other hazards of operation in a revolutionary environment.

On April 7, 1976, a long-awaited foreign investment code that appeared designed to attract foreign capital in several respects was issued by the government. The most favorable aspect of the code was the guarantee of an annual transfer abroad of dividends and profits up to 12 percent of invested capital and up to 20 percent in the case of a company that exports more than 50 percent of its production. This was something of an improvement over the terms set forth in the program of February 20, 1975. Repatriation of proceeds from the sale or liquidation of foreign investment assets was also guaranteed, although it could not exceed 20 percent of the total in any year. For both profits and capital repatriation the Bank of Portugal was authorized to consider transactions beyond these limitations.

Employment of foreign personnel was to be allowed during an indefinite period for training of an adequate number of Portuguese to fill technical and administrative positions. New investment would be approved on the basis of such considerations as creation of new jobs, contributions to balance of payments, production of items not heretofore manufactured in Portugal, introduction of advanced technology, transformation of national resources, regional development, and low industrial pollution. Although existing investments would not be affected, new foreign capital participation would not be permitted in defense industries, public services, banks and other financial institutions, publicity and communications media, the nationalized industry sectors, or other areas of national interest as they might be defined by decree. Negotiations and authorizations were placed under the responsibility of a new agency, the Institute of Foreign Investment (Instituto de Investimento Estrangeivo). With respect to external arbitration of investment questions, consideration was to be given to Portugal's subscribing to the conventions of the International Center for Settlement of Investment Disputes.

FOREIGN AID

Because of Salazar's suspicion of foreign influences, Portugal had received only a small amount in loans and grant aid from the United States under the various postwar economic and military aid programs. Only US$160 million in economic aid was furnished by the United States to Portugal between 1945 and 1974. US$51.2 million of this was extended before 1954 under the Marshall Plan, and virtually all the balance was under the Food for Peace program. In addition US$345.8 million in military aid grants was given to Portugal by the United States. During the same 1945-74 period the United States Export-Import Bank extended loans totaling US$117.3 to Portugal. Portugal borrowed the equivalent of US$57.5 million from the World Bank through 1974 and received US$400,000 under miscellaneous United Nations allocation programs.

Since the coup Portuguese governments have been less reluctant to accept foreign aid. The reluctance has been rather on the part of some potential doners wary about the ultimate political cast of the Portuguese government. Although the United States had authorized several emergency aid packages for refugees and temporary relief of food shortages, long-range development aid has been held in abeyance pending a clearer view of possible political developments. The European Economic Community (EEC, also called the Common Market) was more forthcoming in 1975 with offers of financial aid totaling more than US$200 million in loans and interest rebates, as well as agreements to renegotiate the terms of the existing trade agreement with Portugal and to send food aid for refugees from Angola.

An affiliate of the EEC, the European Investment Bank, agreed in October 1975 to extend loans amounting to 150 million units of account (equivalent to about US$175 million). In early 1976 Portugal was granted emergency loans by the IMF (US$85.5 million), the Swiss National Bank (US$50 million), and the West German Bundesbank (US$250 million). These loans were secured by Portugal's still-substantial gold holdings, valued at nearly US$4 billion at current gold prices. In late 1975 Portugal's partners in EFTA also agreed to assist with a variety of technical aid projects and an industrial development fund of US$150 million.

Altogether the amount available in committed and anticipated grants and credits was estimated in early 1976 as close to US$1 billion. Whether this would be adequate and appropriately applied was far from certain, pending the establishment of a constitutionally authorized government and the issuance of the long-awaited development plan.

BALANCE OF PAYMENTS

Portugal's balance of payments—which had been in surplus for many years, creating steadily increasing reserves since 1962—registered a deficit in 1974 as a decline in tourist receipts and a slowing of emigrant remittances failed to offset the usual trade deficit, which almost doubled in 1974 (see ch. 14). With a balance-of-payments deficit of US$648 million in 1974 and over US$1 billion in 1975, Portugal's traditionally strong reserve position also worsened.

One of the few bright spots in the Portuguese economic picture during the Salazar-Caetano years was the growing hoard of international reserve holdings—the result of Salazar's mercantilist economic policies. These reserves reached a peak of US$2.8 billion in 1973, when they equaled more than a year's merchandise imports in value and thus a much higher proportion of reserves to imports than modern nations customarily maintain. The worsening economic conditions in 1974 and 1975 brought about significant losses in reserve holdings. At the end of 1975 the estimated total was about US$1.5 billion. Most of the gold component remained, however, since gold reserves, which had an official value of US$1.1 billion at the end of 1973, had been drawn down by only US$27 million by the end of 1975. Since gold holdings are officially valued at special drawing rights (SDR) 35 (about US$41) per ounce, the market value of Portugal's gold reserves at the end of 1975 was probably close to US$3.5 billion. This reserve has provided a basis for credit extensions. Significant portions of Portugal's gold holdings were being pledged as security for foreign loans during this critical period.

THE BUDGET

Portugal's annual budgets traditionally and by law remained in balance through Salazar's regime. Thus the 1975 budget, which projected a 15.8 billion escudo deficit, was the first in many years to show a significant deficit. Revenues were forecast at 59.6 billion escudos, compared with 53.2 billion escudos in 1974, and expenditures of 75.4 billion escudos were planned, 43 percent above 1974.

Although the new development plan was still in abeyance when this budget was issued, some of the planned expenditures in the capital portion of the budget were indications of development priorities. Planned capital expenditures amounted to 21.4 billion escudos, a 67 percent increase over 1974; 3.9 billion escudos were earmarked for overseas development aid. The top domestic priority item was 100,000 housing units, followed by construction of clinics, schools, rural market roads, railroad renovation, and electrical systems. It was indicated also that the Sines industrial complex, a major element of the Fourth Development Plan, would proceed on a somewhat reduced scale.

The 1976 budget provided for revenues of 70.7 billion escudos and expenditures of 105.5 billion escudos. A detailed breakdown of expenditures was not available.

INFLATION

Inflation, which in the mid-1970s was a worldwide problem, has been unusually severe in Portugal. Prices on the overall index, including food, fuel, clothing, and rent, doubled between 1970 and 1975. In the previous five-year period they had risen by only 25 percent. In 1974 the rate of increase was 25 percent, surpassed among OECD nations only by Iceland (42.9 percent) and Greece (26.9 percent). In 1975 the rate of increase was estimated to be between 25 and 30 percent—again one of the highest in the Western world.

The price rises of 1974 and 1975 occurred in the face of efforts to hold inflation in check, primarily because of rising wages and falling productivity. Average wages increased 40 percent in 1975 on top of increases on a similar scale in 1974. Because of this and declining production—officially announced as 15 percent but widely estimated at double that figure—many businesses have had to be supported by the banking system in order to continue. This has required a rapid increase in the money supply. In the two years ending in December 1975 coins and notes in circulation rose from the equivalent of US$1.1 billion to US$3.7 billion while short-term bank credit (that is, discounted commercial paper) rose by a factor of twelve, from US$290 million to US$3.9 billion. These credit extensions primarily represented loans to businesses to cover the heavy wage demands of the period while they attempted to operate with frozen prices.

ECONOMIC IMPACT OF DECOLONIZATION

Placing a cost figure on the painful decolonization process that Portugal has undergone in the mid-1970s is a difficult task. The resettlement and rehabilitation of over 800,000 refugees from the colonies was much more than an economic problem. The lost profits from investments in the colonies, both present and future, must also be taken into account. The loss of colonial markets was probably less serious than had been predicted because the colonies had been taking a dwindling share of Portugal's exports and these markets were not necessarily entirely lost (see ch. 14). Portugal's trade deficit with its African territories soared to over US$200 million in 1974 under the pressure of rising oil prices.

The cutback in military spending was an advantage and, although providing employment for demobilized soldiers, became an immediate problem; in the long run a return to economic health could find the pool of skills and manpower an advantage. Although in the mid-1970s Portugal suffered from a decline in remittances from Portuguese overseas, this problem related more to the diminished returns from emigrant workers in Western Europe than from colonials, since the latter tended to consist of whole family units with few ties in metropolitan Portugal requiring support.

The actual measurable costs would presumably cover such factors as repayments on loans for projects initiated before decolonization as well as Portuguese guarantees on loans taken over by the new governments. A certain amount of technical assistance and even financial aid was apparently to be extended to the new governments, and many of the colonial assets of Portuguese companies that were nationalized in metropolitan Portugal in the spring of 1975—either directly or as a result of bank nationalizations—were apparently to be ceded to the new governments. A loss of royalties and tax revenues formerly levied on foreign concessions was expected.

The *Financial Times* made a rough estimate of about US$3.6 billion as the tangible bill for decolonization, most of it spread over a period of years because of staggered loan payments. This figure would, of course, be significantly raised by inclusion of such intangible costs as the resettlement of refugees.

In the spring of 1976 Angola was reported to be carrying out a wholesale nationalization of Portuguese plantations and factories. These included the principal cement and steel producers as well as textile and sugar companies. Although judgments are difficult as to how far reaching and irreversible such takeovers might be and estimates of the size of investment losses are equally so, there appeared to be a possibility for at least some Portuguese technicians and managers to return to useful occupations in Africa. In fact some 40,000 to 50,000 were believed to have remained behind after independence in anticipation of such a possibility. As of May 1976 the Angolan holdings of non-Portuguese, including the American-owned Cabinda Gulf Oil Company and the British-South African diamond concession, had not been disturbed.

Although many unsolved problems with respect to Portugal's economic relations with its former overseas possessions remained . in the spring of 1976, compromise solutions to these problems when politically possible could leave Portugal with a considerable role in Africa. In Angola, for example, a number of small Portuguese industries could continue in operation, and all sectors of the Angolan economy could benefit from the skills of Portuguese experienced in operations in the Angolan environment. Whether these possibilities can be realized will depend, first, on determination of the rights and safeguards made available to those Portuguese who decide to remain or to return to Angola and, second, on determination of appropriate compensation for Angola's nationalization of Portuguese banks and firms. Similar possibilities and problems existed in varying degrees in the other territories.

LABOR

Portugal's labor force under Salazar was chronically underpaid and underemployed. The underemployment problem was partially solved by exporting it in the flow of emigrant workers to the more industrialized countries of northern Europe in the 1960s and early 1970s (see ch.4). This outlet for Portugal's surplus workers was being cut off in the mid-1970s as the recession led the recipient countries to become increasingly restrictive in their acceptance of foreign workers. The estimated net migration from Portugal in 1974 was down to about 70,000 from a peak of about 180,000 in 1970.

Compounding the unemployment problem created by internal economic disorders and by slowing emigration was the inflow of refugees from the African territories. Estimates of the total number of refugees made in 1975 reached 500,000, but press reports in early 1976 escalated the figure to 1 million. Whatever the actual number, the refugee population added a formidable burden to the already overtaxed housing and welfare services and to the unemployment totals, which had reached an estimated 500,000—not counting refugees—at the end of 1975 (see ch. 4).

The chronically low wages paid to Portuguese workers were not regarded as a problem by Portugal's economic and political elite during the Salazar-Caetano period or by the foreign industry that flowed into the country in the 1960s, encouraged by the low wage scales and the apparently docile labor force. This appearance of docility was, of course, the result of laws forbidding strikes and limiting the organizing and collective bargaining rights to the carefully controlled syndicates of the corporate structure of Salazar's New State (Estado Novo), which were under the close supervision of the employers' groups and of the state authorities (see ch. 8).

Although there was some loosening of controls over labor organization in the brief Caetano regime, industrywide unions were forbidden.

Organization was also fragmented within each industry by craft, which was presumed to prevent any one industry's workers from becoming too powerful. It appears also to have made it easier for clandestine communist organizers to operate, since soon after the coup in April 1974 an apparently well-organized and communist-controlled central union organization, Intersindical, emerged. Intersindical demand that it be named the only legal federation for the labor unions, which then numbered over 300. The monopolistic role claimed by Intersindical was opposed by the Socialists, who favored independent unions on the French model. The communist argument that only through an all-embracing federation could labor discipline be maintained was apparently bolstered by the sporadic outbreaks of strikes in defiance of government decree and communist opposition in the months after the coup. In any event the conflict was decided in the Communists' favor when the Council of the Revolution voted by a narrow margin on January 21, 1975, to recognize Intersindical as the only authorized labor federation.

The trade union bill of that date was not, however, a complete victory for the Communists. Although the communist-dominated Intersindical was given a monopoly over the trade union structure, the secret ballot for union elections was retained, and neither union membership nor subscription was compulsory. A majority vote was necessary before a union was required to joint the federation.

Upon being freed from the restrictions of the Salazar-Caetano regime, workers were not long in pressing their grievances. A government grant in May 1974 of a monthly minimum wage of 3,300 escudos was regarded as inadequate, and a wave of strikes broke out with demands for a minimum wage of 6,000 escudos (about US$250) per month, a forty-hour workweek, and the purging from managerial ranks of all who could be identified with the former regime. This last demand resulted in the widespread establishment of workers' committees with the reluctant acquiescence of the government. It also resulted in the loss of trained managerial personnel as well as the all-too-rare engineers and technicians. The few state administrators who replaced the managers have been an inadequate substitute, and management by committees of workers, who have neither the experience nor the inclination to balance worker benefits with concepts of costs and productivity, was another burden on the faltering economy. Even when management was retained or, in a few cases, accepted invitations to return, the workers' committees continued to exercise scrutiny over operations under government-inspired exhortations to maintain "revolutionary diligence." Foreign enterprises, though spared formal takeover, suffered from this form of harassment along with the domestic firms. The forced acceptance of escalating wage demands and other benefits regardless of productivity and income affected both foreign and domestic enterprise impartially.

CURRENCY

The basic unit of currency is the escudo, which is divided into 100 centavos. The customary symbol for the escudo is $, which appears after the escudo amount and before the centavo amount. Thus 10$50 is read "ten escudos fifty centavos." The escudo has also been the currency unit in all overseas territories except Macao, where the local currency unit is the pataca—pegged to the Hong Kong dollar. On March 26, 1973, the value of the pataca was established at 5.015 escudos per pataca.

The escudo had an initial par value of 0.0309103 gram of fine gold, established on June 1, 1962, or 28.75 escudos per US$1. The dollar value was changed on December 21, 1971, to 27.25 escudos per US$1, a rate that prevailed until February 14, 1973, after which it fluctuated within a range of 24.60 to 27.25. During 1975 its value averaged about twenty-five escudos per US$1. One thousand escudos is called a con-to—a term in common use in presenting financial and economic data.

As of late 1975 the escudo was a free-floating currency, convertible into other currencies under existing IMF agreements. Because of the government's substantial gold holdings, its value on international markets was comparatively stable and failed to reflect sharply rising prices in domestic markets. Official devaluation to promote exports remained a possibility, but the adverse effect on the prices of needed imports made this a difficult policy option to accept.

All exchange transactions were subject to Bank of Portugal approval. This included interest and royalty payments, loan repayments, and settlements of trade accounts. The remittance of dividends and profits and the repatriation of capital were allowed provided that the Bank of Portugal had initially authorized the importation of capital that was the original source of the transaction.

CHAPTER 13

AGRICULTURE AND INDUSTRY

Industry and agriculture (including forestry and fishing) were the origin of an estimated 59 percent of Portugal's gross domestic product (GDP) at factor cost in 1974. This constitutes a slightly larger proportion than is found in more developed countries having advanced services sectors. The 62.7 percent of the total work force employed in the agriculture and industry sectors in 1974 was also somewhat larger than in more advanced economies. Of the two sectors agriculture has been growing at a much slower rate and actually lost a considerable number of workers in the 1960s and early 1970s.

Agriculture and industry have tended to complement each other, the agricultural sector providing the raw materials for Portugal's traditional industries—food processing and cork and wood processing. The country's newer industries, however, developed after World War II and have been much more dependent on imports.

Both sectors have been handicapped by a lack of investment capital. Agriculture in particular has failed to keep pace with the rest of Western Europe in acquiring the necessary inputs to maintain yields; the result is that increasing agricultural imports have been necessary. Industry has depended on retained profits for much of its new investment. This source has been inadequate for the smaller establishments, and the larger firms have tended to monopolize access to the domestic banking system. Before the revolution of April 1974 the banking system was closely linked to the larger industrial enterprises through the close-knit family ties that have characterized Portuguese society and have had a repressive influence on the economy. Foreign investment sources, which became significant only in the later years of Prime Minister António de Oliveira Salazar's regime, have also been restricted to the larger established enterprises, leaving most of the country's 47,000 enterprises with little access to the capital resources necessary for modernization.

Both agriculture and industry have been structurally in upheaval since April 1974 because of widespread expropriation of the traditional agricultural estates in the southern third of the country and even more widespread nationalization of industries. In the case of agriculture an orderly transfer of large estates, a plan contemplated by earlier agrarian reform legislation, was upset by the precipitous takeover

333

of many estates by the farmworkers. Much of the nationalization of industry was also a legalization of hasty takeovers by workers before procedural or organizational guidelines had been developed. Although these changes were presumably aimed at eliminating economic hardships and inequities, during the first two years of revolutionary upheaval they were accompanied by rampant inflation, growing unemployment, and political unrest, all of which made it difficult to evaluate either the permanence of the new institutions or their ultimate effect on the economic fortunes of Portugal.

THE ROLE OF AGRICULTURE IN THE ECONOMY

In the mid-1970s agriculture, forestry, and fishing contributed about 16 percent to GDP at factor cost and employed about 27 percent of the working population. These figures compare with a contribution to the GDP of about 22 percent in 1963 and employment by this sector of about 39 percent in the same year. Also in the mid-1970s the sector accounted for about 33 percent of commodity exports, of which one-half were forest products. Agricultural production was fairly diversified, although sugar and tobacco have not been grown on mainland Portugal, primarily because these products were traditionally reserved for the Azores, Madeira, and the overseas possessions. Presumably with the relinquishment of most of the colonies the mainland can look to such products as a means of further diversifying agriculture and increasing potential production.

In spite of the dwindling share that this sector contributed to the GDP, it has been a vital foreign exchange earner. Agricultural and forest products, notably tomato paste, wine, paper, pulp, and cork, provided about one-third of the total value of exports in 1973, and preliminary estimates for 1974 and 1975 suggested that this fraction was increasing (see ch. 14). At the same time, the failure of the sector to contribute more to domestic food needs meant that about 17 percent of imports consisted of foodstuffs, a proportion that appears to have been increasing rapidly in 1974 and 1975.

Although exports and imports of food were roughly in balance in the early 1960s—exports, 3.2 billion escudos (for value of the escudo —see Glossary), and imports, 3.1 billion escudos, in 1963—an increasing deficit was characteristic in the mid-1970s. In 1974, for example, food exports were 8 billion escudos, and food imports were 11.8 billion escudos. This deficit reflected not only the slow growth of agriculture but also changing food tastes. Consumption of animal products grew rapidly in the 1960s and early 1970s while cereals became less important. Per capital meat consumption of thirty kilograms (1 kilogram equals 2.2 pounds) per annum, however, was the lowest in Western Europe in 1974 and only about half the average among members of the European Communities (EC).

334

The poor growth record of agriculture in the 1960s and 1970s was more marked in crops than in livestock. Taking the 1961-65 average as equal to 100, the crop production index was only 94 in 1974 while the livestock index rose to 145, resulting in an overall agricultural production index of 112. The depressed state of Portuguese agriculture has several causes. Soil, topography, and climatic conditions are considerably less than ideal. These natural handicaps are aggravated by traditional landholding patterns that are ill suited to modern agriculture and by the inadequacy of investment in agriculture. Government encouragement of cereal production to attain self-sufficiency has resulted in the cultivation of submarginal lands and in low overall yields. Although some of the natural handicaps defy solution, there is considerable potential for improvement through increased irrigation—particularly in the drier areas of the Alentejo—and through conversion of marginal croplands to forest development or pasture and the introduction of such crops as sugar beets, more appropriate to soil and climatic conditions.

Land Use

Of mainland Portugal's 8.9 million hectares (one hectare equals 2.47 acres), 4.4 million (about 50 percent) were in crops in the early 1970s, 0.5 million (about 6 percent) in meadows and pastures, 2.5 million (about 28 percent) in forests, and the balance either developed or wasteland. Although a shortage of good natural pasture existed, there was much mixed farming in which stockraising was combined with cork oak stands and wheat growing in the south and with maize (corn) and rye cultivation in the north (see fig. 25).

As in Spain and many Latin American countries, landowning patterns have characteristically run to extremes. In the north and central regions small holdings and fragmented plots prevail. These small farms are handicapped by uneconomic size and outmoded farming techniques, the remedy for which includes the easing of agricultural credit and the improvement of government agricultural extension services. In the south, where large landholdings (latifundios) are common, land use is also uneconomic, and inadequate farm credit has been compounded by the unwillingness of wealthy absentee landlords to invest in modern agricultural machinery and employ modern methods. Investment in agriculture declined from about 9 percent of total investment in 1963 to about 4 percent in 1973.

These landholding patterns are based on historical antecedents. The north and central regions have been areas of small proprietorship and subdivision by inheritance, reflecting the practices brought by the Germanic invaders of the fifth and sixth centuries A.D. The region south of the Rio Tejo reflected the original Roman estate system, perpetuated at the time of the Reconquest, when medieval rulers re-

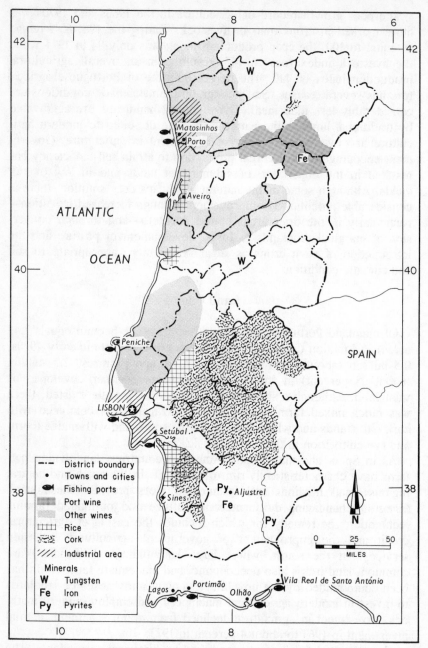

Figure 25. Portugal, Economic Activity, 1974

warded the warrior nobles and the Roman Catholic Church for their valor against the Moors. Widespread confiscation of church lands in the eighteenth and nineteenth centuries resulted in the sale of many estates to the rising bourgeoisie and perpetuated the absentee landlord system that has characterized this region in the twentieth century. Similar patterns of landownership based on similar historical antecedents are found in comparable regions of Spain.

An agricultural survey taken in 1968 revealed a total of 816,000 farms, of which 500,000 were over one hectare in size. Of these, 71 percent were less than five hectares and accounted for only 16 percent of the agricultural area. Medium-sized farms, those between twenty and 100 hectares, occupied only 15 percent of the total agricultural area, whereas the 0.9 percent of the farms that were over 100 hectares occupied 46 percent of the total agricultural area. In the north and central regions where small holdings prevailed, fragmentation was common, averaging 6.27 plots per farm in the north and 7.74 plots per farm in the central region. The land tenure system in 1968 consisted of 63 percent of the farms being worked by owners, 18.6 percent by stock farm associations, 13.4 percent by tenant farmers, 1.5 percent by sharecroppers, and the balance by mixed-tenure arrangements.

Agricultural Labor Force

Although the country's total labor force was declining in the 1960s and early 1970s, the number of independent farmers and farmworkers had been decreasing at an even faster rate. In 1960 about 42 percent of the labor force, 1.4 million people, worked on farms. By 1970 the number of farmworkers had dropped to 898,000, and in the 1972-73 period it was estimated to be 798,000—only 27 percent of the labor force. Within the agricultural work force the number of wage earners dropped even more sharply, from 814,000 in 1960 to 593,000 in 1970, presumably a reflection of the relatively greater ease with which a wage earner could pull up stakes than could the landowners and tenant farmers. Within the latter group it was apparent that the sons of farmers were leaving the farms in quantity since the average age of farmworkers had been rising. There were 45.6 percent of the farmworkers over age forty in 1960 and 64.3 percent in 1970. In the same decade the number of female farmworkers rose by 20 percent, and the number of males fell by 43.4 percent.

These statistics reflect the lack of economic opportunity on farms and the correspondingly greater employment opportunities in the cities and towns, but the major impetus came from the opportunities available for workers willing to emigrate. Of the 1.4 million people who left the rural areas between 1961 and 1971, only 410,000 appear to have gone to the larger urban areas—Lisbon, Porto, and Setúbal—and most of the remainder went to the industrialized countries of Western Europe (see ch. 4).

The migration of rural workers created a growing shortage of agricultural labor in the 1960s, which in turn brought sharp rises in farm wages. These rises averaged about 10 percent annually from 1960 to 1970 but were even greater in the early 1970s, reaching 16 percent in 1973. As a result fewer farmers could afford to hire labor. Of those farmers who had hired labor in 1960, some 77 percent had ceased to do so by 1970. Certain crops—particularly those, such as olives, that depend on seasonal hired labor—suffered in output as a result.

There was considerable underemployment on the farm not only because of the backward state of Portuguese agriculture but also because of the peculiar nature of several major crops. Cork and olives, which are principal cash crops in the dry southern regions, require little attention except during their brief harvest periods. Cork trees are trimmed only once a decade, and olive trees—particularly those that do not benefit from irrgation and fertilizer—often can be harvested only every other year. In the north, although agriculture is more intensive, farm plots tend to be too small to provide full-time employment or an adequate livelihood for the farmer and his family.

Agricultural Investment

The small investment in the agricultural sector was reflected by the low ratio of gross fixed asset formation in agriculture to gross agricultural production. This was only 7.4 percent in 1972, compared with 12 percent in Spain and 17 percent in Greece. Also, the sector's share of total national gross fixed asset formation was only 4.1 percent in 1972. Symptomatic of the official neglect of agriculture was the sharp decline in the proportion of agricultural investment by government departments compared with that by the private sector. This fell from 32 percent in 1970 to only 16 percent in 1971 and 18 percent in 1972.

The chief sources of private agricultural credit have been the Agrarian Reorganization Institute (Instituto de Reorganização Agraria —IRA), the General Savings Bank (Caixa Geral de Depositos), the National Development Bank (Banco de Fomento Nacional), and local mutual agricultural credit banks (see ch. 12). None of these sources has been adequate. For example, in 1974 the IRA issued only 242 million escudos in loans. After the nationalization of banks in March 1975 the government announced a 5-billion-escudo credit extension to small farmers, but during the balance of the year there was little implementation because of staff inadequacy.

Inadequate agricultural investment has resulted in a low proportion of irrigated land relative to need and potential as well as inadequate use of fertilizer and farm machinery. The area under irrigation in 1970 was 683,000 hectares, constituting only a 10-percent increase in the period since 1955 and only 14 percent of the total agricultural area. Irrigation is particularly lacking in the arid southern area, which recorded only 3.3 percent irrigated area in 1970 compared with 27 percent in the north.

Fertilizer consumption, although increasing significantly in the late 1960s and early 1970s, was only 47 kilograms per hectare—considerably below the West European average. Farm machinery use was also low. In 1972 there were 7.2 tractors per 1,000 hectares, less than one-half the number used in Spain and Greece and only one-sixth of those in use per 1,000 hectares in Italy. There was also a great need, particularly in the area of small farms, for garden-type power cultivators.

MAJOR CROPS

Cereals

Wheat is the leading grain crop and predominantes in the Alentejo (Beja, Evora, and Portalegre districts) (see fig. 1). The area under wheat cultivation totaled 469,000 hectares in 1974, and production that year was 511,000 tons.

Maize is grown primarily on the small farms of the north, where rainfall is more plentiful. The principal districts for this crop are Porto, Aveiro, and Braga. The area devoted to maize has been declining. Although 455,000 hectares were the recorded average area in the 1962-71 period, only 372,000 hectares were so recorded in 1974. Production averaged 533,000 tons in the 1970-74 period.

Rice, although occupying less than one-tenth of the area of either wheat or maize, is a significant grain crop. Its average 1970-73 production of 176,000 tons made Portugal Europe's third largest producer of this crop, after Italy and Spain. Because rice requires an abundance of water, its cultivation is confined to about 35,000 hectares in the floodable alluvial areas—chiefly the valleys of the Sorraia, Tejo, and Mondego rivers and the Setúbal peninsula.

Rye is grown chiefly in the drier mountainous areas of the Trás-os-Montes region. Its principal districts are Bragança and Vila Real. Production averaged 156,000 tons on about 220,000 hectares.

Of somewhat lesser importance are oats and barley, which are grown in the same general area as wheat. Annual crops for each are less than 100,000 tons. Portugal's grain-crop yields are generally the lowest in Western Europe, reflecting the inefficient use of the land and the inadequate use of fertilizers, irrigation, and modern agricultural technologies (see table 11). As a result of low yields, substantial grain imports are needed to supplement domestic supplies. In 1974 Portugal imported 380,000 tons of wheat and 983,000 tons of maize.

Vegetables

Portugal produces a variety of horticultural crops, some of which make a contribution to its export capability. Among these the most important has been tomatoes. In 1974 the country ranked fourth in

Table 11. Portugal, Grain-crop Yields Compared with
Selected West European Countires, 1974
(in kilograms per hectare)[1]

Crop	Portugal	Spain	Greece	Average All EEC[2] Countries
Wheat	1,140	1,410	2,430	4,030
Maize (corn).......	1,320	3,810	3,910	4,960
Oats	560	1,180	1,490	3,560
Barley...........	840	1,790	2,350	3,970
Rye	800	1,020	1,500	3,480
Rice	4,240	5,750	5,150	5,140

[1] One kilogram equals 2.2 pounds; one hectare equals 2.47 acres.
[2] European Economic Community.

Source: Based on information from U.S. Department of Agriculture, Foreign
Agricultural Service, *World Agricultural Production and Trade: Statistical Report*, Washington, October 1975 and December 1975.

the world as a processor of tomatoes and was the leading exporter of
tomato paste. This industry grew rapidly in the 1960s and 1970s, and
production of tomatoes rose from 67,000 tons in 1960 to 855,000 tons
in 1972. Other vegetables of significance, for both local consumption
and export, are potatoes, onions, chick-peas, French beans, and
broad beans.

The Azores and Madeira contribute to the country's agricultural
variety through a number of tropical products. In addition to its
world-famous wine, Madeira produces bananas and sugarcane. It is
said to have been the site of the world's first sugarcane plantation.
Sugar beets, rather than cane, are grown in the Azores, which also
produce tea and pineapples. Both island groups produce sweet potatoes, yams, and fruits and table vegetables similar to those grown on
the mainland.

Wine Grapes

In the mid-1970s about 356,000 hectares were in vineyards, and
Portugal was Western Europe's fourth largest producer of wines. The
most important vineyards are in the northern two-thirds of the country, north of the Rio Tejo, but vineyards are also found in the Algarve region and the Setúbal peninsula as well as scattered elsewhere.

Relative to its size Portugal allegedly produces a greater variety of
wines than any other country in the world. It is also claimed that the
Portuguese "southern" sun and obdurate granite soils give a particular character to Portuguese wines. Especially well known are the dessert wines—port, Madeira, and muscatel—and the rosé wines, notably
Mateus. Portuguese red and white table wines are not so well known

abroad, but their export and reputation have been increasing. It is said that the promotion of wine exports was a particular preoccupation of Salazar, who was the son of a winegrower from Santa Comba Dão, one of the leading table wine areas.

Table wines are classified as young or light wines *(vinhos verdes)* and mature or full-bodied wines *(vinhos maduros)*. The former are grown mostly between the Rio Minho and the Rio Douro and the latter in the Rio Dão area as well as in the Estremadura and Ribatejo regions. The best known sparkling rosé wines are from the Mateus and Lamego areas of the Rio Douro valley.

About 10 percent of the annual production is exported. Wine exports in 1974 were about 26 million gallons compared with about 80 million gallons for Spain, 160 million for France, and 190 million for Italy. Wine is the leading agricultural export and contributed about 6 percent by value to Portugal's total exports in 1974 (see ch. 14).

Port

Port wine, officially known in the United States as *porto* or *vinho do porto* in order to distinguish it from American port wines, is produced primarily for export, the Portuguese having a preference for lighter domestic wines. The only wine entitled to use the above appellations or the name *port* in export trade is that defined by the Anglo-Portuguese Treaty of 1916 as "a fortified wine produced in the delimited Douro region and exported through the Bar of Oporto." The region so delimited is a hilly area about sixty miles long, located on both sides of the Rio Douro, and varying in width from about ten to thirty miles. This area is about sixty miles upriver from Porto, starting just west of Peso de Régua, the administrative center for the wine trade, and extending to the Spanish border. The terraced vineyards of the region produce ten to fifteen varieties of grape, which after harvesting in the fall are pressed together, traditionally by barefoot treading but in the modern era increasingly by mechanical means. Fermentation is carefully monitored and stopped at the prescribed moment by the addition of brandy, which brings the alcohol content of the final product to about 20 percent. The next spring the wine is shipped downriver in casks, known as pipes, carried by rail or trucks and, more traditionally, by picturesque boats *(barco rabelo)* to Porto or Vila Nova de Gaia, its suburb at the mouth of the river, for storage until maturity, which may take as long as twenty years for the rarer vintages.

Madeira

Portugal's other internationally known wine is produced solely on the island of Madeira, from which it takes its name. Although not particularly popular in modern times it was the most fashionable wine in colonial America, gradually losing its popularity in the nineteenth century. Its early popularity stemmed not only from its intrinsic merits but also from the practice of the sailing ships' stopping at the island on the westward passage for water and provisions, of which Madeira wine constituted a significant portion.

Madeira wine grapes are grown intensively on irrigated terraces. The harvest is carefully monitored to ensure that the grapes are picked at the height of ripeness. The juice is expressed by treading and, unlike the practice in Spain, the bare foot is used, as it is in the processing of port. After fermentation and the addition of fortifying brandy the wine is matured in hothouses for several weeks, a practice that also stems from the colonial era, when the long ocean voyage in the warm holds of sailing ships was credited with giving Madeira wine its special characteristics. Although this wine no longer enjoys its former popularity as an aperitif or as a dessert wine, it is widely used in French cookery and in the modern era finds its largest export market in France.

Tree Crops

Portugal's most important edible tree crop is olive oil. The country usually stands about fifth in world production. In 1973 about 11 million gallons were produced, and about the same amount was estimated for 1974. These figures are, however, significantly below the annual average of 18 million gallons for the 1965-69 period and 14.5 million gallons for the 1970-73 period. Although olive groves are found over a wide area, the most important production districts are Beja, Portalegre, and Evora.

The olive tree is among the world's oldest cultivated crops. It flourishes in a number of Mediterranean countries because it can endure drought and poor soil conditions. Markedly improved yields can be obtained, however, from irrigation, good soil, and appropriate fertilizers, all of which have been scarce in the Portuguese environment. Alternate yearly bearings are thus the rule where irrigation and fertilization are not carried out, and this is one explanation for the wide fluctuations in annual yields.

The decline in output in the 1970s is attributable to the rising cost of seasonal labor and to an increase in the production of substitutes—other edible oilseeds, such as safflower and sunflower. In spite of the importance of olive oil for the economy and the increasing production of other oilseed crops, Portugal has become a net importer of vegetable fats and oils. In 1973 about one-sixth of all food and animal feed imports were in this category.

Other significant tree crops are figs, nuts, and citrus fruits. Portugal often leads the world in fig production. In 1973 it produced 195,000 tons, about 18 percent of world production. In the same year its production of almonds, 21,000 tons, was about 4 percent of the world total, and the 68,000 tons of chestnuts were about 20 percent of the world supply.

LIVESTOCK

Although there is a scarcity of good pastureland, livestock constitutes a significant part of the agricultural economy. About one-third of the value of agricultural production in 1973 came from animal products. According to a 1972 census there were 1.1 million cattle, an increase of 25 percent over the census figures for 1955. Pig raising increased by 40 percent in the same period, reaching nearly 2 million head in 1972. Cattle, which are widely used as draft animals, are found particularly in the north, where Braga, Porto, and Aveiro are the leading districts. Pigs are more common in central Portugal, where acorns from the cork and holm oaks provide a significant source of pig fodder.

Poultry production also expanded in the 1960s and early 1970s. The average annual production of poultry meat reached 61,000 tons in the 1968-72 period compared with about 27,000 tons in the 1960-64 period. Egg production went up about 10 percent over the same span of years.

In 1972 the number of sheep—2.4 million—represented a decline of about one-third during the time between the two animal censuses; the number of goats remained substantially the same at about 700,000. Wool production dropped significantly from an annual average of 11,945 tons in the 1961-65 period to an estimated 8,200 in 1973.

The demand for animal products in the 1960s and early 1970s led to a decrease in Portuguese self-sufficiency in the livestock sector. Domestic production amounted to only 71 percent of beef, 89 percent of pork, 86 percent of cheese, and 33 percent of butter consumption in 1975.

FORESTRY

Miscellaneous

About one-fifth of the country is forest, primarily pine, oak, and eucalyptus. There is also a wide variety of tropical woods, such as palm and jacaranda, as well as more typically European growth, including chestnut, lime, elm, and poplar. Pine, covering about 1.3 million hectares, is most common on the sandy coastal areas and on mountain slopes in the north; oak is found principally in Ribatejo and Alentejo. About one-half of the oak stand is cork oak *(Quercus suber)*; much of the balance is holm oak *(Quercus ilex)*. Acorns from both varieties are a significant source of pig food.

The natural forest stands are augmented by such crops as fruit, nut, olive, and carob trees, bringing the total wooded area to about 3 million hectares, one-third of the area of Portugal. This could be increased by afforestation to about 5 million hectares, using land that is poorly suited for agriculture. Forest products provide about 15 percent of commodity exports.

The commercially valuable timber stands include pine, which is used not only for timber but also for resin, pitch, and turpentine. Particularly in the north pine is mixed with eucalyptus—a fast-growing import from Australia—which is a prime source of wood pulp and paper. Eucalyptus also grows well in the sandy, less fertile soils of the southern provinces. Portugal's most important forest product, however, is cork; it produces more than one-half of the world's supply.

Cork

The cork oak predominates in the south-central region, the Alentejo. The annual harvest of about 200,000 tons represents the growth of only about 10 percent of the trees as the bark can be stripped from an individual tree only about once in ten years. Stripping is by hand and requires great skill and care to avoid injury to the tree. The initial stripping from young trees occurs when they are about twenty years old. The first and second strippings produce a low-quality cork, which is usually ground for industrial use, whereas the best quality cork, which comes from mature trees, is reserved for bottle stoppers and other specialty uses. Cork's unique characteristics of elasticity, impermeability, and buoyancy give it a wide range of uses. These include insulation; water and chemical resistance; use in flotation equipment, soundproofing, and cushioning; and wear resistance. These industrial applications as well as its decorative uses appear to provide it with an assured continuing market, although many plastics and other synthetic substances are a continuing threat. The processing of cork continues to be an important component of the manufacturing sector (see Industry, this ch.).

Forest Management

Public forests (national and local) amounted to only about 12 percent of all forestlands at the time of the revolution, and there is no information about subsequent nationalization. In mid-1975 a national forestry law reportedly was being prepared, authorizing management by the Forest Service of the Ministry of Agriculture of local forestlands and the provision of management assistance to private owners. Since most private forests belong to owners of small subsistence farms in the mountainous areas, the obstacles to effective management, either on a cooperative basis or through nationalization, appear formidable. There is a lack of management services and technological resources for any such program on a national scale, although since the mid-1960s there has been in operation the Fund for Forestry Development, which has a small program of technical assistance and low-interest credits for the establishment of new forestlands.

FISHERIES

Portugal has traditionally been a major fish-consuming and -producing country. Fish consumption of nearly 50 kilograms per capita is one of the highest in the world—although third after Iceland and Norway among West European countries. The country's preeminence as a fishing nation was undoubtedly a major factor in its role as a maritime power and in the exploration feats during the Age of Discovery. In modern times the industry has been in something of a decline, the number of persons employed in fishing trending downward from about 55,000 in the mid-1960s to about 27,000 in 1974. The peak catch since 1960 was 429,000 tons in 1965, but the average landed catch in the years between 1960 and 1973 was about 350,000 tons. In 1974 the landed catch was provisionally estimated at 289,000 tons and valued at 3.6 billion escudos.

Although canning of fish, particularly sardines, which constitute more than one-quarter of the catch, is an important export-oriented industry, Portugal is a net importer of fish and fish products. In 1974 imports exceeded exports by about 40,000 tons and about 1 billion escudos in value. The potential for improving the fish catch is limited by the narrow continental shelf and the lack of any continental shelf in the Azores, but it is chiefly handicapped by antiquated techniques and equipment. The major fishing ports on the west coast are Matosinhos, a center of the canning industry, Porto, Aveiro, Peniche, Lisbon, and Setúbal, and on the south coast, Vila Real de Santo António, Olhão, Portimão, and Lagos.

Fishing activity is of several major kinds. Coastal fishing, which provides the bulk of the sardine catch, is the source of tuna, anchovies, and mackerel. Trawl fishing, mostly off the African coast, is primarily for whiting, pargo, and sea bream. Cod, a Portuguese dietary staple, is caught off the Grand Banks of Newfoundland and near Greenland. Whaling is carried on primarily in local waters near the Azores and Maedira, where the hand-launched harpoon is still in use.

AGRICULTURAL COOPERATIVES

Before the April 1974 revolution, group farming and other forms of agricultural cooperation had made little progress. Some 143 groups, comprising only 965 members and controlling only 12,500 hectares, were reported in the mid-1970s. Marketing cooperatives were somewhat more in evidence but still involved only 3 or 4 percent of the farmers, mostly those with larger holdings. The Fourth Development Plan (1974-79), published in November 1973, indicated official encouragement for the formation of farm cooperatives and consolidation of landholdings in the area of small and medium-sized farms. Presumably this plan was superseded by the three-year economic and social program approved by the provisional government in February 1975. This program, however, also called for the granting of financial and technical support to agricultural cooperatives.

AGRICULTURAL PLANNING

Agriculture received little more than lip service in the several development plans set forth by the Salazar and Marcello Caetano regimes (see ch. 12). The first plan (1953-58) emphasized infrastructure development, and the second plan (1959-64) stressed industry. The third plan (1968-73) at least enunciated certain goals of agricultural policy, such as increasing production of both domestically needed foodstuffs and export goods and raising rural standards of living. The projected increase in agricultural production was, however, only 3 percent annually, and in the fourth plan this goal was lowered to 2 percent. An indication of the low priority characteristically accorded to agriculture is the approximately 6 percent of investment allocated to this sector in 1973—a decline from the 8 percent of a decade earlier. Thus while total investment increased by 138 percent from 1963 to 1973, investment in agriculture increased by only 57 percent.

Although the fourth development plan also described in some detail a number of structural reforms, marketing arrangements, price guarantees and control mechanisms, and other institutional measures designed to ease the burdens of the long-neglected agricultural sector, the overthrow of the Caetano regime rendered much of this plan academic. The subsequent piecemeal efforts at agrarian reform and the hasty takeovers of land in the south during 1974 and 1975 made it apparent that some maintenance of political order and consensus would be necessary before comprehensive agricultural planning could be carried out.

THE AGRARIAN REFORM MOVEMENT

Before the revolution of April 1974 the latifundios that characterized agricultural holdings in the Alentejo—Portugal's south-central region, where wheat, olives, and cork are the major crops—were held largely by about 500 absentee landlords who used the lands as much for hunting preserves and summer vacation spots as for economically productive assets. Cultivation on these estates was primitive because

346

the landlords were unwilling to make the capital investments necessary for farm equipment, fertilizers, and other inputs necessary to bring production up to economic levels. The chief exceptions might have been a few showplace or pilot ventures, where investment had been subsidized by the government, and a few foreign-owned estates. In addition to the latifundio owners, whose holdings totaled about 500,000 hectares, the area had a number of middle-level farmers with holdings of 200 to 400 hectares; about 300,000 small farmers, mostly tenants, with holdings of thirty hectares or less; and a group of landless agricultural workers.

The 1975 agrarian reform was based on a body of legislation, culminating in a July 29, 1975, law that authorized the expropriation and nationalization of landholdings on the basis of a point system reflecting the number of hectares, kind of land, and crops. Holdings were to be limited to 500 hectares of dry land or fifty hectares of irrigated land. Landowners were to be compensated for expropriated property, but the terms of compensation were not defined in the enabling legislation. Expropriations did not, however, await the orderly procedures anticipated in the legislation. Between July and December 1975, according to government estimates, land seizures totaled about 300,000 hectares in Beja, 235,000 hectares in Evora, and 200,000 hectares in Portalegre.

The pace of the seizures was much too rapid for effective control by the government, which was inadequately staffed with agricultural technicians and swamped with bureaucratic paperwork. It has been alleged that the communist-dominated farmworkers' union was forcing the takeover of the estates at a pace beyond the government's ability to control in order to discredit the socialist minister of agriculture and the government generally (see ch. 9).

Late in 1975 there appeared to be a reaction to the land seizures sweeping through the area south of the Rio Tejo. Protest rallies of farmers in the more conservative north called for a revision of the agrarian reform program and a return of the occupied farms. The protesting farmers also called for a purge of left-wingers from the staffs of the agrarian reform offices and the removal of the agriculture minister, António Lopes Cardoso, who was apparently anathema to both sides. Presumably in response to these rising protests the government announced on December 13, 1975, that it would conduct a review of the agrarian reform legislation.

It was anticipated at the end of 1975 that the forthcoming crop would suffer from the overzealous pace of farm seizures and occupations. Not only was the area under cultivation reported to be reduced, but the slaughtering of livestock, including dairy and breeding herds, had been drastic. Ministry of Agriculture predictions for 1976 were that agricultural production might be below that of 1975 by as much as 30 percent.

By the end of 1975 the future pattern of landholding and farm operation had yet to emerge. It appeared clear that the latifundio system had received a mortal blow, but it remained for national political developments to determine whether the new format would be collective farms on the Soviet model, private ownership with production cooperatives such as have developed in some Western democracies, or a uniquely Portuguese structure.

INDUSTRY

Before World War II Portuguese industry had been concentrated on traditional processed items, such as wine, cork and other forest products, canned fish, textiles, glassware, pottery, and a few simple metallurgical products. The war made it necessary to broaden the industrial base, particularly in import-substitution industries—a necessity that was continued in the postwar period as a matter of conscious government policy. The manufacturing enterprises that date from this period ranged from steel construction to the fabrication of electronic components. Production of the more traditional items also continued with some broadening of scope and modernization of techniques.

Under the first and second development plans modern industries that were given particular emphasis included mining and metallurgy, shipbuilding, chemicals, electrical equipment, machine tools, fertilizers, paper, and pulp (see ch. 12). Between 1953 and 1960 the average annual growth rate for industry was 8.1 percent, one of the highest rates in Western Europe.

Although the initial drive for greater diversity in production was designed to meet the needs of a protected domestic market, by the 1960s and early 1970s it was becoming more export oriented. The production of manufactured goods in total exports rose from 30 percent in 1953 to over 60 percent in the 1970s.

Much of this growth was in textiles, clothing, and footwear, but other significant manufactures entering the export market were cellulose and wood pulp, machine tools, pharmaceuticals, fertilizer, and electrical machinery and appliances. This resulted from a government policy of abandoning self-sufficiency and concentrating in those lines where Portugal could hope to enjoy a competitive advantage. The industries that were accordingly encouraged included chemicals and chemical metallurgy, certain agricultural products (tomato paste and other preserved and prepared fruits and vegetables), and forestry products (cork, wood pulp, cellulose, paper, and paper products). Heavy industry, including steel manufacturing, shipbuilding, and industrial and transportation equipment manufacturing, have also been stressed. Portugal has, for example, taken a growing segment of the world market for iron castings, because in a situation of worldwide shortage of foundry capacity, aggravated by difficult working conditions and strict pollution controls, Portugal has had both the available labor and modern plants with adequate pollution-prevention facilities.

Industrial Areas

Industry is concentrated in two major industrial areas: Lisbon-Setúbal in the south-central region and the Porto-Aveiro-Braga region in the north. These two areas are estimated to have accounted for about three-quarters of the net output in 1970.

The Lisbon area includes such major industries as iron and steel, ship building and repair, oil refining, machinery, chemicals, cement, electronics, and food and beverages. Setúbal, about fifty miles to the southeast of Lisbon, also has a large shipyard, automobile assembly and machine industry plants, cement, woodpulp and cork processing, and some food processing. Porto is primarily a center of light industry, including textiles, footwear, furniture, wine, and food processing. It also has an oil refinery and some machinery manufacture. Aveiro specializes in wood pulp and other wood products and also produces footwear and machinery; Braga is a center for light industry, specializing in textiles and clothing, cutlery, furniture, and electronics.

Among the factors contributing to industrial concentration near the major ports is the dependence of modern industry on imports of raw materials, fuel, and equipment. Among the more traditional industries textiles rely primarily on imported raw materials, but fruit and vegetable processing, winemaking, and fish canning find much of their raw material needs in the vicinity of the major industrial centers. Fish processing is also, of course, of importance in the extreme south, the Algarve, where some significant fishing ports are located.

For such native specialties as cork production local processing near the raw material source is common. Thus many of the 300-odd small factories that process cork are in Portalegre, Evora, and Beja districts.

The Salazar-Caetano regime had embarked on an ambitious 41-billion-escudo development project—10 billion escudos of which was to be provided by the public sector—for a new industrial complex at Sines, about ninety miles south of Lisbon. The project was to be based on an oil refinery with a capacity of 10 million tons and associated petrochemical and fertilizer industries. There were also to be a railroad car plant and miscellaneous light industries. The plan called for substantial development of Sines as a deepwater port for tankers and general cargo carriers. The port is expected to serve as a transshipment point as well as an export facility for the export-oriented industries planned for the complex. Although some aspects of the project have been cut back by the new government, as of early 1976 much of it was going forward with a target date for completion in mid-1977.

349

Manufacturing

Growth in the manufacturing sector was significant in the last years of the Salazar-Caetano regime, averaging 10 percent during the 1963-73 period. In 1974 manufacturing accounted for 36 percent of GDP at current prices compared with 31 percent in 1963. Because much of the growth represented capital-intensive industry's replacing more traditional labor-intensive activity, however, the favorable growth was not reflected in similar rates of growth in industrial employment. The estimated total employment in manufacturing in 1974 was 702,600 compared with 655,400 in 1960, an increase of only 7.5 percent for the fourteen-year period. Employment in the traditional food, textiles, clothing, and footwear industries showed an absolute decline over the period, and there were major increases in the basic metals industries.

Although there are a number of large modern enterprises that have been responsible for most of the growth in industry, Portugal's economy remains one of many small enterprises characterized by obsolete technology. Of the over 40,000 manufacturing enterprises, about three-quarters had fewer than five employees, and fewer than 200 establishments employed more than 500 people. The small firm is characteristic not only in traditional segments, such as food, beverages, textiles, clothing, footwear, wood, and cork products, but also in some of the metalworking and machine tool manufactures. Each of these subsectors typically was dominated by a few large firms, usually family owned and managed through financial ties to a banking system, similarly dominated by a small number of families. Thus access to new investment funds that might enable small enterprises to modernize has been difficult to achieve (see ch. 12).

The rapid nationalization of significant sectors of industry and of the banks themselves after April 1974 has held the promise of more equitable treatment of all industry with respect to access to investment capital (see ch. 12). As of late 1975, however, the instability of the economic and political situation made it difficult to foresee any safe haven for investment capital in Portugal. Private foreign investment in particular could find little that was favorable in Portugal compared with opportunities in other countries. Thus it appeared that for some indeterminate period there would be little encouragement for new industrial investment. Government in the meantime has been hard put to it to provide the minimum of capital and credit resources to keep existing industries operating at levels necessary to maintain employment.

Heavy Industry

One of the fruits of the drive for industrialization in the postwar period is the National Steelworks (Siderurgia Nacional) located at

Seixal, across the Rio Tejo from Lisbon. This is the nucleus of the country's heavy industrial complex, which includes machine tool factories, engineering industries, and ship building and repair facilities. Pig iron production was only 387,000 tons and steel output only 459,000 tons in 1973, however, and most of the raw materials have to be imported.

Ship building and repair constitute one of the country's most significant industries. This activity is the largest employer in heavy industry; there were about 16,000 in the work force in 1975. Two major installations, one operated by the Lisbon Shipyards (Estaleiros Navais de Lisboa—LISNAVE) and one by Setúbal Shipyards (Estaleiros Navais de Setúbal—SETENAVE), provided nine dry docks, one of which was the largest in the world in 1975, having the capacity to accommodate a 1-million-ton ship. The older of the yards, LISNAVE, prospered during the worldwide supertanker boom after the closing of the Suez Canal in 1967, but during the tanker glut period of 1974 and 1975 these yards were less fortunate. Long-run prospects, at least for repair and service activities, appear good, however, because of Portugal's ideal geographic location for serving the tanker trade. Not only is it on the direct route from the Middle East to the major West European oil tanker terminals, but it is about three days distance from those in Northern Europe, for example, Rotterdam, providing just the right sailing time for an empty giant tanker to disperse accumulated gases before it is cleaned.

Portugal's shipyards are modern, LISNAVE having opened in 1967 and SETENAVE in the early 1970s. Although foreign equipment played an important role in the original outfitting of the yards, much of the equipment was of Portuguese origin. The yards have thus provided a stimulus to domestic engineering and heavy equipment industries. With the slowdown caused by the worldwide recession and the unsettled domestic situation in the mid-1970s, both shipyards and associated heavy industrial units have experienced considerable excess capacity and as of early 1976 were awaiting an upturn of economic activity.

Light Industry

The great majority of industrial enterprises and employment opportunities were in the field of light industry. The greatest number of enterprises—12,358—were in food, beverage, and tobacco processing, but according to the 1972 industrial census 10,501 of these employed fewer than five persons. The textile, clothing, and footwear industries had 9,926 enterprises with 220,100 employees; these sectors gave employment to more than four times as many persons as the food-processing industries. Wood and cork products, 7,819 enterprises, provided employment for about 100,000 workers. These figures did not include the paper, paper products, and printing industry, which totaled 1,380 enterprises and 29,800 employees.

Although no separate statistics were available for handicraft industries, it was apparent from the small size of the vast majority of the enterprises listed in the 1972 census—more than 30,000 of the 42,588 manufacturing establishments listed had fewer than five employees—that many were little more than handicraft operations. Among Portuguese handicraft products that have attracted some international recognition are cork manufactures, pottery and tile, jewelry, and Madeira needlework and basketry

Construction Industry

Construction has been an important element of the country's industrial growth pattern with a 9-percent per annum growth record during the 1963-73 period. Because it was providing employment to about 275,000 people in 1974 and associated industries employed another 100,000, it was also an important contributor of employment opportunities. There were about 11,000 enterprises in this sector. As of 1975 many of these firms were feeling the pinch from lagging investment, which brought industrial construction to a virtual halt, as well as from the decline of the tourist industry and the slow pace of housing starts. One of the early government actions after April 1974 was a rent freeze, which discouraged private investment in housing. There was an estimated deficit of about 500,000 dwelling units in mid-1975, which the government was planning to meet with a public housing program. Plans called for a 5-billion-escudo allocation from the development budget for this purpose. Together with anticipated privately financed building, the program had a target of an average of 76,000 new dwelling units per annum through 1994, a substantial increase over the average of 36,600 between 1970 and 1973.

Energy Industry

About 82 percent of the country's energy requirements in 1973 came from petroleum and petroleum products, 8 percent from water power, 7 percent from coal, and 3 percent from other sources. As in a number of other European countries the dependence on petroleum imports exacerbated Portugal's economic problems after the oil crisis of 1973. The cost of petroleum imports rose from US$137 million in 1973 to US$480 million in 1974.

Total energy requirements have been the lowest in Western Europe on a per capita basis—about 890 kilograms in petroleum equivalents compared with 2,100 kilograms in Italy in 1973. Annual energy consumption rose at an average rate of 7.7 percent between 1960 and 1973.

352

Although no significant oil deposits have been found in metropolitan Portugal, there were two oil refineries, both owned by the Portuguese Petroleum Refining Corporation (Sociedade Anónima Concessionária de Refinação de Petróleos em Portugal—SACOR). The largest is at Porto and had a crude capacity of 70,000 barrels per day as of January 1974; the other is at Lisbon and has a crude capacity of 40,000 barrels per day. As of late 1975 the Portuguese Petroleum Company (Sociedade Portuguesa de Petróleos—Petrosul) was planning to construct an oil refinery at the new industrial complex at Sines and had arranged a loan of US$4.5 million (at 8 percent interest) from the United States Export-Import Bank for purchase of equipment and services. When the company begins operations, the monopoly held by SACOR will cease. This is planned for 1977, when Petrosul is expected to take over about 60 percent of the domestic market.

Annual petroleum consumption in the internal market was 5.4 million tons in 1973, and about an additional 1 million tons were used for refueling ships or for reexport. Imports were 6.3 million tons—about one-third of which were refined products and the balance crude. Refining capacity at the end of 1973 was 4.8 million tons. No significant domestic sources of petroleum have been discovered, although intensive efforts have been made in the mid-1970s to discover oil beneath Portugal's offshore waters. About twenty-seven concessions for prospecting on the continental shelf have been granted, involving six groups of companies. The concessionary arrangements call for Portugal to receive 50 percent of the profits and to have a majority representation through a state company in the exploitation of any wells that are found.

The hydroelectric potential of the country was developed extensively during the rule of Prime Minister Salazar, exploiting about 60 percent of the technologically feasible resources and achieving about 93 percent of total electric power production by 1963. In the late 1960s and early 1970s additional thermal plants were constructed, and by 1975 about 28 percent of the total electric power needs were being met by thermal plants. Because of the limited possibilities of further hydroelectrical production and the high cost of fuel for thermal production, nuclear power production has been under consideration.

Although at the time of the revolution there were no nuclear plants in operation, plans were in progress to develop such plants. In addition to enriched uranium promised by the United States these plants would use domestic uranium supplies—two deposits were being exploited in the mid-1970s, and active prospecting for additional deposits was proceeding. Annual production in both 1973 and 1974 was ninety-five tons of uranium oxide concentrate. Tentative plans called for four nuclear reactors to be brought into operation every two years between 1981 and 1987.

Mining and Quarrying

The mining sector provided only a small and diminishing portion of GDP—less than 1 percent in 1973—and employment in the sector declined from 26,000 in 1960 to an estimated 12,000 in 1973, about 0.04 percent of the labor force. Although there were many small mining establishments in existence in mid-1975, only seven produced more than 25 million escudos in value per annum. The only active coal mine in 1974 was in Aveiro. Its 230,000-ton production provided only about 20 percent of the country's coal needs in 1974—down from about 40 percent in 1960. Other exploited mineral deposits included iron and copper pyrites and iron ore (hematite and ferromanganese ores). Major nonferrous metals include tungsten, tin, copper, manganese, uranium, and small amounts of lead, zinc, gold, and silver. Nonmetallic minerals included gypsum, talc, kaolin, quartz, and salt. In addition to the rock salt deposits, about 25 percent of the salt was produced by seawater evaporation in the coastal areas. The quarrying of building materials (stone, clay, and sand) has been of equal significance with mining, accounting for 51 percent of the value of extractive industrial production in 1973. Considerable amounts of this production are exported, particularly marble slabs and building tiles.

Wolframite, the major tungsten ore, has been a rather significant mineral for Portugal because of its strategic use in wartime. In World War II Portugal's handling of its supply of wolframite—selling to both sides under a complex and changing system of quotas until just before the Allies' landing in France—has been both admired and criticized as a bit of "tightrope diplomacy" that played an important role in Salazar's strategy of maintaining his country's neutrality and economic viability throughout the war.

Portugal is Western Europe's largest producer of tungsten and is fifth in importance in the noncommunist world as a producer of this strategic metal, accounting for about 5 percent of the world's production in 1970. Wolframite production accounted for about 75 percent of the country's nonferrous metallic ore production by value in 1974.

The major pyrite deposits are at Aljustrel, fifty miles from the new industrial complex at Sines. As part of the development plans for this complex, new investment for the intensive exploitation of these deposits was announced in September 1975. Portugal is also a minor source of ilmenite, a titanium ore, producing about 220 short tons in 1969. Although not significant on a world scale, Portugal's tin production of around 500 tons annually ranks it second in Western Europe, after the United Kingdom.

Industrial Labor Force

The industrial labor force in continental Portugal totaled about 1 million people in 1974, constituting 34.6 percent of the total working population. Slightly over 700,000 were in manufacturing, 267,000 in construction and public works, 17,000 in public utilities, and 12,000 in mining and quarrying. Within the manufacturing sector the largest employer was the textile, clothing, and footwear component, followed by metal products, machinery, and transport equipment (see ch. 12).

CHAPTER 14

TRADE, TRANSPORTATION, AND SERVICES

In 1974 the services sector of the Portuguese economy, including trade, transportation, housing, public administration, banking, and miscellaneous services, contributed 40.8 percent to gross domestic product (GDP—see Glossary) at current prices compared with 38.8 percent in 1963. Although this appeared to represent a small steady gain over the 1963-74 period, there is reason to believe that the gain primarily reflected sharper price increases in this sector than in industry and agriculture. When measured in constant 1963 prices, the sector contributed only 36.8 percent in 1974—an actual decline from the 1963 level. In any event the proportion of services to GDP in Portugal is one of the lowest among countries of the Organization for Economic Cooperation and Development (OECD). Only Luxembourg had a lower proportion in 1973, and the other major countries of southern Europe were significantly higher; Spain registered 51.8 percent, Italy 50.0 percent, and Greece 47.2 percent in that year.

Employment in the services sector engaged about 37.4 percent of the work force in 1973 compared with about 30 percent in 1963. In this respect the contrast with other countries of southern Europe was less striking. Spain had a slightly lower share, 35.5 percent; Italy had 38.6 percent and Greece 40.2 percent. Many advanced economies characteristically register half or more of their employed persons in the services sector; the United States, for example, had 64.2 percent so employed in 1973.

The Portuguese economy is marked by a considerable dependence on foreign trade, particularly imports. In 1974, for example, imports equaled about one-third of GDP compared with only about one-fourth as the average for all OECD countries. Exports equaled about one-sixth of GDP, which was close to the average of 17.8 percent for all OECD countries. It is apparent from these ratios that a considerable trade deficit existed, and this has been characteristic of Portuguese foreign trade throughout the post-World War II period.

The trade deficit was offset by net revenues from tourism and by remittances from Portuguese emigrants abroad in most years during the 1960s and early 1970s. In 1974, however, income from both these sources declined considerably, and the trade deficit virtually doubled.

For the first time in many years Portugal had an unfavorable current balance of payments and an unfavorable overall balance.

Except for a few department stores and specialty shops in the larger cities, domestic trade is relatively unsophisticated and is dominated by many small retail outlets. Wholesale and retail trade contributed about 13 percent to GDP in 1972 and, together with banking and insurance, employed about 11 percent of the working population.

The transportation and communications sector employed about 5 percent of the working population and contributed about 6 percent to GDP in 1972. Although the road and rail networks are adequate to reach virtually all populated areas, they are poorly maintained. Railroads play a minor role in both domestic and international transport. Domestic shipment of goods is primarily by road or coastal carrier and to a limited extent by inland waterway. Most goods in international trade are carried by sea. Portuguese traveling within the country go by road; international travel is about one-third by air, otherwise largely by car.

FOREIGN TRADE

Portugal's trade relations and policies have been carried out in the context of the obligations and advantages that accrue from its membership in the European Free Trade Association (EFTA), the General Agreement on Tariffs and Trade (GATT), and the International Monetary Fund (IMF) and its association with the European Economic Community (EEC, also called the Common Market). Portugal was also influenced for many years by ties with its overseas possessions. Although the formal ties had been largely given up by the end of 1975, it was expected that, in the absence of political barriers, previously established trade relations with the former colonies would be maintained to some degree. Unless otherwise stated or apparent from the context, all foreign trade data in this chapter include trade between Portugal and its present or former overseas possessions.

Both exports and imports increased steadily in the 1960s and the early 1970s, and imports outpaced exports in every year. Imports reached the equivalent of US$4.2 billion in 1974, almost double exports, which were about US$2.2 billion. These were the equivalent of 33 percent and 17 percent respectively of GDP.

The trade deficit also showed a steady increase in the 1960s and 1970s. In 1959, the last year before EFTA was in operation, the deficit was US$184 million; by 1972 it had reached US$899 million. In 1973, the last year before the trade deficit was further aggravated by skyrocketing oil prices and the associated inflation in prices of many other goods, it was US$1.1 billion. In 1974 the impact of those factors brought the deficit to US$2.2 billion. In the first nine months of 1975 imports were 9 percent higher than in 1974, whereas exports were only 1.5 percent higher. Thus the trade deficit for that year, already at US$1.4 billion, was expected to reach a possible US$2.5 billion.

Until 1974 the trade deficit had been offset in most years by tourist receipts, remittances from Portuguese abroad, and other net inflows (see ch. 12). Because of these favorable factors Portugal's foreign reserves had increased steadily until 1973. During 1974 and 1975 these reserves were drawn down, and some of the country's gold holdings were liquidated in order to provide necessary imports. In 1975 and early 1976 gold was also pledged as security for a number of emergency loans from foreign central banks.

Also creating difficulties for Portuguese foreign trade balances in the mid-1970s was a reversal in the terms of trade. From 1963 to 1973 Portuguese export prices rose at a slightly faster rate than import prices to reach a favorable terms-of-trade ratio of 112 in 1973 (on a base of 100 in 1963). In 1974 sharply rising oil prices reversed this trend, and the terms of trade declined to an estimated 100.7.

Thus the estimated increase of over 50 percent in the value of imports in 1974 reflected little, if any, increase in volume. This was largely the result of higher import prices led by crude oil and also substantially influenced by food products and industrial raw materials. The value of exports in 1974 showed a significantly smaller increase— about 26 percent—again largely reflecting increased prices rather than increased volume.

Special Trade Relations

European Free Trade Association

Portugal is a charter member of EFTA, which was established in November 1959 by those major West European nations that for one reason or another did not become members of EEC. The other charter members of EFTA were Austria, Denmark, Norway, Sweden, Switzerland, and the United Kingdom. In December 1972 Denmark and the United Kingdom withdrew from EFTA to join EEC. In the meantime Iceland had become a full member of EFTA and Finland an associate.

Over a period extending from 1960 to 1967 EFTA undertook the gradual elimination of customs duties and quantitative trade restrictions on industrial goods among member countries. The timetable for tariff elimination excepted certain tariffs on industrial exports maintained by Portugal because, as the least developed industrially of EFTA members, Portugal was considered in need of a greater degree of protection for its developing industries.

Portugal's basic tariff rates were to be cut to 30 percent by January 1, 1975, to 20 percent by January 1, 1977, and to zero by January 1, 1980. In May 1975, however, the Portuguese government informed EFTA that additional import surcharges of 20 to 30 percent on a number of goods would be necessary to alleviate the balance-of-payments problems. These were imposed as of June 1, 1975. Portugal also placed before EFTA a request for technical assistance, concessions on certain agricultural exports, and the establishment of an industrial development fund. These requests were acted upon favorably by EFTA in November 1975. An industrial development fund of US$100 million over five years was agreed upon, Sweden and Switzerland putting up 30 percent and 25.5 percent respectively and the other member countries lesser amounts. Each member country also offered technical assistance, of which Norway's program of fisheries research aid was noteworthy. In addition the prolongation of the Portuguese timetable for tariff elimination and the granting of concessions to encourage the export of Portuguese agricultural goods were accepted.

European Economic Community

In July 1972 an agreement was signed between Portugal and EEC calling for a gradual reduction of tariffs on imported industrial goods through 1980 for most items and through 1985 for a few specialized items. The agreement had two major objectives for Portugal: protection of its domestic industries during a transitional period in anticipation of free trade with EEC countries and maintenance of its markets in the United Kingdom and Denmark in anticipation of the departure of those countries from EFTA and their membership in EEC.

As of early 1976 negotiations were expected to extend the 1972 free-trade agreements between Portugal and EEC. It was also expected that Portugal would be offered higher ceilings on textile exports and greater access to European markets for Portuguese wine as well as industrial and technological cooperation programs and the extension of social security benefits to Portuguese workers and their families on an equal basis with other workers in the states where they reside. In addition to the consideration of longer term trade concessions, which appeared to be leading to ultimate Portuguese membership in EEC, the nine community members agreed in October 1975 to extend about US$200 million in emergency aid to Portugal.

Major Trading Partners

From 1960 through 1972 the largest percentage of Portugal's exports went to its EFTA partners, followed in some years by the overseas territories and in other years by the member countries of EEC. The latter usually provided the largest portion of imports, even before the United Kingdom and Denmark moved from EFTA to EEC in December 1972. Since 1972 EEC has dominated both exports and imports. Among the members of EFTA remaining after the departure of the United Kingdom and Denmark, the leading trading partner has been Sweden, which provided 4.3 percent of imports and took 5.8 percent of exports in 1973. Switzerland was of about equal importance as a supplier but of considerably less significance on the export side, providing 4.1 percent of imports and taking 3 percent of exports in that year.

Another significant shift in the importance of trading partners in the 1970s occurred in 1974, when the value of imports from the Middle Eastern oil-exporting countries rose to US$321 million from an average value of US$100 million in the preceding four years. Of these countries the major suppliers were Iran and Iraq with US$153 million and US$140 million respectively. Imports from Angola, whose share of Portugal's oil imports rose from about 7 percent in 1973 to over 30 percent in 1974, rose in value to US$357 million from an average value of US$171 million over the preceding four years, also obviously reflecting the rise in crude oil prices.

Before the oil crisis years trade with the overseas possessions had been declining. The overseas possessions had traditionally been the largest market for Portuguese chemicals, machinery, electrical equipment, and transport equipment and a chief source of crude oil, cotton, iron ore, coffee, sisal, and other tropical agricultural products. This trade usually resulted in a considerable trade surplus for Portugal, and opponents of the colonial structure have alleged that the mother country exploited the colonies by taking their raw materials at lower than world market prices and selling the colonies manufactured goods that were unmarketable elsewhere. Evidence for this point of view is not wholly convincing, but there is no doubt that special tariff structures and ties between parent companies and their colonial subsidiaries had encouraged intra-escudo-area trade. Although Portugal's surplus in trade exchange with the colonies totaled nearly 20 billion escudos (for value of the escudo—see Glossary), by 1970 trade was approximately in balance; but in the early 1970s the exchange reversed, and the surplus favored the colonies. Exports to the colonies were about one-third of total exports in 1964 but dwindled to 23 percent in 1971 and 11 percent in 1974. On the import side the colonial share dropped from about 15 percent in 1964 to 6.5 percent in 1973. The influence of rapidly rising oil prices is again reflected in the rise of the colonial share of imports to 10.6 percent in 1974.

Close economic relations with England have been maintained for centuries, reflecting the world's oldest alliance, which dates from the Treaty of Windsor in 1386 (see ch. 2). Although there had been some dilution of these economic ties, the United Kingdom in the mid-1970s had the largest number of foreign companies in Portugal and remained the leading trading partner. In 1973 the United Kingdom absorbed US$442 million worth of Portuguese exports, amounting to 23.8 percent of the total. Although leading in exports, the United Kingdom took second place to the Federal Republic of Germany (West Germany) as an importer, its US$349 million constituting an 11.4-percent

361

share of Portugal's imports, compared with West Germany's 14.5 percent.

West Germany, although the leading source of imports, took only 7.5 percent of exports in 1973, ranking third after the United Kingdom and the United States. West Germany has also been an important source of foreign capital for Portugal, ranking above both France and the United Kingdom in the early 1970s (see ch. 12).

Economic relations between Portugal and France have traditionally been close—particularly in the post-World War II period. French trade and investment in Portugal grew significantly in the 1960s, marked by the financing of the Salazar Bridge across the Tejo estuary as well as such projects in the overseas possessions as the Cabora Bassa Dam in Mozambique. In 1973 France was the source of 7 percent of imports and took 5.2 percent of exports. France has also taken the largest number of Portuguese emigrant workers, replacing Brazil, which until the 1960s had been the major destination for jobless emigrants (see ch. 4).

Economic ties with Brazil are not as strong as they were in the nineteenth century, presumably because each country has more natural ties with its hemispheric neighbors. In 1973 Brazil was the source of 2.9 percent of imports and took 1 percent of exports. The Luso-Brazilian Center for Economic Cooperation was set up in 1969 in an effort to encourage closer economic ties. There is reportedly a considerable Brazilian investment in Portuguese real estate.

Economic relations with Spain are also weaker than might be expected, possibly reflecting some Portuguese reluctance to be tied too closely to its large neighbor. The two countries also tend to produce the same commodities and must compete for export markets. In 1973 Spain supplied 5.4 percent of Portugal's imports and took 2.2 percent of exports. There have been periodic discussions of a joint project to bridge the Rio Guadiana, which in its lower course forms the border of the two countries between the Gulf of Cadiz and the Portuguese village of Pomarão, about thirty miles from the gulf. In early 1976 it was reported that the discussions had been resumed.

Trade with the United States has been significant, amounting to about 8.2 percent of imports and 9.8 percent of exports in 1973. Principal import items were grains (corn and wheat), other agricultural products, machinery and transport equipment, and chemicals. The major exports to the United States were wine, canned and preserved vegetables and fish, and electronic components. Portugal ranked fifth as a supplier of wine to the United States, after France, Italy, Spain, and West Germany.

Trade with Communist Countries

Before 1975 trade with communist countries was of little significance, accounting for about 1.2 percent of Portugal's imports and 0.9

percent of its exports in 1974. Major communist trading partners for that year were Romania and Cuba. In 1975 there was a marked increase in imports from the Soviet Union, apparently reflecting a trade agreement signed in December 1974 that called for the Soviet Union to supply 1 million tons of oil to Portugal in 1975. Although in 1974 only US$2.7 million in imports was received from the Soviet Union, the first six months of 1975 produced over US$20 million. It was primarily this increase from the Soviet Union that accounted for communist countries' increasing their share of Portuguese imports from 1.2 percent in 1974 to 3.2 percent for the first six months of 1975.

Other East European states that concluded trade agreements with Portugal between April 1974 and December 1975 included the German Democratic Republic (East Germany), Hungary, Poland, Czechoslovakia, Bulgaria, and Romania. These general agreements were followed—in the cases of Poland and East Germany—by more specific agreements involving Portugal's shipbuilding and ship repair facilities (see ch. 10). As of late 1975, however, significant increases in actual trade reflecting these agreements had not become apparent.

Composition of Trade

Exports

Portugal's traditional exports—wine, cork, textiles, and processed fish—constituted from one-half to three-fourths of the value of exports in the 1950s. Although these remain important, other products have made increasing contributions since the early 1960s. Only textiles among the traditional products have increased their share of the export market since 1963. In the decade between 1963 and 1973 exports of textiles and footwear rose in value from US$112 million to US$545 million and from about 26 percent of total exports to 31 percent. In the same period food and agricultural products rose from US$112 million in value to US$332 million but declined from 26 percent of the total to 19 percent. Timber and cork exports more than doubled in value from US$70 million to US$166 million but declined from 16 percent of total exports to 9.5 percent. Portugal's cork exports remained, however, the largest in the world, constituting about 75 percent of the market for cork manufactures and 60 percent of the market for raw cork.

The most significant rise in exports over the 1963-73 period was in machinery and equipment—from US$14 million to US$231 million and from about 3 percent of the total to about 13 percent. A number of such other relatively new products as tomato paste, chemicals, wood pulp, and paper have also found promising export markets, but their individual contributions have been statistically less significant than that of machinery and equipment.

363

The largest category of imports in 1973 was machinery and equipment, valued at US$850 million and constituting 29 percent of total imports as compared with 23.5 percent in 1963. Imported food and agricultural products were valued at US$500 million and made up 17 percent of total imports in 1973. Although by 1963 Portugal had become a slight net importer of such products (US$4 million), in 1973 its deficit had increased to more than US$162 million. Marked increases within the overall category were in cereal grains and processed foods. Other major import categories and their values and percentages of total imports in 1973 were chemical products valued at US$390 million, 13 percent; textiles and footwear valued at US$312 million, 10.5 percent; metals and metal products valued at US$235 million, 8 percent; and mineral products valued at US$162 million, 5.5 percent. The bulk of mineral products was crude oil, valued at US$130 million. This item soared in 1974 as the full effect of the oil embargo and subsequent price increases imposed by the Organization of Petroleum Exporting Countries (OPEC) was felt. The estimated cost of oil imports in 1974 was US$486 million, constituting over 10 percent of total imports.

Tariffs and Licenses

Portugal's tariff structure is based on the Brussels Tariff Nomenclature, a classification system adopted by most of the world's trading nations, and on its obligations as a member of GATT and EFTA and its association with EEC. Administration of the customs and trade control procedures is conducted by the Directorate General of Customs of the Ministry of Finance in accordance with the various international customs conventions to which Portugal is a party. Duties are low on most raw materials and on manufactured goods that do not compete with local industry and, as indicated, duties on industrial imports from other EFTA members and from EEC members are being gradually reduced under a schedule that calls for virtual free trade in such goods by 1985.

Import licenses, issued by the Bureau of Foreign Commerce of the Ministry of Economic Coordination or by specialized agencies for certain products, such as pharmaceuticals, chemicals, livestock, and cereal grains, also serve as foreign exchange permits. Foreign exchange is made available to the import license holder through the Bank of Portugal, which acts as an agent for the Ministry of Finance in the control of foreign transactions. Although there are no export duties, export licenses are required for transactions valued at more than 2,500 escudos, and the foreign exchange proceeds of export sales must be sold promptly to an authorized bank. Certain exports are restricted to prevent shortages or depletion of goods on the domestic market.

DOMESTIC TRADE

Because of Portugal's small size and relatively undeveloped markets, the distribution of goods on the domestic market is largely dominated by small retail outlets, including many outdoor stalls and markets. One estimate states that there is one retail shop for every sixty-five people, which would mean a total of about 138,000 shops. A small cooperative movement handles some domestic marketing in the Lisbon, Setúbal, and Porto regions. Imported consumer goods are usually received by firms that combine operations as importers and wholesalers or retailers, whereas industrial and raw material imports are usually made directly by the industrial end user. Lisbon and Porto are centers for the distribution of goods. The few large mercantile establishments based in these cities characteristically have their own branch offices and sales agents in the rest of continental Portugal, Madeira, the Azores and the remaining and former overseas possessions.

Trade fairs are important promotional and distributional activities. Large industrial and commercial displays are set up at these fairs in Lisbon and Porto, and agricultural fairs are held annually at Braga, Tomar, and Santarém. Such distribution techniques as direct mail and door-to-door sales have not been accepted. Franchising, leasing, and installment sales, although not prohibited, are of little significance as marketing methods. When installment sales take place—as occasionally for automobiles and large appliances—they are subject to regulation as to minimum down payment and maximum time period, but credit facilities for this kind of transaction are rare. The most significant advertising media are television, radio, and newspapers. Magazine advertising and billboards are also used (see ch. 11).

TOURISM

As in neighboring Spain, tourism became a booming business in the 1960s. Sun- and sand-seeking vacationers from northern Europe flocked to the Iberian Peninsula, attracted by the comparatively low-cost resort facilities. The more than 100 beaches along the southern coast of the Algarve and the short stretch—the so-called Sun Coast—running westward from Lisbon to Cabo Raso at the mouth of the Rio Tejo and including the Costa de Cabarica south of the river are major attractions, but each area of the country has tourist sites. In addition to other west coast beaches and many historical and cultural points of interest throughout the country, one guidebook lists over fifty widely scattered health spas with mineral springs whose waters are alleged to have curative properties for a wide variety of disorders from skin diseases to kidney stones. Madeira, although almost completely lacking in sandy beaches, is also a prominent holiday and tourist location, featuring an ambience of Edwardian nostalgia. Five of the country's twenty top-rated luxury hotels are located there. In the period of political and social unrest on the mainland after the April 1974 revolution Madeira's relative calm enabled it to record increases in tourist traffic and revenues.

There was an average annual increase of 15 percent in the number of foreign visitors to Portugal between 1968 and 1971, slowing to about 1.5 percent in 1972 and 3.9 percent in 1973. The number of visitors reached 4.1 million in 1973, but a decline to 2.6 million in 1974 reflected not only the worldwide recession and the energy shortage but also the unsettled Portuguese political situation. Earnings attributed to tourism amounted to 18 percent of total income from the export of goods and services in 1972, doubling the proportion recorded in 1962. Only Spain, Austria, and Greece among OECD reporting countries topped Portugal in this respect.

Of the 2.6 million foreigners who crossed Portugal's border in 1974, about 1.5 million came by land, 700,000 by air, and 400,000 by sea. Of those who came by sea, however, only 34,000 disembarked in Portugal, the others being classified as in transit. Although the largest number of visitors was from Spain—1.3 million—about two-thirds were classified as excursionists rather than tourists. By OECD definition excursionists are temporary visitors staying for a period of less than twenty-four hours. This distinction is made by analysts of tourist data in order to distinguish between casual, one-day visitors from neighboring countries (who presumably contribute little to tourist revenues) and bona fide tourists. Excepting those from Spain, the largest numbers of tourists in 1974 were from the United Kingdom (383,000), the United States (216,000), West Germany (167,000), and France (153,000).

Steady increases in tourist traffic and revenues have been recorded since the tourist boom started in the late 1950s, reaching a peak in 1973. Of the 4.1 million recorded visitors in that year, 2.4 million were classified as tourists. Tourist earnings in 1973 were US$492 million, 26-percent increase over the previous year. There is considerable seasonal variation in the visits, the peak months being July and August and the low months November and December.

The decline in tourists in 1974 continued into 1975, reflecting not only the worldwide recession but also the unsettled conditions in mainland Portugal. In the January-to-June period 864,000 foreigners visited Portugal, 30 percent fewer than in the comparable six-month period of 1974. Madeira, however, was enjoying a record year for visitors in 1975. Other countries in Europe that were fortunate enough to avoid political unrest also enjoyed high tourist earnings in 1975: Greece, for example, improved its tourist earnings over 1974 by 42 percent.

The hotel industry, including inns and boardinghouses *(pensoãs)*, employed about 30,000 people in 1973, nearly half the estimated 62,000 people classified as employed in miscellaneous services that year. Of the 1,332 establishments providing 75,458 beds, 211 were hotels, twenty of which were given five-star or deluxe ratings. The majority of the establishments were classified as boardinghouses. Other tourist accomodations were provided by some seventy privately operated inns *(estalagems)* and twenty-one government-operated inns *(pousadas)*. A number of the latter are former castles or other historic or architectural landmarks. All establishments are under strict government control and, as in Spain, each is required to maintain an official complaint book for tourists' use to advise government inspectors of the establishment's performance.

The development of tourist facilities was a prominent feature of economic planning under the Salazar-Caetano regime, emphasizing the seaside resort potential of the Algarve, the Azores, and Madeira. Priority tourist-related projects received preferential tax treatment, which included exemption from taxes for the first ten years of operation and a 50-percent reduction of taxes for the next fifteen years. In addition loans with soft terms were granted by the Tourism Fund (Fundo do Turismo) and the General Savings Bank (Caixa Geral de Depositos). Vocational training programs, giving priority to the training of interpreter-guides and travel agency personnel, were conducted under the aegis of the National Center for Tourist and Hotel Development (Centro Nacional de Formaçã Turistica e Hoteleira). In recognition of the importance of tourism to the economy, in December 1975 the State Institute for the Development of Tourism was established.

TRANSPORTATION

In the mid-1970s private automobiles accounted for almost 74 percent of passenger land travel within the country, buses about 15 percent, and trains only about 11 percent. Railroads are also of low importance in the handling of domestic freight, having an estimated share of less than 10 percent in the 1970s. Domestic air travel was statistically insignificant but was increasing rapidly in the 1970s, with an annual increase of about 19 percent in the number of domestic departures from Portela Airport in Lisbon.

Highway Transport

The predominant use of highways for land transportation of both goods and passengers exists despite an inadequately maintained highway network, a small number of motor vehicles, and the high costs of gasoline and other motor transport expenses. At the equivalent of US$2.80 per gallon, the price of premium gasoline in mid-1976 was among the highest in Western Europe. The road network in 1973 consisted of 11,340 miles of national highways—about one-third of which were rated first class, the balance being second and third class or gravel roads—and 8,450 miles of municipal and rural roads. This network provides access to most parts of the country and is a result of a government program during the Salazar-Caetano regime of linking each village of 100 or more inhabitants to the main network (see fig. 26). Road construction and continued maintenance have been poorly sustained, however, and road surfaces, drainage, and other facilities are inadequate.

Total expenditures on national highways and municipal roads in 1973 was only an estimated 800 million escudos, despite 5,730 million escudos collected from gasoline taxes and other highway charges. Highway upkeep has been labor intensive, providing a degree of much-needed rural employment but suffering from a lack of heavy equipment and material.

There are seven principal highway entry points from Spain. The major one is at Vilar Formoso on the highway from both Madrid and the French border, which provides the shortest route to Lisbon through Guarda and Coimbra. In 1973 there were about 890,000 passenger and commercial light automobiles, 70,000 motorcycles, 6,000 buses, and 38,000 heavy trucks and trailers. The passenger car ownership of about one to every 13.5 inhabitants in 1971 compared with one to twelve in Spain and one to thirty-three in Greece.

A spectacular feature of the national highway system is the Salazar Bridge, which spans the Rio Tejo, linking Lisbon with its industrial suburbs on the south bank. The bridge, which in the mid-1970s was said to be the longest suspension bridge in Europe, was completed in 1966 at an estimated cost of US$75 million. French banks put up most of the capital, but construction was carried out primarily by the United States Steel Corporation. Although the bridge fills an obvious need, substantially cutting transportation time between Lisbon and the south, critics of the Salazar-Caetano regime contend that the money could have been used for more urgent needs, such as the long-planned irrigation project in the Alentejo.

In the mid-1970s the only modern dual expressways were in the environs of Lisbon and Porto. A building program calling for the construction of about 300 miles of toll expressways was begun in October 1973 and was expected to provide express highway service from Porto to Lisbon and Setúbal. In late 1975, however, it was reported that the program had been postponed pending the preparation of a master highway plan.

Maritime Transport

In spite of overland access through Spain, the international movement of goods to and from Portugal is overwhelmingly by sea. In

Figure 26. Portugal, Principal Roads, Railroads, Airports, and Ports

369

1973, of the 11.9 million tons of goods entering the country, 11.5 million came by sea.

According to the United States Maritime Administration the Portuguese merchant fleet in 1974 consisted of 114 vessels, totaling 1.2 million gross registered tons. In the fleet were twenty-five tankers, fourteen combined passenger and cargo vessels, sixty-nine freighters, and six bulk carriers. Ships of some 63.2 million registered tonnage entered Portuguese ports in 1973, unloading 14.4 million tons and loading 5.8 million tons.

Although there are a number of small ports that handle coastal shipping and fishing activities, the bulk of international cargo is handled either at Lisbon and its satellite port of Setúbal or at the ports of Douro and Leixões about 30 percent, and Setúbal about 7 percent. About 18 percent of the freight handled at these ports is from coastal shipping.

The port of Lisbon is on one of the world's great natural harbors and is well equipped with over twenty miles of docks, quayside berths, warehouse facilities, shipyards, and dry docks. Porto is handicapped by the silting of the Rio Douro, and its port of Douro is of limited capacity. The major port facilities in the Porto area are provided by the artificial harbor of Leixões located on the coast about three miles north of the river mouth. The major ports serving Madeira and the Azores are located at Funchal and Ponta Delgada respectively. Regular freight and passenger service is provided to the Azores and Madeira and less regular service to Brazil, North America, and the former overseas possessions in Africa.

Inland Water Transport

Inland water transportation is rather limited, because rivers are generally shallow and erratic in their flow. Small craft carry on some local commercial activity on the lower navigable portions of several rivers, notably the Minho, Douro, Mondego, Tejo, and Guadiana. The Douro, particularly in former times, was heavily used for local transportation—not only for the port wine shipments from Peso de Regua to Vila Nova de Gaia and Porto but also for a variety of other cargo.

Railroads

The railroad network is operated by the Portuguese Railway Company (Companhia Caminos de Ferro Portugueses), a private concern —until it was nationalized after the revolution of April 1974—that was set up by the merger of leased concessions in 1951. Although its 2,225 miles (except for 475 miles of narrow-gauge track) the compatible with Spain's, they are of a different gauge (5 feet, 6 inches) from the standard gauge (4 feet, 8 1/2 inches) of the other railroads of Europe. This is a contributing factor to the railroad system's relatively minor role in international rail traffic. Probably more important is the low volume of trade with Spain and the inadequate equipment and maintenance of facilities in both countries. Freight traffic in 1973 was 4.7 million tons, and the average haul was 113.6 miles per ton. This is estimated as less than 10 percent of the domestic freight total. In 1973 the system also carried 166 million passengers, but the average trip was only 15.3 miles, suggesting that most of the passenger rail traffic was suburban service around Lisbon and Porto. There is regular electric train service from Lisbon to Cascais, and a subway system in Lisbon with about 7.5 miles of track and twenty stations serves the commercial district of Rossio in the center of the city and the northern suburbs.

The railroad, which is electrified between Lisbon and Porto and in the suburban areas of each city for about 10 percent of its total trackage, is gradually replacing steam operation in other areas with diesel. The number of steam locomotives declined from 328 to 121 between 1963 and 1973, and the number of diesel locomotives rose from eighty to 223 in that period. Electric locomotives totaled fifty-eight in 1973, rising from only nineteen in 1963. The rolling-stock inventory fell substantially in this period: passenger cars from 1,026 to 715 and freight wagons from 10,027 to 8,746.

Civil Aviation

The international airline Portuguese Air Transports (Transportes Aéreos Portugueses—TAP) was started in 1944 as a government airline. From June 1, 1953, it was operated as a quasi-private company under government control. Forty-four percent of the capital was owned by the Portuguese government, and the airline was nationalized in April 1975 along with other major transport facilities. Its fleet of three Boeing 747s, ten Boeing 707s, seven Boeing 727s, and three Caravelles—reported in April 1975—provided domestic services and international services to the rest of Europe and to Africa, North America, and South America. Seventeen international airlines (including Trans World Airlines and Pan American World Airways) also serve Portugal, and the Azores Air Transport Association (Sociedade Açoreana de Transportes Aéros—SATA), partially owned by TAP, operates an interisland fleet in the Azores.

There are three airports in continental Portugal handling regularly scheduled traffic. All transatlantic and most other international flights use Portela Airport at Lisbon. Domestic flights and some summer international traffic use the Pedras Rubras Airport at Porto and the airport at Faro in the Algarve. Regular air service, both domestic and international, is maintained also at Santa Catarina Airport in Funchal, Madeira, and Santa Maria Airport in the Azores. Traffic at Portela Airport was about two-thirds international and one-third domestic in 1973. The 2.3 million arrivals and departures in that year constituted a

12.8-percent increase over 1972, and the airport ranked twenty-first in traffic volume in Western Europe.

In mid-1975 it was reported that the Ministry of Transportation was undertaking a review of transport problems, policies, and regulations in order to arrive at a master plan for the transportation sector. It was also reported that some of the plans of the previous regime for renovation and expansion of transport facilities had been canceled or postponed, including the shelving of a project to build a new international airport at Lisbon and the suspension of much of the planned superhighway construction.

SECTION IV. NATIONAL SECURITY

CHAPTER 15

THE ARMED FORCES

The Portuguese armed forces by mid-1976 had undergone a drastic reduction in size from the very high levels attained during the counter-insurgency warfare in the African territories. In thirteen years of war —1961 to 1974—the army had tripled in size, and the navy and air force had more than doubled. In early 1974 strength was estimated at about 220,000, the army accounting for over 80 percent of the total. In June 1976, however, military strength was down to about 46,000, and the army had more than 50 percent of the total.

The inconclusive colonial wars had created strains in the military as well as in the society in general. Dissatisfaction among junior career officers fighting those wars led to the formation of a dissident group of army officers known as the Captains' Movement, which eventually spread to other services and became the Armed Forces Movement (Movimento das Forças Armadas—MFA). The MFA was initially concerned with professional grievances but, as disaffection grew within the military and the government failed to provide a solution to the continuing wars, the MFA became more politicized and on April 25, 1974, staged a coup d'etat that ended the authoritarian regime that had controlled Portugal for almost fifty years. The coup engendered a revolution that dismantled the repressive system established by António de Oliveira Salazar and maintained by his successor, Marcello Caetano. Since April 1974 the armed forces have remained the dominant element in a political system that has been torn by internal strife and turmoil. Unusual among military groups that have taken control of political systems, the MFA in 1976 planned to relinquish authority to the legislature elected in April and to the president to be elected in June.

Portugal was one of the original members of the North Atlantic Treaty Organization (NATO), and the revolutionary provisional governments have continued that membership. One of the two army divisions maintained in the homeland during the colonial wars was committed to NATO for the defense of southern Europe, and the other was committed to the defense of the Iberian Peninsula in conjunction with Spanish forces under the terms of a long-standing treaty known as the Iberian Pact. Both divisions were maintained at manning levels much below their authorized strength. Both the air force and the navy were also committed to NATO and Iberian defense. After reductions in force and the restructuring of the army, the new government announced that it would maintain a brigade-size force at authorized strength that would be earmarked for NATO duty.

HISTORICAL BACKGROUND

The military has played a major role in the development of Portugal throughout the country's history. During the Middle Ages the armed forces drove the Moors out of the country and resisted Spanish attempts to end Portugal's newly won independence. During the Renaissance Portuguese navigators and explorers established settlements and trade routes around the world, and the armed forces played an important role in establishing and maintaining the greatest empire then known (see ch. 2).

The glories of conquest and riches of trade were short lived. A military disaster took place when King Sebastião led his poorly prepared army into destruction and defeat in Morocco in 1578. Sebastião was killed along with half of the army, and Portugal was left leaderless without a legitimate heir and quickly fell under Spanish control in 1580. While under Spanish domination Portugal not only lost most of its navy, which sailed with the Spanish Armada against Portugal's former ally, England, but also lost much of its empire in the Far East. After regaining independence in 1640, Portugal renewed its alliance with England and was subsequently drawn into many European wars in the seventeenth and eighteenth centuries. Portugal became a battleground during the Napoleonic Wars. The country was occupied by French troops in 1807. British forces came to Portugal's aid and drove the French out of the country and then, using Portugal as a base of operations, out of Spain in 1813. During the middle and late nineteenth century the armed forces were important in the exploration and effective occupation of Angola and Mozambique.

A military revolt ended the Portuguese monarchy in 1910. Portugal attempted to maintain neutrality during World War I but was drawn into the conflict both in Europe and in Africa and fought on the side of the Allies. The early 1920s were years of instability, military revolts, and a parliamentary government that was unable to bring order to the country. Eventually the military successfully intervened, and a dictatorship was established in 1926. After two years of military rule the president, General António Oscar de Fragoso Carmona, invited Salazar, a conservative economics professor, to become minister of finance. From the initial appointment Salazar built a base of power and influence, became prime minister, and developed an authoritarian

374

regime that he called the New State (Estado Novo) and over which he assumed dictatorial powers. Although there was some anti-Salazar sentiment among the military, the regime successfully depoliticized the career officers and ensured their allegiance to the New State.

The possibility that the Spanish republican forces would succeed during the Spanish civil war led Salazar to send 18,000 Portuguese troops to fight on the side of Francisco Franco's nationalist forces. At the end of the civil war in 1939 Portugal and Spain negotiated the Iberian Pact, which committed the two countries to mutual defense of the peninsula and helped to ensure Iberian neutrality during World War II. In 1943, mindful of German defeats and Portugal's treaties with England, Salazar acceded to Great Britain's request for naval and air facilities in the Azores. Shortly thereafter the United States was also permitted to establish military facilities in the Azores. Portugal became one of the twelve charter members of NATO in 1949 and has retained its membership, which has proved beneficial to the armed forces through the acquisition of arms, ships, and aircraft from the United States and other NATO-member countries and through advanced training made available for officers and noncommissioned officers in the United States.

Counterinsurgency Warfare in Africa

Angola

Rebellion in the form of guerrilla warfare broke out in Angola in March 1961 when Bakongo tribesmen in the extreme north of the then-Portuguese province attacked several coffee plantations, killing white Portuguese owners and their families as well as black African workers who refused to cooperate. Portuguese armed forces in Angola at the time of the insurrection numbered 9,000, of whom about 3,000 were European and 6,000 locally conscripted. Within a month after the first guerrilla attacks Salazar had shaken up his military commands and had personally taken over the Ministry of Defense. He also initiated an airlift to take 10,000 additional troops to Angola and to bring out refugee women and children.

From the outset the insurgents, under the leadership of Holden Roberto, found sanctuary across Angola's northern and northeastern borders in the Democratic Republic of the Congo (present-day Zaire). Roberto's group eventually became the National Front for the Liberation of Angola (Frente Nacional de Libertação de Angola—FNLA), one of the three major anti-Portuguese guerrilla forces. The FNLA had the support of the United States. Fighting was largely contained in the northwestern sector of the province where Portuguese forces, relying heavily on aerial bombardment and strafing attacks, caused an exodus of villagers toward the Congo. During the remainder of 1961 and throughout 1962, when Portuguese forces managed to stabilize the military situation in the northwest and confine most of the fighting to that area, they employed as many as three-quarters of their force in what they called a psychosocial campaign to resettle and pacify African refugees. To this end they brought large segments of the population into *aldeamentos* (controlled villages) similar to the strategic hamlets used during the Vietnam conflict. By the end of 1962 Salazar felt confident enough to relinquish the defense porfolio to his chief of staff of the armed forces, General Manuel Gomes de Araújo.

Although the government counterinsurgency efforts were moderately successful, the guerrilla attacks could not be completely stamped out because of the sanctuaries in neighboring countries, and large numbers of Portuguese troops were involved in trying to hold terrorist attacks to a minimum. As the intermittent warfare dragged on into the mid-1960s, as many as 50,000 troops (half of them European and half African) were involved in the Angolan conflict. Meanwhile a second major anti-Portuguese movement, the Popular Movement for the Liberation of Angola (Movimento Popular de Libertação de Angola—MPLA), had become active in the strife. The MPLA was communist oriented and was supported with arms, equipment, and advisers from communist countries, mainly the Soviet Union. The FNLA and the MPLA, although sharing the goal of Angolan independence, were rivals as far as tribal affiliations and ideological beliefs were concerned. Because they rarely met on the same ground, their rivalry did little to help the government forces, that had to fight both groups. By 1966 a third insurgent group, the National Union for the Total Independence of Angola (União Nacional para a Independência Total de Angola—UNITA), had formed. Once again factional rivalry, now among three groups instead of two, did not materially assist the government forces.

From the mid-1960s until the overthrow of the government in Lisbon in April 1974, the warfare in Angola dragged on; the government forces were generally in control, but they could not end the insurgency. Even though most of the money to carry on the war was coming from Angolan resources—coffee, diamonds, and oil—the long years of conflict had wearied a large segment of the Portuguese people, and there was a definite desire to end the strife. A few months after the revolutionary government came to power, it negotiated with the Angolan factions to grant full independence to the province on November 11, 1975. Portuguese losses in Angola were 1,526 killed in action and 1,465 noncombat deaths.

Portuguese Guinea

The war in Portuguese Guinea (present-day Guinea-Bissau) began in 1961 with guerrilla attacks by members of the African Party for the Independence of Guinea and Cape Verde (Partido Africano de Independência de Guiné e Cabo Verde—PAIGC). At the time of the outbreak of hostilities Portugal maintained a force of about 5,000 troops in the province; half of them were European and half African.

From 1961 until 1973 the insurgency was directed by Amilcar Cabral, an avowed Marxist who accepted the Maoist idea of revolution among the rural peasants rather than among workers in towns where the armed forces were too powerful. Cabral lived much of the time in the neighboring Republic of Guinea, directing attacks from that country and from Senegal into Portuguese Guinea.

Cabral's guerrillas were often successful militarily and became quite adept at psychological warfare, effectively propagandizing the rural population. PAIGC was considered a model for other African insurgent groups because of its efficient organization and its successful operations. By 1968 PAIGC was claiming control over more than half of the province, the Portuguese being confined principally to the towns and major villages. In that year, however, General António de Spínola became governor of the province and commander of the armed forces. Under his leadership the armed forces successfully countered much of the insurgency, and Spínola, who was convinced that a purely military solution was impossible, inaugurated a civic-action program that included some political and governmental reforms. His troops constructed roads and bridges, houses and schools, and medical clinics, all for the benefit of local populations. Cabral, meanwhile, bided his time, kept up the pressure of guerrilla raids from the safety of Senegal and the Republic of Guinea, and accumulated quantities of weapons and equipment from various communist countries. Soviet surface-to-air missiles (SAMs) fired from across the borders brought down several Portuguese Air Force jets. Portugal lost control of the air and consequently the capability of using aircraft to attack raiding parties.

In mid-1973 Spínola returned to a hero's welcome in Lisbon and the presentation of the country's highest military award by President Américo Tomás. Despite Spínola's military and civic successes during his years in Portuguese Guinea, the military situation was still a virtual standoff between the insurgents and the armed forces. Moreover Portuguese morale suffered after the departure of the popular general because the forces felt that they were fighting an unwinnable war. Cabral was assassinated in early 1973, but the PAIGC, which he had led for seventeen years, remained steadfast in its drive toward independence. Later that year, when the PAIGC unilaterally declared the independence of Guinea-Bissau, the Caetano government denounced the declaration as a propaganda ploy, but several African states and Yugoslavia recognized the new state. A few months later, after the revolutionary government had come to power in Portugal, negotiations began for the withdrawal of Portuguese troops from the former province, and Lisbon recognized Guinea-Bissau as an independent state in September 1974 (see ch. 10). Portuguese losses in Portuguese Guinea were 1,656 killed in action and 696 noncombat deaths.

The insurgency in Mozambique began in the extreme northern section of that province in 1964 and was led by guerrilla forces of the Front for the Liberation of Mozambique (Frente de Libertação de Moçambique—FRELIMO), a dissident group that was formed in 1962 and had found refuge across the border in Tanzania. FRELIMO was well armed with weapons from various communist countries, and for some time before the first attacks its guerrilla fighters had been trained and advised by Communist Chinese technicians. Despite early successes in northern Mozambique, the insurgents were not able to press their advantage and move southward, partly because of tribal enmities between FRELIMO forces and tribes living away from the border area and partly because of Portuguese tactics learned in three years of difficult warfare in Angola. At the time of the outbreak of hostilities Portugal had about 16,000 troops in the province, all deployed in the north where the FRELIMO attacks were expected.

For the next several years Portuguese forces fought a classic counterinsurgency war, containing the incursions of the guerrillas and preventing the spread of violence. The government troops, however, were unable to end the warfare because the guerrillas had a sanctuary to which they could retreat and a constant source of arms and equipment. The Portuguese established *aldeamentos* as they had in Angola to control and protect the population. Although almost 1.5 million people were living in *aldeamentos* in the early 1970s, most were in the north where the Portuguese forces were concentrated. With great difficulty the guerrillas eventually skirted the Portuguese strength in the north and began incursions into the relatively unprotected center.

At the time of the overthrow of the Lisbon government about 60,000 government troops were involved in the Mozambique counterinsurgency. Of these about 35,000 were black Africans, 10,000 were white Africans, and the remaining 15,000 were from Portugal. This relatively large force was being tied down by approximately 7,000 guerrillas. The new Portuguese government would have preferred some sort of commonwealth for the African provinces but, as with the other insurgent movements, FRELIMO wanted nothing less than complete independence. Negotiations finally provided for the withdrawal of Portuguese troops, and in June 1975 the former province became independent as the People's Republic of Mozambique. Portuguese losses in Mozambique were 1,606 killed in action and 724 noncombat deaths.

Dissension in the Armed Forces

The inconclusive colonial wars of the 1960s and early 1970s created a great deal of dissension among career officers of the armed forces, eventually leading to the military coup d'etat of April 25, 1974. In addition to overthrowing the government the coup initiated a revolution that set the stage for the decolonization of Portugal's African provinces and altered the role of the military in Portuguese life.

Before the outbreak of the colonial wars the military had been politically apathetic. A military coup in the mid-1920s deposed the republican government and laid the groundwork for Salazar's authoritarian regime. Under Salazar the military was generally loyal. Traditionally the officer corps had been the preserve of younger sons of wealthy families and sons of officers who could afford the tuition charged by the Military Academy in Lisbon. Given the sponsorship of a wealthy individual or a high-ranking officer, however, an exceptionally talented son of a poor family sometimes managed an appointment to the Military Academy or to the Naval School at Alfeite. Military careers were sought by wealthy candidates more for prestige than reward because pay was relatively poor compared with other professions. The low salaries of senior officers, however, were often augmented by remunerative sinecures as corporation board members, held concurrently with their military positions.

In 1958 the Military Academy, failing to attract anywhere near the numbers of cadets needed for the army, ended its tuition requirements, and henceforth the student body was dominated by sons of bureaucrats, small landholders, merchants, and even the sons of some workers. This new class of cadets expected that after graduation they would enter the peaceful garrison life at home or in the colonies that the Portuguese army had known for generations. Instead they were thrown directly into the colonial wars and eventually became the disgruntled captains who instigated the revolution.

After decade of fighting in Angola and almost as long in Portuguese Guinea and Mozambique, even senior officers had begun to show dissatisfaction with the conduct of the warfare. In the upper echelons of the army dissent in the early 1970s centered in two groups: the moderates or reformists associated with generals Francisco de Costa Gomes and Spínola and the rightists associated with General Kaulza de Arriaga. The moderates favored negotiations to end the guerrilla wars in Africa, and the rightists sought a military solution. Prime Minister Caetano and President Tomás favored the latter group.

It was among junior career officers, however, that most of the dissatisfaction with the government was manifested, and during 1973 that dissatisfaction led to the formation of the Captains' Movement. The Captains' Movement was initially an ad hoc committee of career officers—mostly captains—who banded together to give voice to their professional grievances. The Caetano government had just issued Decree Law 353-73, which career officers felt undermined their status in the army as well as in society. Expansion of the armed forces, particularly the army, to fight the African wars necessitated the augmentation of the officer corps with civilian university graduates who were commissioned after a short course by the army. The decree law stated that the nonregular officers were entitled to receive the same consideration for promotion as those who had graduated from the Military Academy.

It was this narrowly based complaint that spurred the formation of the Captains' Movement. Once organized, the captains soon discovered that they had many more grievances—low pay, long separations from families during combat tours, and poorly equipped units. In a short time the captains found that their complaints were shared not only by career officers of the navy and the air force but also by the noncareer officers of all services. The Captains' Movement became the MFA, and by November 1973 it was a full-blown dissident group whose clandestine membership ranged across the political spectrum.

In addition to the question of professional status, officers were disturbed over their inability to secure modern equipment to match that held by African insurgents. Well aware of the sophisticated equipment furnished to the guerrillas by the Soviet Union, the East European countries, and the People's Republic of China, Portuguese officers complained that their soliders were unable to fight with the antiquated equipment furnished to them. Shortly after the outbreak of the Angolan hostilities in 1961, the United States imposed an embargo on arms shipments to the combatants, which was also imposed by several other NATO allies. A near-mutiny occurred in Evora in the late summer of 1973 when a battalion mobilized for duty in Portuguese Guinea was equipped with obsolete weapons. At the same time, the Portuguese Air Force had been virtually grounded in Portuguese Guinea because the PAIGC had obtained Soviet SAM-6 missiles, which were operated by Cuban technicians. Although countermissile techniques had been developed by Portuguese pilots, their obsolete fighter-bombers did not have sophisticated jamming devices and were easy prey for the SAM-6.

By November 1973 the MFA had attracted the attention of General Arriaga, who demanded that Caetano take action against the dissident officers. Failing to impress the government, Arriaga reportedly tried to enlist the support of Costa Gomes and Spínola in a right-wing coup d'etat, but those generals were not interested in such a conspiracy. In his prerevolution book, *Portugal and the Future,* Spínola put forth his view that military victory in Africa was impossible and that the government should seek political solutions to the problems of Angola, Portuguese Guinea, and Mozambique. Such views were anathema to the right wing but found ready acceptance among many members of the MFA as well as among the war-weary public.

As the MFA increased its membership and the situation in Africa seemed to deteriorate, the organization became increasingly radicalized. The rightists became more strident in their demands for a military solution in the African provinces. Caetano feared that his government was in danger from the right; and when Spínola and Costa Gomes failed to appear at a public ceremony in which the military hierarchy was to repledge its allegiance to the government, Caetano fired both of them. Dismissal of the two generals brought on a protest meeting of the MFA, which was broken up by police. In March a military putsch was aborted when loyal troops turned back a military column marching on Lisbon from the north. Five weeks later, on April 25, 1974, the MFA deposed the Caetano government and initiated a full-scale revolution.

During the overthrow there were few casualties; the armed forces still loyal to Caetano offered little or no resistance, and in a very short time the MFA was in complete control. The MFA quickly appointed General Spínola president and named a board of officers—the Junta of National Salvation—to assist him in running the country according to the MFA program. Within days political prisoners were being released from prisons, and long-exiled opposition leaders were returning to Portugal. In the meantime the military was heavily involved in politics for the first time in almost fifty years.

Friction developed almost immediately between the then-anonymous leadership of the MFA and President Spínola's junta over the issue of the pace and direction of decolonization. The MFA favored immediate dissolution of the links with the colonies and withdrawal of Portuguese forces, whereas Spínola favored a gradual solution based on self-determination, which would leave Portugal some economic control. At the same time the labor movement began pressuring for increased salaries and making other demands. Increasing unrest within the MFA led to a change in government whereby the supporters of Spínola were outflanked by radicals within the MFA. Rising political and labor violence by July 1974 led to the formation of an elite military organization—Continental Operations Command (Comando de Operações do Continente—COPCON) composed of paratroopers, marines, and army commandos—with the mission of maintaining public order (see ch. 16).

During the summer of 1974 Spínola attempted to gather support for his moderate policies, and in late September a crisis developed when the radicals within the MFA combined with leftist civilians to blockade Lisbon. To avoid a civil disorder Spínola resigned, and Costa Gomes became president. Spínola essentially had underestimated popular support for the MFA as well as his ability to have orders obeyed without question.

In late 1974 the MFA began to institutionalize itself by creating the Council of the Twenty, which included its seven-member coordinating commission, members of the junta, and military officers who were cabinet ministers. Several weeks before the elections of April 25, 1975—to select a constituent assembly—General Spínola was involved in an unsuccessful right-wing coup d'etat attempt and fled the country. It has been suggested that the coup attempt was sparked by radicals within the MFA, allegedly aided by the Communists, who wanted to discredit moderates in the MFA as well as Spínola.

As of early 1976 a special commission was investigating the coup attempt, but the extent of Spínola's involvement had not been determined (see ch. 16). The radicals in the MFA then created the Council of the Revolution, giving it supreme legislative and administrative powers. A wave of nationalizations of banks and insurance companies followed, as well as arrests of supposed counterrevolutionaries and a further purge of officers from the armed forces. The assembly of the MFA was increased from 200 to 240 to add radical members, and barracks assemblies thought to be loyal to Spínola were abolished. The MFA enforced a policy of requiring the retirement of officers accused of not supporting its program.

In 1975 dissension within the military continued on an unprecedented scale, and political factions attempted to find allies within the armed forces to support their goals. At the same time there was a drastic reduction in force; soldiers returning from Africa were discharged, and conscription was curtailed. To prevent any concentration of power by moderates, radicals abolished the Armed Forces General Staff. Military discipline during most of 1975 depended on the popularity of each unit's commanding officer. Many officers were rejected by the men they were assigned to command. Some units voted whether or not to obey orders. Soldiers sent to end illegal worker-occupations of industrial plants often disobeyed orders and aided the workers.

During the summer of 1975 there was an ongoing crisis within the military over the continuation of Brigadier Vasco dos Santos Gonçalves as prime minister. Gonçalves was linked to the Portuguese Communist Party (Partido Communista Português—PCP) and was supported by Brigadier Otelo Saraiva de Carvalho, commander of COPCON and the key Military Region of Lisbon. Although Gonçalves was eased from office, huge demonstrations took place, and extreme leftists found support for a government based on councils of workers and soldiers. Competing groups within the armed forces issued manifestos favoring radical or moderate positions. The government was obliged to diminish COPCON by removing marines from its control after some units disobeyed orders and when another unit failed to protect the Spanish embassy during anti-Franco riots. A new unit, the Military Inventervention Group (Agrupação Militar de Intervenção—AMI), was established on October 20, 1975.

The dismissal of Brigadier Carvalho, a supporter of the extreme left, as commander of the Military Region of Lisbon was a factor in the attempted coup d'etat of November 25, 1975. Disgruntled paratroopers, facing the disbanding of COPCON and encouraged by support from extreme left-wing parties and elements of the communist party, plotted to overthrow the government. The paratroopers were supported by the Soldiers United Will Win (Soldados Unidos Vencerão—SUV) movement. During November 1975 there were violent confrontations between members of SUV and the armed militias of the conservative political parties. The attempted coup failed when leftist civilians did not aid the military insurrection and units loyal to the government surrounded the air bases the paratroopers had seized; army commandos defeated the leftist military police unit in Lisbon. COPCON was dissolved after the attempted coup, and Carvalho was later reduced in rank.

The suppression of the attempted leftist coup allowed moderates to reatin power in the government and the MFA. Extreme leftists were purged from the armed forces, and large numbers of soldiers were discharged, resulting in an army strength of 40,000 by April 1976. The air force and the navy were also in the process of reducing their manning levels to about 10,000 men each. The moderates in the MFA established a new role for the armed forces in Portugal by the issuance of a constitutional law, the Fundamental Basis for the Reorganization of the Amred Forces, on December 11, 1975. This law made the armed forces the guarantor of national sovereignty and the defender of socialism and democracy in Portugal.

By early 1976 the Council of the Revolution had planned to relinquish legislative power to the National Assembly elected on April 25, 1976, and executive power was scheduled to be handed over to an elected president. Moderates within the armed forces in early 1976 had set in motion the process of disengagement from politics, establishing checks that would prevent further military intervention in political matters.

MISSION, ORGANIZATION, AND OPERATIONS

Less than two years after the coup d'etat of April 1974 the composition, mission, structure, and goals of the armed forces in Portugal had changed. Once the mission of defending the African territories was terminated, the size of the armed forces was reduced to slightly more than 20 percent of its wartime strength. During two years of revolutionary turmoil in Portugal the armed forces had exercised an internal security mission. The newly adopted 1976 Constitution, however, provided social and economic duties for the armed forces.

Constitutional Bases

The 1933 Constitution, which had provided the legal framework for the Salazar and Caetano regimes, remained in effect for almost two years after the revolution before being superseded by the 1976 Constitution. In the old constitution the state guaranteed the existence of armed forces sufficient to the task of defending the country and its territories and "the keeping of order and public peace." Military service was to be general and compulsory for male citizens, and civil service jobs were denied to those who did not fulfill their military obligations. During the interim between the overthrow of the old government in April 1974 and the promulgation of the Constitution in April 1976, the Portuguese armed forces, whose MFA members had been the prime movers of the revolution, had operated under existing statutes and the decrees enacted by the revolutionary governments. From 1975 the Council of the Revolution controlled the armed forces as well as the legislative and executive functions of the government.

The 1976 Constitution retained several basic features of the earlier document concerning the role of the armed forces in national life. It codified the duties of military personnel in the postrevolution republic and reconfirmed the president as commander in chief. The Council of the Revolution was named to act as a collective commander in chief until the election of a president later in 1976. Universal conscription was reinstated, but provisions were made for conscientious objectors, and alternate service was prescribed for some categories of personnel who would not serve in the military.

The Constitution decreed the MFA and the people dual guarantors of national sovereignty; moreover the MFA in combination with the political parties and democratic movements was designated an instrument for peaceful development of the revolution. The armed forces, therefore, assumed duties beyond those of defending the national territory as codified in the 1933 Constitution; they were to be the supervisors of the newly elected members of the democratic government. Although the Council of the Revolution retained power until the presidential election, the armed forces had previously signed a pact with the political parties to guarantee virtual veto power over the government until 1980. Hence the Constitution assigned the armed forces the task of maintaining conditions to allow the "peaceful and pluralistic transition of Portuguese society toward socialism and democracy." The armed forces were placed beyond the realm of political interference and were obliged to serve the people and the political parties.

Army

The organizational basis of the Portuguese Army is territorial. In 1976 there were four military regions in continental Portugal and three independent territorial commands overseas (the Azores, Madeira, and Macao). In early 1976 the government announced plans to abolish the independent territorial command of Macao. The boundaries of the four military regions corresponded generally to those of existing administrative divisions. The Military Region of Lisbon is the most important command and contains most of the country's military bases. In early 1976 there were plans to establish special military intervention zones in various parts of the country in order to coordinate military activities with those of police units. Commanders of military regions were usually brigadier generals or senior colonels. Commanders of military regions and the independent territorial commands were directly responsible to the chief of staff of the army.

In 1974 and 1975, during the period of decolonization, the army had the dual mission of maintaining order in the colonies and evacuating civilians. The bulk of the army was committed to fighting in Africa in the 1960s and early 1970s. Two infantry divisions stationed in Portugal were assigned to missions provided by international treaties: one to NATO and the other to joint defense, with Spanish forces, of the Iberian Peninsula. In practice, however, both divisions were maintained at less than full strength.

The army has modern scout cars and armored personnel carriers but lacks modern tanks and heavy artillery, which would be necessary in present-day land warfare. The army uses American M41 and M47 tanks and 105-mm howitzers. The infantry is equipped with the Portuguese-manufactured G3 automatic rifle, which uses the standard 7.62-mm NATO cartridge. The army does not have a computerized artillery fire-control network and lacks modern antiaircraft and antitank artillery.

By mid-1976 the army's strength was 26,000, and there were plans to retrain the army for conventional warfare. Portugal was reconsidering its tactical commitment to NATO, with the probability that the army's contribution would be reduced to a standing force of about 10,000 men in an airmobile brigade comprising infantry, artillery, engineer, and support units to be placed at the disposal of the Supreme Allied Commander Europe (SACEUR). This Portuguese army brigade would have its headquarters at Santa Margarida, the NATO training camp. Its air support would be located nearby at Tancos.

During the revolutionary period after the April 1974 coup, the army became involved in the political infighting that plagued the nation. In order to prove its value to the people the army assumed the task of bringing health and welfare services to rural parts of metropolitan Portugal. In late 1975 the army began to provide helicopter service to islands in the Azores that were formerly difficult to reach. After the unsuccessful coup attempt in November 1975 by extreme leftists in the army, moderates regained control of the army. By early 1976 they were preparing to use the army in major national economic projects in which private as well as state-owned enterprises were to participate.

Navy

The Portuguese Navy was reorganized after April 1974. The provisional government established a new command structure for the navy under the provisons of Law 4-74, July 1, 1974, which placed the chief of staff of the navy over twenty-four tactical and support commands. The chief of staff also held the position of minister of marine (navy), and the new position of vice chief of staff was created to allow the chief of staff to attend to those additional duties. The duties of the vice chief of staff encompassed supervision of all naval affairs except those of the adjutant to the chief of staff, who had responsibility for finances, and the superintendent of naval supplies, who had responsibility for ship construction and repair.

The operational emphasis of the navy has shifted since 1974 from guerrilla interdiction on rivers, coasts, and lakes in Africa to a concentration of effort on its assigned NATO patrol duties in the Iberian Atlantic Command (IBERLANT) zone of operations. The IBERLANT zone extends from the Strait of Gibraltar westward 700 miles and from northern Portugal southward to the Tropic of Cancer. Gibraltar and the Madeira Islands are part of the IBERLANT zone of operations. In 1976 the navy operated antisubmarine warfare (ASW) patrols in the IBERLANT zone and also from the Azores. The Portuguese obligation was to provide IBERLANT with six escort vessels beginning in 1970, but because of operational necessities of the African wars only three vessels were assigned.

At the end of 1974 the navy had forty operational fighting vessels. The navy's inventory was greatly expanded during the 1950s by the acquisition of modern minesweepers, small patrol vessels, fast frigates, and corvettes obtained through the United States-supported Military Defense Assistance Program. The Dutch and French governments financed construction of vessels in the 1960s. At the end of 1975 four 1200-ton-displacement frigates were on order from Spain. In early 1976 there was concern over the high cost of maintaining four French-built Daphne-class submarines that had been acquired since the mid-1960s, and their future in the navy's inventory was uncertain.

Portuguese naval facilities are available to NATO forces, and continental Portugal, the Azores, and the Madeira Islands all provide excellent port facilities. The Alfeite base on the Rio Tejo estuary has repair facilities and is home port for a six-vessel NATO flotilla. There are additional facilities at Montijo for naval aircraft and important fuel storage areas at Trafaria (near Lisbon) and at Ponta Delgada in the Azores.

By June 1976 navy strength had been reduced from its wartime high of about 19,000 officers and men (including 3,400 marines) to a total of about 12,000. Year-end strength was projected at 10,000 to 11,000 of which about 2,000 would be marines. Naval officers have been prominent in several provisional governments but were expected, along with other officers, to relinquish power to an elected civilian government in mid-1976.

Air Force

Although a separate air force was not established until 1952, the Portuguese military has had a role in aviation since its earliest days. Portuguese pilots flew combat missions in World War I and again in Spain during that country's civil war; others participated in early transatlantic flights to Brazil and the United States.

Since 1949 Portugal, as a member of NATO, has received aircraft from other member countries to strengthen the air arms of the army and navy. In 1952 most of the air capability was drawn together into the Portuguese Air Force. At the time of the revolution both civil and military aviation came under the purview of the Secretariat of Aviation, an office of the Ministry of Defense. The postrevolution government placed the secretariat under the control of the chief of staff of the air force, where it remained in early 1976.

The air force, which was extensively involved in combat, combat support, and medical evacuation during the colonial wars, increased in strength from about 12,500 in 1962 to 21,000 in 1973. The total was down slightly to 19,500 (including 3,300 paratroopers) in early 1974. By mid-1976 almost all paratroopers had been discharged—they had been deeply involved in the coup attempt of the previous November —and air force strength was down to about 8,000 but expected to level off at about 10,000 by the end of the year. The paratroop base and training center was deactivated in April 1976. The aircraft inventory in early 1976 amounted to 130 planes, most of which were obsolete or obsolescent. Despite its aged and aging aircraft, Portugal managed to fly ASW patrols in fulfillment of its assigned NATO mission. In 1976 Portugal had American F-86, T-33, and T-37, and Italian Fiat G-91 jet aircraft and a number of propeller-driven models. Orders for new aircraft that had been placed before the revolution were canceled by the revolutionary authorities. Spain had already delivered a few transport aircraft against a total of twenty-eight, but the remainder of the order was canceled as was an order for 110 trainers from Brazil. A joint endeavor with France for the development of a short-takeoff-and-landing (STOL) transport was also suspended.

The air force provides facilities for NATO aircraft at Montijo and Ovar (north of Aveiro) air bases in continental Portugal and at Lajes on Terceira Island in the Azores. The United States has maintained air facilities at the Portuguese air base at Lajes since World War II. American transports refueled at Lajes en route to the Middle East during the October 1973 war. There were about 2,000 United States Air Force personnel in the Azores in 1976. Under a long-term contract with the Portuguese Air Force, repair facilities at Alverca are used by West German and American aircraft.

MANPOWER, SUPPORT, AND CONDITIONS OF SERVICE

At the end of the colonial wars the Portuguese armed forces had a strength of 220,000 men including about 65,000 Africans, most of whom served in the army. Excluding Africans the Portuguese in the armed forces represented 12.6 percent of the 1.2 million men between eighteen and forty-five who were eligible for military service. By the end of 1975 many men had been discharged from active duty and many placed in the inactive reserve, which numbered 562,000. Because of the manpower requirements of the armed forces during the colonial wars, physical and mental standards for recruits had been lowered, but in early 1976 prewar standards were reimposed, and the pool of men eligible for conscription was thereby reduced.

Service Obligations

Terms of service for the army, navy, and air force were two, four, and three years respectively, but during the colonial wars it was not uncommon for as many as two additional years to be required of individuals serving tours of duty in Africa. Conscription had been the major source of manpower, but the end of the colonial wars and the dissolution of the empire greatly reduced the number of men needed. Conscription was partially suspended, as the services had no problem securing recruits from the growing ranks of the unemployed. By 1976 terms of service had been reduced to eighteen months for all conscripts, and a further reduction to fifteen months was projected for the end of the year. The army is responsible for filling all manpower needs and operates through the Army Recruitment Service to secure recruits for the three services. Since 1969 women have been permitted to enlist for noncombatant positions.

Training

During the colonial wars training in all services emphasized the requirements of counterinsurgency warfare. Decolonization and the reduction in force have necessitated a reorientation toward conventional training. Recruits undergo nine-week basic training courses, before being assigned to specialized training based on aptitude tests and civilian skills. When the armed forces lowered their standards, they received large numbers of personnel deficient in basic education, necessitating special training courses to prepare them for military duties.

Air force and army noncommissioned officers often are trained at army schools, but the navy maintains its own specialized gunnery and communications schools. Noncommissioned officers from the three services have been trained to use advanced equipment by NATO missions or on extended courses in NATO countries, including the United States. The navy maintains schools for lighthouse keepers, merchant seamen and officers, and marines. The air force has special training schools for paratroopers and helicopter pilots.

The Military Academy and the Naval School are the Portuguese counterparts of the United States Military Academy at West Point and the United States Naval Academy at Annapolis. Both service academies offer four-year courses emphasizing the physical and engineering sciences and leading to commissions in the armed forces. In the late 1950s tuition fees at the Military Academy were dropped, and military careers were opened to all levels of the society. The long colonial wars and increased opportunities in private industry made military careers less attractive by the 1970s, and in 1973 there were applications to fill only about 100 of the 400 places available in the Military Academy. The Naval School did not encounter the same difficulties as the Military Academy and in early 1976 continued to train as many as 300 students a year. In late 1975 there were proposals to combine the service academies to form an armed forces academy as part of a general reorganization of the armed forces.

Career army officers attend the Institute of High Military Studies, which was founded in 1911 at Pedrouços near Lisbon. In order to be considered for promotion to field grade, officers must successfully complete the course. The Institute of High National Defense Studies, created in 1967, conducts study groups on national economic development and defense strategy for military and civilian personnel with outstanding records. It survived the military reorganization that followed the coup of April 1974 and is expected to have a role in directing nationalized industries and economic planning.

Military Justice

The Portuguese armed forces are regulated by the Code of Military Justice promulgated in 1925. The Code of Naval Justice continues to be applicable in certain instances to naval personnel at sea. The Code of Military Justice is the Portuguese equivalent of the United States Universal Code of Military Justice. The major difference between the two systems of military justice is that decisions by Portuguese military tribunals are not subject to review by civilian courts. Military courts in the military regions and independent territorial commands consist of a president, two judges, a defense attorney, and a prosecution attorney, all of whom are officers. The Military Supreme Court, presided over by a general or an admiral, reviews sentences of lower tribunals; it also approves promotions and recommendations for military medals and reviews petitions concerning reserve status.

Military tribunals also process the cases of returning deserters who fled during the colonial wars and have rehabilitated some military personnel who rebelled against the Salazar regime. A special military commission was established in 1974 to try former members of the secret police for crimes of murder and torture, but no cases had been tried as of early 1976 (see ch. 16).

After the coup of 1974 and during the period of radical disturbances the Code of Military Justice came under attack by enlisted personnel and noncareer officers. Radical groups of soldiers and saliors, such as SUV, denigrated military discipline, refused to obey orders, favored the formation of a government of soldiers and workers on a Soviet pattern, and eventually precipitated a coup attempt in November 1975. In early 1976, however, discipline had been restored.

Morale and Conditions of Service

During the colonial war there was a deterioration of morale among enlisted men, noncommissioned officers, and junior officers. There were long and frequently repetitive tours of duty in Africa alternating with short periods in Portugal. A military career was not considered prestigious during the late 1960s and early 1970s. The low pay and growing chasm between military and civilian pay was a source of complaint among junior officers, who often resigned their commissions or were obliged to take part-time jobs. To offset low pay there were benefits such as low-cost elementary and high school tuition for children of officers and enlisted men and special medical aid for family members.

The revolutionary euphoria of 1974 brought a great deal of prestige for the armed forces. The military-political process brought the armed forces into contact with the public for the first time through the politically inspired cultural dynamization campaigns and military management of nationalized enterprises. The people also approved overwhelmingly of decolonization. Growing unemployment and economic stagnation in 1976, however, led to complaints that the armed forces had become a privileged sector of the society. The public began to resent the fact that the army had hospitals for its personnel that were superior to civilian-sponsored institutions, that officers and enlisted personnel had access to discount-priced gasoline, and that there were special commissaries and buyers' clubs for active-duty and retired personnel.

Salaries and Pensions

In 1974 salaries of armed forces personnel were raised. At the same time many high-ranking officers were retired and junior officers promoted. At the end of 1975 the base pay of an army captain was 10,400 escudos (for value of the escudo—see Glossary) per month. For married officers there were extra allowances for housing, food, and travel plus special grants for housing in such high-cost areas as Lisbon. The monthly pay for a general of the army was 18,500 escudos per month, but all general officers and admirals received special bonuses in addition to the family allowances given all married personnel. During the colonial wars and the period of decolonization special pay of as much as 100 percent above usual pay was authorized for service in isolated or hardship posts. Enlisted men fared less well than officers; a sergeant received a base pay of 2,400 escudos a month and a recruit less than 1,000 escudos per month.

Each service has a general pension fund. Career officers and noncommissioned officers pay 6 percent of their salaries into it. Retirement pay is determined by a formula rather than by a fixed percentage of active duty pay for the number of years in service. The formula is Y times n divided by 40; Y is the active-duty base pay at the time of retirement, and n is the number of years of service up to forty. Therefore it benefits career personnel to remain on active duty for forty years, but service beyond forty years is not permissible. After the revolution of April 1974 officers unwilling to swear loyalty to the MFA program, which established postcoup authority and set revolutionary goals, were retired or given reserve status. By late 1975, however, many of those forced out during the wave of revolutionary fervor had been reintegrated upon petition. Others were allowed to retire under a sliding-scale pension system based on retirement at age forty or after twenty years of active duty.

Uniforms, Ranks, and Insignia

The official grade structure of the Portuguese armed forces shows nine officer ranks for the army and the air force and ten for the navy (see fig. 27). In practice army and air force general officers serving as chiefs of staff of their respective services, chief of staff of the armed forces, or president of the Supreme Military Tribunal, wear four stars and correspond in rank to the navy vice admiral. The army and the air force each have eight enlisted ranks, but the navy uses only seven. Rank insignia are quite similar to those used by many other countries—bars and stars for commissioned officers of the army and air force, stripes of varying width for naval officers, and chevrons for noncommissioned officers of all services.

Portuguese uniforms are similar to those of the armed forces of the United States and other NATO member nations. The army's uniforms are made of rough wool and are khaki colored, the air force's are of a light fabric and are light blue, and the navy's vary from white to dark blue and are also made of a light fabric. Army fatigue uniforms are olive green, and enlisted men wear headgear with front and rear sun

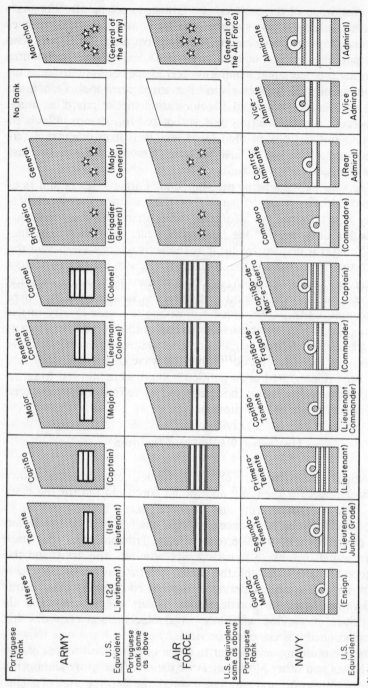

Portuguese Rank	Alferes	Tenente	Capitão	Major	Tenente-Coronel	Coronel	Brigadeiro	General	No Rank	Marechal
ARMY										
U.S. Equivalent	(2d Lieutenant)	(1st Lieutenant)	(Captain)	(Major)	(Lieutenant Colonel)	(Colonel)	(Brigadier General)	(Major General)		(General of the Army)
Portuguese rank same as above										
AIR FORCE										
U.S. equivalent same as above										(General of the Air Force)
Portuguese Rank	Guarda-Marinha	Segundo-Tenente	Primeiro-Tenente	Capitão-Tenente	Capitão-de-Fragata	Capitão-de-Mar-e-Guerra	Comodoro	Contra-Almirante	Vice-Almirante	Almirante
NAVY										
U.S. Equivalent	(Ensign)	(Lieutenant Junior Grade)	(Lieutenant)	(Lieutenant Commander)	(Commander)	(Captain)	(Commodore)	(Rear Admiral)	(Vice Admiral)	(Admiral)

Note--Marechals wear gold stars.

Figure 27. Portugal, Armed Forces, Insignia of Officers' Ranks

visors. A more common uniform for enlisted men and officers is a woolen, waist-length jacket worn over shirt and tie. Soldiers tuck their trouser legs into their boots. Headgear consists of a brown beret with a band bearing the national colors, red and green. Commandos wear distinctive camouflage uniforms and black berets. Air force enlisted personnel wear uniforms similar in appearance to those of army enlisted personnel, but a peaked service cap is the standard headgear. Paratroopers wear camouflage uniforms with green berets. Navy enlisted personnel wear either blue wool or white cotton uniforms for shore or sea duty. In either case pullover blouses are standard. Navy enlisted men's headgear is similar to that of other European navies—round caps with the name of the ship sewn on the front of the headband.

Officers wear full-dress uniforms on ceremonial occasions, but none are authorized for enlisted personnel. Officers generally wear uniforms with suit jackets for staff duty but may wear waist-length jackets similar to those worn by enlisted men when on duty. All officers wear insignia of rank on the sleeves at the cuff, and noncommissioned officers wear them on the sleeves near the shoulders or on shoulder tabs.

Decorations and Awards

During the colonial wars the armed forces awarded large numbers of medals for valor and meritorious service to soldiers in combat as well as to those engaged in civic action. Civilians also received decorations for public service, and foreign scholars were often decorated. A large number of the MFA's future leaders received medals for valor in Africa. During the revolutionary period some medals were awarded for service in Africa, but public ceremonies were no longer common.

Members of the armed forces wear all decorations above the left breast pocket on one or more rows in an established order of precedence from right to left. The national decorations in order of precedence are: Military Order of the Tower and Sword; Military Valor; War Cross; Distinguished Service; Military Merit; Military Order of Aviz; Military Order of Christ; Military Order of Saint James of the Sword; Order of the Empire; Order of Prince Henry; Order of Public Instruction; Order of Beneficence; Order of Agricultural and Industrial Merit; Class of Industrial Merit; Promotion for Distinction; Exemplary Conduct; Victory; Foreign; Portuguese Legion; Lifesaving; Red Cross; and Commemorative. The Portuguese Legion was abolished after April 25, 1974, and although no order forbidding it has been issued, wearing the legion's medal in the political climate of early 1976 would have been considered counterrevolutionary.

The Military Order of the Tower and Sword was instituted in 1495 to reward knights who served in campaigns in North Africa. In modern times it has been awarded for courage on the battlefield, loyalty, and meritorious service in command of troops on campaign. It was awarded in five degrees: Grand Cross, Grand Officer, Commander, Officer, and Member. About fifty Portuguese officers possess this award. In 1976 General Spínola, the former president, was the only living recipient of Portugal's highest military award, the Military Order of the Tower and Sword with Palm, which he received in 1973 on his return from Africa.

The Military Valor medal is awarded for extraordinary deeds of heroism, self-sacrifice, valor, and courage during war or peace under circumstances that endanger the life of the person concerned. The War Cross is awarded for acts and deeds of bravery carried out in campaign by Portuguese and foreign soldiers and civilians when no other medal or decoration has been awarded for the same deeds. The Distinguished Service medal is awarded for military services that are outstanding or noteworthy, resulting in honor and glory for the homeland or for the military institutions of Portugal. The Military Merit medal is awarded to soldiers who show exceptional qualities of a military nature. Of the four classes the first two are for officers only, the third for any rank, and the fourth for sergeants and other ranks.

The Military Order of Aviz is the oldest of the Portuguese military orders, established in 1162 by Portugal's first king, Afonso Henriques. After 1789 its award was limited to members of the armed forces and given in five degrees: Grand Cross, Grand Officer, Commander, Officer, and Member. Only a few active-duty general officers possess this award. The Military Order of Christ was founded in 1318 by King Dinís; it is awarded for distinguished and outstanding service to Portugal and to mankind. It has five degrees and may be awarded to foreigners.

The Promotion for Distinction medal is awarded to disabled servicemen and to civilians on military duties who are promoted for distinction in combat. The Exemplary Conduct medal is awarded to officers, sergeants, and other ranks for long service and exemplary moral and disciplinary conduct. It has three classes: gold, silver, and copper, awarded according to the number of years of active military service free from any disciplinary charge.

The Victory medal was created in 1919 at the suggestion of Marshall Ferdinand Foch during the Versailles Conference. It was intended for all Allied combatants who had participated in World War I. In order of precedence foreign awards are after the Victory medal and before the Portuguese Legion, Life Saving, and Red Cross awards. Commemorative medals are awarded to members of the military forces and civilians who take part in campaigns or expeditions, on Portuguese soil or abroad, during wartime or when there is imminent danger of war, against external enemies or on operations or expeditions to safeguard national sovereignty. A number of privately made medallions commemorate the MFA and the revolution of 1974, but no official medals have been awarded for that military action or subsequent actions.

THE ARMED FORCES AND THE NATIONAL ECONOMY

The armed forces consumed a disproportionately large share of the national budget during the colonial wars in comparison with expenditures for education, housing, and health. Portugal's military expenditures were also the highest in proportion to gross national product (GNP) of any country in Europe. Taxes, foreign investments in Portugal and its colonies, and tourism as well as remittances from emigrants helped finance the war budgets. At the start of the wars the military budget was 5.7 billion escudos, which represented 6.9 percent of GNP. Military spending doubled in ten years to 11.5 billion escudos in 1972, which represented 5.1 percent of GNP and a per capita expenditure of 20,000 escudos. In 1975 the government released figures showing the total cost of the wars in Africa to have been 120 billion escudos.

The end of the colonial wars brought a slight decline in military spending as the armed forces were undergoing a reduction in size. The 1975 military budget amounted to 17.1 billion escudos; though higher in total amount expended, it represented a smaller percentage (29.1 percent) of government expenditure than during the war. In early 1976 there were plans to reorganize the armed forces and reduce spending further. The armed forces were to have a role in improving the rail and road networks as well as providing services to rural areas, utilizing skills acquired in Africa.

FOREIGN INFLUENCE

Since Portugal joined NATO in 1949, the major foreign influence in terms of organization, equipment, and training of its armed forces has been the United States. Some Portuguese officers and noncommissioned officers have trained in the United Kingdom, France, and the Federal Republic of Germany (West Germany) or have been trained by military missions from those countries, but their numbers were small compared with the more than 2,000 who either received training in the United States or were trained in Portugal by the United States Military Advisory and Assistance Group since the early 1950s. In early 1975, during a period of revolutionary furor, Portuguese officers being trained in the United States were recalled, but by early 1976 they were again attending those specialized courses. During the period when Communists were in the Portugal cabinet and pro-Communists occupied key military positions, Portugal was excluded from membership on some NATO committees.

During 1974 and 1975 senior officers of the MFA as well as those who were members of the provisional government visited Cuba, Peru, Algeria, and East European communist nations in search of new models for the Portuguese armed forces. Some officers who were demoted or forced to retire in late 1975 had openly advocated the establishment of a government with a worker-soldier base. By early 1976 conditions had shifted in favor of moderate officers, and West European socialism became the ideological goal of the MFA.

****

There are a number of excellent articles on the origins and development of the MFA in Portugal as well as the revolutionary events of the 1974-76 period. Concise summaries can be found in George W. Grayson's "Portugal and the Armed Forces Movement" and Philippe Schmitter's "Liberation by Golpe: Retrospective Thoughts on the Demise of Authoritarian Rule in Portugal." There are also several books on Portugal's involvement in Africa and the role of NATO countries in supplying Portugal's armed forces, such as Luc Crollen's *Portugal, the U.S., and NATO* and William Minter's *Portuguese Africa and the West*. (For further information see Bibliography.)

CHAPTER 16

PUBLIC ORDER AND INTERNAL SECURITY

The military coup d'etat that ended the long rule of the authoritarian regime in Portugal in April 1974 engendered a revolution that affected the entire fabric of life in the country. The system of justice underwent only minor changes immediately after the coup, and few judges or prosecutors were removed by the revolutionary government. The system of internal security, however, was reorganized. The Public Security Police (Polícia de Segurança Pública) and the National Republican Guard (Guarda Nacional Republicana—GNR) were considered to have been active supporters of the regime, and they were temporarily put under military command. Rising social and political disorder early in the revolutionary process led to the formation of new elite military intervention units, which were in essence additional national police forces under the control of the president of the republic. Revulsion concerning activities of the disbanded secret police was expressed almost daily in Portuguese newspapers. The public knowledge and outrage over prolonged detention and torture of accused terrorists and opposition politicians ensured a long investigation of the former secret police and trial of its agents.

The revolutionary turmoil, lasting more than two years, brought a severe challenge to the maintenance of law and order. Politically inspired disorder was commonplace from 1974 and continued in early 1976, placing a severe strain on the military and paramilitary police. In addition to occasional violence by leftist and rightist ideological groups, a serious threat to the territorial integrity of Portugal emerged in the Azores through the activities of separatist groups. Several separatist groups also emerged in Madeira. With unemployment growing among youth as well as among discharged soldiers and refugees returning from Africa, the potential for violence from those familiar with the instruments of war had increased considerably by early 1976.

POLICE SYSTEM

In early 1976 law enforcement was provided by paramilitary police organizations—the GNR, the Public Security Police, and the Fiscal Guard (Guarda Fiscal)—in which armed forces officers were detailed to fill key administrative and command positions. Although the main duties of the police had always been prevention, detection, and investigation of crime and the maintenance of public order, their involvement under successive governments in breaking up political and labor organizations left a lasting reservoir of fear, hatred, and mistrust among the Portuguese people. The authority of the police, which was identified with the old regime, was seriously undermined by the April 1974 revolution. The months after the revolution were marked by public disorder related to unrest in the military and among workers. During the same period there was a sharp increase in crimes of all kinds owing not only to rising unemployment but also in significant degree to the virtual disappearance of the social and moral constraints imposed by tradition and reinforced by the authoritarian regime. To cope with growing disorder and disregard for law, armed forces security units assumed responsibility for internal security until the civilian police forces, disarmed after the revolution, could be reorganized and retrained to operate in Portugal's new political environment. By early 1976 control of the police apparatus and responsibility for law enforcement had been returned to civilian authorities in the Ministry of Internal Administration, formerly the Ministry of Interior.

National Republican Guard

The GNR was formed in 1913 as a heavily armed paramilitary constabulary organized in units of up to battalion strength to replace the old Civil Guard, which had functioned under the monarchy. It was intended as a check against the military and was first employed to confront monarchist-inspired revolts within the ranks of the armed forces. Although its essential mission was one of maintaining order in the countryside, the GNR's activities were subsequently extended to those of aiding the urban police in controlling demonstrations and quelling labor unrest. With the increase of motor traffic the GNR was assigned to patrolling highways.

In 1976 the GNR numbered approximately 7,000 officers and men (authorized strength—9,000) assigned to five battalions with jurisdiction in areas corresponding roughly to the four military regions. One battalion was stationed in Lisbon and a second outside the city with its companies deployed in suburban municipalities. Three squadrons of horse cavalry supplemented the Lisbon garrison, and an additional mounted squadron was quartered in nearby Barreiro, the site of frequent labor disturbances. A third battalion with headquarters in Porto was responsible for the northern districts and was reinforced by a motorized heavy-weapons detachment. A battalion with headquarters in Coimbra covered the central region and was supported by a motorized reconnaissance detachment and a cavalry platoon. Another battalion was headquartered at Evora; its jurisdiction covered the Alentejo and the Algarve. The Transit Brigade, formerly a separate highway patrol force, was integrated into the GNR in 1974.

Reserve and career officers from all branches of the armed forces were regularly seconded to tours of duty in the GNR. Reservists who were university graduates could apply to continue as GNR officers upon completion of their regular military service. Recruits to the ranks had to have fulfilled their military obligation.

After the April 1974 revolution the GNR was placed directly under the control of the army. Its personnel were relieved of heavy weapons after the temporary seizure of the GNR's Lisbon headquarters during an unsuccessful coup by supporters of General António de Spínola in March 1975. By the end of the year automatic weapons had been returned to the GNR, but their use was restricted to the defense of police barracks.

Public Security Police

The Public Security Police was reorganized in 1953 as a paramilitary police force under the jurisdiction of the Ministry of Interior with criminal investigation, protection of property, and public security in urban areas as its basic mission. Before that date the urban police had been under the control of provincial governors. Under the authoritarian regime the security police were frequently called upon to deploy their mobile assault companies with GNR units to civil disturbances. During the colonial wars, security police assault units were dispatched to Africa, where they participated in combat operations against guerrilla forces. The Public Security Police was reorganized and retrained in 1975 and its heavy equipment turned over to the army. Crowd control remained one of its functions.

Public Security Police detachments operated in each of the twenty-two districts of continental Portugal, the Azores, and Madeira. Manpower was drawn from among former servicemen, and since the early 1970s women had also been recruited for plainclothes investigation and traffic control details. In 1976 there were 12,000 officers and other ranks in the security police, 5,000 of them stationed in the Lisbon area. Armed forces officers were assigned to the Public Security Police upon request of the Ministry of Internal Administration, and in 1974 and 1975 a general officer of the army was placed in temporary command of both the security police and the GNR. Special military advisers had also assisted the security police in training operations.

Several proposals were submitted to the government in 1975 concerning the future organization of both the Public Security Police and the GNR. Suggestions were made concerning a joint command or a merger of the two separate police forces. A third proposal envisioned the fusion of the two with the Fiscal Guard. In the event of a union of the Public Security Police and the GNR a new unit, the General

Staff of the Security Forces, would be established with headquarters in Lisbon.

Fiscal Guard

The Fiscal Guard was a customs and tax service charged with investigating smuggling, tax evasion, and illegal financial transactions, particularly those involving the import-export business and currency exchange, as well as with customs inspection and the collection of duty. In 1976 many of its 5,800 uniformed and plainclothes policemen were stationed at border crossings and ports and terminals of entry.

Lisbon Police

The City Council of Lisbon operated its own small police force separate from the national urban police. The Municipal Police of Lisbon (Polícia Municipal de Lisboa), which numbered fewer than 300 men, had an army officer as commandant. There was also a smaller police force responsible to the administrator general of the Port of Lisbon.

The Secret Police

The existence in Portugal of a secret police apparatus used for political surveillance was as old as the modern state and dated at least from the sixteenth century. It was in the twentieth century, however, that political and social conditions within an authoritarian state permitted the development of a secret police organization as extensive and pervasive in its influence as that maintained by the regime of António de Oliveira Salazar. Although the secret police, operating under various titles, remained under the jurisdiction of the Ministry of Interior, it was after 1932 controlled directly by Salazar, who held at different periods the portfolio of minister of interior in addition to that of prime minister, and it became a formidable component of his regime (see table 12).

After the fall of the parliamentary republic in 1926, the secret police was employed to uncover plots against the regime by military dissidents, Communists and anarchists, and right-wing extremists. Portuguese security forces assisted the Nationalists during the Spanish civil war (1936-39) in support of Salazar's pro-Franco policies, and it has been charged that the secret police cooperated closely with German agents during World War II. In 1945 the existing secret police apparatus was renamed and reorganized as the International Police for the Defense of the State (Polícia Internacional e de Defesa do Estado—PIDE); a statute of habeas corpus was also introduced into the legal code at that time, supposedly as a check on arbitrary arrests

Table 12. *Portugal, Development of the Secret Police, 1926-74*

Date	Event
May 28, 1926	Dictatorship established by military coup
1926-27	Secret Police of Lisbon (Polícia Secreta de Lisboa); Secret Police of Porto (Polícia Secreta de Porto)
1931	Portuguese International Police (Polícia Internacional Portuguesa—PIP); special section for political and social surveillance
January 1933	Police for Political and Social Defense (Polícia de Defesa Política e Social—PDPS); replaced special PIP section for political and social surveillance
July 1933	Police for Vigilance and Defense of the State (Polícia de Vigilância e Defesa do Estado—PVDE); combined PIP and PDPS
1945	International Police for the Defense of the State (Polícia Internacional e de Defesa do Estado—PIDE)
1969	General Security Directorate (Direção Geral de Segurança—DGS); essentially the same organization with a new name
April 26, 1974	DGS abolished in continental Portugal one day after military coup by Junta of National Salvation; functions assumed in Portugal by Judicial Police (Polícia Judiciária) and in the colonies by the armed forces

by the secret police. In practice, however, secret police methods of operation remained unaltered.

Modifications in the law after 1954 conferred judicial status on PIDE inspectors, allowing them to act as inquiring magistrates with authority to bind over for trial persons suspected of crimes against the state. Suspects were routinely arrested without warrants and were sometimes held for months without having specific charges brought against them and without access to legal assistance. Some of those arrested by the PIDE simply disappeared. Torture was commonplace, and it has been alleged that the PIDE was responsible for the assassination of enemies of the regime who had fled abroad. More than 20,000 people are believed to have died or been tortured at the PIDE's hands.

The PIDE is estimated to have employed more than 20,000 agents, informers, and support staff. Agents successfully infiltrated the clandestine communist organization, disrupted its activities, and brought about the arrest of key party leaders. The secret police carried out covert operations within the government-run labor movement, the armed forces, and in the universities, where communist subversion was suspected. The PIDE also maintained agents and informers in

Portuguese emigrant communities abroad, controlled passage across the country's frontier, and exercised police jurisdiction over foreigners in Portugal.

During the 1960s and early 1970s the secret police directed its efforts toward suppressing opposition to the war effort in the African colonies, particularly on the university campuses, where its activities provoked student riots. During the same period the PIDE was active in tracking down antiregime terrorists who had been held responsible for bombings at military installations and telecommunications facilities. In Africa the PIDE trained and commanded counterinsurgency units composed of black troops who were former guerrillas (see ch. 15).

In an obvious attempt to escape the onus attached to the common identification of the Salazar regime with the excesses of the PIDE, Marcello Caetano's government renamed the secret police shortly after succeeding to power in 1969. Newly styled the General Security Directorate (Direção Geral de Segurança—DGS), it retained its old image, and the people called it PIDE-DGS. It was abolished in Portugal the day after the Caetano regime was toppled, and its investigative functions were taken over by the Judicial Police (Polícia Judiciária), an agency controlled by the Ministry of Justice and somewhat comparable to the Federal Bureau of Investigation in the United States. The entire staff of the PIDE-DGS was placed under arrest, and a commission of armed forces officers was established to investigate the past operations of the secret police and to bring charges against officials found to have committed criminal acts against political prisoners. Some of the policemen held in this manner subsequently escaped from prison, and many clerical employees were released after a time, but in early 1976 none of those still held had been brought to trial. In Africa PIDE-DGS operations were not immediately suspended, but their direction passed to the military command.

Postcoup Police

Deterioration of the internal security situation during the summer of 1974 led the second provisional government to establish the Continental Operations Command (Comando de Operações do Continente—COPCON) to deal with labor unrest, political demonstrations, and mutiny in the armed forces. COPCON, which in effect became a national police force, taking precedence over the GNR and the Public Security Police, was composed of selected units from the three military services. Some units within COPCON became heavily politicized and were openly sympathetic to left-wing movements. COPCON was disbanded and its personnel were discharged from service in November 1975 after detachments had consistently refused to obey orders to control leftist opposition groups. The Military Intervention Group

402

(Agrupação Militar de Intervenção—AMI), formed from an elite group of army commandos who were chosen especially for their loyalty to the government, became a replacement for COPCON, but its mandate was more restricted and it was not politicized.

INCIDENCE OF CRIME

In general the Portuguese are a law-abiding people who respect the virtue of honesty. Emigration has served traditionally as the release for social pressures in both rural and urban areas of the country. Decolonization in Africa has brought over 800,000 unemployed refugees to Portugal, some of whom have become involved in crime. There are many other young adults and discharged soldiers who are both unemployed and unable to emigrate, and some of these have also become involved in crime. Economic conditions and the weakening of traditional moral values have contributed to a rise in prostitution in Lisbon and other urban areas. The revolutionary turmoil, though tapering off by early 1976, gave rise to seizures of land and occupation of private property, such as houses, by peasants and workers. The use of drugs among teenagers and young adults increased during the revolutionary period. Statistics for the first year of the revolution (1974) show an apparent decline in the rate of crime, but it is uncertain whether the decline was real or reflected an inability of the police to apprehend criminals.

Violent crimes, though not unknown in Portugal, are rare. Murders are infrequently associated with crimes of robbery and are generally crimes of passion. There was, however, a rise in both the number of persons accused of homicide and the number of convictions in the 1970s. There was a decline in the number of convictions for attacks on persons (generally different degrees of assault and battery) from 1972 to 1974. Growing disrespect for the police and antigovernment sentiment, especially on university campuses, resulted in 1,381 convictions for resisting arrest and for attacks against the police out of 1,860 cases tried in 1972. Many cases were dismissed for lack of evidence.

Various categories of theft were the most serious crimes not involving violence against persons both before and after the fall of the old regime. Petty larceny, housebreaking, and other kinds of theft were the crimes most frequently prosecuted in early 1976. In 1972 there were 1,992 persons convicted of theft, and in 1974 there were 1,823. Although the number of convictions declined, the total number of persons brought to trial for theft increased. Other forms of crime, such as commercial fraud, reckless driving resulting in death or injury, and economic crimes, increased. There was a considerable decline in the number of persons tried for arson during 1974 compared with previous years. Portuguese newspaper reports indicated an increase in the number of armed robberies during 1975 and early 1976.

Prostitution was legally tolerated in Portugal until the early 1960s. In the revolutionary climate of the mid-1970s prostitution became an explosive social issue but, with rising unemployment, teenagers turned to prostitution as a sole source of livelihood. Much in evidence in early 1976 was the increased number of beggars in public places in Lisbon, but they were not so prevalent in Porto. Juvenile delinquency was also growing. The juvenile supervision courts had placed an average of 1,600 children and teenagers a year in homes, medical institutions, or reform shcools between 1972 and 1974. Many children were placed in state institutions because of parental neglect. There were over 12,000 cases involving minors brought to the court in 1974, and over 10 percent of those were for some form of crime, generally petty theft.

Most persons convicted of either violent crimes or crimes against property in Portugal were not professional criminals. Persons convicted of fraud or economic crimes were usually officeworkers or businessmen. Such violent crimes as homicide and assault were most often committed by manual workers and farmworkers. There did not appear to be a significant number of repeat offenders convicted in 1974 of theft or violent crimes. Seasonally unemployed rural workers have often taken to petty theft on large estates, but during 1975 and early 1976 there was an increase in theft, housebreaking, and other forms of crime that Portuguese authorities attributed to rising unemployment (see ch. 4).

Biannual statistics show that a relatively small percentage of persons arrested are eventually brought to trial. A substantial number of cases are resolved by the municipal council or special tribunals, such as those concerned with taxation or public health. Lisbon and other large cities are comparatively peaceful, but increasingly large numbers of people are arrested for disturbing the peace and other minor offenses in some rural districts, such as Portalegre, and in Setúbal, a rapidly growing industrial area. Over 300,000 traffic summonses are issued annually for moving violations, especially careless and drunk driving, and other infractions, but these do not appear to have had any measurable effect in lessening the high incidence of traffic accidents in Portugal.

LEGAL CODE

The Portuguese legal code, grounded in the Roman law, has been subject to major revision in the nineteenth and twentieth centuries. Crimes against persons and property are considered serious offenses, but in theory punishment is strictly graduated according to the gravity of injuries done to the victims or the value of property stolen or damaged. Early penal reform was motivated by the belief that exaggerated penalties did not act as a deterrent to crime. The death penalty was abolished in Portugal in 1867, well before it was in most other European states. Premeditated homicide is punishable by a prison sentence of from sixteen to twenty years, although mitigating circumstances have led to reduced terms. Statutory sentences may be increased, however, for particularly heinous crimes. Homicide committed during a robbery can draw an additional four-year sentence over the maximum statutory prison term. Attacks on government officials, police officers, and foreign diplomats are considered crimes against the state and fall under the jurisdiction of military tribunals.

Larcency, arson, and willful destruction of crops and business establishments are the most common forms of crime directed against property. Petty larceny is defined as the theft of money or goods not exceeding 2,000 escudos (for value of the escudo—see Glossary) in value and is punishable by a jail sentence of up to six months. The theft of food by seasonally unemployed peasants in the countryside, however, commonly goes unpunished (see ch. 4). Grand larceny of property valued between 2,000 and 40,000 escudos is punishable by up to two years in prison, of property valued at from 40,000 to 1 million escudos by two to eight years, and of property valued at more than 1 million escudos by eight to twelve years. Nearly 2,500 suspects were convicted of theft in 1974, including more than 400 arraigned on charges of automobile theft, a figure constantly rising in crime statistics.

Laws covering so-called economic crimes were enacted during the Salazar regime. These included certain categories of speculation, hoarding, falsification of contents, adulteration or dilution of food products, and fraud connected with export goods. Typically, however, prosecutors were concerned with the low-level conspiracies of middlemen and warehouse owners to drive up prices on basic consumer commodities. Strikes and lockouts were considered conspiracies to raise or lower salaries during the Salazar years and were classified as economic crimes.

Under the authoritarian regime persons accused of offenses defined as crimes against the state could be legally detained for periods of from six months to three years without being charged. Suspects convicted of crimes against the state could he held in prison for renewable three-year terms, which could result essentially in life imprisonment. Others considered of less immediate danger were exiled to an overseas territory or were obliged to post large bonds as guarantees of acceptable conduct in the future. Acts of espionage, service with a foreign power, verbal or written defamation of Portugal, and acts and conspiracies involving the military or civilians against the constitutional form of government then in force were severely prosecuted during the Salazar regime. Advocacy or activity in favor of African

liberation movements, for instance, was considered a political offense to be tried as a crime against the state on the grounds that the
overseas terriroties were an integral part of Portugal.

Illegal emigration was categorized as a political crime inasmuch as
the drain of Portuguese manpower was judged to be contrary to the
best interests of the state; however, although unsanctioned emigration
remained on the books as a crime, it continued to be a very common
phenomenon and was tacitly accepted by the government, which regularly issued passports to citizens after they had gone abroad illegally.
Participation in a strike, inciting others to strike, and taking part in
violence associated with a strike were punishable under similar laws
with jail terms of from two to eight years. Conspiracy to participate
in antigovernment demonstrations was also a serious crime. A legal
escape clause existed for persons who desisted from committing an
intended crime against the state or who aided the authorities in appre-
hending suspected subversives. Membership in the Portuguese Communist Party (Partido Comunista Português—PCP) or in any group
dedicated to the violent overthrow of the government was prohibited.
It was also assumed that an individual joined a subversive organization with full knowledge of its aims and ideology. After the revolution, specific laws against the PCP, which had operated underground
from 1926 to 1974, were voided, allowing the party to participate fully
in Portugal's political life.

1976 CONSTITUTION

Restrictions on freedom of assembly and of the press, on the rights
of association and of public protest, and on the right of workers to
strike were removed with the promulgation of the new Constitution in
April 1976. The only restrictions remaining on political activity barred
simultaneous membership in more than one party and prohibited political parties from using emblems similar to those of other parties or
likely to be confused with religious symbols.

The 1976 Constitution emphasized the commitment of the revolution to creating a just society and reinforced the earlier proscriptions
against economic crimes. Illegal transfer of capital from the country
was specifically cited. The property of persons found guilty of such
crimes was made liable to confiscation.

To protect civil rights the role of the police was drastically altered
in the Constitution. Guidelines for criminal investigation and treatment of suspects were laid down. The 1976 Constitution specified that
no person could be held without trial or imprisoned without a definite
sentence. Individuals could not be deprived of citizenship for political
reasons. The principle of habeas corpus was restated and was applied
without exceptions to both civilian criminal courts and military tribunals. A petition for a writ of habeas corpus was to be answered by a

judge within eight days. Torture and inhumane detention were made illegal; moreover confessions obtained under duress and any material obtained by illegal means were declared inadmissible as evidence in criminal proceedings. The inviolability of the home, personal correspondence, and telephone communications was also guaranteed in the Constitution.

JUDICIAL PROCEDURES

The Portuguese criminal justice system is organized on a national basis. The Ministry of Justice has control over the court system, the office of the attorney general, the Judicial Police, and the prisons.

The office of the attorney general has a hierarchy parallel to that of the judiciary; its representatives prosecute cases in each of Portugal's 171 judicial districts and their subdivisions. More specifically the assistant deputy attorney general prosecutes cases before the municipal court at the local level, or municipality (concelho). At the district level, above the municipality, the deputy attorney general represents the state before the district court, which uses a panel of one to three judges to determine guilt or innocence and decide the sentence. The panel may allow the convicted person conditional liberty, decide to what kind of prison he is to be sent, or commit him to a mental or alcoholic rehabilitation asylum.

There are three judicial regions in Portugal, each with an appeals court having appellate jurisdiction over cases tried in the municipal and district courts in its geographical area. There is a court of appeal (tribunal da relação) in Lisbon, in Porto, and in Coimbra. Appeals are made only on the basis of judicial error in the original proceedings. Cases tried in a district court are automatically reviewed after sentencing by the appeals court of the region. The Ministry of Justice reviews all cases and may intervene to initiate a formal appeal. Because the appeals process is often lengthy, bail is frequently allowed the accused during the proceeding, except in cases involving homicide, serious assault, or grand larceny or when it is probable that the accused will flee.

The Portuguese legal system recognizes that all persons are equal before the law although, as in other societies, those able to afford the best legal assistance often fare better than those who are not. An accused person is considered innocent until proved guilty.

In general persons apprehended while committing a crime are held in preventive detention and are usually not considered eligible for conditional liberty. Persons not caught in the commission of a crime are usually given conditional liberty on presentation of a fiança (a bail bond or other article of value). An individual taken into custody cannot be held for more than forty-eight hours without being brought before an inquiring magistrate, who is empowered to order persons held for trial on the basis of the inquiry. Under the law a person accused of a crime has to be tried within three months. The protection of habeas corpus is recognized in nonpolitical cases.

An individual unable to afford an attorney has one appointed by the court from a list furnished by the Order of Advocates (Ordem dos Advogados). Once an attorney is appointed, he cannot pass the case on to another lawyer. The indictment is made available to the accused and his attorney, and charges may be answered in a brief by the defense attorney. A presiding judge may dismiss a case on the basis of a defense attorney's brief or continue the trial at his own discretion. A case can also be dismissed while under way for lack of evidence. Verdicts of guilty or innocent are the only ones permitted.

Minors under eighteen years of age are protected under the law. Juvenile delinquents come under the purview of the juvenile supervision courts, in which the state is represented by a special officer from the attorney general's office called the children's guardian. Children under sixteen are not considered legally responsible for their actions. Rather than being imprisoned delinquent minors are assigned to special public or private institutions or to a family guardian. There are special reformatories for minors between the ages of sixteen and eighteen.

The April 1974 revolution did not cause official changes in the established procedure for handling ordinary or nonpolitical crimes. The administration of justice was reported, however, to have been usurped by local councils in some areas. Large-scale illegal land seizures occurred in the southern part of the country, and there the courts ceased to exercise their function of protecting property rights. Some accounts indicated that large numbers of lawyers and judges left the country after the revolution, though there was no centrally directed purge. The situation was further confused by the June 1974 amnesty, which was declared by the first provisional government to cover those serving prison sentences of less than two years. The amnesty was apparently invoked because the revolutionary regime considered that the former government's criminal processes had been oppressive, and many inmates had received overly harsh sentences for relatively minor offenses. Many of those paroled, however, were apparently rearrested shortly after receiving their freedom.

The 1976 Constitution reaffirmed the basic guarantee of a fair trial and stipulated that trials were to be public except in morals cases, when the judge could close the proceedings. To avoid the abuses practiced during the authoritarian Salazar-Caetano regime, when agents of the secret police exercised the power of magistrates, strict judicial supervision over indictments and trial procedure was provided. Further constitutional provisions prohibited the use of improperly obtained evidence, use of torture, interception of mail, and interference in an individual's private life.

A particularly significant innovation in the 1976 Constitution was its provision for a jury system. The Portuguese jury would consist of a panel of judges or lay jurors. It could be used when requested by the prosecution or the defense in serious cases involving a possible sentence of two or more years' imprisonment.

Attempts by various military and civilian groups to unseat one or more of the provisional governments since 1974 have resulted in several waves of arrests. In addition there were a large number of individuals associated with the former authoritarian government arrested after the coup d'etat of April 1974 and held in preventive detention without specific charges, but most were soon released. The record of the military rulers in Portugal concerning human rights of political detainees has been exemplary in comparison with other military regimes of recent vintage. Persons detained by the military are subject to trial by a military tribunal, and sentences cannot be appealed to a higher civilian court. Although public trials were planned, the preliminary hearings were to be closed. Defense attorneys have full access to materials and to their clients.

Three separate military commissions were established to deal with political prisoners. One commission was investigating agents of the former secret police and members of the former Portuguese Legion. There was some question whether the agents could be fairly tried, since many of their activities, illegal after the revolution, had been legal under the Salazar-Caetano regime. Investigations of the former secret police continued into April 1976, and trials were planned for persons accused of murder, torture, and deprivation of human rights, offenses all legally punishable under the prerevolutionary regime. Such employees of the secret police as clerks and chauffeurs were released from detention.

In April 1976 a second commission was still investigating the activities of military men involved in the March 1975 right-wing coup attempt. Some of the accused fled the country but later returned. They were subsequently charged, though most were released after posting bond. The third commission was investigating those involved in the unsuccessful left-wing coup attempt of November 1975. In January 1976 laws were promulgated expelling military men implicated in the November coup from the armed forces. Expulsion carried with it the loss of political rights for twenty years. Several other persons, including high officials of the Salazar-Caetano regime, had been taken into custody after the April 1974 revolution. Most of them were released, however, in early 1976. As of May 1976 no political detainees had actually been brought to trial.

PENAL SYSTEM

The Portuguese penal system is under the control of the minister of justice. There is a system of local jails in each judicial district. The jails are supervised by the deputy attorney general in each district, who is in turn responsible to the Directorate General of Prison Services of the Ministry of Justice. The deputy attorney general makes weekly visits to the jail to hear complaints of prisoners concerning their cases, treatment at the jail, and other matters; moreover he can discipline the jailers for infractions of jail regulations.

The kind of prison regime to which an offender is sentenced is designated by the district punishment court upon conviction. Youthful offenders are given opportunities to learn trades. The mastery of a trade while in prison and good behavior may be considered in reducing time spent in prison. Individuals convicted three times of the same crime are considered a danger to society and are not usually eligible for parole. Unlike other prisoners, who may be allowed to do farmwork, they may be kept in a strict prison regime. All prisoners earn money for their work while in prison, and work is considered a necessary part of the rehabilitation process.

Some observers have indicated that prison conditions are not very good, especially in Lisbon and Porto; they may be better in rural areas where there are smaller prison populations. In late 1975 plans for changing the structure of the penal system to correct serious problems were proposed, but the lack of money for physical rehabilitation of the prisons has prevented implementation. Special studies have also recommended transferring responsibility for prisons from the Directorate General for Prison Services to the Social Rehabilitation Service, which would work to turn the prisons into reeducation centers to prepare inmates for release into society.

BIBLIOGRAPHY

Section I. Social

Abshire, David M., and Michael A. Samuels (eds.). *Portuguese Africa: A Handbook.* (Handbooks of the Modern World Series.) New York: Praeger, 1969.

Alcoforado, Marianna. *The Letters of a Portuguese Nun.* (Trans., Edgar Prestage.) London: D. Nutt, 1897.

Alden, Dauril. "Vicissitudes of Trade in the Portuguese Atlantic Empire During the First Half of the Eighteenth Century: A Review Article," *Americas,* 32, No. 2, October 1975, 284-304.

Algeria, M. Fernanda. "Documentos Para o Ensino: Estrutura Etária da População de Portugal, Continental em 1970," *Finisterra* [Lisbon], IX, No. 17, 1974, 161-169.

Almeida, Manuel P. de. "The Conservatism of Eça de Queiroz," *Journal of the American-Portuguese Cultural Society,* 3, No. 4, 1969, 52-57.

Anderson, Robert T. *Modern Europe: An Anthropological Perspective.* Pacific Palisades: Goodyear Publishing, 1973, 81-85.

Antunes, M.L. Marinho. "Twenty Years' Emigration from Portugal," *Migration News* [Geneva], 22, No. 1, January-February 1973, 35-38.

Anuário Demográfico, 1966. Lisbon: Instituto Nacional de Estatística, 1967.

Anuário Estatístico, 1950. Lisbon: Instituto Nacional de Estatística, 1951.

Anuário Estatístico, 1960. Lisbon: Instituto Nacional de Estatística, 1961.

Anuário Estatístico, 1961. Lisbon: Instituto Nacional de Estatística, 1962.

Anuário Estatístico, 1962. Lisbon: Instituto Nacional de Estatística, 1963.

Anuário Estatístico, 1963. Lisbon: Instituto Nacional de Estatística, 1964.

Anuário Estatístico, 1970. Lisbon: Instituto Nacional de Estatística, 1971.

Anuário Estatístico, 1971. Lisbon: Instituto Nacional de Estatística, 1972.

Anuário Estatístico, 1972. Lisbon: Instituto Nacional de Estatística, 1973.

Anuário Estatístico, 1973. Lisbon: Instituto Nacional de Estatística, 1974.

Atkinson, William C. *A History of Spain and Portugal.* Harmondsworth, England: Penguin, 1960.

Bailey, Norman A., and William J. Simon. "Portugal: Four Myths of a Curious Revolution," *Columbia Forum,* 3, No. 4, Fall 1974, 24-30.

Barnes, W.J. *Portugal: Gateway to Greatness.* London: Edward Stanford, 1950.

Barreno, Maria Isabel, Maria Teresa Horta, and Maria Fátima Velho da Costa. *The Three Marias: New Portuguese Letters.* (Trans., Helen R. Lane.) Garden City: Doubleday, 1975.

Bell, Aubrey F.G. *In Portugal.* New York: John Lane, 1912.

———. *Portugal of the Portuguese.* London: Isaac Pitman and Sons, 1915.

———. *Portuguese Literature.* (Rev. ed.) Oxford: Clarendon Press, 1970.

———. *Portuguese Portraits.* Oxford: B.H. Blackwell, 1917.

Bell, Aubrey F.G. (ed. and trans.) *The Lyrics of Gil Vicente.* New York: Longmans Green, 1914.

Bereday, George Z.F. "Reflections on Reforms of Teacher Training in Portugal," *Comparative Education* [London], 9, No. 2, June 1973, 55-60.

Bernstein, Harry. "Alexandre Herculano: Portuguese Historian and Historical Novelist," *Journal of the American-Portuguese Cultural Society,* 2, Nos. 1-3, 1968, 65-93.

Blair, Jonathan, and Veronica Thomas. "Madeira, Like Its Wine, Improves with Age." *National Geographic,* 143, No. 4, April 1973, 488-513.

Blanshard, Paul. *Freedom and Catholic Power in Spain and Portugal: An American Interpretation.* Boston: Beacon Press, 1962.

Boletim Anual 1973. Lisbon: Secretariado Nacional da Emigração, 1974.

Bosgra, S.J. "Colonization and Settlement in Portuguese Africa," *Migration Today* [Geneva], 15, Autumn 1970, 34-42.

Boxer, Charles R. "Pombal's Dictatorship and the Great Lisbon Earthquake, 1755," *History Today* [London], 5, No. 11, November 1955, 729-736.

———. *The Portuguese Seaborne Empire, 1415-1825.* (History of Human Society Series.) New York: Knopf, 1970.

———. *Portuguese Society in the Tropics: The Municipal Councils of Goa, Bahia, and Luanda, 1510-1800.* Madison: University of Wisconsin Press, 1965.

———. *Two Pioneers of Tropical Medicine: Garcia d'Orta and Nicolás Monardes.* London: Hispanic and Luso-Brazilian Councils, 1963.

Bradford, Sarah. *Portugal.* New York: Walker, 1973.

Bridge, Ann, and Susan Lowndes. *The Selective Traveller in Portugal.* New York: McGraw-Hill, 1967.

Brooks, Mary Elizabeth. *A King for Portugal: The Madrigal Conspiracy, 1594-1595.* Madison: University of Wisconsin Press, 1964.

Bruce, Neil. *Portugal: The Last Empire.* New York: John Wiley and Sons, 1975.

Bruneau, Thomas C. "Portugal: The Search for a New Political Regime," *World Today* [London], 31, No. 12, December 1975, 478-487.

Bryans, Robin. *The Azores.* London: Faber and Faber, 1963.

------. *Madeira, Pearl of the Atlantic.* London: Robert Hale, 1959.

Callixto, Vasco. *Pelas Estrades dos Açores (2 milhares de Quilómetros Através de 9 Ilhas)* (On the Roads of the Azores [Two Thousand Kilometers Across Nine Islands]). (Author's edition.) Lisbon: 1973.

Camara, J. Mattoso. *The Portuguese Language* (Trans., Anthony J. Naro.) (The History and Structure of Language Series.) Chicago: University of Chicago Press, 1972.

Camoens, Luís de (Camões, Luís de). *The Lusiads.* (Trans., W.C. Atkinson.) Baltimore: Penguin, 1972.

Campbell, Roy. *Portugal.* London: Max Reinhardt, 1957.

Carew, Dorothy. *Portugal.* New York: Macmillan, 1969.

Cavaco, Carminda. "Migrações internacionalis de trabalhodores do sotavento do Algarve" (International Migration of Workers from the Eastern Algarve), *Finisterra* [Lisbon], 6, No. 11, 1971, 41-83.

Chapman, Patrick. "Portugal's Economy Bred Revolution," *Washington Post,* April 6, 1975.

"Churches Score Portuguese Colonial Rule," *Brooklyn Tablet.* April 11, 1974.

Costa Ramalho, América da. "The Classical Tradition in Os Lusíadas," *Journal of the American-Portuguese Cultural Society,* 8, No. 1, 1974, 1-21.

Cowan, Paul. "Portugal Moves Right—and Closer to Civil War," *Village Voice,* October 6, 1975, 9.

Cutileiro, José. *A Portuguese Rural Society.* Oxford: Clarendon Press, 1971.

Demographic Yearbook, 1973. New York: Statistical Office, Department of Economics and Social Affairs, United Nations, 1974.

Dervenn, Claude. *The Azores.* London: Harrap, 1956.

Dias, A. Jorge. *Portuguese Contribution to Cultural Anthropology.* Johannesburg: Witwatersrand University Press, 1964.

Dos Passos, John. *The Portugal Story: Three Centuries of Exploration and Discovery.* New York: Doubleday, 1969.

Drain, Michel. *Géographie de la Péninsule Ibérique.* (3d ed.) Paris: Presses Universitaires de France, 1972.

413

Duncan, T. Bentley. *Atlantic Islands: Madeira, the Azores, and Cape Verdes in Seventeenth Century Commerce and Navigation.* Chicago: University of Chicago Press, 1972.

E.A.G. (Baron de Santá Anna). *Notes on Portugal.* Philadelphia: Philadelphia Catholic Publishing, 1876.

Eça de Queiroz, José Maria de. *The City and the Mountains.* (Trans., Roy Campbell.) Athens: University of Ohio Press, 1955.

————. *Cousin Basilio.* (Trans., Roy Campbell.) London: Max Reinhardt, 1955.

————. *The Illustrious House of Ramires.* (Trans., Ann Stevens.) Athens: Ohio University Press, 1968.

————. *Letters from England.* (Trans., Ann Stevens.) London: Bodley Head, 1970.

————. *The Maias.* (Trans., Patricia McGowan Pinheiro and Ann Stevens.) London: Bodley Head, 1965.

————. *The Mandarin and Other Stories.* (Trans., Richard Franko Goldman.) London: Bodley Head, 1966.

————. *The Relic.* (Trans., Aubrey F.G. Bell.) London: Max Reinhardt, 1966.

————. *The Sin of Father Amaro.* (Trans., Nan Flanagan.) London: Max Reinhardt, 1962.

Eder, Richard. "Rural Portugal Changes in the Revolution, But Not All That Much," *New York Times,* March 31, 1975, 18.

Eppstein, John. *Portugal: The Country and Its People.* London: Queen Ann Press, 1967.

Estatísticas da Saúde, 1969. Lisbon: Instituto Nacional de Estatística, 1970.

Estatísticas da Saúde, 1971. Lisbon: Instituto Nacional de Estatística, 1972.

Estatísticas da Saúde, 1973. Lisbon: Instituto Nacional de Estatística, 1973.

The Europa Year Book, 1975: A World Survey. London: Europa Publications, 1975.

Evans, Robert P. *Let Europe Hear.* Chicago: Moody Press, 1963.

Fernandez, Maria Palmira. "Inquiry in Portuguese Emigrants' Departure Districts," *Migration News* [Geneva], 17, No. 4, 1968, 11-14.

Ferreira, Eduardo de Sousa. "The Present Role of the Portuguese Resettlement Policy," *Africa Today,* 21, No. 1, Winter 1974, 47-55.

Ferreira de Castro, José Maria. *Emigrants.* (Trans., Dorothy Ball.) New York: Macmillan, 1962.

————. *Jungle.* (Trans., Charles Duff.) London: L. Dickson, 1934.

Fieldhouse, David K. *The Colonial Empires: A Comparative Survey from the Eighteenth Century.* London: Weidenfeld and Nicolson, 1966.

Fodor, Eugene (ed.). *Fodor's Portugal, 1974.* New York: David McKay, 1974.

414

Franco, A. de Sousa. "Consequences of Portuguese Emigration," *Migration News* [Geneva], 23, No. 3, 1974, 12-16.

Freitas Branco, João de. "Six Glances at Portuguese Music: Past and Present," *Journal of the American-Portuguese Cultural Society*, 4, Nos. 1-2, Winter-Spring 1970, 18-42.

Fryer, Peter, and Patricia McGowan Pinheiro. *Oldest Ally: A Portrait of Salazar's Portugal.* London: Dennis Dobson, 1961.

Gallagher, Mary A. "Padre António Vieira and the Role of the New Christians in Portugal, 1640-1668," *Journal of the American-Portuguese Cultural Society*, 4, Nos. 3-4, Summer-Fall 1970, 1430.

Gallop, Rodney. *Portugal: A Book of Folk-Ways.* Cambridge: Cambridge University Press, 1936.

Garcia, Rubén. "The Unexpected Affinities: W.B. Yeats and Fernando Pessoa." *Journal of the American-Portuguese Cultural Society*, 10, No. 1, Spring 1976, 29-37.

Gaspar, Jorge. "Os Resultados Preliminares do 11. Recenseamento da População" (The Preliminary Results of the Eleventh Census of the Population), *Finisterra* [Lisbon], VI, No. 12, 1971, 295-300.

Gil Vicente. *Four Plays of Gil Vicente.* (Trans., Aubrey F.G. Bell.) Cambridge: Cambridge University Press, 1920.

———. *Lyrics of Gil Vicente.* (Trans., Aubrey F.G. Bell.) Oxford: B.H. Blackwell, 1914.

Giniger, Henry. "Portugal Day by Day: On the Edge of Chaos," *New York Times*, June 29, 1975.

Girão, Aristides de Amorin. *Geografia de Portugal.* Porto: Portucalence Editoria, 1941.

Giradon, Anne. "Reception in France of Wives of Portuguese Migrants," *Migration News* [Geneval], 17, No. 4, July-August 1968, 7-10.

Gonçalves, Rui Mário. "Brief Notes on Contemporary Portuguese Painting," *Journal of the American-Portuguese Cultural Society*, 5, Nos. 1 and 2, Winter-Spring 1971, 1-21.

Granada, Aurelio. "Emigration of Families from the [sic] Portugal," *Migration News* [Geneva], 23, No. 1, January-February 1974, 17-22.

Great Britain. Admiralty. Naval Intelligence Division. *Spain and Portugal, I: The Peninsula.* (Geographical Handbook Series.) London: 1941.

———. *Spain and Portugal, II: Portugal.* (Geographical Handbook Series.) London: 1942.

———. *Spain and Portugal, IV: The Atlantic Islands.* (Geographical Handbook Series.) London: 1945.

Hale, John R. *Renaissance Exploration.* New York: W.W. Norton, 1968.

Hammond, R.J. *Portugal and Africa, 1815-1910.* Stanford: Stanford University Press, 1966.

Harrison, Paul. "Portugal: A Social Revolution?" *New Society* [London], 29, No. 615, July 18, 1974, 138-143.

Hart, Henry M. *Luís de Camoens and the Epic of the Lusiads.* Norman: University of Oklahoma Press, 1962.

Henige, David P. (ed.) *Colonial Governors from the Fifteenth Century to the Present.* Madison: University of Wisconsin Press, 1970.

Henry, Carl F.H. "Signs of Awakening in Portugal," *Christianity Today,* No. 5, December 6, 1963.

Herman, Stewart Winfield. *Report from Christian Europe.* New York: Friendship Press, 1953.

Herzlich, Guy. "Literacy and 'Self-Service'," *Manchester Guardian Weekly* [London], November 30, 1975, 4.

Hirsch, Elisabeth Feist. *Damião de Góis: The Life and Thought of a Portuguese Humanist, 1502-1574.* (International Archives of the History of Ideas, No. 19.) The Hague: Martinus Nijhoff, 1967.

Hopkins, Garland Evans. "Report on Portugal," *Christian Century,* 66, No. 28, July 13, 1949, 842-843.

Houston, J.M. *The Western Mediterranean World: An Introduction to Its Regional Landscape.* New York: Praeger, 1967.

Howe, Marvine. "Portugal Losing Educated Elite," *New York Times,* September 12, 1975.

Institute of Jewish Affairs. *The Jewish Communities of the World.* (3d ed., rev.) London: André Deutsch, 1971.

Isaacman, Allen F. *Mozambique: The Africanization of a European Institution—The Zambesi Prazos, 1750-1902.* Madison: University of Wisconsin Press, 1975.

Jewish Year Book, 1975. London: Greenberg, 1975, 5735-5736.

Kay, Hugh. *Salazar and Modern Portugal.* New York: Hawthorne Books, 1970.

Kearney, Vincent S. "Colonialism's Last Stand," *America,* 129, No. 15, November 10, 1973, 350-352.

Kendrick, Thomas D. *The Lisbon Earthquake.* Philadelphia: J.B. Lippincott, 1955.

Kidder Smith, George E. *The New Architecture of Europe.* (Meridian Books.) New York: World Publishing, 1961, 290-294.

Kubler, George. *Portuguese Plain Architecture: Between Spices and Diamonds, 1521-1706.* Middletown, Connecticut: Wesleyan University Press, 1972.

Kubler, George, and Martin Soria. *Art and Architecture in Spain and Portugal and Their American Dominions, 1500-1800.* Baltimore: Penguin, 1959.

La Fay, Howard, and Volkmar Wentzel. "Portugal at the Crossroads," *National Geographic,* 128, No. 4, October 1965, 453-501.

Lautensach, Herman. "A Indivualidade Geográfica de Portugal no Conjunto da Peninsula Ibérica" (The Geographic Individuality of Portugal in the Context of the Iberian Peninsula), *Boletim da Socie-*

dade de Geografia de Lisboa [Lisbon], XXXI, Nos. 9 and 10, September-October 1931, 362-409.

Lefcourt, Charles R. "The Portuguese Letters: Fact or Fable?" *Journal of the American-Portuguese Cultural Society*, 9, No. 1, Spring-Summer 1975, 29-32.

Liss, Robert E. *Bazak Guide to Portugal*. New York: Bazak Israel Guidebook Publishers, 1975.

Livermore, Harold V. *A New History of Portugal*. Cambridge: Cambridge University Press, 1969.

Livermore, Harold V. (ed.) *Portugal and Brazil: An Introduction*. Oxford: Clarendon Press, 1953.

Livi Bacci, Massimo. *A Century of Portuguese Fertility*. Princeton: Princeton University Press, 1971.

Longland, Jean R. (ed. and trans.) *Selections from Contemporary Portuguese Poetry*. New York: Hispanic Society of America, 1966.

Lopes de Oliveira, A. *Arquipélago da Madeira, Epopéia Humana* (The Archipelago of Madeira, Human Epoch). Braga: Editora Pax, 1969.

Macaulay, Rose. *They Went to Portugal*. London: Jonathan Cape, 1946.

McMahon, Francis E. "Salazar and the Church," *Commonweal*, 70, No. 16, July 31, 1959, 393-394.

Madariaga, Salvador de. "Portugal." Chapter 19 in *Spain: A Modern History*. New York: Frederick A. Praeger, 1958.

Makler, Harry M. "A Case Study of the Portuguese Business Elite, 1964-1966." Pages 228-241 in Raymond S. Sayers (ed.), *Portugal and Brazil in Transition*. Minneapolis: University of Minnesota Press, 1968.

———. "The Portuguese Industrial Elite." Unpublished Ph.D. dissertation. New York: Columbia University, 1968.

———. "The Portuguese Industrial Elite and Its Corporative Relations: A Study of Compartmentalization in an Authoritarian Regime," *Economic Development and Cultural Change*, 24, No. 3, April 1976, 495-526.

Marques, António Henrique R. de Oliveira. *Daily Life in Portugal in the Late Middle Ages*. Madison: University of Wisconsin Press, 1971.

———. *A History of Portugal*. 2 vols. New York: Columbia University Press, 1972.

———. "Revolution and Counterrevolution in Portugal: Problems of Portuguese History, 1900-1930." Pages 403-418 in Manfred Kossok (ed.), *Studien über die Revolution*. (East) Berlin: Akademie-Verlag, 1969.

Martins, Herminio. "Portugal." Pages 60-89 in Margaret Scotford Archer and Salvador Giner (eds.), *Contemporary Europe: Class, Status, and Power*. London: Weidenfeld and Nicolson, 1971.

————. "Portugal." Pages 302-336 in S.J. Woolf (ed.), *European Fascism.* New York: Random House, 1968.

Maxwell, Kenneth. "The Thorns of the Portuguese Revolution," *Foreign Affairs,* 54, No. 2, January 1976, 250-270.

Mendonça Dias, Urbano de. *História dos Açores (Compêndio)* (History of the Azores [Compendium]). (2d ed., rev.) Vila Franca do Campo: Crença, 1942.

Michelin Guide to Portugal. London: Dickens Press, 1970.

"Migration Facts and Figures," *Migration News* [Geneva], 11, No. 1, January-February 1962, 29-32.

"Migration Facts and Figures: Emigration from Portugal, 1957-1966," *Migration News* [Geneva], 17, No. 4, Statistical Supplement No. 63, July-August 1968.

"Migration Facts and Figures: Portuguese Emigration, 1961-1972," *Migration News* [Geneva], 22, No. 4, July-August 1973, 35-38.

Miller, Jon. *Mountains in the Sea.* New York: Vantage Press, 1972.

Miranda, J. David. "A População Universitaria e a População Portuguesa: Um Confronto da sua Composição Social" (The University Population and the Portuguese Population: A Comparison of Their Social Composition), *Analise Social* [Lisbon], 7, Nos. 25 and 26, 1969, 158-165. (Abstracted in *Sociological Abstracts,* 20, No. 3, 1972, Area 1800, 25.)

Montero, Adolfo Casais. "Theory of Impersonality: Fernando Pessoa and T.S. Eliot." (Adapted by Jean R. Longland.) *Journal of the American-Portuguese Cultural Society,* 6-7, 1972-73, 40-45.

Moreira, Eduardo. *The Significance of Portugal: A Survey of Evangelical Progress.* (The World Dominion Survey Series.) New York: World Dominion Press, 1933.

Moser, Don. "The Azores, Nine Islands in Search of a Future," *National Geographic,* 149, No. 2, February 1976, 261-288.

Namora, Fernando. *Fields of Fate.* (Trans., Dorothy Ball.) New York: Crown Publishers, 1970.

1976 Catholic Almanac. Huntington, Indiana: Our Sunday Visitor, 1975.

"Notes and Notices: Causes of the Portuguese Emigration," *Migration News* [Geneva], 17, No. 4, July-August 1968, 18-22.

Novinsky, Anita, and Amilcar Paulo. "The Last Marranos," *Commentary,* 43, No. 5, May 1967, 76-81.

Nowell, Charles E. *Portugal.* (The Modern Nations in Historical Perspective Series.) Englewood Cliffs: Prentice-Hall, 1973.

Nunes, A. Sedas, and J. David Miranda. "A Composição Social da População Portuguêsa: Alguns Aspectos e Implicaçoes" (The Social Composition of the Portuguese Population: Some Aspects and Implications), *Analise Social* [Lisbon], 7, Nos. 27 and 28, 1969, 333-81. (Abstracted in *Sociological Abstracts,* 20, No. 2, Area 1000, 36.)

Organization for Economic Cooperation and Development. *Education in OECD Developing Countries: Trends and Perspectives.* Paris: 1974.

——. *Portugal.* (Economic Surveys.) Paris: July 1974.

Oxford Book of Portuguese Verse: 12th Century to 20th Century. (2d ed.) (Ed., B. Vidigal.) New York: Oxford University Press, 1953.

Parker, John M. (trans.) *Three Twentieth Century Portuguese Poets.* Johannesburg: Witwatersrand University Press, 1960.

Parry, John H. *The Age of Reconnaissance.* (Mentor Book.) New York: New American Library, 1964.

——. *The Discovery of the Sea.* New York: Dial Press, 1974.

Pattee, Richard. *Portugal and the Portuguese World.* Milwaukee: Bruce Publishing, 1957.

Payne, Stanley G. *A History of Spain and Portugal.* 2 vols. Madison: University of Wisconsin Press, 1973.

Pei, Mario. *The Story of Latin and the Romance Languages.* New York: Harper and Row, 1976.

Pereira Neto, João Baptista Nunes. "Social Evolution in Portugal since 1945." Pages 212-227 in Raymond S. Sayers (ed.), *Portugal and Brazil in Transition.* Minneapolis: University of Minnesota Press, 1968.

Pessoa, Fernando. *Fernando Pessoa I-IV* (Trans., Jonathan Griffin.) Oxford: Carcanet Press, 1971.

——. *Selected Poems.* (Trans., Jonathan Griffin.) Baltimore: Penguin, 1974.

——. *Selected Poems.* (Trans., Peter Rickard.) Edinburgh: Edinburgh University Press, 1975.

——. *Selected Poems by Fernando Pessoa.* (Trans., Edwin Honig.) Chicago: Swallow Press, 1971.

——. *Sixty Portuguese Poems.* (Trans., F.E.G. Quintanilha.) Cardiff: University of Wales Press, 1971.

——. "Twelve Poems." (Trans., Thomas Merton.) Pages 299-307 in J. Laughlin (ed.), *New Directions in Prose and Poetry 19.* New York: New Directions, 1966.

Pevsner, Nikolaus. *An Outline of European Architecture.* Harmondsworth, England: Penguin, 1967.

Portugal. Instituto Nacional de Estatística. *X Recenseamento Geral da Populacão* (Tenth General Census of the Population). I, No. 3 (1960 Census Figures.) Lisbon: Instituto Nacional de Estatística, n.d.

Portugal. Ministry of Mass Communication. *Freedom Is Also an Act of Will.* Lisbon: General Directorate for Information and Diffusion, November 1975.

Portugal. Ministry of National Education. *Guidelines for the Reform of Higher Education.* Lisbon: Ramos, Afonso, and Moita, 1971.

————. *Projected Educational System.* Lisbon: Ramos, Afonso, and Moita, 1971.

————. "Projected Educational System," *Western European Education* [London], 4, No. 3, Fall 1972, 180-195.

"Portugal." Pages 136-141 in *Jewish Encyclopedia,* X. 4th ed.) New York: Funk and Wagnalls, 1916.

"Portugal." Pages 607-614 in *New Catholic Encyclopedia,* XI. (Catholic University of America Editorial Staff.) New York: McGraw-Hill, 1967.

"Portugal." Pages 138-141 in *The New Schaff-Herzog Encyclopedia of Religious Knowledge,* IX. Grand Rapids, Michigan: Baker Book House, 1969.

"Portugal." Page 1112 in *Oxford Dictionary of the Christian Church.* (2d ed.) London: Oxford University Press, 1974.

"Portugal: A Blaze of Freedom," *Big Flame* [Birmingham, England], 1975.

"Portuguese Constitution of April 11, 1933, as amended on August 1, 1935." Pages 509-516 in Sidney Z. Elher and John B. Morrall (eds.), *Church and State Through the Centuries.* New York: Biblo and Tannen, 1967.

Potter, Bonnie. "The Revolutions in Portugal: Chaos after the Coup," *New Leader,* 58, No. 21, October 27, 1975, 7-9.

Prestage, Edgar. "The Chivalry of Portugal." Pages 141-166 in Edgar Prestage (ed.), *Chivalry: A Series of Studies to Illustrate Its Historical Significance and Civilizing Influence.* London: Kegan Paul, Trench, Trubner, 1928.

Pro Mundi Vita Society. *Government Policy and the Church in the Portuguese Territories of Africa.* (Monograph Series, No. 43.) Brussels: Pro Mundi Vita International Research and Information Center, 1972.

Raud, G.P. *Inside Facts on Europe.* New York: European Christian Mission, 1946.

Rebello, Luis Francisco. "Modern Portuguese Theatre: A Survey," *Journal of the American-Portuguese Cultural Society,* 3, No. 3, 1969, 33-42.

Rebelo, Luis de Sousa, and Alice Sedgwick Wohl. "Three Excerpts from the Crónica de Dom Pedro I by Fernão Lopes," *Journal of the American-Portuguese Cultural Society,* 9, No. 1, Spring-Summer 1975, 18-28.

Redol, António Alves. *The Man with Seven Names.* (Trans., Linton Lomas Barret.) New York: Knopf, 1964.

Ribeiro, Aquilino. *When the Wolves Howl.* (Trans., Patricia McGowan Pinheiro.) New York: Macmillan, 1963.

Ribeiro, Orlando. *Geográfica de España y Portugal,* V: Portugal. (Ed., Manuel de Terán.) Barcelona: Montaner y Simón, 1955.

———. *Portugal, o mediterraneo e o atlántico*. Coimbra: Coimbra Editora, 1945.

Riegelhaupt, Joyce F. "Festas and Padres: The Organization of Religious Action in a Portuguese Parish," *American Anthropologist*, 75, No. 3, June 1973, 835-852.

———. "In the Shadow of the City: Integration of a Portuguese Village." Unpublished Ph.D. dissertation. New York: Department of Anthropology, Columbia University, 1964.

———. "Saloio Women: An Analysis of Informal and Formal Political and Economic Roles of Portuguese Peasant Women," *Anthropological Quarterly*, 40, No. 3, July 1967, 109-126.

Roberts, William H. "Notes on the Poetry of Teixeira de Pascoais," *Journal of the American-Portuguese Cultural Society*, 9, No. 1, Spring-Summer 1975, 9-17.

Rosado Fernandes, Raul. "Satire, Irony, and Self-Destruction in Portuguese Modernism," *Journal of the American-Portuguese Cultural Society*, 2, Nos. 1-3, Winter-Spring-Summer 1968, 23-41.

Sayers, Raymond S. (ed.) *Portugal and Brazil in Transition*. Minneapolis: University of Minnesota Press, 1968.

Schweitzer, Frederick M., and Harry E. Wedeck. *Dictionary of the Renaissance*. New York: Philosophical Library, 1967.

Sideri, S. *Trade and Power: Informal Colonialism in Anglo-Portuguese Relations*. Rotterdam: Rotterdam University Press, 1970.

Siegel, Bernard J. "Conflict, Parochialism, and Social Differentiation in Portuguese Society," *Journal of Conflict Resolution*, V, No. 1, March 1961, 35-42.

———. "Social Structure and the Medical Practitioner in Rural Brazil and Portugal." *Sociologia* [São Paulo], 20, No. 4, October 1958, 463-476.

Simon, William Joel. "Scientific Expeditions in the Portuguese Overseas Territories, 1783-1808: The Role of Lisbon in the Intellectual-Scientific Community in the Late Eighteenth Century." Unpublished Ph.D. dissertation (74-20, 843). New York: City University of New York, 1974.

Sitwell, Sacheverell. *Gothic Europe*. New York: Holt, Rinehart and Winston, 1969.

———. *Monks, Nuns, and Monasteries*. New York: Holt, Rinehart and Winston, 1965.

———. *Portugal and Madeira*. London: B.T. Batsford, 1957.

Slavin, Neal. *Portugal*. New York: Listrum Press, 1971.

Smith, Robert C. "André Soares: The Rebirth of an Architect," *Journal of the American-Portuguese Cultural Society*, 3, No. 3, Fall 1969, 6-22.

———. *The Art of Portugal, 1500-1800*. New York: Meredith Press, 1968.

————. "Azulejos of Cascais." *Journal of the American-Portuguese Cultural Society*, 2, No. 4, Fall 1968, 1-15.

————. "Some Lisbon Tiles in Estremoz," *Journal of the American-Portuguese Cultural Society*, 9, No. 2, Fall 1975, 1-17.

————. "Some Manueline Church Doorways," *Journal of the American-Portuguese Cultural Society*, 3, No. 4, Winter 1969, 1-15.

Smith, T. Lynn. "The Social Relationships of Man to the Land in Portugal," *Sociologia* [São Paulo], 25, No. 4, December 1963, 319-343.

Smithsonian Institution. *Contemporary Portuguese Architecture, 1958.* Washington: 1958.

Stanislawski, Dan. *The Individuality of Portugal: A Study in Historical-Political Geography.* Austin: University of Texas Press, 1959. (Reprinted, New York: Greenwood Press, 1969.)

————. *Portugal's Other Kingdom: The Algarve.* Austin: University of Texas Press, 1963.

Stathatos, Constantine Christopher. *A Critical Edition of Gil Vicente's 'Floresta de Enganes.'* (Studies in the Romance Languages and Literatures Series, No. 125.) Chapel Hill: University of North Carolina Press, 1962.

Stephens, Henry Morse. *The Study of Portugal.* (Reprint.) New York: Ams Press, 1971.

Stern, Irwin. "Júlio Denis: The Novelist as Social Historian and Social Critic." *Journal of the American-Portuguese Cultural Society*, 6-7, 1972-73, 46-50.

Stevenson, Robert. "Portuguese Music: A Historical Résumé." *Journal of the American-Portuguese Cultural Society*, 4, Nos. 3 and 4, Summer-Fall 1970, 1013.

Thorlby, Anthony (ed.). *The Penguin Companion to European Literature.* New York: McGraw-Hill, 1969.

Tomlins, Jack E. "Toward an Aesthetic of Gil Vicente's Drama," *Journal of the American-Portuguese Cultural Society*, 2, Nos. 1-3, Winter-Spring-Summer 1968, 42-64.

Trask, Willard. "Some Galician-Portuguese Lyrics of the Middle Ages: Men's Songs: Cantigas d'Amor and other Genres," *Journal of the American-Portuguese Cultural Society*, 8, No. 1, Spring-Summer 1974.

Trend, J.B. *Portugal.* London: Ernest Benn, 1957.

Tuulse, Armin. *Castles of the Western World.* London: Thames and Hudson, 1958.

U.S. Department of State. *Portugal: Post Report,* February 1974.

Vasão, Diamantino P., and António Cruz. "Difficulties and Requirements of Assistance to Portuguese Workers in Europe," *Migration News* [Geneva], 17, No. 4, July-August 1968, 1-6.

Willems, Emilio. "On Portuguese Family Structure," *International Journal of Comparative Society* [Dharwar, India], 3, No. 1, September 1962, 65-79.

Winston, Alexander. "Iberia: Evangelicals in a Cage," *The Christian Century*, 79, No. 1, January 3, 1962, 10-12.

Wolff, Philippe. *Western Languages, AD 1000-1500*. (Trans., Frances Partridge.) (World University Library Series.) New York: McGraw-Hill, 1971.

Woodrow, Alain. "The Church Turns Its Coat," *Commonweal*, 100, No. 14, June 14, 1974, 327-329.

World Christian Handbook. London: World Dominion Press, 1962.

Year Book of Labour Statistics, 1959. (19th ed.) Geneva: International Labour Office, 1959.

Year Book of Labour Statistics, 1969, (29th ed.) Geneva: International Labour Office, 1969.

Year Book of Labour Statistics, 1974. (34th ed.) Geneva: International Labour Office, 1974.

(Various issues of the following periodicals were also used in the preparation of this section: *America* [New York], November 20, 1965-May 4, 1974; *Christian Century* [Chicago], October 18, 1944-May 22, 1974; *Christianity Today* [Washington], December 6, 1963-November 21, 1975; *Christian Science Monitor* [Boston] December 22, 1975-January 13, 1976; *Commonweal* [New York], July 31, 1959-June 14, 1974; *Financial Times* [London], April 13-July 14, 1975; *Manchester Guardian Weekly* [London], September-December 1975; *New York Times*, March 1975-March 1976; and *Washington Post*, March 1, 1975-March 1, 1976).

Section II. Political

Abshire, David M., and Michael A. Samuels (eds.). *Portuguese Africa: A Handbook*. (Handbooks of the Modern World Series.) New York: Praeger, 1969.

Acoca, Miguel. "Chronicle of a Doomed Coup," *Washington Post*, March 20, 1975, A-23.

———. "Lisbon Move to Ease out Leftist Seen," *Washington Post*, August 1, 1975, A-1, A-30.

Adam, Thomas R. *Government and Politics in Africa South of the Sahara*. (3d ed., rev.) New York: Random House, 1967.

Bailey, Norman A., and William J. Simon. "Portugal: Four Myths of a Curious Revolution," *Columbia Forum*, 3, No. 4, Fall 1974, 24-30.

Ball, Robert. "Portugal on the Brink," *Fortune*, XCII, No. 2, August 1975, 126-129, 206, 208, 210-211.

Bemis, Samuel Flagg. *A Diplomatic History of the United States*. New York: Holt, Rinehart and Winston, 1965.

Binder, David. "Washington Sets Up $85-Million Package to Aid Portugal," *New York Times*, October 11, 1975, 11.

Bradford, Sarah. *Portugal*. New York: Walker, 1973.

423

Bruce, Neil. *Portugal: The Last Empire.* New York: John Wiley and Sons, 1975.

Bruneau, Thomas C. "Portugal: The Search for a New Political Regime," *World Today* [London], 31, No. 12, December 1975, 478-487.

———. "The Portuguese Coup: Causes and Probable Consequences," *World Today* [london], 30, No. 7, July 1974, 277-288.

Caetano, Marcello. *Manual de Direito Administrativo.* (7th ed.) Lisbon: Coimbra Editora, 1965.

Chapman, Brian. *The Profession of Government: The Public Service in Europe.* London: Unwin University Books, 1971.

Clark, Joseph. "For Portugal: 'Democracy, Period'," *Dissent,* XXII, No. 3, Summer 1975, 225-226.

"Constituent Assembly Approves New Structure for Revolution Council," *Foreign Broadcast Information Service: Western Europe,* VII, No. 49, (FBIS-WEU-76-49) March 11, 1976, M-1.

"Council of Revolution Discusses Order of Elections," *Foreign Broadcast Information Service: Western Europe,* VII, No. 19, (FBIS-WEU-76-19) January 28, 1976, M-1.

Cutileiro, José. *A Portuguese Rural Society.* Oxford: Clarendon Press, 1971.

"Diario de Noticias Carries Apparent Text of MFA-Parties Pact," *Foreign Broadcast Information Service: Western Europe,* VII, No. 45, (FBIS-WEU-76-45) March 5, 1976, M1-6.

"Draft Program of the Revolutionary Party of the Proletariat—Revolutionary Brigades." Pages 26-31 in *Portugal: Key Documents of the Revolutionary Process.* Berkeley: Peoples Translation Service, October 1975.

Economist Intelligence Unit. "Portugal's Plans for Angola Go Awry," *Foreign Report* [London], April 23, 1975, 4-5.

Emery, Walter B. *National and International Systems of Broadcasting: Their History, Operation, and Control.* East Lansing: Michigan State University Press, 1969.

"The End of the Portuguese Empire." *Orbis,* 19, No. 2, Summer 1975, 330-333.

The Europa Year Book, 1974: A World Survey, I. London: Europa Publications, 1974, 1154.

The Europa Year Book, 1975: A World Survey, I. London: Europa Publications, 1975, 1059-1082.

The Europa Yearbook, 1976: A World Survey, I. London: Europa Publications, 1976, 1014-1037.

Figueiredo, António de. *Portugal: Fifty Years of Dictatorship.* Harmondsworth, England: Penguin Books, 1975.

———. "The Portuguese Dilemma," *World Today* [London], 31, No. 2, February 1975, 66-72.

Fryer, Peter, and Patricia McGowan Pinheiro. *Oldest Ally: A Portrait of Salazar's Portugal.* London: Dennis Dobson, 1961.

Grayson, George W. "Portugal and the Armed Forces Movement," *Orbis*, XIX, No. 2, Summer 1975, 335-378.

Great Britain. British Information Services. *Western Co-operation in Brief*. London: 1962.

Green, Gil. *Portugal's Revolution*. New York: International Publishers, 1976.

"Guidelines to the Alliance Between the People and the MFA." Pages 4-8 in *Portugal: Key Documents of the Revolutionary Process*. Berkeley: Peoples Translation Service, October 1975.

Harsgor, Michael. *Portugal in the Revolution*. (The Washington Papers, No. 32.) Beverly Hills: Sage Publications, 1976.

Hartmann, Frederick H. *The Relations of Nations*. (2d ed.) New York: Macmillan, 1962.

Hendriksen, Thomas. "End of an Empire: Portugal's Collapse in Africa," *Current History*, 68, No. 405, May 1975, 211-215.

Hottinger, Arnold. "The Rise of Portugal's Communists," *Problems of Communism*, XXIV, No. 4, July-August 1975, 1-17.

Howe, Marvine. "Portugal Finding Allies Warmer," *New York Times*, December 17, 1975, 7.

Institute for the Study of Conflict. *Portugal: Revolution and Backlash*. (Conflict Study, No. 61.) London: September 1975.

International Commission of Jurists. "Portugal—the Revolution and the Rule of Law." *Review* [Geneva], 7, No. 15, December 1975, 11-20.

International Literary Market Place: 1973-74. New York: R.R. Bowker, 1972.

International Year Book and Statesmen's Who's Who 1974. London: Mercury House, 1974, 343-352.

International Year Book and Statesmen's Who's Who, 1975. (Comp., Robert N. Bradford.) Kingston on Thames, Surrey: Kelly's Directories, 1975, 349-357.

Kay, Hugh. *Salazar and Modern Portugal*. New York: Hawthorne Books, 1970.

"Many-Sided Economic Crisis Attracts as Many Cures as Lisbon Has Parties," *New York Times*, April 21, 1976, 14.

Marques, António Henrique R. de Oliveira. *A History of Portugal*, II: From Empire to Corporate State. New York: Columbia University Press, 1972.

Maxwell, Kenneth. "The Thorns of the Portuguese Revolution," *Foreign Affairs*, 54, No. 2, January 1976, 250-270.

"The 'Melo Antunes' Document." Pages 11-14 in *Portugal: Key Documents of the Revolutionary Process*. Berkeley: Peoples Translation Service, October 1975.

Miller, Joseph C. "Politics of Decolonization in Portuguese Africa," *African Affairs* [London], 74, No. 295, April 1975, 135-147.

Moser, Don. "The Azores, Nine Islands in Search of a Future," *National Geographic*, 149, No. 2, February 1976, 261-288.

Nevins, Lawrence. "The Portuguese Revolution: Massive Change and Much Confusion," *Worldview*, XVIII, Nos. 7 and 8, July-August 1975, 40-47.

Nogueira, Franco. *Portuguese Foreign Policy*. Lisbon: Ministry of Foreign Affairs, 1965.

————. *The United Nations and Portugal: A Study of Anti-Colonialism*. London: Sidgwick and Jackson, 1963.

North Atlantic Treaty Organization Information Service. "Conference on Security and Cooperation in Europe—Some Views of Alliance Leaders," *NATO Review* [Brussels], 23, No. 5, October 1975, 3-9.

Paulu, Burton. *Radio and Television Broadcasting on the European Continent*. Minneapolis: University of Minnesota Press, 1967.

Payne, Stanley G. *A History of Spain and Portugal*, II. Madison: University of Wisconsin Press, 1973.

Peaslee, Amos J. *Constitutions of Nations*, III. (3d ed., rev.) The Hague: Martinus Nijhoff, 1968.

Pires, José Cardoso. "Changing a Nation's Way of Thinking," *Index on Censorship* [London], 2, No. 3, Spring 1975, 93-106.

Plastrik, Stanley. "Portugal's Dangling Revolution," *Dissent*, XXII, No. 4, Fall 1975, 331-335, 338-344.

Political Handbook of the World, 1975. (Ed., Arthur S. Banks.) New York: McGraw-Hill, 1975, 273-278.

Portugal. Ministry of Foreign Affairs. *Portugal Replies to the United Nations*. Lisbon: n.d.

Portugal. Ministry of Mass Communication. *Freedom Is Also an Act of Will*. Lisbon: General Directorate for Information and Diffusion, November 1975.

————. *Political Action Plan of the A.F.M.* Lisbon: July 1975.

————. *Portugal Information* [Lisbon], No. 1, March 1975.

————. *Portugal Information* [Lisbon], No. 2, May 1975.

————. *Portugal Information* [Lisbon], No. 3, July 1975.

Portugal. Office of the Secretary of State for Information and Tourism. *The Portuguese Cinema*. Lisbon: 1973.

Portugal. Secretariado da Propaganda Nacional. *Political Constitution of the Portuguese Republic*. Lisbon: SPN Editions, 1937.

"Portugal." Pages 274-288 in *Encyclopaedia Britannica*, XVIII. Chicago: William Benton, 1969.

"Portugal." Chapter in *Law and Judicial Systems of Nations*. Washington: World Peace Through Law Center, 1968.

"Portugal: A Blaze of Freedom," *Big Flame* [Birmingham, England], 1975.

"Portugal: La Question des Açores," *Défense Nationale* [Paris], 31, No. 4, November 1975, 138-139.

"Portugal—Those Friendly Russians," *Time*, April 21, 1975, 38-39.

"President Swears in New Government Ombudsman," *Foreign Broadcast Information Service: Western Europe*, VII, No. 54, (FBIS-WEU-76-54) March 18, 1976, M-1.

"Program for a Revolutionary Transitional Government—Revolutionary Councils of Workers, Soldiers and Sailors." Pages 20-25 in *Portugal: Key Documents of the Revolutionary Process*. Berkeley: Peoples Translation Service, October 1975.

Saldanha Sanches, J.L. *O.M.R.P.P., Instrumento da Contra-Revolucão*. Lisbon: Ulmerio, 1975.

Schmitter, Philippe C. *Corporatism and Public Policy in Authoritarian Portugal*, I. (Contemporary Political Sociology Series, No. 06-011.) Beverly Hills: Sage Publications, 1975.

Smith, Dianna. "Turmoil in Portugal," *Index on Censorship* [London], 4, No. 4, Winter 1975, 15-22.

———. "What Next in Lisbon?" *Index on Censorship* [London], 4, No. 3, Autumn 1975, 26-32.

Soares, Mário. *Portugal's Struggle for Liberty*. London: Allen and Unwin, 1975.

"Soldiers United Will Win (SUV): Manifesto." Pages 37-38 in *Portugal: Key Documents of the Revolutionary Process*. Berkeley: Peoples Translation Service, October 1975.

Spínola, António de. *Portugal and the Future*. Johannesburg: Perskor Publications, 1974.

The Statesman's Year-Book, 1975-1976. (Ed., John Paxton.) New York: St. Martin's Press, 1975, 1252-1262.

Stern, Irwin. "Suppressed Portuguese Fiction: 1926-1974," *Books Abroad: An International Literary Quarterly*, 50, No. 1, Winter 1976, 54-60.

Sunday Times Insight Team. *Insight on Portugal: The Year of the Captains*. London: André Deutsch, 1975.

Szulc, Tad. "Lisbon and Washington: Behind the Portuguese Revolution," *Foreign Policy*, No. 21, Winter 1975-76, 3-62.

U.S. Congress. 94th, 1st Session. House of Representatives. Committee on International Relations. Subcommittee on International Political and Military Affairs. *United States Policy Toward Portugal*. Washington: GPO, 1975.

U.S. Congress. 94th, 1st Session. House of Representatives. Select Committee on Intelligence. *U.S. Intelligence Agencies and Activities: The Performance of the Intelligence Community*, Pt. 2. Washington: GPO, 1975.

U.S. Congress. 94th, 1st Session. Senate. Committee on Foreign Relations. *Portugal in Transition*. (A report by Senator Mike Mansfield.) Washington: GPO, 1975.

"U.S. in a Major Policy Switch, Offers Portugal Economic Aid," *New York Times*, December 14, 1974, 1-4.

427

Wilson, Harold. *A Personal Record: The Labour Government, 1964-1970.* Boston: Little, Brown, 1971.

World Communications. New York: Unipub, 1975.

World Radio-TV Handbook, 1976. (30th ed.) (Ed., J.M. Frost.) Hvidovre, Denmark: World Radio-TV Handbook, 1976.

The World This Year, 1973. (Eds., Richard Stebbins and Alba Amoia.) (Supplement to *The Political Handbook and Atlas of the World.*) New York: Council on Foreign Relations, 1973, 92-95.

Yearbook of International Organizations, XV. Brussels: Union of International Associations, 1974.

(Various issues of the following periodicals were also used in the preparation of this section: Economist [London], January 1975-May 1976; *Financial Times* [London], January 1975-May 1976; *Foreign Broadcast Information Service: Western Europe* [Washington], January 1975-May 1976; *Keesing's Contemporary Archives* [London], November 1973-May 1976; *Manchester Guardian Weekly* [London], January 1975-May 1976; *New York Times,* April 1974-June 1976; and *Washington Post,* April 1974-June 1976).

Section III. Economic

Allen, H. Warner. *The Wines of Portugal.* New York: McGraw-Hill, 1963.

Annual Bulletin of Transport Statistics for Europe, 1974. New York: United Nations, 1975.

Anuário Estatístico, 1973. Lisbon: Instituto Nacional de Estatística, 1974.

Bailey, Norman A., and William J. Simon. "Portugal: Four Myths of a Curious Revolution," *Columbia Forum,* 3, No. 4, Fall 1974, 24-30.

Ball, Robert. "Portugal on the Brink," *Fortune,* XCII, No. 2, August 1975, 126-129, 206, 208, 210-211.

Banco Português do Atlântico. *Some Data about Portugal.* Lisbon: n.d.

Beckinsale, Monica, and Robert Beckinsale. *Southern Europe.* New York: Holmes and Meier, 1975.

Bradford, Sarah. *Portugal.* New York: Walker, 1973.

Bruce, Neil. *Portugal: The Last Empire.* New York: John Wiley and Sons, 1975.

Coull, James R. *The Fisheries of Europe.* London: G. Bell and Sons, 1972.

Crollen, Luc. *Portugal, the U.S., and NATO.* (Studies in International Relations Series.) Leuven, Belgium: Leuven University Press, 1973.

Da Cunha, Tristão. "Financial and Money Markets in Portugal,"

Journal of the American-Portuguese Cultural Society, VIII, No. 1, Spring-Summer 1974, 54-61.

Economist Intelligence Unit. *Quarterly Economic Review, Portugal* [London], No. 2, 1975.

Estatísticas do Turismo, 1974. Lisbon: Instituto Nacional de Estatística, 1975.

European Free Trade Association. *Thirteenth Annual Report of the European Free Trade Association (1972-73)*. Geneva: September 1973.

———. *Fourteenth Annual Report of the European Free Trade Association (1973-74)*. Geneva: September 1974.

———. *Fifteenth Annual Report of the European Free Trade Association (1974-75)*. Geneva: September 1975.

Figueiredo, António de. *Portugal: Fifty Years of Dictatorship*. Harmondsworth, England: Penguin Books, 1975.

Food and Agriculture Organization. *Monthly Bulletin of Agricultural Economics and Statistics* [Rome], XXIV, November 1975.

Georges, Pierre. "The Battle for Alentejo," *Manchester Guardian Weekly* [London], 113, No. 19, November 8, 1975, 13-15.

Grayson, George W. "Portugal and the Armed Forces Movement," *Orbis*, XIX, No. 2, Summer 1975, 335-378.

Grossman, Harold J. *Grossman's Guide to Wines, Spirits, and Beers*. New York: Charles Scribner's Sons, 1974.

Gutkind, Erwin. *Urban Development in Southern Europe: Spain and Portugal*. New York: Free Press, 1969.

Harsgor, Michael. *Portugal in the Revolution*. (The Washington Papers, No. 32.) Beverly Hills: Sage Publications, 1976

Institute for the Study of Conflict. *Portugal: Revolution and Backlash*. (Conflict Study, No. 61.) London: September 1975.

Jane's World Railways, 1972-73. (Ed., Henry Sampson.) New York: McGraw-Hill, 1972.

Kay, Hugh. *Salazar and Modern Portugal*. New York: Hawthorne Books, 1970.

Kramer, Jane. "The Reporter at Large: The Portuguese Revolution," *The New Yorker*, December 15, 1975, 92.

Larousse Encyclopedia of World Geography. New York: Odyssey Press, 1965.

Mercier, Pierre. "Portugal's Long Tightrope March," *Vision* [Geneva], No. 64, March 1976, 41-44.

Michelin Guide to Portugal. London: Dickens Press, 1970.

Moss, Robert. "Portugal's Revolutionary Course," *The Banker* [London], 125, No. 590, April 1975, 411-420.

Nowell, Charles E. *Portugal*. (The Modern Nations in Historical Perspective Series.) Englewood Cliffs: Prentice-Hall, 1973.

Organization for Economic Cooperation and Development. *Agricultural Policy in Portugal*. Paris: 1975.

————. *Portugal.* (Economic Surveys.) Paris: July 1974.

————. *Review of Fisheries in OECD Member Countries, 1974.* Paris: 1975.

————. *Tourism Policy and International Tourism in OECD Member Countries.* Paris: 1974.

Payne, Stanley G. *A History of Spain and Portugal.* 2 vols. Madison: University of Wisconsin Press, 1973.

Pintado, V. Xavier. *Structure and Growth of the Portuguese Econo-.my.* Geneva: European Free Trade Association, July 1964.

Ports of the World, 1976. London: Benn Brothers, 1976.

Price Waterhouse. *Current Foreign Exchange Information.* New York: 1976, 113-114.

Production Year Book, 1973. Rome: Food and Agriculture Organization, 1974.

Sociedade Financiera Portuguêsa. *Economic Indicators.* Lisbon: August 1975.

Stanislawski, Dan. *The Individuality of Portugal: A Study in Historical-Political Geography.* Austin: University of Texas Press, 1959. (Reprinted, New York: Greenwood Press, 1969.)

Statistical Yearbook, 1974. (26th ed.) New York: Statistical Office, Department of Economic and Social Affairs, United Nations, 1975.

Szulc, Tad. "Lisbon and Washington: Behind the Portuguese Revolution," *Foreign Policy,* No. 21, Winter 1975-76, 3-62.

U.S. Department of Agriculture. Economic Research Service. *The Agricultural Situation in Western Europe: Review of 1974 and Outlook for 1975.* (Foreign Agricultural Economic Report, No. 100.) Washington: GPO, April 1975.

U.S. Department of Agriculture. Foreign Agricultural Service. *World Agricultural Production and Trade: Statistical Report.* Washington: GPO, October 1975.

————. *World Agricultural Production and Trade: Statistical Report.* Washington: GPO, December 1975.

U.S. Department of Commerce. Bureau of International Commerce. *Marketing in Portugal,* by Ann Corro. (Overseas Business Reports, OBR 74-52.) Washington: GPO, October 1974.

U.S. Department of Commerce. Bureau of International Commerce. Office of International Marketing. "Portugal." Page 18 in *Market Profiles for Western Europe and Canada.* (Overseas Business Reports, OBR 75-59.) Washington: GPO, 1975.

U.S. Department of Commerce. Domestic and International Business Administration. Bureau of International Commerce. *Foreign Economic Trends and Their Implications for the United States: Portugal.* (FET-75-093.) Washington: GPO, 1975.

U.S. Department of State. Agency for International Development. Office of Financial Management. Statistical Reports Division. *U.S.*

Overseas Loans and Grants (July 1, 1945-June 30, 1974.) Washington: GPO, n.d.

U.S. Department of the Interior. Bureau of Mines. *Mineral Trade Notes*, 72, No. 9, September 1975.

"World-Wide Oil at a Glance," *Oil and Gas Journal*, December 31, 1973, 86.

Yearbook of International Trade Statistics, 1974. New York: United Nations, 1975.

(Various issues of the following periodicals were also used in the preparation of this section : *Bank of London and South America Review* [London], January 1970-May 1976; *Economist* [London], December 1975-April 1976; *EFTA Bulletin* [Geneva], December 1973-January 1976; *Financial Times* [London], October 22, 1975-April 1976; *New York Times*, December 16, 1975-April 1976; and *OECD Observer* [Paris], February 1974-February 1976.)

Section IV. National Security

Amaro, José. "Spínola considerou supérflua a existência do MFA como centro de poder" (Spínola Considered the MFA Superfluous as a Power Center), *O Século Ilustrado* [Lisbon], XXXVII, No. 1924, November 23, 1975, 11-15.

"Angola." Pages 515-527 in Colin Legum, Elizabeth Clements, and Richard Synge (eds.), *Africa Contemporary Record: Annual Survey and Documents 1973-1974*, VI. New York: Africana Publishing, 1974.

"Angola." Pages 527-543 in Colin Legum (ed.), *Africa Contemporary Record: Annual Survey and Documents 1974-1975*, VII. New York: Africana Publishing, 1975.

Araújo, Laurentino da Silva, and Vítor António Duarte Faveiro. *Código Penal Português, anotado* (Portuguese Penal Code, Annotated). (7th ed.) Coimbra: Coimbra Editora, 1971.

Bailey, Norman A., and William J. Simon. "Portugal: Four Myths of a Curious Revolution," *Columbia Forum*, 3, No. 4, Fall 1974, 24-30.

Banazol, Luís Ataíde. *A origem do movimento das forças armadas* (The Origin of the Armed Forces Movement). Lisbon: Prêlo, 1974.

Bosgra, S.J., and Chr. van Krimper. *Portugal and NATO.* (3d ed., rev.) Amsterdam: Angola Comité, 1972.

Bruce, Neil. *Portugal: The Last Empire.* New York: John Wiley and Sons, 1975.

Bruneau, Thomas C. "The Portuguese Coup: Causes and Probable Consequences," *World Today* [London], 30, No. 7, July 1974, 277-288.

Caetano, Marcello. *Depoimento* (Deposition). Rio de Janeiro: Record, 1974.

"Coming in from the Cold." *The Economist* [London], 258, No. 6915, March 6, 1976, 15-16.

"Constituçõ da República Portuguêsa." Pages 738-755 in *Diário da República:* Lisbon: National Press, April 10, 1976.

Continental Operations Command. "COPCON: Working Paper for a Political Program." Pages 15-19 in *Portugal: Key Documents of the Revolutionary Process.* Berkeley: Peoples Translation Service, October 1975.

Crollen, Luc. *Portugal, the U.S., and NATO.* (Studies in International Relations Series.) Leuven, Belgium: Leuven University Press, 1973.

Delgado, Humberto da Silva. *The Memoirs of General Delgado.* London: Cassell, 1974.

Duran Clemente, Manuel. *Elementos para a compreensão do 25 de Novembro* (Elements for the Comprehension of November 25). Lisbon: Edições Sociais, 1975.

Ferreira, J. Diniz. *Aeronáutica Portuguêsa (Elementos Básicos de História)* (Portuguese Aeronautics [Basic Historic Elements]). Lisbon: Author's Edition, 1961.

Figueiredo, António de. *Portugal: Fifty Years of Dictatorship.* Harmondsworth, England: Penguin Books, 1975.

Força Aerea Portuguêsa. Lisbon: Fernandes, 1966.

Galvão, Henrique. *Santa Maria: My Crusade for Portugal.* (Trans., William Longfellow.) Cleveland: World Publishing, 1961.

Getler, Michael. "NATO Seen Warming to Portugal," *Washington Post,* April 2, 1976, 1, 10.

Giniger, Henry. "Portuguese Army Plans a New Role: Reorganization Is Intended to Make Military Obedient to Rule by Civilians," *New York Times,* March 29, 1976, 7.

Gonçalves, Manuel Lopes Maia. *Código de Processo Penal, Anotado e Comentado* (Penal Code, Annotated and Discussed). Coimbra: Almedina, 1972.

Grayson, George W. "Portugal and the Armed Forces Movement," *Orbis,* XIX, No. 2, Summer 1975, 335-378.

"Guidelines to the Alliance Between the People and the MFA." Pages 4-8 in *Portugal: Key Documents of the Revolutionary Process.* Berkeley: Peoples Translation Service, October 1975.

Herrick, Allison Butler, et al. *Area Handbook for Angola.* (DA Pam 550-59.) Washington: GPO for Foreign Area Studies, The American University, 1967.

Howe, Marvine. "Lisbon Rebuffed on Azores Plan: Autonomy Proposals Called 'Clearly Unsatisfactory,'" *New York Times,* May 6, 1976, 7.

------. "Portugal's New Army Chief, António Ramalho Eanes," *New York Times,* December 10, 1975, 3.

Lewis, Flora. "Lisbon Navy Chief Is Looking to Full Role in NATO," *New York Times*, April 28, 1976, 3.

Lourenço, Eduardo. *Os militares e o Poder* (The Military and the Power). Lisbon: Arcádia, 1975.

Martins, Ferreira. *História do Exército Português* (History of the Portuguese Army). Lisbon: Editional Inquérito, n.d.

Maurício, Artur. *Crimes Políticos e Habeas Corpos*. (Cadernos Portugália Series.) Lisbon: Portugália, 1974.

"The 'Melo Antunes' Document." Pages 11-14 in *Portugal: Key Documents of the Revolutionary Process*. Berkeley: Peoples Translation Service, October 1975.

The Military Balance 1974-1975. London: International Institute for Strategic Studies, 1975, 25-26.

The Military Balance 1975-1976. London: International Institute for Strategic Studies, 1976, 25-26.

Minter, William. *Portuguese Africa and the West.* New York: Monthly Review Press, 1972.

"Mozambique." Pages 528-542 in Colin Legum, Elizabeth Clements, and Richard Synge (eds.), *Africa Contemporary Record: Annual Survey and Documents 1973-1974*, VI. New York: Africana Publishing, 1974.

"Mozambique." Pages 385-403 in Colin Legum (ed.), *Africa Contemporary Record: Annual Survey and Documents 1974-1975*, VII. New York: Africana Publishing, 1975.

Nowell, Charles E. *Portugal.* (The Modern Nations in Historical Perspective Series.) Englewood Cliffs: Prentice-Hall, 1973.

Nuno, Vasco. "O brigadeiro Saraiva de Carvalho: Sou un militar que cumpriu seu dever" (Brigadier Saraiva de Carvalho: I Am a Military Man Who Did His Duty), *Jornal do Exército* [Lisbon], 15, No. 176, August 1974, 16-21.

O'Ballance, Edward. "The War Potential of Portugal," *Military Review*, 44, August 1964, 84-90.

"O Povo Unidos Jamais Sera Vencido" (The People United Will Never Be Defeated), *O Século Ilustrado* [Lisbon], No. 1896, May 5, 1974, 25.

Portugal. Council of the Revolution. "Bases Fundamentais para a reorganização das Forças Armadas" (Fundamental Basis for the Reorganization of the Armed Forces), *Baluarte* [Lisbon], I, No. 1, January 1976, 8.

Portugal. General Staff of the Armed Forces. Fifth Division. "Relatório Preliminar sobre o glope contra-revolucionário de 11 de março de 1975" (Preliminary Report on the Counterrevolutionary Coup of March 11, 1975), *Movimento-boletim informativo das Forças Armadas* [Lisbon], April 23, 1975.

Portugal. Instituto Nacional de Estatística. Serviços Centrais. *Estatísticas da Justiça, Continente e Ilhas Adjacentes, 1972* (Statistics on

Justice, Continental and Adjacent Islands.) Lisbon: Sociedade Tipográfica, 1973.

————. *Estatísticas da Justiça, Continente e Ilhas Adjacentes, 1973* (Statistics on Justice, Continental and Adjacent Islands.) Lisbon: Sociedade Tipográfica, 1974.

Portugal. Ministry of Marine (Navy). Superintendent of Personnel Services. *Lista da Armada* (Navy List). Lisbon, 1974.

Portugal. Ministry of the Army. Personnel Directorate. *Almanaque do Exército* (Army Almanac). Lisbon: Papelaria Fernandes, July 1, 1975.

"Portugal: A Blaze of Freedom," *Big Flame* [Birmingham, England], 1975.

"Portugal's Year in Africa." Pages 93-97 in Colin Legum and Anthony Hughes (eds.), *Africa Contemporary Record: Annual Survey and Documents, 1970-1971*, III. London: Rex Collings, 1971.

"Portugal's Year in Africa." Pages 120-125 in Colin Legum and Anthony Hughes (eds.), *Africa Contemporary Record: Annual Survey and Documents, 1971-1972*, IV. New York: Africana Publishing, 1972.

"Portugal's Year in Africa." Pages 83-89 in Colin Legum, Elizabeth Clements, and Richard Synge (eds.), *Africa Contemporary Record: Annual Survey and Documents, 1973-1974*, VI. New York: Africana Publishing, 1974.

"Portugal's Year in Africa." Pages 69-73 in Colin Legum (ed.), *Africa Contemporary Record: Annual Survey and Documents, 1974-1975*, VII. New York: Africana Publishing, 1975.

"Portugal—the Revolution and the Rule of Law," *Review of the International Commission of Jurists*, 15, December 1975, 11-20.

Pouchin, Dominique. "Disenchantment in Portugal," *Manchester Guardian Weekly* [London], April 18, 1976, 12-13.

Praça, Afonso. *25 de Abril.* (2d ed., rev.) Lisbon: Casa Viva, 1974.

"Program for a Revolutionary Transitional Government—Revolutionary Councils of Workers, Soldiers and Sailors." Pages 20-25 in *Portugal: Key Documents of the Revolutionary Process.* Berkeley: Peoples Translation Service, October 1975.

"Refugees in Lisbon Threaten Violence if Aid Isn't Received," *New York Times*, May 6, 1976, 7.

Schmitter, Philippe. "Liberation by Golpe: Retrospective Thoughts on the Demise of Authoritarian Rule in Portugal," *Armed Forces and Society*, 2, No. 1, Fall 1975, 5-33.

Selcher, Wayne A. "Brazilian Relations with Portuguese Africa in the Context of the Elusive 'Luso-Brazilian Community'," *Journal of Interamerican Studies and World Affairs*, 18, No. 1, February 1976.

Soares, Fernando Luso. *PIDE/DGS: an estado dentro do estado* (PIDE/DGS: A State Within the State). (Cadernos Portugália Series.) Lisbon: Portugália, 1974.

Spínola, António de. *Portugal and the Future.* Johannesburg: Perskor Publications, 1974.

Sweezy, Paul M. "Class Struggles in Portugal," Pt. 1, *Monthly Review*, 27, No. 4, September 1975, 1-26.

———. "Class Struggles in Portugal," Pt. 2, *Monthly Review*, 27, No. 5, October 1975, 1-15.

Vicente, Leonel Martins. *Codigo de Justiça Militar.* (7th ed.) Lisbon: 1960.

Wilkinson, Anthony R. "Angola and Mozambique: The Implications of Local Power," *Survival* [London], September-October 1975, 217-227.

GLOSSARY

ADITLA—Associação Democrática para a Integração do Timor do Leste na Australia (Democratic Association for the Integration of Eastern Timor in Australia).

APODETI—Associação Popular Democrática Timorense (Timorese People's Democratic Association).

ASDT—Associação Social Democrática Timorense (Timorese Social Democratic Association).

bairro—Ward. An administrative unit between the parish *(freguesia— q.v.)* and the municipality *(concelho—q.v.)* in Lisbon and Porto.

CDS—Partido do Centro Democrático Social (Social Democratic Center Party). A center-right party similar to such others in Western Europe as the British Conservative Party.

concelho (pl., *concelhos*)—A municipality in metropolitan Portugal; a small administrative area in Portugal's former African territories.

COREMO—Comitê Revolucionário para Moçambique (Revolutionary Committee for Mozambique).

escudo—Basic currency unit. One escudo equals 100 centavos. From 1962 to December 21, 1971, one escudo equaled US$0.035. Average annual exchange values in subsequent years were: 1972—one escudo equaled US$0.037; 1973—one escudo equaled US$0.041; 1974— one escudo equaled US$0.041; 1975—one escudo equaled US$0.040.

FICO—Frente para Independência e Continuidade com o Occidente (Front for Independence and Continuity with the West); in Mozambique.

fiscal year—Calendar year.

FLEC—Frente para a Libertação do Enclavo de Cabinda (Front for the Liberation of the Enclave of Cabinda). A small movement that sought Cabinda's independence from Angola, FLEC was defeated by MPLA (*q.v.*).

FLING—Frente para Libertação e Independência da Guiné Português (Front for the Liberty and Independence of Protuguese Guinea).

FNLA—Frente Nacional de Libertação de Angola (National Front for the Liberation of Angola). An independence movement that was supported by the United States, Zaire, and the People's Republic of China, FNLA attempted an alliance with UNITA (*q.v.*), but both were defeated by MPLA (*q.v.*).

437

freguesia (pl., *freguesias*)—Literally, parish. Administrative unit of local government; usually corresponds in area to ecclesiastical unit.

FRELIMO—Frent de Libertação de Moçambique (Front for the Liberation of Mozambique). The ruling party in Mozambique.

FRETLIN—Frente Revolucionária para Timor do Leste Independente (Revolutionary Front for an Independent East Timor).

GDP—Gross domestic product. The value at market prices of all domestically produced goods and services during a specified period.

GNP—Gross national product. The GDP (*q.v.*) adjusted for net factor income received from abroad.

GUMO—Grupo Unido de Moçambique (United Group of Mozambique).

hectare—10,000 square meters. Equal to 2.47 acres.

Intersindical—A collection of several unions and craft groups in the major urban areas; dominated by the PCP (*q.v.*), it was declared the single official body of organized labor in January 1975.

latifundio (pl., latifundios)—Large landed estate, characteristic of southern region of Portugal.

metric ton—1,000 kilograms. Equal to 1.1 short tons or 2,204.6 pounds.

MFA—Movimento das Forças Armadas (Armed Forces Movement). The organized revolutionary element of the Portuguese armed forces, which overthrew the ruling regime in April 1974.

MLSTP—Movimento para a Libertação de São Tomé e Príncipe (Freedom Movement for São Tomé and Príncipe). The ruling party in São Tomé and Príncipe.

MPLA—Movimento Popular de Libertação de Angola (Popular Movement for the Liberation of Angola). The ruling party in Angola, MPLA was supported by the Soviet Union and Cuba in a civil war against FNLA (*q.v.*) and UNITA (*q.v.*).

PAIGC—Partido Africano da Independência da Guiné e Cabo Verde (African Party for the Independence of Guinea and Cape Verde). The ruling party in Guinea-Bissau (formerly Portuguese Guinea) and the Cape Verde Islands.

PCP—Partido Comunista Português (Portuguese Communist Party). Rigidly dogmatic, with a pro-Moscow orientation, the PCP's main support came from some labor unions and from landless peasants in the Alentejo region southwest of Lisbon. Much of the PCP's popularity came from its long opposition to the prerevolutionary regime.

PPD—Partido Popular Deomcrático (Popular Democratic Party). A reformist, center-left party, similar to such others in Western Europe as the British Liberal Party.

PSP—Partido Socialista Português (Portuguese Socialist Party). The single most popular party in Portugal in mid-1976, the PSP was a social democratic party with views similar to those held by the left wings of other West European social democratic parties.

438

PSP—Polícia de Seguarança Pública (Public Security Police). A para-military police force; duties include criminal investigation, property protection, and urban public security.

saneamento—Literally, cleansing or purging. The informal replacement of prerevolutionary officials and industrial managers after the April 1974 revolution.

terms of trade—The ratio of the index of export prices to the index of import prices.

UDCV—União Democrática do Cabo Verde (Democratic Union of the Cape Verde Islands).

UDP—União Democrática Popular (Popular Democratic Union). Formed in 1974 by Stalinist hardliners from the PCP (*q.v.*), UDP was not a single party but rather a common front composed of three separate Marxist-Leninist groups.

UDT—União Democrática Timorense (Timorese Democratic Union).

ultramar—Literally, overseas. The Portuguese overseas territories.

UNITA—União Nacional para a Independência Total de Angola (National Union for the Total Independence of Angola). An independence movement that was supported by the United States, the People's Republic of China, and South Africa, UNITA attempted an alliance with FNLA (*q.v.*), but both were defeated by MPLA (*q.v.*).

UPICV—União dos Povos das Ilhas do Cabo Verde (Union of the Peoples of the Cape Verde Islands).

World Bank—The International Bank for Reconstruction and Development (IBRD).

INDEX

adult education: 170
adultery: 135
advertising: 300, 301, 303, 308, 309, 365
Afonso, Jorge: 185
Afonso Henriques (king): 20, 21, 22, 140, 163, 394
Afonso III: 21, 163
Afonso IV: 24
Afonso V: 30, 178, 183
Afonso VI: 39
Africa (see also decolonization; overseas territories): 40, 47, 292
African Party for the Independence of Guinea and Cape Verde (PAIGC): 264, 265, 267, 268, 269, 376, 377, 380
agriculture (see also land ownership; land use): viii, 23, 26, 40, 65, 159, 314, 333-348; Azores, 77; government policy, 208; work force 92, 94, 333
air force: 373, 380, 383, 387, 388, 391; in politics, 233, 234, 235
airlines and airports: 367, 369, 371-372; military aircraft, 386 387
Ajuda Library: 310
al-Andalus: 18, 19, 22
Albania: 105
Albuquerque, Afonso d': 33
Alcobaça monastery: 188
Alcoforado, Marianna: 180, 183
Alentejo: 16, 22, 34, 59, 108, 175; agriculture, 73, 113, 335, 339, 344; climate, 69; industry, 74, 75, 191; politics, 249; province, 60, 61, 62, 66, 72; social structure, 126, 133
Alexander VI of Spain. See Line of 1493
Algarve: 16, 19, 22, 34, 59, 67, 73, 108; climate, 68, 69; province, 60, 61, 62, 72; tourism, 365, 367
Aljubarrota battle: 27
Alliance of Workers and Peasants (AOC): 230, 239, 241, 251, 252
Almeida Garrett: 180-181
Alves, Vitor: 234

Amaral, Diogo Pinto de Freitas do: 7, 248
Amaro, Adelino: 248
Amieira castle: 187
Anderson, Sofia de Mello Breyner: 182
Angola: 40, 47, 55, 56, 99, 258, 259; church in, 145, 146, 148; independence, 260, 263, 265, 272, 328, 375-376; oil from, 361
Angra do Heroísmo: 76, 78, 216; population, 84, 86, 102
ANP. See National Popular Action
Anthony of Padua. See Santo António
anthropologists (see also Cutileiro, José): 165
antisubmarine warfare: 386, 387
AOC. See Alliance of Workers and Peasants
Arade River: 72
Araújo, Manuel Gomes de: 376
archeology: 14, 15, 187
architecture: 187-189
Argentina: 95, 98
armed forces (see also air force, Armed Forces Movement; army; navy): 93, 236, 397-398; in politics, 50, 213, 223, 224, 226, 227, 237, 245, 255, 378-383
Armed Forces Movement (MFA) (see also revolution of April 1974): 3, 4, 5, 6, 8, 9, 57, 176, 209, 210, 211, 212, 218, 220, 289; church and, 151-152; foreign policy, 257, 263, 264; leadership role, 224, 225, 226, 229, 230, 231, 232, 250; politics and, 222, 223, 237, 373, 380, 381, 382, 383, 384, 391, 395, 396; press and, 305
Armed Revolutionary Action (ARA): 250
army: 373, 379, 383, 384-385, 388, 391, 399; in politics, 233, 234
Arraiolas rugs: 191
Arriaga, Kaulza de: 379
arts: 34, 38, 167, 185-191
Assembly of the Republic: 219, 239

Atlantic Gothic style: 188
attorneys: 206
Austria: 247, 359
Ave River: 70
Aveiro: xiv, 65, 102, 190, 216; agriculture, 339; industry, 74, 349, 354; 339; population, 84, 89, 90; Ria de Aveiro, 66, 75, 71; university, 170
Aviz: house of, 27-28, 36, 39, 178; military order of, 24, 394
Azevedo, José Pinheiro de: 9, 173, 223, 234, 235, 242, 244, 299
Azores: 29, 54, 59, 60, 75-78, 175, 259, 307, 308, 370; agriculture, 340; banks, 322; emigration, 102, 103, 104; government, 223; military in, 384, 385, 386; politics, 242, 243, 244; tourism, 113, 367,371; U.S. base, 273, 275, 288, 289, 291, 292, 375
azulejos: 187, 189, 190-191

Baetica: 18
Baixo Alentejo (see also Alentejo): 62
balance of payments: 223, 312, 323, 326, 359-360
Balsemão, Francisco: 248, 304
Bank of Portugal: 284, 322, 323, 324, 331, 364
banks: 313, 321-323; nationalization, 229, 284, 299, 301, 317, 319, 322-323, 350, 382; overseas issuing bank, 268, 322
Baptista, Manuel: 187
Baptists: 162
Barbosa, Aires: 191
Barca d'Alva: 63, 70
Barnes, W. J.: 157
barracas: 81, 109, 127
Barreno, Maria Isabel: 183
Barros, Alfonso de: 252
Barros, João de: 178, 191
Beira: 60, 61, 62, 65, 66, 71, 87, 164, 182
Beja: xiv, 16, 21, 67, 216; agriculture, 342, 347; emigration, 103, 104; population, 86, 88, 89
Belem monastery: 188
births: 90, 91
Bissau: 56
Black Death: 26
Black Horse Square: 190
Bocage, Manuel Maria Barbosa du: 180
Bomtempo, João Domingos: 184
borders: 1, 13, 60, 61, 63; customs, 400
Borges Irmão family: 320
Bradford, Sarah: 127
Braga: xiv, 65, 68, 183, 216, 339, 349, 365; ecclesiastical province, 153, 189;

emigration, 103, 104; history, 16, 17; population, 85, 86, 88, 89, 90; university, 175
Braga, Teófilo: 49, 181
Bragança: xiv, 65, 68, 69, 187, 216, 339; emigration, 102, 103, 104; population, 84, 86, 88, 89
Bragança, House of: 28, 39-42; Catherine of, 40; duke of, 30
Brandão, Raul: 182
Brazil: 2, 31, 40, 42, 190, 370; emigration to, 95, 97, 314; relations with, 34, 35, 263, 283-284, 362, 387
broadcast media. See radio and television
budget: 315, 326-327; armed forces, 395; colonial wars, 262; education, 172; highways, 368
Bulgaria: 280, 363
bullfighting: 112

Cabinda: 55, 56, 258; status, 265, 274, 275
cabinet. See ministries
Cabora Bassa: 56
Cabral, Amilcar: 267, 377
Cabral, Luis: 265, 267, 269
Cabral, Pedro Alvares da: 31
Cabral, Vasco: 267
Cabreira, Serra da: 64
Caetano, Marcello: 3, 55-57, 119, 123, 150, 151, 193, 209, 218, 221, 224, 246, 284, 285, 289, 291, 300, 381; church and state, 163; economy under, 317, 329; education under, 172; foreign policy, 260, 261, 269, 377
Caldeirão, Serra do: 64, 67, 69
Camões, Luís de: 27, 167, 177, 179
Canada: 95, 96, 98
Canary Islands: 244
cancer: 105
Cão, Diogo: 31, 32
Cape Bojador: 29, 32
Cape Verde Islands: 30, 258, 290; independence, 264, 265, 267, 268-269; islanders in Portugal, 101-102
capital investment (see also foreign investment): 312, 333; in agriculture, 335, 338, 346; in industry, 350
capital punishment: 203, 405
Captain's Movement: 4, 373, 379, 380
Cardoso, Amadeu da Souza: 186
Cardoso, António Lopes: 347
Cardoso, Manuel: 184
Carlucci, Frank: 232
Carmo, Isabel do: 253

Carmona, António Oscar de Fragoso: 51, 374
carob trees: 73, 344
Carvalho, João de Sousa: 184
Carvalho, Joaquim: 270
Carvalho, Otelo Saraiva de: 9, 10, 222, 225, 232, 233, 235, 236, 242, 253, 382, 383
Carvalho e Melo, Sebastião José de. *See* Pombal, Marquis of
Castanheda, Fernão Lopes de: 178
Castelo Branco: xiv, 65, 68, 74, 216; emigration, 103, 104; population, 86, 88, 89
Castelo Branco, Camilo: 181
Castile: 29; language, 177, 180
Catalonia: 38
Catholic University of Lisbon: 170
Cávado River: 70
CDS. *See* Social Democratic Center Party
Ceausescu, Nicolae: 281, 282
Celtic invaders: 15
censorship: viii, 177, 260, 299, 300, 301, 406; films, 309
censuses: 81, 82; animal, 343; industrial, 351; religious, 164
ceramics: 190
Cerejeira, Manuel Gonçalves: 143, 151
Champalimaud Group: 320, 323
Chança River: 63
children (*see also* juvenile deliquency): 105, 130, 157; rights, 408
China, People's Republic of: 252, 258, 272, 279, 378, 380
China, Republic of: 279
china and pottery industries: 74
Chipenda, Daniel: 272
Christian Democratic Party (PDC): 228, 230, 239, 240, 241, 247, 252, 256
Christianity (*see also* Protestants; Roman Catholic Church): 16, 19
church and state: 50, 53, 140-152, 154, 162-163; land confiscated, 118
círio festa: 113, 156, 160
Cistercian architecture: 188
citizenship: 46, 406; Brazilians, 283
civil rights: (*see also* censorship): 4, 52, 196, 206, 233, 237, 238, 245, 406-409; freedom of worship, viii, 19, 163, 164
civil service: 124, 200, 217-218, 384
class. *See* elite class; middle classes; working class
clergy (*see also* Jesuits): anticlericalism, 142; foreigners, 145; parish priests, 154, 155, 156, 162; political power,

117, 141, 249; religious orders, 44, 117, 141, 142, 146
climate: vii, 68-69; Azores, 77; Madeira, 78
coal: 74, 354
codfish: 108, 313, 345
coffee: 108, 111, 361
Coimbra: xiv, 17, 21, 68, 106, 229, 309, 407; cathedral, 187, 190; district, 65, 216; emigration, 102, 103, 104; police, 398; population, 86, 88, 89; schools, 168
Coimbra University: 51, 169, 170, 192
Coina River: 71
Columbus, Christopher: 31
Commandos for the Defense of Western Civilization: 254
communications (*see also* newspapers; publishing; radio and television): 135, 299-310, 358
communism (*see also* left-wing parties): 159, 173, 225, 227, 228; union organizers, 291, 330, 347
communist countries: 11, 280-283, 396; trade with, 362-363
Communist Electoral Front/Marxist-Leninist (FEC-ML): 230, 239, 241, 252
communist-oriented political parties (*see also* Portuguese Communist Party (PCP): 218, 246, 247, 289, 290, 376
Confederation of Portuguese Farmers: 255
Congo: 274, 292
conscription of soldiers: 382, 384, 388
Constituent Assembly: 7, 213, 222, 223, 229, 237, 252, 290
Constitution of 1933: 52, 60, 132, 143, 162, 193, 196-199, 219, 239, 259, 383
Constitution of 1976: viii, 7, 55, 136, 223, 229, 237, 238, 239, 240, 383-384; civil rights, 406-407; communications, 299, 301; economy, 313
constitutions: 195-209; of 1822, 43; Charter of 1826, 43, 164; Concordat of 1940, 143; of 1911, 49, 50
construction: 312, 317, 352, 355
consumerism: 95, 124, 206; fraud, 405
Continental Operations Command (COPCON): 10, 222, 225, 227, 231, 235, 381, 382, 383, 402
cooperatives: 307; marketing, 345, 346, 365
copper mines: 72, 74
Cordova: 19
cork: viii, 66, 67, 73, 336, 338, 343, 363; production, 344, 349, 351

Corporative Chamber: 52, 198, 202, 210
corporative system: 116, 127-129, 194-195, 200, 202
Correia, Fernão Gomes: 183
Correia, Gaspar: 178
Cortes (parliament): 23, 24, 28, 39, 43, 44
Corvo island: 76, 77
Costa, Afonso: 49
Costa, Manuel Pinto da: 265, 272
Costa, Noronha da: 187
Costa de Cabarica: 365
Costa Gomes, Francisco da: 9, 219, 222, 226, 229, 231, 232, 233, 234, 235, 379, 381; foreign policy, 257, 267, 274, 281, 282, 283, 288, 292, 293
Council of Ministers: 198, 199, 200, 201, 323
Council of State: 198, 199, 224
Council of the Revolution: 211, 212, 213, 219, 220, 222, 223, 228, 229, 231, 234, 235, 236, 237, 239, 240, 242, 304, 330, 382, 383, 384
coup d'état attempts: 222; left-wing (November 1975), 10, 223, 235, 382, 390, 409; right-wing (March 1975), 9, 211, 227, 290, 381, 399, 409
coup of 1926: 51
coup of 1974. See revolution of April 1974
Coura River: 70
courts. See judicial structure
Couto, Diogo do: 178
Covilhão, Pedro da: 31
Cravinho, João: 280
Crespo, Victor: 270
crime and punishment: 197, 398, 403-404; robbery, 111, 253, 405
crops: 66, 67, 71, 73, 339-343; Azores, 77
Crusades: 22, 29
Cruz, Wenceslau Pompilio da: 9, 242, 256
Cuba: 240, 261, 272, 275, 280, 396; embassy bombed, 254; trade, 363
cunha: 131
Cunhal, Álvaro: 7, 250, 251, 281, 310
currency: 331
Cutileiro, José: 105, 107, 111, 126, 127, 128, 130, 131, 135, 157, 158, 159
Czechoslovakia: 249, 280, 363

Dadra: 258, 276
da Gama, Vasco: 31, 32, 35, 36, 179
Dahomey: 258
Damão: 258, 276
Dão River: 71
Day of the Red Carnations: 57

deaths: causes, 105-106, 376, 410; rate, 92
decolonization (see also refugees): 262-279, 292, 327-329, 385, 388
decorations and awards, military: 389, 393-395
Delgado, Humberto: 52
de Mello, António Vasco: 320
de Mello family: 320, 323
Democratic Electoral Commission (CDE): 252
Democratic Movement for the Liberation of Portugal (MDLP): 254, 286
Democratic Women's Movement: 255
Denmark: 247, 359, 360
Deus, João de: 169
development planning: 316, 318-319, 322, 327, 360; agriculture, 346; industry, 348; National Development Bank, 338
Diário do Notícias: 237, 302, 303
Dias, Bartolomeu: 31
diet: 107-109, 334, 364; fish, 345, 349
Dinís (king): 23, 26, 146, 168, 178, 394
Dinís, Júlio. See Gomes Coelho, Joaquim Guilherme
diseases: 82, 105, 106
districts (see also provinces): viii, xiv, 60, 65, 86; emigration, 103, 104; government, 207, 208, 216
Diu: 258, 276
divorce: 92, 144, 152
Document of the Nine: 223, 232, 234
domestic trade: 358, 365
Dorotheans (church order): 154
Dourado, Fernão Vaz: 185
Douro region: 62, 87
Douro River: xiv, 63, 70, 341, 370

earthquakes: 67-68, 189, 191
East Germany: 280
Eça de Queirós, José Maria de: 177, 181
economy (see also balance of payments): 54, 223, 311-331; public debt, 53; role of agriculture, 334-339
education (see also higher education; schools): viii, 53, 115, 121, 132, 167-176; in the colonies, 145; radio and television, 307, 308; Roman Catholic Church and, 142
EFTA: See European Free Trade Association
elections (see also suffrage): 47, 152, 214-216, 217, 227, 230; communists and, 250; voter turnout, 240, 245
electricity: 109, 316, 353

444

Elisío, Filinto. See Nascimento, Manuel do
elite class: 115, 121-123, 132, 134, 138, 203
emigration (see also immigration): 54, 55, 56, 81, 83, 92, 95-102, 314, 329, 403; illegal, 96, 98, 406; remittances sent back, 323, 328, 357, 359; to Brazil, 283; to France, 288, 362
energy industry: 109, 289, 316, 352-353
England. See Great Britain
ENR. See National Radio System
ERP. See Portuguese Radio System
escudo: 331
Espírito Santo family: 320, 323
Esposende: 70
Estrêla, Serra da: 64, 66, 68, 74
Estremadura: 60, 61, 62, 87; círios, 113, 160; district, 65, 66, 67
ethnic groups: viii, 13-14, 21, 176-177
eucalyptus trees: 343, 344
European Economic Community (EEC): 288, 294, 325, 358, 359, 360, 364
European Free Trade Association (EFTA): viii, 294, 316, 326, 358, 359, 364
Evangelical Alliance: 162
Evora: xiv, 19, 153, 184, 187, 216; agriculture, 342, 347; district, 67; emigration, 103, 104; police, 398; population, 85, 86, 88, 91; university, 168, 170, 175, 189
exploration and trade: 23, 26, 27, 30-32, 33, 35, 39, 188
exports (see also wines): viii, 357, 359, 361, 363; commodities, 45, 334, 344; fish, 75, 345; manufactured goods, 348
Expresso: 302, 304
expropriation of estates: 6, 137, 138, 229, 236-237, 333, 346, 347, 348; Mozambique, 271

fados: 113, 185
Faial island: 76, 77
Fallaci, Oriana: 250
family and kinship: 116, 122, 132-136, 194
Faro: xiv; district, 67, 68, 73, 216; emigration, 103, 104; population, 86, 87, 88, 91
Fatima shrine: 50, 142, 147, 159
FEC-ML. See Communist Electoral Front/Marxist-Leninist
Felipe I: 36, 37
Felipe III: 38
Ferdinand and Isabella: 34, 164

Fernandes, Grão Vasco: 185
Ferreira, José Medeiros: 286, 291, 295
Ferreira de Castro, José Maria: 183
fertilizer: 339
fig production: 342
films: 300, 309
Finland: 359
Fiscal Guard: 397, 399, 400
fishing: 66, 67, 71, 75, 78, 108, 160, 349; industry, 285, 322, 336, 345, 360
Flanders: 185
Flores island: 76, 77
FNLA. See National Front for the Liberation of Angola
folk health: 107
folk religion: 156, 157-158
Fonseca, António Manuel da: 184, 186
footwear: 363, 364
Ford, President Gerald: 290, 296
foreign affairs (see also treaties and agreements): 54, 229, 257-297
foreign aid (see also United States): 267, 288, 295, 312, 323, 325-326, 360
foreign enterprises: 229, 323, 330
foreign investment: 313, 315, 317, 319, 323-325, 350; by Brazilians, 283
foreign trade (see also exploration and trade; exports): 294, 312, 316, 358-364; with Africa, 292; with Brazil, 283; with England, 41, 287
foreigners: 145, 366; influence on armed forces, 395-396; Jews, 164; jurisdiction of, 402, 405; medals and awards, 394
forests and forest products: 72-73, 334, 335, 343, 344
Formigas Rocks: 75
France: 118, 186, 247, 287-288, 395; aid from, 386, 387; emigration to, 92, 95, 98, 102; language, 180; trade, 342, 362, 366, 368
Franco, Francisco (sculptor): 190
Franco, Francisco (Spain): 54, 285, 375
FRELIMO. See Front for the Liberation of Mozambique
Frondoni, Angelo: 184
Front for Independence and Continuity with the West (FICO): 265, 269
Front for the Liberation of Mozambique (FRELIMO): 265, 269, 270, 293, 378
Front for the Liberation of the Enclave of Cabinda (FLEC): 265, 274
Front for the Liberty and Independence of Portuguese Guinea (FLING): 264, 265
FSP. See Popular Socialist Front

Funchal district: 60, 78, 79, 106, 216, 371; population, 84, 86
FUR. *See* United Revolutionary Front

Galicia: 18, 21, 68; language, 176, 178
Gama, Eurico: 184
Garcão, Pedro António Correia: 180-181
General Agreement on Tariffs and Trade (GATT): 293, 316, 358, 364
Generation of 1870: 181
Gerez, Serra do: 64, 68
Gibraltar: 286, 386
Giscard D'Estaing, Valéry: 288, 295
GNR. *See* National Republican Guard
Goa: 33, 39, 54, 147, 258, 276, 287
Góis, Damião de: 161, 192
gold: 30, 36, 39, 40, 41, 311, 315, 326, 331; reserves, 359
Gomes, António Ferreira: 147, 148, 149
Gomes Coelho, Joaquim Guilherme: 181
Gonçalves, Nuno: 185
Gonçalves, Vasco dos Santos: 9, 10, 222, 223, 225, 226, 232, 233, 234, 282, 292, 296, 382
Gouveia, André de: 168
government (*see also* constitutions; elections; legislative assemblies): viii, 185, 193-220; overseas territories, 261-262; role in communications, 300-301
Graciosa island: 76, 77
grain production: 335, 339
Granada: 29
Grândola, Serra de: 64, 67-68
graphics: 187
Great Britain: 247, 249, 286-287, 395; EEC and, 359, 360; migration to, 95; Mozambique and, 270; relationship with, 13, 14, 27, 40, 161, 313; stonemasons, 188, 190; trade with, 294, 324, 361, 366
gross domestic product: viii, 311, 333, 334, 350, 357
Guadiana River: xiv, 63, 72, 370; bridge project, 362
Guarda: xiv, 65, 68, 74, 216; emigration, 103, 104; population, 83, 85, 86, 88
guilds: 128, 129, 199, 202
Guimarães: 21, 89
Guinea. *See* Portuguese Guinea
Guinea-Bissau: 99, 263, 264, 265, 267, 268
Gulbenkian Foundation: 185, 189
Gulf of Cadiz: 62, 63

habeas corpus: 203, 400, 406, 408
handicrafts: 190, 191, 352; Madeira, 78

health: 82, 102, 105, 107, 123, 155; folk healing, 157
Henry the Navigator: 28, 29-30, 190
Herculano, Alexandre: 180-181
higher education (*see also* Lisbon University): 26, 121, 123, 137, 169, 171; reform, 173, 174; women in, 136
history: 13-57; armed forces, 374-378; foreign relations, 257-260; major political events, 222-223
holidays: 132, 158, 159, 160
d'Hondt, Victor: 215
Hong Kong: 279, 331
horses: 113
Horta: 76, 78; population, 82, 86, 102
Horta, Maria Teresa: 183
hotel industry: 366, 367
houses of the people (*casas do povo*): 111, 128, 199, 202
housing: 89, 109-110, 189, 352, 391; Mozambique, 271
Hungary: 280, 363
hunting: 74

Iberian Atlantic Command (IBERLANT): 54, 386
Iberian Pact: 285, 374, 375
Iberians: 1, 15
Iceland: 359
Ilhas Desertas: 78, 79
immigration (*see also* refugees): 78
imports: 75, 319, 333, 351, 357, 360, 361, 362, 363, 365; food, 334, 339, 342, 364; import-substitution industries, 348; petroleum, 353
Inacio, Herminio da Palma: 253
income: 315, 317
India: 54, 258, 276, 287
Indonesia: 277, 278
industry: viii, 95, 121, 317, 348-355; family owned conglomerates, 320; work force, 93, 94
infant and child mortality: 105
Infante Santo project: 189
inflation: 57, 82, 110, 312, 314, 317, 327, 334, 358
Ingles, Carlos Aboim: 250
inheritance: 92, 110, 133
Inquisition: 34-35, 140, 141, 142, 164, 168; arts and, 179, 184, 192
interest groups: 255-256
International Communist League (LCI): 230, 239, 241, 251
international memberships: viii
International Monetary Fund (IMF): 293, 311, 316, 326, 358

446

International Police for the Defense of the State (PIDE): 400, 401, 402
Intersindical: 226, 304, 330
iron castings: 348, 361
irrigation: 69, 73, 335, 338

Japan: 33, 54
Jesuino, Jorge; 300, 301, 304
Jesuits: 34, 42, 141, 142, 154, 168, 184; university, 189, 192
Jews: 19, 34, 35, 140, 141, 161, 163, 164
João I: 27, 28, 178, 185, 188, 190
João II: 30, 34, 164
João III: 35, 164
João IV: 38, 39, 40
João V: 41, 184, 189
João VI: 42, 43
João de Deus project: 189
João Franco: 47, 48
John of Gaunt: 27
John XXI, Pope: 26, 191
John XXIII, Pope: 147
José (king): 41, 184, 190
judicial structure (see also military justice): viii, 199, 203-206, 211, 218, 407-410
Julião, Pedro. See John XXI, Pope
Júnior, Joaquim Casimiro: 184
Junqueiro, Abílio: 181
Junta of National Salvation: 4, 5, 210, 217, 224, 381, 401
juvenile delinquency: 205, 403, 404, 408, 410

Kaunda, Kenneth: 293
Keil, Alfredo: 184
Kennedy, John F.: 288
Kissinger, Henry: 290, 291, 295

labor (see also unemployment and underemployment): 55, 173, 202, 205, 329-330
labor force (see also trade unions): 93-94, 333, 334, 357; agriculture, 337-338; industry, 6, 350, 351, 352, 354-355; transportation, 358
Lagos: 68
Laingen, L. Bruce: 290
Lajes air base: 291, 387
land ownership (see also expropriation of estates; latifundio system): 17, 24, 25, 26, 44, 45, 115, 121, 125, 128, 312, 337, 346-348; interest groups, 255; Madeira, 78
land use: 117, 122, 124, 335-337

languages (see also Latin language; Portuguese language): viii, 13, 176-178; radio broadcasts, 307
latifundio system (see also expropriation of estates): 6, 26, 67, 122, 126, 130, 320
Latin language: 17, 176, 192
LCI. See International Communist League
Leal, António Duarte Gomes: 182
Leão, Duarte Nunes de: 191
left-wing parties (see also Marxist-Leninist parties): 221, 223, 230, 236, 246; far left groups, 225, 226, 229, 230, 233, 239, 240, 246, 251, 252, 253, 254, 256, 269; press, 302, 303, 304
legislative assemblies (see also Constituent Assembly; Corporative Chamber; National Assembly): 7, 199, 202, 210, 219, 238, 239
Leiria: xiv, 66, 216; emigration, 102, 103, 104; population, 84, 86, 88
Leixões: 70
Lezíria island: 71
libraries: 306, 310
Lima River: xiv, 70
Line of 1493: spheres of influence, 31, 32
Lisbon: xiv, 13, 59, 60, 66, 143, 153, 175, 184, 216, 365, 371, 385; architecture, 187, 190; Bank of Lisbon, 313; earthquake, 41, 68, 189; emigration, 102, 103, 104; government, 208; history, 16, 18, 19, 22; industry, 95, 229, 349, 351, 353; Jews, 164; law enforcement, 398, 400, 404, 407; libraries, 310; living conditions, 106, 108, 109, 113, military region, 385; population, 84, 85, 86, 88, 89; press, 302, 303, 305, 309
Lisbon University: 56, 136, 168, 169, 170
literacy: viii, 167, 173, 175-176; illiteracy rate, 168, 209, 309; voting requirement, 49, 134
literature: 34, 38, 177-183
livestock production: 66, 67, 69, 335, 343, 347
Livi Bacci, Massimo: 90, 91
living standards: 312
Lobo, Duarte: 184
Lopes, Fernão: 178
Lopes, Teixeira: 190
Lourenço Marques: 46, 47, 56
Lupi, Miguel: 186
Lusitania: 1, 13, 14-20
Lusitania news agency: 306
Lusitanian Community: 263
A Luta: 302, 303, 304

Macao: 54, 216, 230, 258, 266, 279, 331, 384
Machado de Castro, Joachim: 189, 190
Machel, Samora: 265, 270
Madariaga, Salvador de: 13
Madeira Islands: 29, 30, 59, 60, 78-79, 259, 308, 370,384, 386; banks, 322; emigration, 102, 103, 104; politics, 223, 242, 243, 244; Soviet base, 229, 282, 296; tourism, 365, 366, 367
Madeira wine: 78, 340, 341
Mafra palace: 189, 190
Magalhaes Mota, Joaquim: 248, 255
Makler, Harry M.: 121, 122, 128, 129, 130
Malhoa, João: 186
Malik, Adam: 278
Manta, João Abel: 187
Manuel I: 164, 179; Manueline design, 188, 190
manufacturing: 312, 316, 344, 350, 351; labor force, 355
Maranos: 164, 165
Mar de Palha: 71
marriage (see also divorce): 33, 90, 91, 134; legal ones, 144, 162; within social classes, 123, 126, 132-133
Martins, Herminio: 120, 127, 136
Martins, Joaquim: 181
Martins, José da Costa: 281
Marxist-Leninist parties: 221, 227, 264, 310, 377
Mateus wines: 340, 341
Mboumoua, William Eteki: 275
MDP. See Portuguese Democratic Movement
medical personnel and facilities: 106-107, 123; military hospitals, 390
Melo, Francisco Manuel de: 180
Melo Antunes, Ernesto Augusto de: 232, 233, 234, 237, 291
Mendes Pinto, Fernão: 179
Mérida: 18, 19
MES. See Movement of the Socialist Left
Mesas, Serra das: 63, 64
MFA. See Armed Forces Movement
middle classes: 44, 115, 118, 119, 120, 123-125; education, 167
migration (see also emigration; immigration): 95; internal, 65, 337
Miguel, Dom: 43, 44
military coup d'état. See coup d'état attempts; coup of 1926; revolution of April 1974
military justice: 205, 218, 383, 389-390

military role in politics. See armed forces
minerals: 74-75, 336, 348, 354; mining and quarrying, 355
Minho province: 60, 61, 62, 65, 67; university, 170
Minho River: xiv, 63, 70, 370
ministries: 200, 210, 214, 215, 238, 240; Ministry of Agriculture, 201, 344, 347; Ministry of Agriculture and Fishing, 215; Ministry of Commerce, 201; Ministry of Commerce and Tourism, 215; Ministry of Communications, 201; Ministry of Cooperation, 210, 215, 264; Ministry of Corporations, 111; Ministry of Corporations and Social Security, 201; Ministry of Defense, 214, 375, 387; Ministry of Economic Coordination, 322, 364; Ministry of Economic Planning, 201; Ministry of Economy, 201, 210; Ministry of Education, 169, 172, 173, 174, 201; Ministry of Education and Culture, 210; Ministry of Education and Scientific Investigation, 215; Ministry of External Trade, 11; Ministry of Finance, 11, 201, 210, 215, 314, 321, 364; Ministry of Foreign Affairs, 201, 210, 261; Ministry of Foreign Relations, 215; Ministry of Health and Welfare, 201; Ministry of Industry, 215; Ministry of Industry and Power, 201; Ministry of Information, 282; Ministry of Internal Administration, 210, 215, 398, 399; Ministry of Internal Commerce, 215; Ministry of Interior, 398, 399, 400; Ministry of Justice, 201, 210, 215, 219, 402, 407, 409; Ministry of Labor, 94, 205, 210, 215; Ministry of Mass Communication, 211, 231, 283; Ministry of National Defense, 201, 210; Ministry of Overseas Provinces, 20, 261, 279; Ministry of Public Works, 201; Ministry of Social Affairs, 111, 215, 255; Ministry of Social Affairs and Social Communication, 210; Ministry of Social Communication and Culture, 215, 299, 301, 302, 304, 305, 307, 308; Ministry of Social Equipment and Environment, 210, 215; Ministry of Transportation, 215, 372
Mira River: 72
Miranda, J. David: 120
Mirandela: 69
missionaries (see also Jesuits): 34, 145, 148, 161
Mobutu Sese Seko: 272, 274
monarchy: 2, 13, 23-24

Monchique, Serra de: 64, 67, 69, 73
Mondego River: xiv, 66, 71, 339, 370
Moors: 1, 17-20, 67, 187, 191
Morocco: 28, 29, 36
Moslems: 161
motor vehicles: 339, 367, 368, 369, 404, 405
mountain ranges: 64, 66
Moura, Francisco Pereira de: 252
Movement for the Reorganization of the Party of the Proletariat (MRPP): 227, 230, 239, 240, 241, 251
Movement for the Self-Determination of the Azorean People (FLA): 244
Movement of National Unity: 52
Movement of the Socialist Left (MES): 227, 239, 241, 252
Mozambique: 39, 46, 49, 55, 56, 216, 260, 287, 362; church in, 145, 146, 148, 150; Europeans in, 99, 100; independence, 263, 265, 269-271, 275, 293, 378; voting rights, 230
Mozarabs: 19, 20
MPLA. See Popular Movement for the Liberation of Angola
MRPP. See Movement for the Reorganization of the Party of the Proletariat
music: 183-185

Nagar-Aveli: 258, 276
names: vii, 13; Azores, 77; inheritance, 133; titles, 123
Namora, Fernando: 183
Nascimento, Manuel do: 180
Nasoni, Nicolau: 189
national anthem: 184
National Assembly: 52, 197, 198, 199, 200, 248, 252, 258
National Front for the Liberation of Angola (FNLA): 265, 272 273, 274, 275, 375
National Institute of Statistics: 82
National Overseas Bank (BNU): 268, 322
National Popular Action (ANP): 209, 217
National Radio System (ENR): 185, 307, 308
National Republican Guard (GNR): 397, 398, 399, 402
National Steelworks: 71, 75, 350
national syndicates: 199, 202
National Union: 3, 52, 53, 195, 209
National Union for the Total Independence of Angola (UNITA): 265, 272, 273, 274, 275, 376
national unity: 21, 115, 194, 196

nationalization of industry (see also banks): viii, 138, 224, 229, 237, 248, 319, 320, 328, 333; radio and television, 152, 236, 300, 307, 308; railroads, 370
nationalization of landholdings. See expropriation of estates
navy: 373, 374, 382, 383, 386, 388, 389, 391
Nery, Eduardo: 187
Netherlands: 38, 40, 247, 248, 267; aid, 386; Dutch influence on art, 186, 191
Neto, Agostinho: 272
Neto, João Baptista Nunes Pereira: 124
New Christians: 34, 35, 37, 164
New State: 3, 51-57, 194, 195, 329, 375; social structure under, 119, 127, 129, 131, 132
New University of Lisbon: 175
news agencies: 305-306
newspapers (see also República): 299, 301-305
Nixon, Richard M.: 289, 295
North Atlantic Treaty Organization (NATO): viii, 10, 54, 227, 229, 239, 250, 261, 282, 289, 290, 295, 315, 373, 374, 375, 385, 389, 395
Norway: 247, 359, 360
nuclear power: 289, 353
Nunes, A. Sedas: 119
Nzita, Henriques Tiago: 274

OAU. See Organization of African Unity
Obidos, Josefa de: 186
Ocussi Ambeno: 278
OECD. See Organization for Economic Cooperation and Development
O Jornal: 302, 304-305
Olisipo. See Lisbon
olives: 66, 67, 69, 338; oil, 342
ombudsman: 219, 238
O'Neill, Alexandre: 182
opera: 184-185
o povo: the people, 6, 116
Organization for Economic Cooperation and Development (OECD): viii, 172, 294, 311, 357
Organization of African Unity (OAU): 264, 275, 292
Ortega y Gasset, José: 28
Ortigão, José: 181
Osorio, Eduardo Sanches: 252
overseas territories: 2, 13, 46, 47, 54-55, 56, 225, 265-266; church in 144-145

449

PAIGC. *See* African Party for the Independence of Guinea and Cape Verde
painting: 185-187
Pais, Sidónio: 49, 50
Palma Carlos, Adelino da: 9, 225, 289
Palme, Olof: 8
Palolo, António: 187
papacy (*see also* Line of 1493): 26, 141, 145, 146, 147, 148, 152, 168; Concordat of 1940, 143, 153
paratroops: 10, 383, 387, 393
parliamentary republic: 48-51, 300
Pascoais, Teixeira de: 182
passage to India: 31, 32, 35, 178
Pato, Octavio: 8-9, 242
patron saints: 156, 159, 160
patronage relationships: 129-131, 135; church and state, 145, 146
Paul VI, Pope: 147, 148
Payne, Stanley: 117, 118
PCP. *See* Portuguese Communist Party
PDC. *See* Christian Democratic Party
peasants: 5, 6, 26, 116, 133, 134
Pedro, Dom: 30, 43
Pedro I: 24, 190
Pedro II: 39
Pereira, Aristides: 265, 267, 269
periodicals: 306
Pessoa, Fernando: 182
petroleum: 352, 353; imports, 361, 363; prices, 358, 359, 364
Philip II (Spain). *See* Felipe I
Philip IV (Spain). *See* Felipe III
Philippa of Lancaster: 27
Pico island: 76, 77
Pinheiro, Columbano Berdal: 186
Pintado, Valentin: 248
Pinto, Heitor: 192
Pinto, Manuel Vieira: 150, 151
Pinto, Serpa: 46
Pinto, Sousa: 186
Pires, Vasco: 184
Plastrik, Stanley: 245-246
poetry: 177, 182
Poland: 280, 363
police system (*see also* secret police): 206, 397-403
political crimes: 401, 405, 406, 409; police torture, 407, 408; political prisoners, 52, 219, 381, 402
political parties (*see also* communist-oriented political parties; left-wing parties; right-wing parties, socialist parties): 7, 45, 48, 49, 50, 195, 211, 212, 213, 215, 221; banned, 52, 246; newspapers identified with, 302-305
political violence: 228, 230, 231, 232, 233, 235, 240, 245, 250, 253, 398
Pombal, Marquis of: 41-42, 118, 142, 168; architecture, 189, 191
Ponta Delgada: 76, 78, 216, 288, 370; population, 84, 86, 102
Popular Democratic Party (PPD): 7, 8, 217, 226, 227, 228, 229, 230, 232, 233, 234, 235, 239, 240, 241, 242, 244, 246, 248, 249, 255, 256, 275, 304, 305
Popular Democratic Union (UDP): 230, 236, 239, 241, 246, 251
Popular Monarchist Party (PPM): 230, 239, 240, 241, 252, 256
Popular Movement for the Liberation of Angola (MPLA): 271, 272, 273, 376
Popular Socialist Front (FSP): 230, 239, 241, 252
Popular Unity Party (PUP): 230, 239, 241, 252
population: viii, 81-94, 127; social structure, 118, 120
Portalegre: xiv, 67, 85, 216; agriculture, 342, 347; emigration, 103, 104; population, 86, 88, 91
Portela Airport: 367, 371
Portimão: 68
Porto: xiv, 13, 60, 65, 106, 175, 208, 339, 407; cathedral, 187; history, 16, 18, 20; industry, 74, 349, 353; Jews in, 164; labor, 95, 229; library, 310; police, 398; population, 89, 90, 92; press, 302, 303, 305, 309; trade, 365; university, 169, 170
Porto, Silva: 186
Porto Santo island: 78, 79
porto wine: 65, 69, 341, 336, 370
ports and harbors: 70, 71, 72, 336, 369
Portugal and the Future (Spínola): 263
Portuguese Air Transports (TAP): 371
Portuguese Anticommunist Movement: 254
Portuguese Communist Marxist-Leninist Organization: 252
Portuguese Communist Party (PCP): 7, 221, 225, 226, 227, 228, 230, 231, 232, 234, 235, 236, 239, 240, 241, 242, 245, 246, 247, 248, 249-251, 253, 254, 255, 256, 281, 284, 289, 305, 321, 382, 383, 401, 406
Portuguese Communist Party/Marxist-Leninist (PCP-ML): 239, 241, 252
Portuguese Democratic Movement (MDP): 228, 230, 239, 241, 252, 305

Portuguese Guinea (*see also* Guinea-Bissau): 55, 258, 376, 380
Portuguese Inter-Ecclesiastical Commission: 162
Portuguese language: 23, 39, 176, 179, 191; literature in, 176-183
Portuguese Legion: 195, 251, 393
Portuguese Liberation Army (ELP): 254, 286
Portuguese Radio System (ERP): 300, 307
Portuguese Socialist Party (PSP): 7, 8, 222, 227, 228, 229, 230, 231, 232, 233, 234, 235, 238, 239, 240, 241, 242, 245, 246, 248, 249, 255, 256, 296, 304; press, 303, 305
Portuguese State of India: 258, 276, 287
Portuguese Television (RTP): 300, 308
Portuguese Youth: 195
PPD. *See* Popular Democratic Party
PPM. *See* Popular Monarchist Party
presidency: viii, 52, 198, 199, 209, 212, 214, 217, 229, 238, 240; constitutional powers, 197
Prester John: 29
prestige. *See* social prestige
prices: 94, 109, 318, 327; freeze, 95, 317
primary schools: 168, 169
prime minister, office of: viii, 9, 52, 196, 198, 199, 209, 212, 239, 240; constitutional powers, 197
Príncipe. *See* São Tomé and Príncipe
prostitution: 403, 404
Protestants: 140, 148, 155, 161-163
provinces (*see also* districts): 61, 62, 208; term used, 259
Provincia Portucalense: 20, 21
PRP-BR. *See* Revolutionary Party of the Proletariat-Revolutionary Brigades
PRT. *See* Revolutionary Workers' Party
PSP. *See* Portuguese Socialist Party
public demonstrations and disorder. *See* political violence
Public Security Police: 397, 399, 402
publishing: 300, 309-310
PUP. *See* Popular Unity Party

Quental, Antero de: 181
Quina family: 320

radio and television: viii, 173, 185, 235, 236, 300, 306-308
Rádio Renascença: 152, 236, 300, 307
railroads: 367, 369, 370
rainfall: 68, 69, 73; Azores, 77
Ramalho Eanes, António: 8, 242

Reconquest: 19, 22-23, 28
recreation and sports: 111-114, 306
refugees: colonial, 100-102, 224, 242, 255, 256, 312, 325, 328, 329, 403; from Angola, 273, 274, 291, 376; from Mozambique, 270-271
Regnerators: 45, 48
Rêgo, Raul: 304
Reis, Soares dos: 190
religion (*see also* New Christians; Roman Catholic Church): viii, 16, 19, 34-35, 91, 139-140; rituals and festas, 113, 158-160
República: 222, 231, 302, 304
research: 281, 310, 360, 381
Resende, André de: 191
Resende, Antero Silva: 252
Resende, Garcia de: 178
Resende, Júlio: 187
revolution of April 1974: 3, 5, 57, 137, 221, 301, 378
Revolutionary Committee for Mozambique (COREMO): 265, 269
Revolutionary Councils of Workers, Soldiers, and Sailors: 253
Revolutionary Front for an Independent East Timor (FRETLIN): 266, 276, 277, 278
Revolutionary Organization of the Armed Forces (ORFA): 255
Revolutionary Party of the Proletariat-Revolutionary Brigades (PRP-BR): 236, 253, 254
Revolutionary Workers' Party (PRT): 239, 241, 251
Ribatejo: 62, 66, 71, 87; agriculture, 113
Ribeiro, António: 151
Ribeiro, Aquilino: 182
Ribeiro, Bernardim: 178
rice: 336, 339
Riegelhaupt, Joyce F.: 125, 135
right-wing parties: 251, 252, 254
rights and freedoms. *See* civil rights
rivers: xiv, 70
roads and highways (*see also* motor vehicles): 367-368, 369, 395, 398
Roberto, Holden: 272, 375
Roman Catholic Church (*see also* clergy; church and state; missionaries; papacy; Rádio Renascença): 26, 44, 139-140, 142-152
Romania: 280, 281, 363
Romans: 16, 17, 18, 187, 335; law, viii, 203, 404
RTP. *See* Portuguese Television

Sá Borges, Jorge de Carvalho: 248
Sá Carneiro, Francisco: 7, 240, 248, 255
Sá de Miranda, Francisco de: 179
Sado River: xiv, 70, 72, 75
Saint Vincent retable: 185
Salazar, António de Oliveira: 2, 51-57,
    193, 194, 195, 196, 198, 200, 209, 217,
    219, 221, 246, 249, 373, 375, 376; arts
    and letters under, 187, 192; civil rights
    under, 300, 309, 400; economy under,
    311, 314-317, 323, 353; foreign rela-
    tions, 258, 260, 261, 276, 285, 354;
    Roman Catholic church and, 139, 142-
    144; social stratification under, 119-127
Salazar Bridge: 362, 368
Saldanha Sanches, J. L.: 252
salt industry: 72, 75
Sancho II: 21, 22
sanitation: 109-110
Santa Maria island: 76, 77
Santarém (see also Fatima shrine): xiv,
    66, 71, 74, 216; emigration, 103, 104;
    population, 85, 86, 88
Santiago, Francisco de: 184
Santo António: 26, 160, 191
Santos, António Almeida: 302
São João: 160
São João Baptista de Ajudá: 258
São Jorge island: 76, 77
São Miguel island: 76, 77, 243, 244
São Pedro: 160
São Tomé and Príncipe: 258, 265, 271
sardines: 75
Savimbi, Jonas: 272
Scarlatti, Domenico: 184
scholarship: 191-192
schools: 162, 261, 388; military schools,
    379, 388, 389
sculpture: 190
Sebastião (king): 36, 37, 142, 374; Sebas-
    tianism, 177
secondary schools: 168, 169, 171, 173;
    conservatories, 170
secret police: 3, 4, 218, 249, 254, 284,
    390, 400-402, 408, 409
Seixas, Carlos: 184
Selvagen Islands: 59
Sena, Jorge de: 182
Senegal: 292
Sequeira, Domingos António: 186
service industries: 317; work force, 93,
    94, 357
Setúbal: xiv, 66, 68, 216, 339; church of
    Jesu, 188, 189; emigration, 103, 104;
    industry, 317, 349, 351, 370; popula-
    tion, 84, 85, 86, 88

shantytowns. See barracas
ships and shipbuilding: 280, 281, 317,
    348, 351, 363; navy, 386
Silva, José da: 184
Silva, Maria Arlete Vieira da: 9
Silva, Maria Helena Vieira da: 187
Silveira, Bento Coelho da: 186
Simão, José Veiga: 262
sindicatos: 128
Sines industrial complex: 316, 327, 349,
    353
Sintra-Mafra area: 74
size: vii, 59
slavery: 30, 39, 46, 164
Soames, Christopher: 294
Soares, Mário: 7, 8, 228, 231, 232, 240,
    242, 246, 247, 256, 267, 276, 281, 292;
    press and, 302
social customs and cultural development:
    19, 24, 158
Social Democratic Center Party (CDS):
    7, 8, 227, 229, 230, 239, 240, 241, 242,
    245, 246, 248, 255, 256, 305
Social Democratic Movement: 248
social prestige (see also class): landown-
    ership, 117, 122, 125, 126, 134; mobili-
    ty, 115, 121, 123; occupations, 121,
    124, 171, 261, 379, 390
social security: 205, 206, 322, 360; mili-
    tary pensions, 391
social services. See social security; wel-
    fare
Social State: 57
social system: 5, 115-138, 145, 146
socialist parties (see also Portuguese So-
    cialist Party): 222, 226, 227, 246, 247-
    248, 254; socialism, 233, 238, 247
Society for the Study of Social and Eco-
    nomic Development (SEDES): 255
soils: 72-74
Soldiers United Will Win (SUV): 255,
    383, 390
South Africa: 95, 272
Soviet Union: Angola and, 272, 376;
    Madeira and, 229; military equipment,
    377, 380; relations with, 54, 247, 280,
    281, 282; trade, 363
Spain: 95, 315, 337, 366, 370, 386; early
    history, 2, 13, 14, 18, 24, 29, 38, 60;
    relations with, 54, 254, 285-286, 362,
    368
Spanish language: 37, 177
spice trade: 31, 35
Spínola, António de: 5, 9, 57, 222, 224,
    225, 227, 228, 252, 254, 284, 286, 377,
    379, 381; book, 380; foreign policy,

452

263, 267, 289, 292, 295; military award, 394
strikes: 318, 329, 330, 405
students: 120, 402, 403
suffrage: 45, 49, 50, 136, 200, 209, 214; electoral law, 47, 48; reciprocity with Brazil, 97; women, 52, 134
sugar cane: 334, 340
Supreme Allied Commander Europe (SACEUR): 385
Supreme Court of Justice: 198, 203, 204
SUV. See Soldiers United Will Win
Swabians: 13, 17, 18
Sweden: 95, 247, 248, 267, 359, 360; trade, 360
Switzerland: 95, 359, 360; Swiss National Bank, 326

tariffs: 359, 364
taxes: 145, 163, 242, 400
teacher training: 169, 170, 171
Technical University of Lisbon: 169, 170
Tejo River: xiv, 22, 63, 66, 71, 190, 339, 370
telephones: 286, 312, 321, 407
Temple of Diana: 187
Tengarrinka, José Manuel: 253
Terceira island: 76; American air base, 77, 387
textiles: 363, 364
theater: 179
Timor: 54, 254, 263, 266, 276-278
Timorese People's Democratic Association (APODETI): 266, 276 277, 278
tin: 74, 75
tobacco: 334
Tomás, Américo: 52, 56, 57, 377, 379
tomatoes: 339-340, 363
topography: vii, 63-68
Torga, Miguel: 182
Torre do Tombo archives: 310
tourism: 78, 160, 280, 281, 352, 365-367; revenues from tourists, 311, 312, 316, 326, 357, 359
trade. See domestic trade; foreign trade
trade unions: 52, 176, 229, 330; communists in, 226, 231, 235, 249
transportation (see also motor vehicles): 358, 367-372
Trás-os-Montes: 23, 25, 60, 61, 62, 65, 87, 164, 339
treaties and agreements: 54, 60, 145, 385; former colonies, 267, 268, 273, 276; France, 98; Great Britain, 288; Spain, 285; trade, 280, 281, 282, 292-293, 363;

United States, 288-290, 292; Vatican, 143
trees. See forests and forest products
trial by jury: 218
tuberculosis: 105
tungsten: 336, 354

UDP. See Popular Democratic Union
unemployment and underemployment: 94, 110, 224, 312, 329, 338
United Group of Mozambique (GUMO): 265, 269
United Kingdom of Portugal, Brazil, and the Algarve: 42
United League for Revolutionary Action (LUAR): 253, 254
United Nations: 55, 244, 259, 293; independence of colonies and, 264, 267, 268, 277, 278; membership, 54
United Revolutionary Front (FUR): 236, 254
United States: aid, 101, 239-240, 273, 315, 325, 380; Azores bases, 54, 77, 243, 261, 288, 291, 375, 387; emigration to, 95, 98; films from, 309; military aid, 386, 387, 395; multinational firms, 323; trade, 324, 362, 366
United States Export-Import Bank: 289, 325, 353
United States Military Advisory and Assistance Group: 395
United States Steel Corporation: 368
universities and colleges. See higher education and names of specific schools
uranium: 75

Vandals and Visigoths: 17, 19
Vasconcelos, Mário Cesarinez de: 182
Vaz, Fátima: 187
Velho da Costa, Maria Fátima: 183
Venezuela: 98
Viana do Castelo: 65, 68, 216; emigration, 103, 104; population, 84, 86, 88
Vicente, Gil: 161, 179, 184
Vieira, Domingos: 186
Vila Franca de Xira: 71
Vila Real: xiv, 68, 69, 75, 216, 339; emigration, 102, 103, 104; population, 84, 86, 88, 89, 90
Vila Real de Santo António: 63, 72
Villela, Manuel Serra António Lobo: 252
Viseu: xiv, 65, 216; emigration, 102, 103, 104; minerals, 74, 75; population, 86, 88, 89

453

vocational training: 169, 170, 171
Vouga River: 71, 75

wages and salaries: 11, 94-95, 136, 312, 317, 321, 327; military pay, 390; minimum wage, 95, 330
Waldheim, Kurt: 278
wars: 49, 54, 374, 375
water transport (*see also* ports and harbors): 368-370
welfare: 110-111, 128, 148, 317
Wellington, Duke of: 42
Wengorovius, Victor: 252
West Germany: 247, 248, 387; aid, 326; emigration to, 92, 95, 98, 102, 395; trade, 295, 324, 361, 366
wildlife: 74
wines (*see also porto* wine): viii, 66, 78; exports, 41, 340, 341, 360

witchcraft: 130, 140, 157
wolframite: 74, 75, 354
women (*see also* marriage): 131, 133, 180, 183; employment, 92, 93, 106, 116, 262, 337, 388, 399; in population, 81, 84, 85; leisure, 112, 306; life expectancy, 102; religion, 154, 156, 157; sex discrimination, 135, 136, 255; voting rights, 52, 134, 209
working class (*see also* peasants): 6, 26, 53, 120, 125, 126, 133
World Bank: 293, 311, 316, 325
World Council of Churches: 148

Yugoslavia: 280, 377

Zaire: 95, 272, 274, 375
Zambia: 293
Zurara, Gomes Eanes de: 178

PUBLISHED AREA HANDBOOKS

550-65	Afghanistan	550-151	Honduras
550-98	Albania	550-165	Hungary
550-44	Algeria	550-21	India
550-59	Angola	550-154	Indian Ocean Territories
550-73	Argentina	550-39	Indonesia
550-169	Australia	550-68	Iran
550-176	Austria	550-31	Iraq
550-175	Bangladesh	550-25	Israel
550-170	Belgium	550-69	Ivory Coast
550-66	Bolivia	550-177	Jamaica
550-20	Brazil	550-30	Japan
550-168	Bulgaria	550-34	Jordan
550-61	Burma	550-56	Kenya
550-83	Burundi	550-50	Khmer Republic (Cambodia)
550-166	Cameroon	550-81	Korea, North
550-96	Ceylon	550-41	Korea, Republic of
550-159	Chad	550-58	Laos
550-77	Chile	550-24	Lebanon
550-60	China, People's Republic of	550-38	Liberia
550-63	China, Republic of	550-85	Libya
550-26	Colombia	550-163	Malagasy Republic
550-67	Congo, Democratic Republic of (Zaire)	550-172	Malawi
		550-45	Malaysia
550-91	Congo, People's Republic of	550-161	Mauritania
550-90	Costa Rica	550-79	Mexico
550-152	Cuba	550-76	Mongolia
550-22	Cyprus	550-49	Morocco
550-158	Czechoslovakia	550-64	Mozambique
550-54	Dominican Republic	550-35	Nepal, Bhutan and Sikkim
550-52	Ecuador	550-88	Nicaragua
550-43	Egypt	550-157	Nigeria
550-150	El Salvador	550-94	Oceania
550-28	Ethiopia	550-48	Pakistan
550-167	Finland	550-46	Panama
550-29	Germany	550-156	Paraguay
550-155	Germany, East	550-92	Peripheral States of the Arabian Peninsula
550-173	Germany, Federal Republic of		
550-153	Ghana	550-42	Peru
550-87	Greece	550-72	Philippines
550-78	Guatemala	550-162	Poland
550-174	Guinea	550-181	Portugal
550-82	Guyana	550-160	Romania
550-164	Haiti	550-84	Rwanda

550-51	Saudi Arabia	550-53	Thailand
550-70	Senegal	550-178	Trinidad and Tobago
550-180	Sierra Leone	550-89	Tunisia, Republic of
550-86	Somalia	550-80	Turkey
550-93	South Africa, Republic of	550-74	Uganda
550-171	Southern Rhodesia	550-97	Uruguay
550-95	Soviet Union	550-71	Venezuela
550-179	Spain	550-57	Vietnam, North
550-27	Sudan, Democratic Republic of	550-55	Vietnam, South
550-47	Syria	550-99	Yugoslavia
550-62	Tanzania	550-75	Zambia

☆ U.S. GOVERNMENT PRINTING OFFICE : 1977—O—241-555/5